CONGREGATIONAL CHURCH, 1902

A Memorial History

OF

Hampstead, New Hampshire

VOLUME II

CONGREGATIONAL CHURCH

1752 - 1902

WITH AN APPENDIX TO VOL. I

———

ILLUSTRATED

———

BY

HARRIETTE ELIZA NOYES

(*Member New England Historic Genealogical Society, New Hampshire Historical Society; Author Memorial History of the Town of Hampstead; Contributor to the "Annual," Hampstead, England.*)

———

BOSTON, MASS.
GEORGE B. REED, 4 PARK STREET
1903

PRESS OF NEWCOMB & GAUSS.

TO

The Committee of Arrangements

for the

One Hundred and Fiftieth Anniversary of
the Founding

of the

Congregational Church in Hampstead,
New Hampshire,

July 2, 1902.

To the Members and Friends of the Church

THIS MEMORIAL

IS

RESPECTFULLY INSCRIBED.

CONTENTS.

ILLUSTRATIONS.

ILLUSTRATIONS.

INTRODUCTION.

TO MY FRIENDS :—

After the Memorial History of Hampstead was received by the public in the winter of 1899, many valuable records and interesting items came to me from people who were in some way interested in our town, which suggested the thought of preparing an Appendix to the history, which, if not published, could be preserved in the Public Library for the use of future generations.

The facts and records were safely treasured with that aim in view, until the greatly appreciated honor was extended to me to be the historian of the church at its one hundred and fiftieth anniversary. In accepting the invitation my efforts to search deeper into the annals and traditions of the town were increased, and a resolve was made to prepare Volume II, as a Memorial of the Church, to include an Appendix to the town history.

In the preparation of this work many family and town histories have been consulted ; professional genealogists have rallied to my aid ; and people in town and out have been earnest in extending words of encouragement and help. Nearly eight hundred letters have been sent to past and present members of the church and descendants, soliciting records, or to verify data, with the result that only three requests have remained unanswered. While a few members have asked that their ages be not recorded, and other persons have requested a brief mention, all have sent best wishes for the success of my undertaking.

But for this generous aid and kindly interest from pastors, members and friends of the church and society, my work would have been almost impossible, not being a member or connected with any church organization, and residing away from even the sound of the church bell.

I extend to all who have aided me by records, photographs or illustrations, or by cheering words of encouragement, my sincere thanks.

The memorial histories of the town and of the church were not prepared with the idea of pecuniary profit, but their publication has afforded the broader contribution of giving and receiving of knowledge and of pleasure.

The first volume has found a place in the homes of nine hundred residents, natives or friends of Hampstead, residing in nearly every State and Territory of the Union, and in England, France, and Germany, eliciting expressions complimentary to its value, as well as words of hearty approval.

Thomas Fuller, D. D., described as "a man of excellent learning and great benevolence," wrote more than two hundred and fifty years ago, "History is an interesting study, and a recreation work." I trust that this volume, the compiling of which has been a pleasurable recreation, may at least find friends who can view its possible errors with kindly discrimination.

> " Whoever thinks a faultless piece to see;
> Thinks what ne'er was, nor is, nor ne'er will be."

With renewed feelings of friendship for you all, with affection for my native town, with great respect for the lives and character of the founders of the Congregational Church, and with becoming pride in its history and historical associations, I am,

Sincerely yours,

HARRIETTE E. NOYES.

HAMPSTEAD, N. H., June 15, 1903.

THE OLD CHURCH.

The Old Church on the hilltop sleeps,
   Through storms and sunny weather.
About its walls the wild wind sweeps,
The drifting rain its grey roof steeps,
Or mellowing sunbeam silent creeps,
   In cold or heat together.

Around its tower that stately rears,
   An ever warning finger,
Like Minaret whence the faithful hears
At morn and eve, the call to prayers.
The pale moon flings her silver spears,
   And rosy sunsets linger.

Within are timbers brown and bare,
   The pulpits high insistence,
And circling gallery rising fair,
O'er empty pews now silent there,
In sunlight that through windows bare
   Streams in without resistance.

The Deacons' seat stands well in view,
   With sounding board above it,
And just before their narrow pew
The table bare where they renew
From month to month their promise true
   To church, and vow to love it.

On sunny summer day when long
   We sit in idle dreaming,
We hear the strains of sacred song
From pew and gallery rising strong,
And stately parson drones along,
   His words with terrors teeming.

Around, the circumjacent air
   Is full of spirit faces.
The old, with visage lined with care,
The happy child, the maiden fair,
And tottering age with silver hair,
   Filling their old time places.

Dear Old New England, proud and stern,
   Thy old traditions keeping,
Thine ancient creed failed to discern
The love that made the Man Christ yearn
O'er sinful souls, nor could you learn
   The Godhead, in them sleeping.

A broader faith for human need
   To-day thy pulpit preaches.
The bulwarks of thy iron creed
Have sunk so low that all may read
The promise given, and claim the meed
   Thy heavenly message teaches.

But yet through all New England strong
   Thy influence still we cherish,
The love for right, hatred of wrong,
Fair freedom's high and holy song,
Faith in that truth that suffered long
   That naught that lives shall perish.

All praise to those who wisely laid
   Foundations past upheaving,
Who through grim forests undismayed,
By sea and mountain lonely strayed,
And with their blood and labor made
   The blessings we're receiving.

Their forms in lonely graveyards rest,
   A mossy headstone telling,
Unlettered for the searcher's quest,
Nor heed they friend or stranger guest
No answers give to their request,
   But yet they're with us dwelling.

We see them in the fertile land
  Its richest harvests giving.
We feel them in each strong right hand,
The pulpit voices their command,
And public schools a record stand,
  As tokens of their living.

What lessons do the rolling years,
Filled full of labor and of tears,
So swiftly waning day by day,
Leave with us as they glide away ?

Our fathers chose the better part,
In living near to Nature's heart.
Contented in their humble lot,
Though now in later years forgot.

What matters though their earthly name
Live not upon the roll of fame ?
They labored for each passing day,
Then silently they stole away.

They counted their life work well done
If they could say at set of sun,
To-day I've seen Thy power increase,
Lord, let Thy servant go in peace.

What though the narrow way they made
Still narrower for the feet that strayed,
The eye that saw a sparrow fall
A constant watch kept over all.

With ostentation, pomp and din,
We seek the way to enter in,
The weak ones crowding to the wall,
What wonder that so many fall.

What use in all this constant strain,
This toil and trouble, care and pain,
Unequal fighting with our lot,
Appearing to be what we're not ?

What matters when our work is done
And we have reached life's setting sun,
If sleep we 'neath the lowly sod,
Forgotten by all else but God ?

Our need is for a simpler life,
With more of Nature's teachings rife,
The nearer we to Nature stand
We surer feel God's guiding hand.

Beneath the rush of busy marts
We lose the beat of suffering hearts.
And where the flag of freedom waves
We congregate, a race of slaves.

Slaves to the eager rush of gain,
Slaves 'neath strenuous labor's strain,
Slaves to ambition's stern command,
Slaves e'en to pleasure's beckoning hand.

With many corded lash they smite,
And ever urge us in the fight,
Not that dread whip that scores the back,
But want and greed and passions pack.

Their lashes take no bloody toll,
But striking inward sear the soul,
And while they leave no throbbing scar,
Our whole eternal welfare mar.

We need less madness in the strife,
More dignity in daily life,
Remembering that the Father's gaze,
Unruffled, sees our devious ways.

Well knowing, when the strife is past,
His love will fold us safe at last.
And close 'neath His protecting arms,
No more we'll fear the world's alarms.

GEORGE ROBY BENNETTE, M. D.

EARLY HISTORY—1620-1733.

In 1640, it was said, "the events of history, in New England, are recorded with ever increasing rapidity, and give promise of surprising changes."

The emigration of the Puritans to New England, as shown by the historians of early days, began about ten years after the landing of the Pilgrims at Plymouth. Few attempts were made to form other settlements until seventeen ships, with more than a thousand persons, came in 1630. More and more the exodus increased, until 1640, when twenty-three thousand representatives of English blood settled on lands adjacent to Massachusetts Bay.

They were men and women who had left their homes, their friends, and their native land, for an abode in a bleak and lonely wilderness, that they might enjoy in peace an austere religion which they regarded more highly than all of the comforts and pleasures of the world.

At a session of the General Court held in Boston May 11, 1640, a petition was received from " Mr. Nathaniel Ward and Newberry men " for permission " to begin a settlement on the Merrimack." The right was granted them to consider Pentucket (Haverhill), or Cochichawick (Andover), provided they give answer in three weeks and build before the next Court." Mr. Ward and his associates chose Pentucket, and commenced a settlement before the following October.

The first company of settlers were William White, Samuel Gile, James Davis, Henry Palmer, John Robinson, John Williams, Christopher Hussey, and Richard Littlehale of Newbury, Abraham Tyler, Daniel Ladd, Joseph Merrie, and Job Clement of Ipswich, all of whom had come to America within a short time.

Rev. John Ward, son of Mr. Nathaniel Ward, the petitioner for the location, and grandson of Rev. John Ward, a worthy and distinguished minister of Haverhill, England, took up his residence with them as soon as they could break ground for the new settlement and prepare for the coming of a minister.

The settlers received the deed of the land of Pentucket Nov. 12, 1642, from the Indians Passaquo and Saggahew with the consent of Passaconaway, which they named Haverhill, in honor of Haverhill, England, the birthplace of Rev. John Ward, and as a token of respect and thankfulness for his settling with them in the work of the ministry. The deed of the land of Pentucket gives the bounds " eight miles in length westward, six miles northward, and six miles eastward, with ye Ileand in ye rivver, that ye Ileand stands in, that is fourteen miles in length, for and in consideration of sum of three pounds and ten shillings."

In the autumn of 1641 they gathered their first church, consisting of fourteen members, eight males and six females.

Tradition says " they assembled the first seven years for prayer and public worship beneath the branches of a large tree which stood in what is now the Old Pentucket burial ground, and at their homes, which were all in the immediate vicinity."

They erected in 1648 a rough one-story building of hewn logs. The house was twenty-six feet in length by twenty feet in width, as their meeting house, and in which also to execute all town and civic affairs, " at ye Lower End of ye Mill Lott," now occupied by the Pentucket and Linwood cemeteries.

During the winter of 1655 Thomas Davis was allowed three pounds by the town " to gound pin and daub it," on condition that he " provide the stone and clay for the underpinning," the town to be at their own expense to bring the clay into place, and " ye plaitering of ye walls up to ye beams."

The house was enlarged and repaired, seats and a gallery added a few years after. In 1672 a store house to secure the stock of powder and ammunition and a stockade of smooth poles sixteen feet tall were set close together for a more secure defence against the Indian attacks. The watch-house and whipping post were in front of the meeting house; the pound for cattle occupied a corner of the lot, and the "nooning house," with the big fireplace beside which the more distant families could eat their lunch during intermission. The burial ground was behind the meeting house.

In September, 1642, the town voted to give Mr. Ward, their teacher, a salary of £50, and in 1645 Richard Little-hale was selected to beat a drum to call the people together, but "in 1652 Abraham Tyler was chosen to blow his horn in the most convenient place, for the same purpose, every Lord's day, about one-half hour before meeting time, and also on lecture days, for which he was to have a peck of corn from every family for the year ensuing." In 1652 the herds-man, James George, was "not permitted to turn the flock of cattle into the common herd until after the second beating of the drum."

One of the duties of the Selectmen in 1674 was to have the meeting house "swept duly, decently, and orderly."

In 1681 the question of building a new meeting house was raised, and a compromise of erecting a new gallery on the east side was made,

Rev. John Ward, the first pastor of the church, became enfeebled with age, and Rev. Benjamin Rolfe, of Newbury, Mass., began to preach in the autumn of 1689 as an assistant of Mr. Ward. The town voted " to pay him forty pounds per annum, in wheat, rye, and Indian, and his diet and board," and " that Mr. Ward should have his full salary, provided he boarded Mr. Rolfe at his own cost." Mr. Ward died Dec. 27th, 1693, "just entering his eightieth eighth year," and his assistant for four years was ordained pastor, April

29, 1693, "at a salary of £60 in wheat, rye, and Indian, and he to find personal quarters for himself as he shall think good," and " there shall be paid him a sufficient quantity and stock of good sweet dry, and sound hay, for the keeping his horse through the winter, at such place in Haverhill as he shall appoint."

The question of repairing the old house, or building a new meeting house, came up in town meeting in 1694, and by a vote of thirty-five for the old place to fifty-three votes against it, and for a location on "the Commons."

It was voted in 1697 " to build a new meeting house, near the Watch house and school house, which had been built on what is now City Hall Park, July 28, 1697. The committee chosen reported that "they had been abroad at several places, taking dimensions, of several meeting houses, and having an account of the cost of them, and after bartering with several workmen, had found Sergeant John Haseltine the most inclinable to build of any one." He offered to " build a meeting house, fifty feet long and forty feet wide, and eighteen feet stud, finishing the same, within and without, with seats, pulpit, galleries, windows, doors, and stairs, after the pattern of the Beverly meeting house, and doing the sides after the styles of the Reading meeting house, finding all materials, for four hundred pounds money," even to " the turning of the key, and building a turret for a bell."

The town by a unanimous vote granted the acceptance of the new house Oct. 24, 1799, and to "dispose of ye old meeting house, for ye public benefit of ye said town for ye use of a school house, or a watch house, or a house of shelter, or a shed to keep horses in, or any other way as they can meet with chapmen."

The people were seated in the house Nov. 20, 1699, by a committee chosen " to place or seat the people in the new meeting house so that they may know where to sit & not disorderly to crowd upon one another, and be uncivil in the time of God's worship."

This house had a door in the end, six windows on each side, and a watch house and school house connected to it. A porch and steeple were built about 1760.

In 1709 several persons were given permission to "build seats for themselves to sit in, in the hind seat of the west gallery, if not built so high as to hinder or damnify the light of them windows in the west end."

Permission was given in 1713 to "build a women's pew in the meeting house."

The first church bell in Haverhill was purchased for this parish in London in 1748, and a belfry was built on the ridge of the meeting house, and the bell rope descended to the broad aisle, and it was voted "to Ring the bell, at one of ye clock, every day, and at nine every night, and on Sabbaths and Lectures," and one hundred pounds were raised (old tenor) towards defraying "the charges of building the steeple and Ringing ye bell."

The meeting house became too small for the parish, and as it was much decayed it was finally decided to build a new one in 1765, and an appropriation of three hundred pounds was granted, but more than one thousand pounds were used for the purpose.

The dimensions of the new house were not to exceed sixty-six feet in length and forty-eight feet in breadth. The whole of the ground floor (excepting the aisles) was occupied by pews, which were built by the parish, appraised by the committee, and sold at auction. The "men's seats" and "women's seats" were then confined to the galleries.

This meeting house, when built, was set "at the northerly side of the old meeting house, as near to it as may be convenient, and was on the Common, about midway between Main and Winter streets, a little north of the foot of Pleasant street, with the principal end to the northeast." This house remained standing till 1887, when it was taken down.

From 1765 to 1770 Baptists were continually asking for a release of their minister rates towards the First Parish Orthodox preacher. Denominational troubles were becoming numerous in the parish from time to time until 1828, which finally led to a separation and division, the Orthodox portion founding the Centre Congregational Church, and the Universalists and Unitarians, being in the majority by five votes, removed the old meeting house in 1837, and built their new house on the site of the present First Parish Unitarian Church, north of City Hall Park.

Rev. Benjamin Rolfe, their pastor, was slain, with his wife and daughter Mehitable, Sunday morning, August 20, 1708, by a desperate band of French and Indians, at the door of his house, which stood near the north corner of Main and Summer streets. They were buried in one grave near the south end of the old Pentucket burial ground, over which the ladies of Haverhill erected a neat and substantial monument in 1847.

" This worthy man was born in Newbury, Mass., in 1662, was graduated from Cambridge 1684. A pious and upright man, ardently devoting his time and talents to forward the cause of his Saviour." " He was beloved and respected by his people."

Sept. 15, 1708, a committee was chosen to "supply ye pulpit for ye present & for ye coming winter."

Mr. Nicholas Seaver preached regularly till the next February, when he was thanked for his pains and labors among them, and a call for a continuation of the labor, which proposal was declined. He was succeeded by Rev. Richard Brown, and after he preached twenty-four Sabbaths, he was also given a call, but declined. They then purchased "the house for a parsonage where Mr. Rolfe was killed, and invited Mr. Joshua Gardner to settle with them, at a salary of £70 per annum, one-half in good passable money, one-half in merchantable corn at money price, and the use of all of the parsonage, and housing & lands, & meadows."

He was ordained Jan. 11, 1711, but died of consumption March 21, 1715, at the age of twenty-eight years.

During his ministry "he admitted 48 persons, baptized 150, and 17 owned the Covenant." He was eminently distinguished for piety in early life. He became a hopeful subject for divine grace at the age of thirteen years, and soon after began to prepare himself to preach the gospel. He entered Harvard College at the age of sixteen, and graduated at twenty; commenced preaching at the age of twenty-one, and was ordained at twenty-three.

Upon his stone the following epitaph is inscribed, "A good man, betimes, and full of the Holy Ghost and faith, of an excellent temper, of good integrity, having faithfully performed his talents, fell asleep in Jesus, and went triumphantly to receive his Reward in Heaven."

At his death the town voted " to pay the funeral expenses, amounting to thirty pounds and nine shillings and six pence. William White made a journey to Boston to get supplies for the funeral, and among the items of expense was " one Bbl. of Cyder."

After Mr. Gardner's death the church was supplied for four years by Mr. Jonathan Cushing, Robert Stanton, Rev. Joseph Parsons, and Mr. Samuel Chickley, all declining proposals to settle with them, until Mr. John Brown of Little Cambridge (now Brighton) was ordained as their minister, May 13, 1719, and served them until his death, of consumption, after twenty years of ill health, Dec. 2, 1742.

Rev. Edward Barnard, a graduate of Harvard College in 1736, son of Rev. John Barnard of Andover, Mass., and grandson of Rev. Thomas Barnard of Andover, all of whom were graduates of Harvard College, was ordained pastor April 17, 1743, having assisted Mr. Brown during his long illness. He served them successfully thirty-one years, during which time he baptized 908 persons, married 211 couples, 94 persons were admitted to church membership, 96 " owned the Covenant." He died in Haverhill January 26, 1774, aged 54 years.

Rev. Mr. Barnard has been spoken of as a man " of distinction and real worth, his sermons correct and finished, his compositions instructive, plain and practical, and as a watchful, affectionate, and unwearied pastor."

From the cessation of the Indian troubles, in 1709, settlements of land to the east, west or northward were rapidly taken, and in 1712 we find a vote on record, " to abate one-half of the ministry rates of several persons on account of the great distance they lived from the town."

The town of Methuen was set off from the First Parish in 1725, and fifty acres of land given to their first settled minister, Rev. Christopher Sargent, and Oct. 24, 1732, twenty-nine members were given permission to embody themselves into a church body in Salem, N. H., with Rev. Abner Bailey as pastor.

In 1734 the inhabitants of the East or " shad " parish petitioned for a new parish, with Rev. Benjamin Parker as pastor, and in the autumn of that same year Rev. Samuel Bachellor was given forty acres of land, and the West Parish given a parsonage of forty acres more, and seventy-seven members were dismissed to form the West Parish Congregational Church.

The northerly part of Haverhill was erected into a parish originally styled " Church of the North Precinct of Haverhill " in 1728, and a meeting house erected on the spot now occupied by the " North Parish and Plaistow Congregational Church."

The church was organized November 4, 1730, with Rev. James Cushing, a graduate of Harvard College in 1725, son of Rev. Caleb Cushing of Salisbury, Mass., as pastor, with

fifty-nine members, and ten others soon after, from the First
Parish church.

The church was granted on condition "that they should
determine within one month where their meeting house
should be erected, and settle an Orthodox minister as soon
as possible." Many of the members favored the location
near where the "Church of the Holy Angels" at West-
ville, N. H., now stands, as this parish was in the "Haverhill District" of New Hampshire in 1741, and included
Plaistow, Atkinson, and Hampstead, and, when organized,
two-thirds of the members resided north of the meeting
house. Rev. Mr. Cushing was granted twenty-nine acres of
land and rent from the parsonage farm, which was the farm
now owned by Mr. James C. Merrill.

The meeting house in the North Parish was built in 1728
to 1730, and has been described "as built of very heavy
timbers; one of the cross-beams was sufficiently large to be
sawn into quarters to make the upright standards of the
present steeple."

The house was not plastered for years, nor had it a steeple. "The bats and swallows mistook it for a barn," and, it
was said that when Rev. Giles Merrill, successor to Rev.
James Cushing, preached, his children saw the swallows build
their nests on the rafters, and not improbable somewhat
changed the 84th Psalm to suit the occasion, "Yea, the
swallow hath built a nest for herself where she may lay her
young, even thy rafters, O Lord of Hosts."

Rev. Mr. Cushing was ordained on "a day of fasting and
prayer, especially appointed." His ministry continued thirty-
three years, without disturbance to the harmony of the
church, during which time one hundred and sixty-four persons were united with the church, two hundred "owned the
covenant," and twelve hundred and seventy-five infants were
baptized. He married two hundred and twenty-four couples.

He died May 13, 1764, aged fifty-nine years. "He was a

solid and fervent preacher, prudent, steady, patient, condescending and candid, and preserved for thirty-four years the most unruffled tranquility, peace and harmony in the society."

HOUSES FOR PUBLIC WORSHIP, 1733-1902.

In the winter of 1738 a petition was sent to the church at the North Precinct, from twenty-five families who had moved to Timberlane, now Hampstead, "that by reason of the great distance of their dwellings from the meeting house they undergo many and great difficulties in attending the public worship of Almighty God," and asked permission to hold meetings by themselves in the winter season, in a log house probably patterned after the meeting houses of the early Puritans, with its thatched roof of hay or straw, and rough hewn logs for pulpit and seats.

It was built where Daniel Emerson's house now stands They probably hired some neighboring minister to assist them in the service, or carried it on among themselves, until after 1746, when it seems that they laid plans for a more commodious meeting house, which was raised and covered before 1748.

Immediately after the incorporation of the town, in 1749, the building was made more comfortable, "the floors finished, the windows glazed, ends and back of the house clapboarded, the doors made and hung."

Votes as recorded on the town records concerning the finishing of the house, not given on pages 22, 23 and 24 in the Memorial History of Hampstead, Vol. 1, are as follows:—

Feb. 22, 1753, "To see if ye town will consent to paint ye pulpit and front of ye galleries in ye meeting house."

(Deed of the land on which the meeting house stands, see p. 25, Memorial History, Vol. 1.)

April 21, 1761, " to see if ye town will vote to plaister ye meeting house this year." It was voted "to plaister the meeting house over head and under the galleries and on the sides, & that John Muzzey, Dea. Benj. Kimball, John Webster, Wm. Marshall, and Col. Jacob Bailey be a Committee to plaister it." But in March, 1765, it was again voted "to see if ye town will allow the same com. to plaister it, or by a new Comittee."

Again, January, 1768, "it was voted to plaister the meeting house this year," and voted to " call five feet from the side of the pews forward, when the hind seats are now on the men's and women's sides of the Body of the house and to let the highest bidder be the purchaser, and to take such materials of the men that purchase pews as is necessary for plaistering of said house, and that Esq. Webster, Nathan Goodwin, Benj. Little were chosen to be a Com. for the same."

Sales of pews were made as follows:—

March, 1767, "to see if the town will purchase of the proprietors or owners of the pews, and the privilege for a pew in the front gallery, in order to make a number of square pews."

" Know all men by these presents that I Jesse Johnson of Hampstead, in the province of New Hampshire, Gentleman, Do give up to the town of Hampstead all my right interest or property that I have for a privilege for a pue in the meeting house on the men's stairs that was bid of by me sometime past, and that the s'd town may have full power to Dispose of the same as they please as though I had not purchased the same " this 5th day of Dec. 1768."

Apr., 1761, Voted to sell ye pews over the two pairs of stairs."

The following pews were sold by auction March, 1794 :—

" The pews below where the men's seats stand & woman's side."

" The pew at the right hand next to the broad alley before Col Emerson's & Dudley Kimball's to Dudley Kimball."

" Roberts Emerson's pew to John True."

" The pew at the right hand before Abner Rogers pew, to Thomas Hoit."

" The pew at the left hand before Dr. John Bonds pew to Moses Atwood."

Apr. 30, 1788, John Calfe, John Harriman & David Moulton, Selectmen, were authorized to "see if they will agree to purchase the privilege of a long pew in the gallery at the east end of the meeting house, of the present owners, and give up the hindermost seat in addition thereto for room to build square pews at said east end, also to see if they will agree to shorten the long seats so much as to make square pews at the end thereof next to the back side of the meeting house down to the front of the gallery, and if so agreed, to choose a committee to make the sale thereof."

Copy of Deed of Pew No. 3: "Know all men by these presents that I Jabez Holt of Hampstead, in the County of Rockingham and State of New Hampshire—Yeoman—for and in consideration of the sum of Five dollars paid me by Thomas Reed of said Hampstead, Gentleman, do hereby grant bargain and sell, unto him the said Thomas Reed, his heirs and executors, the privilege of a square pew in the east gallery in Hampstead meeting house No. 3, which was bid off by me at a vendue held in said Hampstead for the purpose of selling a number of pews in said meeting house. To have and to hold said granted privilege with all privileges and appurtenances to the same belonging to me."

In witness thereof I have hereunto set my hand and seal this 3d day of May, 1797.

JABEZ HOIT [Seal].

In presence of Micajah Little, Joseph Merrick.

Mr. Tristram Little and Mr. Job Tabor made a measurement of the timbers of the Town House (old meeting house) August 18, 1901, and found the building to be 50 feet long and 40 feet wide. The outside sills are of white oak and eight inches square. The posts are about ten inches square, of white oak; the braces are 7 feet long and 11 inches thick. The beams are of pine and 8 by 12 inches, and 9 1-2 feet in the lower story; the inner posts are twenty-eight feet high by twenty inches square.

About 1792 the meeting house, which "had become decayed and in a wasting condition, and almost without a covering, was repaired partly by subscription, but the arrears were in later years added to the minister's tax by the selectmen.

The porch and steeple were built by Abner Rogers and Col. Thomas Reed in 1793. It is eleven feet square, with posts eighteen inches. The distance from the ground to the bell is forty-eight feet, and from there to the top of the spire is fifty feet. The wooden weather vane which surmounted the top of the spire from 1793 to 1882 was made by Stephen Colby of Haverhill, Mass., under the direction of Daniel Nickols, Sen., and in 1882 was replaced by the present vane.

Moses Little, father of Mr. Tristram Little, went up a rod in 1793, drew up a ladder, confined it, and painted the weather vane after it was placed in position. The chimney was built about 1824.

1745 MEETING HOUSE 1837.

The inside of the house had originally, or in the early years, until 1856, a high pulpit on the north side of the room. a broad aisle leading from the front door directly to it. It was eleven feet from the floor, with winding stairs on the west side of it, and a broad step to the minister's seat. A

sounding board eight feet in diameter, of octagon shape,
overhanging the pulpit and about six feet above it. .

.The deacon's seat was underneath the pulpit and facing
the people. A half round board hung from the deacons' seat
on hinges to form a table, to be used at sacramental seasons
.and town meeting days.

There were three galleries, one in front, one on either end,
with long rows of plank seats about fifteen or twenty feet in
length, the seats in front lower than those near the sides of
the room. In the east and west corners of the room was a
winding stairway leading to the galleries. In the main floor
were several long seats and others box shaped, six or eight

feet square and "three feet stud," with a door fastened with a wooden hasp; some of the square pews had a plank seat on the sides of the pew, also, and would accommodate several persons in a seat.

The pews and galleries had a railing of turned work, about seven inches high, and set about four inches apart, and a narrow rail at the top of the little posts. The pews were deep, and the plank seats in them turned up against the back of the pews, while the people were standing in prayer time, and when "Amen" was said, and as the people were seating themselves again, "click, click, click," was heard for several seconds from all parts of the room until all of the seats fell in place for the worshippers.

There were six pillars, or columns, about twelve feet posts, two under each gallery. They were painted to imitate marble, as was also the front of the pulpit and galleries.

The doors were made of plank and double, with ten panels in each door. Hand-wrought rails were used in the building of both the inside and outside. There was an oval-shaped window at the top, behind the minister's seat, and the other windows were glassed with seven by nine inch glass, sixteen panes in the upper part and twelve in the lower part of the sash. The building was painted for the first time in 1793. The present windows were put in place in 1856.

Stoves were first known about 1790, but did not come into general use for several years. Box stoves for heating churches and school houses were first introduced in 1820. Before that time meeting houses were not heated at all, except such heat as the women carried in their foot stoves.

The following is a copy of the original subscription paper for the purchase of a stove in 1821. It was loaned the writer by the Foote Brothers, formerly of Salisbury, N. H., into whose possession the paper was received several years ago, and will henceforth be deposited in Hampstead Public Library :—

We, the subscribers, believing that a stove for the Meeting-House in this place would conduce to health, as well as the comfort of the community.

Therefore we severally promise to pay the sums afixed to our names for the above object.

N. B.—Should a sufficient sum be subscribed a meeting will be called to which a general invitation will be given to all who subscribe, by a notification at the meeting house and Mr. Isaac Smiths to determine how large a Stove will be necessary and apoint a Committee to purchase the same.

HAMPSTEAD, Dec'r 11, 1821.

Hazen Holt,		$1.50
Joseph Calef,		1.50
Jonathan Collins,		.50
Caleb Emerson,		1.00
John Ordway, Jr.,		1.00
John Ordway,		1.00
Moses Heath,		.75
Jonathan C. Little,		.50
Joseph Chase,		1.00
Isaac Tewksbury,		2.00
Jonathan Page,		.50
David Little,		.50
Thorndike Putnam,		.50
Amassa Eastman,		1.00
Benj. B. Garland,		1.00
Isaac Smith,		1.00
John True,		5.00
Jesse Davis,		1.00
Joshua Eastman,		1.25
James Kimball,		2.50
Jesse Heath,		1.00
Nathaniel Little,		1.00
John Emerson,		1.00
Eliphalet Knight,		1.50
John Kelly,		1.00
Daniel Little,		.50
Stephen Osgood,		1.00
John Little,		.50
Isaac Heath,		3.00
Jesse Gordon,		2.00
Hezekiah Ayer,		1.00
Osgood Taylor,		2.00
James Calef,		

Ralph Brickett,		.50
Isaac Spofford,		.50
Ruth Emerson,		" 0.00 "
Dudley George,		1.00
Henry George,		1.00
Samuel Smith,		1.00
William Tenney,		.50
Joseph Chase,		.50
Ephraim Tewksbury,		.50
Joseph Welch,		2.00
John F. Peabody,		.50
Justus Jones,		.50
James Knight,		1.00
James Brown,		1.00
Enos Brown,		.50
Daniel Brown,		.50
Job Kent,		.50
Jonathan Kent,		1.00
Henry Welch,		1.00
James Brickett,		1.00
Jabez Holt,		.50
John Smith,		.50
Received from J. Eastman's subscribers of last year:		
James Smith,		.25
Osgood Taylor,		.25
Osgood Taylor's sons,		.12
Call on Thorndike Putnam for		1.00
Jonathan Page,		.50
Joseph Chandler,		.25
Lorenzo Batchelder,		.50
Total sum,		$50.37

It would seem from the above paper that some of the people of Hampstead made an effort to procure a stove for their meeting house in 1820, but secured pledges of only two dollars and eighty-seven cents toward one. A stove was obtained early in 1822. Mr. Tristram Little and Joshua F. Noyes well remember the first stove as it stood in their childhood days, as they sat in the old box pews and tried to listen to Father Kelly in the high up pulpit. They inform the writer that the stove stood in front of the pulpit and of the deacons' seat. It was a rough, clumsy box stove, large enough to hold a good sized log. There was then no chimney, and the funnel passed up to the second story and branched in either direction and out of the east and west windows.

In the early days it was customary to place a pan of water holding about six quarts upon the stove. Presumably it was thought necessary to have it there to purify the air from the close heat, but the boys said "some were afraid the infernal thing would blow up."

For an account of the Paul Revere bell which to-day rings from the tower of the town hall, placed in position in 1809, see pages 34 and 162 of Mem. Hist., Vol. 1.

As other denominations claimed the use of the meeting house a part of the time, by right given them by the New Hampshire Legislature, the Congregational Church and Society began controlling their affairs aside from the town March 5, 1832, and soon after set about building their own house for public worship which they occupied for the first time October 15, 1837. The new church stood on the spot where the present church now stands. It was built by Capt. James Gibson at a cost of $3000. It was surmounted by a sort of square tower, instead of a tall steeple. It was built by shares, one hundred of them. It was the opinion of the majority of the shareholders to have the church located where Mr. Andrew M. Moulton's house now is, or on the opposite corner, where No. 2 school house stands, but as one of the shareholders now relates, " by a selfish purpose of one of the committee, the wishes of the majority was overruled, and it was located on the present stand," as the record says, " opposite Major Smith's store."

March 7, 1848, voted, " to secure subscriptions and receive donations to repair the new meeting house, and that Joseph Chase, R. K. Brickett and Benj. Sawyer be a Committee for that purpose."

Feb. 20, 1858, it was voted by the Society to " repair the meeting house in a manner that will be safe for public worship."

March 6, 1860, voted, " to ascertain the feelings of the people in regard to the erection of a new meeting house."

At an adjourned meeting, March 17th, voted, " to have a plank fastened to the beams of the meeting house so they will be passable from one end of the church to the other over the plaistering," and that " notice be given to all pewholders in the house to meet April 21, 1860, to see on what terms they will relinquish their rights for the purpose of rebuilding or repairing the same."

April 1, 1861, about two weeks before the civil war was declared, " On motion of Benj. B. Garland it was voted that the Society consent to have their meeting house taken down or disposed of on consideration that a new and more substantial house be erected on the same site," and that " Joseph Chase, Jonathan Kent, William Sanborn, Nelson Ordway, and Hamilton C. Eastman be a committee to look after the interests of the Society in taking down or disposing of the building."

Dea. William Sanborn and Frederick A. Pike were the committee to move the building back of the present location, which was done while the new church was in progress of building, but later it was taken down and moved to Merrimackport, Mass., where it now is rebuilt in as a part of

CHURCH 1861-1901.

True's mill and factory. The same committee to build the new church, in 1861, by carpenters Richard K. Brickett, foreman, and William B. Yeaton of Haverhill, and other young assistants.

June 22, 1886, Albert H. Little, Charles W. Pressey, and William A. Emerson were chosen a committee, on motion of Dea. Wm. H. Davis, "to proceed to build a vestry according to the plans by the architect."

The chapel, or vestry, was built in 1886, at an expense of

VESTRY.

about $2000, and was dedicated, free from debt, Jan. 27, 1887, at 2 o'clock P. M., "in the presence of a large number of persons, filling the vestry to its utmost capacity." The exercises consisted of a report and address by the pastor, dedicatory prayer by Rev. Charles Tenney of Chester, N. H., and an address by Rev. Nehemiah Boynton of Haverhill, Mass. The exercises were interspersed throughout with music.

"Two interesting episodes of the occasion was the unveil-

ing of a picture of our pastor, Rev. Albert Watson, the gift
of Mrs. Mary A. Eastman and her daughter, Mrs. L. Ada
Libbey of Exeter, N. H., and the presentation of a beautiful
Bible from the North Church in Haverhill, Mass., for use in
the vestry. A bountiful supper was provided and a pleasant
time enjoyed by all." (Church records.)

INTERIOR 1894.

Jan. 1, 1887, "Voted, that the one hundred dollars from
the estate of the late Dr. Isaac Tewksbury be used towards
the expenses of the New Vestry." Voted, that "fifty dollars from the communion collections be used to furnish the
New Vestry, and that Dea. Pressey proceed to furnish it at
once." (Church records.)

The vestry has a neatly furnished audience room, with pulpit and organ, chandeliers, etc.; its walls handsomely frescoed and graced with pictures of several of the pastors; a pastor's study, ladies' parlor, dining room, kitchen, and cupboard well filled with dishes, and other conveniences, making the addition to the church appreciative to all.

The church was struck by lightning in the summer of 1894, and considerable damage done to the steeple and inte-

PULPIT—MEMORIAL DAY, 1901.

rior, which necessitated repairs, and at that time the ceiling and walls were frescoed and painted, etc., taking away the panels at the sides of the pulpit as seen in the cut, etc.

The work done to the interior was not satisfactory to the church and society, and it was resolved to make more improvements, and to do so in connection with the organ committee, who asked and were granted leave Feb. 15, 1901, " to make changes in the interior of the church property as will be necessary to place the new organ back of the pulpit, without expense to the Society."

The work was to begin early in July, 1901. We find recorded on the church records :—

"During a heavy thunder shower on the night of Saturday, June 22, 1901, about one thirty o'clock, the church steeple was struck by lightning, which tore away a portion of the steeple, demolished the south corner of the church, tearing out two or three windows, passing through the entire length of the church into the vestry, and doing considerable damage there.

DAMAGED CHURCH.

The next day we held our services in the town hall. During the following week the Supervisors of the Society were able to adjust the damage with the insurance company. They granted $1600 insurance on the building and $100 on furnishings. The church was then cleared of debris, and work begun on the repairs and changes to the interior."

A steel ceiling and newly frescoed walls by the Ladies' Social Circle, and new shades by the C. E. Society, at a cost of $130. The partitions were removed from between the pews so as to pass from one side of the church to the other without going round ; repairs and improvements costing about $3500.

The steeple of the church was prepared for a bell, and

during the last week of August, 1901, a very musical bell was placed in the steeple of the church and presented to the Congregational Church and Society in "the name of Mrs. Rufus P. Gardner." The gift is much appreciated by church and town people.

The rededication of the church occurred Sunday, Sept. 1, 1901, at 10.45 o'clock A. M.

The following order of exercises were rendered :—

1—Organ Voluntary. Mrs. Frank W. Emerson, organist.
2—Doxology.
3—Invocation, Lord's Prayer.
4—Anthem, "Break forth into joy."
5—Responsive reading.
6—Gloria. Choir and congregation.
7—Scripture reading.
8—Prayer.
9—Response, "I cannot do without the Lord," by the choir.
10—Notices and Offering.
11—Solo, Mrs. Albert H. Little, "New Hampshire Home Song."
12—Hymn No. 61.
13—Sermon by the pastor; text, "The Lord is in his sanctuary."
14—Hymn No. 677.
15—Leader—"To the glory of God our Father, to the honor of Jesus
              Christ our Saviour, to the praise of the Holy Ghost our
              Comforter and Guide,"
    Congregation—"We rededicate this church."
    Leader—"For prayer and praise and ministry of the Word,"
    Con.—"We rededicate this church."
    Leader—"For the spiritual good of the community,"
    Con.—"We rededicate this church."
    Leader—"With gratitude for the memory we cherish of the fathers
              and mothers who have worshipped here."
    Con.—"We rededicate this church."
    Leader—"For whatsoever things are true,
              For whatsoever things are honest,
              For whatsoever things are just,
              For whatsoever things are pure,
              For whatsoever things are lovely,
              For whatsoever things are of good report."
    Con.—"We rededicate this church."
    Leader—"In gratitude and love as an offering of thanksgiving and
              praise."

Choir and Congregation—"Glory be to the Father, and to the Son, and to the Holy Ghost. As it was in the beginning, is now, and ever shall be, world without end. Amen."

16—Dedicatory Prayer, Rev. R. P. Gardner.

The choir, composed of William H. Davis, chorister; Mrs. Frank W. Emerson, organist; Mrs. Albert H. Little, Mrs. Henry W. Tabor, Miss Mary G. Davis, Prof. Forrest E. Merrill, C. Park Pressey and H. Clinton Davis, sang the Dedicatory Hymn, to the tune of Coronation, C. M.

"God of the Universe, to thee
This sacred fane we rear,
And now, with songs and bended knee,
Invoke thy presence here.

Long may this echoing dome resound
The praises of thy name;
These hallowed walls to all around
The triune God proclaim.

Here let thy love, thy presence dwell;
Thy glory here made known;
Thy people's home, Oh come and fill,
And seal it as thine own.

When sad with care, by sin oppressed,
Here may the burdened soul
Beneath thy sheltering wing find rest;
Here make the wounded whole.

And when the last long Sabbath morn
Upon the just shall rise,
May all who own thee here be borne
To mansions in the skies.

The church property, valued at more than $10,000, is not excelled by any church in any New England town of equal inhabitants. Church attendants, as well as the entire people of the community, can look to it with pride and satisfaction.

THE CONGREGATIONAL SOCIETY.

The New Hampshire Observer, published at Portsmouth, N. H., in Vol. X., Nos. 27 and 28, on July 2d and 9th, 1828, printed the following :—

" We, the subscribers, inhabitants of Hampstead, and of the Congregational sect or denomination, do hereby associate and form ourselves into a Society assuming the name and style the Congregational Society in Hampstead, to be known and distinguished in law by that name, and do appoint Isaac Smith clerk of this association or society, and do hereby direct him to procure a book of records for the use of the Society, and to record therein this instrument and our names severally subscribed thereto, and to publish in the New Hampshire Observer, a newspaper published in this county, this instrument of association, in order that we may have the benefits, powers, privileges and immunities specified in an act of the Legislature of the State, passed the 3d day of July, 1827, empowering religious associations to assume and exercise co-operate powers, and in order that we, as a corporation, may provide for the support and maintenance of public worship and publick instruction in religion and morality, and for that purpose receive donations, devices, and bequeaths, and raise all necessary monies, and for the purpose, also, of managing any real estate now held by the Congregational Society in Hampstead, or held by any person or body politic for our benefits, or for the purpose of managing any property bequeathed to the Congregational Church and Society in said Hampstead, and that there may be a legal meeting of the Society hereby formed we do hereby authorize Jesse Gordon, Esq., Mr. James Calef and Dea. Jona. Kent, or either of them, to call the first meeting."

" Witness our hands at Hampstead, the twenty-fourth day of December, A. D., 1827. John Emerson, Ralph Brickett, Joseph Chase, Caleb Emerson, John Ordway, Joseph Welch, Joseph Calef, Jonathan Little, Benjamin Garland, James Calef, Isaac Smith, Jona. C. Little, Jona. Kent, Jesse Gordon, Nath'l Little, Isaac Tewksbury, William Tenny, John Currier, Jesse Davis, David D. Irving, Joseph Chase, Jr., James Brickett, Jesse Heath, John Ordway, Jr., John Little, Smith Goodwin, Jona. George, Josiah Webster, Nathan Hadley, Joseph Johnson, Isaac Heath, David Little, Amasa Eastman, Joseph French, Oliver Worthen, Abiel Ordway, Henry George, Samuel Nichols, Henry Welch, Clark Noyes, Humphrey C. Cogswell, Daniel Brown, Benjamin B. Garland Joshua Eastman, Phineas C. Balch, Joshua Eastman, Jr., James Brickett, Jr., Hezekiah Ayer, James Gibson, Jesse Ayer.

Subscribing to this association in later years are the names of :—

Moses Heath, Jonathan Wadleigh, James Durgin, Richard K. Brickett, Thomas Kent, John W. Emerson, Jacob Irving, Benjamin Sawyer, Jabez T. Howard, Isaiah Moody, Lyman Worthen, John Gordon, David Irving, Moody H. Brickett, John Heath, William Sanborn, Dudley George, Nelson Ordway, Nath'l C. Smith, John D. Ordway, Francis J.

Stevens, John C. Drew, Henry Putnam, J. Chase Eastman, John S. Titcomb, Rufus C. Smith, Francis H. Sawyer, Fred T. Kent, Linus L. C. Little, Giles F. Marble.

The first meeting of the Society was held in the meeting house Sept. 22, 1828, with Jesse Gordon, moderator, Isaac Smith, clerk, when it was voted " to sell all of the real estate belonging to John True, Esq., deceased, provided that the widow, Anna True, receive but four and a half per cent. per annum during her natural life on the sum of four thousand dollars that shall be due to the Congregational Society in Hampstead, agreeable to the last will and testament of John True," and voted, " to authorize John Emerson, executor of said Will and Testament, to sell the real estate."

March 19, 1859, a committee—Henry Putnam, Benj. B. Garland and Nelson Ordway—were chosen a committee to report on By-Laws, as follows in part, since revised :

ART. 1. The annual meeting of the Society shall be holden on the first Tuesday of March for the choice of officers and the transaction of other business as may be deemed necessary.

ART. 2 (1902). The officers of the Society shall be a Clerk, three Supervisors, Treasurer, and Trustee and Collector, all of whom shall hold their offices until the next annual meeting and until others are chosen and qualified in their stead, etc., etc.

The names of the members who have subscribed to the foregoing By-Laws are as follows :—

Jona. Kent, Joshua Eastman, Benj. B. Garland, Joseph Chase, Benj. Sawyer, William Sanborn, L. L. C. Little, Nelson Ordway, N. C. Smith, Rufus C. Smith, John C. Drew, Beniah Titcomb, Alvah Alexander, Wm. H. Davis, Francis H. Sawyer, John S. Titcomb, Geo. O. Jenness, Perley H. Shannon, Eliphalet K. Heath, Simon Merrill, J. Chase Eastman, Henry Putnam, Moody H. Brickett, Jesse E. Emerson, Nathan Johnson, Daniel H. Emerson, I. Wm. George, Horace R. Sawyer, Henry C. Little, George E. Merrill, John Jackson, Amos Buck, George W. Eastman, Oliver Putnam, Alfred P. Emerson, Caleb Moulton, Daniel L. Sawyer, Calvin Robinson, Albert Robinson, John H. Clark, Lorenzo Frost, John C. Little, Jacob Irving, Wm. H. Brickett, Silas W. Tenney, C. W. Williams, D. W. George, Alden E. Pillsbury, Jos. G. Brown, Moses B. Little, J. Wm. Sanborn, C. W. Pressey, A. Wm. Griffin, Wm. A. Emerson,

John S. Corson, Rufus H. Bailey, E. W. Foss, Loren M. Chase, Myron P. Dickey, Francis W. Coker, John W. Garland, Orren E. Follansbee, Albert L. Eastman, Charles W. Garland, John W. Tabor, Eben Hoyt, Albert H. Little, John C. Sanborn, Jesse B. Shirley, George G. Williams, Charles H. Emerson, Carlton Barns, W. Amos Fitts, R. C. McNiel, John E. Mills, Albion D. Emerson, Forrest E. Merrill, Charles H. Sweet, Henry L. Eastman, Will S. Griffin, Calvin A. Merrick, Elmer E. Lake, Clarence L. Sawyer, Bradley N. Haynes, Albert E. Haynes, Amasa W. Hunt, Geo. A. F. Picard, Henry W. Tabor.

Officers of the Society, 1902:

Moderator—John S. Corson.
Clerk—Forrest E. Merrill.
Treasurer—James W. Sanborn.
Trustee—Charles W. Garland.
Auditor—John S. Corson.
Supervisors—William A. Emerson, W. Amos Fitts, John S. Corson.

PARSONAGES.

The proprietors of Haverhill gave the inhabitants of "Timberlane" a tract of land for "ye first settled minister in the place." This tract of land was situated on the road which leads from Andrew M. Moulton's to Wadleigh Corner. Troubles arose about the land. April 21, 1753, it was voted "to choose a committee to prosecute Thomas Haynes of Haverhill, to final judgment and Execution, for encroaching on ye parsonage land that was given by the proprietors of Haverhill to Timberlane, or any one who shall hereafter trespass on said parsonage land."

August 18, 1753, voted, "to see if ye town will choose a committee to join with Rev. Mr. True in making a division of ye parsonage, pursuant to ye vote of ye town."

Aug. 31, 1753, Voted, "that Mr. Hazzen, Nathaniel Heath, & John Webster be a committee to divide ye parsonage land, pursuant to ye vote of ye town."

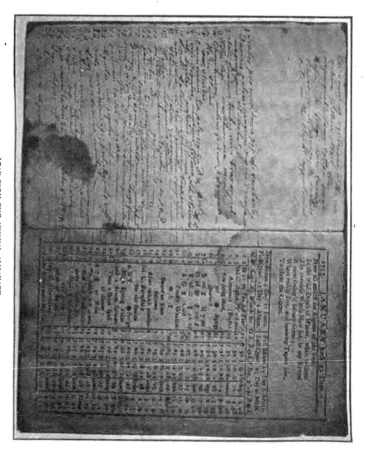

LEAF FROM THE JOURNAL ALMANACK.

Dec. 25, 1853, Voted, "that Lieut. Morse, Capt. Copp, & John Hunkins be a Committee to agree with Flavius Harris of Haverhill, with respect to ye parsonage land that belongs to ye town & the Rev. Mr. True, if they can agree on reasonable terms, or to leave the matter to Referees."

Rev. Mr. True sold his right in the parsonage land at that time for a small sum to Flavius Harris, who, it is said, "made a profitable investment for his money."

Tradition says that Rev. Mr. Phillips and Rev. Mr. Parker and other preachers, when they supplied the church in Hampstead before 1752, made their homes where Mr. Charles Damon now resides, as did also Rev. Henry True from June, 1752, to the spring of 1753, when he became owner of a piece of land where Francis Merrick's house stood, which was burned in 1879.

The Journal Almanac of Rev. Mr. True, in 1753, has recorded in the first line entry in Latin, on January 1st, "Trobes pro mea domo populi secabante," which may be translated to read, "The people cut the timbers for my house." It would seem that the people of Hampstead held a sort of a "Bee" for the purpose of preparing a house for the new minister, to be in readiness for his bride in the following season.

In 1767 Rev. Mr. True built the house now the residence of Francis H. Sawyer, where he lived until his death.

April 22, 1783, Voted, "to sell ye parsonage lands lying in Hampstead, and all other common lands in s'd town, and to choose a Committee to ascertain the bounds of ye parsonage meadow." Major Mooer, Capt. Hezekiah Hutchens and Benjamin Emerson, Jr., were the committee to expend the money arising from the sale aforesaid, and it was voted that "it be appropriated and laid out towards purchasing a place or building spot near the meeting house in Hampstead, suitable for a Gospel minister that may be settled over the church and people, as a parsonage for the use of said minister."

REV. MR. TRUE'S HOUSE, 1767.

The town sold the parsonage lands and purchased the farⁱ " of thirty-five acres, with house and barn on it," which now the farm of Mr. Charles H. Ranlett.

In 1852 the town expended the money, six hundred do lars, arising from the sale of the farm above, for removinⁱ the old pulpit and pews in the old meeting house and makinⁱ a more convenient room for town purposes, and in buildinⁱ the floor to the upper story and fitting up the room for thⁱ use of the Methodists and other denominations, and fo social purposes.

"BRICK HOUSE" AS PARSONAGE.

The parsonage farm became out of repair and unfit foⁱ the use of Rev. Mr. Kelly and his family, and the town noⁱ agreeing to repair it, Rev. John Kelly built for his owⁱ use, with the help of two hundred and three dollarⁱ from friends of the church, in 1808, the house now occupieⁱ by Mrs. Emeline E. Mooer and A. Sydney Little. Here Rev Mr. Kelly lived till his death in 1848. The income of thⁱ parsonage farm was given him " through his natural life."

Rev. J. M. C. Bartley resided during the first years of hiⁱ pastorate where Mr. Orren B. Ranlett now resides, a shorⁱ time where Andrew M. Moulton resides, and later in the brick house known as " Cogswell house," now owned by Dea. C. W. Pressey, houses hired for the use of the minister as a parsonage.

June 4, 1859, it was voted that " the committee chosen to see about a parsonage house report at the next meeting," and July 9, 1859, that " R. K. Brickett, William Sanborn, and Moody H. Brickett be a committee to circulate a paper which B. B. Garland has drawn up to see how much money can be

JACOB TOWNSEND RESIDENCE.

raised towards building a parsonage House to be owned by the Society." Rev. Mr. Pratt at first resided at the present Jacob Townsend residence, which he purchased for himself; and later in the " Brick house."

June 3, 1870, it was voted " to choose a committee to see about procuring a parsonage. Joseph Chase, Nathaniel C. Smith and Amos Buck were the committee, and reported that they had looked at a number of places. June 24, 1870, the committee were empowered to build or purchase, as they thought best.

The committee purchased the farm now the residence of Dr. E. E. Lake, which was occupied by Rev. Mr. Bullard during his pastorate, and also by Rev. Mr. Watson.

The parsonage was then purchased, much through the liberality of Dea. Joseph Chase.

RESIDENCE OF DR. LAKE.—PARSONAGE, 1870 TO 1893.

Oct. 4, 1893, voted, " to purchase the 'Emerson lot' for a new parsonage, and that Dea. C. W. Pressey, John C. Sanborn and John H. Clark be a committee to act as building committee."

The present parsonage was built in 1893, and occupied by Rev. Mr. Gardner from the beginning of his pastorate.

PARSONAGE, BUILT 1893.

RECORDS OF PASTORATES, COVENANTS, ETC.

The church was organized June 3, 1752, with sixty-eight members, who subscribed their names to the following:—

THE CHURCH COVENANT.

We, the subscribers, apprehending ourselves called to unite as Christian Brethren in a particular church in this Place, that we may be built as such on the foundation of the Apostles and Prophets, J. Christ himself being the Corner Stone, do now profess in the Presence of God and his holy Angels his Ministers and People in this Assembly.

That we taking the holy Scriptures called the Bible, to be the rule of our Faith and Practice, believe as followeth; namely, That there is one God, the Maker of Heaven and Earth whose Name is Jehovah revealing himself under the Mysterious Relation of Father, Son and holy Ghost.

And as there is one God so there is one Minister between God and man, the man Christ Jesus, no other than the only begotten of the Father, made flesh, born of the Virgin Mary, who by his Life, Death, Resurrection and Ascension into Heaven, has made way for our Salvation, and from thence he shall come again to Judge the Quick and the Dead.

And that some of the Children of fallen Adam were in Christ chose to Salvation, from the foundation of the world, that they might be delivered from the miseries of the Apostacy, received to the favor of God forfeited thereby, through the everlasting righteousness of Christ, of Christ which is the sole meritorious cause of our Sanctification and acceptance in the sight of God, and preserved in their weak and infirm state by Almighty grace to the Kingdom of Heaven.

That the offers of this Salvation, containing the forgiveness of sin, the Resurrection of the Body and Life everlasting are made to all the members of the holy Catholick Church, that are within the Covenant of grace even Jews and Gentiles as many as are Called. The promise whereof is unto them and their children, and that in a union to Christ our Head, and surely there is a special Communion of Saints, both with God and one another, which is highly promoted in the fellowship of Particular Churches.

And that we may practice according to our holy Rule, we would now in the most devout manner adoring the Divine grace and Condesention

(40)

In taking us into Covenant humbly lay hold on the great Promise thereof through Christ that God Almighty will be a God to every one of us, and to our Seed after us in their generations, and freely Comfort for ourselves and them to be his People forever. And as we have been Taught, and bound by the seals of this Covenant, we will sincerely endeavor to observe all things, whatsoever Christ has Commanded.

And whereas by this Covenant we are in fellowship with the Universal Church, we being all Baptized into one Body, and having been made all to drink unto one spirit, we profess with them to worship God in the Spirit, to rejoice in Christ Jesus, and to have no Confidence in the Flesh, and in our Personal Conduct and Communion with them in all relations, we would walk worthy of the vocation, wherewith we are Called, in all lowliness and in Love endeavoring to keep the unity of the Spirit in the bond of Peace, for there is one Body and one spirit even as we are Called in one hope of our calling.

More particularly. In our personal conduct exercising ourselves we have always a confidence void of offence, towards God and towards man, walking circumspectly not as fools but as wise, and as he who has Called us holy, seeking to be holy in the manner of conversation, not rendering evil to any man, but as we have opportunity doing good unto all men, especially unto them that are of the household of faith.

And in all Political relations, whether domestical, civil or ecclesiastical, to adorn the Doctrine of God and Saviour in all things according as his Grace has appeared unto all men teaching us that designing ungodliness and worldly lusts we should Live soberly, righteously and godly, in the present world. Walking in our Houses agreeably to the Covenant of marriage and the Parental Covenant; resolving that as for us and our Houses we will serve the Lord, Praying together and also instructing and Commanding our children and household to keep the way of the Lord.

And under our civil rulers Living quiet and peaceable Lives in all godliness and Honesty, Rendering to all their dues, Tribute to whom tribute is due, Custom to whom Custom, fear to whom Fear, Honour to whom Honour, to owe no man anything, but to love one another. Praying for the peace of Jerusalem, because they shall prosper that love her. Looking not every man at his own things, but every man also at the things of others.

And in the House of our God, keeping the Ordinances of all things, as delivered to us by Christ and his Apostles, not forsaking the assembling ourselves together, but religiously attending on all Parts of Instituted Worships, whether in the ministry of the Word, or Prayer and praises or in Baptism and the Lord's Supper.

And whereas we are Called to fellowship in a particular Church, wherein we are now to be united, in one Body to maintain a special government within our assembly to which end they have chosen together with us a Pastor, to be over us in the Lord, and admonish us, we promise together as a Church as far as in us lies, that all things shall be done decently and in order with charity unto Edifying, that publick sensures be inflicted on disorderly members, according to the Laws of Christ, for the Destruction of the Flesh, that the spirit may be saved in the Day of the Lord Jesus; And as Bretheren we promise each one for ourselves, that we will not any of us hate our Brother in our hearts, but in any wise rebuke our neighbor and not suffer sin upon him, yet if a man be overtaken in a fault we which are spiritual will restore him with a spirit of meekness, Considering himself lest he also be tempted.

Bearing one anothers Burden and so fulfilling the Law of Christ, even the Law of Charity which covereth a multitude of sins, and in faults that deserve reproof when our Brother trespasses against any one of us, he will go and tell him of his fault alone, that he may gain his Brother, but if he refuse to hear him then take with him one or two more, that in the mouth of two or three witnesses every word may be established and if he refuse to hear them tell the church, and if he hear not the church he shall be unto him as a Heathen and a Publican.

And if there be among us any wicked person polluting the Society we will not be wanting to cast out the old leaven that we may be a new Lump. We will not keep company if any man is Called a Brother, be a fornicator or Covetous, or an Idolitar, or a Railer, or a Drunkard, or an Extortioner, with such an one in our Assembly not to enter.

Shall we not Judge them that are within? and Cast out every wicked person and withdraw from every Brother that walketh disorderly as a busy Body, note that man has no Company with him that he may be ashamed, yet count him not as an enemy but admonish him as a Brother.

And on the other hand when such an offending person shall after censure be sorry unto repentance, then contrary wise we will one and all forgive and Comfort him because sufficient to such is this punishment inflicted of many.

Finally as members of the flock as we shall stand related to our Pastor, we will obey him as having the Rule, and submit ourselves because he shall watch for our souls, as one that must give an account that he may do it with joy and not with grief esteeming him very highly in Love for his works sake, counting an Elder that ruleth well to be worthy of double Honour, especially one that Laboreth with Word and Doctrine for the Scripture, sayeth the Labourer is worthy of his Reward.

To this Covenant we have set our Hands and thus binding ourselves to the Lord, we may keep his Covenant, remembering his Commands to do them that he may establish us a holy People to himself.

Rev. Henry True was ordained June 24, 1752. Rev. Edward Barnard of Haverhill preached the ordination sermon, which was printed as follows :—

"Goodness consider'd as an eminent qualification of a Christian Minister."

"In a sermon preached at the ordination of the Rev. Henry True"

"To the pastorate of the church in Hampstead, in the Province of New Hampshire. June 24, 1752,"

"By Edward Barnard, A. M., Pastor of the Church in Haverhill, Mass."

ORDINATION SERMON.

Acts xi. 24: "For he was a Good Man."

The wisdom of God scarce in anything appears more than raising up persons peculiarly qualified to pronounce the special purposes of his grace. And men never act a juster part than when they engage themselves readily, or employ others in the particular business for which their talents seem most adapted. Such reflections naturally arise from the character of Barnabas in the text, in connection with the context.

The sacred historian in the preceding verses informs us of the happy effect of the fiery Tyral, which came on at Jerusalem, when Stephen was stoned. It tended to the furtherance of the Gospel, through the pious labors of some Christians and the supply of the Spirit of their ascended Lord. For as Christ advised his disciples, when they were persecuted in one city, to flee to another, so many who resided in this seat of blood retired to different places and preached the Gospel to the Jewish inhabitants. At length some natives of Cyprus and Cyrene, having ('tis probable) heard the story of Peter's receiving Cornelius, though a Gentile, into the communion of the church, ventured to preach Jesus Christ to the heathen at Antioch, and to invite them to partake of the blessings of the purchase. This application was followed with a signal success ; a great number believed and turned to the Lord. An event so remarkable in itself, and so favorable to the Christian cause, soon came to the ears of the church at Jerusalem, which seemed to have the care of Christians, particularly lying upon them while in a loose unincorporated state.

Full of grateful surprise at such an unexpected revolution on behalf of Christianity, they concerted measures to forward the good work, and immediately sent Barnabas, one of their body, as the most suitable.

In pursuance of this great end he journeyed for Antioch, and having reached the city he was abundantly rejoiced to see the grace of God in bringing them to the knowledge of Himself and Son, and exhorted them all, that with full purpose of heart they would cleave unto the Lord, for (says the text) he was a good Man, and full of the Holy Ghost and of faith.

He was possessed of a firm and unshaken belief in Christ and the new dispensation which was setting up, grounded upon clear and copious views of the excellency and evidence of both. He was endowed with the graces of the Holy Spirit, which was connected with faith, and the extraordinary gifts which in that day were communicated to believers. Being thus fully persuaded of the truth, and experiencing so largely the advantages of Christianity, he could not but earnestly press upon them steadfastness in their profession. He was a man of benignity, too; his disposition was very kind, and therefore he rejoiced in the prospect of their present and future happiness through the grace of God manifested to them.

Goodness oftentimes in Scripture signifies the special virtue of benevolence. Thus the good man is opposed to the righteous, and goodness is enumerated with righteousness and truth in original terms, the same with the text. So that we may well understand this description of Barnabas to denote, not so much his general moral qualities, as that he was one of a sweet and gentle disposition.

A celebrated writer upon this passage supposes that the Church of Jerusalem pitched upon Barnabas rather than another to repair to Antioch because they imagined the softness of his temper would indispose him to lay any unnecessary burdens of the malice law upon these new converts. Whether they had this particular thought or not, it is certain that in a

more general view they consulted the happiest method to promote the interests of religion among those who were strangers
to it, or had just embraced it, by sending one who would in the
best manner recommend it.

Although the state of the gospel in that early age and the sit
uation of affairs at Antioch might render it specially that a
minister should shine in an eminency of goodness, yet it is a
virtue of vast moment to a person in that office, in every age and
past of the Christian church, and fit to be considered at all
times, most of all upon such an occasion as that of this day.
Here, then, I will attempt:—

I. To illustrate briefly the virtue pointed out in the text.
And then,

II. To show the importance of it on the Christian minister.

In the first place, then, let me briefly illustrate the virtue
pointed out in the text.

This is goodness, which imparts the propensity or inclination
of the soul towards every being who can justly attract it, particularly mankind. It appears in a diversity of lights, agreeable
to the different circumstances of the objects it regards and the
modes of the operation in and upon the passions, and is accordingly variously denominated.

Does it respect the miserable ? Then it flows in compassion.
Are those who are the subjects of it happy ? Then it issues in
a generous satisfaction and delight. Does it meet with provoca-
tion ? It allays a turbulent passion and becomes mildness and
gentleness to the offender, or patience and forgiveness. Considered in relation to near societies is brotherly kindness, but a
reaching forth on a larger extent it is charity.

Goodness is not merely a natural good humor, but a religious
temper. It does not consist only in the original turn of the
mind or a peculiar discipline of the animal frame, but arises
from the principles of the reason and Christianity. The former
being accidental, can scarce be called virtuous; the latter being
matter of choice, is so.

As we are understanding beings, it is fitted that we should be
actuated by the arguments of actual religion to this virtue; and
as we are under the Christian dispensation that we should be

influenced by the additional motives of that. Nor can we be justly deemed the true subjects of either if we have no regard to them.

Goodness is expressly denominated the fruit of the Spirit. It is a production of a divine agent suggesting to and impressing upon the mind such truths as are incentives thereto.

From this representation of it it is plain that it is not an unmanly softness, melting the soul and betraying it, a criminal easiness of conduct, nor blind, disproportionate affection towards all objects alike, or most towards the meanest, or preferring a lower measure of our neighbor's good, or that which is greatly superior. Nor is it a high flush of passion upon sudden good fortune, or an occasional sprightliness of spirit. In opposition to all this, it is a solid disposition exerting itself in an exact conformity to the dictates of judgment and a permanent habitual frame of mind.

But though we thus distinguish between a natural and moral goodness, yet the former is not an apt foundation for, and doubtless is very often connected with an eminency in the later. For it seems at least highly presumable that where God is pleased to set home divine truth upon a tender soul, there will be greater proficiency in goodness than the like operation on another more rigid. Falling into the natural track of the softer powers, it meets with less obstruction than in a more hard and selfish mind, and makes swifter conquest, while this same native temper is refined and sublimated into gracious.

But I hasten to the other general head.

II. To show the importance of this grace or virtue to a Christian minister.

This we may do by two or three considerations. As,

1. Goodness is peculiarly encumbent upon a Christian minister, in respect to his character as an ambassador of Jesus Christ and a preacher of his gospel.

As an ambassador of Christ it is the utmost propriety that he be a good man; yea, an absolute necessity, in order with any consistency with his profession.

Though our Lord Jesus was possessed with universal virtue, yet in none did he shine more illustrious than goodness. All the days of his public ministry were filled with a thousand instances of benevolence. What love and compassion did he breathe in all his discourses? How did he testify it in all his conduct? He went about doing good to the bodies of men by healing all manner of diseases; to their souls by preaching the doctrines of the kingdom of heaven; and in a variety of pungent addresses endeavoring to bring sinners under his wings. And to crown all, he poured out his soul unto death, and offered himself upon the cross an oblation for our offences. An amazing act of grace this! which was thought worthy by perfect wisdom of perpetual memorial by a standing ordinance in the church, and which is an endless source of the most elevated ascriptions to the Lamb from the various orders of glorified spirits throughout the immense regions of light.

Now Christ is a pattern for all Christians in all periods of time, for he has left us an example that we should follow his steps. But his ministers are under superior obligations to imitate him in this divine virtue, as they are brought nearer to him by relation and communion than others. Do they represent his person? how absurd is this without a remembrance of his temper. Are they his peculiar servants? how odious is the appellation without a conformity to his image. Agreeably we find our Lord exhorting his apostles to condescending goodness by his example. Whosoever will be great among you, let him be your minister, and whosoever will be chief among you let him be your servant; even as the Son of Man came not to be ministered unto, but to minister, and to give his life a ransom for many.

From the character of Christ let us proceed to his gospel, and we shall find it a powerful argument for goodness in a minister as he is a preacher of it. This is a dispensation of grace, and it proclaims peace on earth, good will towards men. The glad tidings it brings by introducing joy and gratitude tends to calm every rougher passion and to put the whole soul into an easy, gracious temper; besides that, the love of God therein displayed is the strongest obligation upon us to love one another.

And then, further, it is the law of love, and presses upon us a new commandment, even that we exercise charity, much fuller and clearer and by more cogent measures than by any religious scheme before. So that upon all these accounts it is in a very singular and extraordinary manner calculated to promote goodness, and in the loudest and most peremptory language demands it.

A coldness and indifference, therefore, unto men, is a great and obvious incongruity in any professor of the gospel, most of all in the minister of it. Does he publish the news of salvation as master of great joy, yet does a sullen, uneasy temper deform his brow? Does he urge his hearers to look to the things of others, because of the kind aspect of the gospel upon them, yet is he of a stingy spirit; does he insist upon goodness as a necessary subjection to the Christian religion, yet is he impatient or vindictive? What a palpable contradiction is this! In what a monstrous light must such a minister appear!

II. Goodness is of vast consequence to a minister's usefulness. And this considered in a larger or more limited view.

I. Goodness renders a minister extensively serviceable. A contracted mind is fitted only for a narrow sphere, and is oftentimes confined within it. But the generous soul, like the sun, scatters blessings far and wide, and sends a copious influence.

A good minister adorns the doctrine of God, and proposes it in the most attractive light. His temper disinclines him to embrace the extreme of any controversy in religion, nor will he form his notions by the little rules of bigotry. Much less will he make the gospel an engine of contention, and be fond of bickering about such things as are hard to be understood, well remembering the apostle's instructions to Timothy, that the servant of the Lord must not needlessly strive, but be gentle towards all men. He abhors persecution even in the lowest forms, and maintains the least molestation for religious sentiments to be unwarrantable where they are not inconsistent with the rights of society. He persists not upon a precise uniformity in doctrine or manner of worship in order to his kind regards, but readily discharges the offices of humanity to such as differ most widely from him, and joins in sacred fellowship with those who profess and practice nothing incompatible with the being and happiness of a Christian, or the regular exercise of social acts of worship, endeavoring to keep the unity of spirit in the bonds of peace. In short, a generous temper runs through every branch of his conduct. He is given to hospitality, and his heart and house are open to every worthy guest so far as is consistent with his worldly circumstances and the duties of his station. He shows mercy to the distressed by his personal benefactions, according to his ability, and in stirring up others to be rich in good works; by this means upholding the fatherless, comforting the widow, clothing the naked, feeding the hungry, and becoming in a vast variety of respects a minister of God for good.

Hence he holds forth the Word of Life, in its original colors, as a system calculated to sweeten men's tempers and soften their manners. The religion of Jesus being thus delineated in its native attire, looks glorious and lovely, and can scarce fail of obtaining much influence over the heart of mankind. Such a clergyman must appear to the warmest unbeliever at least unworthy of the severe imputations cast upon the priesthood, and he will be ready to deem the religion which he inculcates and lives as worthy to be true, if it is not really, while those of weaker prejudices, not being able to resist so many charms, fully and cheerfully embrace Christianity, and give themselves up to its excellent dictates.

A good minister promotes the Kingdom of Christ in general by encouraging the hearts and strengthening the hands of those in the same order with himself.

He is so far from magnifying every small mistake in his brother to a fundamental and dangerous error, that though he wishes they might all think the same things, yet he willingly bears with a different judgment and embraces him as his fellow-laborer (finding in him a serious temper and godly life), and esteems him as acceptable to Christ, and worthy to be esteemed by man, and says with the apostle, Whereunto we have attained let us walk by the same rule, let us mind the same thing.

As he indulges no unreasonable suspicions concerning his brother, so he insinuates none in the minds of his people, nor fulfils prejudice or heightens disaffection by exposing failings in private conduct, or exaggerating such as have been observed in public, which are reconcilable with integrity. Well knowing how dear every man's reputation is to him and what weight a minister's is to his usefulness, he studiously endeavors to confirm and increase it.

He will not invade another's charge to serve a cause of a party, or gratify a spirit of curiosity or malignity, but rather reprove such as are restless and uneasy under their pastor, who is faithful to his post, and assiduously labor to recover their affections to him, being conscious that this must tend much more to the good of those souls committed to his sacred care than any single ministration of his own under those disadvantageous circumstances.

In fine, the good minister is ready at all times to counsel and advise his brethren under difficulties, and assist in all exigencies.

Goodness multiplies a minister's opportunities of service by turning the eyes of societies upon him under embarrassments. He will be sought to for the repairing breaches, cementing parties, and restoring unity. Men even of impetuous tempers will find the necessity of calling in the mild and pacifick to heal the disorders which their wrath hath occasioned.

But I proceed to say, a goodness is of eminent advantage to a minister's usefulness among his own flock.

Here his chief business lies, and here his virtue is chiefly to be exerted. Let me be somewhat particular in the consideration of this head.

1. Goodness is a powerful incentive to continued diligence in his work. "The soul, considered abstractively from its passions, is slow in its resolves, and languishing in its executions. But the passions stir it up to action in forcing the will and making the whole man more vigorous in the prosecution of his designs.' Now goodness being attended with a desire of the happiness of its object, must stimulate to go through the hardest duties, and to surmount the greatest obstacles to accomplish it, especially where nothing less than a blessed eternity depends upon its efforts. Many waters cannot quench this love, nor floods drown it ; and a minister whose bosom glows with this flame will spend and be spent for souls. But it is further to be considered that goodness engrosses other passions in its cause, particularly fear

and hope, two mighty springs of action. The former takes an alarm at every danger of a soul's miscarrying in the important affairs of salvation, the latter gives vivacity to the spirits in every prospect of refusing it from death, or carrying it on to sublimer heights of virtue. Both combine to waft the minister forward in his business and to prompt him to the discharge of his errand with unwearied ardor.

2. Goodness inclines the minister to the best methods of promoting religion.

Hereby will he be incited to treat chiefly upon such subjects in his publick preaching wherein the generality of Christians are agreed, and with which the salvation of souls is most intimately connected. The great and substantial things which are the most frequent subject of the Word of God will be oftenest insisted upon in his discourses. It will refrain him from making the pulpit a theatre of war. And when, in the course of his teaching, he handles such points as he judges subservient to godliness, but have been understood in a different sense, he will do it in so calm and rational a way as may enlighten, without exasperating. This will engage him to press the conditions of the gospel covenant and duties of the Christian religion with life and fervency. Being touched with the coal from the altar, and burning with love to souls, he will set the arguments of Revelation in the most moving light he is capable, and represent them in all the language of perfection, and speak with the tongue of a seraph, sent on an embassy from heaven.

As he is to go before his people in the administration of discipline, goodness will cause him solicitously to labor, that it be not attended with unnecessary rigor, and that nothing of a vindictive nature intermix itself therewith. He will be concerned that such a degree of tenderness be exercised with ecclesiastical censure as shall bid fair to impress it upon the heart of the offender, and recover him to a godly sorrow and amendment of life.

This virtue renders him easy of access at all times. It throws off anything haughty, severe, or any ways forbidding, and invites the burdened heart to open its nearest concern and discharge its grief.

This will not suffer him to become a party to civil broils where he can possibly escape ; yet will it put him upon the office of a peacemaker, from an abhorrence of contention and a prospect of its retarding the success of his ministry.

Do errors arise ? This will incline him to instruct in meekness those who oppose themselves, if peradventure God will give them repentance, in the acknowledgment of the truth, and that they may recover themselves out of the snare of the devil who are led captive by him at his will.

This will not allow him to hate his brother in his heart by neglecting to reprove him ; yet where the fault and the temper require it, he will of choice discharge the duty with so much meekness of wisdom as to render the rebuke a real kindness and like an excellent oil.

In sum, this disposes the minister to speak a suitable word to weary souls. To encourage the despondent sinner to pursue his highest welfare, and wait upon God to fulfil the good pleasure of his goodness, " to revive the spirit of the contrite and heal the broken in heart," to dispense needed support to the afflicted, the good minister is a son of consolation, and delights to give it to fit subjects. His tongue drops manna ; he can't use harshness and severity with the trembling and bowed down ; he overlooks weakness, despises not the day of small things, but cultivates what is good, even as his Master brake not the bruised reed and quenched not the smoking flame.

3. Goodness conciliates the respect and affection of a people to their minister, which is an happy foundation for the success of his labor.

When this virtue is exercised with judgment it gives a dignity to a character, as well as beauty, and nothing in the whole circle of Christian graces yields so bright a lustre, or seizes or draws the mind with such irresistible power. A minister, therefore, who hath in this manner captivated his audience, is in the best condition to do them real service. Their ears are open to take the whole counsel of God ; their attention to it is doubled ; every word comes with its due emphasis. Then, if ever, may we expect they will give divine truths their proper weight, and receive into their souls the engrafted Word which is able to save them.

Thus largely have I considered the tendency of goodness to a minister's usefulness. I might now go on to show:

3. That a minister's comfort much depends upon and is promoted by goodness.

It secures him greatly from enemies and gains him friends. It keeps his mind serene under the difficulties of his post, and the opposition and reproach he may sometimes meet with in the conscientious discharge of his duty. It qualifies him to taste the true pleasures of society, while a consciousness of it in his course of ministerial action is a spring of continual high satisfaction. But I hasten to add:

4. Goodness is of great importance to the glorious rewards of a minister.

The exercise of the various offices of love is effectual to true religion. Nor are there any greater commandments than those which respect it. But it is those only who do the will of God from the heart that shall enter into the kingdom of heaven. This is not only necessary by the wise appointment of God, but in the nature of the thing, particularly with respect to the virtue before us.

For love is a constituent of the happiness of the kingdom of glory, which results very much from the blissful society there. So whoever has no affection to intelligent beings here cannot enjoy them there. Goodness, therefore, is absolutely requisite to a minister in his special work, in order to his giving up his account with joy and participating in the blessedness of the upper world, reserved for the peculiar servants of Christ. For this is an universal principle, and leads men to a diversity of duties agreeable to the calls of Providence and their character. In consequence it is as encumbent upon a minister that he performs the peculiar business assigned him under the habitual influence of goodness, in order to the rewards of grace, as that the private Christian discharge the more common duties of his station from a regard to the welfare of mankind. Nor otherwise does he fulfil his ministry, nor can he ever expect the approbation of his Master and an admission into his everlasting kingdom. But 'tis time that I proceed to some improvement of this subject.

And will the ministers of Christ here present, in the exercise of that goodness which I have been recommending, forgive me while, forgetful one moment of my age, I apply this discourse to them. It is very natural for you (my fathers and brethren) to compare the spirit and conduct which hath been considered with that, which your acquaintance with ecclesiastical history must suggest to you hath prevailed in the church of Christ. And it is a very melancholy reflection which you must make, that goodness has been almost as much neglected by the greater part of professing Christians as though it was no branch of our religion.

This in connection with the predictions of the Scriptures concerning the prosperous reign of Christ in the later days inclines you to expect and pray for a better state of things. But to prayers should not their attempts be added which bid fair for the hastening so delightful a scene,—particularly by the cultivation and exercise of moderation and charity, which will be grand ingredients in the glory of that illustrious period. For, as a great divine of the last age hath observed, " The true happiness of that season is not to be measured by formalities and opinions; unshaken devotion, purity of heart and innocence of life, by faithfulness, common charity, cheerful obedience to superiors, abundance of kindness and discreet condescension one to another, in unspotted righteousness and unshaken peace, in the removal of every unjust yoke, in mutual forbearance, and bearing up one another as living stones of that temple where there is not to be heard the noise of axe or hammer, no squabble or clamor about forms and opinions, but a peaceable study and endeavor of provoking one another to love and good works."

But however strong the general argument to goodness is, yet there are others which come nearer home and more particularly urge us to it.

The present circumstances of the church in this land address us to act under the most lively influence of this heavenly disposition.

We have been greatly afflicted, tossed with tempest, and are comforted. The divisions and factions among us have been high and numerous, and though they are much abated, yet there some uneasiness and the voice of complaining, like the hoarse murmurs of the sea after a long storm. Goodness, guided by discretion, must hush the angry passions and calm the discontents which still remain.

Suffer me to remind you, my fathers, of the low ebb of vital virtue amongst us. A generous, kind treatment of one another is a rare thing. Now what shall we do to revive the primitive spirit and practice of Christianity ? Is it enough that we preach its excellency and inculcate its necessity ? Will this be likely to succeed without we go before our people in shining instances of benevolence and illustrate its beauty by our own example ? And particularly as to that part of charity which goes under the denomination of alms (in which even professing Christians are very deficient, notwithstanding the solemn declaration of Scripture on this head). Of what consequence is it that we incite them to it by forwarding all publick schemes of this nature, as well as by our benefactions to particular persons in their exigencies ? And could we, in the visitation to the poor of our flocks, under their distress in addition to the spiritual things which we dispense, communicate to them our carnal, it would be acting in character, and might be of eminent service to their souls, as well as bodies. How happy it would be for us, and our people, if our worldly circumstance would admit of large donations. But let even those in the meanest situation do what they can, being willing to deny themselves some pleasures of life for this end, that Christ may say to them, as to the angels of the church of Christ, "I know thy poverty, but thou art rich."

Let me hint to you that our lot has fallen in an age when revealed religion is looked upon by some in a very contemptible light, and the ministers of Christ as a publick nuisance. Is it not worthy of inquiry whether this hath not greatly arose from the narrow spirit of some ministers and the contentions amongst ourselves. And if so, nothing will tend so much to recover the credit of the gospel and the preachers of it as catholicism and love. This will do more than all the engines of craft or power.

Shall I renew your sorrow by mentioning the removal of sundry ministers of Christ as a quickening motive to goodness. The fathers, where are they ? and the prophets, do they live forever ? It is not long since the venerable Cushing was taken

from our head, as it were, to lead the way to others who were
younger. Peabody soon followed, with Jefferds, his contemporary. And must I add Peabody the son, in whom we hope to
see the father long surviving? These were men who seemed to
have imbibed much of the genius of the gospel. Their faces
shone not more with wisdom than benignity; the law of kindness was upon their tongues, and their whole deportment was
candor and generous. Their fellow-laborers in the gospel, by
the loss of so much goodness to the church, are stimulated to
exercise it more intensely themselves;. while methinks these
ascended servants of God, in the perfection of his grace and a
fullness of joy, are loudly calling to us from the excellent glory
to pursue their steps.

But I must hasten to address myself to you, sir, who are to
presently take part in the gospel ministry with us.

The subject which hath been proposed as matter of our
thoughts cannot be judged by you, who are acquainted with the
gospel, either trifling in itself or impertinent to the tradition
before you. May it sink deep into your heart, and have a happy
influence upon your whole conduct. Your abilities to teach are
well known and approved of by such as hear you. But the
brightest talents, without goodness, constitute but a very low
ministerial character. Though I speak with the tongues of men
and angels (says the apostle), and have not charity, I am become
as sounding brass and a tinkling cymbal. And though I have
the gift of prophecy and understand all mysteries and all knowledge, and have no charity, I am nothing. But we hope better
things of you, sir, even that with gifts you have this grace, also,
yet would I put you in remembrance that you stir it up. To this
end you must converse much with the gospel, not only with a
view to your people, but your personal virtue, and by incessant
prayer be drawing down the influences of the divine spirit.

It was your happiness in your younger years to sit under the
ministry of one remarkable for this amiable quality, the late
Rev. Caleb Cushing of Salisbury. Should not you account your
past situation a talent improvable to great proficiency in this
virtue, inasmuch as the earliest impressions are generally deep
and lasting, and the example of one who is looked upon as a
father must be peculiarly striking.

The work you are engaging in is full of difficulties, but goodness will arm you with fortitude in meeting them, and even inspire you with alacrity in going through them. Nothing is like it to make your work easy.

May the spirit which descended on your Lord and Master, like a gentle dove, on the day of his inauguration into his public ministry, fall on you this day, that, being full of goodness, your life may be exceedingly fruitful in the acts of it. And may you at length reach the world above, where your charity shall exist to immortal ages, where your faith is expired in virtue, and your hope is swallowed up in enjoyment.

From the pastor elect of this people I may, by an easy transition, proceed to apply myself to them who are presently to be committed to his care.

Beloved Brethren: As this is the day of the gladness of your hearts, on account of your happy prospects, so do we rejoice in your behalf. A good minister is a rich blessing; and such we hope you are about to receive. As he is to labor among you in the offices of goodness, so in return show kindness to him. Your affections seem warm towards him now; let them continue so. Time is apt to cool the love of a people to their teacher; let yours grow warmer, as the longer he ministers to you in fidelity the more worthy he will be of it. Overlook his failings in the performance of his duty, for he pretends not to perfection. Comfort him under troubles; make the best of his services. There are some so abandoned as even to trample on goodness. God forbid it should be so here. Yet if such arise, and set themselves carelessly against your minister, take his part, and leave him not to combat the sons of darkness alone. Encourage him in perplexities.

Your beginning in this place, my brethren, was small, but your latter end hath heartily increased. And now you are honoring the Lord with your substance, by making a good provision for the support of his servant; yet let me ask it of you, superadd your private benefactions. Even the smallest presents from parishioners, as they are testimonials of respect and love, are exceedingly pleasant. Let him be always remembered in your prayers. This I dare say he judges the true goodness, and

earnestly desires of you. Be solicitous to gladden his heart by
profiting under his ministry. Let the peace of God rule in your
hearts, in which ye are called in one body. Maintain that union
in him which at present is so grateful to us all, and must be so
advantageous to yourselves. Let me leave with you the words
of the apostle to the Thessalonians : " We beseech you, brethren,
to know them who labor among you and are over you in the
Lord and admonish you ; and to esteem them very highly in
love for their works' sake, and be at peace among yourselves."

I will now conclude with a word to the people of various
flocks convened on this occasion in this house.

You are very forward, my brethren, to attend such solemnities
as this, I would hope from an aim of receiving some benefit yourselves. By the discourses at such seasons you cannot but per-
ceive that we do not lay burdens upon you, which we think ourselves excused from touching with one of our fingers. Instead
of this, although we affirm your obligations to virtue to be indis-
pensible, yet we allow that there are additional ones lying upon
us of peculiar force. Perhaps, therefore, you may the more
readily hearken to the exhortation to goodness, after you have
heard it dispensed to your minister.

Let me, then, repeat the charge that has been often given to
you, to put on charity, which is the bond of perfectness. Detest
a little spirit, concerned for none but yourselves. Love not
every man as his own things, but every man also at the things of
others. Let the same mind be in you which was in Christ Jesus.
Abound in a liberal distribution to the necessitous, even as Christ,
who was rich, for our sakes became poor, that we, through his
poverty, might be rich. Put on, as the elect of God, holy and
beloved, bowels of mercies, kindness, humbleness of mind, meekness, long suffering, forbearing one another in love if any man
have a quarrel against any, even as Christ hath forgiven you,
so also do ye. And walk in universal love, as Christ hath also
loved you, and given himself for you, an offering to God, of a
sweet smelling savor.

Were these evangelical precepts complied with, what a pleasant revolution there would be among us ! All men would be as
brethren, and all contiguous societies as one family. A contin-

ued series of good offices would make a life pass away in a rapture, and earth would resemble heaven.

And necessity is laid upon you thus to comply with these exhortations of the gospel, as ever you would be denominated or accepted as the true subjects of it.

Your faith is vain if it does not work by love; your devotion is hypocrisy if it is not attended with charity; your profession is a lie if you walk not in him who was full of grace. O, then, be concerned that your souls be purified in obeying the truth, through the spirit of unfeigned love of the brethren. See to it that ye love one another, with a pure heart, fervently. Then, being followers of God, who is love, and Jesus Christ, who is his express image, you shall at length arrive at the seat of the blessed, and associating with myriads of angels and saints, with all of the endearments of refined and perfect friendship, you shall with them ascribe blessing and honor, and glory and power, unto Him that sitteth upon the throne, and to the Lamb, for ever and ever.

During the pastorate of Rev. Henry True, eighty-three members were received to the church. He died suddenly Tuesday morning, May 22, 1782, having preached the Sunday before.

From 1782 to 1792 the church called five ministers, who all declined the charge, as follows :—

July 9, 1786, voted, " to invite Mr. Tilly Howe to take the pastoral care and oversight of this church."

Oct. 10, 1787, voted "unanimously to join with the Congregation to giving Mr. Joshua Langdon a call to settle with us in the work of the Ministry."

Aug. 1, 1788, voted, " to make choice of Mr. Jacob Cram to be the pastor of this church."

Feb. 19, 1789, voted, " to make choice of Rev'd John Wilbur as pastor of this church."

Nov. 24, 1789, voted, " Invited Rev. Ashabi Allen to settle in the work of the ministry and to take the oversight of this church."

SECOND PASTORATE.

Sept. 21, 1792, voted and unanimously made choice of Rev. John Kelly as pastor of the church. (The letters of acceptance of Rev. Henry True and Rev. John Kelly are given on pages 208, 209, Memorial History, Vol. 1.)

November 14th, 1792, at a church meeting held at the house of Major Moses Little, "Voted, that John Calfe be moderator."

2d. "Voted, to join in the following council in the ordination of Mr. John Kelly, viz: The church in Chester, E. Flagg, pastor; the church in Salem, A. Bayley, P.; the 1st chh. in Wells, M. Hemmenway, D. D., P.; the North chh. in Haverhill & Plaistow, Giles Merrill, pastor; the chh. in Southampton, N. Noyes, P.; the chh. in Haverhill, West Parish, P. Adams, P.; the chh. in Kingston, E. Thayer, P.; the 1st chh. in Haverhill, J. Shaw, P.; the chh. in Atkinson, S. Peabody, P.; the 1st chh. in Bradford, J. Allen, P.; the 1st chh. in Boxford, P. Eaton, pastor; the 2d chh. in Amesbury, F. Welch, pastor."

"The ordination appointed to be on Wednesday, the 5th day of December, 1792."

"On the 5th day of December, 1792, all of the churches who had received letters from the church sent their pastors and delegates, except the church in Southampton and the church in Kingston. (These two were called to dismiss the Rev'd Mr. Tappan.) The council then convened, chose the Rev'd Ebenezer Flagg, moderator, the Rev'd Jonathan Allen, scribe, and the Rev'd Abner Bayley made a prayer preceding any further transaction of the council.

And then, after the usual business of such ecclesiastical councils was attended to, they proceeded to the meeting house, and there the Rev. Mr. Flagg, as moderator, desired the church to renew the call and the pastor elect to renew his answer, which was accordingly done.

Rev. Mr. Shaw introduced the solemnity of prayer, Rev.

Mr. Hemmenway preached the sermon, Rev. Mr. Adams made the ordaining prayer, Rev. Mr. Merrill gave the charge, Rev. Mr. Peabody gave the right hand of fellowship, and the Rev. Mr. Allen concluded with prayer."

" The sermon preached by Moses Hemmenway, D. D., pastor of the First Church in Wells, Mass. (now Maine), MDCCXCIII., at the ordination of Rev. John Kelly, which was printed in Dover by Eliphalet Ladd, at his printing house near the Court House."

PREFACE.

The author hopes that the candid reader will excuse the liberty he has taken in inserting some passages in this discourse, which, for want of time, were not delivered.

AN ORDINATION SERMON.

" Yea, doubtless, and I count all things but lost for the excellency of the knowledge of Christ Jesus my Lord."—Philippians iii. 8.

The father of spirits has not only given us an understanding superior to the beasts and fowls, but has also implanted within us a strong desire of knowledge. The knowledge of truth is indeed the end of our intellectual faculties, and the common sense of mankind accords with that ancient and divine maxim, " That the heart be without knowledge it is not good."

But is it unhappiness of many, that while they imagine themselves pursuing knowledge with success, they are only chasing a phantom ? The treasures of wisdom with which they imagine .themselves enriched are indeed nuisances, encumbering and debasing their minds. A great part of what passes for valuable knowledge is false or useless notions, and even that which might be useful, if rightly improved, often becomes useless and even hurtful, for want of that governing and directing wisdom which is the principal thing.

It is, then, a capital point of true wisdom to understand that knowledge is the most excellent and of greatest importance to us—a point on which mankind have been much divided in judgment.

And if it now be asked to which of the saints or sages we now shall turn that we may consult them on this great question, methinks the judgment of our apostle Paul is highly worthy of our attention. A man so well acquainted not only with the Christian doctrine, but also with the learning which was most esteemed and cultivated, but who was besides enlightened and moved by divine inspiration. We have his judgment plainly expressed in our text—" I count all things but lost for the excellency of the knowledge of Christ Jesus our Lord."

It was not from ignorance of the nature and value of those accomplishments which men are wont to esteem that he speaks of them in such disparaging terms, for he was bold to declare that if any thought they had whereof they might glory in the flesh he would vie with them. But when he became acquainted with the character of Christ, and the manifold wisdom and glory of God as displayed in the gospel, those things which before were gain to him and matter of glory, he then counted but lost for Christ. " He held them in vile esteem."

For a man of such accomplishments to thus undervalue as dross and dung as soon as he obtained the knowledge of Christ, willing to suffer the loss of all things that he might win him, is something so remarkable that it seems worthy to be inquired into and examined. May I not then rely upon your attention while I shall, First, endeavor to explain and state the true meaning of the assertion in the text, and then,

Secondly, Examine the grounds of it whether it appears the apostle had reason on his side, and wherein spake the words of truth and soberness. And,

Finally, Offer some reflections which may be pertinent to the argument and adapted to the present occasion.

That we may rightly apprehend the spirit and meaning of the apostle's words, it is to be observed that the knowledge of Christ, in the sense here intended, comprehended the whole gospel-doctrine. As Christ is the Author, so is he the great subject of the Gospel. All its doctrine and precepts have respect to him and serve to display the excellent glory of his person, character, operations and achievements. It is from Christ, the Son of righteousness as exhibited in the Gospel, that light shines in upon this dark world.

We may further note that though the truths exhibited to our view in the Gospel are matters of truth, our assent to them being grounded upon the testimony of God, yet a divine thing is knowledge in the account of the apostles. The distinction which some make between knowledge and faith is not admitted in the sacred writings. The knowledge of Christ and the faith of Christ signify the same. True Christians are described as those who believe and know the truth. And Peter, professing his faith, says we believe and are sure or know that thou art the Christ. The testament of God affirming the truth of the Gospel is assured a foundation of assent as any demonstration. The apostle's faith in Christ was not a wavering, doubtful opinion. It was knowledge. And they who have obtained precious faith who believe in Christ and the truth of the Gospel on proper evidence, no longer being in sceptical suspense, but may say say with the apostle, " I know whom I have believed."

It was not then a dead, inefficient faith, which has no sanctifying influence upon the heart and life, but it was such a knowledge of the true God and of Jesus Christ, as is eternal life, as which the worth of our text are to be understood—such a knowledge as is the effect of a special illumination and teaching of the spirit of God, enabling believers to discern spiritual things in a spiritual manner; to discern the excellency, as well as the certainty, of the great truths of the Gospel.

This, then, I conceive was that knowledge of Christ of which the apostle is speaking, and which he esteemed so excellent that in comparison with it he despised all things in which men are wont to glory, accounting them but as dross and dung.

Such were the sentiments of the apostles ; such the sentiments of every true Christian. Very different indeed from the apprehensions of some, who have no mean opinion of their own understanding. Give me leave now to examine a little as was proposed in the second place, what reasons the apostles had in the sentiments here expressed, and whether reason, being judge, he spoke the words of truth and soberness.

Reason must appear that that knowledge is the most excellent which has the most excellent, important, and joyful truths for its object, which is sufficient to direct and enable us to attain the highest end and perfection of our natures, that is to be wise to salvation, which is conveyed to us in such a way and with such evidences as are best adapted to answer the most excellent and desirable purposes, and which has been most effective to deliver mankind from sin and misery and make them good and happy.

In the knowledge of Christ and those truths which are brought to light by the Gospel appear to have all the excellencies meeting and concentrating in us the apostle has had reason to set a low value on all other knowledge and accomplishments in comparison with this. And not to be ashamed of the Gospel of Christ, in which are hidden all treasures of wisdom and knowledge, and which is the power of God to salvation, to every one that believeth; but on the contrary, determine not to know anything but Jesus Christ and him crucified.

1. The knowledge of Christ has for its object the most excellent and important truths, an acquaintance with which yields more benefit and comfort to us than any other about which our minds can be occupied. This knowledge is indeed the one thing needful which crowns and perfects all other knowledge and renders it really valuable and useful and a matter of joy to us. He who is ignorant of the great truths contained in the Gospel has no knowledge of the sake of which it were desirable to have the understanding of a man.

Every man of reason and reflection will agree that the knowledge of God and ourselves is the most excellent and important and necessary that our minds are capable of. Our rational faculties were given to us chiefly to this end, that we might acquaint ourselves with God, glorify and delight ourselves in him. And it is impossible for us to know ourselves while ignorant of God. For our relations to and concerns with him give us all of our importance. Unless we view ourselves as the creatures of God, under his moral government, we cannot understand the end of which our distinguishing faculties and capacities are designed—our natures, our very existence must appear utterly vain, unaccountable, of no importance.

Now it is from the Gospel alone that we derive all that knowledge of God and ourselves which can give us true comfort or benefit.

It is from the manifestation which God has made of himself in the gospel that we obtain the true knowledge of him; such a knowledge I mean as is needful to direct and encourage us to render to him an acceptable worship and service and be happy in his favor. If we know more concerning God than the light of nature discovers, we are ignorant of the most glorious part of the divine character; ignorant of his grandest and most beautiful works, in which he has abounded in all wisdom and prudence; ignorant of that revelation of his will which alone furnishes us with a solid foundation of comfort in this life and hope beyond the grave, and directs us in what way eternal blessedness is to be sought and may be obtained by the children of men.

It is true the heavens declare the glory of God. His eternal power and God-head are clearly to be seen from the works of creation. The light of nature furnishes us with certain evidence that there is a God, a great first cause of all things, who is eternal, independent, powerful, intelligent and wise, and that he is also righteous and good; that he exercises all moral government over mankind, who have the work of moral law written in their hearts. The dictates of natural conscience are the voice of God declaring what is the duty which he requires of us, and what we are to expect as a reward of our obedience or disobedience to his laws thus notified to us. This is for substance what reason discovers concerning the perfections, character and will of God. And if mankind were perfectly righteous this character of the deity might be a proper object, or delightful contemplation, worship and communion to them.

But it is a plain, stubborn fact, that mankind are in a state of moral depravity. All have sinned and come short of the glory of God. And whatever some pretend of the sufficiency of the light of reason to direct men to virtue and happiness, they have been generally so stupidly blind and inattentive that if the knowledge of God and the principles of natural religion had not been preserved by means of supernatural revelation, it would seem as if there was danger of its being quite lost out of the world. But however this may be, if a sinner knows no more concerning God than what nature teaches, his knowledge will yield him no comfort or benefit. To know that he is in the hands of a holy and just God, of whose righteous law he is a transgressor, whose nature and will are in the strongest opposition to sin, who upholds a sinner with great displeasure, and judges him worthy of death, and has condemned him by the sentence of his conscience, this must be so far from being a matter of comfort to him that it must make him extremely miserable. Reason teaches that there is a just God, who is very angry with the wicked, able and ready to punish them according to their deserts, but it makes no discovery of pardoning mercy. Now such a view of God must not only fill a sinner with most fearful and tormenting apprehensions, but it carries no invitations and encouragements to repentance, to hopes of pardon, and a recovering of a divine favor. It would rather tend to increase the sinner's aversion to him as an enemy, and to dispose him to shun all acquaintance with him.

The light of nature indeed teaches us that God is good and merciful, as well as just, and some are ready to presume that they have nothing to fear from a good and merciful God. But goodness stands in the strongest opposition to sin, as inimical to the happiness of the universe. It burns with resentment and abhorrence against it, and its sword is no less terrible and flaming than the sword of justice ; and though we see that God is merciful to sinners, and is long suffering towards them, yet whether it be consistent with honor of his moral character, and the interest of his kingdom, that sinners be forgiven and to escape that punishment which they deserve, reason cannot determine. If men imagine to themselves a God of such goodness and mercy as not to be displeased at sin, or punish it with all of that severity with which his honor and the general good requires, it is not right reason, but vain presumption that has suggested such a notion.

That view of the perfection and character of God which the light of reason exhibits is indeed exceeding glorious and majestic. But this glory and majesty appears so terrible to a guilty creature that he cannot bear to behold it. It is death and hell to such a one to know that there is a holy and just God, who is highly and justly displeased with the wicked, and that to him belong vengeance and recompense. So that though reason in discovering the being and perfection of God, discovers a most glorious and excellent object, yet that knowledge of God which a sinner has answerable to these discoveries, if he knows not that there is forgiveness with him, which most important and amiable art of the divine character is brought to light only by the gospel. The sinner's mere natural knowledge of God, I say, could be no comfort and benefit to him, but rather fill him with tormenting remorse, anguish, dread and aversion. .

How far the light of nature can help us to the knowledge of God has been considered. Let us now inquire how far it can help us to know ourselves. It discovers, indeed, very clearly that we are moral agents, uuder the moral government of God, capable of happiness, or misery, sinful mortals, etc. But without giving a detail of the observation which philosophers have made on the nature and state of mankind, the knowledge of these things can afford us no substantial comfort or benefit unless we could find good reason to hope that we may be delivered from that state of sin, guilt and misery in which we find ourselves, and attain to a state of true righteousness and blessedness in the favor of God. But such a ground of hope, reason discovers not—whatever presumptions and probabilities it may suggest in favor of a future life after death, it gives no information of a state of happiness for a sinner beyond the grave, but rather suggests the justest grounds for most anxious and fearful apprehensions to a guilty conscience. The more we know of ourselves by the mere light of nature the more our fears and sorrows must naturally increase.

How much reason have we, then, to highly prize the gospel, which alone furnishes sinners with such knowledge of God and themselves as not only most excellent and important in itself, but quite changes that sad and alarming aspect of things exhibited. The gospel not only contains plainer and more distinct revelation and perfections of the will of God than reason can discern by the light of nature, but has also brought to view a most glorious and amiable part of the divine character which nature's light did not reveal, the knowledge of which was necessary in order to our taking true comfort or deriving substantial benefit from all our other knowledge necessary to relieve a sin-

ner under anguish, arising from a sense of guilt, necessary to
his drawing near to God, beholding his glory, contemplating his
perfections, and having delightful acquaintance and communion
with him. And that is that there is forgiveness with him, that
he retaineth not his anger forever, for he delighteth in mercy,
that he is in Christ the father of mercies, reconciling the world
to himself, not imputing their trespasses to them. It is the gospel only that teaches us that the just God is the Saviour. Here
only we find the gracious, inviting name of God, which holds
forth encouragement to us to return to him by repentance, to rejoice in the hope of his favor, to trust in him, and fly to the
shadow of his wings for protection. To the gospel, then, we are
beholden for our most glorious and amiable views of the divine
character, and indeed for all of that knowledgi of God which
can give comfort and joy, that knowledge which throws light
on the dark side of things. In the gospel we see light breaking
forth and shining out of darkness, and that God is light and no
darkness at all. Well, then, may the believer say with exalting
joy, "This God is our God forever, our God, our glory." That
knowledge which is the only true God, the eternal life, includes
in it the knowledge of Jesus Christ, whom he has sent, and in
whom he alone he has truly revealed himself as the object of
our faith, worship and happiness. Unbelievers are accordingly
described in Scripture as those who know not God and have not
seen him.

The gospel opens to view the scheme of Providence in which
the divine perfection and character appear in the general majesty, glory and beauty. If we consider the work of our redemption by Christ in its distinct parts, and these parts in the connection and relation to each other and to the whole scheme, and
forming one grand system. If we contemplate the glory of the
divine redeemer, his person, character, offices, performances,
with the issue and results of the whole, the great salvation
which he has effected, the way and means by which he has procured and in which it is applied, how effectually the son of God
is destroying the work of the devil, and has opened a way in
which the richest of divine grace and beauty are flowing down
on the guilty and miserable, raising them from the abyss of

wretchedness and death to glory, honor and immortality, raising a new and more glorious creation from the confusion and chaos of a ruined world, and all to the glory of God the Father, what sublime, glorious, and important discoveries are these! With the knowledge of these the soul of the believer is fed, is feasted, is exalted and ennobled.

Every one of right state must be greatly delighted with the knowledge of such excellent and sublime truths. If our private interest had been less concerned in them we should have reason to highly esteem the knowledge of Christ as furnishing us with the matter of a most noble and delightful contemplation. The angels desire to look into these things, but we have the more reason to value their knowledge above all others since the great work of redemption was planned for the salvation of man. The great Immanuel is our redeemer, and the Saviour assumed our nature; labored and suffered for us, was delivered for our offences, and ruled again for our justification. The gospel shows us the way in which alone we can be delivered from a state of sin and misery and obtain true righteousness and felicity. In precepts are the law of our lives, its promises and doctrines the foundation of our joy and hopes beyond death—in a word, it is a charter of our privileges. It is the instrument in the mind of the holy spirit by which the divine life is generated and maintained and we are prepared for heaven.

By the help of that light which the gospel holds forth a Christian may also know himself to his comfort and advantage, but though by sin he is a child of death, yet through faith in the righteousness of Christ he is so united to him as to receive righteousness and life from him, and so is pardoned and restored to the favor of God, and as an adopted child is a joint heir with Christ to the heavenly inheritance. That the mortal wound which by sin he has given himself is healing,—that sin and death will at length be abolished in him and swallowed up in victory,—by a gospel, too, as a rule and faithful mirror, we may be informed by our true character and state by looking into this law of liberty and comparing ourselves with it we may learn what manner of persons we are.

How much such a knowledge of themselves as Christians

might obtain by the light of gospel truth would be for their comfort and improvement cannot now be further insisted on.

II. The excellency of the gospel and the knowledge of Christ therein exhibited therein appears, in that it is sufficient to direct, is how we may escape from the misery and wretchedness of a state of sin and attain to a state of complete, everlasting holiness and blessedness. If we have this knowledge it will make us truly wise. It will guide and enable us to obtain the highest good, perfection, and end of our nature. Other knowledge, however useful it may be to subserve the lower purposes and occupations of life, yet will eventually be of no substantial advantage to those who miss of salvation, and to perish miserably. Without this wisdom, which is the principal thing, all our knowledge and accomplishments become vain and worthless to us, and must soon perish with us. The insufficiency of the light of nature to guide a sinner to true virtue and happiness has been noticed. And therefore, though the knowledge of the principles of natural religion is of great importance and use, when joined with the knowledge of Christ and the truths of the gospel, and since it gives a sinner no assurance that salvation is obtainable, or in what way he has encouragement to seek or hope for acceptance with God, natural religion is therefore insufficient, as a rule, to direct us how we may have peace with God and be happy in his favor, without a well grounded persuasion of the pardoning mercy of God, of which the gospel only assures us of our knowledge of the principles of natural religion, instead of showing how we may obtain happiness, can only discover our sin and misery, and so increase our sorrow. But the gospel is a complete and sufficient rule of faith and practice. It contains all the instruction we need in order to our salvation. It assures us that there is salvation for the chief of sinners through Christ. It teaches us how God is just in justifying them for the sake of the Redeemer's merits, that it is by faith in him that we have access to his grace. Our obligations and encouragements to repent of sin and turn to God, to deny ungodliness and every worldly lust, and live soberly, righteously and godly in the world, are fully and plainly and most forcibly represented. The manner in which we may worship God acceptably, the ordinances and instrumental duties in which we are to seek him, and in which he will draw near to us and bless us, are here fully declared. In a word, the doctrines, precepts, promises and threatenings of the gospel are sufficient to instruct a Christian fully in his religious and spiritual discernments, and furnish him with all of the duties and enjoyments of his heavenly calling. In this respect the knowledge of Christ and the mysteries of the kingdom of heaven far surpasses in excellence all the wisdom of the children of men.

III. It is a further argument or evidence of the excellency in the gospel that the truths it reveals are proposed to us in such a manner, confirmed with such evidence, and accompanied with such divine influence on the minds and hearts of the children of men.

It may be counted an excellency of the gospel revelation that God, in his goodness and wisdom, has proposed and delivered his will in writing, moving and inspiring holy men to record divine oracles as a rule of faith and practice for all succeeding ages. This is much better adapted than oral tradition to preserve a divine revelation and transmit it, uncorrupt, to remote nations and successive generations; and if men expected immediate revelations, impostures and enthusiasts would have a great advantage to deceive mankind with vain pretences. The plainness with which those things are delivered which are of the greatest and most general importance is also to be noticed as an excellency of the Christian revelation, whereby it is fitted to convey that instruction to persons of weak understanding which is most necessary for them.

And though some truths which are also of great use are more darkly proposed, but plain truths are sometimes expressed in a way not easy to our understanding, this does not lessen the excellence and usefulness of the gospel revelation. But several important advantages arise from this very circumstance which some are ready to complain of.

I say this is no objection to the divine excellency and divine original, unless it be, though an objection against the divine wisdom and goodness of providence, that many points of knowledge for the great use and improvement, comfort, and even preservation of life, are not acquired without much attention and diligence. And unless reason, principles of and the natural religion be objected to, because many important truths in morality will not be discovered or understood without careful and close attention. It must indeed be difficult for low, stupid, gross minds to understand sublime, heavenly and spiritual doctrines, however plainly they are expressed. Nor will it be easy for those who are children of knowledge, and have scarce learned the rudiments of Christianity, to digest the strong meat which is provided for men of full age; the forms of expression in ancient writings will also seem hard to those who are not acquainted with them. And we all know how prejudice darkens the mind. But we may also suppose that some truths are more darkly expressed to exercise our diligence in searching them out, for it is the will of God that we seek for wisdom as for silver, and dig for it as for hidden treasures. And this leads me to observe that the more obscure passages are productive of important advantages beyond what a revelation plain in all of its parts to a meanest capacity could have afforded. For by searching the Scriptures we find out what we do not understand, we become better acquainted and furnished with what we do understand.

And besides, we find that the knowledge acquired by close and painful attention is ordinarily more firmly fixed and thoroughly wrought into our minds, and further, it was fit that suitable instruction be adapted to different capacities. It may be added that some things, particularly in the prophecies which are yet to be fulfilled, seem to have been obscurely expressed, because it was not designed that they should be distinctly understood till they should be explained by the events of Providence. The sublime majesty and force of language which distinguishes many parts of the inspired writings might also be mentioned as an excellency in the manner in which divine truths are proposed to us, and a mark of the heavenly original. Which leads us to observe that the evidence confirming the truth of the gospel which conveys to us the knowledge of Christ is a great argument of its excellency. This evidence is the testimony of God himself to the truth of it. No argument can be plainer, none more convincing and conclusive. A child can understand and feel the force of it, and the greatest master of reasoning can propose no stronger or more perfect demonstration. The testimony God has given in the clearest and most striking manner, by a visible descent of the Holy Ghost upon Christ, by a voice from heaven, "This is my beloved son, in whom I am well pleased; hear him." By the miracles wrought by Christ, by raising him from the dead, by receiving him up into heaven by the light of many spectators, by enabling the apostles to speak all manner of tongues and work the most astonishing miracles in the name of Jesus, by giving the gospel a miraculous propagation, without any external compulsion or worldly allurements or advantages, and by instruments weak, mean and contemptible in the eyes of the world, and that in opposition to all of the vices, lusts, prejudices, false philosophy, superstition, witchcraft, and state policy in the world, supported by the civil authority with all of the terrors of penal and sanguinary laws executed upon the Christians in numberless influences, with unexampled severity and cruelty.

These it is to be remembered are facts which, upon the severest examinations, are found to be supported with accumulated evidence. They are reflected by many eye witnesses, whose writings exhibit the marks of a sound, good understanding, strict integrity, sincere and fervent piety, who at last sealed their testimony with their blood. They are facts which the ancient adversaries of Christianity never, that we can find, undertook to confute, or even ventured to deny many of the most important of them, though they had every advantage and inducement to have done this if they had not been incontestibly true, and some of the most intelligent of them did even acknowledge the miracles wrought in confirmation of Christianity, as their writing declare.

I might add that the efficacy which the gospel has upon the temper and lives by whom it has been received in faith and love is a most important evidence that it is from God. A divine power has attended it, working a great and divine change in the hearts of men, turning them from the darkness to light, and from the power of satan to God, making them new creatures, raising the most wretched slaves of sin to a heavenly temper and conversation, filling them with the fruits of the Spirit, in all goodness, righteousness and truth. A true Christian has a witness in himself that the gospel is divine truth. The blessed change which he finds in himself leaves no room to doubt that the gospel, by means that has been effected, is the power of God to salvation to every one that believeth, to conversion of a sinner to God, is a glorious work of divine power, by which he gives testimony to the truth of Christianity. But this will hereafter be further considered.

Besides the eternal proofs of the truths of the Christian doctrine, the gospel carries in and upon itself the evidences of its divine original. The consistency of the Christian scheme with itself and with every other known truth is a strong presumption that it is true and divine, for by certain fatality the reveries of enthusiasts and the devices of impostors will run crooked and inconsistent. That the gospel is not calculated to serve the selfish views of pride, covetousness and sensuality, but is utterly opposed to them, is a strong evidence that it is no contrivance of worldly craft, which is a further and great presumption in its favor; the purity and the holiness of its precepts and practical rules, which teach us to deny all ungodliness and every worldly lust, and live soberly, righteously and godly in this present world, shows that it is worthy of God according to the clearest and surest of notions which we can form of him, and is calculated to form mankind to such a right temper and behavior as the reason and conscience of every man must approve. Whence then could such a religion be thought to derive its original but from God, the stamp of whose moral perfections is so plainly visible upon it, but the transcendentally generous and amiable character of God, which is displayed and demonstrated by the doctrines and facts exhibited in the gospel, a character in which infinite wisdom, power, holiness and goodness are joined with grace and mercy, which grants pardon and salvation to the most guilty and miserable—a character which right reason must acknowledge surpasses in glory all that is called God, all that the light of nature can discover, which is such an evidence of the divinity of the gospel as must carry conviction to every rational mind that duly attends to it. For what can be more absurd than to imagine that imposture or enthusiasm can draw a more amiable and perfect character of God than reason itself ? Finally, the prophecies of future events, which are utterly beyond the discernments of human sagacity, and which the history and present state of the world shows to have been exactly fulfilled, these are such a seal of the divine inspiration of the Scriptures as cannot be counterfeited, for it is as impossible for an inspired man to be the author of these prophecies as it is for chance to create a world.

So that if we will but duly attend to the contents of the Christian revelation we need be at no loss who is its author. Like the creation, it is a work that fathers itself, and the blindness of infidels who see not these evidences of divinity no more prove that they are not real and visible than the blindness of atheists proves that the power and wisdom of God are not seen in the works of creation.

But though the evidences of the truth and divinity of the gospel are so clear and strong, yet they are not apprehended so as to force conviction upon the minds of all to whom they are proposed, for the minds of men are so blinded and their hearts so hardened in sin that there must be a special influence of grace and spirit of God to give them a saving knowledge of Christ and the truth as is in him. An honest heart, a right spirit, a fair mind, is the effect of this divine influence ; without the truth will not be embraced with faith and love. But when the mind is opened, and the heart reconciled to the light of the truth, its evidence will no longer appear dim and doubtful— it will shine like the oracle of Urim and Thummim. And how excellent must that knowledge be which is conveyed to the mind by the enlightening influence of the Holy Spirit. But for those who hate the light which reproves their evil deeds, and to harden themselves against conviction and resist the Holy Ghost, the evidence of the truth will answer an important and even against them—it will show what they are, and leave them without a reasonable excuse as unreasonable men. If it does not work conviction in them, it will serve, however, as a touchstone to discover their character.

IV. The influence and effect which by the divine blessing the gospel and knowledge which it conveys has had upon the

hearts and lives of men, is a further argument of its appalling
excellency. This influence and efficacy has been mentioned before as an evidence of the truth and divinity of the gospel, but
it is again called up to view as manifesting the excellency
thereof. Other knowledge, however it may civilize and polish
the minds and manners of men, yet leave them under the guilt
and power of sin and in a most miserable condition. But the
gospel has brought to light a righteousness of the knowledge of
faith, of which sinners are justified with a knowledge of God,
are received into his favor and adopted as his children, and so
are the heirs of eternal life. The gospel is also the instrument
of delivering a sinner from the power and dominion of sin, and
quickening those who were in a state of spiritual death. It is
by the word of truth, by the gospel and by the knowledge of
Christ which it conveys, that we are begotten and sanctified and
made wise for eternity. The power of the Holy Spirit goes with
it, changing the soul into the image of God from glory to glory,
to deliver the mind from the darkness in which it was bewil-
dered with respect to the change of its everlasting peace—a
spiritual view of the excellency of Christ and the glorious objects which the gospel reveals as simulates the believer to the
image of Christ. Our souls, by beholding, contemplating, and
being conversant with such glorious truths, take a heavenly
aspect and bias, and our lives esteemed in love by Christians, for
their works' sake, according to an apostolic canon for that purpose.

Will my reverend fathers and brethren suffer a word of address
from one, however unworthy, who has heartily cast in a lot
with them. The excellency of the gospel, the dispensation of
which is committed to us, has been in some manner represented,
indeed in a very imperfect manner, but your more exact, com-
prehensive and penetrating views will easily supply what is
amiss and correct what is wanting in the representation. Should
it not be then our desire, prayer and endeavor that we may be
yet more fully acquainted with those mysteries of divine wisdom
and grace which are exhibited in the gospel ? that we may grow
in grace and in the knowledge of Christ, and have our minds
more illuminated, our hearts more affected and transformed by

it into the image of Christ, and cast in the mould of evangelical truth, wisdom, holiness and joy ?

The ministers of the gospel undertake a trust of very great importance, of no small difficulty. They are entrusted with the dispensation and are set for the defence of the gospel, and who is sufficient for these things ? How rich a treasure is put into these earthen vessels. But then, the vessels containing such a sacred treasure should be clean ones, sanctified and meet for the Master's use. They should be such as have been sweetened and consecrated by the unctions of the Holy One—the stewards of the house of God, who are to feed his household with knowledge and understanding, should be both wise and faithful. They only are qualified, as they ought, have grace as well as gifts, who receive the truth not only in the notion and form, but also in the power and love of it, and experience the sanctifying influence of the knowledge of Christ upon their hearts, though we should cover the best gifts and seek to excel in them for the purposes of edification, yet, unless we are sanctified through the truth, we are not sanctified thoroughly for this great work to which we have been separated. Be it then our care to have our graces in lively exercise, and while we deal out the bread of life to others, not neglect to partake thereof ourselves.

Grace, indeed, is absolutely necessary to one's having a divine call and mission to the evangelical ministry. Nor does the validity or efficacy of divine administration depend on the good attentions of the administrator. This popish error has been constantly rejected by the Protestants. If true saints can have a valid call or mission, then such only are authorized by Christ, and consequently the administration of such only are valid. How, then, could a church know whether they have a valid ministry or ordinance, as since they cannot know the heart or state of another ? However, though Christ may send his messages of grace by whomsoever he will, yet without grace his call and mission will not be sincerely or faithfully obeyed, and whatever good such may be instrumental of doing to others, no real benefit or comfort will thence accrue to the unworthy instruments, nor does it seem likely that the work of God should prosper in an unfaithful hand.

If we should hope to have our ministry comfortable to ourselves or profitable to others, our aim must be to cultivate in
ourselves that most excellent knowledge which has been spoken
of and hold forth to others in the plainest and most affecting
view we can, the pure, unadulterated truths of the gospel, not
shunning to declare all the counsel of God, but still insisting
chiefly on faith and repentance, those practical truths and duties
by which the Christians live, and endeavor to promote the holiness of the truth, without which no man shall see the Lord.
Though our work is difficult, and we are insufficient, yet it is
very good work and pleasant to a Christian, and our great encouragement is that we have a good and kind Master, who had
a feeling of our infirmities, and has promised to be with his
faithful ministers to the end of the world.

It is upon this, our encouragement, that this, our brother, who
is about to be separated to the ministerial office and pastoral
care of the church in this place, now offers himself willingly to
this service, and we cannot but rejoice, dear sir, that the great
Head of the Church, who has, we trust, furnished you with
needful graces and gifts for the work, has also opened an inviting door for you to enter upon it, and inclined you to accept the
invitation which has been tendered to you with so much unanimity.

The step you are taking and the prospect which lies before
you must strike you with a serious awe. You are about to be
an ambassador of Christ to men, in his name to beseech them to
be reconciled to God, and administer his holy ordinances. You
are about to take a commission under the captain of our salvation, the duties of which will require diligent care, patience,
condescension, as well as courage and firmness. You are to
stand as a light in a golden candlestick, yea, as a star in the
firmament of the church, to diffuse the light of knowledge and
holiness before men to the glory of God, and as the star which
went before the wise men in the east, you are to lead them to
Christ, once more. You are to be an angel of the church—so
gospel ministers are styled. And as the angels which appeared
to the shepherds, you are to be a messenger of glad tidings concerning Christ the Saviour. Like the angel who appeared in

the vision flying through the midst of heaven, you are to preach the everlasting gospel to them who dwell on the earth, and your views, temper and deportment must be angelical, answerable to the sublime and dignified title, and I must also add you must be the servant of all, and in this, too, your business is to be like that of the angels, who are ministering spirits to the heirs of salvation.

The work you are entering upon, whatever the world may think of it, is noble and excellent—a work that carries a rich reward in it to those who engage in it and pursue it with the true spirit of Christianity. Your business will be to search out, contemplate, enjoy and communicate to most excellent knowledge, to drink abundantly of that fountain the streams thereof make glad the city of God, to feel the light and truth break in with increasing brightness and energy, to make many rich by dealing out to them those treasures of heavenly wisdom which are more precious than fine gold. Nor need you fear that your distributions in this way will impoverish you. This is a way of scattering which greatly increaseth; your gifts and graces will, like the widow's oil, multiply and increase by being drawn and poured out for the benefit of others, and by profiting them you will profit yourself, for to him that hath shall be given.

As to the hardships and difficulties in the warfare upon which you are entering I shall not say much. You know these things are to be expected and prepared for. And I trust you have counted the cost and are so much of a Christian hero that you can say deliberately and firmly, "None of these things move me." The greatest difficulty we find is to keep our hearts always in frame for the duties of our sacred calling. But for this our dependence is on Christ, whose grace is sufficient for us. If the prospect of straightened worldly circumstances should arise to view, "seek first the kingdom of heaven and his righteousness," and all of these things shall be added to you. If the messengers of Satan should buffet you with the scourge of the tongue, I trust you will find yourself so well armed and mounted that a little barking (pardon the expression) will rather enliven than intimidate you.

Go forth boldly, then, in the strength of Christ, your leader ;

go forth and war a good warfare, put on the whole armor of God and fear not. Heaven is on the side of truth and righteousness, and Christianity; it will be supported; it will prevail; it will triumph over all opposition; be faithful unto death in promoting this glorious cause, and you shall enjoy and share the triumph and receive a crown of life and immortality.

It has given concern to those who have the cause of Christianity at heart that so many societies of professed Christians amongst us should remain so long without a settled ministry among them, but it gives us much joy that so many laborers have lately been sent into the harvest, and this society, which (since the sorrowful breach it suffered in the death of the late worthy pastor, whose memory is blessed), has been so long as a flock without a shepherd, will allow us to express our joy in meeting you here to-day, on so happy an occasion, and that God has at length disposed you with so much unanimity to elect one for your pastor in whose ordination we can so heartily concur and assist.

From present agreeable facts we are encouraged to hope that the important transactions of this day will be remembered by you and him with much satisfaction and thankfulness; that he and you will be a comfort and blessing to each other, and that by your devout and increasing prayers for him, by concurring with and assisting him in his endeavors to maintain the faith, holiness, worship and discipline of the gospel, by taking in good part his labors for your spiritual edification and profiting by them, and contributing freely for his temporal support and comfort, and treating him with Christian candor, kindness, and respect, suitable to his character, you will encourage his heart and strengthen his hands in his great and difficult work, and so be fellow-helpers to the truth.

As this is the first time, and possibly may be the last, in which I shall have an occasion to address for the greater part this large assembly, give me leave before we part to suggest one thing for your serious consideration.

Since the knowledge of Christ and his glorious gospel is, as you have heard, so excellent, ought not Christians to profess their faith without fear or shame? My brethren, is not our gospel the foundation of all our joy and hope? Shall any who hope for salvation through the merits of the Redeemer, be of so base a spirit as to dissemble their faith and religion for the sake of humoring or courting the favor of infidels, and act as if they would steal into heaven in disguise?

Let us show that we are not ashamed of Christ and the gospel by making an open profession of our faith and attending the holy ordinances, and above all, by a holy life. By thus causing our light to shine before man, we shall most commend our holy religion to their consciences. That we may all thus adorn the doctrine of God, our Saviour, may God in his infinite mercy grant. To him I commend you, and to the word of his grace, which is able to build you up and give you an inheritance among them that are sanctified.

Amen.

Charge by the Rev. Mr. Merrill, minister of Plaistow and a part of Haverhill.

In the name and by the authority of Jesus Christ, the great head of the church we his ministers, who now lay our hands upon your head, do by this solemn rite, and in virtue of our office separate and adorn you, Mr. John Kelly, to the office and work of the gospel ministry.

And as you are called of God in the course of his providence to the pastoral care of this Christian society, the church and congregation of Hampstead, we therefore commit unto you the oversight of this flock in particular, declaring you to be invested with all of the distinguishing powers, of the evangelical ministry, to preach the word, to pray with and for the people, and to bless them in the name of the Lord, or administer the holy institutions of the new testament, to bind and loose in the house of God, according to the laws of his kingdom, and, when regularly called and fit occasions arise, to ordain others to the same great and important work.

Take thou then the oversight of this flock, not my constraint, but willingly, not by sordid ends for filthy lucre, or vain ambition, but of a ready mind, a mind sincerely disposed to promote the glory of God, the kingdom of Christ, and the great spiritual interest of immortal souls.

And permit us dear sir, to lay our solemn exhortations and charges upon you before God, who seeth all things, and the Lord Jesus Christ who shall judge the quick and the dead before the elect angels, and this whole assembly that thou take heed to thyself, and to the ministry which thou hast received in the Lord to fulfil it.

Take good heed to thyself, imbibe and exhibit largely, the spirit and genius of the excellent religion which you are to recommend to others, be solicitous to feel its transforming power and to transcribe its amiable virtues, watch in all things—keep under thy body, be sober, just, holy and temperate, lest having preached to others you yourself should be a castaway.

Take heed unto the ministry, which thou hast received in the Lord to fulfil it.

In this view study the sacred scriptures, give thyself to reading and meditation, make the word of God the man of your counsel, the standard of your faith, practice and standard of your preaching, the invariable rule of your administration in the whole compass of your duty.

Preach the word. Be instant in season, and out of season and reprove, rebuke and exhort with all long suffering and doctrine.

Preach not yourself but Christ Jesus the Lord, Preach the truth as it is in Jesus. Testify repentance towards God, the faith towards our Lord Jesus Christ. Represent the necessity of a temper formed on evangelical principles, and regularly operating into a life of obedience and submission to the great Lord and lawgiver of the church. Shun not to declare the whole counsel of God—keep back nothing that is profitable—keep thyself pure from the blood of all men. Do thy diligence to instruct the ignorant, to refute the erroneous, to establish the wavering, to convince the gain sayers, to warn the unruly, to awaken the secure, to direct the awakened into the path of safety. In one word preach the unsearchable riches of Christ, and in connection therewith affirm constantly, that they who believe in God, be careful to maintain good works.   '

Feed the sheep, and feed the lambs, with the sincere milk of

the word, that they may grow thereby. Study to approve thyself
to God, a workman who needed not to be ashamed, rightly
dividing the word of truth, and giving to every one his portion
of meat in due season.

Let your preaching be enforced by a corresponding practice,
Go before the flock in a amiable and attractive example, be an
example unto believers in word, in conversation, in charity, in
spirit, in faith and in purity.

Administer the sacrament of the new testament, baptism and
the Lord's supper to the proper subjects of them.

Let all of your addresses to heaven be adapted to assist to the
devotion of those, who join with you in social worship.

As a ruler in the house of God, preside with dignity, integrity
and discretion.

Exhibit a benevolent spirit, aim an extensive usefulness, endeavor to serve the interest of the churches at large, to preserve
their purity, their stability, their order, their renown, their peace
and their prosperity.

When to call to introduce others into the sacred ministry, act
with fidelity, prudence and caution, lay hands suddenly on no
man, but the things which thou hath received before many witnesses, the same commit thou to faithful men, who shall also be
able to teach others. To sum up the whole as a watchman fail
not to give faithful and seasonable warning of approaching dangers; as an ambassador let all your wisdom, fidelity and address
be exerted in negotiating a treaty of reconciliation between God
and men; as a bishop take heed to yourself, and all of the
flock over which the Holy Ghost has made you an overseer; as a
shepherd or pastor, feed the church of God which he hast purchased, with his own blood and lead them to the green pastures,
and the salutary waters of the sanctuary; as an householder
give to every one his portion of meat in due season, as an angel
to be like a flame of fire, all alive in delivering the messages of
the Lord of hosts; as a star be not eccentric, cross not the
spheres but move on and shine in your proper orbit, diffusing
the salutary rays of gospel light, and as a good soldier of Jesus
Christ, endure hardiness, take to yourself the whole armour of
God, fight the good fight of faith, let not the weapons of your

warfare be carnal, but spiritual that they may be mighty, through God to pull down the strongholds of sin and satan.

Thus we have presented before you a summary of your duties annexed to your office and station and which in the gospel, are injoined in its ministration.

As motives to perform them, need we any more at this time than to suggest, that the honour of God, and the success of the gospel, the salvation of souls for whom Christ died, and your own present, future and everlasting happiness are all interested in your fidelity, let the consideration of the awful solemnities of death, judgment, heaven, hell and eternity, serve strongly to enforce on you and every minister discharge of our duty, and may God add the effectual energy of his grace.

In prospect of these arduous, official duties you are doubtless ready to exclaim, who is sufficient for these things? Your work is great, your difficulties probably will be too. But be strong dear sir, in the grace which is in Christ Jesus. Look by faith and prayer to the everlasting hills, to the rock that is higher than you, for direction and assistance, for support and success in your great undertaking. He will be with you, while you be with Him. He will never leave or forsake you. If you obtain mercy of the Lord to be faithful, if you keep this good thing committed unto you, by the Holy Ghost which dwelleth in us, when the chief shepherd shall appear, then shall thou receive a crown of life which passeth not away. And this may God, in his infinite mercy grant you, through our Lord Jesus Christ, to whom be glory, in his church throughout all ages, world without end. Amen.

The right hand of fellowship, given by the Rev. Mr. Peabody of Atkinson.

However a careless world may neglect and despise the blessed gospel, the glorious salvation, it offers to men the regular means of grace enjoyed in a land of light: yet the happy effects of those distinguished blessings have been so conspicuous as to strike conviction into the minds of every serious, judicious observer.

These being acknowledged privileges, every effort to preserve and increase them cannot fail of giving satisfaction and pleasure to such as are well wishers to the religion of Jesus, and to every friend of society.

The present prospects in this place, after a long interruption of the regularly stated means of religious instruction, are agreeable and encouraging. They produce sensations of joy, my Christian brethren of this church and society, in the hearts of all of your friends and in the minds of all who are the true friends of gospel order.

We would now most heartily congratulate you upon the present occasion upon your union and harmony, and your having a pastor, who, we trust, is faithful, solemnly set over you, to minister unto you on the things pertaining to God and godliness, and to assist you in your most important interests, that you may no longer remain as a sheep without a shepherd.

May the Great Head of the Church, who walks in the midst of his golden candlesticks, increase your love, increase your union, and enrich you with all of the special and excellent graces of the gospel.

Friendship and brotherly affections are such necessary ingredients in a true Christian character that an exhibition of them should not be omitted by sister churches, in regular standing, upon all proper occasions. Giving the right hand of fellowship, apostolic example, and the universal custom of the churches in the States of America, has been rendered familiar upon all ordination solemnities.

As this part of the public exercises devolves upon me, I now, dear sir, in the name and by the direction of this venerable council, give you my right hand, hereby publicly testifying our entire approbation of you, as one regularly introduced into the work of the gospel ministry, and manifesting our most ardent desires that mutual love, friendship and communion may ever be found subsisting between us.

We rejoice with you upon your happy settlement in this place, and that you are engaged to preach the unsearchable riches of Christ. We most cheerfully leave with you the divine presence and direction in all the labors to which you have been called.

January 16, 1793, the church met to fix upon a receptive covenant, and accordingly the following was fixed upon.

"You do now, in the presence of God, of the elect angels, and of this assembly, devoutly and solemnly devote yourself to the eternal God, who is the Father, Son and Holy Ghost, receiving him as your God and portion, desiring by his special aid to live to his glory.

You do likewise give up yourself to the Lord Jesus Christ, and as God manifest in the flesh, who is the Head of the Church.

And you receive him as made of God into you wisdom, righteousness, sanctification and redemption.

You do also own your baptismal covenant. You do likewise give yourself to the Church of Christ in this place, engaging with this help to attend upon the ordinances of the Gospel, and watchfully to avoid every sinful course and everything which shall have a tendency to bring a scandal upon the holy religion which we profess.

You engage also to worship God in your family, to devote your children to God, and to bring them up in the nurture and admonishing of the Lord.

This you promise.

We, then, the Church of Christ in this place, do receive you into our fellowship, and promise, by His assistance, to watch over you, and to treat you with that affection which our sacred relation requires.

This we do, imploring of our Lord that both we and you together may obtain mercy to be faithful in His Covenant, and to glorify Him with that holiness which becomes his house forever."

" At a church meeting at the meeting house, September 29, 1796, unanimously voted the following to be the receptive Covenant of this Church, instead of the one adopted in 1793, and confirmed the same by a unanimous voice again May 3d, 1804."

FORM OF THE COVENANT.

" You do here, in the presence of God and this assembly, own and profess your serious belief of the Christian religion as it is contained in the Holy Scriptures.

And professing your repentance towards God, and faith towards our Lord Jesus Christ, you do give up yourself to the Lord Jehovah, who is the Father, Son, and the Holy Ghost, and receive him as your God and portion.

You do give up yourself to the Lord Jesus Christ and put your whole trust and confidence in him alone for salvation, and receive him as your all-sufficient Saviour, and rely upon him as the Great Head of the Church in the Covenant of grace, and as your Prophet, Priest and King forever.

You do also own your baptismal covenant and your engagements thereby to be the Lord's.

You submit to the laws of his kingdom as they are administered among his people.

You do also give yourself in solemn covenant to this church of Christ, engaging with his help to submit to all of the ordinances of the Gospel."

" To this you submit."

" I, then, as a minister of Jesus Christ, do in his name and in behalf of the Church, acknowledge you to be a member of the Church of Christ, to be admitted to all the special ordinances and privileges for the communion of saints, and do promise that we will receive you and watch over you as such in the Lord.

This we do, imploring of our divine Lord that both we and you may obtain mercy, to be faithful in the Covenant, and glorify him in that holiness which becometh his house forever."

" And now unto him, who is able to keep you from falling," etc.—
Jude 24: 25.

Rev. Mr. Kelly was pastor of the church forty-four years, "lacking eight weeks." He was dismissed Oct. 12, 1836, when seventy-three years of age. For a sketch of his life and other facts see pages 27 to 55 of Memorial History, Vol. I, or sketch of church members.

February 10th 1837.

John Kelly of

Hampstead N.H.

Rev. Mr. Kelly preached the following sermon on the occasion of leaving the old meeting house for the new church, as printed at the time :—

"UNION AND COMMUNION OF SAINTS."

A SERMON DELIVERED AT HAMPSTEAD, N. H., OCT. 13, 1837,
TO THE CONGREGATIONAL CHURCH AND SOCIETY ON LEAV-
ING THE OLD MEETING HOUSE AND REPAIRING TO THE
NEW ONE, BY JOHN KELLY, A. M., LATE PASTOR OF THE
CHURCH AND SOCIETY ABOUT FORTY-FOUR YEARS.

*"This Sermon is Dedicated to the Inhabitants of Hampstead, in
grateful remembrance of the uniform respect and kindness
shown to the Author for a long series of years."*

"Fulfill ye my joy, that ye be like-minded, having the same love,
being of one accord, of one mind ; let nothing be done through strife or
vain glory; but in loveliness of mind, let each esteem the other better
than themselves."—*Philippians 11 : 2, 3.*

These words of the great apostle to the Gentiles were
addressed in the most affectionate manner to the church at Philippi, which was one of the most endeared to his heart, on
account of their exemplary faith and patience, and their affectionate regard to his own person, in ministering to his necessi-
ties, while some others have been neglectful of supplying his
wants.

About twelve years before this epistle was written at Rome,
the apostle had preached the Gospel at Philippi, and was driven
from thence by the hand of persecution. But he could not forget to edify and comfort those precious souls who had been
brought to believe and obey the gospel by his ministrations.

So does the faithful minister love and cherish the souls of
those to whom he has for years ministered in holy things, even
though the more he has loved them the less he is loved by them.

And now, my hearers, since I have constantly preached the
Gospel in this house, with the exception of a few days, thirteen
years longer than St. Paul preached the Gospel in the whole of
his ministry, which continued only thirty-one years, you will
bear with me to speak to you once more.

And with a view of improving the words of the text, it is
proposed :

1. To show how all professors of religion ought to have the same love and to be of one accord, of one mind.

2. To consider some of the urgent reasons why all of God's people ought to comply to the exhortation in the text.

3. To consider the unreasonableness of doing anything through strife or vain glory.

4. To consider the duty of esteeming others better than ourselves, and the happy consequences of a lovely mind.

1. I am first to show how all professors of religion ought to have the same love and to be of the same accord and one mind.

In the first place, doubtless the apostle himself and the spirit of God by which he wrote, intended that we should have the same love to God, and toward our neighbor as the law of God demands.

And it is required that we should all be agreed in the cordial belief of all of the doctrines which are according to godliness. Because, as every science has its first principles, without which it cannot subsist, and upon which its faith and practice its votaries are founded, so in a special manner there must be certain first principles or doctrines of religion which all must admit and hold, or be chargeable of having no religion.

These doctrines, or first principles, are both the foundation and criterion of every man's character, in a religious point of view. If he has no religious principles it has decidedly no religion. If he has false principles, it has a false religion; if he has false ideas of the divine character, he worships a false God, or is an idolator, or an atheist. "As a man thinketh in his heart, so he is." So it is important that we should have correct views of the doctrines of religion.

Here it may not be amiss briefly to state some of the essential doctrines of the Gospel in the belief of which all the true disciples of Christ are agreed.

These are the following :—

That there is one eternal and unchangeable God, revealed to us under the name of the Father, the Son, and the Holy Ghost, to each of whom there is ascribed a peculiar agency in the work of creation and redemption. And yet these are united in one God-head, whose name alone is Jehovah, which means the sum and source of being. Accordingly Moses said, "Hear, O Israel, the Lord, our God, is one Lord," that is, as in the original Hebrews, "The Jehovah, our Aluchinow, is one Jehovah." One of these words is in the plural number and the other in the singular. And this corresponds with the divine nature as more clearly revealed in the New Testament, where the Father, the Son or Word, and the Holy Ghost are declared to be mixed in One in the work of creation and redemption.

For while it is revealed that he who built all things is God, it is also declared that, "By the word of the Lord were the Heavens made, and all the hosts of them by the breath of his mouth." And all things are declared to have been made by Jesus Christ, the Word or Son of God. So, then, according to the Scriptures, God is one in three or three in One.

This God created, upholds and governs all worlds in the most wise, righteous, and most holy manner, according to his most holy and eternal purpose.

He made man at first upright, in his own image and favor, but man soon fell into a state of depravity and alienation from God, and so became justly exposed to the wrath of God forever.

But God, foreknowing this defection, did from eternity constitute his own Son to be a Mediator between God and man.

And God the Father did stipulate to give his Son a seed to serve him from among the human race, as a reward for his sufferings and dying for our sins, that we might be redeemed from all iniquity and become a peculiar people zealous of all good works.

This Saviour was sent to men as lost creatures, wholly depraved and wholly condemned by the righteous sentence of the Divine law. Hence Christ first demanded that men should repent or change their minds, and turn to God through faith in his atoning blood for the remission of their sins.

But though men have all the natural powers of understanding, reason and conscience sufficient to serve God, if they would, yet such is the wickedness of their hearts that nothing of duty will be complied with till a change is wrought in them by the spirit of God, first convincing the soul of its depravity, and then giving a new heart, new desires and affection of heart towards God, by faith in Jesus Christ, the way, the truth, and the life.

In connection with the above doctrines the following truths may be adduced, and are expressly revealed in the word of God.

The election of grace, according to the foreknowledge in which the people of God were chosen in Christ Jesus, before the foundation of the world, that they should become holy and without blame before him in love.   Eph. 4.

The doctrine of the perseverance of the saints is also revealed and made certain.

For the gifts and calling of God are things of which he does not repent.

And Christ says, " My sheep hear my voice, and they follow me, and I give unto them eternal life, and no man shall pluck them out of my hands.   John 10.

The doctrine of justification, sanctification and adoption, also are true and certain, for the Scripture says, " Moreover, whom he did predestinate, them he also called, and when he called them he also justified, and when he justified them he also glorified.   Romans 8 : 30.

It is also made certain that all who believe and obey the gospel shall be saved, and all who believe not shall be forever lost.

These are the doctrines according to godliness, which all must and will admit who are taught by the word and spirit of God to feel our entire dependence on the grace of our Lord Jesus Christ.

And be it remembered, as Luther says, every minister, and every other man who would be a Christian, must be certain of his doctrine that it is exactly according to God's word.

2.   We may notice again, in the second place, that the disciples of Christ must be united as of one accord, of one mind, in the affections of their hearts.

They should love God according to his true character as it is revealed in the Holy Scripture; they should love the Lord Jesus Christ in sincerity, and love one another fervently.

" By this," says Christ, " shall all men know that ye are my disciples, if ye love one to another."

And " if we love not our brother whom we have seen, how can we love God whom we have not seen ? "

" We know that we have passed from death unto life, because we love the brethren."

The heathen said of the primitive Christians, "Behold, how these Christians love one another."

3. In the third place, all Christians should be of one accord and one mind in design.

This design should be to the glory of God and the good of immortal souls.

This is the badge of distinction to know who are true Christians and who are not, without any regard to denominations or professions.

4. In the fourth place all Christians should have the same love and be of one accord, of one mind in the communion of Divine ordinances.

It does not seem necessary that they should have the same mode or manner of performance. For instance, it is not absolutely necessary that all should stand or kneel in prayer, but it is necessary that all should pray to God and that all should have the spirit of Christ. If we have evidence that any soul has communion and fellowship with the Father and His Son Jesus Christ, we ought also to receive him to our fellowship; for otherwise we cannot expect to commune with the saints in heaven.

II. We proceed now, secondly, to consider some of the urgent reasons why all of God's people ought to comply with the exhortation of the apostle in the text.

A general reason may be grounded on the nature of the relation of true believers to God and one another.

By faith in Christ, which implies the regeneration of the heart, all true Christians became the children of God and fellow heirs to the Kingdom of Heaven,—partakers of the Divine nature—and have an earnest of the inheritance of saints in light.

"And by one spirit they have all been baptized into one body, whether bond or free, Jews or Gentiles, and they have all been made to drink into one spirit." I Cor. 12 : 13.

Hence it is according to their very natures as new creatures to be united into one body, and to worship and commune together as the time and place may make it convenient, to the comfort and edification of their souls, in love to Christ and one another.

In the first place, the prayer of Christ, as recorded in the 17th chapter of John, should urge every new born soul to have communion with those who have the same spirit.

Another reason is the command of Christ to love one another. He was so intent upon this important subject that he made this the criterion by which others might know whether we are his disciples or not.

Another argument to urge the duty of Christians to be united in love and to be of one accord of one mind, is what their inspired apostles have said and written on this subject.

To the Romans the apostle says, " Be of the same mind one towards another." Now the God of patience and consolation grant you to be like minded one towards another, according to Christ Jesus, that ye may with one mind and one mouth glorify God, even the father of our Lord Jesus Christ.

Wherefore receive ye one another, as Christ also received us to the glory of God.

To the Corinthians he writes, " Now I beseech you, brethren, by the name of our Lord Jesus Christ, that ye all speak the same thing, that there be no division among you; but be ye perfectly joined together in the same mind and in the same judgment."

Another argument for the union and communion of saints is the example of the primitive Christians in the days of the apostles and martyrs of Jesus.

" These all continued with one accord in prayer and supplication with the women, and Mary, the mother of Jesus, and the brethren."

" And the multitude of them that believed, after the day of Pentecost, were of one heart and one soul."

And it appears that the more they were persecuted, as the children of Israel were in Egypt, the more they increased in love and good works.

III. We now come, thirdly, to consider the unreasonableness of doing anything through strife and vain glory.

In the first place this course is unreasonable because it originates from an unreasonable, wicked, and proud heart.

Strife, contention and malignity come from the dark regions of sin and misery, where no good thing dwells, but only evil, and that continually.

In the next place, strife and vain glory are no manner of benefit to those who are so base and wicked as to practice them. The gainers in this enterprise are always the greatest losers, for though they may seem to gain their point in the first onset, yet at the best their glory is only vain glory still, and in the end there is nothing gained but guilt, shame and confusion forever.

We may once more observe that strife and vain glory are unreasonable because no good is done to the agent or object, but great damage to both, and especially to the agents of this work of confusion and ruin. A swelling always indicates some disease, and climbing always endangers the life by a fall.

In any case pride must have a fall, and he who demands more honors than others are willing to bestow upon him must suffer disappointment and disgrace. God and man will frown upon him.

IV. We come now, fourthly, to consider the duty of esteeming others better than ourselves, and the happy consequences of a lowly mind.

Esteeming others better than ourselves does not imply that we should deny any favor, spiritual or temporal, which God has of his mercy and goodness bestowed upon us more than he has upon some others; but it implies that we should think so much more of our own faults than of the faults of others that we should be so much humbled before God as to think better of others, of whose sins we do not know so much as we do our own. For we never ought to judge more unfavorably of any man than we have evidence against him. Charity thinketh no evil where there is no evidence of evil.

This lowliness of mind we owe to God, to ourselves, and to our fellow-creatures, for we have sinned against all these, and especially we have sinned against our Maker and Redeemer, and ought to prostrate ourselves in the dust before him. Because, first, we have made ourselves vile and mean, poor and wretched, blind and naked by sinning against God.

And so we are wholly dependent on God for every good thing, for soul and body, for time and eternity.

We have also the example of the Lord Jesus Christ and of all of the saints from the beginning of the world to urge us to be of a lowly mind, that we may find rest to our souls.

We are now prepared more directly to consider the happy consequences of a lowly mind.

This may be a settled and universal truth, that it is impossible for a man to be happy without a humble and lowly mind. There is no heaven without humility.

So soon as some of the angels entertained the spirit of pride they were cast down from heaven and reserved under chains of darkness unto the great day of judgment and perdition of ungodly men.

And as soon as man aspired to be good he was cast out of Paradise, and a flaming sword was placed, which was pointed every way to keep him from the tree of life.

And even now, since the Saviour has come into the world to seek and to save that which was lost, no man can enter into heaven unless he is converted and becomes penitent and humble as a little child.

It is a happy thing to be of a lowly mind, or to walk humbly with God, because it is a safe way. It is more safe to walk on the ground than to rise into an airy region, or upon the top of a mast, or upon the crag of a mountain that hangs over an abyss below.

It is a happy thing to be of a meek and lowly mind, because those who are of this spirit are free from any affronts and disappointments of which proud and wicked men are heirs.

How miserable was proud and malicious Haman, who could neither eat nor sleep with any comfort as long as Mordecai would not bow to him.

But how happy was Moses, the meekest of men, and David, who was one of the humblest of men that ever lived upon earth.

St. Paul, too, was joyful in all his tribulations, because he esteemed himself less than the least of all saints.

And to crown the whole, it is a happy thing to be of a lowly mind because God has made all his promises of grace and glory to the humble souls.

"Blessed are the poor in spirit, for their's is the kingdom of heaven."

" He that humbleth himself shall be exalted."

" And thus said the High and Lofty One that inhabiteth eter-

nity, whose name is holy, I dwell in the High and Holy place,
with him also that is of a humble and contrite spirit, to revive
the heart of the humble, and to revive the heart of the contrite
ones."

IMPROVEMENT.

In the application of this subject we remark : First, That
there is no greater evidence of the Christian spirit and temper
in professors of religion than to unite in the doctrines, duties,
and affections which are peculiar to the gospel, and which are
expressly commanded and interceded for by our blessed Lord and
Saviour, Jesus Christ. For as only by pride cometh contention,
so it is only by humiliation, meekness and love, that true Christians are united by faith and fellowship of the gospel.

2. It may also be remarked, secondly, in application to the
brethren and sisters of this church, that the proof and comfort
of this union under God will greatly depend on your temper
towards one another and towards those who are without.

Your whole heart and soul and life must be to endeavor to
keep the unity of spirit in the bond of peace. And as much as
in you lies to live peaceably with all men, follow peace with all
and holiness. Without this no man can see the Lord.

The remaining part of this discourse will chiefly consist in
addresses to the several classes of this assembly upon leaving
the house to repair to the new one.

I would say, then, that though there is no record to be found
in regard to the erection of this house, yet, in comparing the
dates of other events, that it was raised in the year 1748,
eighty-nine years ago this summer, and it was long in finishing ;
I believe it was not plastered till twenty years after it was
erected.

In the year 1792, when the second minister was ordained, its
surface was all out of repair, and the "minister people," as the
Congregational Church and Society were then called, repaired
the house and built the steeple and porch, and painted all of
them at their own cost the first time.

The first minister settled in this place was Rev. Henry True,
from Salisbury, Mass., on the twenty-fourth day of June, 1752.

He continued thirty years, lacking a few days, and died suddenly on Tuesday morning, May 22, 1782, aged fifty-six years and two months. He had preached the Sabbath before, as well as usual.

According with the text (Acts 11: 24), preached upon at his ordination by Rev. Edward Barnard of Haverhill, " he was a good man."

After Mr. True's decease this church and society were destitute more than ten years. No attempt was made to settle a minister for four years. In the next six years calls were extended to five different candidates, but none of them would accept, for fear of infidels and poverty.

At last he who is now speaking to you was urged to come here, when he was under a request to go to another place; but not having promised to go, he came here, and he soon had a call to settle, without a dissenting voice. And as he could not make money his leading object, he could not deny the request of a depressed and almost discouraged people. He was accordingly ordained in this house (the first he preached in alone), on the fifth day of December, 1792. Here he remained pastor forty-four years, lacking eight weeks.

But he was dismissed one year and three days ago; but for what reason I cannot say, though some have asked me in other places why was this man dismissed!

I know the causes, but not the reasons. And though I might dwell upon grievances, I will dismiss them all, and rejoice that the Lord reigneth, remembering that my Saviour, who never said nor did anything amiss, only said, " Why smitest thou me?" and " Father, forgive them, for they know not what they do."

To the Church and Society usually worshipping in this house, from the days of your fathers, eighty-five years, who are about to leave this house and repair to the new one, I would say, do not leave this house because you have no rights here.

If any people have any rights to this house certainly you have. For your Puritan Congregational fathers built it, and they and you have mostly kept it in repair and added to it. And most of the pews belong to you by inheritance or by purchase. It will be asked, then, why do you leave it ?

The answer is, like the Congregational Puritan Orthodox people of England, who first settled New England, you wish to have a place to worship God in peace, where you have no temptation to disturb others, nor be intruded upon by them.

If this be not your motive I am sorry; for otherwise you cannot expect to prosper. I beseech you, let no unhallowed feelings arise in your hearts against other denominations or individuals living in the world. Fulfil ye my joy, that ye be like-minded with Christ and all the saints, having the same love, being of one accord and one mind; let nothing be done through strife or vain glory, but in lowliness of mind let each esteem others better than themselves.

To the young men and women I would say, that on your character in some sense depends mine own honor or disgrace. For it is agreed that among the most accurate observers of human society that the character of the rising generation is, in a great measure, formed by the influence which the minister of the place has upon them.

And now, beloved young men, be ye sober-minded, devout, humble and fervent, serving the Lord. Let not the pleasant village or town of Hampstead be anything like a scene of coarse ribaldry, noise or strife. Fall not in with the clownish or illiberal manners of the times. Avoid all stimulating aliment. Touch not, taste not, handle not the poisonous cup nor noxious plant of the south.

To the respected young women, I would say, that if you are delicate, modest and amiable, you will need no better ornaments than a meek and quiet spirit, which is of great price in the sight of the Lord.

To both classes, I would say, it is very important that you should become acquainted with the doctrines and duties of the word of God. And the way to learn these is to read the Scriptures more diligently and prayerfully than you have ever done. And to help you to a more accurate knowledge of the gospel I advise you to procure a Doctrinal Tract, written by Rev. Dr. Thayer, late of Kingston, N. H., or one more recently and well written by Dr. William Cogswell of Boston.

Towards the children of this assembly I cannot find language to express, in any adequate degree, the feeling of my heart. When I think of these precious and immortal souls, that will never cease to exist, and yet are liable to be lost forever, I cannot endure the thought. Oh, then, my dearly beloved children, the sons and daughters of these parents, and especially dear to me as the offspring of those grandparents, who were my best friends, now in the grave, and I hope in heaven, " Remember now thy Creator in the days of thy youth," and hear the voice of him who says, " I love them that love me, and those who seek me early shall find me." Whatever you forget, forget not your souls.

This whole assembly and this whole town, could they or would they hear my voice, I would ask them to accept my thanks for all the kindness and candor shown me by almost every man, woman and child for the space of forty-five years.

But one to my knowledge has spoken to my character, and that will do me more good than his praise.

Let me once more lift my warning voice before it is lost in death to entreat and beseech every one of you, old and young, great and small, rich and poor, to secure the one thing needful; for everything else will elude your grasp and disappoint your hopes, and turn to your everlasting ruin, if you do not lay hold on the hope set before you in the gospel and so escape the wrath to come.

You may be glad to leave this house and go to the new one; but think, oh think, that you must go one step further, and you will be glad to leave that and go to the house appointed for all of the living. To be prepared for this, see that you seek a house not made with hands, eternal in the heavens.

THIRD PASTORATE.

Voted Aug. 11, 1836, " to extend a call to the Rev. John M. C. Bartley to be the pastor of this church," and that " James Calef, James Brickett and Nathaniel Little be a committee to unite with the Congregational Society in extending the call."

The installation of Rev. Mr. Bartley was holden on Wednesday, Oct. 12, 1836. " Rev. John Kelly, Dea. John Emerson and Dea. Kent were a committee to call a council by letters missive."

" Voted, that the following churches and ministers compose the council to dismiss and recommend the pastor now in office and to install the pastor-elect. Atkinson, Brentwood, Candia, Chester, E. Chester, W. Derry, Londonderry, Newburyport 2d Pres. Chh., Pelham, Plaistow, Raymond, Windham, and Rev'd Leonard Wood, D. D., Rev'd John W. Church, D. D., Rev'd John Kelly of the Chh. in Hampstead."

" The following ministers and churches only were sent to attend the installation of Rev. John M. C. Bartley, viz.: John W. Church of Pelham, churches in Atkinson, Brentwood, Candia, Chester, East Derry, Londonderry, 2d Pres. Chh. in Newburyport, Pelham, Plaistow, and Windham, and Rev'd John Kelly, the pastor to be dismissed. Hampstead, Oct. 8th, 1836."

Pursuant to letters missive sent from Rev'd John Kelly and the Congregational Church in Hampstead, an ecclesiastical council convened at the house of Mr. Joshua Eastman, in Hampstead, Oct. 12th, 1836.

Present from Second Presbyterian Church in Newburyport, Rev'd Daniel Dana, D. D., pastor; Brother Isaac Stone, delegate; Rev'd John W. Church, D. D. Pelham Church in Derry, Rev. E. L. Parker, pastor; Elder John Humphrey, delegate. Church in Atkinson, Rev'd Samuel H. Tolman, acting pastor; Brother Franklin Gilbert, delegate. Church in Londonderry, Rev'd John R. Adams, pastor; Elder John Holmes, delegate. Church in Brentwood, Rev'd Francis Welch, pastor. Church in Plaistow, Rev'd S. N. Peckham, pastor. Church in Chester, Rev'd Jonathan Clement, pastor; Brother William Tenney, delegate. Church in Candia, Brother Coffin M. French, delegate.

The following parts at the installation were assigned;

"Introductory prayer, by Rev. Sam'l H. Tolman ; sermon, by Rev. Dr. Daniel Dana; installing prayer, Rev. Mr. Peckham; charge to the pastor, Rev. Mr. Church; right hand of fellowship, Rev. Mr. Adams ; address to the church and people, Rev. E. L. Parker ; concluding prayer, Rev. Mr. Clement; benediction, Rev. J. M. C. Bartley, pastor."

Jan. 20, 1848. " At a church meeting of the male members of the church previously appointed notifies that Rev. Mr. Bartley made a request, mainly on the state of his health, that the pastoral relations be dissolved, but after much mutual exchange of views and feelings, it was voted to defer the action for a time."

March, 1848, it was voted " that in consequence of the improved state of health of the pastor, to ask the pastor to withdraw his resignation."

Oct. 17, 1859, Rev. Mr. Bartley asked for a dismissal, which was accepted.

The council of dismissal convened at the church Dec. 9, 1859, composed of Rev. Charles Tenney of Plaistow, N. H., Rev. Jesse Page of Atkinson, Rev. William Page of South Salem, N. H., Rev. Lorenzo Thayer of Windham, N. H., Rev. Mr. Parsons of Derry Village, Rev. Hidden Shute of East Derry, with their delegates.

FOURTH PASTORATE.

June 2, 1859. The church met with Benj. B. Garland, moderator, and voted " to extend a call to Rev. Theodore C. Pratt, and chose Dea. John Kent, Dea. William Sanborn and Joseph Chase a committee." His letter of acceptance was received June 11, 1859, and the installation service was voted to occur Tuesday, June 21, 1859.

The following is a copy of the records of the council :—

HAMPSTEAD, June 21, 1859.

In pursuant of letters missive from the Congregational Church and Society in this place, an Ecclesiastical Council assembled, composed as follows: From Atkinson, Rev. Jesse Page, pastor; Bro. Jesse Little, Dele. Winter St. Chh., Haverhill, Rev. Leonard S. Parker, Pastor, and Bro. Francis Butters, Dele. 2d Cong. Chh., Weymouth, Mass., Rev. J. P. Terry, Pastor. Union Chh., Braintree, Mass., and Weymouth, Rev. Jonas Perkins, Pastor; Dea. John P. Nash, Dele. Chester, Rev. H. O. Howland, Pastor; Dea. William Tenney, Dele. Derry 1st Chh., Rev. E. N. Hidden, Pastor; Dea. Benj. Poore, Dele. Windham Pres. Chh., Rev. Loren Thayer, Pastor. Auburn, Rev. James Holmes, Pastor; Dea. J. Russell, Dele.

Council organized by the choice of Rev. Mr. Hidden, moderator; James Holmes, Scribe.

The usual papers were presented, and it was voted to proceed to the examination of the candidate, Mr. Theodore C. Pratt, for ordination as pastor of this Church and Society.

Mr. Pratt read a brief statement of his doctrinal belief. After a full examination and a statement of his religious experience and reasons for entering the ministry, it was unanimously voted that the examination be considered satisfactory, and that we proceed to assign the parts for the public exercises, which were as follows:—

Invocation and reading of the Scriptures—Rev. H. O. Howland.

Prayer—Rev. Loren Thayer.

Sermon—Rev. J. P. Terry. Text, Acts 10. Theme, " The Christian Pulpit."

Ordaining Prayer—Rev. Jonas Perkins.

Charge to the Pastor—Rev. L. S. Parker.

Fellowship of Churches—Rev. Jesse Page.

Address to the People—Rev. E. N. Hidden.

Concluding Prayer—Rev. James Holmes.

Benediction by the Pastor.

Jan. 1, 1861, Rev. Mr. Pratt compiled the Articles of Faith and Covenant, as follows :—

ARTICLES OF FAITH.

I.   We believe there is one God, the Creator, Preserver, and Moral Governor of the Universe; a Being of infinite power, knowledge, wisdom, justice, goodness and truth; the self-existent, independent, and immutable Fountain of Good.

References—Deut. 6: 4; Rev. 4: 8; Is. 42: 8; I John 5: 7; Heb. 3: 4; John 1: 3; Neh. 9: 6; Heb. 3: 4; Prov. 16: 33; Is. 9: 6; Phil. 2: 13; Eph. 1: 11; Rom. 10: 27; Col. 2: 3; Ex. 34, 6: 7; Ps. 90: 2; Ps. 1: 3 ,6; John 3: 27; James 1: 17.

II. We believe that the Scriptures of the Old and New Testaments were given by inspiration of God; that they are profitable for doctrine, for correction, for reproof, and for instruction in righteousness, and that they are our only rule of doctrinal belief and religious practice.

Ref.—II Tim. 3: 16; II Pet. 1: 21; Heb. 1: 1; I Pet. 1: 11; Is. 8: 20; Acts 17: 11; Ps. 19: 7, 8; Matt. 22: 29; Mark 7: 7, 8; Gal. 1: 8, 9; Rev. 22: 18. 19.

III. We believe that the mode of divine existence is such as lays a foundation for a distinction into three persons, the Father, the Son, and the Holy Ghost; and that these three are one in essence, and equal in power and glory.

Ref.—Matt. 28: 19; John 1: 1-3; 1 John 5: 7; John 8: 19; Heb. 1: 3, 8; Acts 5: 3, 4; Rom. 8: 26, 27.

IV. We believe that God has made all things for himself; that known unto him are all his works from the beginning; and that he governs all things according to the counsel of his own will.

Ref.—Prov. 16: 4; Acts 15: 18; Dan. 4: 35; Is. 43: 6, 7; Rom. 11: 36; Col. 1: 16; Acts 2: 23; Col. 2: 3; Eph. 1: 11; Ps. 33: 11; Rev. 17: 17.

V. We believe that the divine law and the principle and administration of the divine government are perfectly holy, just and good; and that all rational beings are bound to approve of them as such.

Ref.—Rom. 7: 12; Gen. 18: 25; Matt. 22: 37-40; Deut. 32: 4; Job 8: 3; Ps. 89: 14, and 145: 17; Rev. 19: 2.

VI. We believe that God at first created man in his own image, in a state of rectitude and holiness, and that he fell from that state by transgressing the divine command in the article of forbidden fruit.

Ref.—Gen. 1: 17; Eccl. 7: 29; Gen. 3: 3 and 6.

VII. We believe that in consequence of the first apostacy the heart of man in his natural state is destitute of all holiness, and in a state of positive disaffection with the law, character and government of God; and that all men, previous to regeneration, are dead in trespasses and sins.

Ref.—Rom. 5: 12; Rom. 8: 7; Eph. 2: 1; Gen. 6: 5; II Cor. 3: 14; Ec. 8: 11; Is. 1: 3, John 1: 42; Col. 2: 13.

VIII. We believe that Christ, the Son of God, has, by his obedience, sufferings and death, made atonement for sins; that he is the only Redeemer of sinners; and that all who are saved will be altogether indebted to the grace and mercy of God for their salvation.

Ref.—Matt. 26: 28; I Cor. 7: 23; Titus 3: 7; Rom. 8: 32; I Cor. 6: 20; I Pet. 1: 18, 19; Gal. 3: 13; Rom. 3: 24; Phil. 2: 8; Eph. 2: 5, 8; Heb. 2: 9; John 1: 16; Tim. 1: 9; I Pet. 5: 10; Titus 2: 11.

IX. We believe that, although the invitation of the Gospel is such that whosoever will may come and take of the water of life freely, yet the depravity of the human heart is such that no man will come to Christ, except the Father, by the special and efficacious influence of his Spirit, draw him,

Ref.—Rev. 22: 17; John 6: 41; John 4: 10, 14; Rev. 21: 6; II Cor. 5: 14; Heb. 2: 3, 9; John 5: 6; Rom. 8: 30; Gal. 5: 15; Eph. 1: 19; II Pet. 1: 20; Ezek. 11: 19.

X. We believe that those who embrace the Gospel were chosen in Christ before the foundation of the world, that they should be holy and without blame before him in love, and that they are saved not by works of righteousness which they have done, but according to the distinguishing mercy of God, through sanctification of the spirit and belief of the truth.

Ref.—Eph. 1: 4, 5; Luke 18: 7; Acts 13: 48; Rom. 8: 28, 30; Matt. 24: 22, 24; Col. 3: 12; I Thes. 1: 4; Titus 1: 1; I Pet. 1: 2; Rev. 13: 8; Rom. 3: 20; Gal. 2: 16.

XI. We believe that those who cordially embrace Christ, although they may be left to fall into sin, never will be left finally to fall away and perish; but will be kept by the mighty power of God through faith unto salvation.

Ref.—John 4: 14; 6: 37; 10: 27, 28; Rom. 8: 1; I Pet. 1: 5; I Thes. 5: 9, 10; Phil. 1: 6; I Cor. 1: 8, 9, 10; Job 17: 9; Ps. 125: 2; Matt. 1: 14; Col. 3: 3; Heb. 10: 30.

XII. We believe that there will be a general resurrection of the bodies, both of the just and unjust.

Ref.—I Cor. 15: 21, 22; Job 19: 20; Is. 26: 19; Hos. 13: 14; Matt. 22: 29-33; John 11: 23-25; Matt. 16: 21; John 5: 28, 29; Acts 4: 2; Rev. 20: 12.

XIII. We believe that all mankind must one day stand before the judgment seat of Christ to receive a just and final sentence of retribution, according to the deeds done in the body; and that, at the day of judgment, the state of all will be unalterably fixed, and that the punishment of the wicked and the happiness of the righteous will be endless.

Ref.—Ec. 12: 14; Matt. 25: 34, 41; Ps. 50: 6; Ec. 11: 9; John 5: 22; Acts 10: 42; Matt. 8: 1; 13: 40; 24: 50; Luke 13: 23-28; Rev. 22: 14; II Tim. 4: 7; Rom. 6: 23; I Cor. 2: 9; Rev. 2: 10; Dan. 12: 2, 3.

XIV. We believe that Christ has a visible church in the world into which none in the sight of God but real believers, and none in the sight of men but visible believers, have right of admission.

Ref.—Matt. 16: 18; 18: 17; Acts 2: 47; Cor. 6: 14-18; Cor. 1: 2; I Cor. 1: 1; I Thes. 1: 1, 2, 3; Ps. 50: 16.

XV. We believe that the sacraments of the New Testament are baptism and the Lord's Supper; that believers in regular church standing only can consistently partake of the Lord's Supper; and that visible believers and their households only can consistently be admitted to the ordinance of Baptism.

Ref.—Matt. 28: 19; Acts 2: 39; 10: 15. Matt. 26: 26-30; Gen. 17: 10; Rom. 4: 11; 11: 17-24; Acts 15: 1, 24-29; Gal. 5: 1-2; I Pet. 3: 21; Luke 18: 15, 16; I Cor. 1: 16; Heb. 9: 10.

COVENANT.

You do now, in the presence of God and men, avouch the Lord Jehovah, Father, Son, and Holy Ghost, to be your God, the supreme object of your affection, and your chosen portion forever.

You humbly and cheerfully devote yourself to God in his gracious covenant, you consecrate all your powers and faculties in his service, and you promise by the aid of His Spirit to cleave to him as your chief good.

You do now cordially join yourself to this as a church of Christ, covenanting to walk with its members in Christian fellowship and in due attendance on all the institutions of Christ.

Thus, in the presence of God, you solemnly covenant and promise.

In consequence of these professions and promises (the church rise), we do now receive you into our communion, and promise to watch over you with Christian affection and tenderness, ever treating you in love as a member of the body of Christ, who is Head over all things to the Church.

And now, beloved in the Lord, let it be impressed upon your mind that you have entered into solemn circumstance, from which you can never escape. Wherever you go these vows will be with you. They will follow you to the bar of God, and in whatever world you may be fixed, will abide upon you to eternity. You can never again be as you have been. You have unalterably committed yourself, and henceforth you must be the servant of God. The eyes of the world will be upon you; and as you demean yourself so religion will be honored or disgraced. Yet be not overwhelmed. Jesus Christ is your helper. May he guide and preserve you till death, and at last receive you and us to that blessed world where our love and joy shall be forever perfect. Amen.

From Church Records

June 26, 1860, voted, " to devote the entire afternoon to the communion service, commencing September next." The vote was " cordial, neither brother or sister voting in the negative."

Sept. 2, 1860. "The communion service took the place of the afternoon service. The congregation were present and gave attention."

May 2, 1862. Voted, "that the church stand during prayer in church and request the people to do the same."

Dec. 12, 1869. "Rev. Mr. Pratt sent a letter of resignation to the church and society, which was accepted, and a council met June 4, 1870. The churches represented were Free Church of Andover, Mass., Rev. James P. Lane, Pastor, Dea. Thomas Clark, Dele. First Parish Church of Methuen, Mass., Thomas J. Grassie, Pastor, Joseph Howe, Dele. Pres. Ch., Windham, N. H., Joseph Lannan, Pastor, Joseph Park, Dele."

The pastoral relations were dissolved, and took effect Jan. 9, 1870.

FIFTH PASTORATE.

Rev. E. W. Bullard had supplied the pulpit for several weeks, and Nov. 23, 1870, on motion of Dea. Sanborn, it was voted "to extend a call to him to become the pastor."

The committee chosen to make necessary arrangements for his installation were William H. Davis, Dea. William Sanborn and John C. Little.

The installation occurred Dec. 14, 1879, "and an Ecclesiastical Council convened in the Congregational meeting house to examine, and, if advisable, to install Rev. E. W. Bullard, consisting of Rev. Jesse Page of Atkinson, N. H., Dele.; Rev. Calvin M. Terry, Pastor, No. Plaistow and Haverhill, Wm. B. Carlton, Dele. Rev. S. Bixby, Pastor, Dea. E. S. Judkins of Kingston. Rev. M. A. Gates, Pastor, Moses Kelly, Dele., of Salem, N. H. Rev. R. Seeley, D. D., Pastor, and B. F. Brickett, Dele., North Church, Haverhill, Mass. Rev. J. C. Paine, Pastor, B. E. Merrill, Dele., Groveland, Mass. Isaac W. Smith, Dele., Franklin St. church, Manchester, N. II. Rev. Thomas J. Grassie, Pastor, Wm. C. Sleeper, Dele., Methuen, Mass. Rev. Joseph Lannan, Pastor, Rev. James P. Lane, without charge.

The following exercises were given: Reading Scripture and prayer, by Rev. Joseph Lannan; sermon, Rev. R. H. Seeley, D. D.; installation prayer, Rev. Calvin Terry; charge to the pastor, Rev. Thos. J. Grassie; right hand of fellowship, Rev. J. C. Paine; address to the people, Rev. J. P. Lane; concluding prayer, Rev. S. Bixby; benediction, Rev. E. W. Bullard, pastor elect.

Failing health compelled Rev. E. W. Bullard to send a letter of resignation to the church and society, Oct. 9, 1875, which, under the circumstances, was accepted, and Oct. 25, 1875, Rev. Jesse Page of Atkinson, N.H., Rev. Charles Tenney of Chester, Rev. William Page of Windham, Rev. E. W. Haskins of Derry, N. H., Dea. Wm. Ambrose, delegate, united in the council for dismissal at that time. Rev. E. W. Bullard gave utterance to his friendly feelings toward his people, and the hope that he had ever cherished of "dying in the harness" seemed destined of God to fail of fulfilment.

SIXTH PASTORATE.

Feb. 21, 1876, Dea. William Sanborn, Dea. Caleb Williams and Bro. Jacob Irving were chosen a committee to unite with the Society Committee in extending a call to Rev. Albert Watson to become their pastor.

Feb. 29, 1876, Rev. Albert Watson sent a letter of acceptance. The council convened at the meeting house Thursday, March 23, 1876, for his installation. Rev. Charles Tenney, Pastor, and John A. Hasleton, Dele., Chester, N. H. Atkinson, Rev. C. T. Melvin, Pastor; Dea. Bailey Knight, Dele. Derry, Rev. R. W. Haskins, Pastor; Bro. H. R. Underhill, Dele. East Derry, Rev. E. S. Huntress, Pastor; Bro. Jonas

Herrick, Dele. Salem, N. H., Rev. Samuel Bowker, Pastor; Albert Robinson, Dele. So. Lawrence, Mass., Rev. Clark Carter, Pastor. Olive St. Church, Nashua, N. H., Bro. T. W. H. Hussey, Dele.

Rev. David Bremmer, Rev. Mr. Winslow, and Rev. Joseph Kimball were invited to sit with the council.

Rev. E. W. Bullard of Stockbridge, Mass., was invited, but was unable to be present.

The installation exercises were: Introductory service, Rev. David Bremmer; sermon, Rev. Clark Carter; prayer installing, Rev. Samuel Bowker; charge to the pastor, Rev. E. W. Huntress; right hand of fellowship, Rev. R. W. Haskins; charge to the people, Rev. Charles Tenney; benediction, by Rev. Albert Watson, pastor elect."

July 1, 1876, voted, "to accept the report of the church committee, Bros. Sanborn, Williams, Irving, Watson, Titcomb and Davis, and strike out the 10th article of the creed." (See Articles of Faith, 1861.)

"July 1, 1876, voted, "to discontinue the use of fermented wine at the communion table and use unfermented wine instead."

Sept. 5, 1879, "the committee chosen to consider the advisability of adopting some new methods of discipline, made the report, after careful deliberation, your committee feel that it would not be advisable to make any new law or adopt any new methods of discipline at present, but would recommend:

1st. That all of the officers and members of the church do their best, with a loving spirit, to restore such as may have been overtaken with a fault.

2d. That the present rules of discipline, as laid down in Matthew 18: 15-17, be faithfully enforced with those who persist in an evil course."

Apr. 29, 1880, " The committee on absent members made the following report, which it was voted to print and present a copy to every member of the church :—

HAMPSTEAD, N. II., May 1, 1880.

By-Laws in Relation to Resident Members who Neglect the Meetings of the Church :—

1st. "All resident members of the church who neglect two communion services in succession, except in cases of sickness or other circumstances wholly beyond their control, shall be deemed worthy of discipline."

2d. "All resident members who shall wilfully neglect the prayer meetings or the preaching service of the church for three months in succession, shall also be deemed worthy of discipline; unless a satisfactory explanation is made to the church, action shall be taken at once, according with Matthew 18: 15-17."

"No Christian can wilfully neglect any of the meetings of the church without violating a direct scriptural injunction. See Hebrews 10: 25."

NOTE.—It should be distinctly understood that while these by-laws have reference only to those who neglect the meetings of the church, the rule of discipline is still in force in relation to those who fail to fulfil their vows, and especially to those who are guilty of immoral conduct."

By-Laws in Relation to Church Members :—

1st. Any absent member who neglects to communicate with the church, or attend any of its meetings for twelve months, shall be temporarily suspended from the church by a vote of the church."

2d. "If the address of such negligent absent member is known, the clerk shall immediately notify him of the action of the church in relation to his case."

3d. "If a satisfactory explanation is made, the church shall at once restore him to membership."

4th. But in case no such explanation is made in six months, his name shall be dropped from the record, and he shall no longer be considered as a member of the church."

Feb. 24, 1884, the following resolutions were adopted:—

"Whereas, gambling, lotteries and gift entertainments have become very prevalent throughout our land, to the great detriment of good morals and the well being of society, we hereby

Resolve 1st. That we, as a Christian church, consider it our doing to resist all evil and do everything in our power to promote righteousness and the best interests of society at large. We therefore,

Resolve 2d. That we will steadfastly oppose the above-named evils with precept and example.

Resolve 3d. That we are in hearty sympathy with all societies and organizations which have for their object the uplifting of man and the relieving of distress, and will co-operate to the extent of our ability and all legitimate means for the promotion of their welfare."

Oct. 30, 1884, voted, "to grant the request of Dea. Sanborn to resign at the expiration of his twenty-five years of service as deacon, and that hereafter all deacons should be chosen for a term of three years."

July 2, 1885, "A motion was made to discontinue the afternoon service for the rest of the church year," but July 9, voted, "to discontinue the afternoon service for an indefinite time."

Nov. 17, 1887, voted, "to accept the report of the church committee and have 300 copies of the church manual printed."

ARTICLES OF FAITH, 1887.

As a church of Jesus Christ, associated in accordance with the teachings of the New Testament for the public worship of God, for the observances of Gospel sacraments and ordinances, for mutual edification and encouragement in the Christian life, and for the advancement of the Redeemer's kingdom, we declare our union in faith and love with all who love our Lord Jesus Christ.

I.   We receive the Scriptures of the Old and New Testament as the Word of God and the only infallible rule of religious faith and practice. Tim. 3: 16; Heb. 1: 1; John 5: 30.

II.   We confess our faith in the one living and true God, revealed as the Father, the Son and the Holy Ghost. Deut. 4: 4; James 1: 17; Matt. 28: 19.

III.   We believe in the universal sinfulness and ruin of our race, since "By one man sin entered into the world, and death by sin, and so death passed unto all men for that all have sinned." Heb. 3: 23; Rom. 6: 23; Eph. 2: 1.

IV.   We believe that the Lord Jesus Christ, the Son of God, having taken upon himself our nature, has, by his obedience, sufferings and death, provided a way of salvation for all mankind, and that, through faith in his name, whosoever will may be saved. John 3: 16; Acts 4: 12; Rev. 12: 17.

V.   We believe that Christ established a visible church in the world, that the sacraments are Baptism and the Lord's Supper, and that professed believers only can consistently partake of the Lord's Supper while they and their children are proper subjects for baptism. Luke 22: 14-20; Acts 11: 14, 47; Acts 14: 15.

VI.   We believe that there will be a general resurrection of the dead, and that all mankind must one day stand before the judgment seat of

Christ to receive a just and final sentence of retribution, according to the deeds done in the body; that at the day of judgment the state of all will be unalterably fixed, and that the wicked "shall go away into everlasting punishment, and the righteous into life eternal." Dan. 12: 2; John 5: 28, 29; Rev. 20: 12-15.

COVENANT.

Dearly Beloved :—In the presence of God and this assembly, you do now freely and cordially enter into the everlasting covenant of grace. You acknowledge the Lord Jehovah, Father, Son, and Holy Ghost to be your God, the supreme object of your affection and your portion forever.

You humbly and heartily consecrate yourself (selves) to God in this Covenant, promising that by divine help you will cleave to him as your chief good, devote your life to his service, hearken to his word, observe his ordinances, and keep his Sabbath; and that henceforth, denying all ungodliness and every worldly lust, you will abstain from the use of all intoxicating drinks as a beverage, discountenance in every appropriate way their sale and use, and endeavor in every respect to live soberly, righteously and godly in the world.

You do cordially join yourself (selves) to this church, and engage to submit to its rules of government and discipline, to do all you can to promote its interests, to strive for its purity, peace and prosperity, and to work with its members in faithfulness and love.

You thus covenant and promise.

We, then, the members of this church (here the members will rise), affectionately receive you to our Christian fellowship. We welcome you in the name of our Lord and Master to a share in the duties, privileges and glories of his church. We pledge to you our love, our sympathy, our counsel, and our prayers. And now, beloved, remember that you are fellow-citizens with the saints and of the household of God. Let your constant prayer be that Christ may dwell in your hearts, and that you may be rooted and grounded in love. The Lord bless you and keep you. The Lord make his face to shine upon you and be gracious unto you. The Lord lift up his countenance upon you and give you peace.

Now unto Him who is able to keep you from falling and to present you faultless before the presence of his glory with exceeding joy to the only wise God our Saviour, be glory and majesty, dominion and peace, both now and forever. Amen.

Sept. 29, 1890. A letter was publicly read presenting the new pulpit furniture to the Congregational Church and Society from Albert L. Eastman and wife.

Oct. 9, 1891, Dea. Caleb W. Williams sent the following request: " Having served you as deacon for nineteen years, and having removed from town, it becomes me to resign my office, praying that you may be led by a true spirit and make a wise choice." His resignation was accepted, and Dea. Sanborn invited to serve out the remainder of the year.

June 26, 1890, voted, " to close the church during the making of some repairs on the church and hold meetings in the vestry."

Oct. 14, 1891, Rev. Albert Watson having received a call to a larger field of labor, sent a letter of resignation, which was voted upon, a council called, and all parties concluded that no justification could be found to admit of the pastoral relations being dissolved, and Rev. Mr. Watson advised to withdraw his resignation, which was happily done, all singing, " Blest be the tie that binds."

May 25, 1893, a communication was received by the church and society asking that the pastoral relations be dissolved, in view of his being called to Mystic Side Congregational Church at Everett, Mass., where his duty called him.

Forrest E. Merrill, Dea. C. Pressey, and Dea. J. W. Garland were chosen a committee to call a council to advise in the matter. The council was composed of J. M. Goodridge, delegate, of Atkinson, N. H.; Rev. J. G. Robertson, pastor, S. O. Morse, delegate, of Chester, N. H.; Rev. H. B. Putnam, pastor, G. M. Barker, delegate, Derry, N. H. ; Rev. R. C. Drisko, pastor, Dea. J. Montgomery, delegate, East Derry, N. H.; Rev. Philip Easterbrook, pastor, Dea. Giles Merrill, delegate, No. Parish, Haverhill, Mass.; Rev. J. B. Moore, pastor, Charles H. Webster, delegate, Salem, N. H.; Rev. S. L. Gerrold, pastor, Hollis, N. H.; and Rev. Albert Watson was released as pastor.

SEVENTH PASTORATE.

Oct. 28, 1893, the committee of the church and society extended to Rev. Rufus P. Gardner of Marion, Mass., a unanimous call to become their pastor, subject to the following conditions: "That the pastor's salary shall be $1000 annually and the use of the parsonage, with three Sundays vacation each year, the call to date from Nov. 1, 1893."

Rev. Rufus P. Gardner accepted the call, and an ecclesiastical council convened at the church at 2 o'clock, Dec. 5, 1893, with the following roll of the council: Atkinson, N. H., Rev. George H. Scott, pastor, Prof. T. B. Rice, delegate; Chester, N. H., Rev. J. G. Robertson, pastor, J. A. Hasleton, delegate; East Derry, N. H., Rev. E. C. Drisko, pastor; No. Parish, Plaistow and Haverhill, Rev. P. Easterbrook, pastor, Charles H. Haseltine, delegate; West Parish, Haverhill, Mass., Rev. J. N. Lowell, pastor, Fred W. Stickney, delegate; Mystic Side Congregational Church, Rev. Albert Watson, pastor; Congregational Church, Marion, Mass., Rev. C. Dryer and W. C. Gibbs, delegates; Congregational Church, Hampstead, Forrest E. Merrill, delegate; Salem, N. H., Rev. S. Sherman Gove, pastor, J. H. Hall, delegate; with invited ministers, Rev. T. C. Pratt, Candia, N. H.; Rev. A. J. McKeon, Amherst, N. H.; and Rev. Dr. George H. Reed of Haverhill, Mass.

The following order of exercises were carried out:—

Organ Voluntary.
Anthem.
Statement of the Moderator.
Minutes of the Council, by Rev. R. C. Drisko, scribe.
Invocation, by Rev. P. Easterbrook.
Scripture Reading, Rev. J. G. Robertson.
Hymn.
Sermon, Rev. Dr. Geo. H. Reed of North Church, Haverhill, Mass.
Anthem.
Prayer of Installation, Rev. T. C. Pratt.
Response, "Hear my prayer."

Charge to the pastor, Rev. A. J. McKeon.
Right hand of fellowship, Rev. R. C. Drisko.
Anthem.
Address to the people, Rev. Albert Watson.
Hymn and benediction by pastor elect, Rev. R. P. Gardner.

At the communion service held June 8, 1898, Rev. R. P.
Gardner, in behalf of Mrs. Mary J. Fellows, presented to the
church a new individual communion service, in memory of
her parents, Mr. and Mrs. Richard K. Brickett, which was
accepted by the church with grateful appreciation.

Sunday, August 4, 1901, Rev. Rufus P. Gardner read his
letter of resignation to the people, having been elected to
assume the duties of superintendent, and Mrs. Gardner as
matron of the New Hampshire State Orphans' Home at
Franklin, N. H., his resignation to take effect Sept. 16, 1901.

August 8, 1901, the resignation was regretfully accepted,
a council of dismissal not to be called until a successor was
installed as pastor of the church.

The clerk read the following letter:—

" *Dear People:*—Will you allow us to present to you a new communion table to take the place of the table that has been used.

Sincerely yours,

Rev. and Mrs. Rufus P. Gardner,
Miss Addie B. and Master Harold P. Gardner.

The gift was kindly acknowledged.

EIGHTH PASTORATE.

A call by the church and society was extended to Rev.
Walter H. Woodsum of Bath, N. H., to become the eighth
pastor, January 24, 1902, to date from the following April 1.

Invitations were sent, April 15, requesting the attendance
of the reverend pastor or acting pastor, with a delegate, to
meet at the church, 29th inst., to act in respect to the dismissal of Rev. Rufus P. Gardner and to assist in the instal-

lation of Rev. W. H. Woodsum. The churches and individuals invited were as follows : The Congregational churches of Chester, Candia, East Derry, Atkinson, Kingston, Salem, Bath, First of Nashua, Union of East Hampstead, Congregational of Plaistow and North Haverhill, and North Church in Haverhill, Mass., with the Rev. Albert Watson of Windham, Rev. T. C. Pratt of Candia, Rev. Andrew Gibson of Boscawen, Rev. A. B. Howard of Danville, Rev. L. N. Fogg of West Hampstead, and Rev. Myron P. Dickey of Milton.

The council convened at 10 o'clock, April 29, 1902. Rev. R. P. Gardner was dismissed from the pastorate. At one o'clock the following programme was enjoyed, and Rev. Walter H. Woodsum installed as pastor :—

1. Organ voluntary, by Mrs. Frank W. Emerson.
2. Anthem, by the choir, William H. Davis, leader.
3. Preliminary statement, by the moderator.
4. Reading of the minutes of the Council, by the scribe.
5. Invocation, by Theodore C. Pratt, Candia.
6. Reading of the Scriptures.
7. Anthem, by the choir.
8. Sermon, by Rev. Cyrus Richardson, D. D., Nashua, whose text was from Gal. 5: 1, and Heb. 13: 7, the last clause from Revised Version; topic, "A Congregational Esprit de Corps," treated under two heads. 1, How is this spirit acquired ? 2, How is it manifested? Especial emphasis was put upon the importance of getting and maintaining our historical bearings, and upon the necessity of keeping our churches in vital touch with each other.
9. Prayer of installation, by Rev. James G. Robertson, Chester.
10. Response, by the choir.
11. Charge to the pastor, by Rev. Albert Watson, Windham.
12. Right hand of fellowship, by Rev. William T. Bartley, Salem.
13. Hymn 679, by the congregation.
14. Charge to the people, by Rev. Rufus P. Gardner, Franklin.
15. Greeting to the people, by Rev. A. B. Howard, Danville.
16. Greeting to the pastor, by Rev. Lewis N. Fogg, West Hampstead.
17. Reception into the fellowship of the church, Rev. and Mrs. Walter H. Woodsum and Mrs. Mary W. Thomas, by the moderator, by vote of the church.
18. Duet, Mrs. Albert H. Little and Miss Mary G. Davis.
19. Concluding prayer, by Rev. John S. Curtis, Candia.
20. Hymn 425, by the congregation.
21. Benediction, by the pastor.

The following manual was approved Oct. 2, 1902:—

ARTICLES OF FAITH.

I.

We believe in the One Living and Personal God, the Father Almighty, the Creator of all things and Preserver of same.

II.

We believe in Jesus Christ, the only begotten Son of God, in whom dwells all the fullness of the Godhead bodily, who became flesh and dwelt among us, taking upon Himself our nature, suffered and died for our sins, He rose again from the dead and ascended into heaven, where He sitteth an Intercessor at the right hand of God, until He shall come again to judge the world in righteousness.

III.

We believe in the Holy Ghost or Spirit, the Lord and giver of life, who is our Comforter, Guide, and Instructor, who operates on men, dead in trespasses and sin, to quicken them to repentance and faith; who witnesses to our hearts that we are the sons of God, and empowers us to rise into the full stature of men in Christ Jesus.

IV.

We believe that the Holy Scriptures of the Old and New Testaments were given by inspiration of God, and are the only authoritative revelation of God, and the only sufficient rule for our faith and practice.

V.

We believe that, according to the Scriptures, God made man upright and in His own image, but that he voluntarily departed from his Maker by transgression, and consequently plunged, not only himself, but all his progeny, into a state of sin and alienation from God.

VI.

We believe that the depravity of man argues the necessity of regeneration in order to become a fit subject for the kingdom of God, that when he is born again, not of blood, nor of the will of the flesh, but of God, he is viewed righteous before God only on account of the merit of our Lord Jesus Christ.

VII.

We believe that Christ has a church militant, and for its benefits hath appointed the ordinances of baptism and the Lord's supper, to be observed in His church, in remembrance of Him, till He comes the second time without sin unto salvation.

VIII.

Finally we believe there will be a resurrection of the dead, both of the just and of the unjust, the righteous to life eternal, but the wicked to everlasting punishment.

THE COVENANT.

In the presence of God, angels and men, we avouch the Lord Jehovah to be our God, the object of our supreme affection and our protection forever. We cordially acknowledge the Lord Jesus Christ in all His mediatorial offices, Prophet, Priest and King, as our only Lord and Saviour and final Judge: and the Holy Spirit as our Sanctifier, Comforter and Guide. We humbly and cheerfully devote ourselves to God in the everlasting covenant of His grace, cleaving to Him as our chief good, consecrating our faculties and powers to His service and glory. We unreservedly covenant and promise through the help of divine grace, without which we can do nothing, that we will give diligent attention to the word and ordinances of God and to prayer: that we will seek the honor of His name and the interests of His kingdom: and that denying ungodliness and worldly lusts, we will live soberly, righteously and godly in this present world. We cordially join ourselves to this church as a true church of Jesus Christ, promising subjection to its rules and discipline, and solemnly covenanting to strive, as much as in us lies, to promote its peace, purity, edification and prosperity, and to walk with its members in christian love, faithfulness, watchfulness, meekness and sobriety.

Trusting in the grace of God, do you thus covenant and engage with us?

FORM OF ADMISSION INTO THE FELLOWSHIP OF THE CHURCH.

The candidates rise, and are addressed by the pastor as follows, or to similar purport:—

Beloved—You present yourselves, in this public manner, to confess Jesus Christ before men, and to unite with His Visible Church. The confession you now make, and the engagements into which you now enter, are of the most solemn moment. May the God of all grace, who hath called you unto His eternal glory, by Christ Jesus, strengthen you, and give unto you the spirit of wisdom and revelation in the knowledge of Him, that you may know what is the hope of His calling, and what the riches of the glory of his inheritance in the saints, and what is the exceeding greatness of His power to us-ward who believe.

Ye are not come unto the mount that burned with fire. But ye are come unto Mount Zion, and unto the city of the living God, the heavenly Jerusalem; and to an innumerable company of angels, to the general assembly and church of the first-born which are written in heaven, and to God the Judge of all, and to Jesus Christ, the Mediator of the new covenant.

Faithful is He that calleth you, who also will do it.

[The Confession of Faith of the church is now read.]

Do you heartily join with us in the substance of this confession, and profess your belief of these things?

You will now enter into covenant with God and with this church.

[The covenant of the church is now read.]

Trusting in the grace of God, do you thus covenant and engage?

In consequence of these confessions and engagements we, the members of this church [here the members of the church rise] affectionately receive you into our holy fellowship in full communion, and promise, in the strength of divine grace, to watch over you and seek your edification with Christian affection and tenderness as long as you shall continue with us.

And now, beloved in the Lord, the vows of God are upon you. Having put on Christ, let it be your care to walk in Him, henceforth, in newness of life. There are given unto you exceeding great and precious promises, that by these ye might be partakers of the divine nature. Be strong in the Lord, and in the power of His might. Take unto you the whole armor of God, that you may be able to stand in the evil day. Be faithful unto death, and you shall receive a crown of life.

Now unto Him that is able to keep you from falling, and to present you faultless before the presence of His glory with exceeding joy, to the only wise God our Saviour, be glory and majesty, dominion and power, both now and ever. Amen.

FORM OF PUBLIC CONSECRATION OF CHILDREN.

The name of the child is to be given to the pastor in writing, with the date of birth, and also the names of its parents.

The children are presented, while some of the following, or similar, selections of Scriptures are read:—

The mercy of the Lord is from everlasting to everlasting upon them that fear Him, and His righteousness unto children's children; to such as keep His covenant, and to those that remember His commandments to do them.—*Ps. ciii* : *17, 18.*

The children of Thy servants shall continue, and their seed shall be established before Thee.—*Ps. cii* : *28.*

I will pour My spirit upon thy seed, and My blessing upon thine offspring.—*Isa. xliv* : *3.*

For the promise is unto you and to your children.—*Acts ii* : *39.*

Jesus said, suffer little children to come unto Me, and forbid them not, for of such is the kingdom of heaven.—*Matt. xix* : *14.*

Believe on the Lord Jesus Christ, and thou shalt be saved and thy house.—*Acts xvi* : *31.*

And when she had weaned him, she took him and brought him to the house of the Lord. And she said, for this child I prayed; and the Lord hath given me my petition which I asked of Him; therefore, also, I have returned him whom I have obtained (marginal rendering) to the Lord. And he worshipped the Lord. And the child did minister unto the Lord, and grew before the Lord.—*I Sam. i : 24, 27, 28, and ii : 11, 21.*

Fathers bring your children up in the nurture and admonition of the Lord.—*Eph. vi : 4.*

Catechise a child in his way (marginal rendering), and when he is old he will not depart from it.—*Prov. xxii : 6.*

I know whom I have believed, and am persuaded that He is able to keep that which I have committed unto Him against that day.—*II Tim. i : 12.*

[To the child.] God grant that, from a child you may know the Holy Scriptures, which are able to make thee wise unto salvation through faith which is in Christ Jesus.—*II Tim. iii : 15.*

Then follows prayer.

Administration of the rite—addressing the parents—Do you hereby honestly and sincerely, believing that you are thus commanded to do by the Lord, consecrate this, your child, unto God, to be His eternally, believing that he accepts this, your gift, which is holy and acceptable in His sight, and considering your child as a holy trust committed unto you of the Lord, you do here promise to lead them in the ways of righteousness, and that they are the Lord's, bringing them up in the nurture and admonition of the Lord?

Then the minister places his hands, moistened in clean water from the font (a symbol of cleansing), upon the head of the child, and makes presentation of the child unto the Lord by consecrating it in the name of the Father, and of the Son, and of the Holy Ghost—Amen.

Following with the concluding prayer.

PRINCIPLES AND RULES OF ORDER.

OF THE CHURCH.

I.

This church desires to be conformed as far as possible to the order and discipline of the Apostolic churches, as set forth in the New Testament.

II.

We believe that Congregationalism is that system of church government in which the Scriptures are recognized as the only authoritative guide respecting church order and discipline, and which maintains that, according to the Scriptures, a church is a company of confessed Christians, who, having covenanted and associated together to worship God and to celebrate religious ordinances, are authorized to elect necessary officers, to make by-laws, to discipline offending members, and to act authoritatively and conclusively upon all appropriate business, independently of the control of any person or persons whatever; at the same time we appreciate the privileges and recognize the duties which belong to the communion of the several congregations of believers. We extend to other churches holding the common faith and maintaining the common order, and receive from them the fellowship and counsel which the New Testament requires: and we seek the promotion of peace and charity with all churches of our Lord, Jesus Christ.

OF THE OFFICERS OF THE CHURCH.

III.

The officers of this church shall consist of a pastor, deacons, clerk, treasurer, and superintendent of the Sunday school, who, together with so many other members, not less than two, as may be determined at each annual meeting for the year ensuing, shall constitute the standing committee.

IV.

1. The pastor of this church shall be a member of it and its standing moderator.

2. In the absence of the pastor, or when church action respecting him is to be taken, the deacon senior in office, who is present, shall preside, unless three members request a moderator be chosen by ballot, when it shall be done.

3. When a pastor is to be chosen, the name of the person proposed shall be presented at least one week before he can be voted for.

4. The vote shall be by ballot.

5. The votes of two-thirds of the members qualified to vote, present and voting at a meeting duly notified for this purpose, shall be necessary to constitute an election.

6. No one shall become pastor of this church who does not assent to its confession of faith and covenant.

V.

1. To the deacons, according to seniority in office, pertains the office of moderator, when necessary: that of assisting in the administration of the Lord's supper, and of aiding the pastor generally in the spiritual care of the church.

2. The number of deacons shall be determined from time to time.

3. Their term of office shall be the number of years that they are deacons, so elected that the term of office of one shall expire each year and a new one be elected each year for the full term.

4. When a deacon is to be chosen to fill a vacancy, the standing committee shall give notice of the proposed election at least one week before the vote shall be taken.

5. The vote shall be by ballot.

6. The votes of two-thirds of the members qualified to vote, present and voting, at a meeting duly notified for this purpose, shall be necessary to constitute an election.

VI.

The standing committee shall examine all applicants for admission to the fellowship of the church and present to it a report of the names of such as they approve, candidates whom they may not approve having the right to appeal to the whole church.

This committee shall also act as a committee of preliminary inquiry in all cases of discipline, and the church will listen to no such case not presented to it by them, except in the way of appeal from their decision. This committee shall also have a general oversight of the affairs of the church, and shall present a report of the conditions of the church and the doings of the committee at each annual meeting.

VII.

The clerk shall keep the records of the church and shall present his records of each church meeting for approval to the standing committee, at their meeting next succeeding that church meeting, whose approval, entered by the chairman on its face, shall validate the records.

VIII.

The treasurer shall have charge of all moneys of the church, and make report at each annual meeting.

IX.

The superintendent of the Sunday school shall have the general oversight of the affairs of the school, and make report of its conditions. doings and prospects at each annual meeting.

X.

The superintendent, assistant superintendent and the superintendents of the various departments of the Sunday school, together with the pastor, shall appoint the secretary, the treasurer, the librarian, and any other necessary officers of the Sunday school, who, together with the superintendents and the pastor, shall constitute a board of government for the school. Plans for raising money and all expenditure of same shall first be submitted to the board of government for their approval. They shall also seek to promote the good and well-being of the Sunday school generally.

XI.

Other officers and committees may be chosen for the convenient ordering of affairs, as the church may see fit.

XII.

1. The qualifications for membership are: First, evidence of repentance and faith in our Lord Jesus Christ; and, second, assent in substance to the confession of faith and covenant of the church; and all persons uniting with the church shall sign its confession of faith, covenant, and rules and by-laws, with their full name, in a book kept for that purpose.

2. All candidates for admission into the church shall be examined by the standing committee.

3. If approved, they shall be propounded to the church at least one week before the vote is to be taken on their reception.

4. Such as have been approved by vote of the church and have been publicly admitted into membership, shall be "members in good and regular standing."

XIII.

1. Members of this church removing from its neighborhood will be expected to take letters of dismission and recommendation to the church with which they worship within one year, or render satisfactory excuse for not doing so, and communicate annually to the church their desire to retain their membership and those who neither take their letters within one year, nor yet communicate once a year their desire to retain their membership, shall have letters of dismission and recommendation as "members in good and regular standing" only to the date of their departure from this place, and their names shall be placed on the "retired list," under the direction of the standing committee.

2. Letters of dismission and recommendation are valid for six months only from their date; dismission shall take effect when notice is received of the reception of the applicant by another church.

3. No letter of dismission and recommendation shall be given by this church except to an individual church of evangelical faith, to be specified in the letter.

XIV.

1. Members of this church who have absented themselves from its worship or ordinances for one year without rendering satisfactory excuse, shall not be considered "members in good and regular standing," and their names shall be placed on the "retired list," under the direction of the standing committee, as long as such habitual absence continues.

2. Members whose names are on the "retired list" shall not vote in business meetings of the church.

3. The church censures are: admonition, suspension from church privileges, and excommunication.

4. As this church regards the object of its discipline and censures to be two-fold, as much for the restoration of the offender as for the justification of the body, it hereby declares its judgment that the acts of "suspension from church privileges," or "excommunication," while they cut off their subject from all church privileges, do not cut him off from any church duty, or from all church relation, leaving him not a member, but a disfranchised member of the spiritual body corporate, as such it will always pray and labor for his return; and the clerk shall keep a record of the names of all from whom the church has withdrawn its communion.

5. This church regards the rule laid down by our Lord in Matthew xviii: 15-17, to be the regular course of procedure in all cases of discipline.

OF THE ORDINANCES OF WORSHIP.

XV.

1. The meetings for public worship shall be at such times, and the order of service shall be so arranged as the church may direct.

2. The sacrament of the Lord's supper shall be administered usually on the first Sabbath of every other month, commencing with January.

3. The admission of members and public consecration of children shall ordinarily be at the same season.

4. A prayer meeting shall be held ordinarily on Thursday evening of each week.

5. The meeting next previous to the Lord's supper shall be preparatory to that sacrament.

6. Other meetings may be appointed from time to time by the church.

BUSINESS AND ANNUAL MEETINGS, ELECTIONS, ETC.

XVI.

1. Business may be legally done at the close of any regular meeting of the church.

2. A special business meeting may be called at any time, when in the opinion of the standing committee it is expedient, or shall be called on the written application to the pastor, or in his absence or refusal, to the deacon senior in office, of five members.

3. Special business shall always be notified from the pulpit the Sabbath previous, or in exigencies where greater haste is expedient, by written or personal notice served upon every resident member and the object of the meeting specified.

4. Members of the church only are entitled to vote upon business before it.

5. All business meetings should be opened with prayer.

XVII.

1. The annual meeting of the church shall be held just previous to the first Sunday in January, on such day as the standing committee may appoint.

2. At the annual meeting the church shall elect necessary officers, vote on the collections for the ensuing year for missionary and benevolent purposes, and act on any other business that may be presented to it at that time.

3. The order of business at the annual meeting shall be as follows:—

   1. Reading of the Scriptures and prayer.
   2. Roll call.
   3. Reading of records of last annual meeting.
   4. Choice of deacon for full term by ballot.
   5. Choice of clerk for ensuing year by ballot.
   6. Report of treasurer and auditor.
   7. Action thereon.
   8. Choice of treasurer for ensuing year by ballot.
   9. Choice of auditor for ensuing year by ballot.
  10. Report of standing committee.
  11. Action thereon—when necessary.
  12. Fixing the number of standing committee for the ensuing year.
  13. Choice of standing committee by ballot.
  14. Report of the superintendents of the Sunday school.
  15. Choice of superintendents by ballot.
  16. Unfinished business.
  17. New business.
  18. Prayer and adjournment.

IN GENERAL.

XVIII.

No alteration shall be made in these rules except at a regular meeting of the church, after notice of the exact nature of the proposed change at a regular meeting of the church at least one week previous, and by vote of three-fourths of the members qualified to vote, present and voting. This rule shall not, however, be so construed as to forbid the suspension of any rule for a single meeting, provided the church shall see fit unanimously to order such suspension.

PASTORS, 1752-1902.

Rev. Henry True, June 3, 1752, to May 22, 1782.

Rev. John Kelly, Dec. 5, 1792, to Oct. 12, 1836.

Rev. John M. C. Bartley, Oct. 12, 1836, to Dec. 9, 1859.
Rev. Theodore C. Pratt, June 11, 1859, to Jan. 6, 1870.
Rev. Ebenezer W. Bullard, Dec. 14, 1870, to Oct. 25, 1875.
Rev. Albert Watson, March 23, 1876, to June 11, 1893.
Rev. Rufus P. Gardner, Nov. 1, 1893, to Sept. 16, 1901.
Rev. Walter H. Woodsum, April 29, 1902.

DEACONS.

Daniel Little,	Aug. 6, 1752
Peter Eastman,	Aug. 6, 1752
Benjamin Kimball,	Jan. 23, 1754
John Calfe,	Apr. 20, 1773
Samuel Currier,	June 1, 1776
Timothy Goodwin,	June 1, 1776
Moses Little,	May 3, 1804
Job Kent,	Apr. 30, 1812
John True,	May 2, 1816
John Emerson,	Mch. 2, 1821
Jonathan Kent,	Dec. 23, 1824
Joshua Eastman,	Nov. 24, 1848
Joseph Chase,	Aug. 16, 1859
William Sanborn,	Aug. 16, 1859
Caleb W. Williams,	Aug. 11, 1872
Charles W. Pressey,	Dec. 31, 1884
John W. Garland,	Dec. 30, 1891
William H. Davis,	Dec. 30, 1896
Forrest E. Merrill,	Dec. 30, 1896
John C. Sanborn,	Dec. 31, 1902

CHURCH OFFICERS, 1902.

Rev. Walter H. Woodsum, Pastor.

Deacons—Pressey, Garland, Davis, and Merrill.

Church and music committee—Dea. C. W. Pressey, Dea. Wm.
H. Davis, Dea. John W. Garland, Dea. Forrest E. Merrill,
Charles W. Garland, Albion D. Emerson and John C. Sanborn.

Supervisors—John C. Sanborn, Albion D. Emerson, Albert H.
Little.

Clerk—John C. Sanborn.

Treasurer—Rev. Rufus P. Gardner, succeeded by Miss Mary E. Spollett.

Organist—Mrs. Frank W. Emerson.

Auditor—Wm. A. Emerson.

Janitor—W. Amos Fitts.

Church service—Morning, 10.45; evening, 7. Sunday school, 12 o'clock.

Junior Endeavor Society, 3.30 P. M. Senior Endeavor Society, 6 P. M.

Midweek prayer meeting, Thursday, 7.45 P. M.

Ladies' Social Circle—Wednesdays, at 2 o'clock P. M.

Sacrament of the Lord's Supper—First Sunday of January, March, May, July, September, and November.

MEMBERS OF THE CONGREGATIONAL CHURCH IN HAMPSTEAD, JUNE, 1902.

The numbers following the names correspond with the number in the list of all members from 1752 to June, 1902. (See "List" and "Sketches of Members.")

Males.

1	William H. Davis,	437	20	W. Amos Fitts,	667
2	Caleb W. Williams,	515	21	Carlton H. Barnes,	672
3	William A. Emerson,	533	22	Forrest E. Merrill,	692
4	Charles W. Garland,	544	23	Lester A. Williams,	686
5	John S. Corson,	546	24	George J. Penneo,	705
6	James W. Sanborn,	548	25	Harlan P. Clark,	700
7	William A. Griffin,	554	26	Horace W. Little,	718
8	Charles W. Pressey,	557	27	Charles F. Foote,	719
9	Ezra W. Foss,	570	28	Edwin L. Corson,	720
10	Rufus A. McNiel,	591	29	Amasa W. Hunt,	727
11	John C. Sanborn,	596	30	Richard Winters,	732
12	John W. Garland,	602	31	Walter A. Johnson,	743
13	Albert H. Little,	604	32	Bradley N. Haynes,	744
14	Frederick Spollett,	610	33	Albert E. Haynes,	746
15	Russell A. Woodward,	619	34	Richard Ordway,	752
16	Ethelbert B. Woodward,	632	35	George A. F. Picard,	770
17	Eugene L. Spinney,	640	36	Rev. Walter H. Wood-	
18	Albion D. Emerson,	652		sum, .	772
19	Giles F. Marble,	665			

Females.

1	Judith S. Eastman,	261
2	Mrs. Caroline M. Chase,	418
3	" Sarah B. Emerson,	439
4	" Mary J. Sanborn,	449
5	" Annie L. Merrick,	465
6	" Lucy A. Adams,	470
7	" Clara A. Davis,	476
8	" Mary M. Irving,	497
9	" Sarah A. Rowe,	503
10	Miss Annie E. George,	473
11	" Abbie M. Stevens,	505
12	Mrs. Lizzie P. Pillsbury,	508
13	" Sarah J. Brown,	509
14	" Mary A. Tabor,	510
15	" Emily Marble,	513
16	" Belinda G. Wilson,	517
17	" Mary E. Eastman,	523
18	" Clara A. Clark,	525
19	" Nellie R. Trow,	531
20	" Mary C. Atwood,	532
21	" Abbie H. Emerson,	534
22	" Mary E. Corson,	547
23	" Flora A. Sanborn,	549
24	" M. Etta Fitts,	550
25	" Mary E. Griffin,	555
26	" Clementine W. Pressey,	558
27	" Sarah E. Chandler,	562
28	" Sabrina D. Noyes,	563
29	" Lydia W. Foss,	571
30	" I. Amanda Cass,	573
31	" Mary A. Masterman	574
32	" Sarah A. Randall,	592
33	" Christie L. McNiel,	578
34	" Mary A. Bragdon,	594
35	" Mary E. Putnam,	600
36	" Hannah B. Griffin,	606

37	Mrs. Emeline E. Mooers,	608
38	Miss Mary E. Spollett,	612
39	Mrs. Eunice A. Hoyt,	616
40	Miss Martha A. Stevens,	618
41	Mrs. Esther S. Bassett,	620
42	Miss Cora M. Bassett,	621
43	Mrs. Minnie C. Steele,	623
44	" Abbie M. Tabor,	624
45	" Ada E. Garland,	625
46	" Abbie I. Little,	631
47	" Alice H. Randall,	657
48	" Laura A. Spinney,	641
49	" Annie G. Sawyer,	643
50	Miss Mary L. Hoyt,	644
51	Mrs. Louisa B. Boyd,	645
52	" Fannie M. Edwards,	647
53	" Etta M. Tupper,	657
54	" Annie L. Eastman,	664
55	" Dora A. Barnes,	673
56	" Fannie E. Little,	674
57	Miss Anna M. Bartlett,	677
58	Mrs. Carrie E. Pressey,	675
59	" Minnie E. Emerson,	679
60	Mrs. Ruth A. Little,	680
61	" Mary L. Noyes,	681
62	" Annie B. Sanborn,	685
63	Miss Agnes C. Millar,	506
64	Mrs. Susan E. Pepper,	688
65	" Annie S. Mills,	689
66	" Annie L. Mills,	689
67	" Alice M. Merrill,	693
68	" Mary S. F. Smith,	694
69	Miss Annie J. Wilson,	695
70	" Lill'n D. Ranlett,	697
71	Mrs. Jane R. Davis,	699
72	Miss Helen E. Spinney,	700
73	" Ethel L. Sanborn,	701

74 Miss Grace M. Bassett, 703
75 Mrs. Josephine Clark, 711
76 " Olivia A. Tabor, 712
77 Miss Gertrude S. Pills-
            bury,   713
78 " Esther B. Kent, 714
79 " Elisabeth M. H.
            Smith,   715
80 Mrs. Josie F. Tabor, 722
81 Miss Mary G. Davis, 723
82 Mrs. Rinda A. Davis, 724
83 Miss Alice G. Spinney, 725
84 Mrs. Lois J. Hunt, 728
85 " Mercy A. Woods, 729
.86 " Clara McD. Hart, 730
87 " Lydia M. Wells, 731
88 " Lilla H. Whittier, 736
89 Miss Fannie F. Davis, 737
90 " Ada M. Ranlett, 738
91 " Sarah O. Brickett, 741
92 " Minnie M. Fitts, 742
93 Mrs. Sarah A. Haynes, 745
94 " Daisy B. Haynes, 747
95 " Hattie M.Cheney, 748

96 Miss Mary F. Heath, 749
97 " Ora L. Ordway, 751
98 Mrs. Mabel E. Butrick,753
99 " Abbie C. Frost, 754
100 " Mary G.Emerson,755
101 " Carrie P. Noyes, 756
102 Miss Alice C. Fitts, 757
103 " Myrta A. Little, 758
104 " Leona C. Garland.759
105 " Mary E. Sherman,760
106 Mrs. Alice E.Pillsbury,761
107 " Maggie C.Conner,772
108 Miss Laura E. Merrill, 763
109 " Agnes F. Osgood, 764
110 " MildredB.Osgood,765
111 " Elsie M. Bartlett, 766
112 " Caroline E. Sher-
            man,   767
113 " Esther G. Bailey, 768
114 " Ida M. Clark, 769
115 Mrs. Florence Picard, 771
116 " Grace Woodsum, 773
117 " Mary W. Thomas,774

THE SUNDAY SCHOOL.

In all ages we find the teacher and the taught. The earliest people, as well as the savages, must have been taught by
observation or by painful experience. In ancient Hebrew
times the rabbi, or wise men, taught the people how to live,
how to act, and how to keep well, but not especially of
death. Antoninus, Plutarch, Confucius, Demosthenes, Sene-
ca, Socrates, and other learned men of the times, taught the
ethical life, the orderly society, and the essentials of happiness. In the so-called mediæval times the teaching was of
ignorance, darkness, and of death. Such teachers as Bacon,

Newton, Kepler, and Humboldt, and in later years Darwin, Spencer, Huxley and Heckel have taught that the ethical and natural life was the only rational life.

All subjects that have engaged the attention of mankind have had teachers and pupils.

Classes have been formed for the study of the Bible since the days of Abraham and Moses, as shown in the book of Nehemiah, which tells of a church school. We read that "Jesus, when twelve years of age, was an earnest scholar within the courts of the Temple."

It is, therefore, probable that a class or school was formed in Hampstead by the earnest band of Christian workers who gathered in the log meeting house fifteen years before the Church of Christ was organized, although we find no authentic account of an organized Sunday school before 1818, and even then, and later to 1875, the records are very imperfect.

The past twenty-five years or more a flourishing Sunday school has been carried on by a corps of faithful teachers and interested pupils.

The officers of the Sunday school are elected annually at the church meeting. The school remembers the Sunday before Christmas with sacred observance, Christmas eve with a tree, Easter and Children's Day with appropriate exercises.

They have a library of 500 volumes. The school has three grades, senior, intermediate, junior or primary, and uses "The Pilgrim Series" of lessons, by M. C. Hazard, Ph. D., and the hymn book, "Heavenly Sunlight," in their service of song.

The school was the first in Rockingham county to observe "Rally Day," in 1898, and annually in October the scholars take special pleasure in their "rallying service."

July, 1902, the officers, teachers and scholars were as follows :—

Superintendent—Forrest E. Merrill.
Assistant Superintendent—John C. Sanborn.
Superintendent Home Department—Miss Mary E. Spollett.
Superintendent Cradle Roll—Mrs. John S. Corson.
Secretary and Treasurer—Miss Myrta A. Little.
Librarians—Fred S. C. Grover and C. Park Pressey.

TEACHERS AND TIME OF SERVICE.

1. Rev. W. H. Woodsum, Senior Class, three months.
2. Mrs. Albert H. Little,   "   "   thirteen years.
3. Prof. F. E. Merrill,   "   "   fifteen   "
4. Mrs. Clara A. Clark,   "   "   six   "
5. Mrs. Jane R. Davis,   "   "   five   "
6. Dea. Wm. H. Davis,   "   "   thirty   "
7. Mrs. Mary E. Eastman,   "   "   five   "
8. Mrs. Sarah J. Brown,   "   "   two   "
9. Mrs. Minnie E. Emerson,   "   "   twelve   "
10. Mary L. Hoyt, Intermediate,   ten   "
11. Minnie M. Fitts, Junior,   three   "
12. Mrs. Inez A. Cass, "   two   "
13. Mrs. Walter H. Woodsum, Junior, three months.

PUPILS OF REV. W. H. WOODSUM.

Bradley N. Haynes,
Albert E. Haynes,
Charles H. Emerson,
Albert H. Little,
Richard Ordway,
James W. Sanborn,
John C. Sanborn,
Albion D. Emerson,
W. Amos Fitts,
W. Alonzo Griffin,

John W. Garland,
Charles W. Garland,
Eugene L. Spinney,
George A. Picard,
Frank N. Pillsbury,
Henry W. Tabor,
Fred S. C. Grover,
C. Park Pressey,
Clinton H. Davis,
Edward M. Noyes.

PUPILS OF MRS. LITTLE.

Howard C. Cass,   .   Howard Putnam,
Will Adams,   Charles Page,

Arthur Hurd,
Thorndike Putnam,
Forrest H. Noyes,
Will W. Bond,

Elbridge Bailey,
Lee W. Noyes,
Clarence Fogg.

PUPILS OF PROF. MERRILL.

Mrs. Bradley N. Haynes,
" Fannie M. Edwards,
" John F. Foss,
" Mary E. Putnam,
" F. E. Merrill,

Mrs. Isaac Randall,
" Angeline Penneo,
" Charles F. Adams,
" W. A. Fitts,
Miss Annie J. Wilson.

PUPILS OF MRS. CLARK.

Mrs. James W. Sanborn,
" John S. Corson,
" George A. Hoyt,
" Chas. H. Emerson,
" Elmer E. Lake,
" Arthur H. Little,

Mrs. Charles W. Garland,
" Henry W. Tabor,
" Carlos W. Noyes,
Miss Mary E. Spollett,
" Aphia Bragdon,
" Annie L. Kimball.

PUPILS OF MRS. DAVIS.

Elsie G. Bartlett,
Ida M. Clark,
Agnes F. Osgood,
Mildred B. Osgood,
Pearl M. Hunt,

Laura M. Spinney,
Alice J. Woods,
Maud B. Foss,
Alice B. Foss.

PUPILS OF DEA. DAVIS.

Mrs. Alden Pillsbury,
" Helen M. Frost,
" Mary J. Sanborn,
" Calvin A. Merrick,
" Mary A. Tabor,
" Job Tabor,

Mrs. C. W. Pressey,
" Sarah A. Rowe,
" Alonzo Griffin,
Miss Ada E. Nichols,
" Anna M. Bartlett,

PUPILS OF MRS. EASTMAN.

Mrs. Aaron Smith,
" Belinda G. Wilson,
" James A. Davis,
" Susan E. Pepper,

Mrs. Wm. H. Woods,
" Benj. G. Hart,
Miss Sarah O. Brickett.

PUPILS OF MRS. BROWN.

Mrs. Emeline E. Mooers, Mrs. Young.
 " Sarah A. Randall,

PUPILS OF MRS. EMERSON.

Mrs. Albion D. Emerson, Miss Gertrude S. Pillsbury,
 " Frank N. Pillsbury,   " Ora L. Ordway,
 " Albert E. Haynes,   " Ethel H. Spinney,
 " George A. F. Pickard, " Alice G. Spinney,
 " Charles Bailey,   " Lillian D. Ranlett,
 " Frank Darling,   " Ida King,
 " John C. Sanborn,   " M. Frances Heath,
 " Richard Ordway,   " Edith Foss,
 " Ellery E. Tabor,   " Grace M. Bassett,
 " George J. Penneo, Jr., " Winifred Winslow,
Miss Esther G. Bailey,   " Elisabeth M. H. Smith,
 " Ethel L. Sanborn,   " Abbie C. Grover,
 " Louise Emery,   " Alice Page,
 " Mary G. Davis,   " Fannie F. Davis.
 " Maud Rowe,

PUPILS OF MISS HOYT.

Margaret Clark,   Carrie E. Sherman,
Bessie Vigneault,   M. Disa King,
Abbie A. Heath,   Glennis F. Ranlett,
Leona C. Garland,   Gladys W. Ranlett,
Pearl G. Ranlett,   Maud S. Putnam,
Laura E. Merrill,   Myrta A. Little,
Nellie F. Adams,   Alice Quimby,
Bernice M. Foss,   Ethel Page.
Alice Clark,

PUPILS OF MISS FITTS.

Ruth N. Bailey,   Gladys Spinney,
Mary Buzzell,   Edith M. Little,
Annie L. Buzzell,   Nettie B. Sherman,
Elsie M. Buzzell,   Louise W. Emerson,

Ethel E. Edwards,
C. Ruth Merrill,
Jeanette E. Merrill,
Flora A. Tabor,
Clara E. Fitts,
Hazel Norton,
Eleanor T. Randall,

Edna Pressey,
George H. Emerson,
Forrest Stickney,
Mary A. Eastman,
Florence Adams,
Marion Adams,
Vida Lake.

PUPILS OF MRS. CASS.

Horace Adams,
Arthur Vigneault,
Fred O. Bailey,
Forrest O. Bailey,
John A. Garland,

Maurice Randall,
Leon Edward,
Wilfred Vigneault,
Forrest Tabor,
Wilfred Stickney.

PUPILS OF MRS. WOODSUM.

Ella M. Emerson,
Alice M. Emerson,
Della Benoit,
Mildred R. Garland,
Florence Merrill,
Mary A. Merrill,
Bessie Buzzell,

Florence Buzzell,
Ethel Hart,
Alta Edwards,
Lucy Adams,
Christie Heath,
Elsie Vigneault.

HOME DEPARTMEMT.

The Home Department was organized Jan. 1, 1898, with fifty-two members. Superintendent, Miss Mary E. Spollett. Assistants, Misses Lillian D. Ranlett, Ethel L. Sanborn. Total number of members, sixty-eight, of whom six have died, fifteen removed from town, six discontinued, and nine transferred to the main school.

The present officers are : Superintendent, Mary E. Spollett; assistants, Mrs. Charles W. Garland and Mrs. Charles O. Cass, with a membership of thirty-one.

THE MEMBERS OF THE HOME DEPARTMENT.

1 Mrs. Cynthia A. Alexander,	35 Mrs. Martha E. Lake,
2 Mrs. Annie N. Beebe,	36 " M. E. Worthen,
3 Anna L. Beede,	37 Miss Lizzie Worthen,
4 Frank J. Beede,	38 " Wilfred Worthen,
5 Clarence Boyce,	39 Harry Worthen.
6 Mrs. Eva Cole,	40 Mrs. Mary George,
7 " Eva Dearborn,	41 " Christia L. McNiel,
8 Miss Jane Mitchell,	42 C. H. Wood,
9 Mrs. John Mills,	43 Mrs. C. P. Noyes,
10 " Herbert W. Mills,	44 Ethel Hart,
11 Carl W. Mills,	45 Isaac W. George,
12 Mrs. Sabrina D. Noyes,	46 Mrs. Nelson Ordway,
13 " Sherman,	47 " Nellie Robbins,
14 " Boyce,	48 Nelson Ordway,
15 " Lydia M. Wells,	49 Mrs. Charles H. Whittier,
16 " Daniel H. Emerson,	50 " Charles W. Bailey,
17 " Sarah A. Emerson,	51 " Alfred P. Emerson,
18 " Anna E. Emerson,	52 " John W. Garland,
19 " Wm. A. Emerson,	53 Miss Lulu J. Corson,
20 " A. A. Webster,	54 Olive M. Noyes,
21 " Harriet A. Stevens,	55 Mrs. B. Frank Rowe,
22 " M. F. S. Smith,	56 Carrie E. Sherman,
23 " Lilla Vigneault,	57 Mrs. Dorcas Brown,
24 " Lydia T. Foote,	58 " William Buzzell,
25 " L. A. Townsend,	59 Florrie Buzzell,
26 " D. A. Barnes,	60 Mrs. Frank Darling,
27 " A. Lyle Eastman,	61 " George Mitchell,
28 " Eliza Cobb,	62 Miss Anna M. Bartlett,
29 " Mary E. Lake,	63 Mrs. B. G. Hart.
30 " Estelle Hayes,	64 Lester A. Williams,
31 " Charles W. Pressey,	65 Harlan P. Clark,
32 " Sarah S. Hoyt,	66 Mrs. Harlan P. Clark,
33 " Mary A. Atwood,	67 " Mary W. Thomas.
34 " Emma A. Marble,	

CRADLE ROLL.

The Hampstead Sunday School was the first in the State to organize a cradle roll in the primary department (Laconia being one mail later) which was formed June 10, 1900, with Mrs. John S. Corson, superintendent, with twenty-eight members. Children retain their membership until the age of five years, when they may be transferred to the main school. The birthdays of the little ones, Christmas and Children's day, are especially remembered for them.

Since the organization eleven have been added to the regular classes, two have died, and one removed from town. Present membership, twenty-nine. Names and dates of birth of the children received to Dec. 1, 1902 :—

Evelyn Worth Randall, b. Nov. 5, 1899.
Marjorie Sanborn, b. April 9, 1900.
Eunice Lake, b. Oct. 22, 1899.
John Edgar Eastman, b. Nov. 6, 1899.
Doris M. Spinney, b. July 31, 1897.
Louise W. Emerson, b. July 6, 1896.
Maurice I. Randall, b. Aug. 17, 1895.
Clara E. Fitts, b. Aug. 19, 1895.
Carrie H. Adams, b. July 3, 1899.
Louis C. Darling, b. Feb. 26, 1898.
Wilfred D. Stickney, b. March 31, 1900.
Verta J. Wilson, b. March 31, 1900.
Lester A. Haynes, b. June 21, 1900; d. Apr. 16, 1901.
Elwin M. Darling, b. May 29, 1900; d. Sept. 15, 1901.
Caroline Darling, b. Sept. 18, 1901.
Adin E. Little, b. Oct. 28, 1898.
George H. Emerson, b. Nov. 15, 1897.
Burton L. Coombs, b. May 11, 1898.
Jessie S. Buzzell, b. Sept. 21, 1899.
Zelda L. Pressey, b. Oct. 11, 1898.
Vera May Coombs, b. Aug. 10, 1900.
Ernest C. Pillsbury, b. Oct. 19, 1900.
Hollis A. Emerson, b. Feb. 4, 1901.

EVELYN W. RANDALL, FIRST MEMBER OF THE CRADLE ROLL.

Esther Picard, b. Feb. 21, 1901.
Perry E. Little, b. Apr. 12, 1901.
Roland C. Emerson, b. Feb. 15, 1902.
Wilbur Herbert Picard, b. Feb. 28, 1902.
Florence Adams, b. Dec. 21, 1895.
Walter I. Tabor, b. Oct. 31, 1896.
Earle E. Haynes, b. Feb. 27, 1896.
Nettie B. Sherman, b. Apr. 20, 1896.
Elizabeth I. Mitchell, b. June 7, 1896.
Vida A. Lake, b. March 10, 1896.
Forrest E. Stickney, b. Oct. 8, 1896.
Albert C. Lake, b. Oct. 18, 1897.
Freda R. Fitts, b. July 21, 1900.
Thalma H. Mitchell, b. July 28, 1900.
Elmer E. Buzzell, b. Feb. 21, 1902.
Donald Fitts Sanborn, b. Sept. 13, 1902.
Everett C. Mills, b. May 25, 1902.
Charles A. Fitts, b. Jan. 9, 1902.

CHRISTIAN ENDEAVOR SOCIETY.

The Christian Endeavor Society connected with the church was organized in Hampstead, May 8, 1894, with twenty-seven members. The following officers were chosen : President, Forrest E. Merrill ; vice-president, Charles W. Garland ; recording secretary, Lillian D. Ranlett ; corresponding secretary, Mrs. Rufus P. Gardner ; treasurer, Edwin L. Corson.

For 1895 : President, Annie J. Wilson ; vice-president, H. Walter Little; recording secretary, Mary G. Davis ; treasurer, Charles T. Foote. Mrs. R. P. Gardner held the office of corresponding secretary until her removal from town, September, 1901.

1896 : President, John C. Sanborn ; vice-president, H. Ethel Spinney ; recording secretary, Esther G. Bailey ; treasurer, Charles T. Foote.

1897: President, Kimball K. Clark; vice-president, Esther G. Bailey; recording secretary, Addie B. Gardner treasurer, Lillian D. Ranlet.

1898: President, Albion D. Emerson; vice-president, Addie B. Gardner; recording secretary, M. Frances Heath; treasurer, Lillian D. Ranlett.

1899: President, Mary E. Spollett; vice-president, M. Frances Heath; recording secretary, Mary G. Davis; treasurer, Richard Ordway.

1900: President, Mrs. Charles O. Cass; vice-president, H. Walter Little; recording secretary, Nellie M. Tabor; treasurer, Richard Ordway.

1901: President, Richard Ordway; vice-president, Mrs. John C. Sanborn; recording secretary, Laura E. Merrill; treasurer, Mrs. Ellery E. Tabor.

Present officers, 1902: President, M. Frances Heath; vice-president, Mary E. Spollett; recording secretary, Abbie A. Heath; corresponding secretary, Mrs. Frank W. Emerson.

LIST OF PRESENT MEMBERS.

1	Forrest E. Merrill,	17	Mary E. Spollett,
2	Mrs. Forrest E. Merrill,	18	Annie J. Wilson,
3	" Frank W. Emerson,	19	Minnie M. Fitts,
4	John C. Sanborn,	20	Richard Ordway,
5	Mrs. John C. Sanborn,	21	Mrs. Albert H. Little,
6	" Calvin A. Merrick,	22	Myrta A. Little,
7	Ethel L. Sanborn,	23	Agnes F. Osgood,
8	H. Ethel Spinney,	24	Laura E. Merrill,
9	H. Walter Little,	25	Elsie G. Bartlett,
10	Mrs. Charles W. Garland.	26	Laura E. Baker,
11	" Ellery E. Tabor,	27	Mildred B. Osgood,
12	Mary G. Davis,	28	Howard C. Cass,
13	Mrs. Charles O. Cass,	29	G. Pearl Ranlett,
14	Esther G. Bailey,	30	Ida M. Clark,
15	Ora L. Ordway,	31	Leona C. Garland,
16	M. Frances Heath,	32	Edith B. Foss,

33 Florence M. Merrill,
34 Alice B. Foss,
35 Bernice M. Foss,
36 Mrs. Isaac Randall,
37 Alice H. Page,
38 Mary A. Merrill,

39 Mrs. Richard Ordway,
40 Rev. W. H. Woodsum,
41 Mrs. W. H. Woodsum,
42 Annie L. Kimball,
43 Alice G. Spinney.

ASSOCIATE MEMBERS.

1. Ella M. Emerson,
2 Alice M. Emerson,
3 Effie Senter,

4 Bernice Senter,
5 Lizzie Worthen.

HONORARY MEMBERS.

1 Wm. H. Davis,
2 Charles W. Garland,
3 Mrs. Mary E. Eastman,
4 W. Amos Fitts,
5 Mrs. W. Amos Fitts,
6 " Wm. H. Woods,
7 " Clara A. Clark,
8 " Belle G. Wilson,
9 Bradley N. Haynes,
10 Mrs. Bradley N. Haynes,
11 " Wm. H. Davis,
12 " Lydia M. Wells,
13 " Charles W. Pressey,
14 " James A. Davis,
15 Miss Sarah O. Brickett,
16 John W. Garland,
17 Clarence H. Wood,

18 Mrs. Mary Tabor,
19 " Emeline E. Mooers,
20 " Job Tabor,
21 James W. Sanborn,
22 Mrs. James W. Sanborn,
23 " Henry W. Tabor,
24 " Harlan P. Clark,
25 " Sarah J. Brown,
26 Miss Mary L. Hoyt,
27 Mrs. Wm. A. Emerson,
28 " Benjamin G. Hart,
29 " Carlos W. Noyes,
30 Albion D. Emerson,
31 Mrs. Albion D. Emerson,
32 Miss Lillian D. Ranlett,
33 Mrs. Mary J. Sanborn.

Mrs. Lillian R. Sanborn, an active member, died May 2, 1897.

Walter H. Moulton, an associate member, died Nov. 5, 1898.

Mrs. Mary J. Fellows, an honorary member, died Aug. 11, 1901; also Mrs. Nelson Ordway, March, 1900; Mrs. John

W. Garland, Feb, 1901, and Mrs. Mary A. Pike, March, 1901.

There have been 100 active members, 32 associate members, and 40 honorary members admitted since the organization of the C. E. Society.

The Junior Christian Endeavor Society was organized June 9, 1898, with twelve members. Officers for the year were: Superintendent, Miss Addie B. Gardner; assistant superintendent, M. Frances Heath; president, Laura E. Merrill; vice president, Abbie A. Heath; secretary, Nellie M. Tabor; treasurer, Bessie A. Vigneault; organist, Mrs. R. P. Gardner.

The meetings are held each Sunday afternoon. The little ones, whose ages range from two to thirteen years, have their officers and committees, and conduct their services in the same manner as the senior society. Once in two weeks they meet at the different homes of the members and have a prayer service, and on alternate Saturdays a time for sewing and making articles for sale.

The members during the year of 1898 were:—

Laura E. Merrill,
Abbie A. Heath,
Nellie M. Tabor,
Bessie A. Vigneault,
Christie R. Heath,
Alta E. Edwards,
Mary A. Merrill,
Elsie O. Vigneault,
Lucy A. Adams,
Ethel E. Edwards,
Florence M. Merrill,
Howard C. Cass,
Harold P. Gardner,
Florence E. Buzzell,
Glennis F. Ranlett,
Gladys W. Ranlett,

G. Pearl Ranlett,
Maud S. Putnam,
Mildred L. Tucker,
Alice M. Emerson,
Ella M. Emerson,
Bernice M. Senter,
Esther M. Hunt,
Emma F. Hunt,
Lottie M. Whittier,
Nellie Adams,
Albert Gates,
Arthur Gates,
Grace Whittier,
Seymour Smith,
Arthur A. Bond.

Officers for 1899 were: President, Laura E. Merrill; vice-president, Mary A. Merrill; secretary, Abbie A. Heath; treasurer, Bessie A. Vigneault; superintendent, Addie B. Gardner; assistant superintendent, M. Frances Heath.

Officers for 1900 were: President, Harold P. Gardner; vice-president, Elsie O. Vigneault; secretary and treasurer, Ella M. Emerson; superintendent, M. Frances Heath; assistant superintendent, Addie B. Gardner.

Officers, 1901: President, Bessie A. Vigneault; vice-president, Florence M. Merrill; secretary, Elsie O. Vigneault; treasurer, Flora A. Tabor; superintendent, M. Frances Heath.

Officers, 1902, same as 1901, with addition of Mrs. Josie F. Tabor as assistant superintendent.

The membership, July, 1902, was as follows;—

Elsie O. Vigneault,	Ethel E. Edwards,
Bessie A. Vigneault,	Florence E. Buzzell,
Florence M. Merrill,	Bessie M. Buzzell,
Ruth C. Merrill,	Arthur A. Bond,
Jeannette C. Merrill,	Bernice M. Senter,
Alice M. Emerson,	Arthur Vigneault,
Ella M. Emerson,	Wilfred U. Vigneault,
Clifford D. Emerson,	Della M. Benoit.
Christie R. Heath,	Flora A. Tabor.
Alta E. Edwards,	

THE LADIES' SOCIETIES.

The Female Cent Society, constituting a branch of the New Hampshire Female Cent Institution, was organized in 1861. Miss Ann M. Howard was chosen treasurer, "and as many solicitors as was deemed needful." In the forty-one years of its existence the ladies have contributed to the New Hampshire Society $1036, an average of $25 annually.

The members in 1861 were :—

Mrs. Benjamin B. Garland,
"   Mary A. Pike,
"   Meribah Putnam,
"   E. Augusta Pratt,
"   Nabby K. Brickett,
"   Susan R. Eastman,
"   Annie J. Smith,
"   Abigail Heath,
"   Martha H. Sanborn,
"   Jonathan Kent,
Miss Ann M. Howard,
"   Abbie R. Heath,
"   Mary J. Heath,
"   Mary A. Merrill,
Mrs. Benj. Pillsbury,
"   John Emerson,
"   Helen Smith,
"   Judith A. Gibson,
"   Mary J. Buck,
"   Sally Marshall,

Mrs. Anna Swan,
"   Susan Merrill,
"   Adeline H. Eastman,
"   Lois Sanborn,
"   Elizabeth Knight,
"   Mary K. Ricker,
"   Elvira P. Howe,
"   Eliza S. Ordway,
"   Louise Ordway,
Miss Nancy R. Marston,
"   Samantha C. Merrill,
"   Abbie A. Currier,
Mrs. James Calef,
"   Enos Colby,
"   Ezekiel Currier,
"   Charles Eastman,
"   Frank Kent,
"   John Jackson,
"   Mary L. Chase.

Members of the Juvenile Society: Mary P. Merrill and Mary Sanborn.

Members in 1902 are :—

Mrs. Sarah J. Brown,
"   Mary A. Tabor,
"   W. Amos Fitts,
"   Mary J. Sanborn,
"   Henry W. Tabor,
"   Emeline E. Mooers,
"   Albion D. Emerson,
"   Sarah Randall,
"   Aaron Smith,
"   Etta M. Tupper,
"   Daniel H. Emerson,
"   Wm. A. Emerson,
"   John S. Corson,

Mrs. James A. Davis,
"   Sabrina D. Noyes,
"   Albert H. Little,
"   Charles W. Garland,
"   Mary E. Putnam,
"   Alden Pillsbury,
"   Frank N. Pillsbury,
"   John C. Sanborn,
"   Lydia M. Wells,
"   Charles W. Pressey,
"   Mary C. Atwood,
"   Belinda G. Wilson,
"   Mary J. Sanborn,

Mrs. Clara A. Clark,
"   Isaac Randall,
"   Mary E. Eastman,
"   Carlton Barnes,
"   W. Alonzo Griffin,
"   Martha (Sanborn) Ord-
        way,

Miss Mary E. Spollett,
"   Mary F. Heath,
"   Annie L. Kimball,
"   Sarah O. Brickett,
"   Gertrude S. Pillsbury.

JUVENILE MEMBERS.

Vera A. Bennett,
Alta Edwards,
Grace I. Leach,

Ethel E. Edwards,
Flora A. Tabor,
Clara E. Fitts.

Honorary member—W. Amos Fitts.

The Woman's Foreign Missionary Society, auxiliary to the N. H. Branch of the Woman's Board of Missions, was organized May 31, 1874, with Miss Ann M. Howard, president, and thirty-three members. Only eleven are living in 1902. Mrs. Mary J. (Heath) Sanborn has been secretary and treasurer from the organization to 1902. The members have contributed in all $452, an average of fifteen dollars annually.

The members in 1902 are :—

Mrs. Martha(Sanborn)Ordway,
 ·   Clara A. Davis,
Miss Sarah O. Brickett,
"   Agnes Millar,
Mrs. Mary C. Atwood,
"   Belinda G. Wilson,
"   Charles O. Cass,
"   James W. Sanborn,
"   Charles W. Pressey,
"   John W. Tabor,
"   Mary E. Eastman,

Mrs. John H. Clark,
"   Isaac Randall,
"   Calvin A. Merrick,
"   Aaron Smith,
"   W. Amos Fitts,
"   Mary J. Sanborn,
Miss Mary E. Spollett,
Mrs. Joseph G. Brown,
"   Sabrina D. Noyes,
"   Alden Pillsbury,
Miss Gertrude S. Pillsbury.

The ladies have, without doubt, added their efforts and aid to every good work through all of the years of the growth of the church, but in attempting to write a history covering a period of years in which no official record seems to have been kept, we can only give a few facts as told by old people, which they had heard from their elders, concerning the work done by the women of the Hampstead church in the early part of the past century. We are told that the ladies in 1830 took great delight in their sewing circle, that they made dickies, both ruffled and plain, stocks, collars and wristbands, which they sold to the gentlemen who joined them at the substantial supper and the social hours of the evening ; that donation parties were an interesting feature of the work of the ladies, and many a sick and needy family in Hampstead was relieved by their kind offerings.

We find no written record of an organization until 1852, when they subscribed their names to the following constitution :—

Article 1. The name of this association shall be the Hampstead Ladies' Charitable Society.

Art. 2. The object of this society shall be to create funds, by work or other approved means, to be appropriated to such objects of charity as shall be agreeable to a majority of the members at any regular meeting.

Art. 3. Any lady contributing annually twenty-five cents to the funds of the association shall be a member.

Art. 4. The officers of the society shall be a superintendent, two assistant superintendents, and secretary, who shall be the treasurer. These shall appoint as many collectors as they shall deem expedient, and shall constitute a board of managers.

Art. 5. There shall be an annual meeting of the association at such time and place as the board of managers shall designate, when a report shall be presented by the secretary, officers elected for the ensuing year, and such other business transacted to promote the objects of the association.

ART. 6. The society shall meet at least once a month, together or in sections, as may be agreed upon by its members.

ART. 7. This constitution shall be subject to an alteration at only a regular meeting, and upon the recommendation of the board of managers.

The names of the signers of this constitution were :—

Mrs. Susan Bartley,
Susan R. Eastman,
Nabby K. Brickett,
Adeline H. Eastman,
Sally Harriman,
Elizabeth Emerson,
Clarissa Kent,
Susan C. Eastman,
Polly Ayer,
Mary Jane Kimball,
Eliza S. Ordway,
Elvira Ordway,
Emma E. Ordway,
Louisa M. Ordway,
Nancy Ordway,
Hannah H. Chase,
Elizabeth M. Chase,
Betsey E. Eastman,
Susan E. M. Stevens,
Elizabeth Calef,
Martha Jane Adolphus,
Judith S. Eastman,
Sally Heath,
Eliza Jane Nichols,
Lois Sanborn,
Clara Ann Kent,
Elizabeth Ann Smith,
Abigail R. Heath,
Ann M. Howard,
Martha B. Marble,
Sabra F. Tewksbury,
Emily J. Davis,
Priscilla Sawyer.

The proceeds during that year, 1852, were $13.62, of which $6.53 were expended as follows by the society : One piece of cotton cloth, $2.30 ; two spools of cotton and buttons, 14c.; needles, 9c.; chimneys, 25c.; oil, 35c.; one piece of cotton cloth, $2.20 ; a blank book, 20c.; and the remainder of their money was given to the " Seaman's Friend Society " at Portsmouth.

The officers chosen for the year 1852 were : Mrs. Susan Bartley, superintendent; Mrs. Susan Eastman and Mrs. Nabby Brickett, assistants ; Mrs. Adeline H. Eastman, secretary and treasurer.

In 1853 additional members were Esther Bartley, Hannah

Drew, Mary Griffin, Mary J. Heath, Mary S. Kent, Ruth G. Merrill, Mrs. Pillsbury, Angeline Simpson, Ann E. Sawyer, Mary P. Eastman.

June 7, 1852, they met at Mrs. Tappan Eastman's, with fourteen members present, and reorganized by the choice of Miss Esther Bartley as superintendent; Mrs. Tappan Eastman and Miss Mary P. Eastman, assistants ; Mrs. Adeline H. Eastman, secretary and treasurer ; and they also voted to meet at the different houses and take tea, two kinds of food only to be served, and that the proceeds for the year should go to the Home Missionary Society.

Aug. 6, 1853, they met at the house of Mrs. Marble, with thirty-six members present. The meeting was opened by prayer by Mrs. Elizabeth Emerson. Then they cut a piece of cloth into sheets and pillow cases. Mrs. Mount gave them one dollar, and they received from a member who brought her own work, three cents.

Sept. 7, 1853, forty members were present at Mrs. Joseph Chase's. The ladies finished the piece of cloth cut at the last meeting and bound a half set of shoes.

Oct. 5, they met at Mrs. John Heath's, and with thirty-five present made fifteen pairs of overalls, they being cut and fitted by the superintendent previous to the meeting, and shoes were bound amounting to $2.12.

Nov. 8, at Mrs. John D. Ordway's, some of the time was devoted to reading from the Memoirs of Mrs. Greenleaf. Thirty-five ladies made sixteen pairs of overalls, and ladies who brought their own work paid 49 cents.

Dec. 13, forty-five met at Mrs. Kimball Brickett's and bound shoes.

January, 1854, forty-seven present made overalls and bound shoes ; singing and prayers.

Jan. 31, fifty-six met at Mrs. Nelson Ordway's and bound shoes amounting to $2.20.

Feb. 14, seventy-five met at Mrs. N. C. Smith's, where they

sold confections and had many contributions from the gentlemen, and remarks by Mr. Bartley, their pastor.

Feb. 28, eighty met at Mrs. Tristram Little's and bound shoes, etc.

March 8, forty met at Mrs. Drew's and bound shoes.

April, fifty met at Mrs. Bartley's.

May, forty met at Mrs. Silas Griffin's.

June 29, 1854, twenty met at Mrs. Benj. Pillsbury's. The secretary reported as follows of the year's work: The society has met thirteen times, besides the annual meeting. List of articles made by the society and presented · to the "Seaman's Friend Society," Boston: Two and one-half pairs of sheets, $2.65; six pillow cases, $2.10; two pairs shirts, $2.26. Cotton cloth remaining, $2.33; yarn and knitting, 50c.; quilt, $2; money received for work, $47.16, and remaining as avails for the year $50.13, which was appropriated in the following manner: Thirty dollars was given to constitute Rev. Mr. Bartley a life member of the American Home Missionary Society; fifteen dollars to the Mission among the Chinese in California, receipts for which have been received, and also a bundle valued at $6.91 to the Seaman's Home in Boston.

Sept. 6, 1854, sixteen ladies met at the meeting house and listened to a reading by Mrs. Bartley upon being "ready for every good work," after which a new constitution was adopted and a new force of officers elected: Mrs. Esther Bartley, president; Mrs. Hannah J. Drew, vice-president; Miss Judith S. Eastman, secretary; Miss Emma E. Ordway, treasurer; and Mrs. Elizabeth P. Ordway, Mrs. Louisa M. Ordway, Mrs. Nabby K. Brickett, Mrs. Phebe L. Sawyer, Miss Abby R. Heath, were chosen directresses. They adopted as a preamble, "Believing that union is strength, and that voluntary associations for benevolent purposes have a direct tendency to promote and strengthen the kindred feelings we ought to cherish towards each other, the subscribers propose to form themselves into a society, the object of which shall be the extension of the knowledge and influence of the gospel and mutual improvement, and for this purpose we adopt the new constitution."

The new constitution was not materially different from the one formed in 1852, except they were to be governed by a president, vice-president, secretary and treasurer, and five directresses. "That one-half hour of each meeting should be devoted to reading," and that "any gentleman who sustains a good moral character may become a member of this society by paying twenty-five cents annually." The only new members of the forty ladies who signed the constitution were: Marietta Buck, Mary J. Drew, Annette Colby, Julia A. Colby, Betsey P. Little, Mary A. Pike, Lydia A. Ring, Mary J. Titcomb, Sophia A. Greenleaf, Abby B. Spollett.

The work was carried on as in 1853, and Mrs. Susan Bartley was made a life member of the American Home Missionary Society by the payment of thirty dollars from their proceeds for the year 1854.

It was in these years that the society was very dear to its members. (See No. 423, "Sketches of Members.")

In 1856 there were twenty members, but their meetings were largely attended, as in March, 1856, at Mrs. N. C. Smith's, they had seventy present, collected $7.08, and presented Mr. Bartley with twelve dollars as a gift.

Jan. 11, 1860, the society was again reorganized, and their constitution very little changed. The following members signed it for the year :—

Mrs. Susan Batchelder,
  "   R. K. Brickett,
  "   Elizabeth Calef,
Miss Abby Currier,
  "   Julia A. Colby,
Mrs. Jesse Davis,
  "   Adeline Eastman,

Mrs. Thomas K. Little,
  "   William C. Little,
  "   Caleb Moulton,
Miss Nancy Marston,
  "   Nancy Ordway,
Mrs. Nelson Ordway,
  "   J. D. Ordway,

Mrs. Dea. Eastman,
" George W. Eastman,
Miss Sophia A. Greenleaf,
Mrs. Sally Harriman,
" Isaac Heath,
Miss Ann M. Howard,
" Abby R. Heath,
" Mary J. Heath,
Mrs. John Jackson,
" Dea. Kent,
Miss Sarah Little,

Mrs. T. C. Pratt,
" Henry Putnam,
" Benjamin Sawyer,
" William Sanborn,
" John W. Tabor,
" John Ordway,
" John C. Drew,
" Tristram Little,
" Amos Ring,
" Sarah Chandler.

HONORARY MEMBERS.

Rev. T. C. Pratt,
Mr. Amos Buck,
" D. H. Emerson,
" Nelson Ordway,
" N. C. Smith,

Mr. L. W. Frost,
" John S. Titcomb,
" Frank Kent,
" George W. Eastman.

They elected Mrs. John C. Drew, president; Mrs. T. C. Pratt, vice-president; Sophia A. Greenleaf, secretary and treasurer.

Voted, that thirty dollars in their hands be appropriated to constitute Rev. T. C. Pratt a "life member of the American and Foreign Christian Union." There were nearly a hundred persons present.

In 1860 there were forty-four members—thirty-five ladies and nine gentlemen—and they had sixteen meetings, all largely attended.

From 1860 to 1868 the society meetings were well attended, and in the form of a social, with readings and other entertainments in the evenings at various homes. Sept. 8, 1862, it is recorded at a meeting at R. K. Brickett's, "a good number of young people were present, and cheerfulness and sociability prevailed." And Aug. 20, 1862, "a number of the volunteers were present, and addresses made by Mr. Pratt, Messrs. Garland and Buck in a happy manner." Much of the money raised was given to the "Soldiers' Aid Society." Few meetings were holden without at least seventy-five persons present.

In September, 1867, the annual meeting was held at the house of Mrs. Tappan Eastman, with few present, and the reorganization of the Society was effected by voting to take some of the funds collected at the social and purchase materials for work, and that Mrs. T. C. Pratt have charge of the Charitable Society only, and Mrs. J. Henry Clark look after the social gatherings connected with it. The members admitted at that time were :—

Mrs. Mary E. Irving,
" W. H. Brickett,
" J. H. Clark,
" Isaac Smith,
" Mary Brickett,
" J. T. Brickett,
" L. W. Frost,
" Luther Chase,
" Hannah Titcomb,
" Ann Howard,
" T. C. Pratt,
" E. M. Locke,
" Tappan Eastman,
" Sally Harriman,
" Abby Brickett,
" Benjamin Sawyer,
" Lizzie Hunkins,
Miss Mary A. Merrill,

Miss Mary E. Merrill,
" Lucy A. Sawyer,
Mrs. B. F. Herrick,
" Tristram Little,
Miss M. Jennie Little,
" Lizzie Locke,
" Edwina Eaton,
Henry Putnam,
John C. Little,
John Jackson,
Linus H. Little,
George O. Jenness,
Adin T. Little,
Charles Peasley,
Frank H. Sawyer,
B. Frank Herrick,
John H. Clark,
Dea. Jona. Kent.

Nov. 5, 1867, the ladies met for work in the afternoon at Mrs. Kimball Brickett's, and only eleven members present. Knitting was introduced and six pairs of hose commenced, and in the evening of that day the social was held at Mrs. Jesse Emerson's, and about "fifty present and a royal good time enjoyed."

Trouble ensued, and in 1868 only three members would unite with the society—Mrs. E. M. Locke, Mrs. Colby, and Mrs. Nelson Ordway.

We find no records of meetings holden until December, 1870, when a few ladies met at Mrs. John H. Clark's for the purpose of forming a "Ladies' Benevolent Society, which was organized with Mrs. E. W. Bullard as president, Mrs. Mary C. Brickett as vice-president, Mrs. Wm. H. Davis as secretary and treasurer, and a committee in each school district to find places to hold meetings—Mrs. Wm. C. Little, No. 1; Miss Mary J. Heath, No. 2; Miss H. A. Eastman, No. 8; Mrs. M. A. Eastman, No. 4.

The constitution drawn by the committee, Mrs. E. W. Bullard, Mrs. Mary C. Brickett, Mrs. Wm. H. Davis, and Miss Ann M. Howard, was as follows;—

"PREAMBLE.—We, the ladies of the Congregational Church and Society, believing that volunteer association for benevolent purposes has a direct tendency to promote and strengthen the kindred feelings we ought to cherish towards each other, and that we ought to be ready for every good work, we therefore propose to form ourselves into a society with the design to promote these objects. We therefore recommend and agree to be governed by the foregoing constitution.

ART. 1. This Society shall be called "The Hampstead Ladies' Benevolent Society."

ART. 2. The object of this Society shall be to cultivate acquaintance with ladies in different sections of the town, to promote unanimity of feeling on all subjects tending to elevate society generally, and also to procure funds for benevolent purposes.

ART. 3. Any one over fourteen years of age can become a member of this Society by paying twenty-five cents annually.

ART. 6. In order to increase the funds it is expected that all present at any meeting, whether members or not, shall pay five cents.

Articles 4, 5, 7, 8, 9 and 10, relating to business of the officers, etc.

The members belonging to the Benevolent Society were:

Rev. Mr. Bullard,
William H. Davis,
Horace R. Sawyer,
John H. Clark,
R. K. Brickett,
J. S. Titcomb,
Dea. Sanborn,
Joseph Chase,
John W. Tabor,
James Knight,
Nathaniel Smith,
Silas Tenney,
J. D. Ordway,
H. C. Eastman,
J. L. Cunningham,
Nelson Ordway,
Tristram Little,
Rufus Bailey,
Caleb J. Hoyt,
Mrs. E. W. Bullard,
" R. K. Brickett,
" Benjamin Sawyer,
" Amos Buck,
Miss Mary J. Heath,
" Abby R. Heath,
Mrs. C. J. Hoyt,
" J. H. Clark,
" W. H. Davis,
Miss M. E. Clark,
Dr. W. E. Bullard,
Mr. and Mrs. Albert Pressey,
Miss Agnes Millar,

Mrs. George O. Jenness,
" John Titcomb,
Miss Helen A. Eastman,
Mrs. William Sanborn,
" M. Irving,
" Nathaniel Smith,
" Rufus C. Smith,
Miss H. E. Hoyt,
Mrs. M. C. Brickett,
" George W. Eastman,
" H. C. Eastman,
" M. A. Currier,
" Isaac Heath,
Miss Anna L. Heath,
Mrs. E. M. Locke,
" Tristram Little,
" Sally Harriman,
" Sally Hubbard,
Miss A. M. Howard,
" Lucy A. Bullard,
Mrs. Nelson Ordway,
Miss Nancy Ordway,
Mrs. John Jackson,
" Abner Chandler,
" Susan V. Eastman,
Mr. Jacob Irving,
Mr. and Mrs. Alonzo Griffin,
Fannie Williams, infant,
George R. Bennette.
Mrs. J. Kimball,
Mrs. C. J. Sherman.

The members held meetings at the various homes of the members, with afternoon work on quilts, shirts and knitting work, and a social gathering in the evening, interspersed with songs, recitations and games. In 1877 the secretary says: "Less interest has been manifested during the past year and less meetings held than any previous year." Only nine meetings of the Benevolent Society were held in 1878. In May it is recorded that "The Ladies' Sociable met at the Town Hall; prayer by Rev. Albert Watson; 'the Social Gem' was prepared by Misses Cynthia S. Mills and Susie C. Smith, and recitations by Rev. Albert Watson and Master Charlie Grover." They received $4 by admission at the door.

The Benevolent Society held few meetings until Jan. 14, 1880, when the members met with the "Sociable" at Mrs. Alfred Emerson's, Jan. 14, where there were eighty persons present, and the members of the Benevolent Society "excused themselves to elect some new officers."

Very little interest was manifested in the meetings, the "sociable" being the leading attraction for the young people of the parish. The members were:—

Rev. and Mrs. Albert Watson,	Edwin S. Pressey,
Mr. and Mrs. W. A. Emerson,	Mrs. Margaret Marshall,
Dea. and Mrs. C. W. Williams,	" E. M. Locke,
Mr. and Mrs. Chas. W. Pressey,	" Tappan Eastman,
Mr. and Mrs. John H. Clark,	" Laura Corson,
Dea. and Mrs. Wm. Sanborn,	" Belinda G. Wilson,
Mr. and Mrs. Fred A. Pike,	" Mary E. Irving,
Mr. and Mrs. Joseph G. Brown,	" Wm Fellows,
Mr. and Mrs. Moses B. Little,	" Almira Perley,
Mrs. M. E. Corson,	" Lizzie Hunkins,
Mr. and Mrs. Tristram Little,	" Martha E. Lake,
Mr. and Mrs. Nelson Ordway,	" Lizzie Coaker,
Mr. and Mrs. Ezra W. Foss,	" Lizzie Little,
Mrs. R. K. Brickett,	" Abner Chandler,
Jesse B. Shirley,	Miss Abbie F. Chandler,

C. H. Wood,	Miss Abbie Pillsbury,
Daniel H. Emerson,	" Nellie F. Perley,
Mr. and Mrs. P. H. Shannon,	. " Abbie Heath,
Capt. William Griffin,	" Ann M. Howard,
Col. Albert L. Eastman,	" Lucy S. Johnson,
Willie A. Love,	" Abbie A. Johnson,
Arthur Bond,	" Judith Eastman,
Rufus H. Bailey,	" Clara A. Irving,
Fred Clark,	" Annie E. George.

The first four months of 1880 were memorable for the enjoyable evenings spent by the members of the Sociable and their young friends. In January they met with Mrs. Alfred Emerson, with eighty present; February, with Mrs. Charles W. Pressey, thirty-six present; March 8, with Mrs. Charles Osgood, with eighty present; March 19, Mrs. Eben Hoyt's, with twenty-two present; March 31, at Mr. Giles Marble's, with forty-two; April 18, at Mrs. Dea. Sanborn's, fifty-three attending; and April 18, at Mrs. E. M. Coaker's, with fifty-seven present. At each meeting there were various games, charades, recitations, readings and singing by the young people. They then adjourned until autumn, when the parties were again resumed. The secretary, in her annual report for the year ending Oct. 29, 1881, records : "For various reasons it has not been thought best to meet as often as in some years past. We trust, however, that some good has been accomplished, which shall benefit not only those of us who have met together to enjoy a social hour, but some less favored than ourselves." The report of the year showed that they held ten meetings, a membership of fifty-five— thirty-seven ladies and eighteen gentlemen—and raised $81.81 ; that they had sent $10 to foreign missions, two barrels of clothing and two dollars sent to the Kansas refugees, and $19.91 spent for necessary articles for the church.

At that date, Oct. 29, 1881, they voted " to revise the constitution," by a committee consisting of Mrs. E. M.

Coaker, Miss Abbie A. Johnson, and Mrs. Mary E. Eastman, which was adopted at an adjourned meeting, Nov. 9, 1881, at Y. M. C. A. Hall, as follows:—

ART. 1. This society shall be an auxiliary to the Congregational Church at Hampstead, and its name shall be "The Ladies' Social Circle."

ART. 2. The object of this Society shall be to cultivate acquaintance with ladies in different sections of the town, to promote unanimity of feeling on all subjects tending to elevate society generally, and also to raise funds for the benefit of the church and society, and for other objects, as shall from time to time be decided on by a vote of the Society.

ART. 3. Any lady over fourteen years of age may become an active member, and any gentleman over fourteen years of age may become an honorary member by paying twenty-five cents annually.

ART. 4. In order to increase the funds it is expected that all present at any meeting, whether members or not, shall pay five cents.

ART. 5. The officers of the Society shall be a president, vice-president, and secretary, who shall also act as treasurer.

ART. 6. There shall be an annual meeting of the Society early in October, when a report shall be presented by the secretary, officers elected for the ensuing year, and any other business transacted as shall be deemed necessary to promote the objects of the Society.

ART. 7. The officers may at any time call a special meeting by giving due notice in the church.

ART. 8. Eight members shall constitute a quorum for the transaction of business.

ART. 9. This constitution shall be altered or amended by a two-thirds vote of the Society at any regular meeting.

ART. 10. Each meeting shall be closed with prayer.

The officers then chosen were: Mrs. John Page, president; Mrs. Alfred Emerson, vice-president; and Katie E.

Coaker, secretary and treasurer. The members joining the "Ladies' Social Circle" in 1881, Nov. 9, for the following year, were :—

Mrs. E. M. Coaker,
" Mary E. Eastman,
" C. W. Williams,
" John Page,
" J. Henry Clark,
" C. W. Pressey,
" Belinda Wilson,
" Alfred Emerson,
" O. E. Follansbee,
" R. K. Brickett,
" Mary A. Bragdon,
" E. M. Locke,
" Lizzie Little,
" Nellie Ordway,
" Bailey,
" Abner Chandler,
" Nelson Ordway,
" Mary E. Corson,
" Laura A. Corson
" Amanda Cass,
Miss Judith S. Eastman,
" Katie E. Coaker,
" Lizzie Johnson,
" Abbie A. Johnson,
" Lucy Johnson,
" Annie Graham,

Miss Ann M. Howard,
" Nellie Perley,
" Ada Nichols,
" Alice M. Little,
" Mary E. Spollett,
" Agnes Millar,
Rev. and Mrs. Albert Watson,
Mrs. Joseph G. Brown,
" Lewis Little,
" Lizzie Hunkins,
Mr. Wm. H. Davis,
Dea. John Page,
John S. Corson,
J. Henry Clark,
Capt. Moffatt,
Col. A. L. Eastman,
Charles H. Emerson,
Charles W. Garland,
Mariner Chase,
John Lawton,
Isaac Randall,
Forrest E. Merrill,
Dr. Isaac Tewksbury,
George E. Lake,
George G. Williams,
F. W. Coaker.

The first meeting of the "Ladies' Social Circle" was held at Mrs. E. M. Coaker's, with eighty persons present, who were entertained with instrumental music by Susie Stimson and Etta Hunkins, singing by Abbie F. Chandler, Mrs. Coaker, John S. Corson and William H. Davis. Prayer by Rev. Albert Watson. $8.65 was collected, also a present from Miss Hannah Howard of $10.

From this meeting the members of the Social Circle showed an interest in the work from year to year, and during the colder season meetings were held every two weeks at the homes, which were largely attended and enjoyed.

In June, 1886, several deeply interested ladies who were tireless workers, and seeing urgent need of funds to finish and furnish the parlor, kitchen, etc., incident to the new vestry, in a manner creditable to the church organization, pledged themselves to work especially for that cause, but not realizing the extent or how much they might accomplish, no special records were kept, It is, therefore, from the reminiscences of Mrs. G. R. Bennette and other of the ladies interested that we are indebted for items concerning their work.

The first meeting was held in the Town Hall, where a dozen or more ladies met and talked over plans of how they could raise the most money for their purpose, and adjourned to meet with Mrs. E. M. Locke in one week, when many more ladies met with them, and they named themselves the " Vestry Aid Society," which included most of the ladies of the church and society who were conveniently situated to be helpers. They chose Mrs. Mary E. Eastman, Mrs. Mary J. Fellows, Mrs. E. M. Coaker and Mrs. George R. Bennette, directresses to provide work. They also agreed that any person attending should pay five cents and improve every moment doing fancy work for a coming " sale about Christmas." As the year rolled around they saw so many things needed .to beautify the new vestry that with increased interest they kept on busily working to plan how they could increase the funds so much desired. A few more months and the members of the V. A. S. held receipted bills for $365.65, expended as follows : Paid to the building committee, $140 ; for dishes, $50.66 ; for shades, lamps and oyster bowls, $37.80 ; for parlor carpet, $15.47 ; for glassware, $7.50 ; for a mirror, $6.50 ; table for the parlor, $4 ; for mantle, $1.43 ;

incidental expenses to raise the full amount to $400 expended.

The children, under the direction of Mrs. Charles H. Sweet, gave a series of entertainments, realizing the sum of $41.40, and purchased the pulpit and chair, and chandeliers, and six lamps for the chapel, as a worker with the V. A. S., whose members have the satisfaction of seeing the parlor and kitchen of the vestry as pleasant and comfortable as the Society in Hampstead can wish.

Mrs. Mary E. Eastman and Mrs. Albert H. Little solicited funds to assist in building and furnishing the vestry, and collected from one hundred and thirty-six persons the sum of $977.75 towards the object in 1886.

Jan. 3, 1888, the members of the Ladies' Social Circle voted " to unite with the Y. P. S. C. E. in holding sociables." The first was held Jan. 11, 1888, in the vestry, with thirty-nine persons present, who were entertained by readings by Miss Mabel Watson and Jennie Coaker, recitations by Frances Buzzell; singing by a quartette, Messrs. Corson and Spinney, Misses Minnie C. Townsend and Annie L. Kimball of Chester; prayer by Rev. Albert Watson. They collected $2.00, and gave the Y. P. S. C. E. $1.

At the close of the year they voted " to extend a vote of thanks to the Y. P. S. C. E. for their kind and able assistance since the societies united," and credited them with $22.49.

Members in 1890 were :—

Mrs. Albert Watson,	Mrs. Mary J. Sanborn,
Miss Mabel Watson,	" Mary A. Pike,
Mrs. C. W. Pressey,	" Sarah M. Johnson,
" Albert L. Eastman,	" John W. Tabor,
" Orren E. Follansbee,	" M. Etta Fitts,
" R. K. Brickett,	Miss Clara A. Irving,
" Mary J. Fellows,	" Mary E. Spollett,

Mrs. John H. Clark,
" Charles Bassett,
" Carrie A. Moulton,
" Lillian Sanborn,
" Mary E. Corson,
" Abbie M. Tabor,
" Isaac Randall,
" Frank W. Emerson,
" Wm. A. Emerson,
" Nelson Ordway,
" Belinda G. Wilson,
' Mary E. Griffin,
" Mary A. Bragdon,
" Emma A. Little,

Miss Lucy S. Johnson,
" Anna M. Bartlett,
" Abbie A. Johnson,
" Bessie Grover,
" Cora M. Bassett,
" Minnie C. Townsend,
" M. Etta Hunkins,
Rev. Albert Watson,
Edwin H. Whitehill,
John C. Sanborn,
Orren E. Follansbee,
Charles W. Pressey,
I. Wm. George,
W. Alonzo Griffin.

The report of the secretary for the year ending Oct. 81, 1890, says: "Considerable interest has been manifested during the year. We have had very pleasant gatherings, and feel very grateful to our young people for their kind assistance in making them enjoyable. Less meetings than usual have been held, on account of the "Auxiliary" and our present needs. We were all interested in the repairs of our church, and cheerfully gave way for the time, hoping it might in no way lessen our zeal, but by working together we might strengthen our bond of sympathy. We are all laboring for one common cause, and thus best promote the objects of the L. S. C."

The Ladies' Auxiliary was organized April 10, 1890, with the following officers: President, Mrs. William Fellows ; vice-president, Mrs. George R. Bennette ; secretary and treasurer, Miss Mary E. Spollett.

This Society continued until Jan. 20, 1891, when it voted to unite with the "Ladies' Social Circle," and passed over to that organization all the material for aprons, etc., on hand, with the twenty dollars in money which they had unexpended.

During the nine months of its existence six hundred and seventy-three dollars were raised and expended as follows:

For new cushions for the pews, ...	$310 68
For decorating the walls of the church, etc., ...	240 25
For cleaning and varnishing pews, ...	60 00
For ventilators, ...	20 65
For incidentals, ...	12 42
To the Ladies' Social Circle, ...	20 00
	$673 00

The ladies of the "Auxiliary" then desired a new pulpit set, but felt that they must work on until they earned the money to pay for it, when Col. Albert L. Eastman, who was then confined to his bed by his last illness, urged them to select a set and put it in place. When it was done, the following note was received in the last handwriting of Mr. Eastman :—

"*To the Ladies of the Auxiliary Society, Miss Mary E. Spollett, Secretary and Treasurer :—*

The pulpit furniture selected by you for the Congregational Church has been paid for by the undersigned, as per bill enclosed, amounting to $140.21. They now beg leave to present the same, through you, to the Congregational Church and Society of Hampstead, N. H.

Respectfully,

ALBERT L. EASTMAN AND WIFE."

The members of the Auxiliary were :—

Mrs. Orren E. Follansbee,
" Benj. F. Rowe,
" Nelson Ordway,
" W. Alonzo Griffin,
" Emma A. Little,
" John C. Sanborn,
" William Fellows,
" R. K. Brickett,
" E. L. Spinney,
" William Sanborn,

Mrs. Isaac Roundy,
" Horace R. Sawyer,
" John E. Mills,
" Mary A. Pike,
" Belinda G. Wilson,
" Frank W. Emerson,
Miss Abbie A. Johnson,
" Clara A. Irving,
" Anna W. Bartlett,
" Mary E. Spollett,

Mrs. C. W. Pressey,
" Albert L. Eastman,
" Albert Watson,
" George R. Bennette,
" John H. Coark,
" John S. Corson,
" John W. Tabor,
" Charles Tabor,

Miss Lucy S. Johnson,
" Mabel A. Watson,
" Sarah O. Brickett,
" Nettie M. Follansbee,
" Minnie C. Townsend,
Rev. Albert Watson,
Isaac W. George,
Frederick Spollett.

Nov. 4, 1891, the circle met with Mrs. John S. Corson at their annual meeting, and it was voted " to give $40 annually towards parish expenses until otherwise decided."

That the ladies worked assiduously from week to week, from 1890 to 1895, is shown by the following resolutions:—

" *Whereas,* the Ladies' Social Circle, with untiring zeal and industry, and a grand devotion to the interests of the Christian Church and Society with which they are connected, have secured and generously given results of much labor and effort towards the beautifying and adornment of the church edifice; and

Whereas, Mrs. Fellows, Mrs. Eastman, Mrs. Ordway, Mrs. Chandler, and others, with a large spirit of unselfishness, and of lively interest in the well being of the church, have given with unsparing hand to the same beneficent end,

Resolved, That we, the Society of the Hampstead Congregational Church, do hereby express our most hearty appreciation of the lavish expenditures and gifts, and extend to them one and all our hearty thanks for the same.

Respectfully submitted,

F. E. MERRILL,)   *Committee*
W. H. DAVIS,   }   *on*
J. S. CORSON,)   *Resolutions.*
OLIVER PUTNAM, *Clerk.*

During the year ending Dec. 31, 1901, the ladies had met forty afternoons for work, one evening sociable, eight entertainments, one Easter sale, one Christmas sale, and the total cash receipts were $903.61 from all sources.

Early in January, 1901, the ladies residing in District No. 1, being deeply interested in raising funds for the contemplated repairs on the church, but living too far from the

centre to often meet with the L. S. C., organized an auxiliary,
with Mrs. Albert H. Little, vice-president, in charge. Meetings were held weekly at the several homes in the neighborhood, and a similar line of work carried on as in the main
Circle, namely, making quilts, aprons, fancy work, etc. In
the summer, when the church repairs called for money, the
Auxiliary paid the treasurer of the Circle $78.64, as the
result of their work. A particularly interesting feature was
the making of an album quilt containing five hundred or
more names, which netted them $50 at ten cents each. The
quilt was presented to Mrs. Rufus P. Gardner. In soliciting
names for the quilt the largest number secured by any person was one hundred and twenty by Mrs. Benj. F. Rowe.

The members of the Auxiliary in District No. 1 were:—

Mrs. Albert H. Little,	Mrs. Sabrina D. Noyes,
" Helen Frost,	" Henry Noyes,
" Mary E. Putnam,	" Herbert W. Mills,
" Mary A. Pike,	" John Mills,
" John W. Garland,	" Benjamin F. Rowe,
" Charles W. Garland,	Miss Lulu J. Corson,
" Eugene L. Spinney,	" Elisabeth H. M. Smith,
" Charles H. Whittier,	" Mildred R. Garland,
" Amasa W. Hunt,	" Carrie E. Sherman.
" Arthur H. Little,	

With unfaltering zeal, the work by the members of the
Social Circle has been harmoniously and pleasantly carried
on to the completion of the one hundred and fiftieth anniversary of the Congregational Church, and they commence
on another period of existence under the most auspicious
circumstances. The members of the Circle for the years
1901-'02 are:—

Mrs. Mary E. Eastman,	Mrs. L. M. Wells,
" Aaron Smith,	" Isaac Randall,
" Amos Fitts,	" Arthur M. Emerson,

Mrs. Mary A. Tabor,
" Albert H. Little,
" William Fellows (dec'd),
" H. W. Tabor,
" J. W. Sanborn,
" John H. Clark,
" Mary J. Sanborn,
" John S. Corson,
" Frank W. Emerson,
" Sabrina D. Noyes,
" Rufus P. Gardner,
" C. B. Gilman,
" H. D. Huntoon,
" Geo. R. Bennette,

Mrs. Wm. H. Woods,
" Forrest E. Merrill,
" Alden Pillsbury,
" Frank Pillsbury,
" George Hoyt,
" Joseph Frost,
" C. W. Pressey,
" Wm. H. Davis,
" Benjamin Hart,
" Charles W. Garland,
" Amasa W. Hunt,
Miss Mary E. Spollett,
" Gertrude S. Pillsbury,
" M. Lillie Hoyt.

HONORARY MEMBERS.

Rev. R. P. Gardner,
Nathaniel Bartlett,
Maurice Randall,
E. B. Woodward,
W. A. Little,
Harold E. Corson,

Fred S. C. Grover,
H. Walter Little,
Forrest Merrill,
Mahlon D. Currier,
C. W. Pressey,
J. W. Sanborn.

List of the officers from 1852 to 1902, as follows :—

SUPERINTENDENTS AND PRESIDENTS.

Mrs. Susan D. Bartley, 1852.
Miss Esther Bartley, 1853, '54, '55, '56, '57.
Mrs. John C. Drew, 1858, '59, '60.
" Adeline H. Eastman, 1861, '62.
" Fred Kent, 1863.
" E. M. Locke, 1864, '65.
" T. C. Pratt, 1866, '67.
" J. H. Clark, 1868.
" E. W. Bullard, 1870, '71, '72, '73, '74.
" R. K. Brickett, 1875, '76.
" Albert Watson, 1877, '82.
" Mary E. Eastman, 1878, '79, '83, '84, '85, '86, '87, '92, '93,
    '94, '96, '97.

Mrs. C. W. Williams, 1880, '81.
" John Page, 1881.
Miss Mary E. Spollett, 1888.
Mrs. Charles W. Pressey, 1889.
" John S. Corson, 1890, '91.
" R. P. Gardner, 1895.
" James W. Sanborn, 1898, '99, 1900, '01 to '02.

VICE PRESIDENTS AND ASSISTANT SUPERINTENDENTS.

Mrs. Susan R. Eastman, and Mrs. Nabby Brickett, assistant, 1852.
" Hannah J. Drew, 1853, '54, '55, '56, '57.
" F. A. Pike, 1858.
" T. C. Pratt, 1860.
" Wm. Sanborn, 1861, '62.
" David S. Clark, 1863.
" Tristram Little, 1864, '65, '66.
" Clara A. Clark, 1865.
Miss M. Jennie Little, 1868, '69.
Mrs. Mary C. Brickett, 1870, '71, '72.
" E. M. Locke, 1873, '74, '75.
" Mary J. Sanborn, 1876.
" Wm. A. Emerson, 1877, '78, '79.
" C. W. Pressey, 1880, '81.
" Alfred P. Emerson, 1882.
" Nellie T. Ordway, 1883.
" O. E. Follansbee, 1884, '92, '93.
" John S. Corson, 1885, '86, '95, '98, '99.
" Wm. Fellows, 1887.
" Mary E. Eastman, 1888, '89.
" John C. Sanborn, 1890, '91.
" R. P. Gardner, 1894.
" J. Wm. Sanborn, 1896, '97.
" Albert H. Little, 1900.
" Henry W. Tabor, 1901 to '02.

SECRETARIES AND TREASURERS, 1852 TO 1902.

Mrs. Adeline H. Eastman, 1852.
Miss Judith S. Eastman, 1853.
" Emma E. Ordway, 1864, '65, '66.

Mrs. Elizabeth P. Ordway, 1857, '58, '59.
Miss Sophia A. Greenleaf, 1860.
" Ann M. Howard, 1861, '62, '63, '64, '65, '66, '67.
" M. Jennie Little, 1868, '69.
Mrs. Lizzie W. Davis, 1870, '71, '72, '73.
" Mary E. Eastman, 1874, '75, '76, '77.
Miss Annie E. George, 1878.
" Abbie A. Johnson, 1879, '80, '81.
" Katie E. Coaker, 1882.
Mrs. Abbie I. Little, 1883, '84, '85, '86.
Miss Mary E. Spollett, 1887 to 1897.
" M. Etta Tabor, 1888, '89.
Mrs. R. P. Gardner, 1898, '99.
" John S. Corson, 1900, '01, '02.

The money raised by work, sales, annual dues, entertainments, and other means, including free will offerings, year
by year, as accurate as can be taken from the books of the
societies, are as follows :—

1852, to year ending October,					1876,	.	.	.	.	93.81
1853,	.	.	.	.	$13.62	1877,	.	.	.	.	49.05
1854,	.	.	.	.	58.00	1878,	.	.	.	.	49.15
1855,	.	.	.	.	41.02	1879,	.	.	.	.	107.32
1856,	.	.	.	.	32.87	1880,	.	.	.	.	143.29
1857,	.	.	.	.	15.53	1881,	.	.	.	.	149.30
1858-59,	.	.	.	.	54.92	1882,	.	.	.	.	122.00
1860,	.	.	.	.	67.45	1883,	.	.	.	.	74.85
1861,	.	.	.	.	60.72	1884,	.	.	.	.	185.06
1862,	.	.	.	.	34.23	1885,	.	.	.	.	68.74
1863,	.	.	.	.	0.00	1886,	.	.	.	.	1,521.16
1864,	.	.	.	.	33.92	1887,	.	.	.	.	44.38
1865,	.	.	.	.	9.46	1888,	.	.	.	.	67.88
1866-'67,	.	.	.	.	65.05	1889,	.	.	.	.	54.35
1868-'69,	.	.	.	.	10.33	1890,	.	.	.	.	718.25
1870,	.	.	.	.	90.00	1891,	.	.	.	.	122.29
1871,	.	.	.	.	55.40	1892,	.	.	.	.	124.89
1872,	.	.	.	.	37.88	1893-'94,	.	.	.	.	667.17
1873,	.	.	.	.	58.48	1895,	.	.	.	.	163.90
1874, by " Levee," etc.,				253.77	1896,	.	.	.	.	242.00
1875,	.	.	.	.	76.48	1897,		.	.	.	177.71

1898,	.	.	.	.	138.01	1901 to 1902,	.	.	.	908.01
1899,	.	.	.	.	145.90					
1900,	.	.	.	.	400.73	Making a total of				$9,513.16

besides numerous works of charity during the past fifty years.

Of the original members joining the Society in 1852 only Martha J. Adolphus (see No. 637, Church Mem.), Miss Judith S. Eastman (No. 361), Emily S. Davis (No. 235), and Mrs. Clara A. Clark (No. 525), are now living, the latter being the only lady that has retained her membership unbroken during the fifty years.

MUSIC.

The Puritans brought with them for their service of song "The Book of Psalms, English, both in prose and metre," by Henry Ainsworth. The third book published in America was "The Whole Book of Psalms, faithfully translated into English metre." This book had no tunes; the people sang "by rote and varied the melody." Cotton Mather said, "A little more art was found to be necessary," and a revision was made of the Psalms, which edition was called "The New England Psalm Book."

In those days there was no instruction in music. The fathers of the churches remembered the tunes as they had learned them in childhood, and taught their children the same tunes. They all sang the Psalms with variations, and no two churches could sing together the same tune. It is written that "in 1714 the service of song had become an abomination," and that Rev. Thomas Symmes of the church at Bradford, Mass., Rev. John Tufts of the church in New-bury (now West Newbury), and others, introduced singing by note and parts. This method in singing was not looked upon with favor in the churches of New England. "Women fainted, men left the house," and even ministers opposed it " as a work of Satan."

Rev. Mr. Tufts says : " The care of the old time choristers was to set the tune at such a pitch that the people could sing it without squeaking above or grumbling below, and beat the time so that they could reasonably sing together."

" Elder Ruling Tenney stood before the pulpit in the rude meeting house on the brow of the hill in the old Pentucket burial ground and set the tunes, while only four or five could sing them, and they with such torturing and twisting that no one could tell the tune."

In the days of the organization of the church in Hampstead there were few tunes in use—Standish, London, and Eighty-fifth Psalm, St. Mary's, and the like. The words of the hymns were lined out in couplets. The deacons read the first line and pitched the tune, using a sort of whistle, which was " homemade " and could be lengthened or shortened to give lower or sharper sounds, the whole congregation joining in the singing of the line. Another line was read, and again the melody was taken up by the people, and so on to the end of the psalm. This was called " deaconing the hymn."

Nov. 12, 1753, at the house of Deacon Benjamin Kimball, it was voted " to sing Dr. Watts' Psalms at sacramental seasons."

March 31, 1767, it was voted in town meeting " to give eight feet in length and four and one-half feet in width before the deacons' seat for the use of those who lead in singing."

April 14, 1767, voted, " to give one-half of the men's gallery on the west side of the meeting house, in the room of the pew before the deacons' seat, the upper end of said seat, for the use of the singers."

Dec. 6, 1774, voted, " to exchange the two seats that were given the use of the singers and give them an equal privilege in the front gallery."

March 29, 1775, voted, " that one-third of the front gallery be allowed for a seat for those persons that lead in singing, the division to be made as followeth, viz.: Beginning over the pillar standing in the pue belonging to the family of Currier and extending as far as the woman's gallery as to complete one-third of the length of one whole front, and that they may have liberty to build a pue if they see fit to do so at their own charge, and that they may raise the floor in the fore seat on a level with the floor of the second seat, and voted that Jeremiah Ames, John Calfe, Moses Little, Caleb Emerson, Abner Little, Eliphalet Poor, and Jona. Eastman be a committee to seat said pue of singers."

The introduction of musical instruments to aid in the service was in September, 1797, when Rev. John Kelly held a meeting at his own house, and voted " to give leave to the singers to use a bass viol in the meeting house and a tenor one." In some towns the advent of such musical viols was a source of displeasure among the clergy, as well as congregations. One minister is said to have shouted, " Sing the 112th Psalm and fiddle it to your hearts' content."

In Chester, N. H., " Samuel Graham carried his bass viol into the meeting house on Thanksgiving day of 1806, and no sooner did he begin to sound it than Deacon William Wilson and Moody Chase left the house in hot haste."

The first viol used in the Hampstead meeting house was made by the Prescotts of Chester, and as far as research shows the Ayer family brought forth the first musical strains. John Little played the large bass viol for about twenty years in the gallery of the old meeting house. In 1825 " James Brickett bought of Capt. Jesse Ayer one large bass viol for use in the meeting house for $18.00." Occasionally some one, particularly Paul Heald of Atkinson, would assist in the music with some brass instrument.

. The Hampstead Sacred Musical Society was organized Dec. 7, 1840, in " Amos Buck's Hall," which stood where

Daniel Emerson's house now stands. Dr. J. C. Eastman was chosen chairman ; Henry Putnam, secretary ; and Benj. B. Garland, president; Jona. Kent, vice-president ; Jacob Irving, treasurer; A. M. Merrill, first chorister; R. K. Brickett, second chorister. There were twenty-eight men and ten female members, with twenty-two patrons.

The constitution adopted was in part as follows : —

"Deeming it important, in order to secure good music in any surety, that those who are willing to assist should organize and frequently meet for practice, and that they should avail themselves of all of that information and correction which every choir must have in order to sing with accuracy and taste, and that they should be provided with suitable books and instruments, the subscribers, for the purpose of securing good music in the Congregational meeting house in Hampstead, hereby agree to form themselves into a society to be known as the Sacred Music Society, and most honorably pledge ourselves to each other to make every proper exertion to promote the object of the Society."

ART. 1.   The members of this Society shall consist of singers. Other persons who may be willing to assist by advice, votes, and otherwise, shall be styled ' Patrons.' "

Members who signed this constitution, from 1840 to 1880, were as follows :—

A. M. Merrill,
Henry Putnam,
Simon Merrill,
N. H. Little,
Jacob Irving,
Edwin H. Kent,
R. K. Brickett,
John T. Eastman,
Albert W. Ayer,
Ralph Brickett,
E. R. Smiley,
Joseph Eastman,
William Tenney,
Josiah C. Eastman,
E. B. Mooers,

Orren Chandler,
Lorenzo Frost,
Charles W. Pensley,
Josiah S. Page,
John S. Corson,
Rufus H. Bailey,
Edward King,
Andrew M. Moulton,
George H. Rowe,
Mary B. Eastman,
Elizabeth Emerson,
Judith S. Eastman,
Mary Emerson,
Meribah H. Putnam,
Susan E. Putnam,

Benjamin Sargent,
C. P. Ayer,
G. Bartlett,
J. H. Richardson,
D. H. Emerson,
E. H. L. Gibson,
H. L. Hoyt,
J. P. Shannon,
N. C. Smith,
Leonard Hutchens,
Charles W. Grimstone,
William Minot,
J. Chase Eastman,
Isaac W. Smith,
John Jefferson,
J. B. Sanborn,
John A. Renton,
Benjamin F. Merrill,
W. H. Hoyt,
Caleb Moulton,
Paul Heald,
Isaac Tewksbury,
George A. Allen,
John D. Irving,
J. F. Gibson,
J. H. Clark,
F. H. Sawyer,
William H. Davis,
C. N. Stevens,
R. C. Smith,
E. G. Wood,
George O. Jenness,
George W. Eastman,
Joseph K. Harris,
Nathaniel Frost,
E. S. Tenny,
William A. McNiel,
William Jones,

Hannah W. Merrill,
Mary C. Smith,
Hannah H. Palmer,
Belinda A. Sawyer,
Betsey Minot,
Judith A. Sargent,
Almira Sargent,
Mary E. Ayer,
Betsey H. Davis,
C. M. Davis,
Clara A. Kent,
Mary E. Davis,
Mary J. Heath,
Elizabeth Heath,
Sabra F. Tewksbury,
Emily S. Davis,
Mary E. Kent,
Mary J. Brickett,
Martha H. Sanborn,
Mary S. Kent,
S. Lizzie Sawyer,
Julia A. Merrill,
Helen M. Nichols,
Helen M. Putnam,
H. C. Sawyer,
Sarah E. Chandler,
Julia E. Little,
Susan E. Pepper,
Lucy A. Sawyer,
Mary A. Eastman,
Elizabeth M. Locke,
C. M. Chase,
Abbie F. Chandler,
Annie S. Moulton,
Belle Moulton,
Lucy A. Bullard,
Mary E. Clark,
Mattie E. Irving,

Henry S. Sprague,
David Clark,
Paul S. Davis,
John W. Garland,
Jona. C. Little,
Daniel L. Sawyer,

Etta M. Tabor,
Nellie T. Randall,
Eliza S. Page,
Sara A. Little,
Carrie A. Moulton.

PATRONS.

Joshua Eastman,
Rev. John Kelly,
John Emerson,
Isaac Tewksbury,
Benjamin B. Garland,
Isaac Smith,
John M. C. Bartley,
Jona. Kent,
David Irving,
A. M. Marshall,
John P. Stickney,
Lorenzo Babb,
E. R. Smiley,
Ezra Davis,
Edwin Grimston,
S. S. Shannon,
David Irving,
B. L. Merrill,

A. E. Colby,
William Hoyt,
Onslow Bailey,
John B. Richardson,
Henry Putnam,
J. C. Eastman,
Ezekiel Bartlett,
Jesse E. Emerson,
Moses Heath,
M. H. Brickett,
James Gibson,
Enoch Ordway,
Benjamin Sawyer,
Amos Buck,
Clark Noyes,
Horace R. Sawyer,
Charles E. Davis,
Horatio Emerson.

Voted, April 4, 1848, that " the musical instruments belonging to the Society for the use of the choir be under the
care of the chorister, and the Society to keep the instruments
in repair and find lights for the choir when they meet to
sing."

In 1851 an effort was made to provide a more suitable
aid to their music in the form of an organ, which had become
common in most of the New England churches. A subscription paper was circulated among the friends of better music
in the church, and was successful, as follows :—

"We, the subscribers, agree to pay on demand the sums annexed to
our respective names for the purchase of an organ, to be owned and
contracted for by the Congregational Church and Society in Hampstead, to be placed in their house of worship, and to be used for the
benefit of said church and society and the congregation worshipping
with them."

James Calef,	$ 5.00	John W. Garland,	$1.00
Jesse Ayer,	20.00	Amos Ring,	2.00
R. K. Brickett,	5.00	Fred A. Pike,	1.00
N. C. Smith,	5.00	Giles O. Marble,	2.00
W. M. Bartley,	5.00	F. J. Stevens,	2.00
A friend,	5.00	Tristram Little,	2.00
Jonathan Kent,	5.00	Albert W. Ayer,	2.00
Isaac Smith,	15.00	Tappan Eastman,	2.00
Joseph Chase,	20.00	Hiram Nichols,	2.00
Nelson Ordway,	5.00	Benjamin Sawyer,	2.00
J. D. Ordway,	5.00	Hezekiah Ayer,	2.00
H. L. Hoyt,	1.00	Daniel H. Emerson,	2.00
Wm. C. Little,	5.00	Frederick Emerson,	10.00
Silas Griffin,	5.00	James H. Hoyt,	1.00
Wm. Sanborn,	5.00	Dudley Emerson,	10.00
Joshua Eastman,	6.00	Perley Ayer,	2.00
Samuel Pillsbury,	5.00	Giles F. Marble,	1.00
Amos Buck,	2.00	David Little,	2.00
Caleb Moulton,	2.00	Joseph Sargent,	1.00
John Jefferson,	2.00	Benjamin Pillsbury,	2.00
A female friend,	2.00	A. N. Merrill,	.50
E. H. Kent,	2.00	C. E. Woodman,	.50
Daniel Nichols,	2.00	C. H. Shannon,	1.00
Benj. B. Garland,	2.00	A. W. Perley,	1.00
Amasa Eastman,	1.00	Abner Kent,	1.00
Wm. Johnson,	2.00	Dudley George,	1.00
Abial Ordway,	1.00	John Ordway,	5.00
John Jackson,	.50	Enos Colby,	1.00

Jan. 9, 1853, the Orthodox Congregational Society of
Hampstead, N. H., bought of Wm. B. D. Simmons & Co., of
Boston, one second hand parlor organ for $200; also paid R.
K. Brickett for making a false roof for better security of the
organ, $2; Wm. Sanborn, for iron work, $1; and Isaac
Smith, for alpacca and lock, $1.

Simmons & Co. gave the Society an obligation, as follows:

" We hereby obligate to receive as part payment (for an organ of any size which we may build) the organ sold to Mr. Bartley of Hampstead, N. H., and allow for it in part payment for a new one one hundred and fifty dollars, any time within five years, provided it receive no other injury than comes of natural use.

The price of a new organ to be a fair price, such as we now receive say like the organ in the Methodist Church in Cambridgeport, Mass., for six hundred dollars, or according to our price book of 1853."

Miss Mary C. Smith was the first organist, and continued for several years. With the new organ a new impetus was given to singing in the church.

October, 1854, it was voted " that the singers meet once a week in the Town Hall, and that 'Ancient Harmony' be used at the sings.' "

In 1858, Caleb Moulton was chosen "to get up a singing school," and for several years singing schools were held each winter and largely attended.

Oct. 3, 1859, it was voted " that George W. Eastman be requested to ascertain the expense of repairing and fitting up the two bass viols."

In 1862 the organ needed tuning and was much out of repair, which led to desiring a large organ for the gallery. A pipe organ was procured, which after a time was pronounced unsatisfactory, and in 1867 Col. Albert L. Eastman presented the church and society with the organ represented in the cut.

This organ was dedicated with programme as follows:—

" *Grand Concert and Opening of the New Organ in the Congregational Church, on Tuesday Evening, December 10, 1867.*

Organists—Mr. Charles H. Burbank, Mr. S. A. Dow, Mr. J. Q. Adams. Wm. H. Davis, Director.

1. Organ Invocation, Mr. Burbank.
2. Chorus, " Hallelujah to the God of Israel," choir of the church.
3. Chorus, " Heavenly Father," Mr. Dow, director.
4. "How Beautiful," Mrs. Hoyt.
5. "I Waited for the Lord," Mrs. Kent.
6. "Come to the Mountains," Mr. Dow, director.
7. "Protect Me through the Coming Night," Mr. Hopkins, Mrs. Kent, and Miss Dinsmore.

8. "Guide me, O Thou Great Jehovah," quartette from choir.
9. Organ solo.
10. Duet, "The Bird is Loose," Mrs. Little and Miss Chandler.
11. Organ solo, Mr. Burbank.
12. Finale, "Old Hundred." All invited to sing.

Concert to commence at 7 3-4 o'clock.

ORGAN—1867 TO 1901.

March 15, 1870, voted, "that the committee have power to sell the old parlor organ."

In 1867, Mrs. S. Lizzie Hunkins was organist for two years ; Mrs. Mary Ida (Haseltine) Noyes from 1869 to 1874 ; Mrs. Orrie B. (Little) Pressey from 1874 for several years.

March 6, 1880, at a church meeting, "it was recommended that circumstances deem it expedient that the church do henceforth have entire control of the sacred music, according to congregational usage, and not depend upon outside organization. In view of the foregoing the following resolutions were accepted and adopted :—

Resolved 1st. " That the church shall begin at once to assume entire control of her sacred music."

2d. " That the members of the Hampstead Sacred Music Society be respectfully informed of the above action on the part of the church, and that in consequence thereof their services as an organization are no longer required in the conducting of our service of song."

3d. "That we do hereby extend a vote of thanks |to the members of the Hampstead Sacred Music Society for their valuable services."

4th. " That a committee of three be chosen for the year ensuing to have full power to organize a choir to lead us in our service of song."

John S. Corson, Dea. Wm. Sanborn, and Dea. Caleb Williams were chosen.

April, 1893, voted, " that John S. Corson, Eugene L. Spinney, Wm. H. Davis and Forrest E. Merrill be a committee to consider and formulate plans for the training of young voices, in the view of enlarging the choir and to introduce new singing books."

A piano was placed in the church in 1893, through the personal effort of Rev. Mr. Gardner, who obtained subscriptions for the same, beginning with a substantial gift from Mrs. Nelson Ordway. The piano has proved a great help to the church and Sunday school, and is greatly prized in their evening services.

Dec. 20, 1895, Forrest E. Merrill motioned that the old organ used before the new piano was secured be presented to Dea. Wm. H. Davis as a token of esteem for his long service as a faithful chorister, which was done, and cordially accepted.

In the spring of 1901 it was self evident to nearly all of the church people that something should be done with the old organ which for thirty-four years had been in constant use on the Sabbath. It was found upon careful investigation that the organ could only be repaired at a great expense. The pastor, Rev. Rufus P. Gardner, moved to see if they could not have a new organ, and with the repairs which were to be made in the interior of the church, have it placed in front of the church. He brought the matter before his church committee, who approved cordially his plan. With

no subscription paper, but with a quiet invitation to friends
and descendants of the fathers and mothers of the church
during its one hundred and fifty years of existence, he succeeded in securing the necessary funds to procure the beautiful organ as shown in the cut.

The new organ was dedicated Sunday evening, Sept. 1,
1901, when the following programme was pleasantly enjoyed

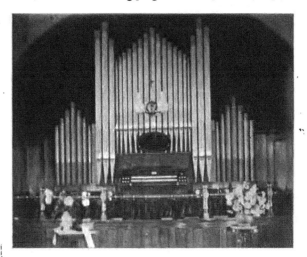

ORGAN 1901.

by a large and appreciative audience, including nine persons
who were present at the dedication of the organ in the gallery, Dec. 10, 1867.

Order of service:—

1. Organ Voluntary, Prof. James W. Hill of Haverhill, Mass.
2. Presentation of the organ, by Rufus P. Gardner, pastor.
3. Acceptance in behalf of the church, by John C. Sanborn, clerk.
4. Prayer of dedication.
5. Organ response, Mrs. Emerson.

6. Response Psalm. Congregation seated.
7. Dedication Hymn, No. 104, choir and congregation.
8. Response Psalm. Congregation seated.
9. Gloria, choir and congregation; Mrs. Emerson, organist.
10. Organ recital, by Prof. James W. Hill, consisting of "Toccata in
      D minor," "Jerusalem the Golden," "Largo," "Spring Song,"
      "Fantasia on Familiar Air," "Benediction," "Pastorale,"
      "Serenata," and "Overture to Straddella."
11. "Praise God from whom all blessings flow."
12. Benediction.

Rev. Mr. Gardner spoke in part as follows: "It has been one of the real pleasures of my life to collect the free will offerings—no one but the auditor to know how much each one has given—enabling me, as chairman of the musical committee, to present this beautiful organ in behalf of the donors, as a piece of property to the church and society. A gift of one hundred and fifty of the friends of the Congregational Church in Hampstead, for the praise of God, and in memory of the fathers and mothers who have worshipped here. And these keys to the faithful organist of the church, Mrs. Minnie E. Emerson, who for nearly fourteen years has played the old organ. We extend to her our grateful appreciation of her willingness to aid in our service of song.

The organ loft and platform have been quite expensive, built by Mr. Horace Bailey in a workmanlike manner of quartered oak finish, and as the organ firm directed, and must give general satisfaction. The organ loft, furnishings, carpet, chairs (excepting the chorister's chair), are gifts of the Sunday School and Home Department.

The chorister's chair is a gift from Mrs. L. Ada Libbey, in the name of her father, Mr. George W. Eastman, who for thirty-six years was a member of the choir and fourteen years as chorister.

The glass upon the organ is the gift of Mrs. Cleveland, wife of ex-President Grover Cleveland.

The lamp is the gift of some of my personal friends, not Hampstead people. The curtain is a gift of the King's Daughters.

May the new organ be very useful."

Nearly one hundred persons have sung in the choir five years or more. The choristers since 1840 have been Amos Merrill, R. Kimball Brickett, a member of the choir for more than fifty years; Jacob Irving, many years; Albert W. Ayer, twenty-two years in the choir; George W. Eastman, thirty-six years in the choir; William McNiel, in the choir nine years; John C. Little, eleven years; Eugene

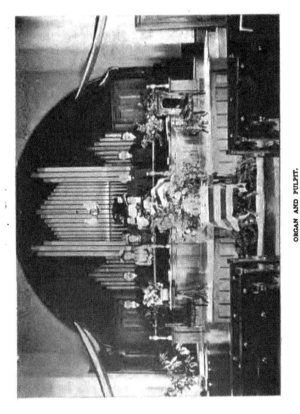

ORGAN AND PULPIT.

L. Spinney, several years; John S. Corson, since 1878; William H. Davis, since 1848.

The choir for 1902: Mrs. Minnie E. Emerson, organist fifteen years; Prof. Forrest E. Merrill, thirteen years. Tenor, William H. Davis, member fifty-two years; C. Park Pressey, eight years, bass; H. Clinton Davis, three years, bass; Mrs. Albert H. Little, nineteen years, soprano; Mrs. Henry W. Tabor, thirteen years, alto; and Miss Mary G. Davis, five years, alto. (For portraits, see "Sketches of Church Members," numbers 679, 692, 437, 558, 699, 681, 624 and 723.)

BAPTISMS.

The list of persons, mostly children, baptized in the "Church of Christ," in Hampstead, Abanno, 1752 to the year 1903 :—

1752.

June 3, Lydia, daughter of Ebenezer Gile.
"   " Mary, daughter of Josiah Davis.
July, David, son of David Copp.
"   Edmund, son of Edmund Eastman.
"   Abiah, daughter of Samuel Stevens.
"   Caleb, son of John Webster.
"   Henry, son of Jacob Eaton.
"   Collins, son of Jacob Eaton.
"   Dorothy, daughter of Jacob Hancock.
August, Mary, daughter of Jonathan Hutchens.
"   Hannah, daughter of Ebenezer Johnson.
"   Moses, son of Benjamin Emerson.
"   John, son of Joseph Little of Plaistow.
Sept., William, son of William Burbank of Plaistow.
"   Ichabod Shaw, son of Lemuel Davis and his wife, who owned the Covenant.
"   Mehitable, daughter of Benjamin Philbrick.
October, Abraham, son of Jonathan Gile.
"   William, son of Joseph Palmer of Plaistow.

1753.

Jan'y,   Mary, daughter of Bartholomew Heath.
    "   Abigail, daughter of Samuel Stevens.
Feb'y,   Phineas, son of James Graves.
March,   John, son of Jacob Tucker (Kingston).
    "   Sarah, daughter of David Eastman.
    "   Mary, daughter of Samuel Worthen.
May,   John, son of Dr. John Bond.
    "   Abigail, daughter of Benjamin Stevens.
June,   Dolley, daughter of Daniel Roberts, Jr.
    "   Sarah, daughter of John Muzzey.
    "   James, son of John Mills.
    "   David, son of John Atwood.
    "   Samuel, son of Thomas Fellows (Kingston).
July,   Isaac, son of Joseph Stevens.
    "   Lemner, daughter of Samuel Hadley.
    "   Hezekiah, son of Benjamin Heath.
August, Lydia, daughter of Daniel Johnson.
    "   Molly, daughter of James Stickney (adopted child).
    "   Susanna, daughter of Peter Eastman.
    "   Eliphalet, son of Samuel Davis.
    "   David, son of David Stevens.
Sept.,   John, son of John Hunkins.
    "   Reuben, son of Nathaniel Heath.
    "   Simeon, son of Ebenezer Kezer.
    "   Mehitabel, daughter of Ebenezer Kezer.
    "   Hannah, daughter of Ebenezer Kezer.
October, William, son of John Mudgett.
    "   Ebenezer, son of George Little.
Nov'r,   Sarah, daughter of Moses Hale.

1754.

Jan'y,   Sarah, daughter of James Graves.
March,   Jonathan, son of Stephen Johnson, Jr.
    "   Nicholas, son of Benjamin Kimball.
    "   Mary, daughter of Leonard Harriman.
April,   Abiah, daughter of Joseph Little of Plaistow.

April,   Abiah, daughter of Otho Stevens.
"   James, son of Jonathan Gile.
"   Moses, son of Theopolis Griffin of Kingston.
June,   Jonathan, son of Joseph Palmer of Plaistow.
"   Jonathan, son of Amos Clark.
"   John, son of John Muggett.
"   Jonathan, son of David Copp.
"   Ruth, daughter of John Johnson.
"   Elizabeth, daughter of John Johnson.
July,   Lydia, daughter of Joseph Thurle.
"   Ark, a black boy under the care of Moses Gile.
"   Thomas, son of William Straw of Kingston.
"   David, son of David Sanborn of Kingston.
"   James, son of John Atwood.
"   Hugh, son of Hugh Tallant.
"   Ruth, daughter of Ebenezer Johnson, Jr. •
"   Susana, daughter of Theopolis Colby.
August, Philemon, son of Joseph Hadley, Jr.
"   Collins, son of Jacob Eaton.
"   Paul Pressey of Kingston, baptized aged 40.
October, Benjamin, son of John Chuet.
Nov'r,   Samuel, son of Nehemiah Stevens.
"   Richard, son of Bartholomew Heath.
Dec'r,   Ichabod, son of Samuel Plummer.
"   Sarah, daughter of Jonathan Hutchens.

1755.

Jan'y,   John, son of Paul Pressey of Kingston.
"   Mary, daughter of Israel Huse of Kingston.
Feb'y,   Sarah, daughter of John Ingals of Plaistow.
March,   Moses, son of Moses Gile.
"   Sarah, daughter of Thomas Little of Plaistow.
"   David, son of Moses Hale, Jr.
April,   Samuel, son of George Little.
"   Mary, daughter of Benjamin Emerson.
"   Truth, daughter of Obediah Davis.
"   Thomas, son of Abraham Dow.

May,	Sarah, daughter of Thomas Williams.
"	Caleb, son of Archelus Stevens.
"	Simon, son of Otho Stevens, Jr.
"	Jonathan, son of Daniel Roberts, Jr.
"	Sarah, daughter of Jacob Tucker of Kingston.
"	Thomas, son of Jonathan Colburne of Kingston.
"	Reuben, son of Jonathan Colburne of Kingston.
"	David, son of David Eastman of Kingston.
"	Josiah, son of Samuel Stevens.
June,	Sarah, daughter of Thomas Crawford.
"	Robert, son of Thomas Crawford.
"	Hannah, daughter of Thomas Fellows of Kingston.
July,	Dolley, daughter of Lemuel Davis.
"	Abigail, daughter of Peter Eastman.
August,	Asa, son of Archelus Stevens.
"	Moses, son of Ebenezer Mudgett.
"	Ruth, daughter of Daniel Johnson.
"	——, son of Obediah Davis.
October,	Jacob, son of Jacob Bayley.
"	Sarah, daughter of Philip Nelson of Plaistow.
"	Nannie, daughter of Elijah Heath.
"	Sarah, daughter of John Mooers.
"	William, son of John Mooers.
"	Richard, son of John Mooers.
"	Nabby, daughter of James Graves.
"	Jemima, daughter of Obediah Wells.
"	Ruth, daughter of Nathaniel Merrill.
"	Phineas, son of ye wife of Jonathan Stevens of Plaistow.
"	Elizabeth, daughter of Jonathan Stevens.
"	Rachel, daughter of Nathaniel Heath.

1756.

Jan'y,	Benjamin, son of Jacob Eaton.
"	Joseph, son of John Mudgett.
"	Daniel, son of Nichodemus Watson.
March,	Moses, son of Benjamin Kimball.

March, Samuel, son of Rev. Henry True.
" Benjamin, son of David Stevens.
" Moses, son of William Eastman.
April, Mary, daughter of Nathan Goodwin.
May, Samuel, son of Stephen Johnson, Jr.
" Joseph, son of John Atwood.
" Lydia, daughter of Paul Dustin.
" Betty, daughter of Paul Dustin.
June, Jonathan, son of widow Sarah Clark.
" James, son of Hugh Tallent.
" ——, son of Ebenezer Johnson.
" Timothy, son of Jacob Wells of Sandown.
" Edward, son of Nathaniel Buzzell.
" Judith, daughter of Nathaniel Eastman.
July, Molly, daughter of Nehemiah Stevens.
" Susanna, daughter of Abraham Davis.
" John Kezer ("tertius atetayis"), aged 28.
" George, son of Joseph Hancock.
" Susanna, daughter of Stephen Colburne.
" Gilbert, son of John Bond.
Nov'r, Rachel, daughter of Obediah Davis.
" Hannah, daughter of John Mooers.
" Jesse, son of Bartholomew Heath.
" Jesse, son of Nathaniel Merrill.
Dec'r, John, son of Thomas Williams.
" Abner, son of Moses Gile.
" Joseph, son of Joseph Hadley, Jr.
" Benjamin, son of Benjamin Tucker of Sandown.
" Ebenezer Fellows, son of Theopolis Eaton of Sandown.

1757.

Feb'y, Joseph, son of Paul Chase, once of Sandown (deceased).
" Deborah, daughter of Benjamin Emerson.
" Abigail, daughter of Ebenezer Johnson.
Mch. 12, Sarah, daughter of Benjamin Philbrick.
" " John, son of John Woodman; David, son of John Woodman (twins).

Mch. 12,   John, son of John Clark.
May   8,   Phebe, daughter of Theopolis Colby (deceased).
"   15,   Jonathan, son of Joshua Haselton.
"   22,   Jesse, son of Otho Stevens, Jr.
"   29,   Hannah, daughter of Rev. Henry True.
"   "   John, son of Theopolis Griffin of Sandown.
June,   Thomas, son of Thomas Hale (deceased).
"   Sarah, daughter of Ebenezer Mudgett.
"   Abigail, daughter of Moses Hale, Jr.
"   Timothy, son of John Clark.
"   Elizabeth, daughter of Thomas Fellows of Sandown.
"   George, son of Joseph Little of Plaistow.
"   James, son of Archelus Stevens.
"   Joseph, son of Joseph Hancock.
Oct.,   James, son of Jacob Bailey.
Nov.,   Martha, daughter of Daniel McClure of Windham.
Dec. 24,   Martha, daughter of James Graves.

1758.

Jan.   5,   Rachel, daughter of Jonathan Stevens of Plaistow.
Feb.,   Elizabeth, daughter of John Ingalls of Plaistow.
Apr.   2,   Henry, son of Jeremiah Allen of Sandown.
"   15,   Dearborn, son of Elijah Heath.
"   23,   Joshua, son of Benjamin Little.
May,   Mary, daughter of John Colbey.
"   Joseph, son of John Colby.
"   John, son of Thomas Crafford.
"   Moses, son of John Hazen.
"   Elizabeth, daughter of widow Mary Stevens.
"   Samuel, son of Reuben Mills.
June,   Mary, daughter of Jesse Harriman.
July,   Judith, daughter of John Johnson.
"   28,   Thomas, son of Stephen Colburne.
"   30,   Abigail, daughter of Joseph Sawyer.
Sept.,   Abijah, son of Nichodemus Watson.
"   Rachel, daughter of Joseph Stevens, Jr.
Oct.   8,   Nanne, daughter of Dr. John Bond.
Nov. 12,   Sarah, daughter of John Chuet.

Dec. 10, Molley, daughter of Nathaniel Merrill.
" 31, Mehitable, daughter of John Atwood.

1759.

Mar. 3, Ebenezer, son of Dea. Benjamin Kimball.
" " Caleb, son of Joseph Little of Plaistow.
" " Mehitabel, daughter of John Ingalls of Plaistow.
Mar. 4, Jacob, son of Jacob Eaton, Jr.
" " Mehitable, daughter of Jacob Eaton, Jr.
" " Bethiah, daughter of Jacob Eaton, Jr.
" 25, James, son of Rev. Henry True, " b. March 3, at 7 o'clock in the morning."
April, Hannah, daughter of Joseph Hadley.
May 6, Moses, son of John Bly.
" " Moses, son of Obediah Davis.
" " George, son of John Kezer, Jr.
" " Betty, daughter of Benjamin Colby of Sandown.
" " Molly, daughter of Edward Colby of Sandown.
" " Sarah, daughter of Joseph Hancock.
" 13, Jacob, son of Otho Stevens, Jr.
" " Elis, daughter of Esq. Benjamin Tucker of Sandown.
" " Moses, son of John Clark.
" " Susan, a daughter of Ebenezer Hale.
" 20, Jacob, son of Michael Gurdy.
" " Elizabeth, daughter of John Haseltine.
" 22, Nicholas, son of Noah White.
Oct., John, son of Jeremiah Allen.

1760.

Feb. 7, Rachel, dau. of Thomas Fellows of Sandown.
" 24, Henry, son of Stephen Johnson.
" " Sarah, daughter of Stephen Johnson.
Mar. 16, Anna, daughter of Benjamin Emerson.
Apr. 4, Nanne, daughter of Josiah Davis.
" " Huldah, daughter of Elijah Heath.
" " John, son of Edward Ordway.
" 30, Benjamin, son of Isaac Foster.
" " Sarah, daughter of Ezekiel Foster.

Apr. 80, Martha, daughter of Ezekiel Foster.
" " Elizabeth, daughter of Edmund Colby.
May 11, Elizabeth, daughter of John Mills.
" " Sarah, daughter of John Mudgett.
" " Susanna, daughter of David Stevens.
" " Hannah, daughter of Archelus Stevens.
July 3, Infant son of Jassaal Harriman.
" " Levi, son of Benjamin Little.
Aug. 3, Jonathan Duston, son of David Cheney.
" 31, Frederick, son of Asa Foster.
Oct. 5, Moses, son of John Ingalls.
" " Phebe, daughter of Stephen Colburne.
" 13, Jabez, son of Rev. Henry True, " b. Oct. 6, at 7 o'clock
in the morning."
" " Jonathan Roberts, son of Ebenezer Hale.
Nov. 16, Joseph, son of Abraham Johnson.
Dec. 7, David, son of David Hale.
" 14, Abigail, daughter of Obediah Davis.
" " Sarah, daughter of Dea. Benjamin Kimball.
" " Amherst, son of Jacob Bailey.
" 28, Jacob, son of Jonathan Stevens (deceased).
" " Elizabeth, daughter of Timothy Stevens.

1761.

Jan. 11, Moses, son of James Emerson.
" 18, Ruth, daughter of Joshua Merrill.
Feb. 8, Otho, son of Samuel Stevens.
Mar. 1, Judith, daughter of Moses Kelly of Plaistow.
" 8, Elizabeth, daughter of Thomas Chase.
Apr. 12, Moses, son of John Atwood.
" 19, Joanna, daughter of Joseph Hadley.
" " Abigail, daughter of Robert Johnson.
" 26, Moses, son of Moses Hale.
" " Anna, daughter of William Eaton.
May 5, Caleb, son of Nichodemus Watson.
" " Phebe, daughter of Edward Ordway.
" 17, Ephraim Carter, son of Aaron French.
" " Judith, daughter of Caleb Heath.

May 17, Susanna, daughter of Caleb Heath.

" " Betty, daughter of Caleb Heath.

" " Mary, wife of Caleb Heath.

" " Juda, daughter of Thomas Wadley.

" " Mary, daughter of Jeremiah Kent.

Sept. 20, Elizabeth, daughter of Jonathan Atwood.

" " Miriam, daughter of Jesse Johnson.

" " Robert, son of Nathaniel Martin of Goffstown.

" " James, son of James Eaton of Goffstown.

" " Katy, daughter of Samuel Richards of Goffstown.

" " Molly, daughter of Leonard Harriman.

Nov. 15, Achsa, son of Ebenezer Mudgett.

Dec. 6, Joseph, son of Dr. John Bond.

" " Joseph, son of Thomas Fellows of Sandown.

1762.

Jan. 3, John, son of Rev. Henry True, " b. Dec. 26, 1761, at 1 o'clock in the morning."

" " Anna, daughter of Joseph Sawyer.

" " ——, son of Abraham Johnson.

May 16, Mary, daughter of Benjamin Emerson.

" " Sarah, daughter of Joseph Little.

" 23, Sarah, daughter of Robert Johnson.

June 13, Asa, son of Simeon Goodwin.

" " Ebenezer Ward, son of John Clark.

" " Hannah, daughter of Daniel Stevens.

" " Elizabeth, daughter of Daniel Cheney.

" 27, Molly, daughter of Josiah Davis.

" " Mary, daughter of Stephen Merrill.

" " John, son of Michael Merrill.

" " Sipio Newton, son of Daniel McClure.

Oct. 19, Nathan, son of Jeremiah Allen.

" " Sarah, daughter of Edmund Colby.

Nov. 14, Sarah, daughter of David Hale.

" " Abigail, daughter of Joshua Merrill.

" 18, Asa, son of John Mills.

" 28, Molley, daughter of Joshua Copp.

" " Hannah, daughter of John Merrill.

" " James, son of James Little.

1763.

Jan. 16, Micajah, son of Benjamin Little.
" 28, Abner, son of Jacob Bailey.
Mar. 20, Molly, daughter of Reuben Mills.
Apr. 17, Martha, daughter of William Page.
" " Miriam, daughter of John Atwood.
" " Relief, daughter of William Eaton.
" 24. Nathan, son of Alpheus Goodwin.
May 21, Peabody, son of Jesse Harriman.
" " Moses, son of widow Rachel Morse.
" 27, ——, son of Timothy Stevens.
" " Hannah, daughter of Moses Wells of Goffstown.
        Baptized ye first Sabbath in June, Jonathan Burbank,
        son of Joseph Ordway of Goffstown.
" " Sarah, daughter of Timothy Ferren of Goffstown.
" " Ruth, daughter of Samuel Richards of Goffstown.
" " Abigail, daughter of James Eaton.
June,   First Sabbath, Margaret, daughter of Thomas Carr of
        Goffstown.
" Judith, daughter of Eben Johnson.
" 6, Eunice, daughter of Moses Gile of Halestown.
" " Susanna, daughter of James Emerson.
" 19, Daniel, son of Joseph Hadley.
" " Samuel, son of —— Ordway of New Salem.
July 9, Ruth, daughter of John Colby.
" " Jesse, son of Jesse Johnson.
" 16, Nathan, son of David Hadley.
" 24, Ithamer, son of Nichodemus Watson.
Aug. 23, John Knight was baptized.
" " Mary, daughter of Joseph Knight.
" " Moses, son of Caleb Johnson.
" " Caleb, son of Caleb Johnson.
Sept. 4, Samuel, son of Ezekiel Currier.
Oct. 16, George, son of Moses Little of New Boston.
" 30, Susanna, daughter of Edmund Eastman.
" " Lois, daughter of John Calfe.
" " Susanna, daughter of Archelus Stevens.
" " David, son of Micajah Morrill.

Nov. 20, Daniel, son of John Trussell.
" " Rebecca, daughter of John Chase.
" 27, Moses, son of Richard Heath.
" " Richard, son of Richard Heath.
" " Abel, son of John Merrill.
" " Child of John Chase of Derry.

1764.

Jan., Isaac, son of Dea. Benjamin Kimball.
" 29, Ephraim, son of John Clark.
Feb. 6, Hannah, daughter of Joseph French, Jr.
" 19, Ruth, daughter of Rev. Henry True, b. Feb. 15, at 6 o'clock in the morning.
" " James, son of Moses Brown.
Mar. 25, Moses, son of Thomas Wadley.
Apr. 8, Ruth, daughter of Robert Johnson,
July 22, Abiah, daughter of Abraham Johnson of Halestown.
" " Daniel, son of Daniel Stevens.
" " Edmund, son of Joshua Kelly.
Aug., ——, daughter of William Hutchens of Halestown.
" Dolly, daughter of Levi Stevens.
" Simeon, son of Levi Stevens.
Sept., Molly, daughter of Moses Little of New Boston.
" Ruth, daughter of Jonathan Atwood of Halestown.
" Betty, daughter of John Mudgett of Halestown.
" John, son of John Ordway of Halestown.
" 14, Ammi Ruhmiah, son of Dr. John Bond.
" 23, Judith, daughter of Bartholomew Heath.
Oct. 1, William, son of Eben Mudgett.
" 21, Jonathan, son of James Clement.
Nov. 14, Joseph, son of Stephen Merrill.
" " Moses, son of John Chase.
" 18, Jedediah Worthen, son of Thomas Cheney.
Dec. 10, Moses, son of Benjamin Little, Jr.
" 11, Susanna, daughter of Edmund Colby.

1766.

Mar., Susanna, daughter of Ezekiel Currier.

Apr. 6, Rachel, daughter of Benjamin Richards.
 "   28, Joseph, son of Joseph French, Jr.
May,   Amos, son of James Little.
 "   Samuel, son of Micajah Morrill.
 "   25, Benjamin, son of Obednum Hall of Candia.
June 1, Walter, son of Benjamin Little.
July 27, Joseph, son of Job Kent.
Aug. 13, Philip, son of Jonathan Atwood of Weare.
 "   " Sarah, daughter of William Hutchens of Weare.
 ·′ 17, Margaret, daughter of Hugh Jamerson of Dunbarton.
 "   25, Thomas, son of Thomas Caldwell of Dunbarton.
Aug. 5, John, son of Timothy Ferren.
 "   " Moses, son of Asa Patten of Goffstown.
 "   " Martha, daughter of John Patten of Goffstown.
 "   " Thomas Stevens, son of Moses Little of New Boston.
 "   11, Enoch, son of Samuel Clark of Candia.
 "   17, Caleb, son of John Ingalls.
 "   24, Ruth Follansbee, daughter of Thomas Fellows of San-
              down.
 "   " Joshua, son of Joshua Little.
 "   31, Sinclear, son of John Clark.
 "   " Eliphalet, son of Daniel Stevens.
Sept. 28, Mary, daughter of Charles Johnston.

1767.

Feb. 17, Patty, daughter of Benjamin Plummer of Derry.
 "   25, Nathaniel, son of Samuel Mooers of Candia.
 "   " Stephen, son of John Merrill of Plaistow.
Mar. 1, Moses, son of Joseph Sawyer.
 "   17, Damaris, son of Timothy Goodwin.
 "   29, Sarah, daughter of Moses Brown.
May 3, Nathaniel, son of James King.
 "   31, Henry, son of Obednum Hall of Candia.
June 7, Sarah, daughter of Rev. Henry True.
July 26, Martha, daughter of Joseph Hadley.
 "   " Rebecca, daughter of Thomas Whittier of Plaistow.
 "   " Tabby, daughter of Thomas Cheney.
Aug. 23, Elizabeth, daughter of Joseph Knight of Plaistow.

Aug. 23, Thomas, son of Job Kent.
Sept. 20, Molley, daughter of Moses Kelly.
"   27, Betty, daughter of Richard Goodwin.

1768.

Jan. 16, Robert, son of William George.
Feb. 20, James, son of Joseph Little.
Apr. 3, Lydia, daughter of Dea. Benjamin Kimball.
"   10, Mary, daughter of Ephraim Webster.
"   "   Moses, son of Moses Poor.
"   "   Jonathan, son of John Ingalls.
May   2, Stephen, son of Moses Whittier of Plaistow.
"   "   Rachel, daughter of Moses Whittier of Plaistow
July,   Child of Timothy Stevens.
"   17, Sarah, daughter of Robert Hunkins.
"   "   Betty, daughter of Robert Hunkins.
"   31, Smith, son of Nathan Goodwin.
"   "   Aaron, son of Thomas Wadley.
"   "   David, son of Brinsley Plummer.
"   "   John, son of John Calfe.
Aug. 13, Jesse, son of Josiah Davis.
"   "   James, son of Reuben Mills.
"   28, Robert, son of Samuel Richards of Goffstown.
"   "   Samuel, son of Samuel Richards of Goffstown.
"   "   Ebenezer, son of Ebenezer Hackett of Goffstown.
"   "   Thomas, son of William Bell of Goffstown.
"   "   David, son of Eleazer Wells of Goffstown.
"   "   Mary, daughter of Eleazer Wells of Goffstown.
"   "   Aaron, son of Philip Ferren of Goffstown.
"   "   Rebecca, daughter of Philip Ferren of Goffstown.
"   "   Nathaniel, son of Joseph Ordway of Goffstown.
"   "   James, son of Benjamin Richards of Goffstown.
"   "   Sarah, daughter of Moses Little of Goffstown.
"   "   Mehitable, daughter of Job Dow of Goffstown.
"   29, Aaron, son of Nathaniel Carr of Weare.
"   "   Rachel, daughter of Joshua Maxfield of Weare.
"   "   James, son of James Emerson of Weare.
Sept. 18, Hannah, daughter of Simeon Morrill.

Sept. 18, Sarah, daughter of Joseph French.
"   " Meribah Farnum, daughter of Eben Hale.
Nov. 5, Philip, son of James King.
"   13, Hannah, daughter of Ezekiel Currier.
"   18, Joshua, son of Richard Heath.

1769.

Jan. 15, ——, daughter of Joseph Sawyer.
"   20, Richard Ferren, son of Benjamin Little.
Mar. 9, Thomas, son of Moses Little of New Boston.
"   16, Jerusha, daughter of Obednum Hall of Candia.
Apr. 5, Elijah, son of Job Rowell.
"   28, Abiah, daughter of Joseph Webster.
May 13, Mary, daughter of Benjamin Little, Jr.
"   31, Jeremiah, son of —— Bean of Candia.
"   "   Samuel, son of Lieut. Samuel Towle of Candia.
"   "   Moses, son of Moses Baker of Candia.
July 16, Polly, daughter of Hezekiah Hutchens.
"   23, Simeon, son of Moses Brown.
"   "   Molly, daughter of Joseph Hadley.
"   30, Rhoda, daughter of Timothy Goodwin.
Aug. 6, Lydia, daughter of Benjamin Hale.
"   12, Ebenezer, son of Joseph Pillsbury.
"   "   Judith, daughter of Moses Clark.
"   26, Susanna, daughter of William Clark of Candia.
"   "   Susanna, daughter of William Dolbey of Candia.
"   "   Mary, daughter of William Sanborn of Deerfield.
Sept. 10, Joseph, son of Joseph Knight of Atkinson.
"   17, Christopher, son of Christopher Rowell.
Oct. 29, Molly, daughter of widow Mary Tirrell.
"   "   Jesse, son of widow Mary Tirrell.
"   "   Sarah, daughter of widow Mary Tirrell.
"   "   Moses, son of Richard Goodwin.
"   "   Mehitabel Emerson, daughter of Samuel Stevens
Nov. 19, John Webster, son of Moody Chase.
Dec. 10, Jacob, son of Jacob Chase.

1770.

Feb. 13, Mary, daughter of Nathaniel Whittier of Raymond.
Apr. 30, Ephraim, son of Thomas Wadley.
May 27, Henry, son of Rev. Henry True.
 " " Jacob, son of Dea. Benjamin Kimball.
June 3, Moses, son of James King.
Aug. 7, Moses, son of Moses Clark.
Oct. 8, Sarah, daughter of Ephraim Webster.
 " 7, Enoch, son of Moses Poor.
 " 28, Miriam, daughter of Joseph French, Jr.

1771.

Feb. 24, Edward, son of Alpheus Goodwin.
May 12, Caleb, son of Obednum Hall of Candia.
 " 19, Mary, daughter of Moody Chase of Chester.
 " 26, Mary, daughter of Benjamin Hale.
June 2, Judith, daughter of Anthony Taylor.
 " 16, Caleb, son of Reuben Mills.
July 1, Lydia, daughter of James Emerson of Weare.
 " " Robert, son of Nathaniel Carr of Weare.
 " 14, Ruth, daughter of Hezekiah Hutchens.
 " " Jacob Morrill, son of Jacob Currier.
 " " Sarah, daughter of Joseph Knight of Atkinson.
 " " Hannah, daughter of Joseph Knight of Atkinson.
 " 28, George, son of Thomas Walker of Rindge.
Aug. 4, Mark, son of —— Present of Raymond.
 " 18, Gore Choate, son of John Clark.
 " " John, son of Joseph Pillsbury.
Nov. 17, Joshua, son of James King.
 " " Ella, daughter of Hannah Grove of Stratham.
 " " John Denny, son of John Porter.
Dec. 29, Aaron, son of Job Rowell.

1772.

Jan. 17, Jabez, son of Dea. Benjamin Kimball.
Apr. 19, James, son of Job Kent.
May 13, Sarah, daughter of Samuel Dodge.
 " " Molly, daughter of Simeon Morrill.

May 23, Molly, daughter of Timothy Goodwin.
June 18, Mary, daughter of Benjamin Little.
July,   Judith, daughter of John Ingalls of Atkinson.
  "   Abigail, daughter of John Ingalls of Atkinson
  "   12, John, son of Christopher Rowell.
  "   27, Mary, daughter of Rev. Henry True.
Oct. 11, Ruth, daughter of William George.
Dec.   6, Moses, son of Ephraim Webster.
  "   " Tamer, daughter of Reuben Mills.

1773.

Jan. 10, James, son of Anthony Taylor.
July 1, Ednah Hale, daughter of Parker Dole.
Aug. 15, William, son of Dea. John Calfe.
  "   29, Molly, daughter of Timothy Stevens.
Oct. 31, Stephen, son of Joseph Webster.
Nov. 7, Robert, son of Moses Little.
  "   15, George, son of James King.

1774.

Apr.,   ——, child of Thomas Wadley.
May 29, Joseph, son of Moody Chase of Chester.
June 2, Lydia, daughter of Simeon Morrill.
  "   26, Miriam Getchell, daughter of Reuben Mills.
  "   29, Richard, son of Hezekiah Hutchens.
July 31, Micajah, son of Christopher Rowell.
Aug. 7, James, son of Joseph Brown.
  "   " Stephen, son of Joseph Brown.
  "   " Hannah, daughter of Joseph Brown.
  "   " Lydia, daughter of Joseph Brown.
  "   10, *Daniel, son of Samuel Worthen of Weare.
  "   " *Samuel, son of Samuel Worthen of Weare.
  "   " Sarah, daughter of Samuel Worthen of Weare.
  "   " *Dolly, daughter of Samuel Worthen of Weare.
  "   " *Ruth, daughter of Samuel Worthen of Weare.
  "   " *Moses, son of Samuel Worthen of Weare.

*These baptized by the Rev. Mr. Marster, as he said.

Aug. 21, Johnson, son of Samuel Dodge.
Oct. 9, Moses, son of William George.
" 19, Micajah, son of Jacob Currier.
" 30, Daniel, son of Waite Stevens (deceased).
" " Sarah, daughter of Waite Stevens (deceased).
Nov. 6, Susanna, daughter of Joseph Brown.

1775.

Jan. 29, Ebenezer, son of Job Kent.
Feb. 19, Bartholomew, son of Moses Stevens.
" " Hester, daughter of Nathaniel Flanders.
Mar. 12, Susanna, daughter of Jeremiah Eames.
Apr. 30, Nathaniel, son of Timothy Goodwin.
June 14, Nanna, daughter of Dea. Benjamin Kimball.
" 25, Sarah, daughter of Job Rowell.
" Dudley, son of Benjamin Little.
Sept. 17, Molly, daughter of James Cheney.
Oct. 5, Mary, wife of Samuel Currier.
" " Ephraim, son of Benjamin Tuksbury.
" " Mary, daughter of John Kinkaed.
" " Aaron, son of Samuel Currier.
" " Samuel, son of Samuel Currier.
" " Daniel, son of Samuel Currier.
" " Molly, daughter of Samuel Currier.
" " Hannah, daughter of Samuel Currier.
Dec. 10, Ruth, daughter of Joseph Pillsbury.

1776.

Apr. 7, Joseph, son of Dea. John Calf.
May 25, Jacob, son of Moody Chase.
June 16, Hannah, daughter of Christopher Rowell.
July 10, Moses, son of Moses Stevens.
Aug. 13, Peter and Betty, twins of John Wicar.
" 25, Sarah, daughter of Joseph Webster.
Oct. 6, Ruth, daughter of Jacob Currier.

1777.

July 23, Hannah, daughter of David Cheney.

July 23, Sarah, daughter of Daniel Cheney.
  "   "   Nanne Abise, daughter of Daniel Cheney.
  "   "   Daniel, son of Daniel Cheney.
  "   "   Thomas, son of Daniel Cheney.
  "   "   John, son of Brinsley Plummer.

1778.

May 16, Elizabeth, daughter of William George.
  " 31, Joseph, son of Joseph Webster.
  "   " Moody, son of Moody Chase of Chester.
June 19, Job, son of Job Kent.
  "   " David, son of Moses Stevens.
July 12, Martha, daughter of John March.
Aug. 23, Henry, son of Thomas Wadley.
Oct. 4, Levi, son of Timothy Stevens.
  "   " Sarah, daughter of Dea. John Calf.
Nov. 8, Hannah, daughter of Joseph Pillsbury.
Dec. 6, Joshua, son of James Cheney.

1779.

Jan. 28, Daniel Little, son of Jacob Currier.
  "   " John, son of Nathaniel Flanders.
  "   " David, son of Samuel Currier.
Oct. 31, Jonathan, son of Moses Brown.
Nov. 7, Ellis, daughter of Moses Brown.

1780.

May,   Nathan, son of Timothy Goodwin.
  "   Moses, son of Moses Brown.
June 17, David, son of Widow Ordway of Goffstown.
Oct. 1, Samuel, son of Moody Chase of Chester.
  "   " Edward, son of Jacob Proctor of Derry.
Nov. 12, Sarah, daughter of Joseph Webster.

1781.

May 20, Ellice, daughter of Ens. John Kent.
  " 27, Jacob, son of Joseph Pillsbury.
  "   " Sargent, son of Abner Rogers.

May 20, Robert, son of Abner Rogers.
" " Abner, son of Abner Rogers.
" " Jacob, son of Abner Rogers.
July 1, Elizabeth, daughter of David Knowlton Ross.
" 9, Dexter, son of John Brown, from Ipswich, Mass.
" 29, Job, son of Job Rowell.
" " Robert Emerson, son of Job Rowell.

1782.

Jan. 12, Ephraim, son of Jonathan Taylor of Alexandria.
" " James, son of Jonathan Taylor of Alexandria.
May 19, James, son of Dea. John Calfe.
" 26, Elizabeth Adams, daughter of Theopolis Goodwin.
June 30, Ellis, daughter of Parker Dodge.
July 9, Sarah, daughter of John Harriman.
" " Betty, daughter of John Harriman.
" " Abigail, daughter of John Harriman.
" " Mary, daughter of John Harriman.
" " Caleb, son of John Harriman.
Aug. 5, Hannah, daughter of Jacob Currier.
" 25, Abner Little, son of Joseph Merrick.
Dec. 4, Tamar, daughter of Moses Kimball.

1783.

Apr. 8, Sarah, daughter of Timothy Goodwin.
" " Suppose Jonathan, son of Jonathan Kent.
" " William, son of Abner Rogers.
May 3, Timothy Dexter, son of John Brown.
" " Child of Parker Dodge.
" " Child of Job Rowell.

1785.

July 2, Sarah Marden, daughter of Barnes Morrill.
Aug. 10, Anna, daughter of Timothy Goodwin.
Sept. 4, Sarah, daughter of John Brown.

1787.

July 27, Sarah, daughter of Job Kent.

1793.

Mar. 27, Elizabeth, Molly, Freeman and Jemima, children of Barnes Morrill of Londonderry.

June 23, Nathaniel, son of Nathaniel Mitchell.

July 7, Henry Welch, son of Joseph Welch.

Aug. 8, Joshua, son of Joshua Eastman.

"   "   Anna, daughter of Joshua Eastman.

"   "   Tappan, son of Joshua Eastman.

"   "   Sally, daughter of Benjamin Chase of Sandown.

"   "   Nabby, daughter of Benjamin Chase of Sandown.

"   "   Samuel, son of Benjamin Chase of Sandown.

"   "   Polly, daughter of Benjamin Chase of Sandown.

"   "   Nancy, daughter of Benjamin Chase of Sandown.

"   "   Elice, daughter of Benjamin Chase of Sandown

1794.

Aug. 17, Henry True, son of Rev. John Kelly.

Oct. 12, Nancy, daughter of Barnes Morrill.

1795.

Oct. 30, Ephraim, son of Amos Mills (deceased), and Mary, his widow.

Dec. 6, Daniel Bodwell, son of Robert Chase.

1796.

Jan. 27, Miriam, daughter of Joseph French, Jr.

"   "   Polly, daughter of Joseph French, Jr.

July 31, Mary, daughter of Joseph Welch.

Oct. 30, Abigail, daughter of Barnes Morrill of Londonderry.

Above was baptized by the Rev. William Morrison, at the meeting house in Londonderry.

1797.

Feb. 5, Nancy, daughter of John Brown.

"   "   John, son of John Brown.

"   "   Jabez, son of John Brown.

July 2, Ruth, daughter of Dr. Joshua Sawyer, and Nabby, or Abigail, his wife.

John, son of Dr. Joshua Sawyer.
George, son of Reuben Mills.
Nathaniel, son of Reuben Mills.
John, son of Reuben Mills.
Amos, son of Reuben Mills.
Betty, daughter of Reuben Mills.
Whettmore, son of Reuben Mills.
Elizabeth, daughter of Parker Dodge of Londonderry.
Joseph, son of Parker Dodge.
Lydia, daughter of Parker Dodge.
Sally, daughter of Joshua Eastman.
Susanna, daughter of widow Abigail Johnson.
Henry, son of Abigail Johnson.
Jesse Terrill, son of Daniel Plummer of Londonderry.
John, son of Daniel Plummer of Londonderry.
Joseph, son of Nathaniel Mitchell, baptized by Rev.
    Mr. Abbott of Haverhill.
Sally, daughter of Joseph Welch.

1798.

John, son of Rev. John Kelly.
Daniel, son of John Little of Goffstown.
Lucinda (twin), dau. of Amos Richards of Goffstown.
Cynthia (twin), dau. of Amos Richards of Goffstown.
Sophia and Clarissa, twin daughters of Mathew Rich-
    ardson of Goffstown.
Lydia, daughter of George Poor of Goffstown.
Cyrus, son of Robert Walker of Goffstown.
Sarah, daughter of Josiah Grover of Hampstead.
Jonathan, son of Rev. True Kimball.
Mary, daughter of David Plummer.
Sarah, daughter of Damarias Goodwin.
Harriet, daughter of Dr. Joshua Sawyer, by the Rev.
    Mr. Abbott of Haverhill.

1799.

Mary Webster, daughter of Joseph Welch.
Ruth, daughter of Benjamin Emerson.

May 5, Maria, daughter of Benjamin Emerson.
  "   "   Benjamin Dudley, son of Benjamin Emerson.
  "   "   Abner, son of Benjamin Emerson.
  "   "   Frederick, son of Benjamin Emerson.
          " Three first offered for baptism."
July 7, Amos, son of Richard Kelly.
Sept. 29, Alpheus, son of Robert Chase.
  "   "   Francis James, son of Barnes Morrill.
Oct. 6, Susanna, daughter of Joseph Grover, baptized by the
          Rev. Mr. Adams of Haverhill.
Dec. 8, Judith, daughter of Richard Kelly.

1800.

Apr. 17, Irene, daughter of Rev. John Kelly. "Day of birth."
May,   ` Ruth, daughter of Reuben Mills.
  "   George, son of Reuben Mills.

1801.

Feb. 14, Francis, son of Rev. John Kelly, drowned in a well,
          June, 1804.
Apr. 11, William, son of Josiah Grover.
Apr. 26, Jane, daughter of True Kimball.
May 3, Irene, daughter of Joseph French, Jr.
  "   "   Francis, son of Joseph Welch.
June 7, Henry Johnson, son of Daniel Plummer.
Nov. 1, Aaron, son of Dr. Joshua Sawyer.

1802.

May 7, Clarissa, daughter of Benjamin Chase of Sandown.
  "   "   Lydia, daughter of Benjamin Chase of Sandown.
  "   26, Jonathan, son of Barnes Morrill of Londonderry.
Oct. 24, Eliza Merrill, daughter of Joseph Welch.

1803.

Feb. 27, Hannah, daughter of Richard Kelly.
Aug. 14, Israel, son of Rev. John Kelly.
Oct. 9, Abigail, daughter of Dr. Joshua Sawyer.
  "   "   Margaret Tilton, daughter of Joseph French, baptized
          by Rev. Mr. Patten.

1804.

May 15, Martha Sageant, daughter of Joseph Welch, at his home; died soon after.

Nov. 4, Mary, daughter of Richard Kelly.

1805.

Feb. 3, Samuel, son of Rev. John Kelly.

May 26, Francis, son of Joseph Welch.

Sept. 29, Mary, daughter of Daniel Plummer, baptized by Rev. Mr. Rowland of Exeter.

Oct. 13, Elizabeth Jenness, daughter of Barnes Morrill.

1806.

July 6, Mary Dearborn, daughter of Rev. John Kelly (day of birth).

Sept. 21, Mary, adult daughter of John Harriman.

"   "   Bayley, son of Silas Tenney of Chester.

"   "   Thomas, son of Silas Tenney of Chester.

"   "   Sewell, son of Silas Tenney of Chester.

"   "   Sally Ann, daughter of Silas Tenney of Chester.

"   20, Sarah Clement, daughter of Dr. Joshua Sawyer.

1807.

June 3, Mary, daughter of Reuben Mills.

"   7, Joseph Kimball, son of Joseph Welch.

Aug. 2, William, son of Silas Tenney.

Sept., Lois, daughter of Richard Kelly.

1808.

Jan. 31, Abigail, daughter of Rev. John Kelly, by Rev. Joseph Smith.

Mar. 27, Mary, wife of Silas Dinsmoor.

"   "   Silas, son of Silas Dinsmoor and Mary, his wife.

Oct. 16, William Pecker, son of Dr. Joshua Sawyer.

1809.

Apr. 10, Eunice, daughter of Reuben Mills.

May, Martha Sargent, daughter of Joseph Welch.

June 25, Mary, daughter of Silas Tenney, by the Rev. Samuel Harriss of Windham.

1810.

Mar. 11, Elizabeth Hoyt, " s." Rev. John Kelly.

May 5, George Washington, son of Joseph Welch.

July 7, Mary Colby, daughter of —— Huse and wife, by the
      grandparents, Dea. Benjamin Colby and wife.

1811.

Oct. 16, Sarah, daughter of Rev. John Kelly and Abigail, his
      wife, 11th ch.

1812.

May 6, Ann, daughter of Dr. Sawyer, and on account of Abi-
      gail, his wife.

  "   10, Harriet, daughter of Silas Tenney.

  "   "   Nathaniel Barre, son of Isaac Colby, on account of his
      wife.

  "   "   Jesse Hoyt, son of Isaac Colby, on account of his wife.

  "   "   Allen, son of Isaac Colby, on account of his wife.

  "   "   Lucy, daughter of Isaac Colby, on account of his wife.

  "   "   James Knight, son of Isaac Colby, on account of his
      wife.

1813.

May 2, Amasa Sargent, son of Joseph Welch, and Martha,
      his wife.

1814.

Apr. 24, Hannah Worth, daughter of Rev. John Kelly, twelfth
      child.

June 10, Joshua Sawyer, baptized at Mr. Reuben Mills' (son of
      Dr. J. Sawyer).

Nov. 6, Charles, son of Silas Tenney and Rebecca, his wife.

1817.

Apr. 20, Daniel, son of Silas Tenney and Rebecca, his wife.

May 4. Mary Heath, aged 17.

  "   18, James, Richard Kimball, Louisa and Moody Hill,
      children of James and Anna Brickett.

June 7, Harriet, daughter of Jesse Davis.
"   "   Horatio Gates, Almira Ann, James Albert, and Harriet
          Newell, children of James and Anna Calef.
"   22, Rufus, son of William Fellows, on account of his
          wife, Hannah F.
Aug. 10, Phebe Little, wife of Jona. C. Little, and five of their
          children, Meribah Hale, Linus Lewis, Carlton, David
          Poor, Phebe, and Nathaniel.
"   17, Anna Safford, aged sixteen, baptized for the Rev. Mr.
          Peabody, who is aged and infirm, and the three chil-
          dren of Jona. Page, Mira, Moody, and Sarah Jane.

1818.

Sept. 20, The wife of Rev. Stephen Peabody, and the four chil-
          dren, Nancy, Leonard, Stephen, and George Augus-
          tus, their sons.

1819.

Apr. 4, Baptized, also, William Smith Shaw, their son.
June 13, Susanna Eastman, wife of Joshua Eastman, Jr.
Nov. 28, Mary Putnam, daughter of Joshua Eastman.

1820.

June 4, Ezra Davis, baptized.
"   30, Jesse Brooks, son of Ezra Davis.
July 30, Lydia Chandler and Joseph Wentworth Batchelder
          were baptized.
Aug. 20, Henry George and Robert Collins Hackett, children of
          Dr. Philip and Elizabeth Hackett, on her account.
Sept. 17, Delia Welch, daughter of Jonathan Brickett.
Oct. 1, Sally Heath, wife of Moses Heath.
"   15, John Emerson, wife Elizabeth, and their children,
          Jesse, Alfred, John Webster, and Robert Henry.
Dec. 31, Edmund Tucker, son of Joshua Eastman, Jr.

1821.

Jan. 7, Moses Heath, aged 41.
"   "   Clarissa, wife of Jonathan Kent.

Feb. 8, Thomas, Nabby Kimball, Lorenzo, Jonathan Page,
          Elbridge Gerry, and Robert Emerson, children of
          Jona. Kent and Clarissa, his wife.
Apr. 8, Leonard, son of Rev. Stephen Peabody, at Atkinson.
June 3, William, son of Joseph Cogswell of Atkinson.
Aug. 19, Elizabeth, daughter of Dea. John Emerson and Eliza-
          beth, his wife.
  "   26, Mary Brown, daughter of Samuel Brown (deceased).
Oct. 20, Lois, daughter of James Calef.
Nov. 18, Joanna, daughter of Ezra Davis.

1823.

Aug. 18, Edwin Alena, son of Jona. Kent.
Nov. 2, Mary, daughter of Dea. John Emerson.

1824.

Mar. 4, John True, son of Joshua Eastman, Jr.
June 7, Charles Henry, son of Ezra Davis.

1825.

Jan. 23, Moses Tyler, son of Henry Welch, " at the house in ye
          evening, as he was very feeble and unable to come
          to ye meeting house."
Apr. 10, Charles Franklin, son of Jona. Brickett and Lydia,
          his wife, baptized by the Rev. E. L. Parker of Lon-
          donderry.
May   8, Jona. K. Little, baptized and admitted to the church.
Sept. 22, Judith Sawyer, daughter of Joshua Eastman, " and
          sick and apparently unto death."

1826.

Jan. 24, Susanna Sawyer, daughter of James Calef and Anna,
          his wife.
Apr. 30, Clarissa Ann True, daughter of Dea. Jona. Kent and
          Clarissa, his wife.
June 11, Charles Roger, son of Jabez Hoyt, and Hannah, his
          wife, on her account.

July   2, Abigail, wife of Nathaniel Little, Jr., baptized and
           admitted.
Apr.   6, Miriam, daughter of George Roger Gilbert, and Mary,
           his wife, members of the church in Candia, but re-
           siding in this town.
Oct.   8, Mary Elizabeth, daughter of Ezra Davis and wife Mary.

1827.

May   6, Elizabeth, daughter of William Tenney and Emma, his
           wife, on her account, as members of the church.
Oct. 28, Milton, son of Henry George.

1828.

Jan.   6, Mary C. Ayer.
  "   "   Mary Babb.
  "   "   Hannah Brown.
  "   "   Sally Brickett.
  "   "   Fanny Tufts.
  "   "   Sarah W. Jaques.
  "   "   Nancy Ordway.
  "   "   Belinda Little.
  "   "   Mary George.
  "   "   Lavina W. Pevear.
  "   "   Delia Welch.
  "   "   Jacob Irving.
  "   "   Thomas K. Little.
  "   "   Lyman Worthen.
  "   "   Josiah F. Heath.
  "   "   Daniel, son of Samuel Nichols.
  "   "   Alice, Frances and Sarah, children of widow Hannah
           Brown.
  "   "   Lorenzo Hale and Mary Ann, children of Mary Babb.
  "   "   Meribah Hale, Albery William and Christopher Per-
           ley, children of Jesse and Mary C. Ayer.
  "   "   Henry Welch, son of Henry Hubbard.
  "   "   Sarah Ordway Rogers, daughter of Ralph and wife
           Sally Brickett.
  "   15, Hiram and Eliza Jane, children of Samuel and Alice
           Nichols.

Jan. 15, Belinda Ann, daughter of Benjamin Sawyer and Pris-
cilla, his wife.
Mar. 2, George, son of Theodore Tarlton.
" " Sarah Noyes.
" " Theodore Tarlton.
" " Daniel Nichols, son of Stephen Nichols (deceased).
" 5, Mary Webster Emerson, daughter of David Lowell
Nichols.
May 4, Mary Webster, wife of Josiah.
" " John Thomas Tarlton.
" " Abigail A. Emerson.
" " Lauretta, daughter of William Tenney.
" " Abiab F. Tewksbury.
" " Samira York.
" " Hannah Johnson.
" " Mary Ann Mooers.
" " George W. Little.
" " Calvin Clifford, son of Josiah Webster.
July 6, Mary, daughter of James Calef.
Sept. 21, Henry Welch, son of Jona. Brickett.
Oct. 26, Benj. Kimball, son of Benj. Sawyer and Priscilla, his
wife, on her account, by the Rev. Mr. Rowland.
Nov. 2, Caroline Matilda, daughter of Ezra Davis.

1829.

July 5, Martha Ann, daughter of James Mann.
Sept. 20, Augusta Ella, daughter of Ralph Brickett, on account
of his wife Sarah.
" 27, Mary Elizabeth, daughter of Jesse Ayer, on account
of his wife.
Nov. 8, Albert William, son of William Tenney, by the Rev.
Mr. Arnold of Chester, on account of Emma M.
Tenney, his wife.
" 5, Ann Eliza, daughter of Josiah Webster and Mary, his
wife, by the Rev. Mr. Cutter of Windham.

1830.

Apr. 10, John Henry, son of Henry George.

May 3, Herbert Kimball, son of Jona. Brickett, by the Rev. Henry True Kelly.

Dec. 5, Samuel Gordon Smith, son of Francis Sawyer and Phebe, his wife, of Portsmouth.

1831.

May 8, Joshua, son of Joshua Eastman.

" 29, Mary Jane, daughter of James Mann.

Sept. 5, In the prayer meeting in the meeting house, Charles Ezra, son of Ezra Davis.

1832.

May 6, Sabra Foster, wife of Dr. Isaac Tewksbury.

" " Mary Emerson, wife of Joseph Johnson.

" " Herman Foster, son of Dr. Tewksbury.

" " Isaac Adolphus, son of Dr. Tewksbury.

" " Sabra Frances, daughter of Dr. Tewksbury.

" " Nathaniel Clarke, son of Isaac Smith, on account of his wife.

" " Mary Clarke, daughter of Isaac Smith, on account of his wife.

" " Isaac William, son of Isaac Smith, on account of his wife.

" " Robert Emerson, son of James Brickett.

" " Lorenzo Emerson, son of Richard K. Brickett, Jr.

" 25, Caroline Priscilla, daughter of Benjamin Sawyer and Priscilla, on her account.

July 1, Sarah Foster, daughter of Thomas Johnson of Derry.

Sept. 2, Harriet Mary, daughter of Dr. Isaac Tewksbury.

Dec. 23, Josiah Crosby, son of Josiah Webster.

1833.

May 5, Ruth A. Howard.

" " Jabez T. Howard.

" 19, Lucretia, daughter of Thomas Kent, by Rev. Mr. Cutter of Windham.

July 14, Mary Elizabeth, daughter of Dea. Jona. Kent.

" 21, Albion Danforth, son of Dr. Isaac Tewksbury.

Nov. 24, John Davis, son of Jacob Irving.

1834.

Aug. 10, Francis Henry, son of Benjamin Sawyer and Priscilla, his wife, on her account.

Sept. 21, Elizabeth Merrill, daughter of Dr. Isaac Tewksbury and wife, by Rev. Mr. Peckham.

July 29, At the house of Capt. Jesse Ayer, baptized Ebenezer Hale Little, on account of Mary, his wife.

"   " Delia Ann Ayer, daughter of Ralph Brickett, on account of Sally, his wife, a member of the church.

"   " Henry Little, son of Francis Sawyer and Phebe, his wife, of Portsmouth.

1835.

Aug. 2, Mary Elizabeth, daughter of Attai Pierce and Mary, his wife.

"   " Thomas, son of Thomas Cogswell, Esq., of Atkinson.

Sept. 13, Enoch Pillsbury, son of William Tenney.

Oct. 11, Baptized Hannah Brown, Lydia, Maria, children of Isaiah P. Moody, on account of his wife, Hannah K.

"   " Harlan, son of Benjamin Pillsbury, on account of his wife, a member of this church.

1836.

Mar. 31, Elizabeth Kelly, daughter of John W. Emerson and Abigail, his wife.

Aug. 2, Emily Susan, daughter of Ezra Kelly, baptized by Rev. Mr. Kelly, pastor.

"   14, Horace Reuben, son of Benjamin Sawyer, on account of his wife, by Mr. Bartley.

1837.

May 18, Rhoda Ann Little, daughter of Linus Lewis Little.

"   " Mary Ann, daughter of Linus Lewis Little.

Oct. 22, William Henry, son of Ezra Davis.

Nov. 6, Ellen Danforth, daughter of Dr. Tewksbury.

"   13, John James, son of Ralph Brickett.

1838.

Jan., Charles Isaiah Moody, infant son of Isaiah P. Moody, Esq.

" 7, Miss Louisa Currier, adult.

July 1, Elbridge G. Little.

" " Mrs. Sally Harriman.

" " Harriet Illsley.

" " Eunice Illsley.

" " Mrs. Ruth Emerson.

" " Miss Sarah George.

" " Miss Abigail Currier.

" " Mrs. Betsey Eastman.

" " Betsey Heath. (All adults.)

" " Daniel Haxen, James Henry, and Horatio Bartlett, children of Daniel Emerson, baptized on account of his wife.

Aug. 12, Jona. Adams, Moses Atkinson, and Harriet Susan, children of widow Harriet Illsley.

Sept. 2, Samuel Gibson, John Heath, Elizabeth Langmain, Abigail Heath, Louisa Heath, Ellen Gordon, Benjamin Atwood, Amos Nelson, Ralph Brickett, Harriet Nelson, Mrs. Mary H. Garland, John Little, Mrs. Louisa Little, Dr. Tewksbury (all adults), were baptized this date.

" " Sarah Abigail, daughter of Dr. Tewksbury.

" " Ezekiel Henry Little, son of Capt. James Gibson.

" " James Franklin, son of Capt. James Gibson.

Nov., Joseph Dana, infant son of Rev. John M. C. Bartley.

1840.

Sept. 13, Sarah Jane, daughter of Ezra Davis.

Nov. 1, Jacob Kimball, infant son of Daniel Emerson.

1841.

June, James Thorndike, infant son of Moody H. Brickett and wife.

Aug. 1, Harriet Ellen, Albert William, Eben Hale, children of Mr. and Mrs. Little.

Nov. 7, Martha, infant of Dea. William Sanborn.

1842.

June,   Eliphalet Harrison, infant son of Mr. and Mrs. Eliphalet Heath.

July,   William Henry, infant son of R. Kimball Brickett.

"   Mary Ann Morrison, infant daughter of Rev. J. M. C. Bartley.

1843.

Apr. 9, Harriet Frances, infant daughter of Rev. Francis Welch.

Sept. 3, Mary Danforth, daughter of Dr. Tewksbury.

"   8, Emma Alice, infant daughter of Mr. Joseph Chase.

Nov. 19, Mary Abbie, infant daughter of Mr. and Mrs. Simon Merrill.

"   "   Sarah Ellen, daughter of Jacob Irving.

1844.

Jan. 4, Charles Richards, son of Capt. Jesse Ayer, on account of his wife.

"   "   Mary Elizabeth, Albert Warren, Julia Ann, children of widow Merrill.*

Sept.,   Susan, infant daughter of Rev. J. M. C. Bartley, baptized by the Rev. Mr. Bodwell of Sanbornton.

"   "   Albert Cushing, son of Mr. Moody H. Brickett.

1846.

June 28, Mary Elizabeth, infant daughter of Joseph Chase.

July,   Jacob H., infant son of Jacob Irving.

Oct.,   Clara Whitman, infant daughter of Dr. Isaac Tewksbury.

1847.

Sept.,   Hannah Eliza, daughter of Simon Merrill, aged 3.

"   3, Mary Stevens, Eliza Frances, Josephine, children of Mr. Jesse Davis.

*John Merrill, b. in Bradford, Mass., Sept. 20, 1788; married Ruth Gould, b. in Topsfield, Mass., Aug. 20, 1833. Their children were: Mary Elizabeth, b. Apr. 9, 1833; Albert Warren, b. Nov. 23, 1834; Julia Ann, b. Nov. 4, 1836; all deceased but the youngest. Sent by Mrs. O. F. Sumner, Goffstown, N. H., a niece of the above, March 4, 1902.

1848.

Feb. 29, Mary Ann, daughter of Thomas and Mary Ann Kent.

Sept., Albert Emerson, son of John and Mary Bradley of Danville.

1850.

June, Joseph, son of Joseph Chase, baptized by Rev. Mr. Page of Atkinson.

July, Clara Louisa, Charles Edwin, children of Jona. and Ann Kent, baptized by the Rev. Mr. Princhild of South Boston.

1852.

June, John Bartley, infant son of Rev. J. M. C. Bartley, baptized at the altar by the Rev. Mr. Daniel Decker.

Oct., Mary Elizabeth, daughter of Wm. and Lois Sanborn.

1853.

July, Twins, infant children of John and Mary Bradley of Danville.

Sept., James William, infant son of William and Lois Sanborn.

" ———, daughter of Mr. Drew of Derry.

" Calvin Webster, son of Moody H. and Laura Brickett.

1857.

Sept., Susan Emma, daughter of Wm. and Lois Sanborn.

1861.

June, Eugene Meader, infant son of Rev. T. C. Pratt.

May 5, Laura Annette, daughter of Daniel H. and Sarah B. Emerson, on account of the mother.

1862.

July 6, Ella Boardman, infant daughter of Rev. T. C. Pratt.

1864.

July 6, John Calef, son of William and Lois (Calef) Sanborn.

" " Lucy Jane, daughter of Mrs. Adams.

Nov. 6, Albert Wallace, infant son of Rev. T. C. Pratt.

1866.

Sept.,   Charles Stacy, son of John S. and Hannah E. Titcomb.

1872.

July 7, Henry Irving, son of John S. and Hannah E. Titcomb.
"   "   Emma Lizzie Tenney, child of Silas and Mary E.
          Tenney.

1876.

May 7, Albert Priestley Watson, son of Rev. Albert Watson
         and Miranda, his wife.

1878.

Sept. 1, Carrie Elsie Davis, daughter of Wm. H. Davis and
          wife, Jane R.

1879.

May 14, Maurice Woodburn Dickey, son of M. P. and Louise
         S. Dickey.

1880.

July 4, Henry Clinton, son of William and Jane R. Davis.

1882.

"   2, Mary Garland, daughter of Wm. and Jane R. Davis.

-1890.

"   6, Ray Everett Fitts, son of W. Amos and Mary Etta
          Fitts.

1891.

Nov. 1, Lee Mahlon, son of W. Amos and Mary Etta Fitts.

1893.

May 7, Mabel Gertrude, daughter of W. Amos and Mary Etta
         Fitts.
"   "   Otto Theodore Anderson, christened at home.

1894.

Sept.,   Charlotte Ruth, daughter of Forrest and Alice Merrill.
"   Janette Edith, daughter of Forrest and Alice Merrill.

1895.

June 6, Clara Emma, daughter of W. Amos and Mary Etta Fitts.

1896.

June 6, Eleanor True Randall, dau. of Isaac and Alice Randall.
"   "   Maurice, son of Isaac and Alice Randall.

1900.

June 3, Evelyn, daughter of Isaac and Alice Randall.
"   "   Earl Haynes, son of Albert and Daisy Haynes.

1901.

Sept.,   Hollis, son of Albion and Mary G. Emerson.
"   Marjorie, daughter of John C. and Annie Sanborn.
"   16, Ernest Colby, son of Frank and Alice Pillsbury.

1902.

Nov. 2, Roland C., son of Albion D. and Mary G. Emerson.

PROCEEDINGS

OF THE

150TH ANNIVERSARY

OF THE

CHURCH.

HAMPSTEAD. NEW HAMPSHIRE.

JULY 2ND, 1902.

150th ANNIVERSARY CELEBRATION.

The celebration of the 150th anniversary of Hampstead as a corporate town July 4, 1899 was an event ever to be remembered by those who were present on that occasion. It broadened our lives, and made us realize that the town in a century and a half of growth, has reached out to the farthermost parts of the earth, and we trust has encouraged us, to feel that life means something even here in an ordinary New England town.

The incorporation of Hampstead in 1749 was followed by the organization of the church three years later in 1752. For ninety years town and church affairs were closely connected.

The church committee in the summer of 1901, with the Rev. Rufus P. Gardner as the leading spirit, acted upon the thought, that the celebration of the anniversary of the town would be recognized only in part, unless the church fittingly remembered its one hundred and fifty years of work, by observing with appropriate exercises the birthday of the church the coming year.

The removal from town of Rev. Mr. Gardner was a serious drawback to the plans, but May 14, 1902 the following committees were chosen to complete the arrangements for a reunion of the friends of the church.

Executive Committee.—Rev. Walter H. Woodsum, Dea. Charles W. Pressey, Dea. William H. Davis, Dea. Forrest E. Merrill, John C. Sanborn, Miss Mary E. Spollett, and Mrs. John S. Corson.

Committee on Invitations.—Dea. Charles W. Pressey, Mrs. Mary E. Eastman, and William A. Emerson.

Committee on Music.—Dea. William H. Davis, Dea. Forrest
E. Merrill, Mrs. Albert H. Little, and Mrs. Frank W.
Emerson.

Committee on Reception.—Mr. and Mrs. Forrest E. Merrill,
Mrs. Isaac Randall, and Mr. Charles Park Pressey.

Committee of Entertainment and Transportation.—John C.
Sanborn, John S. Corson, Albion D. Emerson, Ammasa
W. Hunt, Mrs. Clara Irving Davis, Mrs. William A.
Emerson, and Mrs. James W. Sanborn.

Committee on Decorations.—Miss Mary E. Spollett, Miss
Minnie M. Fitts, and Mrs. Charles O. Cass.

Committee on Banquet.—Mrs. John S. Corson, Mrs. Henry
W. Tabor, and Mrs. William H. Davis.

Wednesday, July 2, 1902, the day chosen for the celebration was a cloudless, cool July day. Invitations had been
sent to past and present members, town people and their
friends, also to the neighboring parishes, and invited guests
to meet at the church in the afternoon and evening.

The auditorium of the church was entered through an
arch of evergreen, bearing the inscription in large white letters nestled among the twigs of the beautiful hemlock,
" Welcome Home."   On the other side of the arch where it
met the eye on leaving the church were the words " Come
in '52 " formed of field daisies. In front of the new organ
and about the pulpit were a mass of ferns and meadow rue,
above which, filling the large room with their delightful fra-
grance were 150 roses of rare varieties, 150 carnations and
other beautiful blossoms from the conservatories of Mrs.
Joseph H. White of Boston who with her sisters, Mrs. Coaker,
Mrs. Jackson and Mrs. Hitchcock, sent the gift as a birthday
remembrance to their former church home. On the piano,
surrounded with roses and maiden hair ferns, was placed a
picture of the church in Hampstead, England, loaned by Mr.
J. T. Rhodes of Haverhill, Mass., a native of Old Hamp-

stead. In front of the new organ hung the word "150th Anniversary," in gilt and snowy white, trimmed with rock ferns and scarlet ramblers.

PROGRAMME.

Afternoon, 1 o'clock.

1. Organ Prelude—Extracts from Lohengrin, . . *R. Wagner*
    Mrs. Frank W. Emerson.
2. Anthem—"O Give Thanks," . . . . . . *Gabriel*
    Chorus—William H. Davis, Director.
3. Reading of Scripture and Invocation.
4. Response Duet—"Through the Gates of Gold." *Maud Anita Hart*
    Mrs. Albert H. Little, Miss Mary G. Davis.
5. Address of Welcome.
    The Pastor, Walter H. Woodsum.
6. Reminiscences of Former Pastors.
    1. Rev. Henry True, 1752-1782. By Henry True, Marion, Ohio.
    2. Rev. John Kelley, 1792-1836. By Rev. George O. Jenness, Charlton, Mass.
    3. Rev. John M. C. Bartley, 1836-1857. By Rev. William T. Bartley, Ph.D., Salem, N. H.
    4. Rev. Theodore C. Pratt, 1859-1870.
    5. Rev. Ebenezer W. Bullard, 1870-1875. By Dr. William E. Bullard, Larchmont, L. I.
    6. Rev. Albert Watson, 1876-1893.
    7. Rev. Rufus P. Gardner, 1893-1901.
7. Solo—"There is a City Bright," . . . . *A. F. Loud*
    Mrs. Forrest E. Merrill.
8. Historical Address.
    Miss Harriette E. Noyes.
9. Singing—"While the Years are Rolling on." *arr. by W. E. Hartwell*
    Double Male Quartette, Forrest E. Merrill, Director.
10. Reminiscences of Past Preceptors.
    1. Rev. Myron P. Dickey, Milton, N. H.
    2. Edward E. Bradley, Lincoln, Mass.
    3. Forrest E. Merrill.
11. Solo—"The Gates of the West," . . *Caroline Lowthian*
    Miss Abbie F. Chandler, Haverhill, Mass.
12. Reminiscences of Past Members.
    1. Miss Fannie B. Williams, Carney, Oklahoma.
    2. Rev. Albert P. Watson, Bedford, N. H.
    3. Henry C. Ordway, Winchester, Mass.
    4. Rev. Kimball K. Clark, Fitzwilliam, N. H.
13. Singing—"Jerusalem the Golden," . . . . *Gabriel*
    Quartette.

14. Greetings from the Mother Church, Plaistow and No. Haverhill.
      Rev. Joseph Kimball.
15. Greetings from Friends,
      Hon. Lyman D. Stevens, Concord, N. H.
16. Song of the Day,   .   .   *James H. Taylor, Dorchester, Mass.*
      Congregation.
17. Organ Postlude—Polish Serenade, ...   *J. Kaffa*
      Mrs. Frank W. Emerson.
   Social Greetings and Banquet.

                Evening, 7.30 o'clock.

1. Organ Prelude—"Sunset Glow,"   .   .   .   *E. L. Ashford*
      Mrs. Frank W. Emerson.
2. Anthem—"Praise ye the Father,"   .   .   .   .   *Gounod*
      Chorus.
3. Reading of Letters from Friends.
4. Singing—"He Knows it All,"   .   .   .   .   *Finley Lyon*
      Double Male Quartette.
5. Poem of the Day.
      Rev. William T. Bartley, Ph. D.
6. Solo—"The Land of Home,"   .   .   .   .   *Hamilton Gray*
      Mrs. Albert H. Little.
7. Address,
      Rev. Burton W. Lockhart, D. D., Manchester, N. H.
8. Anthem—"Ye that Stand in the House of the Lord."   *Walter Spinney*
      Chorus.
9. Prayer.
10. Anniversary Hymn, ...   *James H. Taylor*
      .   Congregation.
11. Benediction.
12. Organ Postlude—March from Tannhauser,   .   .   *R Wagner*
      Mrs. Frank W. Emerson.

At one o'clock the spacious room was filled to overflow-
ing. The exercises opened by an organ prelude, by Mrs.
Frank W. Emerson, followed by anthem, "O give thanks"
by chorus director, Wm. H. Davis; sopranos, Mrs. Albert
H. Little, Mrs. Forrest E. Merrill, Misses Annie L. Kimball,
and Ethel H. Spinney; altos, Mrs. Henry W. Tabor, Mrs.

Frank E. Darling, Misses Mary G. Davis, and Edith Foss;
tenors, William H. Davis, Forrest E. Merrill, John S. Corson, and Lowell M. Clark; basses, Eugene L. Spinney, H.
Clinton Davis, C. Park Pressey, and Albion D. Emerson;
reading of scripture and invocation by Rev. A. B. Howard,
pastor of the First Free Baptist Church, Danville, N. H.;
response duet, "Through the gates of gold," Mrs. Albert H.
Little and Miss Mary G. Davis.

Rev. Walter H. Woodsum then greeted the visitors with
the following words of welcome.

"I think it was Tennyson who said, ' Words partly reveal and partly conceal the soul that is within.' I fully
appreciate the inadequacy of words to express the sublime
sentiments that surge in our hearts as we extend to you this
welcome to the one hundred and fiftieth anniversary of
organized work for God in Hampstead, for what expressions
of words can do justice to the grandeur of a century and a
half of gospel labor of love and self sacrifice?

And yet what an honor to extend a welcome in so glorious a cause, for surely the work of the Gospel of Jesus
Christ stands pre-eminently the grandest that ever engaged
the feeble efforts of men.

And what a pleasure, also, it is to welcome you here to-
day back to the old familiar haunts, to the recollections of
childhood days, to the sacred precincts of God's house, hallowed by memories of devotion and holy worship, where
was learned reverence for God, love for His Son, and true
service for one another.

Truly it gives us genuine pleasure to welcome you to-day
here in this house, and to our homes, our friendships, and
our hospitality, such as we are enabled to give.

We welcome you, pastors of the past, we glory in the
record of noble unselfish service to God and man, which you
have made, and I pray God that as we reap the benefits of
the heritage of good works, so when we shall have closed
our labors as pastor of this people, the standard of service
shall not have been lowered.

We welcome you, the posterity of those early pastors, who
laid the foundations, and stood like the very bulwarks of

God against the assaults of the enemy, truly an ancestry to be proud of.

We welcome you, the preceptors of the high school, which in the wise provision of its founder is in close connection with the church, and the cause of righteousness, to instruct in knowledge, in righteousness and in christian principle is the especial province of the church of Christ.

We welcome you, the members of former years. What a foretaste is this of the great family reunion in the kingdom of God, when from north and south, and from east and west, the children of God in all the ages shall sit down with Abraham and Isaac in that blessed land and talk of all the wonderful goodness of God.

We welcome you, the representatives of our parent church. Surely no greater work can be done by the church of God than the giving of birth, as it were, to children churches who shall carry the glorious gospel into the regions beyond.

And we welcome you, friends and neighbors, one and all. "Come, let us make a joyful noise unto the Lord;" "Come, behold what great things the Lord hath wrought," and let us each one contribute in honoring the past, in giving inspiration to the present and to enlarging the hope for the future.

I extend the welcome to you in behalf of the Executive Committee who have been untiring in their efforts to do justice to this occasion.

I also welcome you in behalf of the church organization standing in its entirety of one hundred and fifty years, and of over seven hundred and seventy members, "The church of the living God, the pillar and ground of the truth."

And finally I welcome you in behalf of the community, which has always done its part willingly and gladly, and has ever shown its respect and esteem for the church to which it should belong, and its regard and reverence for the true religion of Jesus Christ, which it should more emphatically and definitely espouse."

Number six of the programme "Reminiscences of former pastors," followed.

Rev. Henry True was represented by Henry True of Marion, Ohio, a great-grandson and namesake of the first pastor, and his son, Harry Ayer True, who were pleased to be present, and spoke briefly in response. A grand-daughter, Mrs. Mary True Vose and her daughter, Helen A., also revered the memory of their ancestor.

Rev. George O. Jenness of Charlton, Mass., gave the following tribute to the memory of Rev. John Kelly, grand father of Mrs. Jenness.

Ladies and Gentlemen:—

I have been invited to give you a five or ten minutes reminiscent address as a representative of the Rev. John Kelly, the second minister of this town.

I suppose your committee who extended this invitation knew very well that I had no acquaintance personally with good old Father Kelly, but that they also knew that for the last thirty-two years, I have been on familiar terms with his grand-daughter; and so they necessarily expect that what I shall say about him will be but an echo from her. So much has been printed and published in your excellent history of Hampstead concerning Father Kelly, there is very little of a biographical character left which would interest you.

There are, however, two or three very interesting facts about him to which I may, perhaps, call your attention appropriately.

Mr. Kelly was very specially interested in little children, even down to his last years. He was never known to pass one by, even in the streets, without some signal indications of his special love for them.

He delighted to take them on his knees and tell them bible stories. All the children loved and respected him, and when on his pastoral rounds wherever he visited, the children of that home were among the most cordial to gather about and welcome him.

If, as has often been stated, the average minister of his times was generally inclined, like the early disciples who rebuked the Master for paying little children marked attention, and giving them a peculiarly warm place in his heart, it is a most beautiful tribute to the memory of your second minister to be able to refer to him on such an occasion as this, as strikingly endowed with the Master's spirit who said, "Suffer little children to come unto me, and forbid them not."

Father Kelly was also, I think, ahead of his brother ministers of his time, and indeed, I may say, ahead of the average christian man of the period, on the temperance question. On March 4th, 1841, when I was four years old, and he was seventy, he delivered a most remarkably strong sermon before the Hampstead Temperance Society, and also, three years later, repeated the sermon, one evening in the Plaistow Town House, from the text, " Wine is a mocker, strong drink is raging."

Among other things in this sermon, he spoke of the danger of being deceived and snared by using liquor, and also of the criminality of having anything to do in promoting its use in the common concerns of life.

On the first point mentioned, Father Kelly goes on to say, " There is one circumstance which has a great tendency to produce this deception, and that is when the intemperate man first takes down the deadly poison; he immediately feels better at his stomach, because the ingredient produces an excitement which he imagines to be renewed strength, whereas it is nothing more than a movement towards a fall."

When I read this from the pen of your second minister, I couldn't help thinking of that " tired feeling," and the promise of *renewed strength in our day*, by the Patent Medicine vender, who advertises a remedy and compounds it largely of intoxicating liquors.

And on the second point of the criminality of anything to do in promoting the use of intoxicants in the common con cerns of life, he asks, " Is it not a national crime that a large proportion, one third of the best land in France, is taken up in the culture of the vine instead of that of bread corn ? And is it not a national sin that in this country men are suffered to turn bread corn into poison, and a greater sin to give a license to covetous and wicked ones to sell this same poison to whom it will turn the sweetest and best food into poison, and to the ruin of soul and body, or to urge it upon others to the utter ruin of millions of individuals and families is a great sin, an aggravated sin."

Then your second minister was, I am persuaded, far in advance of many of his contemporaries, in his estimate of the importance of music in religious worship. I hold in my hand a sermon of his preached one hundred and two years ago, to the singing school in Hampstead. In this discourse, he argues that music is *a divine institution*. He takes strong grounds in support of instrumental music as helpful in worship. "Singing to the Lord before men," he says, "should be hearty and also reverent." Let me quote to you one or two of his sentences which might well be considered as most excellent advice to singers, even in these times. "It is granted by all," he says, "that regard is to be had to time, concord, distinct pronunciation, and the variety of the subject, but what gives the grace to the music is the unaffected piety of the heart, glowing in the countenance and flowing on the tongue." The apostle says, "I will sing, saith the spirit, I will sing with the understanding also." "And so ought all thus to sing with grace in their hearts, by the assistance of the spirit of God, and with their own mind in spirit engaged in the work; and according to rule, understanding themselves what they sing and how they sing, and as far as they are able singing to the understanding of others, by pronouncing distinctly and in plain language, what they sing." In his closing he says to this singing school, "You will permit me to express my satisfaction with the conduct of many youths in this place, that instead of being engaged in those frivolous occupations which neither improve the head nor the heart, you have turned your attention to one of the most improving and useful sciences, which by divine grace, will enable you to praise God, to aid His people in their devotions, and to enjoy much satisfaction yourselves."

As I look back thirty years to the time when I left Hampstead, my memory recurs to the old singing seats where I used to sit with the Hampstead choir, many of whom have gone to sing the praises of God in the upper and more glorious sanctuary, that I cannot but feel that much of the success and interest which has been a distinguishing feature in the musical part of the Hampstead Congregational Church worship is largely due to the encouragement the singers of the olden days received from the long and faithful ministry of Father Kelly.

Rev. William Tenney Bartlett, Ph. D., pastor of the Congregational Church in Salem, N. H., and grandson of the third minister, Rev. John M. C. Bartley, 1836-1857, referred briefly to his grandfather's life, mentioned dates, spoke of his relation to children, how he would question them on the street, " Do you want to be happy?" and finally would tell them, " Then you must be good "; spoke of his mild, but firm home government, in which the words " I guess I wouldn't " were well understood, and served to frustrate childish plans of which he disapproved. He referred to his grandfather's charity, as when he interested parents in the further education of their sons, or even paid a part of their tuition himself, or when he secured the free services of a Newburyport physician to remove cataracts from the eyes of an indigent parishioner, himself driving to Newburyport to bring the doctor, and driving back to return him to his home ; and of his last words, nearly the last, as, towards morning, after a night of sickness, in which he had paid little attention to surroundings, he asked the watcher who had spent the night at his bedside, " And how is your little family ? " adding almost immediately, " Of which the whole family in heaven and earth is named—one family," thus showing how closely his every day thoughts were with his holy ones.

In closing he suggested that it would be well for every one if the secular were so closely connected in his own life with the divine.

The fourth pastor, Rev. Theodore C. Pratt, was present, and spoke for himself, as follows:—

" When the early spring sap runs from the rock maples it is sweetish. Boiled down it becomes delicious syrup or maple sugar. But this requires time and skill on the part of the sugar-maker. The same holds true of writers and speakers. Time and skill are required to produce the best thoughts in the fewest words. Whether I shall give you sap or syrup remains to be seen.

I came to this church and people after many men had been heard. Candidates and supplies had been tried for more than a year, until some thirty, more or less, had been tested.

Unless a settled pastor was secured within the second year, certain funds in the possession of the Society would perhaps be forfeited. Was this the main reason for the choice they finally made?

The war of the rebellion came on near the close of my second year. When the first gun was fired at Fort Sumter, my way became plain and clear. It had been my method when any important question came up to seek the advice of those wiser than myself. But I had no time nor inclination to confer with others. The government must be sustained, was my immediate decision.

Then came those four years of conflict, of fierce struggles, of successes, and of final victory. This church in those four years never faltered. In God we trusted, and he gave us success.

I spoke out plainly and boldly, in and out of the pulpit, advocating freedom and every movement that aimed to improve the church and people.

In accepting the call to this pastorate I closed my letter with the assurance that I would preach what in my judgment was truth. Hence I was not trammelled. I could not be, if I remained a true man.

Just before the war broke out the people decided to build a new church, which in due time was completed. I preached the sermon of dedication from I Kings 8: 27, "And will God in every deed dwell on the earth? Behold the heaven, and heaven of heavens cannot contain thee : how much less this house that I have builded." God accepted this house as his own, and here for forty years he has manifested his grace, his power to save souls.

The last year of my ministry here was remarkable in my personal experience. Circumstances led me to the investigation of spiritual phenomena, and to deeper, closer thinking, And here, at my home, and in this sanctuary, the angels of God met me. They soon convinced me that they were ministering spirits, strengthening the soul in its conflict with sin and deepening its love for others. Yes, after ten years of labor, I found my love for others increased, and a deeper longing for a knowledge of divine truth. As it had been my practice to utter truth as I saw it, how could I conceal the change in my views and feelings? Did not the angels do much to bring about the change? They met Jacob in olden time and helped him. Is it strange that they helped me?

I frankly spoke of my rich experiences, my love for God, and my deeper longings for personal holiness. In a word, I poured out my whole soul. This course was in such marked contrast with my former teaching that my hearers were surprised. What can it mean? they asked. Afraid that something was wrong, and desirous of doing the right thing, they called a council. I consented, and pastors and delegates met and advised that I spend a while in study at Andover Theological Seminary.

The next year and a half at Andover was rich in its results. The professors were men of ability and truth lovers. I found myself in sympathy with their views of truth. Some were unable to help me in my special investigations. One said he "knew nothing about such matters." Was he not wise to withhold his judgment? I honor him. From Prof. Phelps and his aged father I received much information. The elder man confirmed me in my new views, while the professor indirectly influenced me along the same lines. Prof. Park was absent in Europe, I think, when I arrived. Some one advised me to avoid him. Circumstances never brought us together except for a moment. The faculty of the seminary were very kind and helpful, and I hold them in grateful remembrance.

The application of the church in Tilton, N. H., was handed to me by one of the professors. I answered it, went to Tilton, and, after an interval, was installed as pastor of the Congregational Church. I remained with them five years.

I come back to-day, after thirty-two years of reflection and experience, strengthened in my impressions and belief in the value and power of angelic guidance, and in sympathy with many of my brethren in the ministry—I mean the more conservative thinkers.

My interest in this church and people has not waned. This is the only church that I know well throughout my entire ministry. To see my successors doing good work has gladdened my heart, while the kind attention shown me recently in my age has been most gratifying.

To-day is a rare occasion in my varied experience. Looking backward I see that better work has been done by my successors as one result of the change. And the two men who have toiled here for twenty-four years have received marked blessing from above. For this I hoped, for this I prayed. The improvements made in this house of worship, its enlargement, and its added beauty, have been in keeping with my desire for your good, and I am satisfied.

This church and this people are dear to my heart. Here I began my work as a minister of the gospel. Here I received blessing, enlargement, uplifting.

Three times the angel of life entered our little cottage. Later in a few days death removed the little ones so dear to us. The dust of my wife and four children mingle with the precious dust of those whom you have loved. And by their side is room for me and my remaining daughter. But when this body is laid in yonder cemetery do not think of me as being here. Only the cast-off garment that my soul hast worn will be deposited with you.

I may be with you as an angel of light, with larger power for aiding and strengthening your pastors. If infinite wisdom shall send me here as a helper, I will come on the swift wings of joy and love."

The remarks by Rev. Mr. Pratt were listened to with marked attention, and suggested the following lines, dedicated to him by a friend:—

TO OUR PASTOR.

Thin is the veil that hides the unseen portal
   That leads from out this narrrw place of tears
Into wide fields, the blessed life immortal,
   Where we, rejoicing, spend the eternal years.

We feel a presence rising dark before us,
   A shadow looming dimly on our way,
A gasping cry, and then full shining o'er us,
   The bright effulgence of an endless day.

The death we fear is but the quiet going
   From life's dim chamber into quickening day,
The careful reaping of a lifetime's sowing
   Of seed we scattered on our daily way.

Perhaps with joy we'll find the end we wrought for
   Has yielded gracious store of golden sheaves.
Perchance with tears too late the purpose sought for,
   We find left naught to glean but scattered leaves.

What wonder if, with all these scenes before us,
   We think of loved ones in life's weary day,
In full remembrance of the love they bore us,
   And long to help them on their weary way.

The burning bush that still was not consumed,
   The mighty triad on the mountain grim,
And spirit forms that all the space illumed
   When Christ in anguish paced the garden dim.

The spirit mild that hailed the favored maiden,
   And gave sweet promise of the coming child,
And those who later, with great tidings laden,
   Led the rude shepherds through the pastures wild.

All prove you that with watchful love's persistence,
   We silent guide you on your homeward way,
And when you falter, we, with mild insistence,
   Still lure you onward toward the perfect day.

Sometimes at eventide, when night's descending,
   And you unconscious breathe a silent prayer,
You feel us present o'er you quiet bending,
   And know, unseen, we stand beside you there.

Hope on, dear heart. The hours you spent in sowing
   Along the wayside of each weary day,
Shall come to you in measure deep o'erflowing
   In the rich harvest of the bright alway.

The following letter was read in response to the fifth
pastor, Rev. E. W. Bullard:—

THE BUNGALOW, LARCHMONT-ON-THE SOUND,
NEW YORK, June 26, 1902.

JOHN C. SANBORN, *Clerk of the Hampstead Cong'l Church:*
Dear Sir:—I thank you, and through you the pastor and peo-

ple, for the very kind invitation to be present at your one hundred and fiftieth anniversary.

I shall be with you in spirit, but shall be unable to be present in person.

My late father, Rev. E. W. Bullard, and former pastor of your church, often spoke of his pastorate among you as years of great happiness, due in a large measure to the loyal support that he' received in his work from the church officers and the congregation.

Surely, when any church gives such stalwart aid to the Lord's work, and upholds its pastor's hands, as you did during my father's ministry, then such a church will prosper and be blessed.

I wish you, as a church, congregation and town, all possible joy and happiness in your anniversary, and for the future may God's richest blessings be in store for you.

Very sincerely yours,

WILLIAM E. BULLARD (No. 501).

Rev. Albert Watson, sixth pastor, spoke as follows :—

"In response to the kind and gracious welcome given us, I feel like saying, "thank you" most heartily to this beloved pastor and church, whose guests we are to-day.

Even if this is not exactly the "Mount of Transfiguration," it is good to be here, to listen to the story of the past, to look into each other's faces, to take each other by the hand, and exchange hearty greetings.

Doubtless we all feel like saying, with Tiny Tim, "God bless us, every one."

In giving reminiscences such as are called for this afternoon, there is great danger of the "ego" coming to the front; and yet one can hardly speak of what he saw, heard and felt during a ministry extending a little over seventeen years without using personal pronouns in a manner that is not altogether pleasant to the ear.

This difficulty, combined with the brief time limit allowed the speakers, baffles one and makes him tremble a little as he undertakes to tell his story.

It is not with a view of calling attention to myself, but in simple gratitude to Almighty God to whom all glory belongs, that I now submit to you a few facts and figures.

It was in the early days of 1876 that your attention was called to me, as one who might possibly fit in the vacant place in your church and become your sixth pastor. You sent for me; "I came, I saw, I conquered." A very hearty and unanimous call followed. We were one at the start. The installation took place March 28, 1876. Now as to reminiscences.

The most marked event in my pastorate was the great revival which begun Sunday evening, May 21st, a little less than two months after the installation. We had been singing the well-known hymn, "Pass me not, O Gentle Saviour," when the pastor was moved by an almost invisible impulse to stop the singing and press home the truth that if any were passed by it was their own fault. Surely God was present, and willing and waiting to save there and then.

No need of any being "passed by." The blessing is here, A full, free, complete salvation is offered to all. Will you have it? Will you open your heart, surrender yourselves, and be saved now? If so, please rise at once. Seventeen stood on their feet, as if moved by a common impulse, most of them heads of families now. The spirit of the Lord was with us in mighty power.

A few extra meetings were called, and in less than two weeks over twice as many more were on their feet in our meetings, saying virtually, "We will go with you, for we have heard that God is with you."

The whole town was moved as it had not been before for forty years. In fact, the influence of the revival extended through the whole of my pastorate. It was emphatically the best thing in it, and it was particularly gratifying to me, a few weeks ago, to hear my successor, Brother Gardner, say publicly, that he "had felt its effect all through his ministry here."

I can hardly begin to tell you its effect upon my own heart. It will be enough, perhaps, to say that I never felt so weak or so humble in all my life; it seemed as if God almost took the breath out of me. How utterly insignificant I was! There was no chance whatever for any self-glorification, because, you see, I had done nothing special to bring about such a revival. And yet I had rather have one grand, gracious, God-given revival like that than fifty man-made, machine-like, manufactured articles called by that name, for such things are very likely to be superficial in character, shallow in spirit, and sadly disappointing in results.

Beginning with a membership of seventy-two, the church life and work grew so rapidly that at the end of five years we were able to report a membership of one hundred and sixty-one.

Whole number received during my pastorate was 182, on confession of faith 136, and by letter 46.

Whole number connected with the church during my ministry was 254, of these 98 were removed by letter, death, or discipline.

The attendance on evening meetings was increased fourfold. There was a corresponding increase in benevolence. You gave on an average, during my ministry, $500 a year, besides meeting current expenses.

This includes what you gave for the building of the new vestry, also the church repairs and alterations from time to time. About one half of the above sum, (or $250), represented your average yearly contribution, for missionary and other benevolent purposes.

I may remark, in passing, that I performed the marriage service eighty-nine times. The oldest bridegroom was 78 years of age, and the youngest 18. The oldest bride 71 years and the youngest 15.

Whole number of funerals attended 226. I had thought of mentioning a long list of names ever dear to me, with a view to noting their excellent virtues and characteristics, but time will not permit. To mention a few would, I fear, be invidious, so I deny myself the pleasure of mentioning any.

Permit me to express my thanks, to the whole church and people of this town, for the many kindnesses I received during my ministry.

And as time is rapidly passing, and soon it will be said of each of us, "He is gone," allow me to say another thing to each, and all who felt themselves in the least degree injured by me (through plainness of speech or anything else), I most sincerely and humbly crave your forgiveness.

How small some of these things seem now about which we differed occasionally ; and how grandly the sweeter and better things rise and grow before our eyes !

It is one of the things that gladdens our hearts, this "survival of the fittest." The fact that the weak things, the foolish things, the evil things in life will die (like weeds picked up by the roots) if we give them a fair chance, while the nobler, better, sweeter things of life will live and flourish abundantly; for is it not an eternal truth that no really good thing ever dies?

I wish to express my obligation to the pastors who preceded me, especially, Bros. Bartley, Pratt and Bullard, who did such efficient work and faithful seed sowing, as to make possible the revival which followed. I shall ever hold, also, in grateful remembrance the brotherly love and encouragement I received from neighboring pastors, notably, Rev. Jesse Page of Atkinson, and Rev. Charles Tenney of Chester, both noble men of God, who seemed to deem it a joy to help a young man, and cheer his heart with kind words, now and again.

I should be glad, if time permitted, to speak of the Hampstead Young Men's Christian Association, the Young Ladies Reading Class, The Hampstead Lecture Course, The King's Daughters and the Young People's Society of Christian Endeavor; all of which had their inception during my ministry here.

With varying degrees of success, they all rendered valuable service to the church, and town.

Some of them after serving their desired purpose, very properly fell asleep, or were "merged" into the regular life and work of the church. Others served as distinct organizations and are doing good work to-day.

A prominent New England divine took exception the other day to the common remark "life is a voyage;" he said, "that is poetic nonsense, life is not a voyage, it is building; we cannot sail away from our past, and leave it behind, we take it with us and, build it unto our very being, our life, our character." If that is true, then church life is a building. Paradoxical as it may seem, all that has gone before, remains. It is with us. It is part of the building as we find it to-day. The work of the former pastors, the work of the laity, during these one hundred and fifty years is here. It is the business and high privilege of those who are here to-day, and those who shall come after us, to go on building better and better, rock to rock, grace to grace, power to power, until the structure shall be completed, and the top stone is brought on with shouting, "grace, grace unto it."

It was much regretted that unavoidable official duties prevented the seventh pastor, Rev. Rufus P. Gardner, Supt. of the N. H. Orphans' Home, Webster Place, Franklin, from being present. He, however, sent a most cordial letter, expressing much joy in the remembrance of the part he took in the life of the church for eight years; and recalled with pleasure the loyalty of the church people.

Mrs. Forrest E. Merrill rendered the solo, "There is a City Bright," after which, Miss Harriette E. Noyes was introduced, and occupied the next hour and fifteen minutes in reviewing the history of the church in the following address.

ADDRESS.

The first principle of history is growth. From history in general, we see the development of humanity. From the history of a community, we shall see its growth and development.

The Right Hon. James Bryce says: "The task of history is to trace the march of humanity, and to show the relations which each part of it bears to the others." Vives, the first historian of civilization, desired to chronicle "only the events of peace, and progress, and the acquisitions of intellect." The great historian, Herodotus, wrote only of the prominent people of the world. Other writers have defined history as "the essence of numerous biographies," as fiction immortalized," as a register of successes and disappointments." Prof. Von Helmolt, however, says, "It is not for the historian to discover the scheme of the universe, but to record the facts of human experience." All nations and all people are makers of history, and however writers may differ, historical narrations are always interesting and helpful, whether they be a review of the revolutions of the past centuries, or the evolutions of modern times.

MISS H. E. NOYES,
July 2, 1902.

The year 1899 was the one hundred and fiftieth birth-day of
the town of Hampstead. The year 1902 is the one hundred and
fiftieth birth-day of the Congregational Church of Hampstead.
I was honored, in 1899, by being permitted to relate some
thoughts relative to the history of the town. Today, I am
doubly honored by being invited to present a second chapter, or
some of the history of the church.

During a period of several centuries nearly all the nations of
civilized western Europe had been under the domination of the
Roman Catholic Church. The principles of the Reformation, under
the active propagandism of Luther and Malancthon, in Germany in
the sixteenth century, developed a state of religious discord and
social confusion all over England, which resulted in dividing the
people of that nation into four religious bodies—the Catholics,
the Church of England, the Puritans, and the Pilgrims. The
Puritans and the Pilgrims were especially obnoxious to the reign-
ing monarchs of England. The growing intelligence of the people
of that great realm asserted itself, and about the year 1600 many
counties of old England were visited by a " revival of the vital
religion." Many learned graduates of Oxford and Cambridge
were partakers of the spiritual benefits, and united with the
Puritan cause.

In the early days of the reign of James I., son of Mary,
Queen of Scots, the Hampton Court Conference made an unsuc-
cessful attempt to reconcile the Puritans to the views of the
Catholics, and in July, 1604, more stringent measures were
taken against them. A proclamation was issued commanding
the Puritan clergy " to conform before the last of November, or
dispose of themselves and families in some other way." The
law virtually declared England uninhabitable by " non-conform-
ists " and by " separatists," as the Puritans and Pilgrims were
called.

Persecutions, ruinous fines, imprisonments, and even sentences
of death were imposed, until, seeing no way to worship God
unmolested in their native land, a number of the best families
of England, representing nearly every coat of arms in the Kingdom, emigrated and came to Massachusetts Bay, willing to
endure danger, deprivation, hardship and exile in a strange

land, where they could enjoy the privileges of civil and religious liberty for themselves, and transmit to posterity what they believed to be a pure religion and a more scriptural mode of worship.

In the spring of 1640 we find twelve of those sturdy farmers and their families from Essex county, England, with the Rev. John Ward as their master spirit, forming a new settlement, where no white man had ever trod, in the wild woods of ancient Pentucket, on the northern bank of the Merrimack river, which the following year they named Haverhill, in honor of Haverhill, England, the birthplace of Mr. Ward.

Captain Edward Johnson, in his celebrated history of New England, published in 1654, entitled "Wonder-Working Providence of Zion's Saviour," says, "When they came at once to hopes of being such a competent number of people as might be able to maintain a minister, they then surely seated themselves, and not before, it being as unnatural for a right New England man to live without an able ministry as a smith to work his iron without a fire." He further says: "The town of Haverhill is built upon the fair and large river of Merrimack, the people are wholly bent to improve their labor in tilling the earth and keeping cattle, whose yearly income encourages them to spend their days in these remote parts; the people are labourers in gaining the goods of this life, yet they are not unmindful of the chief end of their coming hither, namely, to be made partakers of the blessed ordinances of Christ, that their souls might be refreshed by the continual income of his rich grace, to which end they gathered into a church body and called to office the Reverend Mr. Ward."

In the month of June of 1641, the General Court of Massachusetts, on consideration that the settlers have six or more dwellings erected, appointed a committee to determine the bounds of the lands which they had purchased of the Indians; which territory comprised a large portion of the present towns of Haverhill and Methuen, in Massachusetts; Salem, Plaistow, Atkinson and Hampstead, in New Hampshire; and in the autumn of that year their church, the twentieth in the Massachusetts Bay Colony, was gathered with fourteen members, eight males and six females.

This faithful band, whose homes were all in the vicinity of what is now called Water street, assembled for worship Sabbath after Sabbath, for seven years, beneath the branches of a noble tree which stood on the brow of the hill in the old Pentucket burial ground.

The Puritan fathers knew no churches, or "houses of the Lord;" but as other Puritans came to the settlement and prospered, they were enabled, in 1648, to build at the "Lower knoll of the Mill Lott," now occupied by the Pentucket and Linwood cemeteries, a rude log house, which they called their "meeting-house, or house to meet in," for prayers and public worship, and also the transaction of all town and civic affairs.

Rev. Rufus P. Gardner, in his historical discourse at the re-dedication service September 1, 1901, gave a descriptive sketch of the several places of worship, pastors, etc., which interested each successive generation, from the pioneers of Haverhill to the worshippers in this church. Therefore in this paper I shall notice more particularly the people and their works.

The fifty years that the inhabitants of Haverhill gathered for worship in their humble house, with its stockade of smooth poles, and armed watch for defence against attacks of a lurking foe, were years of hardship, poverty, dread and peril. The story has been often told of how nearly thirty of their number were murderously slain or taken captive by the Indians, their houses plundered, or reduced to ashes. A whole generation of fathers and mothers had been laid to rest in their burial ground behind the meeting-house, yet at no time do we find them faltering in either Sabbath or family worship.

No man could take the freeman's oath or be invested with power to vote or hold any public office who was not a member of a Congregational church, which was the established church. Thus every family was a family of prayer. They believed in its efficacy, and entered upon no enterprise that they could not commend to heaven by prayer. They sanctified the Sabbath, and felt for that day emotions of peculiar reverence and pleasure. It was the universal custom to gather their children and households about them for morning and evening worship.

Even if famine was at their doors they felt it far safer to

trust in their God than to engage in any doubtful expedient for a supply of corn. Besides the regular Sabbath and family worship, they often devoted whole days to fasting and to prayer, with mutual exhortation and encouragement. They taught the catechism to their children, and dedicated themselves and their children by the ordinances of baptism and the sacrament. They were people of pure morals, of rigid honesty, and of patient, self-denying industry. They had great courage and strong faith.

During that half century men of character, wealth and influence had settled in the town. So that even in those perilous times the pioneers had prospered in their homes and families, in their church and minister, in their town organization, in their mills and mechanics, in their cultivated fields and meadows, and in their horses and cattle. In 1699 they were seated in their new and more commodious meeting-house on the 'Commons,' now known as City Hall Park.

We read of the heroic courage and unfaltering trust which those zealous worshippers possessed, as they saw their beloved pastor, Rev. Benjamin Rolfe, and his wife, with several members of their church, together with the soldiers who had been sent to their relief, ruthlessly slain at their own doors by a desperate band of French and Indians in their march through the town, and of how they spent not only whole days, but weeks, in exhortation, fasting, and prayer, that the Indian troubles might cease.

Their Christian faith and obligation was strengthened when the treaty of peace was signed in 1709, and as less fear and anxiety rested in their hearts the more thrifty and adventurous were eager to take up wild tracts of land in the dense woods in the north, the east, or the westward limits of the town, and establish homes for their families.

As each section of the town prospered, they at once petitioned the mother parish " that as, by reason of the great distance of their dwellings from the meeting-house, they undergo many and great difficulties in attending the public worship of Almighty God," and asked " that they might be permitted to hold meeting by themselves."

In 1730, seventy-six members from the First Parish Church

had selected homes among the neighboring hills and valleys at the north, and were organized into a church body, since known as the "North Parish and Plaistow Congregational Church," with the Rev. James Cushing as their teacher. Two-thirds of those members were residents of what is now Plaistow, Atkinson or Hampstead.

Many of those hardy pioneers, who had separated from the parent church, "gentlemen and yeomen," skilled in all trades, were eager for more land, and the tide of migration rested not near the North Parish meeting house, for in 1733 twenty-five families, from that and neighboring parishes, had braved the hardships and cleared their lands from four to eight miles north from Rev. Mr. Cushing's parish. They had found an ideal location for their homes in the midst of the valuable timber lands, where the lakes and ponds glistened in the sunlight, where the streams abounded in fish, the excellent mill privileges and the rich soil assured them of prosperity and of happiness. They had prepared a house for worship—a simple log building, where Daniel Emerson's house now stands, and humbly asked the North Parish committee to permit them "to hold meetings by themselves during the winter months." This permission was granted them.

Study reveals to us very little concerning their mode of worship for the next fifteen years, or of the exact date when the Church of Christ in Timberlane was gathered; but, as "from the character of the father that of the son may be anticipated," we can readily believe that the families of Little, Hazen, Heath, Johnson, Bailey, Emerson, Stevens, Webster, Eastman, Gile, Morse, Hale, and others, strengthened by the influence of the great religious revival which spread over the settlement in 1741, were as faithful to their Christian obligation and duties of worship, and as earnest to be gathered into a church body, as were their grandparents one hundred years before, when they brought from England their austere rules of worship.

July 29, 1746, Daniel Little, in behalf of the inhabitants, sent a petition to the Governor and His Majesty's Council, giving as a reason for asking to be set off into a distinct parish or township, that "we are so compactly situated, and by the blessings of God have made such improvements, that we are now able to support a gospel minister amongst ourselves," and that " most of us now live far from ye public worship of God (unless carried on amongst ourselves), that we cannot possibly attend upon it without the utmost difficulty and hazard."

The petition of Richard Hazen, May 12, 1748, says : " We have for the greater part of fifteen years, at a very great cost and charge, hired a minister to preach amongst us," and " we have now a suitable place for worship, and ask to be freed from all support of the North Parish minister."

These petitions lead to the belief that three years before the granting of the township or parish of Hampstead, January 19, 1749, the people had their meeting house (our present town house) raised and covered, and perhaps used for public worship.

In the warrant for the first town meeting, called by " Daniel Little, Justice of the Peace," January 24, 1749, as a former historian has said, " every line but one was penned to take measures for the enjoyment of increased privileges in the worship of God and to provide a permanent preacher of His Word."

The history of the town was the history of the church in those days. The church was maintained and the minister supported by rates levied upon the whole town, under the charge of the selectmen. Therefore it was a town meeting question of settling a minister and providing for his support.

The first three years after the incorporation of the township of Hampstead, articles were inserted from time to time in the warrant for town meetings, to " see if the town would vote to extend a call to either Mr. Parker, Mr. Phillips, Mr. Merriam, or other preacher to settle as a gospel minister in town," or " to supply ye pulpit with ye advice of ye neighboring ministers." The voters decided, however, at each attempt to settle a minister, " to provide preaching, with ye advice of ye pastors in ye neighboring parishes." It may seem remarkable that, with their meeting house ready, and with a people able and willing to support a minister, that they did not unite and settle a preacher before three years.

Rev. John Kelly used the expression, " Hampstead had the name of being a difficult people." Their delay in uniting in the choice of a pastor, while numerous candidates came and went, may not have been due to the fact that the people were hard to please. Fifteen families had come to Hampstead from Old Salisbury, Massachusetts, and were watching the progress of their beloved friend, Henry True. Twenty other families were in the Hampstead parish, having come from the First Church in Haverhill, where, under the guidance of their pastor, Rev. Edward Barnard, their friend, Henry True, of Salisbury, fresh from a four years' course at Harvard College, was teaching the village school, and faithfully pursuing his studies for the ministry. When Henry True, the young man of twenty-six years, was ready for the work, the inhabitants of Hampstead were ready to extend to him a unanimous call to become their first settled minister. He sent his letter of acceptance May 3, 1752. He was dismissed from the church in Salisbury, May 31, 1752, having been admitted a member of the Second Church in 1746. The pastor, Rev. Edmund Noyes, granted him a letter from that church, "in order of his being incorporated with ye church of and at Hampstead."

June 3d, 1752, the church was organized with sixty-eight members, fifteen from the First Church in Haverhill, twenty from the North Parish Church, and fourteen from the Second Church of Amesbury and Salisbury, Massachusetts.

Ordination day June 24th, 1752, was doubtless observed with the usual festivities of the times. We do not find a complete record of the event. Rev. Edward Barnard preached the ordination sermon from the eleventh chapter of Acts and the twenty-fourth verse, "For he was a good man, and full of the Holy Ghost."

The church records of Salisbury, under date of June 21, 1752, read, "It was proposed to ye church whether ye would comply with ye church in Hampstead, to assist in ye ordination of Mr. Henry True which was voted in ye affirmative." The names of Rev. Edmund Noyes, Pastor, Moses Merrill, and Nathaniel Fitts are given as delegates, and doubtless they were present. We also find mention of Rev. Ebenezer Flagg of Chester, Rev. Abner Bailey of Salem, Rev. Stephen Bachelor of West Parish of Haverhill, and Rev. James Cushing of the North Parish being present.

The first church in New Hampshire was organized at Dover, in 1700. The Church of Christ in Hampstead was the thirty-second in the Province, but no church had been gathered with more members or with persons of greater influence.

They were Nature's noblemen and women, possessed of courage, integrity, and perseverance. The various votes of the freeholders, as recorded on the town and church books, show the members of the parish to have been unwearied in their efforts to found the system of common schools, to improve and make more comfortable their house of worship, and to firmly establish the principles of the Puritan Congregational faith in town, which have proved such a rich inheritance to their descendants.

The first votes by the early members of the church, under date of August 16, 1752, were the choosing of two deacons, Daniel Little and Peter Eastman, and at the same time voting " that a levy should be made on each communicant to pay five shillings annually for providing for ye elements." November 12, 1753, it was voted "that ye overplus of money that had been raised for ye procuring vessels for ye use of ye church should in part be disposed of to buy a church book; " " that there be five sacraments a year, one every other month, omitting one in ye winter season," and that " ye sing Dr. Watts hymns at sacramental seasons." July 9, 1754, it was voted " to procure ye burying cloth ; " and that " Lieut. Peter Morse, Moses Hale, Stephen Johnson and John Muzzey be chosen a committee to inspect ye lives of professing christians, and if any be found absenting themselves from ye communion table, to know ye reason why."

From Amesbury, Salisbury, Newbury and Haverhill young men and their families came to the town. Most of them had been baptized in their infancy, and at once united with the church, by profession or by letter. Others went before the church officials and accepted certain doctrines. Those that are thus recorded, " Owned the Covenent " and were placed into such relations to the church as to give them rights of citizenship, and their children the ordinance of baptism. One hundred and forty-six persons were so accepted by Rev. Henry True, from 1752 to 1782, and termed " half way members," many of them in later years became members in full communion.

And now that the church in Hampstead is well established, let us in imagination go back and visit the town, and keep Sabbath with its people in their new meeting house, that we may record our observations.

Borne with indescribable velocity on the wings of fancy, through the current of time, we suddenly alight on the Thomas Hale farm, of which the Daniel Ayer homestead is now a part.

It is daylight of a fine Sabbath morning in June, nearly one hundred and fifty years ago. We stand for some moments listening to the howling of the wolves and wildcats over in the "Kingston woods" and as the gruesome sound dies away, and the rosy hue of the morning light spreads up into the heavens, we slowly wend our way along the beaten path towards the meeting house.

A solemn stillness presides over the bright scene which Nature has spread around us. The motions and joyous songs of numerous birds, together with the fragrant odor of the wild blossoms, seem like a morning offering of praise.

Giant trees of oak, elm, chestnut and ash are on each side, broken branches, masses of briers, and often huge logs, lie where storm or decay had strewn them, showing marks of extreme age. Now and then we come to a low framed house of rough boards, and log sheds or other out-buildings, stone walls in progress of making and garden patches in the clearings, where the surface of the meadows and grass lands are clad in richest green.

We silently pass the homes of the Harrimans, Grandmother Copp, Ebenezer Gile, Col. Jacob Bailey, Lemuel Tucker, the Hutchens' home with the sycamore tree in the doorway, and the stately elm opposite, the Merrill lands, the Hazen homestead, and over the log bridge across "Flaggy meadow," from which loads of sweet flag are yearly taken to the ports of Salem and Newbury.

The families are all astir, for on Sabbath mornings the needed work is early done. The warmth of the morning has caused the windows and doors to be opened, and at some dwellings we hear from within, the voices of prayer, at others, groups of little boys and girls are reading to their pious mothers from the Testament or Book of Psalms, or promptly answering the questions of the Puritan Catechism.

Impressed with the sacredness of the scene, we leave the meadows to the right, and enter a narrow bridle path, through a dense forest, with the waters of Rowell's pond glistening at our left. Nearing the ledgy hill with the meeting house in sight, we meet Stephen Johnson, the aged sexton, on his way to open the house of worship. We explain to him that we have come to worship with them for the day, and to learn their way of worship, but our observations will not be disclosed till one hundred and fifty years have passed away.

With a kindly smile he places a massive iron key in the lock of the solid plank door, which springs wide open as if to bid us welcome, and as we stand on the rocky eminence admiring the beautiful landscape before us, he makes several loud blasts from an ox horn, which doubtless are heard to the distant parts of the parish.

He fervently surveys the plain house, newly clapboarded, and with part of the windows glazed, but solid enough to withstand the storms of centuries, remarking, " our house was raised and covered by willing hands, and we have dedicated it to God, and His praise forever."

Several couples come up the hill to the stone horse-mount where the women dismount and the men lead their horses to the stakes among the trees behind the meeting house. "The Morses, Williams, Johnson, and Kezer families from Amesbury Peak, though farthest from the sanctuary," said he, " are always first to arrive. We are thankful to be permitted to be here, and few are late for morning prayer." We are given prominent seats in the meeting house.

A few solemn women glance at us as if we are subjects for church discipline, as we take the opportunity to look about, while the people are gathering. We see the pulpit high up, with its glazed window behind it, the winding stairway leading to it, the octagon shaped sounding board suspended above it, the deacons' seat beneath it, with the sacramental table on hinges in front, the rows of plank seats, the deep box pews and hasped doors, the galleries supported by marble painted pillars, the un-plastered walls and ceiling showing the substantial timbers of which the house was builded.

Ebenezer Gile, Jonathan Hutchens, Moses Hale, Samuel Worthen, and James Graves had been chosen a committee to "seat the meeting house" and the selectmen, Benjamin Emerson, Benjamin Philbrick, and Nathaniel Heath were to seat the committee and their families.

The sittings had been assigned with regard to the amount of taxes each paid, the social position, or according to age.

Facing the pulpit at the east of the broad aisle are the selectmen's seats. Behind them are seated those whose white locks and bending forms betokened them to be the surviving few who had come to Hampstead to take possession of the land. Among them are Michael Johnson, James Mills, Bartholomew Heath, Henry Hale, Stephen Emerson, and Jonathan Eastman.

Next, in crowded ranks, sit the rugged young farmers and mechanics of the town—David Dodge, Josiah Davis, Timothy Goodwin, Samuel and Joseph Little, John Hunkins, Thomas Williams, Otho Stevens, Jr., and many others.

The box pews are occupied by Richard Hazen, Jacob Bailey, Esquire Plummer, Charles Johnston, John Webster, and Edmund Sawyer, whose dignity of bearing and finer clothing are emblems of their importance in the parish.

In the corresponding seats at the west of the aisle are the wives and mothers and sisters, dressed as suited to their rank, many in homespun gingham, with tidy aprons of purest white. The young men and maidens are opposite each other, in the east and west galleries, and on the long benches against the wall are the boys of the parish, David Copp, the tything man, with his rod in hand, near them, to suppress any smile, whisper, or wink, by a rap on the ear.

Nearly three hundred people have arrived, as every inhabitant, not excused for sufficient reasons, must attend public worship.

As the Rev. Mr. True enters the house the whole congregation rise and stand, until the sexton escorts the minister to the pulpit and seats himself on the broad stair: It is nine o'clock. All heads are bowed. Rev. Mr. True rises, and with a clear, earnest voice, commences the service with a short invocation, praising God for the light and privileges of another of His holy days, and fervently imploring His presence and aid in the prayers and praises to be offered, and humbly asking His blessing upon His Word now to be dispensed.

A half hour of reading and explaining the nineteenth Psalm is followed by Deacon Little reading the five stanzas of the fifth Psalm, from the "New England Collection of Psalms, Hymns and Spiritual Songs." Repeating the first line of the Psalm—"Jehovah, to my words give ear"—Deacon Little commences singing in a tremulous voice, to the tune of Windsor," as Deacon Eastman "pitched the tune," when instantly the whole congregation, old and young, without rising, join in the singing. He reads the second line, "My meditation weigh," and the words are caught from his lips, and so on separately, line by line.

There is no harmony in the singing, no perfect keeping of time, yet it is exceedingly interesting and impressive. It is much like a roar of thunder, or the voice of many waters, but the seriousness of the appearance and manner of the people cause a deep solemnity to pervade the whole congregation. "They sing to the Lord, with spirit and understanding."

The sexton passes from seat to seat while the people are rising for the long prayer, and collects the letters or little notes, which are read by the pastor. Widow Elizabeth Johnson wishes prayers from minister and congregation that she may be reconciled in her recent bereavement; Ebenezer Gile would render thanks for manifold mercies which had been given him and Mrs. Gile for the birth of a daughter; John Muzzey and wife wish prayers for relief from the depredations of wild beasts; Nathaniel Heath and his relatives would give thanks to the Lord for relief from the dreaded throat distemper in his family; Ruth Atwood asks prayers for help and wisdom in guiding her family of step-children, and that her troubles may cease; Benjamin Kimball requests prayers that he may be more fully prepared to commune at the Lord's table; and so on till every event of life is made an occasion of prayer and praise.

The prayer commences with acknowledgments of dependence, guilt, and spiritual necessity. The minister spreads before the Lord all the wants, trials, sins and temptations of the people, all of the joys and sorrows in the town during the past week, and with special minuteness of description the thanksgivings and requests of those who have expressly desired particular mention in the prayers of the sanctuary this day, and finally prays that they may be prepared for the final change that awaits them, that they may meet it in peace, with the hope of pardon and acceptance to eternal life, and felicity beyond the grave.

When the long plank seats, which are hung on hinges, and are raised up as the people passed in or out of the pews, or rise for the long prayers, fall into place, the resounding clatter of "click, click, click," from all parts of the room for several seconds, is amusing to our imagination.

The congregation, without any visible signs of weariness or impatience during the long prayer, catch the tune from Deacon Little, as he reads line by line four verses of the sixth Psalm, commencing :—

> "Lord, in thy wrath, rebuke me not,
> Nor in thy hot wrath chasten me.
> Lord, pity me, for I am weak ;
> Lord, heal me, for my bones vex'd be.
> Also my soul is vex'd sore,
> How long, Lord, wilt thou me forsake ?
> Return, O Lord, my soul release,
> O, save me, for thy mercy's sake."

We hear a slight rustling and espy the deacons, selectmen and others, who carry the pens of ready writers, preparing to take the text and heads of the discourse. We are reminded that we may do the same, and note the text as from 2d Timothy 11 : 19, "And let every one that nameth the name of Christ depart from iniquity."

The discourse is divided into seven parts, namely, questions and answers, with occasional points of doctrine, but abounding in practical thoughts and suggestions.

A short prayer for the blessing of God on His Word dispensed and a solemn benediction closes the forenoon service.

An hour intermission is social and of good cheer. Promptly
at one o'clock minister and people are in their seats. Deacon
Eastman reads the one hundred and forty-eighth hymn, and the
melody of each line is caught from the voice of Deacon Little
to the tune of " Old One Hundred and Forty-eighth." A long
prayer follows, observing the same particularity of enumera-
tion and minuteness of description of the mercies implored as
the prayer of the morning. A more exact profession of the pre-
vailing sins among the people, the special intercession for the
country, for all mankind, for the church of God throughout the
world, for the inhabitants of New England, especially those of
Massachusetts Bay, that they may never forget the errand for
which their fathers crossed the ocean to the wilderness, that
righteousness may reign in the whole colony, for blessing and
direction upon the sovereign, King George, and divine benediction upon the high court of Parliament, of the realm of England. Finally the Lord is earnestly besought to hasten the
end of all idolatry, superstition, and imposture.

The singing of the fifteenth Psalm is followed by a long
sermon from the same text as in the morning. In the forenoon
it was noticeably an explanation and defence of the truth of the
text. In the afternoon it is the enforcement of it upon the
conscience and heart.

When the good man closes this labor of love, Deacon Eastman arises and says : " Brethren, if any among you have a word
of exhortation to offer, let him say on." Several of the aged men
speak a few words of admonition to the young people, telling
them of the danger of longer delay, and earnestly entreating
them to " name the name of Christ."

At the close of the service of exhortation, and after singing a
verse of a psalm, several young men hastily arrange rows of
plank tables in the long aisles and in front of the pulpit, and
spread them with linen, and the long seats are moved into
place by the sides of the tables.

The Lord's Supper is, by custom, the social event of the
church, and many visitors from neighboring parishes had come
to partake of the "elements " with them, each stranger going
to the pastor or deacons holding a lead coin marked " A," which

served in keeping any unworthy person from the sacramental table. The aged communicants are seated at the tables first, followed by the next in age or rank.

The whole service is very impressive, and amid much singing of Dr. Watts' Psalms and Hymns, the "elements" are passed from one to another. The pastor and deacons are favored with "elements" of a more choice flavor.

Jeremiah Eaton, who had recently moved to Hampstead from Lynn, Massachusetts, was noted for his musical talents. He had been given permission by a vote in church meeting "to set ye psalms if he saw fit." He became enthusiastic in the singing, and at the close of the supper sings in a very spirited way the interrogative verse so familiar to their parents and grandparents, as sang at their sacramental service :—

"Did Jesus ordain
His supper in vain,
And furnish a feast
For none but His earliest servants to taste?"

The communicants seem to vie with one another as they join Mr. Eaton with their voices and hearts in singing the following words of the chorus or answer :—

"In rapturous bliss
He bid us do this;
The joy it imparts,
Hath witnessed His gracious
Design in our hearts.

Receiving the bread
On Jesus we feed;
It doth not appear,
His manner of working :
But Jesus is here."

Rev. Mr. True gives notice that during the coming week he shall visit the families of Ebenezer Gile, John Kezer, Peter Morse, Benjamin Emerson, Peter Eastman, and David Copp, for the purpose of questioning their children on the points of doctrine, as required in the Westminster Catechism.

A short prayer is then in order, imploring blessings on the services of the day, and a joyous singing of the doxology :—

" To cav'ry hill He bore my load,
And there the Lamb, my Lord and God,
When He came hither nailed
My sin and my iniquity
With His own body on the tree,
And there my pardon sealed."

A scriptural benediction closes the public worship. Rev.
Mr. True descends the pulpit stairs and passes through the
long aisle to the door, bowing right and left to the congregation.
No person moves from his seat until the minister has passed
out of the meeting house. The people then begin departing to
their homes, as it is nearly sundown.

After this vision, we are swiftly transported through space
and over one hundred and fifty years of time. Let us now
revert to the records and traditions of the past.

The thirty years that Rev. Mr. True was pastor of the church
were years of trying experience to minister and people. Early
in his work the New Hampshire Provincial army was calling
for recruits to protect the colonies against the invasion of
France. From 1755 to 1762 thirty-three stalwart sons and
fathers from the parish, who had been taught the qualities and
traditions of the soldier, true to their ancestral training, marched
to Lake George, Crown Point, or other places of defence. Rev.
Mr. True, as their good shepherd, went with them as chaplain
in 1759, and again in 1762. His "Journal of Events," as he
arrived home, reads: "May I never forgit ye goodness of ye
Lord, in ye land of ye living," rejoicing that he was once more
among his people.

In 1756 a "mortal fever" prevailed, and thirty or more
members of the church died. The migrations to the "northern
country" from 1762 to 1770 took one hundred or more inhabitants of Hampstead. Among them were some of the most influential families, but their places were quickly filled by others
imbued with the same religious zeal.

Most of the early settlers of Hampstead were said to be
" rough and hardy, like the soil." Men of that iron mould were
quick to see that a vigorous enforcement of the laws were car-

ried out by the town officials, whereby every inhabitant was required to attend divine service and to give due observance to the ordinances of religion.

With one faith and with one form of worship, it was an ideal church, with none to gainsay its rights, to dispute its doctrines, or to criticise its methods.

For nearly twenty years Rev. Mr. True's pastorate continued, with only one voice of dissent, and that was in the action of John Hogg, Esq., who is supposed to have been a Quaker, and who, in 1752, and years following, caused some trouble by refusing to pay his proportion of the rates towards the support of the ministry and of building the meeting house, under pretence of "his being of a different persuasion from the church and congregation of the town;" but it was voted in town meeting "to instruct the selectmen to make distress on him for his rates," and it was agreed "to stand by the constable and pay reasonable charges for so doing."

From 1765 to 1775 an insatiable thirst for liberty spread over the colonies. The "stamp act" aroused the people to independence, and with the determination to sever allegiance from the British crown and from all political connection with Great Britain, a constantly growing number in the State Church of New England were demanding liberty from the burdensome exactions of the church, believing that not only a free government should prevail, but that religious worship should be voluntary and free to the choice of every man according to the dictates of his own conscience.

Rev. John Kelly, in his sketch of Hampstead, in 1835, says: "About twenty years after Rev. Mr. True's settlement in town, Baptist ministers came into the place, and by zealous and loud speaking they produced a great commotion, but no revival among the people, who were very sanguine and versatile in their dispositions," which "did not unsettle the good minister, or sully his character in the views of any man, but it reduced his salary and reduced the number of his hearers, and greatly injured the character of the people, for almost all of the followers of the new teachers became downright infidels."

In 1762 the town voted "to keep the meeting house doors

shut against all such preachers, whose principles are such that neither Congregational nor Presbyterian churches amongst us can hold communion with or admit as preachers."

John Hogg, Esq., Lieut. Peter Morse, John Muzzey, Esquire Plummer, Deacon Joseph French, Nathaniel Heath, John Kent, Samuel Brown, Daniel Emerson, Joseph Noyes, Edward Prescott, and Reuben Harriman were among the leaders in asking for freedom from the minister rates. They were freed from paying their rates by a vote of the town from 1768 to 1779.

Rev. Mr. True died May 22, 1782. Of the first one hundred members before 1760 all had gone, by death or removal from town, save one, Thomas Williams, who was then eighty years of age.

Eighty-three persons had been added to the church rolls in spite of these serious obstacles, which doubtless were a cause of great grief to the pastor, and may be, hastened his sudden and untimely death at the age of fifty-six years. He was a person whose piety, integrity, learning, and ability none can question.

The next ten years were evidently the darkest days in the history of the church. The depreciation of the currency had made the people poor, and according to the writings of Rev. Mr. Kelly, " this town contained more infidels than any other town in the state, who gave themselves up to reproaching the saints and blaspheming the name of the Saviour."

By infidels he evidently referred to all the followers of the Methodist, the Baptist, or the Universalist preachers who had visited the town. He says, " The goodly number of sober people of the Orthodox faith were in trouble, longing to have a minister to speak the word of truth, and to break the bread of life to them," and that " they sometimes had preaching, but they had not the courage to give any man a call for four years." In 1786 they were obliged to insert in the warrant for town meeting an exemption from paying a minister tax to all those who in other years had been freed by a vote of the town.

September 11, 1786, a call was extended to Mr. Tillison Howe from the Church of Christ at Dartmouth College. He accepted the terms and preached several months in town and united with the church here, but the people judged him as ".morally unsuitable " and withdrew the call.

October 11, 1787, Mr. Joshua Langdon was called, but declined the invitation on account "of the small salary, and open infidels." Mr. Jacob Cram was called the next June, but he was invited elsewhere at a larger salary. February 19, 1789, Reverend John Wilbur was invited, but would not accept the situation. Rev'd Abishai Allen was asked to become their pastor, but later both parties were willing to relinquish the call.

These men were all graduates from either Dartmouth or Harvard Colleges, and were eminently fitted for the duties of the ministry, but the prospects for a living were so meagre that they gave principally that reason for declining to enter the work.

The salary offered was $200 in money annually, the use of the parsonage, two cows and six sheep.

The three following years the people could not get a vote to raise one cent for maintaining a minister, as the agitation for the repeal of the law which recognized only the Orthodox sect, in 1791, shook New Hampshire from seaboard to mountain.

Early in 1792 a subscription was taken for the object of hiring a minister, and this measure opened the way for a unanimous vote of the town to call John Kelly, A. M., of Amesbury Mass., a graduate of Dartmouth College, and a student of Theology under that eminent scholar and divine, Rev. Moses Hemmenway D. D., of Wells, Me.

Mr. Kelly said, " he feared neither poverty or the infidels of Hampstead, and that his death, if not his life, might be the salvation of this people." He was ordained Dec. 5, 1792. His teacher Dr. Hemmenway preached the ordination sermon from Philippians, third chapter, sixth verse: " Count all things as lost, for the excellency of the knowledge of Christ Jesus my Lord."

That Mr. Kelly led a busy and eventful life, cannot be doubted as we read in his Autobiography, of his preaching three thousand written sermons, and many unwritten ones, attending five hundred and three funerals in town, and half as many more in other parishes, uniting nearly two thousand persons in marriage, attending thirty ordaining or other councils, publishing

twenty sermons, discourses or reports, taking an active part in
the various Bible, tract, missionary or educational societies of
New Hampshire, contributing various articles to the newspapers,
teaching the youth abundantly, aiding with his voice in the
service of song, uniting one hundred and sixty-eight persons to
the fellowship of the church, burying or dismissing all except
Deacon Job Kent of the members, and all but Jonathan C. Little and Mr. Hezekiah Ayer of the voters in town, when he was
ordained, besides, as he says, " gaining a victory over the infidels
and enemies of the church."

In 1793 the porch and steeple were added to the meeting
house, mostly by subscription, and numerous repairs were made
to the building, which was in a wasting and miserable condition.

A social library was formed, with a good number of valuable
and interesting volumes, in 1796.

Through the efforts also of Rev. Mr. Kelly, the " Paul
Revere" bell, which rings from the town hall tower, was
secured and placed in position Dec. 19, 1809.

Rev. Mr. Kelly was the leader in the "Moral Society of
Hampstead, Atkinson and Plaistow." This society was organized in Hampstead, Dec. 29, 1814, at the house of John True
Esq., with John True, chairman, and Rev. Mr. Kelly, as secretary, and continued until about 1822.

The society was composed of a very select membership of
seventy-eight men from the three towns, whose duties as members
were to exert their influence to suppress immorality of every
description, particularly Sabbath breaking, profanity, intemper-
ance, falsehood and gaming, and to see that tythingmen of respectable character, in sufficient numbers be chosen and qualified
to carry the law respecting the Christian Sabbath into effect,
" and to openly and dividedly to discountenance profane language, and the improper and unnecessary use of ardent spirits
at funerals and other occasions, and by their example and
advice to encourage the rising generation to a constant attendance on the public worship of God, and in habits of sobriety,
morality and industry."

Quarterly meetings were held in Hampstead at the homes of
John True, Rev. Mr. Kelly, Dr. Jeremiah Spofford, Mr. Jesse
Gordon, and Benjamin Garland.

Annual sermons were given alternately in the three towns in the meeting houses by Rev. Samuel Harris of Windham, Rev. Stephen Peabody of Atkinson, Rev. Edward L. Parker of Londonderry, Rev. John H. Church of Pelham, Rev. John Kelly, and others.

Their favorite texts were "Righteousness exalteth a nation, but sin is a reproach to any people;" and "One sinner destroyeth much good."

Similar societies were formed in Portsmouth, Exeter, Concord, Chester, Londonderry, Candia, and Salem in New Hampshire, and Bradford and Rowley in Massachusetts.

June 13, 1815, it was voted by the society to determine what vice was the most prevalent in Hampstead, and that the secretary consider ways of petitioning Congress to prevent the carrying and opening of the mail on the Lord's day.

September 14, 1818, it was voted "that Silas Tenney be a collector of a subscription to purchase tracts to be distributed among themselves, which was so much of a success that the next December at a meeting at the house of Josiah Grover in Atkinson, Hon. John Vose of that town and Rev. John Kelly were selected to purchase tracts for the public," "that it would be desirable to purchase them from the New England Tract Society of Andover, Massachusetts," and that "the tracts should all treat of the importance of the sanctification of the Sabbath, and should contain as many disasters happening on that day to those who have profaned the Sabbath as can well be collected from authentic records."

August 4, 1819, 7000 tracts were purchased for the $7.00 collected, and were distributed in each town according to the number of the inhabitants. And again in 1820 a great number of tracts were likewise obtained and used.

It was voted, March 13, 1821 "that it would be expedient for the members of the "Moral Society to refrain from the use of ardent spirits at their meetings."

We would hope that this action did not lead to the disbanding of the Society, but so few members attended the next meetings that early the next year they voted "to divide the subscription on hand to the Sabbath schools of the three towns."

The religious toleration bill, which had been pending in the
New Hampshire Legislature for several years, through the
weighty efforts of Ichabod Bartlett, the young and talented
lawyer of Portsmouth, became a law in 1819, and all religious
denominations in the State, by the enactment of that law, were
given equal rights and privileges, in face of the declaration of
the opposer, Mr. Hubbard, who said, "Pass this bill, and the
temples now consecrated to the worship of the Saviour of the
world will soon be deserted and forsaken."

By the passing of that law believers in the doctrines of the
Methodists, the Baptists, and the Universalists in Hampstead,
asked to have their minister tax for the support of Rev. Mr.
Kelly abated, and they claimed from the town the right to have
ministers of their own faith to occupy the meeting house a part
of the time.

This seems to have been a sore trial to Rev. Mr. Kelly and
his friends. The church records show repeated efforts to reclaim
some delinquent members of the parish or family who had
gone over to what was termed "false doctrines"; and January
28, 1828, the church appointed twelve of its members "to visit
every family in Hampstead to call the attention of the people to
the consciences of their souls, and to pray with them from house
to house." "Deacon John Emerson and Jacob Irving to begin
at Enoch Tewksbury's, including all of Kent's farm, Mr. Davis',
Mrs. Stevens', and Mr. Bartlett's families." "Deacon Jonathan
Kent and Thomas K. Little beginning at Nathaniel Heath's and
ending at Mr. Knight's, on the Harriman farm." "Mr. Jesse
Davis and Lyman Worthen to begin at Lieut. Poor's and end at
John Currier's, including the Island." "Mr. Phineas Balch and
Francis Sawyer to begin at the widow Brown's and come around
to Jesse Davis', including James Brickett's." "Mr. Jonathan
Brickett and David Little to take all of the 'Peak' and 'Han-
dle,' so called."

For a period of eighty-three years from the incorporation of
Hampstead the salary of the minister was assessed by the selectmen, and the town collector gathered the assessments and paid
the money and delivered the wood to the minister.

After March 5, 1832, the Congregational Church and Society,

for the first time, held their meetings and transacted their business without a town meeting, and separate from the affairs of the town, and soon made their plans to build their own church, where the present church now stands.

On leaving the old meeting house to occupy the new church, Oct. 13, 1837, Rev. Mr. Kelly preached the farewell sermon, from the second chapter of Philippians, second and third verses, his topic being, "Union and Communion of Saints," which he dedicated "to the inhabitants of the town of Hampstead, in grateful remembrance of the uniform respect and kindness shown to him for a long series of years."

He gave as a reason for leaving the old meeting house of the fathers, "that, like the Congregational Puritan Orthodox people of England, who first settled New England, you wish to have a place to worship God in peace, where you have no temptation to disturb others, nor be intruded on by them."

Mr. Kelly was twenty-nine years of age when he was ordained, and he spent forty-four years as an able minister and faithful friend to the people of Hampstead. He retired from the pastorate at the age of seventy-three years, and died in Hampstead at the age of eighty-five.

Rev. John M. C. Bartley was installed as pastor on the day of Mr. Kelly's dismissal, October 12, 1836. Rev. Dr. Daniel Dana, who was for fifty years pastor of the church in Newburyport, Mass., preached the installation sermon on "Ministerial Firmness," taking his text from the twentieth chapter of Acts and the twenty-fourth verse.

Rev. Mr. Bartley is remembered by many residents of Hampstead, who valued him during his labors of twenty-one years as an affectionate and warm-hearted friend, and as one whose precept and practice were sincere and courteous. Besides fulfilling his bounden duty to the church and to the society, and uniting one hundred and four persons to church membership, he took an active part in whatever would be of benefit to the town. He served sixteen years as superintendent of the public schools, and was instrumental in founding the Emerson High School, as a result of his intimate acquaintance and friendship with Benjamin Dudley Emerson, its benefactor, who was a member of this church under his pastorate.

January 2, 1860, about one year after he relinquished his labors in town, he was laid to rest, at the age of sixty-one years, in the pleasant cemetery at Kittery Point, Maine, where a granite monument marks his grave.

And now we come to the present times, or to the last forty-three years of the history of the church. We come to the pastorates of Reverends Mr. Pratt, Bullard, Watson and Gardner, and the present pastor, Rev. Walter H. Woodsum.

Rev. Mr. Bullard died four years ago, at the ripe age of eighty-eight years. His remains rest in the family burial lot in the beautiful Laurel Hill Cemetery at Fitchburg, Massachusetts.

It is not always well to say much of the living. The work of the several pastors and members of the church and society have all been recorded on the church records or impressed on memory's page.

The past few months it has been our privilege to make an exhaustive study of those records, and the results obtained from the study and from personal research of each individual member will, we trust, be published in a "Memorial of the Church."

The church books record a list of 775 persons who have been admitted to the fellowship of the church, 272 males and 503 females. Nearly 1100 children have received the ordinance of baptism.

Among the members there have been twenty-two ordained ministers. Eleven members have adopted the profession of medicine and five have become lawyers. Fifty-six men have been graduated from some college, and twenty-eight ladies have graduated or attended some college, seminary, normal school, or higher institution of learning. Ninety-seven or more members have been teachers in the public schools of the country, and a goodly number of the teachers have occupied prominent positions. Forty-four members have received diplomas from our High school, and forty-three others have been students there and have nearly or quite completed the prescribed course of study.

The Colonial and Revolutionary wars and the State militia have been represented by one general, two colonels, three lieutenant-colonels, five captains; four majors, three lieutenants, one chaplain, and nine private soldiers. Eleven have served in the civil war, and one member was enlisted as a marine in the Spanish-American war.

Fifty-eight members have served as selectmen in town, and several other members in other towns. Five members have represented the town in the State Legislature, and the various minor town offices have been often filled from the church ranks.

The present membership of the church numbers one hundred and fifty-three, thirty-six males and one hundred and seventeen females, of whom thirty-seven descend directly from the original sixty-eight members. Nine members are descended directly from Richard Hazen, fourteen from Deacon Daniel Little, four from James and Jane Mills. Several others of the present zealous church workers can trace their noblest blood from the founders of the church.

We find that a majority of the members have been faithful to the church covenant and faithful to their Christian obligations, and entirely worthy of the honors which have been bestowed upon them. Also,

> "We find 'tis true there's blood that's blue
> That in their veins was flowing,
> And then we find some other kind,
> O'er which we do no crowing."

As we continue our research to the village cemetery, we are reminded that,—

> "There is a reaper whose name is Death,
> And with his sickle keen
> He reaps the bearded grain at a breath,
> And the flowers that grow between."

There rest the remains of the two earliest pastors, who labored faithfully for the church and town people for eighty-four years, and at least three hundred members of the church, whose lives were characterized by the qualities of true citizenship.

Of the original sixty-eight members, fifty-six or more were buried in town. A goodly number of the deceased members reached the age of seventy years, but we find many of the tiny graves of the children there whose names are on our list of baptisms.

We stand by the tomb that covers the grave of Rev. Henry True, and notice the variety of monuments and other stones, from Nature's simplest boulder to the exquisitely carved granite tablet that marks the family lot. We see the humble monument made of wood, around which the Grand Army of the Republic loyally gather and pay tribute to the memory of their deceased comrades.

But should it seem unbefitting that in the cemetery we find no special tablet inscribed to the memory of the founders of the Congregational Church?

It has been said of one of the world's greatest architects, Sir Christopher Wren, who designed St. Paul's Cathedral and eighty-seven churches, besides hospitals, palaces and monuments in London, England, and who died two hundred years ago, at the age of ninety-one years, that when it was asked concerning him, if he had no monument, the reply was given, "Look around thee; Saint Paul's Cathedral is Sir Christopher's monument; he needs no other."

Would you contemplate the monument to the founders of the Congregational Church in Hampstead, that will stand when many another structure will have crumbled into dust, builded by those noble men and women "whose outward mould was hardship and whose inward bliss was piety"?—"Look around thee!" Go first to the old meeting-house, the early shrine where the pioneer worshippers truly went up to their Jerusalem, upon the level crest of a solid ledge, typical of Zion's foundation! Go to that ancient structure, which has stood more than a century and a half, defiant to storm or decay! There they organized and constructed the Congregational Church, and there they subscribed their names to the covenant; there they laid the foundation of an everlasting monument, whose "pillars are as of lily work."

The Puritan *faith* which they planted in Hampstead is *their* monument. They *need* no other! That faith has been cherished through the long vista of the changing years of progress by five generations of members. With industry in their labors, with perseverance and fidelity in all good works, with love, honesty and honor in their hearts, and with loyalty to their God and to the established forms of worship, the members have, through education and intelligence, builded higher and higher a monument to Hampstead, the Congregational Church, which will stand to glorify posterity and to remain against the inroads of time, a fitting concomitant to the dear old meeting-house.

And while this great world of ours speeds forever on its course, freighted with human joys and sorrows, hopes, aspirations, successes and disappointments, may the present and future members of the Congregational Church and Society deeply feel that it is better to transmit than to inherit a good record of their works.

May they "hold fast to their Puritan heritage," and also may they let the free light of the age,—

> "Its life, its hope, and its sweetness add
> To the sterner faith the fathers had."

The double male quartette—first tenors, Forrest E. Merrill, Lowell M. Clark ; second tenors, William H. Davis, John S. Corson ; first basses, C. Park Pressey, Albion D. Emerson ; second basses, Eugene L. Spinney, H. Clinton Davis—sang " While the Years are Rolling On," which was followed by reminiscent remarks by Rev. Myron P. Dickey, pastor of the Congregational Church at Milton, N. H., and first preceptor of Hampstead High School.

Mr. Chairman and Friends :—

They have a custom in Congress to give leave to print (in the Congressional record) certain speeches for which there is not time for their delivery. I should be inclined at this late hour to ask that privilege if I had any speech to print : not having any prepared speech, I must needs deliver my remarks to find out what they are.

There used to be an eccentric character in my native town of Derry, who insisted that a minister did not need time to study during the week in order to preach Sundays if he preached the *truth.* " The truth is easy " he said, " it takes study to preach lies." I have not found it so. Rather has it seemed to me easy for folks to speak and believe things that are untrue and hard to get at the whole truth.

In my remarks I shall try not to speak untruth, but tell a few of the things which came under my observation in the years of my residence here, 1876 to 1879, and in especial reference to the church in its connection with the High school and its pupils.

I always feels somewhat aged when I come to Hampstead, and to-day I feel that I must be very old, for of the eight pastors this church has had in the one hundred and fifty years of its history, I have had some personal acquaintance with all but the first three, and I almost feel that I have a little acquaintance with the very first pastor, Parson True, since today I sat at the table with his great grandson Henry True, the direct lineal descendant of the Rev. Henry True.

When I was a boy, Pastor Pratt would occasionally exchange with the pastor of my home church in Derry, and I always was pleased to see a new face in the pulpit and wonder if the boys now feel as I did.

The pastor of this church when I came to Hampstead, in 1875, was Rev. E. W. Bullard and as there seems to be no one here to speak for him today, I wish to render to his memory my hearty tribute.

Mr. Bullard was somewhat advanced in years and not in the best of health during his pastorate here. His pastorate was the shortest in the history of the church, and the additions to the membership were not many. But my estimate of Mr. Bullard is that he was a *fine Christian gentleman*, an able preacher, and faithful pastor. He was one of the finest looking men I ever knew. I remember hearing him tell of a lady who sat in the choir behind him where he once preached (it was not so common then for the choir to be behind the pulpit as now), and this lady remarked after the service, " How delighted I've been with it all." Mr. Bullard was curious to know what it was that had made so favorable an impression, and asked what part of the sermon she liked so well. "Oh," she replied, "I didn't hear any part of the sermon, couldn't even tell the text, I was so taken with admiring your beautiful white locks." (Mr. Bullard did not like choirs back of his pulpit.)

Mrs. Bullard was equally delighful with Mr. Bullard, and I think one daughter resided at home. Perhaps they all were at their best in the home circle, and any who enjoyed their hospitality will always cherish it.

Mr. Bullard took great interest in the High school in its first beginnings, and I greatly appreciated his personal kindness and council. Such ministers as Mr. Bullard may not bring out as many new converts as some, but one wonders if any one could make converts, if there were not such fine examples of Christian manhood.

It used to be a common remark that Mr. Bullard sowed seed, the reaping of which was gathered by those who succeeded him.

The coming of Rev. Albert Watson marked a new era in the history of the church. At his coming the membership had not materially increased. Mr. Watson has himself given the account of the revival spirit which manifested itself so markedly in the spring of his first year's pastorate.

That Sunday night manifestation of which he has spoken was a complete surprise to me. The interest from the first was very deep among the pupils of the High school. Mattie Irving was the first to be called to heaven. Hattie Hoyt, Orrie Belle Little, Charles Garland, Sarah Sagar, and many others made their Christian committal, and a different atmosphere, serious, but wholesome and joyous, pervaded the school room, and all about the school premises. For a time a weekly prayer meeting was held at the school.

From that time on through my principalship, the school was decidedly Christian. This revival spirit continued in church and school and doubled the church membership. The prayer meetings especially were of great power.

I recall the night when Joseph Brown made his first attempt to speak in meeting. The tense muscle as he drew himself to his feet, his broken utterance, the deep earnestness which showed on every feature. Some of the Christian people of that time, now gone to their reward, who impressed their ideas on me, are Dea. Sanborn, Jacob Irving, Mr. and Mrs. R. K. Brickett, Mrs. Nelson Ordway, Mrs. Pike, Henry Clarke and many others. These people all had their faults and imperfections, as do all, but in the memory of them, it is their Christian spirit, their sincerity, and devotion to Christ and the church, that have made their names to abide.

In closing I must not fail to express my personal interest in this church. For several years my name was enrolled on its roll of membership. Here my wife made public confession of her Christian faith, and here our first born was baptized into the name of the Father, Son and Holy Ghost.

I have rejoiced in all your prosperity in these recent years. I am glad to join with you today in this celebration, and I pray the future may be even richer than the past in the nurture and perfecting of Christian souls for the eternal habitations."

Prof. Edward E. Bradley of Lincoln, Mass., late teacher of the High school was unable to be present to respond to the part assigned to him.

Prof. Forrest E. Merrill occupied a few minutes in reviewing the school work as connected with the church during the fifteen years in which he had been teacher.

Miss Abbie F. Chandler, a daughter of Hampstead, sang in a pleasing way the solo, "The Gates of the West." In response to the number, "Reminiscences by past members," Miss Fannie B. Williams sent a cordial letter of greeting to the church from the field of her missionory labors in Oklahoma.

Rev. Albert P. Watson, pastor of the Presbyterian Church in Bedford, N. H., was present, and spoke as follows:—

"To speak successfully on reminiscences the one thing absolutely essential is a long and varied experience from which, as a storehouse, memory can draw at will. This I do not possess. The usual introductory remark, "when I was a boy," carries very little weight in this instance, for I seem hardly out of boyhood yet. Any of the circumstances and conditions of former years that I might recall are more familiar to you, than to myself, accordingly I shall not attempt to enlighten you; but shall simply endeavor to pay a very willing tribute to this, the church home of my childhood.

I united with this church at the age of twelve. Three years later I left home to attend school and have not been here since except on brief occasional visits. Although my actual personal fellowship here was so brief, yet I feel that to this church I owe a debt greater than words can tell. It was here that I first felt the power of a Christian faith, and made public confession of the same. Here, by the grace of God, was laid the foundation of a Christian character. It was from the Christian people of this place that I received the kindly sympathy, the words of encouragement, the patience, forbearance and charitable consideration which are of such measureless worth to the young Christian. How much all this has been to me through the intervening years I cannot tell.

The worth of this church, like the worth of any other, has not been wholly due to the clergy. A good deal has been said this afternoon in praise of the noble men of God who have labored here as Christian ministers. I am in hearty sympathy with every word that has been said. But they are not the only ones deserving of our grateful appreciation. I am glad of this opportunity of paying tribute to one whose permanent influence over my life has been greater than she knew. I refer to my first Sunday school teacher, Mrs. Pike. She was my teacher nearly all the time I was in this school. I know we caused her a great deal of trouble and anxiety, but she was always patient and kind. I cannot remember much that she ever said, but I do remember that somehow, through her consecrated service, I learned that God is Love, and that He loves to pity and to save His sinful, erring child. She has now gone home to her reward, but I'm sure she has left with every one of her boys, as she used to call us, a sweet, beautiful, inspiring, and immortal memory, that we shall ever cherish.

The Christian church has not yet done its work. The brightest days for this and every household of faith are yet to come. The eternal living truth of God does not yet permeate humanity. The abundant life is not yet every man's possession. And it is the highest glory of the Christian church to bring close to the human heart the truth of God, that all, old and young, rich and poor, from the least men to the greatest, may know Him, and in that knowledge live.

Henry C. Ordway, of Winchester, Mass., was listened to with close attention. His remarks were :—

".The kind invitation to join with you in this celebration

is appreciated. I am glad to be here and take part in the birthday festivities of the old church.

Hampstead was my birthplace and for many years my home. For nearly a generation, I have been much away. As my visits to Hampstead became infrequent, I was enabled to keep in touch with old friends as we came together here on Sunday. Their cordial welcome and kindly greeting always given to me are pleasant memories of those years.

Your pastor has asked me to say something on this subject—'Personal reminiscences, and anything else you like.' I hope I may be able to stick to the text.

I have always felt when one indulged in reminiscences on such an occasion as this that it implied great age. It is, therefore, a genuine satisfaction for me to state that I can give no account of what happened under Parsons True and Kelly.

Still, candor compels me to admit that I was a contemporary of Rev. Mr. Bartley, though at the time of his dismissal I was only one year old. This will account for my passing lightly over his administration.

I well remember the long ride to church. From the old Watts' and Select Hymns the minister would read:

> " Lord, in the morning Thou shalt hear
> My voice ascending high,
> To Thee will I direct my prayer,
> To Thee lift up mine eye."

Then, as the singing began, right about face turned the congregation. For in those days, the organ and the singers were in the gallery, and the reward of the choir was to behold the faces of the people.

'Twas a good old custom and had much of merit. The minister, freed from the gaze of every eye, relaxed; the people changed their positions, saw who were behind them, and got thoroughly waked up. Pastor and people were refreshed and prepared for the sermon.

Then, as now, the morning service was followed by the Sunday School. William Davis, now Deacon Davis, was one of my teachers. With another boy, I frequently gathered in the pennies, passing my cap from pew to pew. In addition to the Sunday School lesson, we learned Bible verses. Whether you follow our example in this respect I do not know, but I

am credibly informed that the ancient custom of taking up
a collection is still observed.

After Sunday School we youngsters ate our lunch, which
was a great feature of the child's Sunday forty years ago,
for the afternoon services soon began, and dinner was still
far away.

Mr. Pratt was the minister of my childhood days. It was
the custom then to hold prayer meetings occasionally in different parts of the town. On Sunday, the notice might be
given that next Tuesday evening there would be a prayer
meeting at the school house in District No. 4, at half-past
seven, and there the neighbors would gather, taking their
lamps with them.

Of the many excellent things said by Mr. Pratt in this
church, what I am about to relate made the greatest impression on my young mind. He then lived at the village in
the brick house now owned by Deacon Pressey. It sometimes happened that his good helpmeet, burdened with the
cares of the household and the preparation of the children,
was not always in readiness Sunday mornings when the
minister brought the horse to the door. The resulting rush
and hurry were disquieting to one who wished to be "In the
spirit on the Lord's day."

One morning he entered the pulpit promptly, and, flushed
with victory won, told us what he had done, and what
other men might do. It was this: "Instead of waiting
about, finding fault and doing nothing, Sunday mornings,
take hold and help!" Very simple, wasn't it? But to me
it was worth more than a bushel of sermons.

Those were the days of Deacon Chase and Deacon Sanborn.
A tall, spare man was the senior deacon, of tireless energy,
faithful in the discharge of his duties, working always to the
limit of his strength and of the daylight hours. After the
labors of the week, he came to the house of God, and found
the rest which his soul and body alike craved. I count it no
sin for a man to sleep in meeting, if only he is graceful about
it, nodding in the right direction and at the right time. But
I shall never forget the sharp profile of my great uncle's face
as I gazed across to his pew the hot summer afternoons. He
looked neither forward nor backward, but reverently upward,
and his head, bobbing back and forth, was so delicately

poised, I felt that Providence alone prevented the catastrophe that seemed imminent.

Many of you will remember Deacon Sanborn and recall his genial smile and warm hand-grasp. He, too, has done his work and gone to his reward. Associated together for many years, these two men, independent and straightforward, made their impress on the life of the church and the community, doing their duty as they saw it. To-day we honor their memory.

You who are older miss many whose presence on Sunday at that time identified them with this place. The once familiar faces of Deacon Kent, Isaac Smith, John Ordway, Amos Buck, Kimball Brickett, John Drew and Nathan Johnson have long since passed from view.

Then one after another, Frederick Pike, Mrs. Nabby K. Brickett, Oliver Putnam, and many more joined the silent majority. Of those who have more recently entered into the eternal home, I will not speak. The memory of their lives is with us. Their kindly deeds and helpful influence still remain:

Mr. Pratt was followed by Mr. Bullard, a mature and scholarly man, fond of books and fond of nature. He worked not alone in the study, but in the garden and field. Deacon Sanborn said with satisfaction, "Mr. Bullard is a good farmer, he is improving the parsonage property."

The home life of the Bullard family was delightful, and its uplifting, refining influence was a benediction to all whom it reached.

In 1876, after one hundred years of independence, we voluntarily came again under the British yoke, and called Rev. Mr. Watson to come and rule over us. Had England cared for her colonies as well as Mr. Watson cared for the people under his charge, there would have been no wrongs to right, no Declaration of Independence. Not only was Mr. Watson a worker along distinctly religious lines, but he took a deep interest in everything that might stimulate and instruct the people of the town. The Y. M. C. A., with its associate membership open to all, was helpful. The lectures and concerts, the Jubilee singers, were due to his faith and push. It was in Mr. Watson's pastorate that I became a member of this church. The late Mrs. William Fellows joined at the same time.

Of Mr. Gardner I ought not to speak. It would be carrying coals to Newcastle, for you all know better than I what he has accomplished here. However, it may not be amiss for me to say that his success in making all hands march the quickstep the past few years seems rather remarkable.

The outside world has begun to wonder what Hampstead will do next. Only five years ago yonder library building was dedicated. We gathered in this house, proud to welcome to his native town the most distinguished of Hampstead's sons, the eminent jurist, the Christian gentleman, Isaac W. Smith. Three years ago, hundreds of her sons and daughters came back to Hampstead. The civic pride of her citizens had arrayed the mother town in best attire. On the spot where, fifty years before, the one hundredth anniversary had been observed, in the grove by the pond, fitting exercises crowned the third half century of the town's corporate existence. The story of the long life was ably told by Miss Noyes, and has been preserved for us in her " Memorial History of Hampstead."

And this same daughter of Hampstead, loyal, not alone to the interests of the town, but thoughtful of the church as well, has carefully studied its past, and put in permanent form the results of her painstaking research. It is most fortunate for the church that the data relating to its history have been so gathered and preserved. Our gratitude and appreciation go out to Miss Noyes for her labor of love.

Two years pass. The tireless energy of Mr. Gardner, seconded by the lightning and the ladies, works a transformation scene. Within a twelvemonth, the church interior assumes its present attractive and finished appearance. The new organ is welcomed to the front of the church, and is dedicated with appropriate ceremony. In early fall of last year, reluctant farewells are said to Mr. Gardner, and as the blossoms of spring time show once more, Mr. Woodsum is installed.

To-day, at the bidding of the old church, we come again to Hampstead. For one hundred and fifty years, she has stood for those things which are honest and of good report. Three years younger than the town, she has grown with and labored for its welfare. Enriched by the experiences of the past, conserving that which is good, let her be receptive of all that is inspiring and helpful in the life of to-day. Old in

years, she is young in all that tends for effective effort. She
rejoices in what has been accomplished, but her work lies ever
before her. The conflict between right and wrong is always
going on. Let her train the boys and girls to battle for the
right, to have high ideals, to become good citizens.

This church is beautiful for situation; it is unrivalled in
equipment; it is out of debt. It is strong in the affections
of its members. Its pastor comes to his duties full of courage and eager to serve. Cheered by the inspiration of the
past, rejoicing in the abounding life of the present, the old
church looks forward to a future great with promise.

Rev. Kimball Kent Clark, pastor of the M. E. Church at
Fitzwilliam, N. H., recalled his boyhood days in Hampstead,
as follows :—

"It is a great pleasure for me to stand here to-day and
speak a few words. The other day, when I was in Keene,
I had the good fortune to meet Judge Holmes of that city.
He said to me, "Young man, how do you like the ministry ?" I said, "Very much." "Well," said he, "Ministers' sermons and lawyers' pleas ought never to be more
than one-half hour long and leaning towards mercy at that."
It would seem to me, my friends, that there could be no
place as dear to us as the town in which we spend our childhood years. Around this town, therefore, cluster for me
sacred memories and tender associations. It was in the public schools of this town that I received my early education.
How well do I remember the years spent in the High school
under Prof. F. E. Merrill. The Saturday morning remarks,
what a source of blessing in after life ! My life may be spared
many years, but I shall not forget his kindness and timely
words of advice. Hampstead never had a better man than
Prof. Merrill. It has not been my pleasure to know but two
of the pastors of the church, Rev. Albert Watson and Rev.
Rufus P. Gardner. I have the pleasure of an acquaintance
with Rev. Mr. Pratt, but did not live under his ministration.

How well do I remember Mr. Watson. One day in particular, as I was trudging along the street, he came along in
his sleigh and said, "Lad, won't you have a ride ?" I was
pleased to ride, and what a ride we did have ! If you remem-

ber about Mr. Watson's horse, you know how swift he could travel. I suppose he has forgotten the incident, and may be wondering even this moment when he took me to ride. However, he took me to my home, and made a kindly call, and from that day I knew he was my friend, and I certainly was his. Well do I remember when he was about to leave Hampstead that I said to him, " I shall never think as much of another minister as I have of you." " Oh, yes you will," said he. Mr. Watson understood human nature better than I did.

At my charge in East Deering, one of the members of my church, and my next door neighbor, said to me when I left there, " We shall never like another minister as we have liked you." I said, " Yes, you will, I'm sure," and recently I hear that my neighbor has just the same feeling towards the new minister. I am glad it is so, glad for my friend, glad for the new minister, and glad for the church.

Mr. Watson went away and Mr. Gardner came, and to know him was to love him. I did not forget the old pastor, but I learned to honor and respect the new one. There sprang up a peculiar relation between us, that of the pastor with the young man whom he had received into the church. I am sure no man ever endeavored to benefit the young people more than Mr. Gardner.

The Hampstead Congregational Church has had a grand history in the past. The pastors have been men of God. Their lives have been more than their sermons. You have had noble men and women, also, in your midst. Many that were here a short time since are gone. They have heard the words, " Come up higher." Their work on earth is done. They have entered into rest, but their lives are a power still for good. You have to-day men and women who are carrying on the work loyally for Christ and His church. I believe that the best work of the Hampstead church has not been done. Fair and as grand as her history has been in the past, there is a brighter history in the future.

My parting thought is this : Work for the church, not because it is your church, not so much that as because it represents the work of Jesus Christ in this world, and you desire a part in that work, remembering that success depends on God alone. " Man may come and man may go, but I go on forever." Thus sings the mountain brook as it journeys down the side of the mountain. So may we learn the great lesson that we are but instruments in the hands of God. ·May we, knowing this, work earnestly for the upbuilding of His kingdom, which shall one day come to its full fruition, and the kingdoms of this world become the kingdoms of our Lord and the Christ."

The singing of " Jerusalem, the Golden," by the quartette ⌐⌐Mrs. Forrest E. Merrill, soprano ; Miss Mary G. Davis, alto ; Prof. Forrest E. Merrill, tenor ; Mr. H. Clinton Davis, bass—was much enjoyed by the audience.

" Greetings from the Mother Church, Plaistow and North Haverhill," was responded to by Rev. Joseph Kimball, pastor, and was as follows :—

When the settlers of Haverhill had extended a considerable distance to the north, there was reasonably a desire for a new parish, and in the autumn of 1730 the North Parish Church was organized.

Most of its members were from the town church of Haverhill. At length the settlers had extended farther northward, so that another church was desired, and after some twenty-two years the church of Hampstead was formed.

The membership was largely from the North Parish of Haverhill church, which, after the state line of New Hampshire and Massachusetts was established, had become the Congregational Cnurch of Plaistow and the North Parish of Haverhill, Mass.

There appears to have been a number of quite intimate features of relationship between the parent and daughter churches. The first minister of the parent church, Rev. James Cushing, was from Salisbury, Mass., and he may have had some influence in causing that the first minister of the daughter church should be from that town.

The second minister at the parent church, Rev. Giles Merrill, also from Salisbury, is said to have studied for a time with Rev. Henry True, your first minister.

The next minister of your church was a near family relative of a prominently theological family of the parent church.

There continued to be an intimate relationship between

the two churches, aided by the fact that some residents of
the Hampstead parish were from the parent parish, as well
as by the frequent exchange of pulpits that were enjoyed.
Both communities also had various intimate relationships to
Salisbury, Mass.

We are wont to look upon you as fortunate in situation,
upon the sides of the north, free from mar by distractions of
city pastimes, fortunate in your long pastorates, fortunate in
your present beautifully appointed church, fortunate in your
new organ, and fortunate in the presence of a successful
endowed school.

Please accept the cordial congratulations of the parent
church, which, as the years have passed, has become rather
an older sister. May grace, mercy and peace be multiplied
to you abundantly.

Hon. Lyman Dewey Stevens of Concord, N. H., spoke as
follows in response to No. 15 of the programme, " Greetings
from Friends " :—

Brethren and Friends :—

Your programme has assigned to me the pleasant duty of
bringing to the church the greetings of friends. Among
that company I feel that I may properly claim a place, and
the greetings I offer in their behalf are most cordial and
heartfelt.

Here was the home of my ancestors, one of whom was a
member of this church, and their remains now rest in the
ancient cemetery of this town. My father, in his early boyhood, migrated from Hampstead, with the family of my
grandfather, to the northern part of the state, there to spend
the remainder of his life.

I should be destitute of filial affection and a due respect
for my progenitors, did I not feel a deep interest in Hampstead, my ancestral home, and especially in its church, the
corner-stone on which its advancement and growth rest.

On an occasion like this it is necessary to compare the
past with the present, in order to get a correct and full understanding of the day we celebrate, and note carefully the
changes which the lapse of years has wrought.

On whichever side we look it is our happiness to see a

better husbandry, a higher standard of domestic life and comfort, a longer term of life and better health, by reason of improved sanitation; better schools, the establishment of public libraries, and a more general interest in popular education—in short, all the conditions of life have been characterized by such a vast improvement that the subject is not easy of comprehension.

The church has kept step in this grand march of progress. If we take a retrospect of the last one hundred and fifty years, their history informs us that the original home, cold, uncomfortable, possessing none of the appointments of a modern house of worship, and bearing no resemblance to the gate of heaven, except in the sublime faith, the undoubting trust and seal of the worshippers who gathered there.

To-day we find this same church installed in this beautiful and commodious edifice, with its sweet-toned organ and trained choir, and appointments for comfort. We rejoice and are happy over its increase of numbers and the noble work and blessed influence it has contributed to make possible the Hampstead of to-day.

All friends of this church give thanks to God as they contemplate the blessings which his gracious hand has bestowed upon it, while they offer congratulations and pray for its continued growth and enlarged usefulness.

This joyous day is not a celebration of the conclusion of a noble Christian work, but rather to mark and emphasize its progress, and to gather inspiration from the consideration of its past to achieve greater work and more extensive usefulness in the years to come.

It is the ardent desire of all friends of this church who have assembled here to congratulate its members and to rejoice in the prosperity of its past, that when those who shall participate in the three hundredth anniversary of its formation, they shall behold a progress far greater, and a standard of piety and Christian service far higher than the present, gratifying as that surely is.

I can close in no better way than by quoting this sentiment, which is worthy to be held in perpetual remembrance : "To preserve the institutions of our holy religion is a duty which we owe to ourselves who enjoy them, to our pious ancestors who transmitted them down, and to our posterity who will require at our hands these, the noblest gift and the best birthright of mankind."

The congregation joined in the singing of the "Song of the Day," after which Mrs. Frank W. Emerson, organist, rendered an organ postlude, "Polish Serenade," the closing number of the afternoon exercises.

SONG

Written for the occasion by James H. Taylor.

Tune, "Marching Through Georgia.'

Come, ye happy people, come, and let your voices ring
Loud in jubilation as a praise offering ;
Sing in faith and courage as our fathers used to sing—
Filled with a hope everlasting.

CHORUS.

Rejoice, be glad this is our natal day,
Our friends are here to swell the cheerful lay,
Coming from the hills and valleys, many miles away,—
Back to the old church in Hampstead.

Sing of how the joy of life outweighs the grief and tears ;
Sing of all the triumph that on memory's page appears ;
Sing our *church's* record, born of three times fifty years ;
Who would forbid us of praising ?
CHORUS—

Dear familiar faces once again we welcome here—
Pastors we have parted with in sorrowing sincere—
Voices long unheard we now with deepest pleasure hear.
This is a happy occasion.
CHORUS—

Builded like the church of old, upon the solid rock,
Riven by the tempest oft, yet rising from the shock ;
Still the goodly shelter of a persevering flock—
Ever the way mark to Glory.
CHORUS—

Hampstead should for character be strongly underlined.
Nowhere else are people raised so generally kind.
No place where the pastors stay so long you'd ever find
    If you should search the world over.

        Chorus—

Love and loyalty to God : Oh, may these never cease.
Goodwill unto all mankind, here let it not decrease
Till the glory-morning ushers in the day of peace,
    Day of a righteous dominion.

        Final Chorus.

All praise to Him who saw the church begun—
Who viewed the work through many seasons run ;
Grant that all may hear some day the Saviour's glad "Well
    done,"
    Welcoming us home to Glory.

The audience room and kitchen of the vestry which had been draped with crepe paper of delicate tints in artistic designs, served as a banquet hall, where three hundred invited guests repaired to enjoy a lunch and social hour, until the organ prelude, "Sunset Glow," at 7.30 o'clock, announced the opening of the evening entertainment. A large company filled the church. The singing of the anthem, "Praise ye the Lord," by the chorus, was followed by invocation, by Rev. George Hale Scott, pastor of the Congregational church, Atkinson.

By request, Miss Harriette E. Noyes read the following letter from Rev. George B. Spalding, D. D., pastor, First Presbyterian church, Syracuse, N. Y.

" *To the Congregational Church, Hampstead, N. H.*

Greeting :—It is a matter of great regret to me that I am unable to be present at the celebration of the one hundred and fiftieth anniversary of the Congregational Church at Hampstead.

This church, beyond all others, is precious to me, because of the three generations of my ancestors who were connected with it. My great-grandfather, Hezekiah Hutchens, and his wife, Anna Merrill, daughter of Deacon John Merrill, of Newbury, Mass., came to Hampstead about ten years after the organization of the church. Captain Hutchens, when a boy of seventeen years, was a soldier at the capture of Louisburg, June 17, 1745. He won his title of captain by active service in every Indian war from that date to the breaking out of the war of the Revolution.

Here, on the ground before the old church building, he mustered the largest company of soldiers that took part in the great battle at Bunker Hill on June 17th, and as captain of a New Hampshire company he was present at the not less famous battle which ended in the surrender of Burgoyne.

Within the walls of the old church, now your well preserved Town Hall, the old warrior worshipped until with reverent hand his fellow citizens and soldiers laid him away in the cemetery close by, where the pines above his own and wife's graves seem to whisper their ceaseless requiems.

Here in the old homestead, still known as the "Hutchens Tavern," was born my grandmother Patty, whose name as "Polly Hutchens" stands in the baptismal list of the church. I remember her as "grandma" all through my childhood years in her home in Montpelier, Vt. Her virtues of wisdom and large-hearted charity and clear-eyed faith were admired by a large circle of old people, but better to us younger ones were her virtues of constant cheerfulness and sweet laughter and ever-brooding love.

It is a supreme grace of heaven which makes old age lovable to children.

Here in the old church, or more probably in the old tavern, Thomas Reed of Uxbridge, Mass., made this "Polly" his wife. On the hillside now owned by Mr. Tristram Little they made their home. Here my mother was born a century ago. Here she began a growth which matured into a remarkable beauty of person and mingled sweetness and strength of character, and lofty ambition and faith which children and children's children recall with constant praise.

Before my grandfather, Thomas Reed, went from Hampstead to live at Montpelier, he performed a service for the old church which in my visits here, I regard with utmost pleasure and pride.

He was a carpenter and cabinet worker, and he it was who

designed and built the porch and the graceful steeple of the meeting house,—the town hall of to-day.

Pardon me, if in my appreciation of my grandfather's work during his brief sojourn here in Hampstead, I look at this structure of his hands as a monument to his worthy memory, and breathe the prayer that by your preserving care and that of heaven, it may endure in its integrity and beauty through coming generations.

Dear friends of the old church, these fathers and mothers have bequeathed to you a noble heritage in their characters, sacrifices, their prayers, in their clear vision of the surpassing worth of spiritual things over the material.

These last, which we so unduly magnify, they held subordinate. They endured "seeing the invisible."

Let no generation of such ancestors in all their magnificent progress in earthly things forget or miss the heavenly realities for which these fathers and mothers so bravely struggled and which now they forever more possess.

Sincerely and cordially your friend,
GEORGE B. SPALDING.

The double male quartette sung " He knows it All," after which Rev. W. T. Bartley recited the " Poem of the Day," as follows :—

" No pompous deeds of heroes known to fame,
No fulsome eulogies to-day we frame,
But rather humbly thank the Father, God,
For faithful ones that beneath the sod

Repose ; and with them those who still
Abide, and do the Heavenly Father's will.
The world esteems the conquering warriors great,
And bows before the men of princely state ;

Yet far above his name, in heaven's roll,
Is that of him who hath a noble soul.
" The short and simple annals of the poor "
In God's esteem will often times endure.

Till more pretentious records, carved on brass
Or sculptured stone, from recollection pass;
And when "the noiseless tenor of their way"
The faithful keep, nor from their duty stray,

They shall not be as flowers that blush unseen,
But after death their memory shall be green.
With honor deep we turn the backward page,
And with the past our chastened thoughts engage.

Those early saints who kindled heavenly light,
That whosoever would might walk aright
And happy-hearted tread the toilsome road,
Laborious life relieved of half its load.

These were the benefactors of the land;
Their names beside the patriots should stand
Who freed us from the cruel foreign yoke,
Or to the slave the great deliverance spoke.

If he who freed the body labored well,
Then he who freed the spirit from the spell
Of evil, better still performed his part,
His work unmatched by any human art

We honor them to-day, the men of old,
Who prayed that every name might be enrolled
Within the book of life, and praying, reared
A sanctuary fit for those who feared

" The Lord of earth and sky, and sealed the bond
That holds the Christian with affection fond
In that fraternal love and warm accord
Enjoyed by all that know and love the Lord.

We honor, too, the generations five
Who sacrificed, to keep the flame alive
Upon the sacred altar : all their fears,
Their toils laborious and their anxious tears,

Their contest with the evil one, their deeds
That showed how Christ within supplied their needs,
Their prayers at home, their virtues known to men,
We kindle, and our hearts are warm again,

As retrospection brings their worth to light,
And we acknowledge that their day was bright.
A happy church at Hampstead long has stood,
Harmonious, strong, and hospitable, good.

With goodness as a crowning grace of all,
For that which pleases heaven cannot fall
To utter ruin. Had celestial fire
In flame this temple swathed from lofty spire

To stone beneath, or in titantic play
Its solid timbers splintered in a day,
Lamented havoc, still would He who keeps
And cheers His people form those dreadful heaps,

Have helped once more the edifice to rise,
And point another spire to the skies.
Harmonious church, thy people well content
With several pastors several years have spent.

And they who ministered have loved the spot
And thanked the Father for their earthly lot,
An honor both to shepherd and to sheep
That loved each other with affection deep.

Nor looked for failings with too keen a gaze,
But rather trained their kindly lips to praise.
Could I those faithful shepherds call by name,
And into lines poetic fitly frame,

The dissyllabic titles that you've known,
As Kelly, Bartley, Gardner and your own,
From Bath, imported Woodsum, and to that
Should add a Watson, and a genial Pratt.

Brief monosyllables, of sort unique
Among its rivals, man of spirit meek;
And heroes of the faith in earlier days,
Your voice would blend with mine in words of praise.

If faults they had, the faults were well concealed,
And many virtues to the eye revealed.
A part have passed from earth, and some remain,
Have you forgotten him whose heart and brain

Combined their efforts, or the cordial hold
Of loving hand, or ringing voice that rolled
From pulpit up to organ? He was known
All trials to lament except his own.

Another, rich in sparkling mother wit,
Holds honored record here. How oft he hit
The point with language choice, or stirred
The drowsy listener with a mirthful word.

Nor lacks he skill in parliamentry law,
And outlines methods fit without a flaw.
On him who now the sacred office fills
We seek the blessing of the Lord who wills

That all men holy be. The spirit's might
Explaining things divine, and making bright
The shaded life, in him abideth strong,
Abides in all that after goodness long.

Alone in power the church has striven apace,
Nor yet been called to show forgiving grace
To proselyting sects who fain would found
Another church upon pre-empted ground.

Pray why this peace? This undisturbed career?
A twin response I'll whisper in your ear.
The first, surrounding churches have been kind;
The second, never could their eyes be blind

To life and consecrated vigor lent
To God by earnest souls obedient.
The field was bravely fortified ; the shot
At Satan's ramparts was seemly hot,

The captain and the warriors stood their ground,
And needless interruption never found.
The world unites to glorify the wise,
And views inventions with astonished eyes ;

It praises him who journeys towards the pole,
And steers 'mid icebergs with courageous soul,
Reveres the name of him who braved the worst,
To penetrate the Afric jungle first.

Yet equal honors, and as fine a prize,
And exaltation to the very skies
Await the foe of sin, the friend of man,
Who aids the soul of God's appointed plan.

The Christian church's dignity and worth
Are unsurpassed to any on the earth.
The worth and dignity of those who teach
A higher life, and by example preach.

There's none but God their value can appraise,
Enduring work is theirs, and richly pays.
May God perpetuate these altar fires,
And may the sons inherit from their sires

The love of all things good, and may they strive
To keep a true religion here alive,
And let thy blessings on the people rest,
O, Father.   Thus we voice our heart's request.

The solo by Mrs. Albert H. Little, " The Land of Home,"
was well enjoyed, and although the people had listened to
address after address for more than five hours in the after-

noon, they proved their appreciation by their rapt attention
to the discourse from the text, " Upon this rock I will build
my church, and the gates of hell shall not prevail against it,"
by Rev. Burton W. Lockhart, D. D., pastor of the Franklin
Congregational Church, Manchester.

The anthem by the chorus. " Ye that stand in the House
of the Lord," a short prayer, followed by the anniversary
hymn, sang by the congregation, the benediction by the pastor, and the organist with her beautiful " Organ Postlude,"
closed the exercises of the one hundred and fiftieth anniversary of the founding of the church in town, which will be
remembered by its members and friends as one of the happiest days in the life of the church.

ANNIVERSARY HYMN.

Written for the occasion by James H. Taylor.

Tune, " Uxbridge."

Great God, from whose almighty hand
The centuries roll like grains of sand,
Thy power through varying scenes we see
Changeless in glorious majesty.

We praise Thee for our native land ;
This hallowed ground on which we stand ;
Thy care that watches year by year
The church that Thou hast planted here.

Loved preachers of Thy work and word
Have toiled within Thy vineyard, Lord ;
Entreating men to turn and see
The Christ who died on Calvary.

New followers stand where old have stood,
A tribute to redeeming blood ;
The same forgiving love to share,
One voice in praise, one heart in prayer.

Like as the branches to the vine
May we subsist on food divine—
Through Thy blest Bible, freely given,
The light of earth, the guide to Heaven.

Thanks be to Thee for all the past,
Protect, support us to the last,
When we to earthly being lost,
Shall join the everlasting host.
            Amen.

Letters were received as follows:—

METHUCHEN, NEW JERSEY,
June 9, 1902.

REV. W. H. WOODSUM:

My Dear Sir:—Your letter is before me. While I would gladly be with you on July 2d, I have not the courage to undertake the journey. I am in good health, and lead an active life for a man of eighty years, but I do not like to leave my pleasant home to incur the fatigues of travel.

I was never a member of the church in Hampstead, but I used to attend the Sabbath meetings in the old meeting house (now the town hall), under the Rev. John Kelly's pastorate, and in the first new house, Rev. J. M. C. Bartley, pastor.

In 1849 I sailed for Valparaiso, Chile, where I resided about ten years, teaching. I became interested in religion, and united with the Congregational Church, Rev. David Trumbull, pastor, in 1852. Returning from Chile in 1859, I moved to Kingston, N. Y., and then to Methuchen in 1866, where I still reside.

I have all these years been in Sunday school work as teacher or superintendent. I have now an adult Bible class, and find great pleasure in the work. I rejoice in the prosperity of the church at Hampstead, and I am sure it has been a power for good in all these years.

I have had eight children. Four have passed on to the better land; four are doing good work in church and society. All were members of the church.

All or nearly all of those whom I knew in boyhood have gone, and the work which they were doing has fallen to other hands.

I trust you will have a grand time July 2d, and that it will be a prelude to a great spiritual awakening. These are not church reminiscences, but perhaps there may be a few remaining who will be interested to hear from an old resident who has not forgotten the home of his childhood.

I am very truly yours,

A. W. MARSHALL (See 424).

LINCOLN, MASS., June 19, 1902.

My Dear Mrs. Eastman :—

Your very kind remembrance of me with an invitation to attend the exercises celebrating the one hundred and fiftieth anniversary of the Hampstead Church I appreciate very much. I should enjoy exceedingly attending the celebration, but I am intending to attend the Harvard Summer School of Theology in Cambridge from July 1st to 18th, and I am making so much effort to attend these lectures, in addition to carrying on my regular work, that I feel that I must forego the pleasure of going to Hampstead.

I hope most sincerely that the exercises will pass off successfully, and that the result of the celebration will be to endear the church yet more to those who love it, and to exalt it in the community.

With sincere regard to you and all who may remember me,

I remain, very truly yours,

EDW. E. BRADLEY (658).

"ELMHURST," BROOKLINE, MASS.,
July 1st, 1902.

My Dear Mrs. Eastman :—

May the one hundred and fifty roses and one hundred and fifty carnations, and many other bright flowers, express to you and other members of the committee of arrangements the sincere and united interest and sympathy of my sisters, Mrs. Coaker, Mrs. Jackson, and Mrs. Hitchcock, with my own, on this festal day that you celebrate, and our mutual regret that we are unable to personally rejoice with the many who will gather at the historic church.

It is a glorious thing that, through all the changes of the one hundred and fifty years, that this ancient church has not changed except for the better.

My hope and prayer is that God's presence may continue to bless and ever maintain its high standard through this twentieth century.

With sincere and affectionate greetings,
ELLEN DANFORTH WHITE (421).

2261 GORDON AVE., ST. PAUL, MINN.,
June 12, 1902.

REV. WALTER H. WOODSUM :

Dear Brother:—I thank you for the invitation received from you, as chairman of the executive committee, to attend the celebration of the one hundred and fiftieth anniversary of the organization of the Hampstead Congregational Church. I thank you, also, for your invitation to speak on that occasion.

It would give both Mrs. Pressey and myself great and sincere pleasure to be present at that time, but it will be impossible to do so.

Let me say in behalf of both of us, that we remember the old home with a great deal of affection.

Those who have been away from Hampstead nearly all the time for twenty years, as we have, will of course think of the church as it was years ago, more than of it now. We remember very distinctly the days when we were in the Hampstead High School, and attended the various services of the church, and had some part in its different activities.

Mrs. Pressey played the organ for a long time, and I used to teach a class of boys, nearly of my own age, in the Sunday school. It was along in these days that the season of great revival of religious interest came to the church, in the early part of the ministry of the Rev. Albert Watson. It was then that a great many new names were added to the roll of membership, and new forces were added to the working power of the church.

The earnest, emphatic, sometimes severe, more often tender, words of Deacon Sanborn ; the rapid, whole-hearted testimonies of Joseph Brown ; the whole-souled, deep and helpful talks of Mr. Dickey, and the influence of many others, abide with us still.

Very many of those whose voices were heard in the meetings at that time have gone to their reward. Earnest, humble, yes, human and imperfect, too, they yet set in motion influences that will never cease.

Mr. Watson's clear and searching preaching, his business-like methods and his spiritual fervor, had a great and lasting effect, greater and more lasting than many, perhaps, who sat under his ministrations realize even yet.

Others will tell of the great work of the church during the past decade or two, and they will have many good things to relate. By and by those who are children now will speak to one another about the good work of the first decade of the twentieth century, for Hampstead church is very much alive, and its beneficent activities will be continued by new generations.

Very cordially yours,

EDWIN S. PRESSEY (518).

WEST HARTFORD, VT.,
June 18, 1902.

REV. W. H. WOODSUM, HAMPSTEAD, N. H.:

My Dear Sir:—Your esteemed favor of the 5th instant is at hand. I thank you for your kind invitation to be present at the one hundred and fiftieth anniversary of the organization of the Congregational Church and to speak of "personal reminiscences."

Hampstead is the home of my boyhood, and the Congregational Church there is the birthplace of my Christian experience. Nearly two-thirds of my life has been spent in Hampstead as my home, hence I have a feeling of gratitude for what the Congregational Church there has accomplished for me spiritually.

I regret that I cannot be with you, but I wish you Godspeed, and congratulate you on the advent of this birthday.

Most cordially yours,

J. W. WATSON (651).

BURLINGTON, VT., June 13, 1902.

My Dear Mr. Woodsum :—

I thank you for your cordial invitation to be present and to give some personal reminiscences at the celebration of the one hundred and fiftieth anniversary of the Congregational Church in Hampstead.

I regret more than I can express that engagements here in connection with the meeting of the American Institute of Instruction, July 1, 2, and 3, make it impossible to leave Burlington at that time.

My happy twenty years in Hampstead will never be forgotten, and I count it among my life's choicest experiences that in 1855, at the age of sixteen, I became a member of the Hampstead church.

Five things in my life began beyond the limits of my memory, namely, attendance at singing school, day school, Sunday school, the weekly prayer meetings, and the church service. As soon as they came into my consciousness I loved them all, and the habits thus formed have been abiding. I now sing in our festal chorus, teach in the Sunday school and in the Burlington High school, and am rarely absent from church or prayer meeting.

Kind, gentle Mrs. Deacon Eastman was my first Sunday school teacher. In suitable weather on Thursday evenings I took my father's hand, and, like Inlus and Aeneas, we walked with "unequal steps" to the home of either Deacon Kent, Deacon Eastman, or Deacon Emerson, for the weekly prayer meeting, in which the only part I took was in the singing. Even at that early age the meetings were interesting to me.

I am happy to know that you will have present with you a representative in my son, Rev. W. T. Bartley of Salem.

Mrs. Bartley, whose grandfather was once a member of your church, and my daughter Helen, join with me in best wishes for the prosperity of the church and the success of the celebration.

They, with myself, have delightful memories of the late celebration of the settlement of the town, which we were happy to attend.

Very truly yours.

JOSEPH DANA BARTLEY (426).

PLYMPTON, MASS., June 24, 1902.

Dear Mrs. Eastman :—

Mr. Perot unites with me in thanking the committee for the invitations to be present at the celebration of the Hampstead church.

It would be a very enjoyable occasion for us to be with you at that time, but circumstances forbid it. But our best wishes go to you, and hope the occasion will be a grand success and an anniversary long to be remembered.

I have the most pleasant recollections of the dear old church of my younger years in Hampstead, especially the teachers of my class in the Sunday school.

May God bless and prosper you.

"We may build more splendid habitations, fill our homes with paintings and with sculpture, but we cannot buy with gold the *old* associations."

Yours in Christ,

CARRIE F. PEROT (684).

PHILADELPHIA, PA., June 29, 1902.

Mrs. Mary E. Eastman :—

Your kind invitation to be present at the one hundred and fiftieth anniversary of the organization of the Congregational Church was duly received, and I regret to say that I cannot be with you on that occasion, but my thoughts will be with you, and I shall ever pray that the richest blessings of heaven may ever rest on the loved ones of my old New England home.

Knowing as I do the committee of invitations, I am confident that it will not only be a success, but will add another interesting chapter in the history of old Hampstead. With kind regards to all who may have a passing thought to the absent one,

Very truly,

WILL C. WILSON (650).

CHELSEA, MASS., June 27, 1902.

Dear Mrs. Eastman :—

I very much regret that on account of my advanced years I am unable to visit the home of my younger days, and celebrate

with you the one hundred and fiftieth anniversary of the organization of the Congregational Church of Hampstead.

Wishing you prosperity in the future as in the past, I am,
Sincerely yours,
MRS. MARY P. EMERSON (396).

54 V ST. N. W., WASHINGTON, D. C.,
June 26, 1902.

My Dear Mrs. Eastman :—

Accept my thanks for the invitation received to the one hundred and fiftieth anniversary of the Congregational Church in
Hampstead.

There are many pleasant memories connected with the church
of my earlier years, and it would give me great pleasure to be
present at the exercises. The distance is so great, I regret that
I will not be able to attend.

Very sincerely and cordially yours,
EMMA L. LANE (422).

NEW LONDON, CONN., June 23, 1902.

"Miss Elizabeth Muzzey Browne desires to extend to the
committee her best wishes for the success of the celebration of
the one hundred and fiftieth anniversary of the Congregational
Church in Hampstead, and regrets most exceedingly her inability
to attend either the exercises or the banquet. Since her ancestor
was one of its founders, the occasion would be one of extreme
interest."

HAVERHILL, MASS., June 23, 1902.

My Dear Mrs. Eastman :—

My mother wishes to acknowledge the invitation to a gathering of Hampstead people with thanks, and regrets that she will
not be able to accept it.

We are glad to have the assurance of the prosperity of the
church and the interest shown in old-time friends and members.

With cordial wishes for its future well-being and high attain-
ments, in which my mother joins me, I am,

Sincerely yours,
MARY PUTNAM MERRILL (384).

ST. LOUIS, Mo., June 24, 1902.

Dear Mrs. Eastman :—

Many thanks for your kind invitation to attend the celebration of the one hundred and fiftieth anniversary of the church. Much as I would be pleased to be with you, I can only send kind greetings and best hopes for the welfare of the church.

Sincerely,

MRS. FRANK M. CONNER (762).

22 ARLINGTON ST., ROCHESTER, N. Y.,
June 22, 1902.

Dear Mrs. Eastman :—

I regret I cannot accept the invitation to attend the celebration of the one hundred and fiftieth anniversary of the organization of the Congregational Church of Hampstead.

Although I cannot be with you at this time, I have many pleasant memories of my church home, and I hope the many blessings the church has received during the past will be continued.

With best wishes, I am,

Sincerely yours,

LYLE EASTMAN (664).

CHELSEA, MASS., June 25, 1902.

Dear Mrs. Eastman :—

We regret very much our inability to be present at the anniversary exercises and banquet of the Congregational Church, but let us assure you that wherever we may be, we always consider the Hampstead church as our church home.

We would be pleased indeed, to be present on this interesting occasion if circumstances would permit.

Most cordially,

MR. AND MRS. RUFUS C. MCNIEL AND CARRIE C.
(591, 578, 716).

BLUFF LAKE RESORT, REDLANDS, CAL.,
June 29, 1902.

Dear Mrs. Eastman :—

The invitation to be present at the one hundred and fiftieth anniversary of the church at Hampstead is at hand. I regret

that it will be impossible for us to be present. I can never lose
interest in the church and town where my childhood days were
spent, and I extend my best wishes for its prosperity.

For fourteen years my home has been in this beautiful land of
sunshine and flowers. Mr. Thurman and myself are both members of the First Congregational Church at Redlands. We
spend our summers at our mountain resort (Bluff Lake), at an
elevation of 7675 feet above sea level, and our winters at
" Allendale," near Redlands.

> With cordial greetings,
>
> MRS. M. ABBIE (PILLSBURY) THURMAN (433).

Others who sent letters of regret of inability to attend
the celebration, with cordial greetings to the members and
best wishes for the welfare of the church, were Dr. Francis
J. Stevens (419), Boxford, Mass.; Miss Anna M. Bartlett
(677), Sutton, N. H.; Rev. D. W. Morgan, East Barrington,
N. H.; Mr. and Mrs. E. Moody Boynton, West Newbury,
Mass.; Miss Samantha C. Merrill (444), Malden, Mass.; Mr.
and Mrs. Orren Hall (617, 512), Ayers Village, Mass.; Mrs.
Sara A. Little (527), Newburyport, Mass.; Rev. George E.
Lake,(626), Stratham, N. H.; Miss Ellen Gordon (863), Low-
ell, Mass.; Miss Esther B. Kent(714), Lawrence, Mass.; Mr.
and Mrs. Oliver H. Godfrey, Hampton, N. H.; Mrs. Mary
A. Masterman (574), Dea. Daniel Hackett, Linus H. Little,
Mrs. Helen A. Page (590), Mrs. E. E. Ranlett (596), Miss
Alice M. Little (585), Mrs. George F. Carlton (587), Mrs.
Sarah E. Cowdery (514), of Haverhill, Mass.; Rev. R. T.
Wilton, East Derry, N. H.; George Warren Graham, Jr.,
Brooklyn, N. Y.; Mr. Isaac H. Marshall, Still River, Mass.;
Mrs. Dr. S. A. Harris, White Plains, N. Y.; Rev. W. L. An-
derson, Exeter, N. H.; Dr. and Mrs. O. C. B. Nason (655),
Medway, Mass.; Roland Rowell, Esq., Manchester, N. H.;
A. Burnside Atwood, Roxbury, Mass.; Mr. and Mrs. James
P. Johnston, Miss Elizabeth Mussey Browne, New London,
Conn.; Albert W. Tenney, Stoneham, Mass.; Rev. Fannie

B. Williams (542), King Fisher, Okla.; and Rev. John S. Curtis, Candia, N. H.

LIST OF MEMBERS—1752-1902.

See corresponding numbers in the "Sketches of Members."

RECEIVED DURING THE PASTORATE OF REV. HENRY TRUE.

1 Rev. Henry True.
2 Richard Hazen.
3 Sarah Hazen.
4 Jeremiah Eaton.
5 Hannah Eaton.
6 David Dodge.
7 Martha Dodge.
8 Ebenezer Gile.
9 Lydia Gile.
10 Widow Mary Gile.
11 Stephen Johnson.
12 Mary Colby.
13 Daniel Little.
14 Abiah Little.
15 Stephen Emerson.
16 Hannah Emerson.
17 Nathaniel Heath.
18 Sarah Heath.
19 Peter Eastman.
20 Elizabeth Eastman.
21 Benjamin Kimball.
22 Mary Kimball.
23 Stephen Johnson, Jr.
24 Susanna Johnson.
25 Moses Gile.
26 Eunice Gile.
27 Jonathan Hutchens.
28 Mary Hutchens.
29 Mehitable Copp.
30 Sarah Heath.
31 Martha Roberts.
32 Capt. George Little.
33 Elizabeth Little.
34 Jacob Bailey.
35 Peter Morse.
36 Tamosine Morse.
37 Benjamin Emerson.
38 Hannah Emerson.
39 Ruth Stevens.
40 Mehitable Worthen.
41 Widow Eliz'h Johnson.
42 Hannah Kezer.
43 Samuel Hadley.
44 Judith Hadley.
45 Edmund Sawyer.
46 Sarah Sawyer.
47 Nathan Goodwin.
48 Rhoda Goodwin.
49 Amos Clark.
50 Sarah Clark.
51 John Muzzey.
52 John Hunkins.
53 Jerusha Stevens.
54 Hannah Heath.
55 John Bond.
56 Juda Bond.
57 Moses Hale.
58 Elizabeth Hale.

59 James Mills.
60 Jane Mills.
61 James Graves.
62 Sarah Graves.
63 Otho Stevens.
64 Abigail Stevens.
65 Rebecca Tucker.
66 Edmund Eastman.
67 Hannah Eastman.
68 Eleanor Stickney.
69 Joseph Hadley.
70 Susanna Heath.
71 Hannah Copp.
72 Ruth True.
73 Jacob Eaton.
74 Mary Eaton.
75 Thomas Fellows.
76 Ruth Atwood.
77 Thomas Williams.
78 Deliverance Williams.
79 Obediah Wells.
80 Jemima Wells.
81 John Morrill.
82 Judith Morrill.
83 Prudence Bailey.
84 Mehitable Harriman.
85 Elizabeth Webster.
86 Abiah Nellson.
87 Mehitable Hale.
88 Ruth Kezer.
89 William Eaton.
90 Ruth Eaton.
91 Mary Kimball.
92 Jeremiah Allen.
93 Abigail Allen.
94 Phebe Webster.
95 Rachel Morse.
96 Aaron French.

97 Sarah French.
98 Dea. Samuel Currier.
99 Hannah Currier.
100 Dea. Joseph French.
101 Hannah French.
102 Martha Hadley.
103 Joseph French, Jr.
104 Judith French.
105 Samuel Brown.
106 Hannah Brown. .
107 John Calfe.
108 Lois Calfe.
109 Abiah Muzzey.
110 Charles Johnson.
111 Ruth Johnson.
112 Timothy Goodwin.
113 Hannah Goodwin.
114 Sarah Sinclear.
115 Hannah Sinclear.
116 Susanna Johnson.
117 Joseph Sawyer.
118 Judith Sawyer.
119 James King.
120 Job Kent.
121 Alice Kent.
122 Jemima Stevens.
123 Annar Dodge.
124 Elizabeth Cheney.
125 Molly Stevens.
126 Mary Goodwin.
127 Richard Goodwin.
128 Elizabeth Goodwin.
129 Nathaniel Knight.
130 Hannah Sanclear.
131 Simeon Morrill.
132 Sarah Merrill.
133 Widow Jane Worthen.
134 Ephraim Webster.

135 William Kelly.
136 Nehemiah Heath.
137 Abiah Heath.
138 Lydia Williams.
139 Theopolis Goodwin.
140 Abigail Goodwin.
141 Joseph Brown.
142 Susanna Brown.
143 Jonathan Currier.
144 Austin George.
145 Sarah George.
146 Samuel Currier.
147 Mary Currier.
148 Timothy Stevens.
149 James Emerson.

150 Lydia Emerson.
151 Samuel Pillsbury.
152 Abner Rogers.
153 Hannah Rogers.
154 Mary Ely.
155 Mary Cheney.
156 Clark Ely.
157 Lt. John Darling.
158 Hannah Darling.
159 Lt. John Harriman.
160 Abigail Harriman.
161 James True.
162 James Kimball.
163 Tilly Howe.

RECEIVED DURING THE PASTORATE OF REV. JOHN KELLY.

164 Rev. John Kelly.
165 Barnes Morrill,
166 Abigail Morrill.
167 Jonathan C. Little.
168 Martha Welch.
169 Joshua Eastman.
170 Sarah Eastman.
171 Abigail Kelly.
172 Widow Mary Mills.
173 Joseph French, Jr.
174 Molly French.
175 Widow Abigail Johnson.
176 Reuben Mills.
177 Ruth Mills.
178 Daniel Plummer.
179 Abigail Plummer.
180 Moses Little.
181 Mary Little.
182 Nabby Sawyer.
183 Rev. True Kimball.
184 Widow Martha Page.

185 Miriam French.
186 Robert Emerson.
187 Mary Emerson.
188 Sally French.
189 Damarias Goodwin.
190 Benjamin Emerson.
191 Mrs. Ruth Emerson.
192 Ruth Emerson.
193 Maria Emerson.
194 Benjamin Dudley Emerson.
195 Mary Noyes.
196 Richard Kelly.
197 Ruth Wright.
198 Mary Smith.
199 Robert Chase.
200 Samuel Little.
201 Ruth Little.
202 Martha Knight.
203 Silas Tenney.
204 Rebecca Tenney.
205 Mary Poor.

206 Mary Harriman.
207 Mary Dinsmoor.
208 Capt. Simon Merrill.
209 Lucy Colby.
210 Sarah Putnam.
211 Eunice Kelly.
212 Tamer Woodward.
213 Joshua Eastman, Jr.
214 John True, Esq.
215 Widow Susanna Currier.
216 Sarah Gould.
217 Hannah True.
218 Henry True Kelly.
219 Joseph Welch.
220 Benjamin Garland.
221 Mary Garland.
222 Mary Heath.
223 Jesse Davis.
224 James Brickett.
225 Anna Brickett.
226 Mrs. Anna Calef.
227 Phebe Little.
228 Irene Kelly.
229 Emma Chase.
230 Susanna Eastman.
231 John Kelly, Jr.
232 Jonathan Brickett.
233 Lydia Brickett.
234 Ezra Davis.
235 Mary Davis.
236 Lydia Chandler.
237 Jos. Wentworth Batchelder.
238 Elizabeth Hackett.
239 Henry George.
240 Sally Heath.
241 John Emerson.[1]
242 Elizabeth Emerson.
243 Hannah George.

244 Moses Heath
245 Jonathan Kent.
246 Clarissa Kent.
247 Sarah Howard.
248 Mary Brown.
249 Anna True.
250 Samuel Kelly.
251 Major Eliphalet Knight.
252 Jonathan K. Little.
253 Hannah R. Hoyt.
254 Mary Little.
255 Abiah Little.
256 Nathaniel Little, Jr.
257 Jeremiah Tenney.
258 Francis Welch.
259 Almira Ann Calef.
260 Harriet Davis.
261 Sarah Hubbard.
262 Abigail Kelly.
263 Abigail Kent.
264 Phebe Little.
265 Alice Nichols.
266 Mary W. Nichols.
267 Priscilla Sawyer.
268 James Green.
269 Thomas Kent.
270 David P. Little.
271 Francis Sawyer.
272 Mary C. Ayer.
273 Mary Babb.
274 Widow Hannah Brown.
275 Sally Brickett.
276 Mary George.
277 Belinda Little.
278 Sarah W. Jaques.
279 Nancy Ordway.
280 Abigail S. Emerson.
281 Fanny Tufts.

282 Delia Welch.
283 Jacob Irving.
284 Thomas K. Little.
285 Daniel Nichols.
286 Josiah F. Heath.
287 Lyman Worthen.
288 Widow Sarah Noyes.
289 Theodore Tarlton.
290 Daniel Nichols.
291 Richard K. Brickett.
292 Moody H. Brickett.
293 C. Phineas Balch.
294 Lorenzo Kent.
295 Jonathan P. Kent.
296 Widow Sarah Emerson.
297 Louisa Brickett.
298 Caroline French.
299 Josiah Webster.
300 Mary Webster.
301 John W. Emerson.
302 Abiah F. Tewksbury.
303 Hannah Johnson.
304 Lavina York.

305 Mary Ann Mooers.
306 George W. Little.
307 Thomas Tarlton.
308 Jesse Emerson.
309 Nabby K. Calef.
310 Widow Mary Merrill.
311 Mary Tarlton.
312 James Mann.
313 Miriam Mann.
314 Elizabeth Calef.
315 Sally Burnham.
316 James Calef.
317 Sabra F. Tewksbury.
318 Mary C. Smith.
319 Mary E. Johnson.
320 Mary D. Kelly.
321 William Tenney.
322 Abigail J. Page.
323 Ruth A. Howard.
324 Jabez T. Howard.
325 Mary J. Pillsbury.
326 Hannah K. Moody.
327 Lavina W. Pevear.

RECEIVED DURING THE PASTORATE OF REV. JOHN M. C. BARTLEY.

328 Rev. John M. C. Bartley.
329 Elbridge Kent.
330 Robert B. Kent.
331 Edwin Kent.
332 Edmund T. Eastman.
333 Jesse B. Davis.
334 James Brown.
335 Harriet N. Calef.
336 Miss Louisa Currier.
337 Mr. Daniel Jones.
338 Mrs. Jones.
339 Martha Kelly.
340 Mr. Nathaniel Ordway.

341 Mrs. Sarah Harriman.
342 Mrs. Harriet Illsley.
343 Mrs. Ruth Emerson.
344 Mary True.
345 Mary Emerson.
346 Sarah George.
347 Abigail Currier.
348 Mr. Amasa Eastman.
349 Betsey Eastman.
350 Elbridge G. Little.
351 Eunice Kelly.
352 Weld Pecker.
353 Mrs. Betsey Heath.

354 Mrs. Mary S. Emerson.
355 Mrs. Susan D. Bartley.
356 Capt. James Gibson.
357 Mrs. Sarah Gibson.
358 Capt. John Heath.
359 Mrs. Abigail Heath.
360 Miss Louisa Heath.
361 Judith S. Eastman.
362 Elizabeth Langmaid.
363 Ellen Gordon.
364 Benjamin Atwood.
365 Mrs. Hannah W. Merrill.
366 Miss Meribah Ayer.
367 Benjamin B. Garland.
368 Mrs. Mary H. Garland.
369 Mr. John Little.
370 Mrs. Louisa Little.
371 Mrs. Mary Calef.
372 Amos Nelson.
373 Mrs. Harriet Nelson.
374 Mrs. Mary Hoyt.
375 Mrs. Hannah Irving.
376 Mr. Ralph Brickett.
377 Dr. Isaac Tewksbury.
378 Albert A. Little.
379 Dudley George.
380 Mrs. Betsey George.
381 Laura A. Putnam.
382 Albert Grant.
383 Lorenzo H. Babb.
384 Susan E. Putnam.
385 Mrs. Ruth Brickett.
386 Mary Ann Garland.
387 Belinda L. Merrick.
388 Herman F. Tewksbury.
389 Dea. Joseph Chase.
390 William Sanborn.
391 Mrs. Mary Sanborn.

392 Mrs. Martha Ann Little.
393 Mrs. Ann Ordway.
394 Belinda H. Ayer.
395 Benjamin Sawyer.
396 Miss Mary Eastman.
397 Elizabeth Emerson.
398 Mrs. Elizabeth Chase.
399 Polly Ayer.
400 Ann A. Eastman.
401 Caleb Emerson.
402 Mrs. Harrington.
403 Mrs. Hannah Chase.
404 Hannah Emerson.
405 Helen M. Davis.
406 Miss Hannah French.
407 Mrs. Eliza Davis.
408 Mrs. Mary Davis.
409 Mrs. Hannah Mooers.
410 Harlan H. Pillsbury.
411 Eliza J. Nichols.
412 Mrs. Martha B. Marble.
413 Emma E. Ordway.
414 Mrs. Mary J. Buck.
415 Ann E. Sawyer.
416 James Burrill.
417 John Jackson.
418 Mrs. Caroline M. Chase.
419 Dr. F. J. Stevens.
420 Mrs. Susan E. M. Stevens.
421 Helen Tewksbury.
422 Emma L. Pillsbury.
423 Sophia A. Greenleaf.
424 Sally Marshall.
425 Lois Sanborn.
426 Joseph D. Bartley.
427 John C. Drew.
428 Mrs. Hannah Drew.
429 Miss Mary Davis.

430 Mrs. Mary Jackson.
431 Mr. Samuel Atwood.
432 Mrs. Lucretia Jefferson.
433 M. Abbie Pillsbury.

RECEIVED DURING THE PASTORATE OF REV. T. C. PRATT.

434 Rev. Theodore C. Pratt.
435 James T. Brickett.
436 Daniel S. Pillsbury.
437 William H. Davis.
438 Mrs. E. Augusta Pratt.
438 Mrs. Sarah B. Emerson.
440 Mary A. T. Brown.
441 George O. Jenness.
442 Miss Mary B. Eastman.
443 Mrs. Louisa M. Ordway.
444 Samantha C. Merrill.
445 Mary A. Merrill.
446 Martha Sanborn.
447 Maria H. Little.
448 Meribah F. Little.
449 Mary J. Heath.
450 Abby R. Heath.
451 John S. Titcomb.
452 Mrs. Caroline Buck.
453 Huldah A. Hoyt.
454 Mrs. Elizabeth P. Ordway.
455 Mrs. Lydia C. Ring.
456 Nancy R. Marston.
457 Mrs. Elvira P. Howe.
458 Mary E. Chase.
459 Mrs. Maria M. Hale.
460 Mrs. Elizabeth M. Locke.
461 Mrs. Syrena B. Johnson.
462 Abbie A. Johnson.
463 Mrs. Clementine H. Marble.
464 Alice C. Merrill.
465 Anna L. Heath.

466 Mrs. Eliza S. Ordway.
467 Mrs. Rebecca Colby.
468 Mrs. Adeline H. Eastman.
469 Mrs. Julia E. Little.
470 Mrs. Lucy A. Adams.
471 I. William George.
472 Charles W. George.
473 Annie E. George.
474 George H. Titcomb.
475 John C. Little.
476 Clara A. Irving.
477 Juliette E. Batchelder.
478 Annie R. Eaton.
479 Mary A. Eastman.
480 Sarah S. Hoyt.
481 Sarah M. Johnson.
482 Mrs. Hannah E. Titcomb.
483 Ellen A. Hersum.
484 Mary S. Kent.
485 Lizzie G. Little.
486 Mrs. Almira W. Sawyer.
487 Mary E. Emerson.
488 Frank H. Little.
489 Dianna H. Pillsbury.
490 Martha H. Williams.
491 Albert Robinson.
492 Phebe Robinson.
493 Harriet Robinson.
494 Mrs. Abby C. Smith.
495 Mrs. Mary C. Brickett.
496 Mrs. Mary E. Robinson.
497 Mrs. Mary M. Irving.

RECEIVED DURING THE PASTORATE OF REV. E. W. BULLARD.

498 Rev. E. W. Bullard.
499 Mrs. Harriet N. Bullard.
500 Lucy A. Bullard.
501 William E. Bullard.
502 Mrs. Lizzie E. Davis.
503 Mrs. Sarah A. Rowe.
504 Abigail Heath.
505 Abby W. Stevens.
506 Agnes C. Millar.
507 Martha E. Lake.
508 Mrs. Lizzie Pillsbury.
509 Mrs. Sarah J. Brown.
510 Mrs. Mary A. Tabor.
511 Ida M. Tabor.
512 Melissa McN. Marble.
513 Mrs. Emily Marble.
514 Sarah E. Irving.
515 Caleb W. Williams.
516 Margaret B. Marshall.
517 Belinda G. Wilson.
518 Edwin S. Pressey.

RECEIVED DURING THE PASTORATE OF REV. ALBERT WATSON.

519 Rev. Albert Watson.
520 Mrs. Miranda Watson.
521 John F. Brown.
522 Mrs. Annie S. Brown.
523 Mrs. Mary E. Eastman.
524 John H. Clark.
525 Mrs. Clara A. Clark.
526 Moses B. Little.
527 Sara A. Little.
528 Joseph G. Brown.
529 Horace R. Sawyer.
530 Jesse B. Shirley.
531 Nellie R. Williams.
532 Mrs. Mary C. Atwood.
533 William A. Emerson.
534 Abbie H. Emerson.
535 Rufus H. H. Bailey.
536 Mattie Irving.
537 Orrie B. Little.
538 Arthur E. Bond.
539 Sarah Sager.
540 Perley H. Shannon.
541 Mrs. Sarah J. Shannon.
542 Susie C. Smith.
543 Mrs. Laura A. Bailey.
544 Charles W. Garland.
545 Nellie Haseltine.
546 John S. Corsen.
547 Mary E. Corson.
548 James W. Sanborn.
549 Flora A. Sanborn.
550 Mary E. Tabor.
551 William A. Love.
552 William Johnson.
553 George G. Williams.
554 William A. Griffin.
555 Mrs. Mary E. Griffin.
556 Emma F. Chase.
557 Charles W. Pressey.
558 Mrs. ClementineW.Pressey.
559 Lucy S. Johnson.
560 Mrs. S. Lizzie Hunkins.
561 Mrs. Mary F. Follansbee.
562 Mrs. Sarah E. Chandler.
563 Mrs. Sabrina D. Noyes.
564 Nellie T. Randall.

565 Sarah A. Graham.
566 Loren M. Chase.
567 Addie M. Chase.
568 Mrs. Nettie Arnold.
569 Lizzie H. Johnson.
570 Ezra W. Foss.
571 Mrs. Lydia W. Foss.
572 Charles O. Cass.
573 Inez A. Wilson.
574 Mary A. Williams.
575 Mrs. Sarah R. Hoyt.
576 Mrs. Lucy A. Little.
577 Abbie M. Randall.
578 Christie Graham.
579 Francis W. Coaker.
580 Mrs. Elizabeth M. Coaker.
581 Catherine E. Coaker.
582 Emma J. Coaker.
583 Myron P. Dickey.
584 Mrs. Louisa S. Dickey.
585 Alice M. Little.
586 Alice M. Smith.
587 Nellie L. Perley.
588 Lizzie I. Tabor.
589 Lillian R. Griffin.
590 Helen A. Ranlett.
591 Rufus McNiel.
592 Mrs. Sarah A. Randall.
593 Mrs. Flora J. Little.
594 Mrs. Mary A. Bragdon.
595 Mrs. Charlotte E. Townsend
596 Myra C. Townsend.
597 Annie M. Tabor.
598 John C. Sanborn.
599 Annie J. Tabor.
600 Mrs. Mary E. Putnam.
601 Orren E. Follansbee.
602 John W. Garland.

603 Mrs. Emily J. Garland.
604 Albert H. Little.
605 Mrs. Betsey P. Little.
606 Mrs. Hannah B. Griffin.
607 Mrs. Almira Perley.
608 Mrs. Emeline E. Mooers.
609 George W. Bragdon.
610 Frederick Spollett.
611 Mrs. Abbie B. Spollett.
612 Mary E. Spollett.
613 John W. Tabor.
614 Wallace Bailey.
615 Ebenezer Hoyt.
616 Mrs. Eunice Hoyt.
617 Orren Hall.
618 Martha A. Stevens.
619 Russell A. Woodward.
620 Esther S. Bassett.
621 Cora M. Bassett.
622 Mamie C. Lake.
623 Minnie C. Townsend.
624 Abbie M. Corson.
625 Ada E. Emerson.
626 George E. Lake.
627 Mary B. Sargent.
628 Charles H. Blake.
629 Mrs. Angelina Blake.
630 Mrs. Roxanna Tabor.
631 Abbie I. Little.
632 Ethelbert B. Woodward.
633 Seth Bruce.
634 Charles H. Sweet.
635 Osman C. B. Nason.
636 Mrs. Medora T. Nason:
637 Alice H. Spollett.
638 Mrs. Mary J. Fellows.
639 Henry C. Ordway.
640 Eugene L. Spinney.

641 Mrs. Laura A. Spinney.
642 Fannie B. Williams.
643 Annie Graham.
644 Mary L. Hoyt.
645 Louisa B. Griffin.
646 Helen P. Lake.
647 Fannie M. Tabor.
648 Charles M. Colby.
649 Mrs. Sarah J. Colby.
650 Will C. Wilson.
651 John W. Watson.
652 Albion D. Emerson,
653 Fred Marble.
654 Dana G. Marble.
655 Kate F. Chaples.
656 Emma E. Emerson.
657 Etta M. Hunkins.
658 Edward E. Bradley.
659 J. Herbert Emerson.
660 Mrs. Emma J. Card.
661 Edward Colby.
662 Mabel A. Watson.
663 Fred M. Rice.
664 Annie L. Griffin.
665 Giles F. Marble.
666 Nettie M. Follansbee.
667 W. Amos Fitts.

668 Christina Shirley.
669 Harry A. Tucker.
670 George S. Emerson.
671 Albert P. Watson.
672 Carlton H. Barnes.
673 Mrs. Dora A. Barnes.
674 Fannie C. Emerson.
675 Edwin H. Whitehill.
676 Edward F. Perot.
677 Anna M. Bartlett.
678 Carrie E. Ranlett.
679 Minnie E. Emerson.
680 Ruth A. Emerson.
681 Mary L. Emerson.
682 Thomas H. Knight.
683 John Pease.
684 Carrie M. Perot.
685 Annie B. Fitts.
686 Lester A. Williams.
687 Ezra W. Pepper.
688 Mrs. Susan E. Pepper.
689 Mrs. Annie S. Mills.
690 Mrs. Annie L. Mills.
691 William D. Rich.
692 Forrest E. Merrill.
693 Mrs. Alice A. Merrill.

RECEIVED DURING THE PASTORATE OF REV. RUFUS P. GARDNER.

694 Mary S. F. Smith.
695 Annie J. Wilson.
696 Hannah T. Howard.
697 Lillian D. Ranlett.
698 Carrie E. Davis.
699 Mrs. Jane R. Davis.
700 Ethel H. Spinney.
701 Ethel L. Sanborn.
702 Edith S. Griffin.

703 Grace M. Bassett.
704 Kimball K. Clark.
705 George J. Peneo.
706 Rev. R. P. Gardner.
707 Mrs. Belle B. Gardner.
708 Addie B. Gardner.
709 Will S. Griffin.
710 Harlan P. Clark.
711 Mrs. Harlan P. Clark.

712 Mrs. Olivia Tabor.
713 Gertrude S. Pillsbury.
714 Esther B. Kent.
715 Elisabeth M. H. Smith.
716 Carrie E. McNiel.
717 Oliver Putnam.
718 Horace W. Little.
719 Charles F. Foote.
720 Edwin L. Corson.
721 Eugene Barnes.
722 Josie F. Hyde.
723 Mary G. Davis.
724 A. Rinda Osgood.
725 Alice G. Spinney.
726 Mary S. Shirley.
727 Amasa W. Hunt.
728 Mrs. Lois J. Hunt.
729 Mrs. Mercy A. Woods.
730 Clara McD. Hart.
731 Mrs. Lydia M. Wells.
732 Richard Winters.
733 Lizzie S. Hoyt.
734 Calvin A. Merrick.
735 Charles H. Whittier.
736 Mrs. Charles H. Whittier.
737 Fannie F. Davis.
738 Ada M. Ranlett.
739 John T. Whitely.
740 Mrs. John T. Whitely.
741 Sarah O. Brickett.
742 Minnie M. Fitts.

743 Walter A. Johnson.
744 Bradley Haynes.
745 Mrs. Sarah A. Haynes.
746 Albert E. Haynes.
747 Daisey B. Haynes.
748 Hattie M. Haynes.
749 Mary F. Heath.
750 Grace M. Robbins.
751 Ora L. Ordway.
752 Richard Ordway.
753 Mabel E. Mills.
754 Abbie C. Frost.
755 Mary G. Emerson.
756 Mrs. Carrie P. Noyes.
757 Alice C. Fitts.
758 Myrta A. Little.
759 Leona C. Garland.
760 Mary E. Sherman.
761 Alice C. Pillsbury.
762 Mrs. Frank M. Conner.
763 Laura E. Merrill.
764 Agnes F. Osgood.
765 Mildred B. Osgood.
766 Elsie G. Bartlett.
767 Caroline E. Sherman.
768 Esther G. Bailey.
769 Ida May Clark.
770 Lillian G. George.
771 George A. F. Picard.
772 Mrs. Florence Picard.

RECEIVED DURING THE PASTORATE OF REV. WALTER H.
WOODSUM. APRIL 29, 1902.

773 Rev. Walter H. Woodsum. 775 Mrs. Mary W. Thomas.
774 Mrs. Walter H. Woodsum.

MEMBERS ADMITTED SINCE JULY, 1902.

JAN. 4, 1903.

776 Edna Clark Ordway (Mrs. Richard).

777 G. Pearl Ranlett.

778 Charles L. Clement, by letter from M. E. Church, Waterville, Me.

779 Avis Stanley Clement, (Mrs. C. L.), by letter from M. E. Church, Montecello, Me.

780 Lowell M. Clark, by letter from Congregational Church, Orange, Mass.

781 Hattie Fisher Clark (Mrs. L. M.), by letter from Congregational Church, Orange, Mass.

782 Lowell R. Clark, by letter from Congregational Church, Orange, Mass.

783 Marguerite Clark, by letter from Congregational Church, Orange, Mass.

MARCH 1, 1903.

784 Howard C. Cass.

785 Frank J. Beebe.

786 Miss Anna Louise Beebe.

787 Miss Melvina B. Shupe.

788 Miss Alice B. Foss.

789 Miss Bernice M. Foss.

790 Miss Alice Mabel Clark.

791 Miss Abbie Alice Heath.

SKETCHES OF MEMBERS.

When the State is not given in a sketch New Hampshire is meant. The number of the member corresponds with the number in the preceding list of members. Abbreviations: b. for born; d., died; m. or mar., married; adm., admitted; dis. and rec. for dismissed and recommended. Vol. 1 refers to the Memorial History of the town.

No. 1.

Rev. Henry True, b. in Salisbury, Mass., Feb. 27, 1726; a son of Deacon Jabez and Sarah (Tappan) True. His father was elected deacon of the Salisbury church in 1721, and the son Henry was received to the membership of that church, 1746. He was graduated from Harvard College, 1750. After his graduation he taught school in Haverhill, Mass., and studied divinity with the pastor of the First Church, Rev. Edward Barnard.

It is stated that he received an invitation to settle in his native town, but declined, mainly in consequence of the opposition of Henry Eaton, who raised some technical objection, "mainly for the sake of being contrary."

He married Ruth Ayer (72). He was twice chaplain in the "Old French war." His Bible has dates, "Fort Edward, 1759;" "At Crown Point, 1762."

He died suddenly Tuesday morning, May 22, 1782. His "tomb," as represented, is in the village cemetery (see page 308, Vol. 1).

Judging from the manuscript sermons, many of which remain, his teachings abounded in practical thoughts and suggestions.

Henry True had two brothers and seven sisters. His father, Jabez True, b. Oct. 5, 1686, was the youngest of the

eight children of Henry True, b. March 6, 1645, and wife
Jane Bradbury, whose father, Henry True, is the first True
mentioned on the records of Salem, Mass., 1644, and who
married Israel, daughter of John Pike of Langford, England,
and bought lands and house in Salisbury, 1659.

The following incident, evidently believed to be a "warning," is related: "In the house of his brother Samuel, in
Salisbury, an old clock which had not been running for a
long time, began to strike, and struck continually about forty
times at eleven o'clock in the morning. It did this several
times. Samuel's wife Sarah could not stay in the house, and
went to neighbors. Dea. Samuel remarked, "We shall have
bad news." At eleven o'clock that night a messenger from
Hampstead brought the news that his brother Henry had
died that morning at eleven o'clock."

In 1855 Mr. Jesse Davis (223) described Mr. True as he
knew him when he was a boy, "as a venerable looking man,
with light, silvery hair, and, like the most of his family, of
quite large frame, but not inclined to corpulency."

Henry True, of Marion, Ohio, a great-grandson, has in his
possession :—

I. Some forty sermons of the Rev. Henry True, the text
of which is sometimes prefixed in Greek. The handwriting
is microscopic.

II. Four letters to his wife, Ruth Ayer True.

III. Almanack Journal of years 1758, '54.

IV. His journal in 1759 and 1762, reprints of which Mr.
True has deposited in the Public Libraries of Hampstead,
Boston, Mass., and other places. This journal is partly
written in Latin. Mrs. Mary True Vose, of Chelsea, Mass.,
the only living grandchild, says: "Grandpa True was fond
of using Latin in his family, and would ask for his specta-
cles in Latin."

The Almanac Journal of 1758 records accounts of the
erection of his parsonage (see p. 84), alternate with visits

to Haverhill to see Ruth Ayer, and under date of Nov. 29th is the following extract in Latin: " Proscectus ad Haverhill, intergrims connubalia vincula." (See autograph, p. 331, Vol. I.)

No. 2.

Richard Hazen, b. in Haverhill, Mass., July 20, 1686, was son of Lieut. Richard and Mary, dau. of Capt. John and Hannah (Andrews) Peabody. His father, Lieut. Richard Hazen, inherited an immense fortune, for the times, from his stepfather, George Browne, of Haverhill, who adopted him by law. He was the youngest child of the family of ten children of his parents.

Richard Hazen, Jr., was a graduate of Harvard College, in 1717. In 1723 he kept school in Haverhill, " one quarter at the widow Mary Whittier's, and three quarters, for which he received eleven pounds a quarter."

In 1726-7, he, with his brother Moses, were the first proprietors of Pennacook (now Concord), and active in making the early surveys.

In 1726 he was chosen, at a meeting in Ipswich, Mass., Sept. 9, to search out the way from Chester to Pennacook and mark the same.

He was appointed by Gov. Belcher and his Council to survey the western and principal boundary between Massachusetts and New Hampshire.

Some extracts from the journal of Richard Hazen, written while making the survey, which is now in the possession of John W. Garland, of Hampstead, read: " Friday, March 20, 1740, at Eight o'clock forenoon, we set out from my dwelling house in Haverhill, with our provisions on hand sleds, which we hal'd up the Merrimack river, with great difficulty and danger of falling through, most of the falls in the river being broke Open & Rotten, and at eight o'clock at night we came to Mr. Richard Hall's, at Tewksbury, and lodged by his fireside."

On April 26, 1740, he wrote : "I purchased a canoe at Dunstable and come down the Merrimack river at Dracut. We carried Our Canoe Over Pentucket falls. Zechariah Hildrick, another of our company, slept at Dracut, where he belongs. We came down the river to Methuen, where Mr. Caleb Swan, another of our company, who belonged there left us. The rest (46) of us came down to Haverhill, about eight or nine of the clock. After a journey of thirty-seven days, all in perfect health through God's goodness to us."

"N. B. The weather proved so favorable to us that we never slept in the woods for any foul weather, nor did we made a camp for any one night, & stretched our blankets but three times all the journey, but Lodged without any covering save the Heavens and our Blankets. Distance covered in the thirty-seven days was one hundred and nine miles, three-quarters and thirty-eight perches."

He was one of the "Prince subscribers" and representative to the General Court of Massachusetts in 1742. He was an early owner of land in Hampstead, and settled the farm where John W. Garland now resides. He was also owner of a mill on the Merrimack river till his death.

He married Sarah Clement (No. 3). He was a principal member at the organization of the church, being admitted from the First Church in Haverhill.

The Boston Gazette of February 19, 1754, says ; "Richard Hazen, an ingenious surveyor of land, was found dead in the road, at or near Bradford, in the county of Essex. His horse was standing by him. As there were no marks of violence found upon him by the Jury of Inquest, 'tis thought he was seized with a fit, and fell from his horse & dy'd."

The date of his death has been given as February 7 or 9, 1754.

No. 3.

Sarah Clement, b. in Salisbury, Mass., 1697 ; daughter of Fawne and Sarah (Hoyt) Clement. She married Richard

Hazen, Esq. (No. 2), Oct. 22, 1719; children, all b. in Haverhill. She was one of the original members of the church from the First Church in Haverhill, June 8, 1752. In 1723, she, with several other women, asked permission to "erect a pew over the head of the stairs in the meeting house in Haverhill, so as not to damnify the stairway, as they could always find seats if belated to meeting."

The children of Hon. Richard and Sarah (Clement) Hazen were :—

I.   Richard, b. June 12, 1722; m. Miriam, daughter of Robert and Mary (Currier) Hoyt, in 1741.
II.   Sarah, b. Feb. 12, 1723; d. July 29, 1740.
III.   Mary, b. March 10, 1725; d. Nov. 30, 1737.
IV.   Hannah, b. Sept. 17, 1729; m. John Moors (see list "Owned the Covenant.")
V.   Nathaniel, b. July 23, 1732; d. Nov. 19, 1737.
VI.   Elizabeth, b. Sept. 23, 1734; m. Joseph Little of Newburyport, Mass.
VII.   Nathaniel, b. Dec. 9, 1737; d. Dec. 10, 1745.
VIII.   Mary, b. Feb. 2, 1739-40; m. Benjamin, son of Moses and Sarah (Jaques) Little; second, Major Edmund Moors, both of Hampstead. (See Cov.)

No. 4.

Jeremiah Eaton, b. in Reading, Mass., August 10, 1698, was a son of William and Mary (Swain) Eaton of Reading, and who moved to Lynnfield, Mass., where the father died, Nov. 27, 1731.

Jeremiah married, first, Margaret Hawkes of Lynn, March 17, 1721, by whom he had two children, Margaret and Hannah. His wife was b. Feb. 4, 1702, in Lynn, and died there May 25, 1730. He then married Hannah Osgood (No. 5), Nov. 4, 1730, and moved to Hampstead about 1750.

He was a designer and carver of wood for printing purposes, and was also noted for his fine musical voice and singer of psalms. From the church records: "Voted, January 19, 1754, that Jeremiah Eaton should set ye psalms,

if he saw fit;" but in July, 1754, the "prior vote was re-
voked allowing him setting ye psalms." He was admitted
a member of the church from the First Church in Haverhill,
June 8, 1752. He died October 14, 1754, and was buried
in the village cemetery.

Jonathan Eaton m. Mehitable Page in Hamp., April 8,
1784. Three of their children settled in Plymouth. Daniel
reared a large family there. Ruth and Hannah both married
King, son of William and Ruth (Hastings) George, who was
b. in Hamp. (See p. 412, Vol. 1.)

No. 5.

Hannah Osgood, b. in Haverhill, Mass., June 8, 1704;
daughter of Samuel and Hannah (Dane) Osgood, of Andover, Mass., who were married in Haverhill Dec. 28, 1734;
married Jeremiah Eaton (No. 4), "ye 3 or 4 of Nov.,
1730," and the mother of Jeremiah and William, who
d. young; Osgood William, b. April 21, 1743, married
Sarah Farnham, and lived in Fryeburg, Me., where they both
died, and whose children were William, Osgood, Sarah, Hannah, Mary, Jeremiah, Susanna, and Enoch Abbott.

After the death of her husband, she married James Abbott, Feb. 14, 1765, and lived in the West Parish of Haverhill some time.

No. 6.

David Dodge, b. in Ipswich, Mass., 1704, was son of
Antipas and Joanna (Low) Dodge of Ipswich. His mother
married, second, Joseph Hale of Bradford, Mass. David
lived in Boston from 1725 to 1728, and soon after removed
to Haverhill, Mass., where he was a wheelwright. He mar.
Martha Esgate (No. 7) in Haverhill, in 1729. They lived
in Hampstead a few years, but later removed to Londonderry, where he died. He was admitted to the church June 8,
1752, from the First Church in Haverhill.

No. 7.

Martha Esgate, She
married David Dodge (No. 6) in Haverhill, Mass., 1729.
She was adm. to the church from the First Church in Haverhill, June 3, 1752. They had seven children, all born in Haverhill.

I. Susanna, b. Feb. 11, 1730; d. 1731.
II. Joanna, b. Sept. 15, 1732; d. 1735.
III. Mary, b. March 7, 1745.
IV. Antipas, b. March 5, 1738.
V. David, b. Sept. 29, 1740.
VI. Samuel, b. Sept. 13, 1743; mar. Anna Copp (No. 123).
VII. Parker, b. May 3, 1747; mar. Mary, daughter of Thomas and Mary (Bond) Little.

Parker and Mary (Little) Dodge were mar. Jan. 4, 1750, and had nine children, born in Londonderry.

I. Edna, b. Nov. 27, 1771.
II. Martha, b. Jan. 22, 1774.
III. Mary, b. Feb. 12, 1776 (No. 310).
IV. Sarah, b. March 6, 1778.
V. Alice, b. June 5, 1780; mar. Dea. Robert Morse of Derry. (See 398.)
VI. Abigail, b. Jan. 16, 1783.
VII. Elizabeth, b. June 25, 1785.
VIII. Joseph, b. Sept. 23, 1789.
IX. Lydia, b. Nov. 18, 1700.

No. 8.

Ebenezer Gile, b. in Haverhill, Mass., Sept. 11, 1708, was son of Ephraim and Martha (Bradley) Gile of Haverhill. He mar. Lydia Johnson (No. 9), moved to Hampstead 1740, and resided where the " Old Noyes place " was burned (p. 857, Vol. 1). He was a Revolutionary soldier, and active in town affairs. He was admitted a member of the church from the First Church of Haverhill, June 3, 1752. He moved to Henniker in 1765, and then to Hopkinton, where he d. about 1775. He was a large speculator in lands, and in deeds was called " trader."

No. 9.

Lydia Johnson, b. in Haverhill, Mass., 1707 ; a daughter of Thomas and Ruth (Bradley) Johnson, a grandson of John and Elizabeth (Maverick) Johnson. Mirick's History of Haverhill says : "Ruth, wife of Thomas Johnson, was killed by the Indians in 1708, with both of the grandparents of Mr. Johnson, and that the oldest daughter, Lydia, b. 1707, was in her mother's arms when she was slain, a year and six months old. The child strangely escaped the tomahawk, (concealed perhaps in the folds of her dress), grew to womanhood, and in the 25th year of her age married Ebenezer Gile (No. 8). She was admitted to the church from the First Church in Haverhill, June 3, 1752. They had children, the first five b. in Haverhill, the others in Hampstead.

I.   Timothy, b. Feb. 9, 1732; d. young.
II.   Ruth, b. Jan. 12, 1733; d. young.
III.   Thomas, b. Nov. 19, 1734; d. young.
IV.   Anna, b. Jan. 13, 1735.
V.   Abigail, b. March 13, 1737.
VI.   Joshua, b. April 9, 1740; m. Hannah Dustin (?).
VII.   Noah, b. 1745; m. Elizabeth Howe. He was a soldier in the
        Revolutionary war, in Capt. Adams' company from Henni-
        ker; moved to Enfield; ten children.
VIII.   Lydia, b. 1750.
IX.   Johnson, b. 1852; m. Hannah Jewell; six children in Enfield.

No. 10.

Mary Heath, b. in Haverhill, Mass., 1794, a daughter of John and Frances (Hutchens) Heath of Haverhill. She mar. Joseph Guile, a son of James and Ruth (Palmer) Gile of Haverhill, Jan. 9, 1718. They were living in Kingston in 1742. She was a widow in 1752, and was admitted to the church June 3, 1752. "Voted, Dec. 13, 1758, that ye widow Mary Gile should be debarred from communion for being confederate with her daughter in ye affairs of James Stickney in his eloping and carrying off ye daughter of ye widow

Mary Gile." She d. 1754, aged 60 years, and buried in the village cemetery. They had children: Mary; Hannah, b. Jan. 1, 1721; and Abiah (No. 86); Moses (No. 25); Jonathan, b. Dec. 10, 1724, mar. Lydia Colby Nov. 12, 1747, in Hampstead, and had son Jonathan, mar. Sarah Shelborne, and d. in 1818, who, although a mere boy, was a soldier in the French and Indian war, and also in the Revolution; he became a farmer in Canterbury, where he had a family of children and grandchildren ; Sarah, Obediah, and others.

No. 11.

Stephen Johnson, b. in Andover, Mass., 1679, was a son of Lt. Stephen Johnson of Ipswich and his wife Elizabeth, daughter of Rev. Francis Dane, who were mar. in Andover, 1661. Lt. Stephen Johnson died in Andover in 1690, and his wife Elizabeth d. there in 1722. Rev. Francis Dane speaks of his daughter (see Upham's Witchcraft, Vol. 2) : " Concerning my daughter, Elizabeth Johnson, I never had grounds to suspect her. Neither have I heard any other accuse her, till by *spectre* evidence she was brought forth, but this I would say, she was weak & incapacious, tearful, & in that respect I fear she hath falsely accused herself & others—that long before she was sent for she spake as to her own particular that she was sure she was *no witch*. And for her daughter Elizabeth, she is but *simplish* at the best, & I fear the common speech that was ·frequently spread among us of their *liberty* if they would confess, & the like expressions used by some have brought many into a snare. The Lord direct & guide those that are in *place* & give us all submissive *wills*, & lett the Lord do with me & mine what seems good in his eyes." She was condemned to death, but as it was late, escaped the fate of the other condemned *witches*.

Stephen Johnson married, first, Sarah Whittaker of Haverhill, and they had children as follows :—

I.   Sarah, b. Oct. 27, 1700.
II.   Ruth, b. April 27, 1711.
III. Stephen (No. 23).
IV.   Samuel, b. June 2, 1716; mar. Susanna Black. (See No. 116).

His wife died in Haverhill June 14, 1716, and he then married Ruth, daughter of Thomas and Eunice (Singletary) Eaton. She was b. in Haverhill Nov. 21, 1784, and married, first, Ebenezer Kimball, by whom she had children, Sarah, Aaron and Richard, in Ipswich. Her husband died in 1714. She married Stephen Johnson in Haverhill Dec. 13, 1716, and had children:—

I.   Ebenezer, b. Sept. 16, 1717.
II.   Abigail, b. Jan. 29, 1721.
III. Eunice, b. Jan. 19, 1723. (See No. 26.)
IV.   Timothy, b. June 15, 1727; d. 1727.

Ruth, the wife, died April 6, 1750, and he married, August 11, 1750, Priscilla (Farnum), b. in Andover, Mass., 1769, and widow of Ephraim Holt of Andover, who d. 1699. She d. in 1754. He then married widow Sarah Clark of Methuen, Mass., pub. March 15, 1755. He was admitted a member of the church June 8, 1752, from the North Parish Church. He was always prominent in church and affairs in town, and called "the aged sexton" several years.

No. 12.

Mary Chase, b. in Haverhill, Mass., July 8, 1726, was a daughter of Abner and Elizabeth (Whittier) Chase of Haverhill. She married Ebenezer Colby. She was admitted to the church June 8, 1752, and the mother of children:—

I.   Sarah, b. Dec. 8, 1748.
II.   Abner, b. Feb. 10, 1746.
III. Ensign, b. Dec. 13, 1748.
IV.   Daniel, b. Nov. 22, 1754.
V.   Molly, b. Sept. 8, 1754-5.
VI.   Eunice, b. Oct. 20, 1756; d. 1757.

VII. Ebenezer, b. Oct. 20, 1761.
VIII. Reuben, b. Sept. 23, 1764.
IX.   John, b. July 18, 1766.
X.   Elizabeth, b. June 27, 1769.

No. 18.

Daniel Little, b. in Newbury, Mass., Jan. 13, 1692, was a son of Capt. Joseph and Mary (Coffin) Little. He married, first, Abiah Clement (No. 14) of Haverhill, in 1712, by whom he had eleven children. He married, second, Hannah Morrill, widow of Jacob Currier of Hampstead, Feb. 11, 1768. He moved from Newbury to Haverhill about 1716, and resided on what is now the northern side of Arlington street, bordering on Main street, then known as "Bartholomew Path." He was chosen a deacon of the First Church in Haverhill in 1737 or 1738, and also held many important offices of trust in Haverhill. He moved to Timberlane about 1733, having purchased a tract of thirty-six acres, with the dwelling house thereon, March 11, 1733, now known as the "Daniel Mayley place." He was mentioned in the charter of the town, in 1749, to call the first town meeting. He was a tanner by trade. He was a leading and influential citizen, and held public office many years. He also held a magistrate's commission, and solemnized many marriages. He was noted (so relate his descendants) for his extensive knowledge of the Bible. He was a member of the church in Hampstead at its organization, June 3, 1752, from the First Church in Haverhill. He was chosen deacon Aug. 6, 1752, and officiated seventeen years. His will was dated Dec. 31, 1770. In it he gave his son Daniel forty pounds, and divided the household goods between his daughters, Ruth Smith, Sarah Ayer, and the heirs of Elizabeth Kimball. He gave a cow each to his grandsons, John and Joseph Tallant, and the rest of his property, real and personal, to his son Samuel Little. He died November, 1777, aged 85 years, and was buried in the village cemetery.

No. 14.

Abiah Clement, b. in Haverhill, Mass., Sept. 12, 1692, was a daughter of John and Elizabeth (Ayer) Clement of Haverhill. She married Daniel Little (No. 13) in 1712. Her first two children were born in Newbury, Mass., and the others in Haverhill. She was admitted to the church from the First Church in Haverhill, June 8, 1752. She died in Hampstead, August 24, 1766, and was buried in the village cemetery. Her children were :—

I.   Samuel, b. in Newbury, April 27, 1712; m., first, Hannah Sewell; second, Sarah Follansbee.
II.   Joseph, b. Nov. 6, 1715; married, and soon after died, Sept. 6, 1761, and from the inventory of his estate, was of Nottingham, N. H., at that time. His only child died unnamed.
III.   Sarah, b. Nov. 11, 1717; mar. William Ayer of Plaistow; had nine children.
IV.   Elizabeth, b. Nov. 12, 1719; mar. Jonathan Kimball of Plaistow, and had five children.
V.   Mary, b. Oct. 6, 1721; d. young.
VI.   Abiah, b. August 14, 1723; m. Hugh Tallant of Hampstead and Plaistow. She had three children, and died in 1753. Her husband m., second, Mary Dodge. (See No. 7.)
VII.   Daniel, b. July 18, 1724; m. Mary Emerson of Malden, a great aunt of Ralph Waldo Emerson; and, second, Sarah Coffin of Newbury, Mass; had nine children. The degree of A. M. was conferred upon him in 1766 by Harvard College. He studied theology with Rev. Joseph Moody of York, Me., and in March, 1751, was ordained as pastor of the church in Wells, Me., and remained over fifty years, or until his death, Dec. 5, 1801.
VIII.   Hannah, b. June 21, 1725; d. young.
IX.   Judith, b. July 11, 1727; d. young.
X.   Ruth, b. Sept. 14, 1728; m. Moses Smith of Ipswich, Mass. She had four children, and died about 1776.
XI.   Abigail, b. Jan. 19, 1730; d. 1737.
        (See Appendix, Little.)

No. 15.

Stephen Emerson, b. in Haverhill, Mass., Feb. 23, 1701, was a son of Stephen and Elizabeth (Dustin) Emerson, of Jew street, Haverhill. He was one of the original members

of the North Parish Church in 1730, and admitted by letter
from there June 3, 1752. He married Hannah Marden (No.
16). He removed to the east part of Weare, N. H., where
Eben Colby lately resided, about 1762. From the church
records: "May 29, 1761, voted, that Stephen Emerson
should again partake with them on his acknowledgment that
he had gone contrary to ye Gospel in forsaking their communion." He died in Weare, N. H.

No. 16.

Hannah Marden, b. in 1716, in Rye, N. H., daughter of
Samuel and Mary (Rand) Marden; married Stephen Emerson
(No. 15). She was an original member of the North Parish
Church in 1730, and admitted to the church here June 3d,
1752. Her children were:—

I.   Ensign Stephen, who mar. Judith, daughter of Samuel and
        Dorothy (Noyes) Little of Atkinson for his second wife (first
        an Eaton), and had children, Joseph, Samuel, and several
        daughters, settled in Weare.
II.   Lieut. Marden, b. in Hampstead; mar. Anna Carr of Kingston,
        N. H., and settled about two miles east of the oil mills in
        Weare, and had children. 1, Polly, mar. Thomas Marshall of
        Newbury, Vt.; 2, Stephen, m. Anna Gould; 3, Marden, m.
        Polly Dow, resided on the homestead of his father in Weare,
        and had four children; 4, Moses, m. Sarah Shaw, settled in
        Weare, and had one daughter; 5, Obediah, m. Eunice Mar-
        shall; 6, Levi, m. Sarah Pineo; 7, Hannah, who d. young; 8,
        John, who was killed by a log falling on him when young; 9,
        Carr; 10, Hezekiah; and others.
III.   Susanna, b. Dec. 5, 1737; d. Sept. 3, 1737.
IV.   Abigail, b. June 14, 1729; m. Phineas Virgin of Concord, N. H.
V.   Elizabeth, b. Feb. 3, 1730.
VI.   Moses, b. May 21, 1735.
VII.   Mary, b. Jan. 20, 1736.
VIII.   James, b. Jan. 10, 1739; m. Lydia Hoyt (Nos. 149, 150).

No. 17.

Nathaniel Heath, b. in Haverhill, Mass., January 12, 1708,
son of James and widow Mary (Davis) Heath of Haverhill.

His mother was the first wife of Josiah Heath, whom she mar. July 19, 1671. He mar. Sarah Stevens (No. 18). He was received from the North Parish Church June 8, 1752, and removed to Hampstead about 1785. Resided near "Copp's Corner," where he purchased land from Robert Ford, sen. He served as selectman in 1758, and was prominent in town and church affairs. He died in Hampstead, and was buried in the village cemetery.

No. 18.

· Sarah Stevens, b. in Haverhill, Mass., Feb. 21, 1711, was a daughter of Aaron and Mary (Harriss) Stevens of Haverhill. She mar. Nathaniel Heath (No. 17), and was received by letter from the North Parish Church, June 3d, 1752. She had children, b. in Haverhill. She died in Hampstead, and was buried in the village cemetery.

I.   Nathaniel, b. Oct. 2, 1731.
II.   Mary, b. April 15, 1733.
III.   James, b. April 11, 1734.
IV.   Abraham, b. Dec., 1736.

No. 19.

Peter Eastman, b. in Haverhill, Mass., April 20, 1710, was a son of Jonathan and Hannah (Green) Eastman of Haverhill. He removed to Hampstead about 1732, and owned extensive lands in Hampstead on the western shores of the Wash pond, and also, in connection with his father, owned the island, in connection with his uncle, Peter Green, who sold the island to Gov. Benning Wentworth in 1741. He was town clerk of Hampstead in 1758 and 1760. He and his brother William were among the petitioners for the charter of Hampstead. His brother William, b. in Haverhill, Oct. 3d, 1715, mar. Ruth Chase, and, second, Rebecca Jewett. They had three children, b. elsewhere, but the next four children were b. in Hampstead, when they removed to

Bath, N. H., in 1767 (after living a short time in Haverhill, N. H.), where he lived the remainder of his life, and died there. He lies in an old abandoned burying ground, known as "Petty Borough." The railroad crosses his farm in a deep cut about two miles below Lisbon village. He had eleven children. Peter married Elizabeth Harriman (No. 20). He was the first deacon of the church, being elected August, 1758. He was adm. a member, at the organization, from the church in Haverhill, June 3d, 1752.

No. 20.

Elizabeth Harriman, b. in Haverhill, Mass., May 26, 1714, a daughter of Mathew and Martha (Page) Harriman of Haverhill and Plaistow; mar. Peter Eastman (No. 19). She was admitted a member of the church June 3d, 1752. She was the mother of ten children (see p. 409, Vol. 1). Her son Jonathan mar. Esther Morgan. He settled in Hopkinton early in its settlement, and about the time of the Revolutionary war removed to Henniker, on the south side of Crany Hill, where he died Feb. 12, 1827. They had five children.

No. 21.

Benjamin Kimball, b. in Haverhill, Mass., May 8, 1722, was a son of Dea. Benjamin Kimball of Plaistow and Mary, daughter of Joseph and Martha (Toothaker) Emerson, his wife. His parents were members of the church at the North Parish, Haverhill, when it was organized, in 1730, and his father was the first deacon there. It is said that "his father married at the age of eighteen and went three miles north of the river, into the woods, and cleared his farm, now known as the homestead of Nathaniel Wentworth, near the old burial ground in the North Parish of Haverhill, and that his mother was greatly distressed from the danger he run from the Indians."

Jonathan, a son, settled on the old homestead, and mar. Elizabeth, a daughter of Dea. Daniel Little of Hampstead (No. 18), for his first wife, and, second, mar. Abigail True of Salisbury, Mass. Tradition says that "Jonathan was the first person to migrate to that part of the town of Haverhill which is now Hampstead; that he went up into the woods and had twenty men to help him build his log cabin, and that two stood guard against the Indians while the rest worked." He afterwards returned to Plaistow to the old homestead, where he lived and died. He was town clerk of Plaistow twenty-three years, and deacon of the North Parish Church for fifty-seven years, and had nine children.

Benjamin, the subject of our sketch, occupied the cleared farm in Hampstead, which was a large tract, which now includes the homes of Charles B. Gilman (which was the old Kimball homestead), and Dr. Bennette and others in that vicinity, and to the Island pond on the west, and much land bordering on the Wash pond. He married, first, Mary Eaton (No. 22), by whom he had nine children. He mar., second, Mary Hoyt (No. 91), by whom he had seven children. He was adm. a member of the church by letter from the North Parish Church, June 3, 1752, and was elected deacon of the church June 23, 1754, and continued till June 17, 1774. "It was voted to communie with Dea. Benj. Kimball not to officiate any longer as a deacon on accound of an irregularity in his accounts as guardian of Enoch Heath." (*Church records.*)

His gravestone and that of his wife are in the village cemetery not far from the street, near the gate, and bear the inscriptions: "Dea. Benjamin Kimball, died June 22, 1799, aged 77." "Mary, wife of Dea. Benjamin Kimball, died March 10, 1816, aged 84."

No. 22.

Mary Eaton b. in Salisbury, Mass., a daughter of John and Esther (Johnson) Eaton of Salisbury. Married Dea. Benjamin Kimball (No. 21) Dec. 29, 1742. She was adm. a member of the church June 3d, 1752, by letter from the North Parish church. She d. in Hampstead, August 29, 1757, and was the mother of nine children, b. in Hampstead:—

I. Joseph, mar., first, Abiah Muzzey; second, Hannah Gile; third, Dolly Squires, whose oldest child was James (No. 162).
II. Mary, mar. Obedeum Hall (see sketches of Covenant members).
III. Benjamin, d. young.
IV. Caleb, mar. Sarah Sawyer.
V. Andrew; he was a Revolutionary soldier, and in 1775 lived in Goffstown, and with others left Goffstown, and later went to New London, Conn. as a soldier, then to New York and Canada and was discharged at Morristown, N. J. He took part in the battles of Princeton and Trenton, N. J. He was a blacksmith by trade, and lived in Rutland, Ohio, where he received a pension in 1820.
VI. Benjamin, d. young.
VII. Nicholas, d. young.
VIII. Sarah, mar. Stephen Jeffers.
IX. Moses, mar. Hannah ——; lived in Vasselboro', Me.

No. 23.

Stephen Johnson, Jr., b. in Haverhill, Mass., was a son of Stephen and Sarah (Whittaker) Johnson of Haverhill (see No. 11). He married Susanna Lovekin (No. 24). He was adm. from the church at the North Parish by letter June 3d, 1752. He removed to Londonderry about 1768 and mar. 2d, Ruth Johnson, by whom he had two children, b. in Londonderry.

No. 24.

Susanna Lovekin, b. in Haverhill, Mass., Feb. 8, 1739, a daughter of Jonathan and Ruth (Johnson) Lovekin of Haverhill, married Stephen Johnson Jr. (No. 23). She was adm. as member of the church from the North Parish church, June 3d, 1752. She died in Hampstead, 1862. She was a mother of nine children, two pairs of twins, all b. in Hampstead. (p. 416 vol. 1).

No. 25.

Moses Guile, b. Feb. 15, 1720, in Haverhill, Mass., a son of Joseph and Mary (Heath) Gile of Haverhill. Married Eunice Johnson (No. 26) and was received from the Haverhill church (1st) June 3d, 1752. He mar. 2d, Mary Heath, who d. 1793, aged 67 years. He was farmer in town and in 1755 moved to Weare, and in 1770 he sold his farm there of 150 acres and went to Chester, Vt., where he was recorded a freeman in 1779. In 1775 he was chosen a standing committee to ascertain the state of the Colonies and keep the county informed of the doings of the friends of liberty in the different colonies, and took an active part in the events which preceded the Revolution. He owned a farm of rich bottom land in Williams River. He died 1786, and was called the richest man in Chester, his estate being given as £160. He had nine children by 2d wife, prominent in Vt.

Holmes in his annals in 1720 states that tea began to be used in New England, and probably was soon after used in Haverhill, and it has been said that the father of Moses Guile, had a pound of tea sent to him as a present from Boston. His good wife had never tasted of it, and was not acquainted with the way to make it, but thought it must be cooked in some way, so partly filling her large dinner pot with water she hung it over the fire, and put into it the whole pound of tea. To make it more luscious, as she thought, she put in a good piece of beef, for to make "a real dish of tea." After boiling until the meat was tender she removed the tea from the fire, and, as the old man remarked "the liquor was so despot strong they could not drink it, besides it had made a complete jelly of the meat."

No. 26.

Eunice Johnson, b. in Haverhill, Mass., Jan. 19, 1728, a daughter of Stephen and Ruth (Eaton) Johnson of Haverhill (No. 11). She married Moses Guile, Nov. 11, 1741,

(No. 25) and was admitted to the church, from the North Parish Church, June 3d, 1752. She had two children b. in Hampstead, Hannah and Ebenezer (p. 411, vol. 1), and Moses, b. in Haverhill, Feb. 21, 1742. She died in Hampstead, 1756.

No. 27.

Jonathan Hutchens, b. in Haverhill, July 26, 1715, a son of John and Sarah (Page) Hutchens of Haverhill. He married, 1st, Mary Emery (No. 28), and was admitted to the church from the 1st parish church June 3d, 1752. He settled a tract of land east of where Edw. F. Noyes resides and was an uncle of Capt. Hezekiah Hutchens. He was prominent in town and church affairs. He married, 2d, Sarah Watts, and had one child Sarah, bapt. Nov. 1754.

No. 28.

Mary Emery, b. in Haverhill, Mass., 1732, a daughter of James and Ruth (Watson) Emery, of Haverhill. She married Jonathan Hutchens (No. 27), May 29, 1750, in Haverhill and had one child Mary, bapt. Aug., 1752 and died in August, 1752, of childbirth, aged 22 years, and was buried in the village cemetery, where a stone marks her grave.

No. 29.

Mehitable Emerson, b. in Haverhill, Mass., a daughter of Stephen and Elizabeth (Dustin) Emerson, of Haverhill. Married 1st, Peter Griffing, of Haverhill, Feb. 21, 1722. She had one child, Theolopolis, b. Jan. 30, 1723, in Haverhill. After Mr. Griffing's death she married, 2d, Moses Copp, July 17, 1732, and removed to Hampstead, nearly opposite the home of Joshua F. Noyes; some of the family lived at what is now known as Copp's Corner, and others near the east shore of the Wash pond. She was called "Grandmother" for many years. A daughter Elizabeth, b.

in Hampstead, April 1, 1788, mar. John Ingalls, of Hampstead, "June 1, 1770, notified Joshua Copp, Eben Copp and John Ingalls of Hampstead to take care of their grandmother Copp, she being not able to take care of herself." "Old mother Copp was put to board to Bartholmew Heath's at the town's expense July 12, 1770." (Plaistow town record). She was admitted a member of the church June 3d, 1752, from the First church of Haverhill.

No. 30.

Sarah Heath, b. in Haverhill, Mass., a daughter of John and Frances (Hutchens) Heath, of Haverhill. Was admitted a member of the church, June 3d, 1752. Married and went to Dunbarton.

No. 31.

Martha Heath, b. March 21, 1702, in Haverhill, Mass., a daughter of Joseph and Hannah (Bradley) Heath, of Haverhill. Married Daniel Roberts, who died at Lake George while serving in the Indian war, Sept., 1755. She was admitted to the church at its organization June 3d, 1752. She had children (see vol. 1, p. 425). She died in Hampstead, Aug. 3, 1757 and was buried in the village cemetery.

No. 32.

Capt. George Little, b. in Newbury, Mass., Sept. 9, 1718, a son of George and Edna (Hale) Little. His parents moved from Newbury to Atkinson (then Plaistow) to a tract of land in the northwest part of the town, now the homestead of Mr. Albert Little in Atkinson. The old homestead having descended from the parents (George and Edna Little) to the son Thomas, who mar. Mary Bond of Haverhill, Mass., then to their son Thomas, who mar. Abigail Kent, of Newbury, Vt., from them to their son Jesse, who mar. Louisa Read, of Litchfield, and to their son Albert Little, who occu-

pies the farm. The old house stood near the brook north of
the present house.

Capt. George Little, the subject of this sketch, lived near
the Island pond, but owned much land near the center of the
town. He gave the land where the old meeting house was
built, "in consideration of his always having a pew at the
right hand of the fore-door of the house," (see deed Vol. 1,
p. 25). He was a prominent citizen, a farmer, and captain
of the militia, he also held a commission under the king as
justice of the peace and was styled "gentleman" in the
deeds. He with his brother Joseph in 1746, were appointed
by Gov. Wentworth to make a plan of "Timberlane" now
Hampstead. He married 1st, Mary Kimball, July 30, 1734,
who died July 20, 1743 ; they had children.

I.   Benjamin, b. March 18, 1738, mar. Hepsebiah, daughter of
     Samuel and Elizabeth (Searl) Poor, of Hampstead. They had
     five children, Joshua and Levi, who d. young; Ezekial, who
     mar. Mehitable Emery, in 1801; he was a graduate of Harvard
     College, in 1784 and for many years a successful teacher in
     the public schools of Boston, and among his pupils was
     Edward Everett Hale, and many others of note; he was an
     author of an arithmetic called "Usher" published in Exeter
     in 1799. The later part of his life he resided in Atkinson.
     Their daughter Ann Poor, mar. Rev. Jesse Page of Atkin-
     son, parents of Miss Mary Ann Page of that town; Moses, d.
     young, and Mary, who mar. Nathaniel Merrill of Atkinson.
     Benj. Little lived first in West Haverhill, where he had a
     grist mill, and engaged in trade, he then moved to Hampstead
     near the site of our high school building, but later moved to
     Bradford, Vt., where he died in 1809.
II. George, b. Dec. 27, 1739, who d. young.
III. Moses, b. Aug. 3, 1742, mar. Mary Stevens, in 1761. He lived in
     Hampstead, where their first three children were born and
     afterwards in Goffstown and New Boston (see list "owned
     the Covenant.")

Capt. Little m. 2d, Elizabeth Taylor, who had children.

IV. Joseph Taylor, b. Jan. 1, 1745, who d. young.
V.   Mary, b. April 18, 1746, d. young.

VI.   Taylor, b. June 25, 1748, mar. in Hampstead, Elizabeth Morse
       in 1874. He was a farmer, and lived in New Boston, and
       afterwards in Windham and Chester, where he died, Feb. 6,
       1817. They had four children,—Jane, who mar. John Mel-
       vin of Weare; Hepsebiah, who mar. Nathaniel Southwick,—
       Hannah, who mar. Isaac Dinsmoor of Windham, and Anna,
       who mar. Abram Melvin of Weare.

Elizabeth (Taylor) Little died April 7, 1752, and Capt.
George married 8d, Sarah Hale, March 1, 1753, who died
Dec., 1758, and left a child.

VII.   Ebenezer, b. Dec. 20, 1753.

Capt. Little then married Elizabeth (Searl) Poor (No. 33),
and moved to New Boston in 1765, and was living there in
1778. He was a member of the church at its organization
June 8d, 1752, from the first church in Haverhill.

No. 33.

Elizabeth Searl, b. in Rowley, Mass., January 20, 1712, a
daughter of John Searl, of Rowley. She married Samuel
Poor, of Rowley, and had five children b. in Rowley.

I.   Elizabeth, who d. young
II.   Hepsebiah, mar. Benjamin Little (see children of No. 32).
III.   Joseph, a deacon of the church at Byfield, Mass., mar. Margeret
       Bailey.
IV.   Sarah, mar. Joshua Copp of Hampstead.
V.   Eliphalet, mar. Elizabeth Little, both of Hampstead.

Her husband died of "acute fever," Sept. 21, 1748, and
she then married Capt. George Little (No. 32) as his fourth
wife, March 24, 1754 and had one child.

I.   Samuel, b. April 1, 1755, who d. in 1750.

She was a member of the church in Hampstead in 1754.
She died May 28, 1779, in New Boston.

No. 84.

Jacob Bailey, b. in Newbury, Mass., was a son of Joshua and Sarah (Coffin) Bailey, of Newbury. He married Prudence, daughter of Ephraim and Prudence (Stickney) Noyes, of Newbury (No. 83). They removed to Hampstead soon after marriage and resided on his farm of 150 acres, which included the present homesteads of Edward F. Noyes, B. F. Rowe and part of the John Mills' farm. He was influential towards the incorporation of Hampstead and the parish in 1746. He raised a company of soldiers, of which he was the capt., in the French war in 1756. He was at the capture of Fort William Henry and ran the gauntlet of that dreadful massacre that occurred by the violation of the plighted faith of the enemy, in August, 1757, and was one of those who escaped to Fort Edward. He was made a colonel by General Amherst and was with him at the taking of Fort Ticonderoga and Crown Point, in 1759. In 1767 he obtained a charter of a township in "Coos County," and removed to Haverhill, N. H., in 1764. He was there appointed by New York as brig. gen., and soon after, by General Washington, commissionary general of the Northern department, which involved great responsibilities and subjected him to dangers, difficulties and sacrifices. A reward of 500 guineas was offered for his capture, dead or alive, and it required vigilance to escape the scouts sent from Canada to take him. He made a treaty with St. Francis tribe of Indians, and was looked up to by them as a father, and by the friendly Indians. By means of spies he acquired important intelligence respecting the movments of the British, and rendered great service with his purse, pen and person before and at the time of the capture of Burgoyne. Several of his sons served with him against the British. He sacrificed a large estate in the service of his country, o which he never received any compensation. He was judge of probate in Newbury district, in 1778; chief justice of

Orange county court from 1781 to 1791, with the exception
of years 1788 and 1784. He was termed the "father" of
Newbury, Vt., for he was the original grantee, and the prime
mover in all of its enterprises concerning its settlement. He
died in Newbury, March 1, 1810. He was admitted a member of the church June 8d, 1752, and dismissed to Newbury, Vt. in 1764.

No. 85.

Lieut. Peter Morse, b. in Newbury, Mass., October 3, 1701,
a son of William and Sarah (Merrill) Morse, of Newbury,
Married Tamosine Hale (No. 86) and moved to Hampstead,
(see Vol. 1, p. 379). He was a member of the church at its
organization, June 8d, 1752, and died in town, buried in the
old burial ground at East Hampstead. He was early prominent in town and church affairs, and had been called "a
man whose integrity none can question."

No. 86.

Tamosine Hale, b. in Amesbury, Mass., a daughter of Henry
and Sarah (Kelley) Hale, of Amesbury. She married Lieut.
Peter Morse (No. 85), Sept. 30, 1726, adm. to the church
from Amesbury at the organization June 3, 1752. She died
in Hampstead and was buried in the old burial ground at
East Hampstead. She had children (see pp. 879-380,
Vol. 1). Her son Peter, b. July 7, 1739 (the first child said
to be *recorded* on the town records), and mar. Anna Currier;
had children, the first three b. in Hampstead.

I.   Sarah, b. Aug. 6, 1759; mar. Daniel Stickney, and had six chil-
       dren, of whom Wm. W. Stickney, U. S. District Attorney for
       the N. H. district, at Exeter, was a son.
II.   Lois, b. Dec. 17, 1760.
III.   Anna, b. Apr. 17, 1762.
IV.   Hannah, b. Sept. 17, 1764.
V.   Mary, b. May, 1769; d. young.
VI.   James, b. in Hampstead, Sept. 26, 1768.

VII.   Caleb, b. April 8, 1770.
VIII. Nathan, b. July 30, 1772.
IX.   Abigail, b. April 4, 1774.   •
X.   Stephen, b. Feb. 26, 1776; lived in Londonderry.
XI.   Joseph, b. 1778; lived in Shepscott, Me.
XII.   Peter, b. about 1785; mar. Abigail Webster, settled in West
       Haverhill, Mass.

No. 87.

Benjamin Emerson, b. in Haverhill, Mass., May 21, 1716,
a son of Benjamin and Sarah (Philbrick) Emerson of Haverhill. He married Hannah Watts (No. 88). They resided
south of the "Old Brickett place," and had a mill at
"Beaver dam" there. (See Vol. 1, p. 867.) The ancestor
of the Emerson family in Hampstead, and was prominent in
town and church affairs, holding public offices with honor.
He was admitted to the church June 3d, 1752, and to full
fellowship Aug. 6, 1752. "A descendant of the daughter
Abigail, who mar. Otho Stevens, Jr., says there is a tradition
in the family that "Hampstead received its name partly by a
suggestion to Gov. Wentworth from Benjamin Emerson that
it be so named in remembrance of the birthplace of his
grandfather Robert Emerson of England." (Mrs. William
Clark of Littleton, Mass.)

No. 88.

Hannah Watts, b. in Haverhill, Mass., July 23, 1718, a
daughter of Samuel and Abigail (Dustin) Watts of Haverhill. Her parents were in Hampstead in the early years of
the town and raised a company for the French war. She
married Benjamin Emerson, and was adm. to the church
June 3d, 1752, and to full fellowship Aug. 6, 1752. She
was the mother of thirteen children. (See pp. 867, 410,
Vol. 1.)

No. 89.

Ruth Heath, b. in Haverhill, Mass., a daughter of Joseph

and Hannah (Bradley) Heath of Haverhill; mar. Joseph
Stevens. She was adm. to the church June 3d, 1752. She
had three children, b. in Hampstead—Isaac, Ezekiel, and
Abigail.

No. 40.

Mehitable Heath, b. in Haverhill, Mass., May 20, 1710, a
daughter of Joseph and Hannah (Bradley) Heath of Haverhill (a sister to No. 39). She married Samuel Worthen, a
son of Samuel and Deliverance (Heath) Worthen of Haverhill. They lived on "Kent's Farm," and later moved to
Dunbarton, and probably farther north. She was adm. to
the church at its organization, June 8, 1752. She had children—Mehitable, Samuel, Oliver, Amos and Mary.

No. 41.

Elizabeth Page, b. in Haverhill, Mass., Sept. 14, 1769, a
daughter of Cornelius and Martha (Gould) Page of Haverhill. She married Thomas Johnson of Haverhill, May 1,
1799, and moved to the north part of Haverhill soon after
the Indian troubles ceased, to near the North Parish meeting
house, where they were original members in 1730. Her
husband was a son of William Johnson of Charlestown,
Mass., the emigrant of that branch of the Johnson family.
She was a member of this church at its organization, June
3d, 1752, and died at the home of her son, John Johnson,
who mar. Sarah Haynes nine days after the church was con-
stituted, June 12, 1752. She had other children, one of
whom was Cornelius, of Concord, who was a colonel in the
Revolutionary war.

No. 42.

Hannah Moulton, b. in Hampton, June 9, 1725, a daughter of Simon and Hannah (Perkins) Moulton of Hampton;
mar. Ebenezer Kezer of Hampstead, son of John and Judith

Heath) Kezer, of the "Handle." Her father was in the siege of Louisburg. Her husband lived on the homestead sold to William George, in 1756, at West Hampstead, the homestead of the late Isaac Wm. George (No. 471). She was adm. to the church June 3d, 1752, and died in town; had one child, b. in town, Hannah, b. Aug. 28, 1751. (See pp. 361, 362, Vol. 1.)

No. 43.

Samuel Hadley, b. in Amesbury, Mass., May 5, 1707, a son of Samuel and Dorothy (Colby) Hadley of Amesbury. He married Judith Flanders (No. 44), and was adm. to the church June 3d, 1752, by letter from the North Parish Church. His father, Samuel Hadley, was said to have been the first person buried in the village cemetery, having been drowned in the Island pond.

No. 44.

Judith Flanders, b. in South Hampton, Oct. 14, 1709, a daughter of Jonathan and Judith (Merrill) Flanders of South Hampton. She married Samuel Hadley (No. 43), and was adm. by letter from the North Parish Congregational Church, Haverhill, Mass., June 3, 1752.

No. 45.

Edmund Sawyer, b. in Newbury, Mass., Nov. 6, 1714, a son of Samuel and Abigail (Goodridge) Sawyer of Newbury (1, William). His father d. in 1728, and his mother in 1722, so that he was left an orphan at an early age. He was m. to Sarah Rowell (No. 46), by the Rev. Paine Wingate, at the Second Parish of Amesbury, Jan. 1, 1735-6. He joined the church (Second, of Amesbury), June 13, 1736, and, with his wife, was dis. to unite with the church in Hampstead, May 31, 1752. They resided a few years in Amesbury, and moved to Hampstead, to the farm now occupied by Everett

Moulton. He was a selectman of Hampstead in 1758.
He resided in the last part of his life in Sutton, N.H.,
on what is now known as "Eaton Grange," an account of
which is found in the History of Sutton, Vol. 2. In this
book we read: "Edmund Sawyer, a man of devout piety,
passed his last days at the home of his daughter, Mrs. Sarah
Kimball, where he d. Feb. 18, 1807."

No. 46.

Sarah Rowell, b. in Salisbury, Mass., Oct. 4, 1719, said to
be a daughter of Job and Bethiah (Brown) Rowell of Salisbury. Still another record says she was a daughter of
Philip and Sarah (Davis) Rowell of Amesbury, b. Jan. 20,
1704. A Sarah Rowell was adm. to the church in Amesbury by confession of faith, Jan. 14, 1728. The birth and
parentage of Sarah (Rowell) Sawyer is open to question. She
mar. Edmund Sawyer (No. 45), Jan. 1, 1786. She was adm.
to the church in Hampstead, from the Second Church in
Amesbury, June 8, 1752. They had children, b. in Amesbury, Mass.

I.   Joseph (No. 117), m. Judith Kelly (No. 118).
II.   Jacob, b. Oct. 4, 1788; settled in Hampstead.
III. Enoch, b. Dec. 27, 1741; m. Sarah Little. He was a farmer in
      Hampstead until about 1774, when he moved to Goffstown,
      N. H., and in 1794 to Antrim, where he d. in 1817. His wife
      d. in 1829. It is said that nearly all of their twelve children
      and most of their grand-children have been church members.
      Their children were:
        1. Mary, b. March 15, 1766; d. young.
        2. Elizabeth, b. June 29, 1767; m. Jonathan Marsh of
           Hudson.
        3. Samuel, b. July 11, 1771; m. first, Susannah Reed of
           Litchfield; second, Eleanor Orr of Bedford; and he
           had eleven children.
        4. Abigail Peabody, b. March 13, 1774; m. Joshua Hay-
           wood of Alexandria; no children.
        5. Enoch, b. Feb. 21, 1777; m. Lucy Simonds; resided in
           Antrim; six children.

6. Tristram, b. Dec. 31, 1780; m. Mary Ann Templeton of Hillsboro, and had twelve children.

7. Edmund, b. Sept. 17, 1782; m. Jane Taggard of Hillsboro, and left numerous descendants in Hillsboro.

8. Sally, b. July 22, 1785; d., unmarried, 1860.

9. Lucinda, b. Aug. 9, 1788; m. Richard Chase of Hillsboro; no children.

IV. Sarah, b. Jan. 30, 1744; m. Dea. Caleb Kimball, and lived in Sutton, where she d. 1822, aged 77 years. The Kimball Genealogy and History of Sutton gives a record of ten children and families, from which we learn that Caleb Kimball was son of Benjamin and Mary (Hoyt) Kimball (Nos. 21, 22), and was one of the earliest selectmen of Sutton, and one of the heaviest taxpayers. He was one of the committee to erect a meeting house in 1784, and was associated with those who built the first saw mill at the foot of Jones' hill, on Lane Brook, in Sutton. Tradition says he spent a year in town camping in the forest, preparing his farm, before taking his family there. He lived two years in Hampstead after marriage, and eleven years in Goffstown. His wife was said to be "a woman of strong intellect and high purpose, and heartily seconded her husband in all his endeavors for advancement," and "no efforts were spared for their children." They kept tavern in what was first called "Kimball Hill," but now "Eaton Grange," soon after the public roads were built. Their home has been fitted up by the Eaton heirs for their summer residence.

No. 47.

Nathan Goodwin, b. in Amesbury, Mass., 1716, a son of Richard and Esther (Hadley) Goodwin of Amesbury. "Richard Goodwin and son Nathan were in Amesbury Peak, fourteen miles from South Hampton, eight miles from Kingston, and lived near each other, in 1748." Richard d. in Hampstead, March, 1768, aged 84, called "old Mr. Goodwin" on the records. He mar., first, Rhoda Colby (No. 48); second, Mary Smith (No. 126). He was received a member of the church, by letter from North Parish church, June 3, 1752. He resided where Mr. Charles Shannon now has his summer home at East Hampstead.

No. 48.

Rhoda Colby, b. April 16, 1719, in Amesbury, a daughter
of Timothy and Hannah (Heath) Colby of Amesbury ; mar.
Nathan Goodwin (No. 47), and was admitted a member from
the North Parish Church June 3d, 1752. She died Nov. 29,
1765. She was the mother of seven children (see p. 412,
Vol. 1). She was buried in the village cemetery.

No. 49.

Amos Clark, b. in Haverhill, Mass., Jan. 12, 1719, a son
of Jonathan and Priscilla (Whittaker) Clark of Haverhill.
He removed to Hampstead in 1739, and mar. Sarah Kelly
(No. 50), to the farm now owned by his great-granddaugh-
ters, Mary and Sarah A. Clark, where he died. A brother
John mar. Susanna Sinclair, also resided in Hampstead, and
were parents of eight children, b. here (see p. 407, Vol. 1).
Amos Clark was received a member of the church from the
North Parish Church at the organization, June 3d, 1752;
buried in Hampstead, June 4, 1783.

No. 50.

Sarah Kelly, b. in West Newbury, Mass., Oct. 6, 1718; a
daughter of John and Elizabeth (Emery) Kelly of West
Newbury. Her parents resided on the homestead of their
father in West Newbury at the time of the ordination of
Rev. Mr. Tufts, June 30, 1714, and at that time were mem-
bers of the Second Church of Newbury now West New-
bury), and were members in full communion, as they were
fourteen years later. She mar. Amos Clark (No. 49), and
was the mother of eleven children (p. 407, Vol. 1).
Of these Amos settled at the homestead and mar. Hannah
Stevens; died Feb. 18, 1835, aged 84 years. Their son
John mar. Mary Harriman, and their son John H. mar. Sarah
A. Noyes, who were the parents of the Misses Clark of East
Hampstead (p. 374, Vol. 1). Another son, Moses, settled in

Warner, N. H., and Jonathan settled in Alexandria, N. H.
Sarah married, after the death of Mr. Clark, Mr. —— Hadley. She was adm. to the church at its organization, June
3d, 1752, as from the North Parish Church.

No. 51.

John Muzzey, b. in Amesbury, Mass., May 5, 1714, a son
of John and Hannah (Diamond) Muzzey of Salisbury, Mass.
He married Abiah Hunkins (No. 109). He was admitted to
the church June 3d, 1752, from the North Parish Church of
Haverhill. They lived at first in Plaistow, now Atkinson,
on the farm opposite the home of Frank W. Greenough, on
the " East road," and later moved to the homestead where
Giles F. Marble now resides. He was prominent in town
and church affairs (see Vol. 1). He died June 15, 1787,
and was buried in the village cemetery.

No. 52.

John Hunkins, b. in Haverhill, Mass., Dec. 25, 1708, a son
of Robert and Abiah (Page) Hunkins of Haverhill. He m.
Sarah Gile, a daughter of Ephraim and Martha (Bradley)
Gile of Haverhill, and had five children: Robert, b. 1745
(p. 391, Vol. 1); John, b. May 5, 1747; Abiah, b. Nov. 20,
1751; and two that d. young. He was a member of the
church June 3d, 1752, and died in Hampstead, when the
children were very young. His wife died about the same
time.

No. 53.

Jerusha Stevens, b. in Haverhill, Mass., Feb. 18, 1789, a
daughter of Samuel and Jerusha (Dow) Stevens of Haverhill. She was adm. a member of the church June 3, 1752,
and dismissed " by vote of ye church, Oct. 14, 1763, upon
her request of being united by the church of and at Pembroke." She married —— Dorien, and had several children.

No. 54.

Hannah Kelly, b. in Amesbury, Mass., Oct. 12, 1726, a daughter of Richard and Hannah (Bartlett) Kelly of Birch Meadow. She married Bartholomew Heath of Hampstead, a soldier in the French and Indian war. She was a member of the church at its organization, June 3d, 1752, and died in Hampstead in 1810. She was the mother of twelve children (p. 365, Vol. 1). The eighth, Anne, b. in Hampstead, June 29, 1762, married Joseph Colby, Esq., of Amesbury, and settled in New London, and were the parents of Anthony Colby, who was Governor of New Hampshire.

No. 55.

John Bond, b. in Haverhill, Mass., Jan. 14, 1718, a son of John and —— (Hall) Bond of Haverhill. His father was drowned May 21, 1721, in the Merrimac river. He was a doctor in Hampstead for many years, and mention is made on the town records of his caring for the small pox patients in the Sinclear family and of the pest house on the island in 1778. He settled in Kingston, in that part now Sandown, and was one of the petitioners for a separate township for Sandown. Later he built a house in Hampstead, near the homestead of the late Ezekiel Currier. He was one of the original members of the church, June 3d, 1752, from the church at Haverhill. He married Judith Dow (No. 56), and died in Hampstead, and was buried in the West Hampstead cemetery.

From the town records, 1794: " Voted, that the request of Dr. John Bond, for inoculating for small pox for the term of one year, excluding July and August, at the Sinclear house, be granted, he taking the Sinclear Farm for himself, all but the house which is kept as a hospital for the use of ye town in case of need, and for paying the whole of the expense for purchasing said farm all charges, on account of the small pox."

Tradition says this farm was near the Angly pond.

No. 56.

Judith Dow, b. in Haverhill, Mass., Aug. 11, 1721, a daughter of John and Sarah (Browne) Dow of Haverhill. She married John Bond (No. 55), and was the mother of six children, b. in Hampstead (p. 405, Vol. 1). Of these John, Jr., mar. Mary Moulton, and had seven children. Joseph m. Hannah Brown, and lived in Londonderry, where three children were born. Jona. mar. Abigail Rogers and had two children, Judith and Amos, born in Hampstead, where Ezekiel Currier lately resided, and did a large business at one time in getting out the material for braiding poplar stuff for hats. A son, Charles Milton, b. 1798 to '99. She was a member of the church June 3d, 1752, from the First Church of Haverhill. She died in Hampstead, and was buried in the West Hampstead cemetery.

No. 57.

Moses Hale, b. in Newbury, Mass., bapt. Oct. 4, 1708, a son of Thomas and Sarah (Northend) Hale of Newbury, grandson of Thomas and Mary (Hutchinson), and great-grandson of Thomas and Tamosine Hale, the emigrants to America in 1635. He married Elizabeth Wheeler (No. 58). They resided first in Plaistow, now Atkinson, where John B. Mason resides, and there resided when he was admitted to the Hampstead church, June 3, 1752. Later he removed to Hampstead, near where Benj. W. Clark resides.

It is related that " when he left his home in Newburyport his mother felt that it was so far a journey to Plaistow that she would never see him again, and mournfully said, " He has gone to Timberlane to live, and there he will lay his bones."

He was bapt. in Newbury, and removed to Rowley, Mass., in 1729, then to Plaistow, or Hampstead, about 1742, and thence to Rindge, 1760 ; m., in Rowley, by his father, Justice Thomas Hale, Dec. 4, 1727. He was treasurer of Hampstead in 1758, and owned pew No. 7 in the meeting-house. He was a farmer, and in Rindge a merchant. His gravestone in Rindge bears the inscription, " Memento mon." Then a head of a cherubim. " Here lies buried ye body of Mr. Moses Hale; he died June ye 19, 1762, in ye 59 year of his age."

No. 58.

Elizabeth Wheeler, b. in Newbury, Mass., 1706, a daughter of Jethro and Hannah (French) Wheeler of Rowley, Mass. She married Moses Hale, Dec. 4, 1727 (No. 57). She was admitted to the church June 8, 1752, and d. in Rindge, Jan. 9, 1780. They had children, b. in Rowley, except the youngest, b. in Hampstead.

I.   Nathan, b. Jan. 22, 1730; d. young.
II.   Moses, m. Abigail Emerson. (See list "Owned the Covenant.")
III. Enoch, b. Nov. 28, 1733; m. Abigail Stanley. They removed to Jaffrey, and later to Rindge, where he was an extensive land owner and prominent in the town, being selectman many years; member of the N. H. Assembly in 1776 and 1778, and delegate to the Provincial Congress in 1775, high sheriff of Chesboro' 1778 to 1783. He was a colonel of the N. H. militia during the Revolutionary war. He also served in the old French war from Hampstead. He built the first bridge across the river at Bellows Falls, Vt., "and was renowned for his strong intellect." He d. April 9, 1813.
IV.   Elizabeth, b. 1736; m. Jacob Gould; they had nine children.
V.   Eunice, b. July, 1739; m. James Philbrick of Hampstead; nine children.
VI.   Lucy, b. 1741; m. Henry Coffen; six children.
VII. Nathan, b. Sept. 20, 1743, in Hampstead; m. Abigail Grout; seven children.

No. 59.

Nathan Hale, b. in Hampstead, m. Abigail, daughter of Col. John and Joanna (Boynton) Grout, of Lunenburg, Mass. He removed to Rindge with his father before 1760. He was chosen the first constable of Rindge. He was moderator in

1773, '74, '75. As early as 1774 he was captain of a company of "minute-men," and led his company to Lexington on the alarm, April 19, 1775. Four days after he was commissioned major in Col. James Read's company. He was at the battle of Bunker Hill with his regiment. Nov. 8, 1776, he was commissioned lieutenant-colonel, and was appointed colonel of the 2d N. H. regiment, and filled up with three-years' men. He served under Washington in New York, in 1776-7, and under St. Clair, at Ticonderoga, until the evacuation. He was taken prisoner at Hubbardston, July 7, 1777, and discharged on parole, not to serve again, but to return to the enemy's lines if not exchanged in two years. He returned to the enemy in two years, and died a prisoner in the hands of the British forces, at New Utrecht, N. Y., Sept. 23, 1780.

A soldier in his regiment wrote: "Nathan Hale was as brave a man as ever trod shoe leather," and was "always the finest looking man I ever set eyes on."

His widow drew $600 per year from the government as a pension as widow of a colonel. They had children:—

I.   Charlotte, m. Abraham Lowe.
II.   Thomas, m. Hannah Goldsmith.
III.   Nathan, m., first, Eunice Raymond; second, Ruth Tyler; third, Susan C. Black
IV.   A son; d. young.
V.   Eliphalet; m. Abigail Waters.
VI.   Polly; d. young.
VII.   Harry; m. Phebe Adams; second, Lucinda Eddy.

No. 59.

James Mills, b. in 1684, was probably a grandson of Thomas and Mary (Wadleigh) Mills, of Scarboro, Maine, and may be among the people who about 1702 were driven from those northern towns southward "into New Hampshire" by the Indians, who were so treacherously inclined. He early came to Haverhill, Mass., and in 1735 bought a tract of land of Robert Ford, sen. and settled near "Copp's Corner," with his wife Jane —— (No. 60) and a family of children. He was admitted a member of the church, June 3d, 1752. He died in Hampstead, and was buried in the village cemetery.

No. 60.

Jane —— b. 1689, married James Mills (No. 59), and was admitted a member of the church, June 8, 1752. She had children, probably not recorded in the order of birth.

I.   Reuben, b. in 1731, d. in Hampstead, aged 85 years, Dec. 14, 1846.
II.   John, mar. Elizabeth Emerson (see No. 176).
III.   Caleb.
IV.   William.
V.   Sarah.
VI.   Elizabeth, b. 1729 and d. 1757.
VII.   James, m. Jane Fulton.
VIII.   Thomas, b. 1720, who mar. Elizabeth Hogg (or Hoog) (see Appendix), a daughter of John Hogg, of Hampstead. Sept. 14, 1752. They were one of the three first settlers of Dunbarton. Their children, all b. in Dunbarton, were:—
        1. Sarah, b. Feb. 11, 1755 (said to have been the first child born in Dunbarton).
        2. John, b. Jan. 7, 1756, was at the battle of Bunker Hill.
        3. Agnes, b. Jan. 27, 1758.
        4. Thomas, b. Jan. 7, 1761 (see 532).
        5. Caleb, b. June 9, 1765.
        6. Elizabeth, b. Sept. 25, 1767.
        7. Peter, b. Sept. 25, 1769.
        8. James, b. Aug. 25, 1771.
        9. Samuel, b. Dec. 5, 1773, mar. at Medford, Mass., Aug. 23, 1796, Sally Morse, and had a son William, b. May 2, 1812, who mar. Sept. 4, 1831, Laura A. Fisk, and were the parents of William Stowell Mills, LL. B. of Brooklyn, New York, author of "Foundations of Genealogy," "The story of the Western Reserve of Connecticut," "Leaves from Genealogical trees," etc. to whom the writer is indebted for much of the sketch of Mills and Hogg families.

Jane Mills, the mother, d. in Hampstead, Nov. 2, 1762, aged 78, and was buried in the village cemetery.

No. 61.

James Graves, probably b. in Hampton, May 2, 1707, a son of William and Margeret Graves, of Hampton. He married in Haverhill, Mass., Sarah Roberts (No. 62). He was admitted to the church, June 8d, 1752, from the first church of Haverhill and d. " before 1764." He was one of the earliest petitioners for the town of Sandown, and probably lived in town, but near the Angly Pond, in 1756. He was called " of Kingston," in town and church affairs, but of that part set off as Sandown.

No. 62.

Sarah Roberts, b. in Haverhill, Mass., May 7, 1825, a daughter of Ephraim and Hannah (Smith) Roberts of Haverhill. She married James Graves (No. 64), Sept. 1, 1741, in Haverhill. She was admitted to the church, June 8d, 1752. " Voted at church meeting after lecture March 25, 1764, that Sarah Graves be transferred at her request to the church at South Hampton." They had children, bapt. in South Hampton :—

I.   Lucy, b. Aug. 22, 1762.
II.   Molly, b. Oct. 16, 1764.

No. 63.

Ensign Otho Stevens, b. in Gloucester, Mass. (probably) 1702, a son of John and Mary, a daughter of Aquilla Chase. John Stevens took the oath of allegiance in 1669, also in 1678, aged 70 years, and lived in Newbury, Haverhill, Gloucester, and perhaps other towns in Massachusetts. John and Mary Stevens had ten children and perhaps others, three or four born in Haverhill. In his will, dated 1715, he mentions children · by name and age,

" John, aged 19 years, Samuel, aged 16 years, and Otho, aged 18." Otho, mar. first, Abigail Kent (No. 67), and second, mar. Mary ——— (see "Covenant" No. 2). He was a farmer and constable in Hampstead and lived on the eastern shore of the pond. He was admitted to the church June 3d, 1 752. He died in Hampstead, May 4, 1771, aged 69 years. (See Stevens in Appendix).

No. 64.

Abigail Kent, b. July 9, 1797, in Gloucester, Mass., a daughter of Josiah and Mary (Lufkin) Kent, of Gloucester. It is said that she was one-fourth Indian blood. She mar. Otho Stevens, Mar. 21, 1728 (No. 66), and was admitted to the church June 3d, 1752, and d. in Hampstead. She was the mother of children :—

I.   Samuel, b. 1724, mar. Susanna Griffin, and lived in Hampstead, nearly opposite George Braggs' house.
II.   Levi, m. Lydia Hills (see No. 67).
III.   Otho, b. 1726, mar. Abigail Emerson (see No. 748 "Covenant").
IV.   Archelus, b. 1729, mar. Hannah Emerson (see No. 17-18).
V.   Abigail, b. 1731.
VI.   Simeon, b. 1736, mar. Sarah Hadley, in Hampstead, and lived here awhile.
VII.   Josiah.
VIII. Daniel, b. 1742, m. Elizabeth Bryant (see No. 407); second, Hannah Hills (see No. 67).
IX.   Susan.

Archelus and Josiah settled later in Enfield, and d. there. Daniel settled in Haverhill. Simeon, settled in Newbury, Vt., and d. there July 6, 1788, aged 52 years. He mar. first, Sarah Hadley, who d. in Newbury in 1799, and second, he mar. widow Susanah Shepherd, a daughter of Dea. Moses Chamberlain, who after Mr. Stevens' death, mar. James Corliss of Greenboro, Vt., and lived to be over 100 years old. Simeon was one of the first settlers in Newbury, and in the spring of 1762 was a first lieutenant in the first company

of minute men of Newbury, and captain in a company of
Col. Bebell's regiment, from April, 1778 to Nov. 30, 1779,
and also served on several alarms. On his gravestone his
name is spelled Stephens, and he is said to have written it
in that way. He had nine children, 1, Abigail, who d. unm.
2, Otho, mar. widow Sarah Bailey, who was b. in Newbury,
Mass., a daughter of John G. and Abigail Bailey. She mar.
first, James, son of Gen. Jacob and Prudence (Noyes) Bailey
(Nos. 34-83). Her husband James Bailey, served in the
Revolutionary war and was taken prisoner by the party
which had failed to capture his father (see No. 34), in 1782.
He was going home from his father's saw-mill in the dusk of
the evening, barefooted and bareheaded, and was taken to
Canada in that condition, and kept until the close of the war.
Some benevolent people provided him with clothing and shoes.
He died April, 1784. His grandmother said " that he was
killed by accident," but " the oldest people in town " say
that he died " by foul play." His widow then mar. Otho
Stevens (son of Simeon), and lived in Waterford, Vt. 8,
Simeon, mar. Hannah Bailey. 4, Sarah. 5, Levi, mar. Susan
Shepherd, and d. in Greenboro, Vt. 6, Judith, mar. George
W. Stone. 7, Ruth, mar. Mr. Ingalls. 8, Samuel, mar. Au-
gusta Young. 9, Moses, d. young ; and two others, who d.
young. Most of these children lived in Waterford, Vt., and
surrounding towns.

No. 65.

Rebecca Tucker, b. in Kingston, May 4, 1729, a daughter
of Moses and Joanna (Dow) Tucker of Kingston, who were
mar. Sept. 30, 1727, and was in Kingston as one of the early
settlers in 1735, and prominent in the early settlement. She
was admitted to the church June 3, 1752.

No. 66.

Edmund Eastman, b. in Salisbury, Mass., May 21, 1715,

a son of Edmund and Susanna Singletary, who married, for
a second husband, Richard Bartlett, Dec. 8, 1720. She had
three children by Mr. Eastman, of whom Edmund was the
second child. He married widow Hannah Hills (No. 67),
and removed to Hampstead soon after, to the "old Eastman
residence" at West Hampstead, where he died, Oct. 21,
1804, and was buried in the hill cemetery at West Hampstead. He was admitted a member of the church June 3,
1752. (See p. 548, Vol. 1.)

No. 67.

Hannah Hunt, b. in Amesbury, Mass., July 7, 1716, a
daughter of John and Hannah (Clough) Hunt of Amesbury,
"a shoe man" there. She m., first, Joshua, son of Joshua
and Priscilla (Chase) Hills, who was b. in Newbury, Mass.,
March 2, 1718 ; m. Nov. 27, 1739. He d. in Newbury, Nov.
13, 1744. She m., second, Edmund Eastman (No. 66), Mar.
10, 1746. She had children, b. in Hampstead :—

I.   Jemima, mar. Parker Stevens (No. 22).
II.   Edmund, b. April 8, 1752; mar. Mary Davis, b. Mar. 21, 1752, in
       Hampstead, a daughter of Josiah and Dorothy (Colby) Davis,
       and who d. in Corinth, Vt., Aug. 30, 1836, aged 85 years. He
       was a farmer of Corinth, and had nine children born there.
III.   Joshua; mar. Sarah Tucker (Nos. 169 and 170).
IV.   Susannah, b. Oct. 18, 1763; d. unmarried.

Hannah d. in Hampstead, Aug. 21, 1806, and was buried
in the hill cemetery at West Hampstead. She was adm. to
the church June 3, 1752. The Eastman Genealogy and also
Vol. 1 records the fact that widow Hannah Hill was the
grandmother of Governor Hill of New Hampshire, which is
pronounced now (1902), by Guy S. Rix of Concord, author
of Eastman Genealogy, as an error, made by the compiler of
the family and so recorded in the New England Gen. Reg. of
1869. Hannah (Hunt) Hills had children, b. in Newbury :—

I. Lydia, b. Oct. 13, 1740; m. Levi Stevens, and had children b. in
    Hampstead. (See p. 428, Vol. 1.)

II. Hannah, b. May 5, 1742; m. Daniel Stevens. (See also above.)

Both of the above owned the Covenant. (See list.)

Her father, John Hunt, was son of Edward and Ann
(Weed) Hunt of Amesbury, freeman, 1677, possible son of
Edward of Duxbury, Mass., 1635.

No. 68.

Eleanor Davis, b. in Haverhill, Mass., April 13, 1694, a
daughter of Stephen and Mary (Tucker) Davis of Haverhill.
She married James Stickney of Kingston, about 1728, and
was a widow in 1752. They had a daughter Susan, and
Mary, who m. John Dodge of Ipswich, Mass. Admitted to
the church June 3, 1752.

No. 69.

Joseph Hadley, b. in Amesbury, Mass., Dec. 6, 1700, a son
of Samuel and Jane (Martin) Hadley of the West Parish of
Amesbury. His father belonged to the "training band" in
1680, and was a "weaver." They had twelve children, of
whom Joseph was the tenth. Joseph married Hannah Flanders of Amesbury, July 12, 1721. He removed to Hampstead about 1732, to where Mr. Verburght resides, and died
in Hampstead Oct. 11, 1758. They had a number of children, among them Joseph, Jr., who mar. Martha Gile, and
had eleven children, b. in Hampstead (see Vol. 1, p. 413, No.
102). Others were David, who mar. Mary Gile, and Nathan,
who mar. Betsey Hackett, both of whom had children, b. in
town. Joseph Hadley was admitted to the church Aug. 6,
1752.

No. 70.

Susannah Heath, b. in Hampstead, July 27, 1788, a daughter of Ensign James and Dinah (Mudgett) Heath, who was

a widow of William Mudgett of Salisbury, Mass. She was admitted a member of the church Aug. 6, 1752. (See list, Covenant, Nos. 2 and 14.)

No. 71.

Hannah Tucker, b. in Salisbury, Mass., June 4, 1705, a daughter of James and Hannah (True) Tucker of Salisbury. She mar. David Copp of Hampstead, Oct. 27, 1725, and moved here in 1732, near the eastern shore of Wash pond (see p. 15, Vol. 1). She was admitted to the church Aug. 6, 1752, and died in Hampstead, aged 85 years, and was buried in the village cemetery. She had several children, some of whom went to Vermont. One of them, David, mar. Hannah Merrill (widow), in 1768, and mar. second, Mary French of Hampstead ; Moses ; and Joshua, who mar. Sarah Poor, and resided in town, at "Copp's Corner," and had eleven children, b. in town.

No. 72.

Ruth Ayer, b. in Haverhill, Mass., Nov. 7, 1728, a daughter of Deacon James and Mary (White) Ayer of Haverhill. She married Rev. Henry True (No. 1), Nov. 29 or 30, 1753, evidently having made his acquaintance while he was pursuing his studies for the ministry in Haverhill. She was adm. to the church November, 1753, and died in Hampstead, Jan. 1, 1810. (See inscription on tomb of Rev. Mr. True, p. 309, Vol. 1.) She was the mother of children :—

I.   A daughter, b. and d. Nov. 2, 1754.
II.   Samuel, b. March 8, 1756; d. Aug. 5, 1778; in the Revolutionary
        war at Providence.
III.   Hannah (see No. 217).
IV.   Rev. James (see No. 161).
V.   Dr. Jabez, b. Oct. 6, 1760; d. Sept. 5, 1823; mar. at Marietta,
        Ohio. He was one of the first settlers in Marietta. His
        name appears on the first subscription for celebrating July
        4th in the new settlement. He was one of the " Ohio Com-

pany " reaching Marietta in 1788. Harris' History of Ohio
says Dr. True was "one of the early teachers," and "always
foremost in laying the foundations of the educational system
of that part of the State of Ohio." He was a deacon of the
church, and the first Bible society in the Northwest Territory was formed in Mr. True's house in 1812. He had a fine
orchard, and one day going into it he saw a boy in an apple
tree. He said, "My boy, you are in the [wrong tree; that
has not the best; come down, and I will give you some better
apples," which he proceeded to gather, saying, "When you
want some apples again, come to me; you endanger your
limbs by climbing so high a fence." The lad told of it, saying, "I will never steal apples again from so kind a man; I
am ashamed of myself." Dr. True practised his profession,
with a glad desire to relieve distress and pain, not caring
whether the patient could pay; and he cared little for money
except as he could do good with it. He was earnest in support
of all educational, religious, and moral reforms. He was
marked by the usual peculiarities of the New England race,
being frugal, industrious, temperate, and public-spirited. He
went out as a surgeon in the Revolution on board a privateer.

VI.   Deacon John, mar. Mrs. Anna Kimball (Nos. 214 and 249).
VII.   Ruth, mar. Samuel Little (see Nos. 201 and 200).
VIII.   Sarah, mar. John Howard (see No. 247).
IX.   Rev. Henry, b. May 20, 1770; mar. Mary Barrett. He d. April
        17, 1757. He graduated from Dartmouth College 1796. His
        wife was born June 8, 1784; a daughter of Amos Barrett, a
        captain of minute men at Concord; she d. Feb. 18, 1856. Rev.
        Henry True was fitted for college at Atkinson Academy, and
        partly with the Rev. Giles Merrill of North Parish, Haver-
        hill. He taught school after his graduation from Dartmouth
        College, for five or six years, in Salisbury, Beverly and Tyngs-
        borough, and other towns. He studied divinity, partly with
        the Rev. Mr. Lawrence, with whom he boarded in Tyngs-
        borough, and partly with Rev. Dr. Chapin of Groton. He
        preached some at Tewksbury and Dracut, Mass., and one
        summer for the North Parish Church at Plaistow, and during
        one session of Congress for the Rev. Manassah Cutler, at
        Hamilton, Mass. He was trustee of Warren, Mass., Acade-
        my for many years; also chaplain of a regiment, justice of
        the peace and quorum, and town clerk—"none of these
        offices very profitable." He published a sermon delivered by
        him in Hampstead Nov. 15, 1807. He was called as pastor of
        the Congregational Church at Union, Me., Sept. 24, 1806, and
        settled Nov. 11, 1806. The charge at the ordination was

▲

given by Rev. Manassah Cutler of Hamilton. He resigned April, 1810. In the fall of 1849 he moved with his wife to Marion, Ohio, where he resided with his son, Dr. Henry True, three years, when he returned to Union, Me., where he resided with his daughter, Mrs. Vose, until he died, April 17, 1857. Mrs. Mary Barrett (True), his daughter, writes of her father: "He was loving and affectionate to his children, and fond of other children. He retained his love of Latin, Hebrew and Greek to his old age. Our minister would come in often to talk with him in Union on some difficult points in theology, and always found help." Nathan Rice of Union said: "I would trust him with any amount of money uncounted, knowing that every cent would be returned." Mrs. Vose says, "He composed this morning prayer for me ":—

> "Now I awake to see the light,
> In this my God I take delight;
> Guard me this day from every ill,
> And make me know and do thy will."

X.   Mary (No. 344).

The children of Rev. Henry and Mary (Barrett) True were:—

I.   Henry Ayer, b. Aug. 10, 1812; d. Dec. 12, 1870. He was a graduate from Bowdoin College, 1832, and Harvard Medical College; was a doctor, merchant, and banker in Marion, Ohio. and after retiring from active business was ordained a minister by the Presbytery of Marion, Ohio. He was an elder in the First Presbyterian Church of Marion from 1842 to 1870. He married Elizabeth Pierce Reed, daughter of James Reed of Deerfield, Mass. (grand-daughter of Sarah Warren Reed, who was descended from Richard Warren of the Mayflower). They had one child, Henry True, b. Jan. 26, 1848; banker at Marion, Ohio; elder in the Presbyterian Church at Marion, 1891; mar., Sept. 13, 1876, Flora P. Brown. They had children:—

    1.   Mary Alice True, b. Sept. 25, 1877; d. Aug. 12, 1879.

    2.   Henry Ayer True, b. July 26, 1879; was graduated from Princeton University, June 7, 1902.

II.   Mary Barrett True, b. in 1818; m. Elijah Vose, May 16, 1843, who was b. March 19, 1807, and d. at Ipswich, Mass., Aug. 4, 1877. They resided at Union, Me., Ipswich, Mass., Marion, O., and at present Mrs. Vose resides at 38 Cary ave., Chelsea, Mass. Their children were:—

    1.   Helen Ayer Vose, b. March 5, 1844.

    2.   Mary True Vose, b. Dec. 17, 1849; d. March 8, 1855.

3. Amos Barrett, b. July 22, 1825; d. Aug. 6, 1825. The line upon his little gravestone is as follows:—
"Rest here sweet babe till Jesus comes."

(I am indebted to Henry True, Esq., of Marion, Ohio, and Mrs. Mary Barrett (True) Vose, of Chelsea, Mass., for many items concerning the family of Rev. Henry and Ruth (Ayer) True.)

(A letter from Rev. Henry True, of Union, Me., to his sister in Hampstead, in 1849, appears on p. 66, Vol. 1).

No. 73.

Jacob Eaton, b. in Lynn, Mass., Jan. 7, 1708, a son of William and Mary (Swain) Eaton, of Reading, Mass. (brother to No. 4). He mar. Mary Breed (No. 74), and removed to Hampstead, near the Kingston line. He was sometimes called of the Kingston parish. He was adm. to the church June 30, 1756, and d. in Hampstead, Dec. 7, 1768, aged 56 years. He with his wife Mary, " owned the Covenant," Jan., 1756 (see list No. 14).

No. 74.

Mary Breed, b. in Lynn, Mass., a daughter of Jacob and Mehitable Breed, of Lynn, mar. Jacob Eaton (No. 73), Oct. 29, 1737, in Lynn. She was received a member of this church June 30, 1756, by letter from the First church in Lynn. She d. in Medford, Mass., Feb. 16, 1775. She had a daughter Mary, b. and bapt. at the New North church in Boston, Mass., Oct. 14, 1744.

No. 75.

Thomas Fellows, b. in Salisbury, Mass., Jan. 20, 1685, a son of Samuel and Abigail (Barnard) Fellows, of Salisbury, grandson of Samuel and Ann Fellows, the emigrant to Newbury, 1646. He was bapt. and owned the Covenant in Salisbury, Nov. 18, 1705, and was adm. to the church in

Salisbury, 1719, and mar. Dec. 10, 1718, Elizabeth, daughter of Samuel and Elizabeth (Scriven) Eastman, of Salisbury; they had children in Salisbury; they removed to Sandown early. He was adm. to the church in Hampstead, June 30, 1753.

No. 76.

Ruth Whittaker, b. in Haverhill, Mass., April 28, 1720, a daughter of William, Jr., and Mehitable (Harriman) Whittaker, of North Parish, of Haverhill. She mar. John Atwood, of Hampstead, as his second wife, April 18, 1751. She was adm. to the church June, 1753. They had children:—

I.   David, b. 1752, m. Sarah Clement, Nov. 10, 1774. Settled in
        Alexandria, and had a large family of children.
II.   James, b. June 16, 1754; remained at the Atwood homestead in
        Hampstead; mar. Polly Lowell, from Me., Nov. 30, 1775. He
        d. in Hampstead, Nov. 21, 1839; his wife d. Feb. 16, 1839.
        They had thirteen children (see p. 404, Vol. 1).
III.   Joseph, b. April 8, 1756, m. Ruth Cross of Methuen, Mass., 1718;
        settled in Alexandria; no children.
IV.   Mehitable, b. Nov. 12, 1758, m. Moses Williams (see No. 78 and
        p. 429, Vol. 1).
V.   Moses, b. Feb. 25, 1761, m. Judith, daughter of Thomas and
        Margaret (Rowen) Wadleigh, of Hampstead, Feb. 2, 1783;
        they had a large family of children in Hampstead, and later
        moved to Alexandria.
VI.   Merriam, b. June 18, 1763, mar. Thomas Wadleigh of Hamp-
        stead, and later of Perrytown.

No. 77.

Thomas Williams, b. in Amesbury, Mass., Aug. 9, 1709, a son of Richard and Ruth (Rogers) Williams, of Newbury, before 1684. He mar. Deliverance Merrill (No. 78), and moved to Hampstead (near Ellsworth Hadley homestead). He was adm. to the church June 30, 1753 (p. 376, Vol. 1). He mar. second, Lydia (Rideout) Holgate (No. 138). He mar. third, Susannah Johnson, who d. in Hampstead, Dec.

20, 1790, aged 80 years. He d. in Hampstead, Nov. 18, 1789, and was buried in East Hampstead.

No. 78.

Deliverance Merrill, b. in Newbury, Mass., March 15, 1716, a daughter of John Merrill, of Newbury, and his wife Deborah Hazelton, of Haverhill. She mar. Thomas Williams (No. 77), in 1739, and was adm. to the church June 30, 1753. She d. in Hampstead, Jan. 15, 1759. She was the mother of eight children :—

I.   Sarah, b. May 20, 1740, mar. Peltish Wilson, in 1761.
II.   Ruth, b. March 23, 1742, mar. Daniel Gile, in 1764.
III.   Ruhamah, b. August 29, 1743.
IV.   Thomas, b. Feb. 20, 1745.
V.   Mary, b. July 23, 1749.
VI.   Moses, b. July 11, 1751, mar. Mehitable Atwood (see No. 76). Of the eleven children (see p. 429, Vol. 1), James, Ruth and Moses settled and d. in Warren; Dr. Thomas, a graduate of Dartmouth College, mar. Lucinda B. Remington, of Canandaiga, N. Y., where he practised and d. David mar. Sarah Harriman, and lived and d. in Hampstead. Hannah mar. Moses Hoyt of Hampstead (see p. 340, Vol. 1). Jonathan mar. Philena Webster of Hampstead; they removed to Haverhill, Mass., in 1844; d. 1870 and 1873 (four children of Moses and Mehitable (Atwood) d. young).
VII.   Hannah, b. Jan. 2, 1755, mar. Phillip Rowell, in 1776.
VIII.   John, b. Nov. 30, 1756, mar. first, Alice Stevens; second, Rachel Cheney; (first wife sometimes called Eunice Stevens); they had seven children, b. in Hampstead, of whom Benjamin, b. Aug. 26, 1798, mar. Hannah Rowell, and had family (see pp. 376-377, Vol. 1), and church members (No. 515 and family).

Jonathan and Philena (Webster) Williams had children born in Hampstead :—

Harrison, b. July 16, 1819, mar. Louisa Perkins Day; and, second, mar. Julia Morse Tarr. He resided in Groveland and Bradford, Mass. He d. Dec. 31, 1891. They had four children. One, H. Parker Williams, d. Feb., 1903; mar. Eleanor T. Randall (No. 564).

II.   . Stephen Webster, b. June 21, 1821, mar. Nancy Call Fales; and, second, mar. Mary Ann Fales. They resided in Methuen, Mass., and had five children, four sons and an infant daughter, that d. in infancy. He d. Dec. 26, 1808.

III. Julia Woodford, b. June 6, 1823, mar. Benjamin Franklin Sargent. They resided in Merrimac, Mass., and had four children.

IV.   Moses, b. June 20, 1825, mar. Eliza Ann Esterbrook. They resided in West Newbury, Mass., and had four children

V.   Dolly Ann, b. August 22, 1827, mar. Albert Bartlett. They resided at Reading and Dover, Mass., and had two daughters.

VI.   Abigail, b. January 12, 1830, mar. William Sawyer, and lived in Haverhill, Mass.; no issue.

VII. Hannah Hoyt, b. December 3, 1831, mar. John Edwin Bly. They resided in Plaistow; and had one child.

VIII. William Bell, b. Dec. 6, 1833, mar. Eliza (Thompson) Fish (widow). They have no children, and reside in Redwing, Goodhue County, Minn. He served in the tenth Minn. Reg. in the civil war, from 1801 to 1805.

IX.   Joseph, b. Nov. 4, 1835; d. at Baton Rouge, La., April 15, 1863. unmar. He was a member of the 50th Mass. Reg., Co. G.

X.   Mary Bell, b. October 14, 1837, mar. William Clarke Noyes of Atkinson. They have five children.

XI.   Philena, b. January 7, 1840; and d. unmar. May 4, 1803. She was a teacher in the public schools of Haverhill.

Of this family four widowed sisters survive. Mrs. Bartlett was a member of the Cong. Church, at Dover, Mass.; Mrs. Sargent, at present a member of the Cong. Church, at Merrimac, Mass.; Mrs. Sawyer, a member of the Bapt. Church (Portland street), Haverhill, Mass.; and Mrs. Bly and Mrs. Noyes, of the North Parish Cong. Church of Haverhill, Mass.

No. 79.

Obediah Wells, b. in Amesbury, Mass., 1712, a son of Luke and Widow Dorothy (Trull) Wells, of Amesbury. Luke was a son of Rev. Thomas Wells, of Amesbury, and wife Mary Perkins, of the First church of Amesbury. Obediah was adm. a member of the church Nov., 1753, from the First church in Amesbury. He mar. first, Judith Straw, Sept. 6, 1736, and had children.

I.   Dorothy, b. 1788.
II.   Lydia, b. 1740.
III. Sarah, b. 1742.

He mar. second, Jemima Wiburn, of Salisbury (No. 80). He was a resident of Sandown in early years, and d. there. He was called " of Kingston, in 1754."

No. 80.

Jemima Wiburn, b.
She married Obediah Wells (No. 79), in Salisbury, May 25, 1749, and had children, b. in Hampstead : Thomas, b. Feb. 27, 1751, and Jemima, b. Oct. 12, 1755. She was admitted to the church, November, 1758.

No. 81.

John Morrill, b. in Salisbury, Mass., March 28, 1713, a son of Ezekiel and Abigail (Wadleigh) Morrill of Salisbury. He married Judith Morrill (No. 82), and removed to Londonderry. He was received by letter from the Second Church in Salisbury, March, 1756.

No. 82.

Judith Morrill, b. in Amesbury, Mass., July 4, 1719, daughter of Jacob and Elizabeth (Stevens) Morrill of Amesbury. Married John Morrill (No. 81). She was admitted to the church by letter from the Second Church of Christ at Kingston, December, 1755.

No. 83.

Prudence Noyes, b. in Newbury, Mass., April 10, 1725, a daughter of Capt. Ephraim and Prudence (Stickney) Noyes of Newbury. She married Jacob Bayley (No. 84), Oct. 15, 1745, and was admitted to the church Aug. 26, 1758. She died in Newbury, Vt., June 1, 1809. Her children were :

I.   Ephraim, b. Oct. 5, 1746, in Newbury; d. young.

II.   Abigail, b. in Hampstead, Jan. 15, 1748; d. young.

III.   Noyes, b. in Hampstead, Feb. 15, 1750; d. young.

IV.   Joshua, b. in Hampstead, June 11, 1753; married, first, Anna
        Fowler. He was successively a lieutenant, captain, major
        and colonel in the Revolutionary war. He was representa-
        tive from Newbury, Vt., in 1791, 1802-3-4, and 1809. They
        had twelve children, of whom the sons, Jacob, Joshua, John,
        Noyes and Benjamin settled what is now known as Jefferson
        Hill.

V.   Jacob, b. in Hampstead, Oct. 3, 1755; married, first, Ruth Be-
        dell, daughter of Col. Moody Bedell of Haverhill; and mar.,
        second, Mary, daughter of Ezekiel and Mary (Hutchens)
        Ladd of Atkinson. The mother was said to be the first white
        female born in Haverhill. Jacob was the parent of twelve
        children. He spent his life on the Ox-Bow, in Haverhill.

VI.   Ephraim, b. in Hampstead, Oct. 1, 1757; married, first, Anna
        Fowler, and, second, Lucy Hodges. He moved to Newbury,
        Vt., with his father, and in 1790 moved to Littleton, and died
        in Lyman, N. H., July 7, 1825. He served in the Revolution-
        ary war. He had eleven children, some of whom settled in
        Stillwater, and Newbury, and Topsham, Vt.

VII.   James (twin to Ephraim); married Sarah Bailey. (See Nos. 63
        and 64.)

VIII.   Amherst, b, in Hampstead, Dec. 10, 1760; mar. Sally Stevens.

IX.   Abner, b. in Newbury, Vt., Jan. 16, 1762; d. 1783.

X.   John, b. in Newbury, Vt., May 20, 1765; mar., first, Betsey
        Bailey; and, second, Hannah Ladd. They had thirteen chil-
        dren, and resided on Jefferson Hill.

XI.   Isaac, b. in Newbury, June 28, 1767; mar. Betsey, daughter of
        Col. Thomas Johnson of Hampstead, and Newbury, Vt.
        They had eleven children.

No. 84.

Mehitable Putnam, b. March 26, 1727, in Danvers, Mass.,
a daughter of Dea. Nathaniel and Hannah (Roberts) Putnam. She married Reuben Harriman, in Salem, Mass., June
4, 1747, who was b. in Haverhill, Mass., Nov. 5, 1725, son of
Joseph and Lydia (Eaton) Harriman of Haverhill. Reuben
Harriman was a soldier in the Revolutionary war, having
enlisted " in the company to go on an expedition now on
foot to the State of Rhode Island." A torn receipt, which

is preserved in the Record and Pension Bureau at Washington, D. C., shows " that Lieut. Moses Little received 20 pounds for Reuben Harrim— (receipt torn) and another soldier, who were members of his company."

They removed to Hampstead soon after their marriage, to the farm purchased by his grandfather, Nathaniel Harriman, one of the first land-owners in this part of Haverhill. She was admitted to the church by letter from the church at Danvers, Mass., November, 1754. The old farm remained in the family until Jan. 27, 1841, when a grandson, Caleb Harriman, sold the farm to Johnson Noyes, since owned by Stephen Harris, and deeded to Daniel Ayer, April 15, 1861, " excepting and reserving the burial lot at the southerly corner, as walled around, containing fifteen or twenty rods, to myself and heirs forever." In this lot are buried Reuben and Mehitable (Putnam) Harriman, and their colored servant Philo. (See inscriptions on tombstones, p. 313, Vol. 1.) The graves were also marked by memorial trees (noble ash), preserved by the children and grand-children before they left their home, about 1827. Feb. 3, 1902, those family trees, which measured nearly two feet in diameter at the ground and at least fifty feet in height, were felled and removed for lumber by trespassers, and other depredations committed in the burial lot. Prof. F. G. Harriman, for many years a teacher in California, and in 1902 a mining engineer in South America, visited the old yard, June 18, 1902, and counted the *rings* very accurately on the bases of the felled trees, which showed ninety-four rings on the tree cut at the head of Mrs. Harriman's grave, eighty-three at Mr. Harriman's grave, and seventy-nine rings for the servant's memorial tree, which date the ages of the trees.

Their children were all born in Hampstead, and nearly all removed to northern New Hampshire or Vermont. They were :—

I.   Mehitable, b. May 8, 1748; d. young.
II.   Rufus, b. July 8, 1749; d. young.
III.   Laban, b. July 10, 1751; mar. Molly Harriman, and lived for
       several years at the old homestead in the lane south of the
       Ayers house; in later years kept a hotel in Hookset. The
       house in the lane was moved to the street and the present
       house built of it. Laban Harriman's carpenter shop formed
       the north portion. The rocks from the old Harriman cellar
       are a part of C. Frank Noyes' house cellar in Atkinson, and
       the stone door-step is now the street door-step at the home
       of Joshua F. Noyes. Laban d. Mar. 26, 1830; wife d. 1822,
       aged 67 years. They had children :—

        1. William, whose grand-daughter Elizabeth mar. Samuel
           Fellows of Sandown, 1835; whose daughter, Mary
           E., mar. Hon. Oliver Taylor, and son, Croydon
           H. Fellows, both of Haverhill, Mass.

        2. Sarah, mar. Joseph Merrick of Hampstead, son of
           Joseph and Judith (Little) Merrick. He was a
           worker in the U. S. navy yard at Boston. They had
           children : Eliza, mar. Green Hicks Brutus, New
           York; Rufus, m. Sarah Robbins; Laban Harriman,
           twice mar. at Corinth, Vt., and parents of Hon.
           George B. Merrick, author of the Merrick Family
           Genealogy; Joseph, mar. Elizabeth Smart; Silas
           mar. Fanny Miner, and parents of Mr. Fred B.
           Merrick, steel and horseshoe nail manufacturer at
           Brighton, Pa.; George W., m. Lucinda Graves; Sarah,
           m. Spencer Brown; Abigail, m. Wm. Whitney; Mary
           L., d. young; Judith, m. William H. Hutchens; and
           Byron L., m. and d. early.

        3. Mary (No. 206).

        4. Putnam, mar., and resided in Vermont; a son, Fred
           Putnam, now resides in Washington, Vt.

        5. Caleb, mar. Lois Knight (widow of Richard, son of
           Capt. Hezekiah and Mrs. Anne (Swett) Hutchens),
           and lived at the old Hutchens home, now occupied
           by Edw. F. Noyes, and kept tavern there many years.
           He was converted in later life, and travelled through
           the towns preaching the "faith as shown to him."
           His cousins relate hearing him preach, and of his in-
           variably commencing his talks by relating " how he
           was converted," as follows, in a very slow tone and
           drawling accent : "I see in this congregation a good
           many small boys. Once I was a small boy, a poor,
           sinful child, and I caught a blue jay, and I pulled out

all of his tail feathers, and I pulled out all of his
wing feathers, and I laid him on the stone of the
door screaming, as he looked up to heaven, 'Caleb,
Caleb, son of Laban, have mercy on my soul. Amen.' "

IV.   Zeniah, b. Dec. 20, 1754; mar. Caleb, son of Capt. William Marshall of Hampstead, and soon after moved to Northumber-
land. Several forts were built in that section during the
Revolutionary war. One of them was located on the farm
of Caleb Marshall. "Wild consternation filled the hearts of
the settlers, who were scattered. The young wife of Marshall had her household goods hidden away, and with one
child of two years of age and an infant in her arms less than
a month old, mounted a horse and fled to Hampstead, a distance of more than one hundred and fifty miles, arriving in
safety." (Hist. Lancaster, N. H.) (See Marshall, Appendix
of this Vol.)

V.   Hannah, b. Nov. 30, 1757.

VI.   Sarah, b. Jan. 30, 1758; m. Nathaniel Noyes, who resided, until
their three oldest children were born, in Atkinson, where
Joshua A. Richards now resides, and then moved to Boscawen a few years, and then to Landaff, where they died.
Their children were :—

1. Sarah, m. Joseph Hutchens of Bath.
2. Moses, m. Sally Stone of Landaff.
3. Enoch, m. Hannah Morrill, and resided in Landaff. (See
    sketch, p. 201, Vol. 1, by Rev. Henry A. Merrill, a
    grandson.)
4. James, m. Temperance Merrick. (See p. 355, Vol. 1.)
    They resided in Richford, Vt., and had a large family
    of children, several living there now.
5. Eunice, mar. Moses Eastman of Landaff. A large fam-
    ily there; she mar. second, Obediah Eastman.
6. Henry, mar. Priscilla Carlton; second, Asenath Noyes;
    third, Amanda Hildrick. They resided in Haverhill,
    N. H., and Canada.
7. Nathaniel, d., unmarried, in his 18th year, in Landaff.
8. Mary, m. Amos Clark; second, —— Evens; resided in
    Lisbon.
9. Phebe, m. John George, of Franconia.
10. Rufus, m. Hannah Clark, and had children. Amos C.
    m. Rebecca Stewart; resided in Pennsylvania; James
    C. m., first, Betsey Cogswell; second, Maria Bowles;
    resided in Bath. Rufus H. m. Patience Gordon; re-
    sided in Landaff. Charles R. m. Mary Homans; re-
    sided in Pennsylvania. Jane C. m. Willis B. Blandin;

resided in Bath (a son, Amos Noyes Blandin); and Miss Hannah M., unmarried, of Bath, in 1902.

    11. John, mar. Phebe W. Clark. A son, Moses C., resided in Bethlehem (p. 210, Vol. 1). d. Apr. 2, 1908.

VII.   Joseph, b. May 7, 1759; m. Eunice, daughter of Enoch and Phebe (Harriman) Noyes of Atkinson. She was said to have been "the strongest woman in the country," and stories of the many pounds which she could lift with ease are told by the older people who remember her.

VIII.   Archelaus Putnam, b. Nov. 8, 1760; d. young.

IX.   Mehitable, b. Aug. 30, 1762; mar. John Abraham, and went to Vermont.

X.   Mary, b. Oct. 13, 1764; mar. —— Hoyt, and resided in northern New Hampshire.

XI.   Rufus, b. Sept. 28, 1766; mar. Judith Merrick, daughter of Joseph and Judith (Little) Merrick, of Hampstead, Oct. 27, 1786. They kept a tavern in Hooksett for a time, then removed to Vermont; in the vicinity of Bradford and Corinth. Their children, as taken from an "old red morocco note-book, along with formulas for liniments for rheumatism," belonging to the fourth son, Reuben, who "was a cripple for thirty years by reason of rheumatism," were :—

    1. John.
    2. Mary.
    3. Abner.
    4. Reuben, b. Jan. 1, 1799; mar. Abbie Davis, Jan. 20, 1823, and had children—Huldah, George W., Caroline, Lydia, Rufus Putnam (who has sons named Lake Huron and Lake Michigan Harriman, as the father "would have no Bible names in the family "; he called them Lake and Huron, Huron now residing in New York State, John, and Franklin (who mar. Della Lewis), now superintendent of the Milwaukee, Wis., street railway, and has children; Maude, mar. G. V. Leonard of Lawrence, Kansas; Lou B., unmarried; Franklin and Hazel, all of Wauwatosa, Wis.
    5. Joseph.
    6. Nicholas.
    7. Noah.
    8. Eunice.
    9. Rufus Harriman.
    10. Dudley.

No. 85.

Elizabeth Lunt, b. March 8, 1709, in Newbury, Mass., a daughter of Henry, Jr., and Sarah (   ) Lunt of New-

bury, She married John, son of John and Abiah (Shaw)
Webster, of Rye, or Hampton, in 1784. He was b. Feb. 10,
1712–8. She was admitted to the church in 1755. They
lived nearly opposite the house of George Bragg, and died
in Hampstead, and were buried in the Hadley cemetery at
East Hampstead. (See gravestone inscription, p. 813, Vol.
1.) They probably came to Hampstead about 1742-8, as the
first four of their children were born in Newbury. They
had children :—

I.   Sarah, b. March 20, 1785: m. Moses Kimball in 1758, a brother of
       Dea. Benjamin Kimball (No. 21), and resided at Hampstead.
       Their children, b. in Hampstead, were :—
       1. Tamer, b. April 10, 1758.
       2. Nanne, b. July 10, 1760; d., unm., 1794.
       3. Abiah, b. Feb. 10, 1762; m. Jesse, son of Bartholomew
          and Hannah (Kelly) Heath, of Hampstead, and had
          eight children, b. in Hampstead.
       4. Sarah (No. 288).
       5. John, b. Jan. 4, 1766; m. Sarah Dearborn of Chester,
          and were parents of six children.
II.   Abiah, b. April 25, 1787; m. Asa Page of Atkinson.
III.   Joseph, b. March 19, 1789; m. Mary Sawyer; eight children, b.
       in Hampstead (see page 420, Vol. 1).
IV.   Caleb, b. Dec. 17, 1740; probably d. young.
V.   Elizabeth, b. in Hampstead, Feb. 23, 1743; m., first, Jacob Saw-
       yer; second, Edmund Worth; lived in Hampstead with her
       first husband, and in Newbury later.
VI.   John, b. June 20, 1745.
VII.   Mary (No. 187).
VIII. Anna, m. Moody Chase (see list "Owned the Covenant").
IX.   Caleb, b. July 12, 1752; m. Sarah Davis, and had children, b. in
       Hampstead—Sarah, b. Jan. 18, 1777, and others. He mar.,
       second, Joanna Smith; and, third, Mary Smith; and was
       buried in the Hadley cemetery. (See p. 818, Vol. 1.)

No. 86.

· Abiah Gile, b. in Kingston, May 7, 1722, a daughter of
Joseph and Mary (Heath) Gile (No. 10). She mar. Philip
Nelson of Plaistow in 1745. She was admitted to the church
in 1757.

No. 87.

Mehitable Kimball, b. in Plaistow, Aug. 28, 1739, daughter of Dea. Benjamin and Mary (Emerson) Kimball (sister of No. 21). She married, first, Thomas Hale, in 1755, who was b. in 1731, and d. 1756. She married, second, in 1767, Benjamin Pettengill. She was admitted to full communion in 1757.

No. 88.

Ruth Terrill, b. in Amesbury, Mass., July 14, 1734, a daughter of Gideon and Edith (   ) Terrill of Kingston. Married John Kezar, Jan. 4, 1755, son of John Kezar, "the elder," who mar., first, Judith Heath, and had ten children. (See Vol. 1, p. 419.) Ruth Kezar was the mother of

I.   John, b. March 4, 1758.
II.   George, b. July 4, 1750.
III. Molly, b. July 4, 1761.

She was admitted to the church Oct. 16, 1757.

No. 89.

Dea. William Eaton, b. in Lynn, Mass., June 3, 1731, a son of William and Mary (Swain) Eaton of Reading and Lynn (a brother to No. 4). His father d. in 1731 in Lynn. He married Ruth Bradley (No. 90) about 1751, and removed to Hampstead, and later settled on No. 12, P. 2d D., in Chester. He was a soldier in the Revolutionary war, and d. in Candia. He was adm. to the church Oct. 29, 1758.

No. 90.

Ruth Bradley, b. in Haverhill, Mass., June 19, 1739, a daughter of Daniel and Elizabeth (Ayer) Bradley of Haverhill. She married William Eaton (No. 89) about 1751, and was admitted to the church Oct. 29, 1758. She had several children, b. in Candia, where she died in 1789.

No. 91.

Mary Hoyt, b. in Salisbury, Mass., Feb. 2, 1732, daughter of Moses and Mary (Carr) Hoyt of Salisbury, who was a son of Benjamin and Hannah (Pillsbury) Hoyt, and grandson of Thomas. Her parents were both members of the First Church of Salisbury. She married Dea. Benjamin Kimball (No. 21) for his second wife, Feb. 28, 1758. Her parents resided in Epping for some time, were there in 1743, and both d. in Weare. She was admitted a member of the church March 25, 1759, and was buried near the gate in the Centre cemetery at Hampstead. The inscription on the stone reads, "Mary, wife of Dea. Benjamin Kimball, died March 10, 1816, aged 84." Their children were:—

I.   Ebenezer, b. Feb. 17, 1759.

II.   Ruth, b. Nov. 9, 1761; m. Benjamin Brown, and d. July 17, 1818.

III.   Lydia, b. March 15, 1768.

IV.   Isaac, b. July 1, 1764.

V.   Jacob, b. March 20, 1770; m. Ruth, daughter of Enoch Rogers of Amesbury, Dec. 20, 1808. Jacob resided in Hampstead, on the old Kimball farm, where Charles B. Gilman lives. He d. in town, Sept. 1, 1840, and left no issue. He bequeathed his property to the New Hampshire Hospital for the Insane at Concord.

VI.   Jabez, b. Jan. 20, 1772. He was a graduate of Harvard College, class of 1797, and was a tutor in the college from 1800 to 1806. He studied law with Hon. John Prentiss in Londonderry, N. H., and was living in his family when he died, March 10, 1805. He settled in Haverhill in 1805, but ill health compelled him to relinquish his work. He was said to have been a young man of much promise. His funeral sermon was printed.

VII.   Nannie, b. March 10, 1775.

No. 92.

Jeremiah Allen, b. in Salisbury, Mass., Sept. 1, 1718; son of John and Hannah (Weare) Allen of Salisbury. He married Abigail Currier (No. 93) of South Hampton, and was received from the church at Salisbury, May 20, 1759. He was a farmer, and resided in Salisbury until 1758, when he moved to Sandown. The church records call him of Hampstead in 1765. The church records say, Feb. 27, 1774 : "Chh. stopped after Publick worship and voted to consent that Jeremiah Allen and Abigail his wife should be dismissed from this church, upon their being rec'd by the ch. at Greenfield."

No. 93.

Abigail Currier, b. Nov. 20, 1722, in Amesbury, Mass., a daughter of Benjamin and Abigail (Brown) Currier of South Hampton. She married Jeremiah Allen (No. 92) at South Hampton, Oct. 15, 1751, and was admitted to the church May 20, 1759, and was dis. to unite with the church at Greenfield, Feb. 27, 1774. She had children, the oldest three b. in Salisbury.

I.   Betty, b. March 28, 1753.
II.   Benjamin, b. Nov. 1, 1754.
III.   Moses, b. April 5, 1756.
IV.   Nathan, b. in Hampstead, Oct. 12, 1702.
V.   Jeremiah, b. Jan. 8, 1704.

No. 94.

Phebe Parker, b. in Bradford, Mass., June 4, 1732, daughter of Abraham and Hannah (Chase) Parker of Bradford. (This statement is as sent by a relative, but others' research have placed the item as in doubt.) She was married to Ephraim Webster (No. 84), Dec. 21, 1752, in Bradford, by the Rev. Ebenezer Ray. They resided in Chester until about 1760, when they moved to Hampstead, near "Marshall's Corner." She was admitted to the church Oct. 5, 1760, and died in Newbury, Vt., seventeen days after the birth of her son Ebenezer, or May 1, 1775. Her children were:—

I.   Samuel, b. in Chester, Dec. 29, 1753.
II.   Phebe, b. in Chester, 1756.
III.   Asa, b. in Chester, April 25, 1758.
IV.   Susanna, b. in Hampstead, May 16, 1760; d. April 2, 1795.

V. Ephraim, b. in Hampstead, June 30, 1762; enlisted in the Revolutionary war, 1777, as from Newbury, Vt., under Col. Thomas Johnson, late of Hampstead, having been a little over fifteen years old. He married Miss Hannah Banks, Nov. 19, 1796. In a very interesting leaflet, published by the Onondaga Historical Society of Syracuse, N. Y., as read by Rev. George B. Spalding, D. D., LL. D., of Syracuse, Dec. 8, 1899, Ephraim Webster's life is given, and he is called "the hero of Onondaga." (See leaflet No. 21 of that Society.)

VI. Parker, b. at Hampstead, April 5, 1765.

VII. Mary, b. at Hampstead, April 3, 1768.

VIII. Sarah, b. at Hampstead, April 20, 1770.

IX. Moses, b. at Hampstead, Oct. 27, 1772.

X. Ebenezer, b. April 13, 1775, at Newbury, Vt.

No. 95.

Rachel Rowell, b. in Amesbury, Mass., Jan. 12, 1726, a daughter of Philip and Sarah (Davis) Rowell of Amesbury ; married Lieut. Edmund Morse, April 16, 1750, and settled in Hampstead, near the "old mill," as described on pp. 379 and 380, Vol. 1. She was admitted to the church May 29, 1761, "at her own house, as she was unable to attend public worship, to full communion and fellowship." (Church records.) Her children were:—

I. Jacob, b. March 3, 1751.

II. Rachel, b. Aug. 2, 1760.

III. Daniel, b. April 22, 1763.

She died in Hampstead, 1763, and her husband mar., second, Rebecca Carlton (see pp. 421 and 380, Vol. 1). Her daughter Molly m. Abiel Kelly, and were "the enterprising settlers of Kennebec, Me., June 3, 1792."

No. 96.

Aaron French, b. Jan. 21, 1733, in Amesbury, Mass., a son of Joseph and Hannah (Gould) French of Amesbury and Hampstead (see Nos. 100 and 101). Married Sarah Stevens (No. 97). He was admitted to the church by letter from the church at Sandown, May 31, 1761, and resided in Sandown.

No. 97.

Sarah Stevens, b. in Amesbury, Mass., May 26, 1748, a daughter of Rev. Phineas and Mrs. Sarah (Saunders) Stevens of Contoocook. She married Aaron French (No. 96), and resided in Sandown. She was adm. to the church May 31, 1761. She had children, recorded in Hampstead (p. 411, Vol. 1). Daughter Hannah, bapt. Nov. 13, 1757, in South Hampton.

No. 98.

Dea. Samuel Currier, b. in Amesbury, Mass., Feb. 1, 1709, a son of Samuel and Dorothy (Foot) Currier of Amesbury. He married Hannah Morrill (No. 99), and removed to Hampstead, to the old Currier homestead at West Hampstead, about 1760. He was received by letter from the church at South Hampton, July 26, 1761, and died in Hampstead, Sept. 24, 1766 (p. 812, Vol. 1).

No. 99.

Hannah Morrill, b. in Salisbury, Mass., March 16, 1711, a daughter of Capt. Ezekiel and Abigail (Wadleigh) Morrill of Salisbury. She married Samuel Currier (No. 98), Jan. 24, 1731, in Salisbury. She was admitted to the church by letter from the South Hampton church, July 26, 1761, and died at Hampstead. Their children were:—

I.   Samuel, bapt. in South Hampton, Nov. 4, 1744; d. young.
II.   Ezekiel, m. Susanna Emerson. (See p. 306, Vol. 1.)
III.   Samuel, bapt. Jan. 17, 1747 (No. 146).
IV.   Dorothy, bapt. Nov. 5, 1752.

No. 100.

Dea. Joseph French, b. in Salisbury, Mass., Feb. 27, 1702, a son of Dea. Joseph and Abigail (Browne) French of Salisbury. He married Hannah Gould (No. 101), and was received as a member of the church by letter from South Hampton church, July 26, 1761. He resided in Sandown.

(He was called Joseph, 4th, a grandson of Joseph and Sarah (Eastman) French; 2, Joseph and Susanna French; 1, Edward and Ann, of Salisbury, 1642.)

No. 101.

Hannah Gould, b. Nov. 8, 1703, in Amesbury, Mass., a daughter of Samuel and Sarah (Rowell) Gould of Amesbury. She married Joseph French (No. 100), Jan. 10, 1723, and was admitted as a member of the church by letter from the church at South Hampton, July 26, 1761. She had children, b. in Amesbury:—

I.   Sarah, b. March 29, 1725.
II.   ——, b. March 23, 1726.
III. Joseph, b. June 23, 1720; d. young.
IV.   Joseph, b. Feb. 21, 1732; m. Judith Diamond (Nos. 103, 104).
V.   Aaron, b. Jan. 21, 1733; m. Sarah Stevens (96, 97).

No. 102.

Martha Gile, b. 1726, in Plaistow, a daughter of Daniel and Joanna (Heath) Gile of Plaistow. She married Joseph Hadley (No. 69), and moved to Hampstead, where her children were born (p. 413, Vol. 1). She was admitted to the church May 31, 1761, died 1785, and was buried in the Hadley cemetery at East Hampstead.

No. 103.

Joseph French, Jr., b. Feb. 21, 1732, in Amesbury, Mass., son of Dea. Joseph and Hannah (Gould) French, of Hampstead and Amesbury (Nos. 100-101); married Judith Diamond (No. 104). He was received a member of the church by letter from the Church of Christ at South Hampton, June 18, 1762, and died in Hampstead, Nov. 8, 1808, aged 77 years. He was a captain in the militia, and major in the Revolutionary war.

No. 104.

Judith Diamond, b. in South Hampton, 1734, a daughter of Ezekiel and Miriam (Fowler) Diamond, of South Hampton, who emigrated from Devonshire, Eng., about 1725. She married Joseph French (No. 108), Dec. 12, 1752, and was adm. to the church by letter from the Church of Christ of South Hampton, June 18, 1762. She was the mother of children :—

I.   Ezra, bapt. in South Hampton, June 2, 1754.
II.   Hannah, b. Jan. 15, 1764; d., unmarried, in Hampstead, 1859, aged 90 years.
III.   Ephraim, bapt. in South Hamp., Aug. 24, 1755.
IV.   Joseph, m. Molly Tilton (Nos. 173, 174).
V.   Dorothy, bapt. in South Hamp., Nov. 6, 1757.
VI.   Sarah, m. Joshua Stevens (see No. 188).
VII.   Miriam, b. Oct. 27, 1770 (No. 185).

No. 105.

Samuel Browne, b. in Newbury, Mass., July 7, 1712, a son of James and Rebecca (Kelly) Browne of Newbury. He mar. his cousin Hannah Pike (No. 106), and soon after removed to Plaistow; about 1741, removed to Hampstead at the farm lately the home of Joseph G. Brown (No. 527). He was adm. to the church by letter from the church, at Newbury June 27, 1762, and d. in Hampstead about 1780.

No. 106.

Hannah Pike, b. Mar. 13, 1713, in Newbury, Mass., a daughter of Hugh and Hannah (Kelly) Pike of Newbury. Her parents settled in Plaistow before 1741. She mar. her cousin Samuel Browne (No. 105), in 1735, and was received as a member of the church, by letter from the church at Newbury, June 27, 1762. She d. in Hampstead, in 1804, aged " over 90." July 2, 1784, she gave a receipt to the executor of the estate of " Her honored uncle Richard Kelly," for gift of a feather bed, and the receipt was signed with

her mark. Two years later, May 12, 1786, Samuel Browne
and Hannah his wife, signed a receipt to the same executor,
and signed her name in full, with a fair handwriting,
and saying, "she had in the interval of two receipts, obtained a husband, and had also learned to write." She was
the mother of the following children, and perhaps others:—

I.   Moses, m. Sarah Kimball, daughter of Moses and Sarah (Webster) Kimball of Hampstead. They had children, b. in
Hampstead.
>   1. James, b. Aug. 15, 1763, m. Alice Ferren, resided in
>   Hampstead, and had children :—1. Enos, b. Nov.
>   13, 1784, m. Sally Brown, daughter of Samuel and
>   Hannah (George) Brown, his cousin. He d. Nov. 13,
>   1784; she d. Feb. 10, 1786. Their children :—1.
>   James, b. May 10, 1815; d. Nov. 5, 1831. 2. Wil-
>   liam H., b. May 15, 1819; d. Dec. 15, 1895; mar. Mary
>   Ann Hadley; she d. Sept. 8, 1869; children were —1.
>   Prescott W., b. April 14, 1844; d. unm. Aug. 28, 1881.
>   2. Charles H., b. Feb. 19, 1846; d. Jan. 31, 1870. 3.
>   Mary L., b. Aug. 20, 1847; d. unm. July 6, 1868. 4.
>   Sarah J., b. July 6, 1849; d. Dec. 28, 1855. 5. Louisa
>   S., b. July 6, 1849, d. Nov. 24, 1853.
>> 2. Jona. Kimball, b. March 10, 1790, m. Sarah
>> Brown.
>   3. Sarah, b. Oct. 10, 1794.
> 2. Abigail, b. July 4, 1764.
> 3. Sarah, b. March 6, 1767, mar. Daniel Browne (cousin).
> 4. Simeon, b. July 2, 1769, m. Susannah Johnson; had six
> children (p. 406, Vol, 1).
> 5. Jonathan, b. Feb. 22, 1772.
> 6. Alice, b. Feb. 17, 1776, m. Thomas Pierce of Atkinson.
> 7. Moses, b. Mar. 24, 1780.
> 8. Hannah, b. June 23, 1783; d. unm.

II.   Joseph, m. Susanah Johnson (see Nos. 141-142).
III. John, m. Lucy Abbott.
IV. Samuel Jr., m. Hannah or Abigail (George), and had ten children, b. in Hampstead, d. at the old Browne residence. Of
these children, Daniel, b. Nov. 5, 1797, mar. his cousin Sarah
Browne, and had children :—1. Dana. 2. Oscar, b. Jan.
20, 1830, mar. Emily S. Davis (see Nos. 234 and 235), May 1,
1853. He d. in Worcester, Mass., May 7, 1896. They had
two children, George and Marland of Worcester. 3. Harland, d. unm. Joseph, son of Samuel, Jr., and Abigail

Browne, b. Oct. 7, 1851, mar. Sally Greenleaf, who was b.
March 19, 1785, mar. April 14, 1814. He d. Dec. 24, 1850;
she d. Oct. 24, 1851. They had children :—
1. Mary A. O. (No. 440).
2. Serena, mar. Nathan Johnson (No. 461).
3. Abigail A., b. Oct. 25, 1824, 'd. unm. Sept. 8, 1847, in
   Hampstead.
4. Joseph G. (No. 527), mar. Sarah J. Hall (No. 508).

No. 107.

John Calfe, b. in Newbury, Mass., June 13, 1741, was the
oldest son of John and Naomi (Eliot) Calfe of Newbury,
and grandson of John and Deborah (King) Calfe, who
moved to Chester from Newbury, and owned proprietary
rights in several towns in this vicinity, and much land in
Chester, where he held various town offices. The grandfather John, was son of Robert Calef the emigrant, to Boston undoubtedly (who always spelled his name Calef; the
next three or four generations spelled it as did Hon. John
of Hampstead, but all of the name now seem to have gone
back to the original spelling of the name). Robert Calef was
the author of " More Wonders of the Invisible World."
He emigrated to America before 1688, and later became conspicuous through a controversy with Cotton and Increase
Mather, in which he emphatically denounced their witch
craft theories. There have been doubts expressed as to
whether the author was the elder Robert or the son Robert.
Hon Arthur B. Calef, late of Middleton, Conn., who made a
study of the Calef family in America, and collected many
family records, wrote in 1899, " there is no reason to believe
that the son Robert was the author, both by reason of his
probable youth, and also, because there is a copy with the
autograph of the author, in the Lenox Library, at New
York, which was presented by Robert the elder to Gov.
Bellingham, and the writing corresponds with that of
Robert the emigrant, as seen on the records."

A sketch of Hon. John Calfe of Hampstead was published

in Vol. 2, of the N. H. Historical Collection, and Monthly
Literary Journal at Concord, in 1823, by J. B. Moore. The
sermon preached at his funeral, Oct. 30, 1808, by Rev. John
Kelly, is reprinted in Vol. 1, p. 278, and a partial history of
his life is given in that paper. "He was said to have been a
great man in intellect as well as in stature. He was five feet
eight and one-half inches in height, and weighed over three
hundred pounds."

He was admitted a member of the church, Oct. 16, 1763,
and remained a member just forty-five years. He was
elected deacon, in 1773, April 20, and served thirty-five
years. He mar. his cousin Lois Calfe of Kingston (No. 108).
His life work will be found in above mentioned publications.
He resided where Mr. Charles H. Osgood now resides.

No. 108.

Lois Calfe, b. in Newbury, Mass., January 4, 1739, was a
daughter of Deacon William and Lois (Sawyer) Calfe of
Kingston. Her father lived in Newbury, where he mar. his
first wife Sarah Cheney ; she d. leaving him one child, Col.
John, later of Kingston. Her father purchased 15 acres of
land of Obed Elkins of Kingston, April 19, 1739, and
moved to Kingston soon after. He mar. Lois Sawyer, Nov.,
1740, and had ten children, Lois being the second, she was
bapt. in Kingston, Jan. 18, 1740. She was adm. to the
church, Oct. 16, 1763. She mar. her cousin Hon. John
Calfe (No. 107), and was the mother of five sons and four
daughters.

I.   Lois, b. June 27, 1763.
II.   Molly, b. June 27, 1765, m. John Poore of Hampstead.
III.   Child, b. April 7, 1767, d. young.
IV.   John, b. June 13, 1768, d. young.
V.   John, b. Mar. 20, 1771.
VI.   William, b. May 1, 1773, mar. Mary Little (No. 871).
VII.   Joseph, b. Dec. 4, 1775, mar. first, Nabby Kimball, daughter of
        Nathaniel and Susanna (Sawyer) Kimball of Plaistow. Her
        father was ensign in the Revolution, and afterwards was

quartermaster in Col. Cilley's reg., and in 1777, was appointed deputy sheriff of Rockingham county, and coroner in 1794. Joseph and Nabby Calef had one child.

1. Nabby, b. Mar. 31, 1803. His wife d. Oct. 8, 1804, and he mar. second, Margaret McKenzie, July 9, 1807, and had children.
2. John, b. Dec. 9, 1808, m. and resided in Weare; had one son, Robert, and daughters, Etta and Lizzie.
3. Nabby Kimball, b. June 8, 1810 (No. 504).
4. Caroline, b. May 21, 1820, m. John Sanborn; buried in West Hampstead cemetery.
5. Joseph James, b. April 2, 1828, m. Mary F. Batchelder (widow, resided at Haverhill, Mass., 1902), one daughter Margeret Ann, in business in Lawrence, Mass. Mrs. Calef is descended from the first minister in the West Parish.
6. Margeret Ann, b. (twin to Joseph J.), m. Loren Flanders of Sandown. They resided in Nashua.

VIII. Sarah, b. Aug. 6, 1778.
IX.   James, m. Anna Kimball (Nos. 334, 225, 314).

Mrs. Calfe d. in Hampstead, and was buried in the village cemetery.

No. 109.

Abiah Hunkins, b. in Haverhill, Mass., Nov. 9, 1715, a daughter of Robert and Abiah (Page) Hunkins of Haverhill and Bradford, Vt. She married John Muzzey (No. 51), and was admitted to the church March 25, 176., and died in Hampstead. Her children were born in Hampstead (p. 423, Vol. 1). Her son Thomas, b. July 17, 1845-6, married Martha Pearson, and had eight children, b. in Hampstead (see p. 423, Vol. 1) ; second, he mar. Tamer Little (No. 78, Covenant list).

No. 110.

Charles Johnson, b. in Hampstead, May 29, 1737, son of Michael and Mary (Hancock) Johnson. Some records say that Michael Johnson came, in 1730, from North Londonderry, Ireland, to Londonderry, originally from Scotland,

but the birth of a daughter, Abigail, b. in Haverhill, Mass.,
Aug. 31, 1728, would seem to show that he was in Haverhill
early. Their children, born in Hampstead, were:—

I.   Col. Thomas Johnson, of Revolutionary fame in Vermont; m.
Abigail Carlton, daughter of Dudley Carlton, of Bradford,
Mass.

II.   Robert Johnson, m. Abigail Kincaed; had daughter; m., first,
Luther Bailey; second, James Bailey.

III.   Miriam, m. Eben Mudgett of Hampstead and Weare; second,
Capt. Wm. Marshall of Hampstead.

IV.   John Johnson, died in Hampstead, 1756; buried with Michael,
the father, in the village cemetery (p. 309, Vol. 1).

V.   Mary, m. Samuel Kinkead of Windham in 1752.

Charles Johnson was admitted to the church March 25,
1764, and married Ruth Marsh (No. 111). He was dismissed
"upon his own request that they be received by the church
in Newbury." He was a distinguished officer in the Revolutionary army, and captured a sword from a Hessian lieutenant, which has been handed down in his family, and was
recently in the possession of Charles S. Johnson, of Lodi,
N.Y. He removed to Haverhill in 1772, where he was a deacon
of the church, justice of the peace, member of the General
Assembly, and one of the founders and trustees of the Haverhill Library. He died in Haverhill, March 8, 1818.
Many of the descendants of Michael and Mary (Hancock)
Johnson spell their names *Johnston*.

No. 111.

Ruth Marsh, b. in Haverhill, Mass., June 22, 1739, a
daughter of Ephraim and Hannah (Smith) Marsh of Haverhill. She married Charles Johnston (No. 10), in Providence,
Rhode Island, May 13 or 16, 1762. She was admitted to the
church membership March 25, 1764, and was dismissed to be
received by the church at Newbury, at Coos, Feb. 27, 1774.
They had children:—

I.   Capt. Michael, b. in Hampstead, April 19, 1764; married, Sept.
23, 1784, Sarah, daughter of Dea. Joseph and Hannah (Hale)
Atkinson, of Boscawen. She was of the same family as
Nathan Hale, the "martyr spy." Capt. Michael died at
Haverhill, N. H., Oct. 12, 1848; grandparents of Miss Philena
McKeen, for many years principal of Abbott Academy at
Andover, Mass.

II.   Polly, b. in Hampstead, May 13, 1760; m. Henry Burbank in
1785; d. May 17, 1880. Other children were born in Haverhill.

No. 112.

Timothy Goodwin, b. April 24, 1743, in Hampstead, son
of Nathan and Rhoda (Colby) Goodwin (Nos. 47, 48). He
married Anna Gould (No. 113), and was admitted to the
church July 28, 1765. He was prominent in town and
church affairs, and was elected deacon of the church June 1,
1776, and continued until his death, about 1804. He lived
at the present homestead of Henry Morgan, at East Hampstead.

No. 113.

Anna Gould, b. in South Hampton; bapt. June 12, 1743;
daughter of Nathan and Abigail (Stevens) Gould, of Amesbury, Mass. She married Timothy Goodwin (No. 112), and
was admitted to the church July 28, 1765, and died in Hampstead about 1790. She had eight children, b. in Hampstead.
(p. 412, Vol. 1.)

No. 114.

Sarah Sanclear, b. in Kingston, April, 1734, daughter of
George and Hannah (Downer) Sanclear, of Hampstead (No.
130). She was admitted to the church July 28, 1765.

No. 115.

Hannah Sanclear, b. in Kingston in 1738, daughter of
George and Hannah (Downer) Sanclear, of Hampstead (No.
130). She was admitted to the church July 28, 1765, and

married Moses Poore of Hampstead, March 31, 1767, and
had several children, and it has been said lived a while in
Weare.

No. 116.

Susanna Black, b. in Haverhill, Mass., a daughter of John
and Susanna (Davis) Black of Haverhill. She married
Samuel Johnson, April 28, 1843, in Haverhill, son of Stephen
and Sarah (Whittaker) Johnson, of Haverhill and Hampstead (No. 11). She was admitted to the church Sept. 28,
1765, and had children, b. in Haverhill:—

I.   Mary, b. April 10, 1744.
II.   Hannah, b. Dec. 4, 1748.
III. John, b. March 4, 1749.
IV.   Samuel, b. Dec. 2, 1751.

No. 117.

Joseph Sawyer, bapt. in Amesbury, Mass., Oct. 31, 1736
son of Edmund and Sarah (Rowell) Sawyer (Nos. 45 and
46). He came to Hampstead with his father when about
nine years old. He married Judith Kelly, and owned the
covenant in town, July 30, 1759 (see list), and was adm. to
full communion May 25, 1766. He settled on " Darby Hill,"
now called " Jeffers Hill," about 1756, and later moved to
Warner, as one of the earliest settlers. He was a respected
citizen, and was deputed to find the first minister for the
town, and selected his wife's cousin, William Kelly (No.
135), of Hampstead. He was a justice of the peace, and
was always spoken of as " Squire Sawyer." From the New
Hampshire State papers, dated Dec. 16, 1788 : " The petition of us, the subscribers, Humbly sheweth that whereas we
understand that Commissions of the Peace are soon to be
given, We wish that Joseph Sawyer, who has hitherto been
honored with a Justice's Commission and has behaved with
Integrity and Uprightness, may again be favoured with the

Honour of that Office for the Town of Warner, and your petitioners shall ever pray." Nineteen signatures. He d. at Warner, Nov. 29, 1813.

No. 118.

Judith Kelly, b. in Amesbury, Mass., Nov. 17, 1737, a daughter of Richard and Hannah (Bartlett) Kelly, of Birch Meadow (now Merrimac). Her father was an extensive farmer and shoemaker, and during a large portion of his life he took notes of " passing events." Quotations and extracts of his papers have largely aided local historians.

" Her mother, Hannah Bartlett, was a woman of very strong will and almost indescribable power of physical endurance. At one time her pastor made some sensatious remarks about her treatment of a slave, Reuben, and she left his communion and connected herself with the Presbyterian Church in Newburyport, where she would walk every Sabbath, no matter what the weather, a distance of ten miles, attend two services of two hours in length, and if she could find a sick person she would watch all night, walk home, and do burdensome work of a large family wash. Once her husband built a stone wall not where she thought it should be put, and she removed it all with her own hands and built it where she wanted it put, but age wrought its soothing balm, and she became a genial old lady."

Under date of Nov. 3, 1756, Judith's father wrote : " My daughter Judith removed from my house to Darby Hill, so called, in Hampstead, in the Province of New Hampshire, and this is an account of what I gave her, to make her equal to what I have given her sisters in portion." (Then follows a list of goods and value.)

And in 1749 and 1750 he wrote : "The later end of February and the beginning of March was again a very sorrowful time in my family, occasioned by ye canker or throat distemper, of which Judith was first taken and was exceed-

ing bad with it, but through mercy recovered, but Moses and
Richard died; John and William recovered."

Judith married Joseph Sawyer (No. 117), Sept. 9, 1756,
and owned the covenant, July 30, 1758, and was adm. to the
church May 25, 1766.

They had six children, b. in Hampstead (see p. 426, Vol.
1), and then removed to Warner, where others were born
(see History of Warner, Antrim, and Sutton, N. H.) Their
children, b. in Hampstead :—

I.   Abigail, b. May 31, 1757; m. Wells Davis, of Warner.
II.   Edmund, b. Sept. 2, 1750; m. Mehitable Morrill. Their son,
        Jacob Sawyer, was b. in 1794, was the father of J. Herbert
        Sawyer, of Boston, Mass., to whom I am indebted for much
        of the facts in relation to Edmund and Joseph Sawyer and
        their families (Nos. 45, 46, 117, 118).
III.   Anna, b. Dec. 19, 1761; m. Joseph B. Hoyt of Warner.
IV.   Jacob, b. Feb. 8, 1765.
V.   Moses, b. Feb. 27, 1767; m. Lavinia Kelly, daughter of Rev. Wil-
        liam, of Warner.
VI.   Joseph, b. Feb. 2, 1771; m. Ruth Page.
VII.   Judith, b. Oct. 14, 1772; m., first, John Hoyt, of Warner; sec-
        ond, Isaac Dalton; and d. March 2, 1865, aged 93 years.
VIII.   Sally, b. June 11, 1769.
IX.   Hannah, b. in Warner; probably m. Mitchell Gilman of Warner.
X.   Lois.
XI.   Richard Kelly, b. June 25, 1779: m. Polly Bean of Warner.

No. 119.

James King, b.   He
married Deliverance Harriman, of Haverhill, Mass., March 6,
1760, and resided in Haverhill District, now Plaistow, and
was admitted to the church in Hampstead, July 27, 1766
They had three children, b. in Haverhill :—

I.   Sarah, b. April 30, 1761; d. young.
II.   John, b. Jan. 16, 1763.
III.   James, b. May 20, 1765

No. 120.

Job Kent, b. in Haverhill, Mass., March 31, 1743, was a son of John and Mary (Godfrey) Kent, of Haverhill and Hampstead. John Kent lived for a time near the brook by Atkinson Depot, and later moved to the west part of Hampstead, near the home of the late Joseph G. Brown. Job Kent married Alice Little (No. 121), and was admitted to the church July 27, 1766, and remained a member seventy-one years. He was elected a deacon April 30, 1812, and died in Hampstead, Dec. 26, 1837, aged 94 years and 9 months. He served in the Revolution as a private soldier.

Thomas Kent of England came to Gloucester, Mass., prior to 1643. He had a house and land in what is now known as Essex, Mass. His oldest son, Thomas, probably born in England, was among those drafted in King Philip's war, Nov. 30, 1675. He purchased lands at West Gloucester, since known as Kent's Landing. He married Joan ——, and their oldest son was Josiah, b. March 31, 1660, who married Mary Lufkin, at Gloucester, April 17, 1689. Their children, b. at Gloucester, were :—

I.   Mary, b. Jan. 20, 1690; m., probably, John Bond, 1722.
II.   Sarah, b. Aug. 16, 1692.
III. Josiah, b. Aug. 3, 1699; probably moved to Harvard, Mass.
IV.   Abigail (No. 64).
V.   John, b. March 29, 1700; m. Mary Godfrey (above). Their children were : 1, Mary, b. Dec. 20, 1723; 2, Jacob, b. June 12, 1726; Josiah, b. June 23, 1728; Joseph, b. June 7, 1730; James, b. June 31, 1732; John, b. Feb. 11, 1735; Sarah, b. Nov. 12, 1738; Jeremiah (see "owned the covenant," No. 65); Job (No. 120); and Judith, m. Thomas Merrill.

No. 121.

Elice, or Alice, Little, b. in Hampstead, March 18, 1746, a daughter of Thomas and Mary (Bond) Little (see No. 32). She married Job Kent (120), and was admitted to the church July 27, 1766. She died in Hampstead, Oct. 7, 1816, and was buried in the village cemetery. She was the mother of ten children :—

I.   Joseph, b. Jan. 28, 1766.
II.   Thomas, b. Aug. 17, 1767.
III.   Mary, b. June 15, 1769.
IV.   James, b. Feb. 1, 1772.
V.   Elizabeth, b. Jan. 23, 1775; m. Samuel, son of Jeremiah Poore, of Atkinson.
VI.   Job, b. June 17, 1778.
VII.   Alice, m. Samuel Nichols (No. 265).
VIII.   Jonathan, m. Clarissa Page (Nos. 245, 246).
IX.   Sarah, m. Robert Emerson, Jr. (No. 206).
X.   Lydia, m. Jonathan Brickett (Nos. 232, 233).

No. 122.

Jemima Eastman, b. in Hampstead, March 1, 1750, a daughter of Edmund and widow Hannah (Hills) Eastman (Nos. 66, 67). She married Parker Stevens, son of William and Mary (Tucker) Stevens, who came to Hampstead from Gloucester, Mass., and settled north of the Island pond, William Stevens was doubtless a younger son of John and Mary (Chase) Stevens (see No. 68). He married, first, Mary Tucker, Nov. 24, 1744. She died in Hampstead, June 18, 1748. He then married, Elizabeth, daughter of Antepas Dodge, of Ipswich, Mass. (sister to No. 6), Feb. 20, 1749. She died in Hampstead, March 31, 1750, and he married, third, Lydia Gile, Jan. 19, 1769. (Births of children by the three wives, p. 427, Vol. 1.) The oldest son, Parker, b. Nov. 26, 1745, married Jemima Eastman (above), Feb. 10, 1766, they had children, b. in Hampstead :—

I.   Parker, b. Oct. 6, 1767; d. May 12, 1857.
II.   Polly, b. Nov. 13, 1769; d. Nov. 24, 1850, in New York State.
III.   Edmund, b. Feb. 11, 1772; d. Feb. 2, 1849, in Piermont.
IV.   Hannah, b. Feb. 24, 1775; d. Dec. 13, 1857, in Piermont.
V.   John, b. Sept. 25, 1777; d. March 7, 1854.
VI.   Joseph, b. Feb. 19, 1780.
VII.   Caleb, b. Nov. 27, 1782; d. in Concord, March 29, 1870; and was the father of Hon. Lyman Dewey Stevens, of Concord (see address, p. 176, Vol. 1, also remarks at 150th anniversary in this Volume) to whom I am indebted for these items.

Parker Stevens moved from Hampstead to Piermont, with his seven children, in 1787. He died there, Oct. 15, 1818. Jemima died in Hampstead, Feb. 29, 1784, having been admitted to the church July 27, 1766.

No. 123.

Annar Copp, b. in Hampstead, May 5, 1748, a daughter of David and Hannah (Merrill) Copp. She married Samuel Dodge (see No. 6), and was admitted to the church July 27, 1766. They lived later in Londonderry. Samuel Dodge married a second time in Londonderry.

No. 124.

Elizabeth Worthen, b. in Hampstead, April 12, 1735, a daughter of Samuel and Mehitable (Heath) Worthen of Hampstead and Weare. She married Thomas Cheney, son of Thomas and Hannah (Stevens) Cheney, of Plaistow. They owned the covenant, Nov. 18, 1764, and she was admitted to the church, July 27, 1766. She had three children, and died about 1769. Her husband married, third, Hannah Worthen, and a son, Peter, born in Hampstead, July 18, 1770. He was a member of Capt. Newell's company, of Titcomb's regiment, and served in Rhode Island in 1777. They removed to Sutton before 1805.

No. 125.

Molly Heath, b. in Hampstead, Jan. 3, 1752, was a daughter of Bartholomew and Hannah (Kelly) Heath of Hampstead (No. 54). She married Moses Stevens, May 4, 1766 (?) and was admitted to the church July 27, 1766. She had children, b. in Hampstead (p. 426, Vol. 1).

No. 126.

Mary Smith, b. in Salisbury, Mass., 1737, daughter of Samuel and Mary (Gove) Smith, of Hampton. She married Nathan Goodwin as his second wife (No. 47), and was ad-

mitted to the church July 26, 1767. She had a son, born in
Hampstead :—

I.   Smith, b. May 27, 1708; m. Molly Colby. He resided on the
     homestead for a time, and later on the street in Hampstead
     near where Joshua Merrick resides, and was a wheelwright
     by trade (see p. 412, Vol. 1). Their daughter, Peggy, m.
     John Jackson (see No. 417).

No. 127.

Richard Goodwin, b. in Amesbury, Mass., 1746, son of
Daniel and Hannah (Colby) Goodwin, later of Newton. He
married Elizabeth Heath (No. 128), and moved to Hampstead. He was admitted to the church Sept. 27, 1767, then
went to Dunbarton, and later settled in Newport, about 1780,
where he d. in 1821.

No. 128.

Elizabeth Heath, b. in Hampstead, Aug. 27, 1748, a
daughter of Bartholomew and Hannah (Kelly) Heath (No.
54). She married Richard Goodwin (No. 127), in Hampstead, Dec. 19, 1765, and was admitted to the church Sept.
27, 1767. They had children (it may be that the youngest
child was by a second wife) :—

I.   Elizabeth, m. Nathan Gould.
II. Moses, b. Dec. 28, 1768; m. Sarah Stanwood.
III. Benjamin, b. April 26, 1770.
IV. Hannah.
V.   Polly.
VI. Elizabeth, m. Jonathan Wakefield.

No. 129.

Nathaniel Knight, b. in Plaistow (now Atkinson), May,
1724, the second son of Nathaniel and Sarah (Somersby),
Knight, of Atkinson. Nathaniel, Sr., b. in Newbury, Mass.,
Dec. 22, 1688, son of John and Rebecca (Noyes) Knight of
Newbury, mar. Sarah, daughter of Abiel and Jane (Brockle-
bank) Somersby of Newbury. They moved to Plaistow soon

after their marriage, to the farm now owned by John (Knight) Mason (now East road, Atkinson), and were the first couple to live in the town with a family; their oldest son, John, who married Sarah Merrill, being the first child in town, b. in 1722, of which proof has been found. John settled where Harry I. Noyes now resides in Atkinson. Nathaniel Knight, Jr., married Abigail Merrill, and had children, b. in Atkinson:—

I.   Ruth, b. Aug. 19, 1752; m. Moses Harriman.
II.   Abigail, b. Feb. 20, 1755; m. Moses Emery.
III.   Samuel, b. Feb. 21, 1757; settled in Ryegate, Vt., and m. twice.
IV.   Betty, b. Feb. 26, 1759; d. Oct. 3, 1764.
V.   Nathaniel, b. Feb. 28, 1761; m. —— Smith; settled in Ryegate, Vt.
VI..   Elizabeth, b. Aug. 7, 1766; m. Simeon Kelly,

and were the parents of :—

1. John Kelly, Esq., b. July 22, 1790; m. Mary, daughter of Moses and Mary (Noyes) Chase. He was the only lawyer Atkinson ever had to settle in town, and they were the parents of Mary Elizabeth, wife of the late Rev. Charles Tenney (see Nos. 203, 204), and Henry Arthur, unmarried, employed in the P. O. department at Washington, D. C.
2. Dr. Nathaniel Knight Kelly, b. Sept. 14, 1800, of Plaistow.
3. Jacob, b. June 13, 1803; m. Betsey, daughter of Humphrey, Jr., and Judith (Noyes) Noyes of Atkinson.

Elizabeth Kelly, the mother, d. April 2, 1860. It is related by those who remember her that she has told the story of how "she has sat on the doorstep of her home (now where John Brackett Mason lives in Atkinson), and seen bears cross from the west, and also could hear the wolves howling in the Kingston woods."

Nathaniel Knight was admitted to the church Nov. 29, 1767, and died in Atkinson, and was buried in Atkinson cemetery.

No. 130.

Hannah Downer, b. June, 1697, in Newbury, Mass., daughter of Andrew and Susanna (Huntington) Downer of Salisbury. She married George Sinclear, and lived near the Angly pond, in Hampstead, which was the farm taken by the town (see No. 55) for a small pox hospital, in 1794. He died Apri 11, 1767, aged 72 years. Hannah, the wife, was admitted to the church Sept. 27, 1767, and died in Hampstead, Dec. 5, 1768, aged 71 years. She had children:—

I.   Susanna, m. John Clark (p. 407, Vol. 1).
II. Sarah (No. 114).
III. Hannah (No. 115).

No. 131.

Simeon Morrill, b. in Amesbury, Mass., May 9, 1726, a son of William Barnes and Lydia (Pillsbury) Morrill of Amesbury. He married Sarah Morrill (No. 132), and was admitted to the church by letter from the church at South Hampton, May 28, 1769. They moved to Londonderry, later, and probably died there.

No. 132.

Sarah Morrill, b. in South Hampton, bapt. Sept. 11, 1748, daughter of Joseph and Sarah Morrill of South Hampton. She married Simeon Morrill (No. 131), and was admitted to the church by letter from the Church of Christ at South Hampton, Sept. 27, 1769. She had children, b. at South Hampton :—

I.   Barnes, bapt. Jan. 24, 1750; m. Abigail Davis (No. 165).
II. Samuel, bapt. March 17, 1751.
III. William, b. Aug. 5, 1758.
IV. Betty, bapt. April 27, 1755.
V.   Sarah, bapt. Aug. 3, 1755; d. young.
VI. Sarah, bapt. Feb. 21, 1762.

No. 133.

Jane Martin, b. March 10, 1714, in Amesbury, Mass., a daughter of John and Jane (Flanders) Martin of Amesbury. She married Thomas Worthen of Haverhill, Mass., Jan. 3, 1734. She was admitted as a widow Nov. 19, 1769. "She had lived with a niece in town for a few years."

No. 134.

Ephraim Webster, b. in Bradford, Mass., May 13, 1730, a son of Samuel and Mary (Kimball) Webster of Bradford. He mar. Phebe Parker (No. 94), and later moved to Chester, where they resided six years; then they moved to East Hampstead about 1760, where George Plummer now resides. They probably lived there about fifteen years, then moved to Newbury, Vt., where he built a new house in 1773 (or as Clark and other historians say,—"moved to New York State," which then included Vt.). He was admitted to the church by letter from the church at Chester, Oct. 7, 1770, and died at New Chester, Aug. 18, 1803.

No. 135.

William Kelly, b. in West Newbury, Mass., Oct. 11, 1744, was a son of John and Hannah (Hale) Kelly. His parents soon after their marriage moved from West Newbury, to Salem, and lived first near the summit of Spicket Hill, but later, near the southern base of the road leading from Salem village to Scotland Hill, Haverhill, Mass. William graduated from Harvard College in 1767; studied divinity with Rev. Henry True. He was adm. a member of the church May, 1770, and Feb. 5, 1772, was ordained as pastor over the church in Warner.

While an undergraduate in college, he taught school several winters in Atkinson, and for a certain time after his graduation. He mar. Lavina, daughter of Rev. Abner Bayley of Salem, Feb. 24, 1773. He died of apoplexy in Warner, May 18, 1813, and was the parent of five children. From Long's sketch of Warner: "In the spring of 1771, Rev. Mr. Kelly was employed to preach as a candidate, and in November following, he received a call to settle in the ministry with a salary of 40 pounds the first year, to increase 1 pound and ten shillings a year, till it should amount to sixty pounds, and twenty cords of wood annually."

"On the day of his ordination, a Congregational church was gathered, consisting of seven male members." At that time there were but fifteen houses in Warner, and about as many glass windows. "The house built by him, was the first built in Warner with two stories." He was dismissed, at his own request, Mar. 1, 1801, and afterwards preached occasionally in Warner, and vicinity. It is also written of him, that "he was a small-sized, fair-looking man, rather liberal in his religious views, as compared with the orthodoxy of his times."

No. 136.

Nehemiah Heath, b. Nov. 1, 1745, in Hampstead, was a son of Bartholmew and Hannah (Kelly) Heath of Haverhill, Mass., and Hampstead (No. 54). He mar. Abiah Kelly (No. 137). He was adm. to the church May 26, 1771, and went to Warner with Rev. William Kelly to settle, and was a deacon of his church (No. 136).

No. 137.

Abiah Kelly, b. in Amesbury, Mass., Dec. 4, 1743, daughter of Joseph and Elizabeth (Hastings) Kelly of Haverhill; mar. Nehemiah Heath (No. 136), and was adm. to the church May 26, 1771.

No. 138.

Lydia Rideout, b. in Haverhill, Mass., May 1, 1700 (?), a daughter of James and Jemima (Davis) Rideout of Haver-

hill. She mar. first, James Holgate of Haverhill, and
second, Thomas Williams of Hampstead (No. 77), as
his second wife, Aug. 10, 1762. She was adm. to the church
Nov. 28, 1773, and d. in Hampstead, Dec. 2, 1784, aged 84
years.

No. 139.

Theopolis Goodwin, b. in Hampstead, Sept. 21, 1753, a
son of Nathan and Rhoda (Colby) Goodwin (Nos. 47-48).
He mar. Abigail Adams (No. 140), and was adm. to the
church June 19, 1774. He served in the Revolution, at Bunker Hill, and in the expedition to Rhode Island; moved to
Dunbarton and thence to Newport, in 1784. He d. in 1799.

No. 140.

Abigail Adams, b. Sept. 2, 1750, in Rowley, Mass.,
daughter of Israel and Deborah (Searl) Adams of Rowley.
She mar. Theopolis Goodwin (No. 139), March 9, 1773, and
was adm. to the church June 19, 1774. They had children:—

I.   Deborah, b. Dec. 12, 1776; m. Ralph Chamberlain.
II.   Elizabeth, b. Dec. 31; m. 1780.
III.   Polly, b. Feb. 2, 1783; m. Jeremiah Kelsey.
IV.   Molly, b. Mar. 3, 1785.
V.   Rhoda, b. June 13, 1788; m. David Reed.
VI.   Ruth, b. April 30, 1791.
VII.   Israel, b. Feb. 14, 1793; called "Judge."

No. 141.

Joseph Browne, b. in Newbury, Mass., 1737, was a son of
Samuel and Hannah (Pike) Browne (Nos. 105-106). He
mar. Susannah Johnson (No. 142), and resided where the
late Joseph G. Brown resided; was a wheelwright by trade.
He was adm. to the church July 31, 1774, and d. in Hampstead; was buried in the village cemetery.

No. 142.

Susannah Johnson, b. in Hampstead, July 13, 1742, was a daughter of Stephen, Jr., and Susanna (Lovekin) Johnson, of Hampstead and Londonderry (Nos. 23, 24). She married Joseph Browne (No. 141), and was admitted to the church July 31, 1774. She had six children, b. in Hampstead (see p. 405, Vol. 1).

No. 143.

Jonathan Currier, b. in Gloucester, Mass., Nov. 27, 1737, was a son of Samuel and Lydia (Williams) Currier, who later moved to Haverhill. He married Hannah Clark of Haverhill, Mass., Nov. 1, 1778. He was admitted to the church by letter from the church at Methuen, Mass., May 6, 1775. He later was of Piermont.

No. 144.

Austin George, b. in Haverhill, Mass., June 25, 1732, was a son of William and Sarah (Smith) George of Haverhill. He married Sarah Shute (No. 145), Jan. 2, 1755, and moved from Haverhill to Hampstead, to the farm nearly opposite the late residence of I. William George. He was admitted to the church June 25, 1778, and died in Hampstead. His father, b. in Haverhill, June 27, 1705, was a son of John and Ann (Swaddock) George, who had children, b. in Haverhill :—

I.   John Swaddock, b. Dec. 15, 1703; m., first, Alice Robinson; second, widow Sarah English; third, Sarah Colby; and by the three wives had eleven children.
II.   William, b. June 27, 1705; m. Sarah Smith, and they were the parents of ten children, of whom Austin, b. June 26, 1732, m. Sarah Shute (above), (the third), and Jonathan, b. Jan. 2, 1735 (the fourth), mar. Hannah Currier (see No. 243).
III.   Augustin, b. Jan 18, 1708.
IV.   Elizabeth, b. Sept. 20, 1709.

hill. She mar. first, James Holgate of Haverhill, and
second, Thomas Williams of Hampstead (No. 77), as
his second wife, Aug. 10, 1762. She was adm. to the church
Nov. 28, 1773, and d. in Hampstead, Dec. 2, 1784, aged 84
years.

No. 139.

Theopolis Goodwin, b. in Hampstead, Sept. 21, 1753, a
son of Nathan and Rhoda (Colby) Goodwin (Nos. 47-48).
He mar. Abigail Adams (No. 140), and was adm. to the
church June 19, 1774. He served in the Revolution, at Bunker Hill, and in the expedition to Rhode Island; moved to
Dunbarton and thence to Newport, in 1784. He d. in 1799.

No. 140.

Abigail Adams, b. Sept. 2, 1750, in Rowley, Mass.,
daughter of Israel and Deborah (Searl) Adams of Rowley.
She mar. Theopolis Goodwin (No. 139), March 9, 1773, and
was adm. to the church June 19, 1774. They had children :—

I.   Deborah, b. Dec. 12, 1776; m. Ralph Chamberlain.
II.   Elizabeth, b. Dec. 31; m. 1780.
III.   Polly, b. Feb. 2, 1783; m. Jeremiah Kelsey.
IV.   Molly, b. Mar. 3, 1785.
V.   Rhoda, b. June 13, 1788; m. David Reed.
VI.   Ruth, b. April 30, 1791.
VII.   Israel, b. Feb. 14, 1793; called " Judge."

No. 141.

Joseph Browne, b. in Newbury, Mass., 1787, was a son
Samuel and Hannah (Pike) Browne (Nos. 105-106). I
mar. Susannah Johnson (No. 142), and resided where t
late Joseph G. Brown resided; was a wheelwright by tra
He was adm. to the church July 31, 1774, and d. in Ha
stead ; was buried in the village cemetery.

No. 142.

Susanna Johnson, b. in Hampstead, July 12, 1762, was a daughter of Stephen Jr. and Susanna (Jenness) Johnson, of Hampstead and Londonderry (No. 20, 26). She married Joseph Emerson (No. 161), and was removed to ... July 15, 1774. She had no children ... in Hampstead ...

No. 143.

Jonathan Emerson ...

No. 144.

V.   Gideon, b. May 27, 1712; m. Elizabeth Jewett of Rowley, Mass.;
lived in Bradford, where children were born :—

> 1. William, b. in Bradford, Nov. 18, 1737; m. Ruth Has-
> tings, Nov. 20, 1763, and had children : 1, Robert, b.
> April 14, 1764. 2, William, b. April 3, 1766, settled
> in Plymouth, N. H., and was the grandfather of Miss
> Louisa V. George, compiler in part of the History of
> Plymouth, and to whom I am greatly indebted for
> much help in this sketch. William and Ruth (Has-
> tings) George moved to Hampstead for a time, where
> five other children were born. (See p. 412, Vol. 1.)

No. 145.

Sarah Shute, b. in July, 1732, in Haverhill, Mass., was a
daughter of Jacob and Sarah (George) Shute, of Haverhill
and Concord. She married Austin George, 2d, Jan. 1, 1755,
in Haverhill, and was admitted to the church June 25, 1775.
She died Jan. 24, 1830, aged 97 years and 5 months. She
had children, b. in Haverhill :—

I.   Austin, b. Dec. 4, 1755; d. young.
II.   Abigail, b. Oct. 30, 1756.
III. Mary, b. Sept. 30, 1758; d. young.
IV.   Jonathan, b. Sept. 12, 1760; d. young.
V.   Jonathan, b. Nov. 9, 1762.
VI.   Sarah, b. March 5, 1765.
VII. Austin, b. April 25, 1768; m. Sally Marston; d. Dec. 6, 1806, in
      Hampstead. (See p. 412, Vol. 1.)

Jacob Shute, father of Sarah (Shute) George, was of
French origin. He was a son of a French Protestant, or
Huguenot, who fled from Paris on the revocation of the edict
of Nantes, and took refuge in Ireland. When 17 years old,
disliking the trade to which he had been apprenticed, he ran
away, with a man named Dawen, and took secret passage in
a hold of a ship for this country. They remained concealed
till driven out by hunger. On arriving in Newburyport
they, having nothing with which to pay their fare, were sold
(their service, for a time) to pay it. They were both bought
by Capt. Ebenezer Eastman, of Haverhill, and served him

until twenty-one years of age. He married Sarah George, and had children: Sarah, mar. Austin George (above); John and Elizabeth, born at Pennecook. His wife d. January, 1745, and he married a widow, Evan, and had two daughters, that died young. He died in Concord, Feb. 16, 1794, aged 94 years.

According to tradition, Ebenezer Eastman's team of six yoke of oxen was the first to cross the wilderness from Haverhill, Mass,, to Concord, or Pennecook, and Jacob Shute was the driver, who, in order to get safely down Sugar Ball bank, felled a pine tree and chained it top foremost to the cart to stay the motion of it down the precipice (Bouton's History of Concord).

Shute afterwards settled in Pennecook, and was one of the first thirty-six men to settle there.

No. 146.

Samuel Currier, bapt. in South Hampton, Jan. 17, 1747, by the Rev. William Parsons, was a son of Dea. Samuel and Hannah (Morrill) Currier, of Amesbury and Hamp. (see Nos. 98, 99). He mar. Mary Rowell (No. 147), and was adm. to the church Oct. 2, 1775, and elected deacon June 1, 1776, and served till 1804.

No. 147.

Mary Rowell, b. in 1750, in Kingston, a daughter of Daniel and Anne (Currier) Rowell of Kingston. She married Samuel Currier (No. 146), and was admitted to the church Oct. 2, 1775.

No. 148.

Timothy Stevens, b. in Haverhill, Mass., June 20, 1721, a son of John and Mary (Chase) Stevens of Haverhill. He married Elizabeth Huse, who was born Dec. 26, 1840, and moved to Hampstead, near the Derry line, where several

children were born. He was admitted to the church by letter from the Byfield church, June 1, 1776. He died in
Hampstead, June 19, 1801, and was buried in the West
Hampstead cemetery, where his wife Elizabeth and several
of his children lie buried (see p. 311, Vol. 1.). See Appendix, Stevens.)

No. 149.

James Emerson, b. in Haverhill, Mass., Jan. 10, 1739, a
son of Stephen and Hannah (Marden) Emerson (Nos. 15 and
16). He married Lydia Hoyt (No. 150), and was admitted
to the church from Weare, where he went to live when his
father moved to that place. He and his wife owned the
covenant in Hampstead (see list), Jan. 11, 1761. He was a
deacon of the church at Weare, and " was very pious about
keeping the Sabbath." It is related that " one day he was
riding horseback, with his wife behind him, to meeting. As
they jogged along they saw a fox chasing a rabbit, both
jumping over and under a log, the rabbit dodging and very
much frightened. Mrs. Emerson wanted her husband to get
off the horse and scare the fox away. Deacon Emerson said
it would be profaning the Sabbath. God would be angry
with him if he did, and so he rode on and left the poor
bunny to his fate." His wife, in telling the story, said " her
husband was a little particular, but she could not tell this
time whether he was too pious or too lazy." He died in 1814.

No. 150.

Lydia Hoyt, b. in Salisbury, Mass , April 6, or 9, 1740, a
daughter of Moses and Mary (Carr) Hoyt of Salisbury (a
sister of No. 91). She married Dea. James Emerson (No.
149), Sept. 25, 1760, and was admitted to the church from
the church in Weare, Aug. 30, 1778. She owned the covenant in Hampstead (see list), Jan. 11, 1761. She died in
1833, aged 97 years. She had children :—

I. Moses, b. in Hampstead, Sept. 24, 1760, who settled in Weare.
II. James, settled in Bradford.
III. Stephen, m. —— Boynton, and went to Ohio.
IV. Hannah, m. —— Stevens; and, second, m. —— ——.
  And three other children, b. in Weare.

No. 151.

Samuel Pillsbury, b. in Rowley, Mass., Dec. 22, 1752, son of John and Ruth (Brocklebank) Pillsbury, both of Rowley, m. March 16, 1742. He married Elizabeth Pingree, of New Chester, Nov. 27, 1776, and lived for a time in Chester, and soon after moved to Salisbury, where they had ten children. He was admitted to the church by letter from the Third Church at Newbury, Mass., May 3, 1779.

No. 152.

Abner Rogers, b. April 14, 1739, in Amesbury, Mass., son of Robert and Hannah (Sargent) Rogers, of Amesbury and Newbury. He married Hannah Rowell (No. 153), and was admitted to the church Oct. 29, 1780. He was a carpenter by trade, and lived at what is known as the "old Brickett place," near the Hog Hill brook. He, in company with Lieut. Thomas Reed, "built the porch and steeple to the old meeting house, in 1793, and took two pews as part payment for the work" (p. 161, Vol. 1).

No. 153.

Hannah Rowell, b. July 7, 1732, in Amesbury, Mass., a daughter of Philip and Elizabeth (Puddington) Rowell, of Amesbury; married Abner Rogers (No. 152), and was admitted to the church Oct. 29, 1780. Their children were:—

I. Sargent, b. Oct. 21, 1770.
II. Robert, b. Dec. 5, 1772; graduated from Harvard College in 1802; was a merchant in France at one time, but resided in Boston in 1837.

Cheney of Plaistow, Nov. 23, 1780. He was b. Dec. 5, 1756, in Plaistow. He was in Capt. Jere. Gilman's company, of Col. John Nixon's regiment. In 1779, July 7, he bought one-fourth of lot No. 46 in the second division of Perry-town (Sutton), and was one of the original petitioners for the incorporation of Sutton, May 21, 1783. In 1823 he was in Jefferson county, N. Y., and reported to be 63 years old at the issue of pensions in 1819, and received a pension for services in the Revolution, on the Massachusetts line. Mary Cheney was admitted to the church and baptized Feb. 1, 1781, and soon after moved to Canaan to reside.

No. 156.

Clark Ela, b. in Haverhill, Mass., July 14, 1756, son of Samuel and Mary (Homans) Ela (No. 154,) of Haverhill and Londonderry. He married —— Fulton, of Londonderry, and had one son, b. in L. He was admitted to the church by baptism, Feb. 17, 1781, and died in Derry.

No. 157.

Lieut. John Darling, b. in Amesbury, Mass., Sept. 27, 1716, was a son of John and Mary (Brown) Darling. He married, first, Phebe Roberts, daughter of Daniel, Jr., and Mehitable (Davis) Roberts, and had five children, b. in Hampstead (see p. 409, Vol. 1.). He married, second, Hannah Roberts (No. 158), and was admitted to the church by letter from the church in Hopkinton, June 24, 1781. He removed to Hopkinton, from Hampstead, about 1760.

No. 158.

Hannah Roberts, b. in Hampstead, April 19, 1740, a daughter of Daniel and Martha (Heath) Roberts (No. 81). She married Lieut. John Darling (No. 157), and was admitted to the church by letter from the church at Hopkinton, June 24, 1781.

No. 159.

Lieut. John Harriman, b. in Haverhill, Mass., Feb. 14, 1788, a son of Abner and Sarah (Merrill) Harriman, of Haverhill and Hampstead. His father was one of the first settlers in Hampstead, the father of Jassael Harriman mentioned on p. 309, Vol. 1. Abner Harriman was a son of Matthew and Elizabeth (Swan) Harriman, son of Leonard Harriman, the emigrant, of Rowley, Mass. He was admitted to the church May 26, 1788. He resided at the " Moulton homestead." Lieut. John Harriman d. Aug. 6, 1822, and was buried in the Hadley cemetery. (Page 313, Vol. 1.)

No. 160.

Abigail Clement, b. in Haverhill, Mass., March 7, 1748, fifth daughter of Benjamin and Mary (Bartlett) Clement, of Haverhill. She married Lieut. John Harriman (No. 159), and was admitted to the church May 26, 1788. She had children, b. in Hampstead:—

I.   Sarah, b. July 8, 1760; m. William Moulton, 1787 (see p. 372, Vol. 1).
II.   Abigail, b. April 10, 1774.
III.   Betty, b. Aug. 4, 1777.
IV.   Mary, b. April 10, 1780; m. John Clark (see p. 374, Vol. 1).

She died in Hampstead, Aug. 15, 1812, and was buried in the Hadley cemetery.

No. 161.

James True, b. in Hampstead, March 23, 1759, a son of Rev. Henry and Ruth (Ayer) True (Nos. 1 and 72). He was a graduate from Harvard College, 1780. He preached in Virginia and in Portland, Me. He died unmarried, Jan. 6, 1795. He was admitted to the church June 6, 1785.

No. 162.

James Kimball, b. in Hampstead, Feb. 19, 1770, a son of Joseph and Abiah (Muzzey) Kimball, and grandson of Dea. Benjamin and Mary (Eaton) Kimball (No. 22). He was admitted to the church June 17, 1785, and died in Hampstead, unmarried, March 2, 1790, and was buried in the village cemetery.

No. 163.

Rev. Tillius Howe, b. in Henniker, May 1, 1750, a son of Jonathan and Lydia (Bingham) Howe. He was a graduate of Dartmouth College, April 17, 1787, and received a call to Hampstead, which he accepted, and preached several months, but was dismissed "as not suitable for the place." He married a daughter of Anthony and Ruth Stickney, of Chester and Pembroke. He was pastor of a church at Sharon, Vt., and died in Fryeburg, Me., September, 1830.

No. 164.

Rev. John Kelly, b. in Amesbury, Mass., Feb. 22, 1763, a son of John and Elizabeth (Hoyt) Kelly, of Amesbury. (See Autobiography, by Rev. John Kelly, p. 46, Vol. 1.) He married Abigail Dearborn (No. 171). He was admitted by letter from the Second Church at Amesbury, Dec. 5, 1792. He died in Hampstead, Nov. 28, 1848, and was buried in the village cemetery.

No. 165.

Barnes Morrill, b. in South Hampton, bapt. Jan. 24, 1750, a son of Simeon and Sarah (Morrill) Morrill, of South Hampton, and later of Hampstead (Nos. 181 and 182). He married Abigail Davis (No. 166), and was admitted to the church by letter from the church at Londonderry, Jan. 27, 1798, and was buried in the village cemetery.

No. 166.

Abigail Davis, b. Dec. 9, 1760, in Hampstead, daughter of Obediah and Sarah (Colby) Davis of Hampstead. She married Barnes Morrill (No. 165), and was admitted to the church from the Londonderry church, Jan. 27, 1798. She died in Hampstead, Feb. 29, 1844, and was buried in the village cemetery. She had children, buried in the village cemetery at Hampstead:—

I.   Francis, d. Sept. 22, 1794, aged 4 years.
II.   Betsey, d. Feb. 4, 1803, aged 16 years.
III.   Francis, d. Dec. 7, 1805, aged 5 years.
IV.   Betsey, d. April 2, 1809, aged 4 years.
V.   Joseph G. Morrill, d. Oct. 2, 1845, aged 41 years.

No. 167.

Jonathan Carlton Little, b. in Plaistow, June 29, 1769, a son of Nathaniel and Mary (Carlton) Little (see p. 351, Vol. 1). He married, first, Meribah Farnum Hale, in April, 1793, a daughter of Ebenezer and Meribah (Roberts) Hale, of Hampstead. She died Nov. 14, 1801, aged 33 years. He then married his cousin, Phebe Poor (No. 227). During his father's absence in the Revolutionary war, though only nine years old, he had entire charge of the large farm, with his younger brother Nathaniel (No. 256). Capt. Jonathan Little was very regular in his habits, and it has been said that he rose every morning before the sun for forty years in succession. He voted at every presidential election, from that of Washington to his decease (Feb. 10, 1856). He attended the annual town meeting for fifty-six years, with but four exceptions. He served several years as selectman. He took great delight in the Bible, which he read habitually, and the sanctuary was his unfailing resort on the Sabbath until he was detained by the infirmities of age. He had children by his first wife:—

I. Eben Hale, b. June 12, 1794; married, first, Elizabeth Gibbon, who d. Dec. 26, 1874; and, second, mar. Jerusha Palmer. He was a cooper by trade, and for many years was an inspector of fish in Boston. He d. in Haverhill, Mass., May 31, 1876 (see p. 65, Vol. 1).
II. Mary Carlton, mar. Capt. Jesse Ayer (No. 272).

No. 168.

Martha Sargent, b. in Amesbury, Mass., Dec. 25, 1771, a daughter of Amassa and Mary (Webster) Sargent, of Amesbury. She married Joseph Welch (No. 219), of Enfield, March 13, 1791, and was admitted to the church by letter from the Second Church at Amesbury, July 5, 1793. She d. in Perry, Me., May 16, 1838. She had children, b. in Hampstead:—

I. Henry, b. April 20, 1793; mar. Delia Brickett (No. 282).
II. Sally, mar. Henry Hubbard (see No. 261).
III. Mary W. (No. 266).
IV. Eliza Merrill, b. Aug. 10, 1802; d. July 11, 1821.
V. Francis (No. 258).
VI. Joseph, b. April 12, 1807; mar. Louisa Choate.
VII. Martha Sargent, b. Dec. 5, 1808; mar. James Nichols, whose first wife was her sister, Mary W.
VIII. George Washington, b. Feb. 2, 1811; d. Dec. 2, 1826.
IX. Amassa, b. Nov. 1, 1815; married Martha Whittier; resided in Lawrence, Mass., where he died, March 12, 1881.

No. 169.

Joshua Eastman, b. in Hampstead, a son of Edmund and widow Hannah Hills (Nos. 66, 67). He married Sarah Tucker (No. 170), and was admitted to the church Aug. 4, 1793. He died in Hampstead, Feb. 1, 1841, and was buried in the West Hampstead cemetery.

No. 170.

Sarah Tucker, b. in Kingston (now Sandown), Jan. 18, 1755, a daughter of Jacob and Lydia (Lunt) Tucker, of Kingston and South Hampton. She married Joshua East-

man (No. 169), Dec. 4, 1780, and was admitted to the
church Aug. 4, 1798, and d. Aug. 22, 1827, and was buried
in West Hampstead cemetery. She had children, b. in
Hampstead :—

I.   Joshua (No. 213), mar. Susanna Chase (No. 230).
II.   Amassa (No. 348), mar. Betsey Tucker (No. 149).
III.   Tappan, b. Nov 23, 1790; mar. Susan K. Boyington, Dec. 28,
       1813. He died in Hampstead, Sept. 13, 1864. They had an
       only son, Albert L., born in Hampstead, Oct. 17, 1815; mar.
       Mary E. (Kent) Irving (No. 523).
IV.   Sally, b. Jan. 10, 1793; mar. George Moores of Derry, and had
       three daughters.

No. 171.

Abigail Dearborn, b. in Chester, July 9, 1770, a daughter
of Dea. John S. and Mary (Emerson) Dearborn, of Chester,
who resided on what was the Robie place in 1778, originally
the Blake farm (tanyard). Dea. Dearborn was given the
farm by his parents, Thomas and Dorothy (Sanborn) Dearborn, in 1751. She married Rev. John Kelly (No. 164), and
was admitted to the church in Hampstead, Jan. 29, 1794.
She died in Hampstead, May 28, 1850, and was buried in the
village cemetery. She had children, b. in Hampstead (See
p. 417, Vol. 1.) :—

I.   Henry True (No. 218).
II.   John (No. 231).
III.   Daughter, d. young.
IV.   Irene (No. 228).
V.   Francis, drowned in a well, June, 1804.
VI.   Israel, d. young.
VII.   Samuel (No. 250).
VIII. Mary D., d. young.
IX.   Abigail (No. 262).
X.   Elizabeth Hoyt, d. unmarried.
XI.   Sarah, d. unmarried.
XII.   Hannah Worth (No. 365).

No. 172.

Mary Dow, b. in Salem, N. H., July 7, 1776, a daughter of Abraham and Susannah (Hoyt) Dow of Salem. She mar. Amos Mills of Hampstead, and was adm. to the church as a widow, Oct. 25, 1795. She was dismissed to the church at Dunbarton, in 1834. She had one son b. in Hampstead :—

I.   Ephraim, b. June 8, 1790.

No. 173.

Joseph French, Jr., b. April 20, 1766, in Hampstead, a son of Capt. Joseph and Judith (Diamond) French (Nos. 103-104). He mar. Molly Tilton (No. 174), and was adm. to the church June 10, 1796. He d. in Hampstead, March 7, 1844, and was buried in the village cemetery.

No. 174.

Molly Tilton, b. in Sandown, Feb. 17, 1770, a daughter of Daniel and Miriam (French) Tilton of South Hampton, and Piermont, N. H., and at one time of Sandown. She mar. Joseph French, Jr. (No. 173), 1788, and was adm. to the church June 10, 1796. She d. in Hampstead, July 9, 1852, aged 82 years, and 4 months, and was buried in the village cemetery. She had children :—

I.   Miriam, b. Dec. 21, 1789; m.
II.   Polly, b. Dec. 18, 1792.
III.   Judith, b. Nov. 11, 1795.
IV.   Irene, b. Feb. 4, 1801; d. aged 18 mos.
V.   Margritta Tilton, b. Oct. 10, 1803.
VI.   Caroline (No. 208).

No. 175.

Abigail Plummer, b. in Londonderry, daughter of Daniel and Abigail (   ) Plummer (Nos. 178-179). She mar., first, Henry, son of Stephen, Jr., and Susanna (Lovekin) Johnson (Nos. 23-24), Nov. 28, 1786, and had children b. in

Hampstead (see p. 416, Vol. 1). Mr. Johnson d. Aug. 21,
1795. She was adm. to the church as a widow, June 4,
1799. She mar., second, Joseph Warner Burroughs of
Hampstead, June 3, 1799. The church records show that
she was disciplined, May 6, 1798, but "appeared before the
church, and asked pardon and forgiveness of God ; and expressed her desire to be continued in the fellowship and communion of the church, and was freely accepted; and may
God forgive, accept of her, and save her, through the Redeemer of his word." On June 12, 1831, she was again
disciplined for a neglect of public worship, and as she expressed no desire ever again to attend the worship of that
denomination, she was separated from the church.

No. 176.

Reuben Mills, b. in Plaistow (now Atkinson) in 1760, a
son of John and Abigail (Emerson) Mills (see No. 60) of
Hampstead. He mar., first, Betsey Burns, who had two
children b. in Hampstead (see p. 422, Vol. 1). She d. Dec.
11, 1784, and he then mar., second, Ruth Kelly (No. 177).
He was adm. to the church Aug. 13, 1797. He was dismissed to the church at Dunbarton, before 1834. He d. at
the home of a son-in-law, Thomas Wilson, at Dunbarton,
July 17, 1847, aged 87 years. It is said that, "during his
life, he read the Bible through 100 times."

No. 177.

Ruth Kelly, b. in Kingston, March 12, 1764, a daughter of
Samuel and Elizabeth (Heath) Kelly of Birch Meadow,
Amesbury. She mar. Reuben Mills (No. 176), published
Nov. 10, 1784, and was adm. to the church Aug. 13, 1797.
She d. in Dunbarton, June 22, 1828. She was dismissed to
the Dunbarton church Feb. 24, 1824. She was the mother
of children :—

I.   Nathaniel Whitmore, b. July 6, 1786; d. Sept. 16, 1815.
II.   John, b. Sept. 9, 1788; m. Alice Williams of Hampstead, and d.
        in Dunbarton, Feb. 12, 1831.
III.   Robert, b. Feb. 9, 1791; d. Oct., 1795..
IV.   Amos, b. Dec. 23, 1793; resided in Dunbarton, where he d. June
        29, 1878; m. Betsey, daughter of Thomas, son of Thomas and
        Elizabeth (Hogg) Mills (see Nos. 60, 532).
V.   Betsey, b. Feb. 10, 1799 (No. 362).
VI.   Ruth, b. Aug. 19, 1800; d. Oct. 22, 1818.
VII.   George, b. March 15, 1802; lived in Lynn, Mass., and d. of can-
        cer, Jan. 26, 1870.
VIII.   Mary, b. Feb. 3, 1807; m. Thomas Wilson of Dunbarton.
IX.   Eunice, b. Jan. 24, 1809; m. Lewis Wilson of Dunbarton.

No. 178.

Daniel Plummer, b. in Gloucester, Mass. He mar. widow
Abigail Plummer (No. 179), second wife, and. was adm. to
the church, from the Londonderry church June 25, 1797.
He and his wife were received into the church "without the
indulgence of communing at the Lord's Table, until they
could more clearly ascertain their fitness for the ordinance."

No. 179.

Abigail Plummer, widow.

She mar. Daniel Plummer (No. 178), and was adm. to the
church June 25, 1797, from the Londonderry church.
Daughter Abigail (No. 175).

No. 180.

Moses Little, b. in Plaistow, Sept. 9, 1739, a son of
Samuel and Hannah (Sewell) Little of Plaistow (now Atkinson) (see No. 14). He mar. Mary Noyes of Atkinson (No.
181). He was adm. to the church July 1, 1797, and was elected
deacon, May 3, 1804, and continued till his death, March
26, 1816. He was a carpenter and builder, and resided
where William A. Emerson now resides. He was also
prominent in town affairs, and served on the committees of
the town in the Revolution.

No. 181.

Mary Noyes, b. in Atkinson, in 1742, a daughter of Capt. James and Sarah (Little) Noyes of Atkinson, who resided where the late James Henry Noyes resided. She mar. Moses Little (No. 180), and was adm. to the church July 2, 1797. She d. Oct. 23, 1823, in Hampstead. She had no children.

No. 182.

Abigail (or, Nabby) Patten, b. in Amesbury, Mass., bapt. Oct. 15, 1772, a daughter of John and Ruth (Pillsbury) Patten, of Amesbury. She married Dr. Joshua Sawyer of Hampstead, who d. in Hampstead, Nov. 2, 1829, aged 62 years. She was admitted to the church July 2, 1797, and was dismissed, and afterwards received to the Congregational Church of Haverhill, Mass., Sept. 25, 1848. She d. March 4, 1847. A daughter, b. in Hampstead—Anna, b. 1810; d. in 1815.

No. 183.

Rev. True Kimball, b. in Plaistow, Jan. 28, 1757, a son of Jonathan and Abigail (True) Kimball, who was elected deacon of the North Parish Church in 1789 (see No. 21). He was graduated in the class of 1778, at Harvard College, and studied for the ministry. He preached in Amherst and Newbury, Mass., and his final charge was at Hampstead as a supply, where he died. For several months before his death he was partially deranged, and was complained of by Dea. Joseph French "as walking disorderly before the church." He "was placed on probation" several times for the "fault of neglecting the public worship and ordinances of the gospel." "Deacon French said in church meeting that ' Brother True Kimball told him that he denied the entire depravity of human nature, and has also said, as nearly as I can remember, that the devils in hell are not wholly depraved.' On account of these things it is my desire that the church will admonish and deal with my brother Kimball according to the rules of the gospel."

On April 20, 1814, the committee of the church, Moses Little, Abner Rogers, and John True, presented resolutions recommending dismissal from the church fellowship, which was done.

The following account of his death appears on the church records: "On the 17th day of July, 1816, about 10 o'clock A. M., Mr. Kimball put an end to his life in his barn, with the long reins of his chaise, without being supposed of such a design, only as he seemed to be inclined to Universalism and infidelity."

He married Jane Short, at Newbury, Mass., who was b. in 1761, and who died in Hampstead, Jan. 22, 1841, at the house now occupied by John Eastman, known as "the Jane Kimball house." They had children :—

I.   James, b. 1785; d. April 26, 1846, unmarried.
II.   Jane, b. 1792; d. March 18, 1800.
III.   Jonathan P., b. Dec., 1794; d. Sept., 1797.
IV.   Jonathan Sewell, b. Aug. 10, 1798; m. Betsey George, and resided in Hampstead, where they had one son, Joshua, b. June, 1840; d. young.
V.   Mary Jane, b. April 20, 1801; d., unmarried, at Hampstead.
VI.   Joshua, b. ——; mar. Betsey ——; lived in Beverly, Mass., where they had children :—
        1. Mary Jane, d. young.
        2. Joshua Sewell.
        3. Charles E.; mar. Julia Teague, and had five children.
        4. Sarah E., mar. Isaac B. Stevens.
        5. James K., mar. Betsey A. Gray, and had five children.

Joseph Kimball, son of Jonathan and Abigail (True) Kimball (see No. 21), mar. Anna, daughter of Joseph Welch of Plaistow. They resided in Plaistow, on the home farm now residence of Nathaniel Wentworth. They had children :—

I.   Elizabeth, b. Dec. 15, 1781; m. James Knight of Atkinson
        (grandfather of No. 689).

II.   Sarah Welch, b. Dec. 20, 1786; m. William Foster of Andover,
        Mass.

III.   True, b. June 11, 1790, in Hampstead; m. Betsey Chase in 1818.
        His father died before he was 17 years old, and the entire care
        of the homestead fell to him. They had children :—

        1. Moses C., mar. Amanda M. Stevens; resided at the
           homestead in Plaistow. He died Oct. 3, 1876. He
           was clerk and treasurer of the church and Sunday
           school for many years, and superintendent of the
           Sunday school. He was a deacon of the North Par-
           ish Church from 1862 to his death. They had one
           child, Charles William, b. in 1865, d. young (see 407).
        2. Elizabeth Ann, d. unmarried, in 1860, an invalid for
           many years.
        3. Mary Noyes, d. an infant.
        4. Rev. Joseph, b. in Plaistow; prepared for college at
           Andover, Mass.; graduated from Amherst College in
           1857. He has been principal of an academy in Mifflin-
           burg, Pa., an instructor at Phillips Andover Acade-
           my, superintendent of schools at Massalon, O., coun-
           ty examiner of teachers and an instructor at Mobile,
           Ala. He was ordained as an evangelist at Lynnfield,
           Mass., in 1883, and as pastor of the First Evangelist
           Church at Hampton Falls, in September, 1884, to
           1901. He is the present pastor of the North Parish
           of Haverhill Congregational Church. (See 150th
           anniversary proceedings.)
        5. Anna, d. in Andover, Mass., unmarried.
        6. Sophia, m. Charles Tufts of Andover.

No. 184.

Martha Burns, b. in Andover, Mass., 1789, a daughter of
Joseph and Martha (French) Burns, of Andover. She married Stephen Page of Hampstead, in 1760, and was admitted
to the church as a widow May 6, 1798.

No. 185.

Miriam French, b. in Hampstead, Oct. 27, 1770, a daughter of Joseph, Jr., and Judith (Diamond) French (Nos. 103,
104). She married Samuel Little (No. 200) as his third

wife, Feb. 18, 1818, and was admitted to the church May 6, 1798. She died in Hampstead, Sept. 26, 1859, aged 89 years. She had no children.

No. 186.

Robert Emerson, b. in Hampstead, July 9, 1746, a son of Benjamin and Hannah (Watts) Emerson of Hampstead. (Nos. 37 and 38.) He married Mary Webster (No. 187), and was admitted to the church May 20, 1798. He resided at the Moody Brickett place, now occupied by Mr. John F. Brown (No. 521). He died Nov. 18, 1809, and was buried in the village cemetery.

No. 187.

Mary Webster, b. in Hampstead, March 20, 1747, a daughter of John and Elizabeth (Lunt) Webster (No. 85). She married Robert Emerson (No. 186), and was admitted to the church May 20, 1798. She was the mother of eight children (pp. 411 and 367, Vol. 1). She died in Hampstead, and was buried in the village cemetery.

No. 188.

Sally French, b. in Hampstead, Sept. 15, 1768, a daughter of Joseph, Jr., and Judith (Diamond) French (Nos. 103, 104). She married Joshua, son of Samuel and Susannah (Griffin) Stevens (see Nos. 63 and 64). They removed to Enfield. She was admitted to the church Nov. 1, 1798, and asked for dismissal to the church at Canaan in 1824, but the request was denied her, upon complaint of her brother, Dea. Joseph French, that she had not satisfactorily settled the estate of their mother, and refused full share to the brother, Ezra French. (Church records.)

No. 189.

Demarias Goodwin, b. in Hampstead, March 27, 1767, a son of Timothy and Hannah (Gould) Goodwin (Nos. 112

and 113). He married Polly Heath, and was admitted to the church Nov. 4, 1798, and " moved to the upper country."

No. 190.

Col. Benjamin Emerson, b. in Hampstead, April 2, 1740, a son of Benjamin and Hannah (Watts) Emerson (Nos. 37, 38). He married Mary Tucker (No. 191), and was admitted to the church May 5, 1799. He was owner of a mill, and resided where the late Dr. J. C. Eastman resided. He died April 21, 1811, and was buried in Hampstead village cemetery (see p. 369, Vol. 1).

No. 191.

· Mary Tucker, b. in Kingston, May 5, 1750, daughter of Jacob and Lydia (Lunt) Tucker. She married Col. Benjamin Emerson (No. 190), and was admitted to the church May 5, 1799, but to " full communion," as a widow, Sept. 1, 1811.

I.   Hannah, b. Nov. 4, 1771.
II.   Ruth (No. 192).
III.   Maria (No. 193).
IV.   Benjamin Dudley (No. 194).
V.   Abner, b. March 20, 1775; graduated from Dartmouth College in 1805. He was a teacher, and died in Somerville, Mass., Dec. 12, 1836.
VI.   Frederick, b. Nov. 28, 1789. He was the author of the North American arithmetics and spelling books, and a teacher many years in Boston public schools.

No. 192.

Ruth Emerson, b. in Hampstead, Sept. 14, 1775, a daughter of Col. Benjamin and Ruth (Tucker) Emerson (Nos. 190 and 191.) She was admitted to the church May 5, 1799, aged 24 years, but " without the indulgence of communing at the Lord's table until she could more clearly ascertain her fitness for that ordinance."

No. 193.

Maria Emerson, b. in Hampstead, Oct. 5, 1777, daughter
of Col. Benjamin and Ruth (Tucker) Emerson (Nos. 190,
191). She was admitted to the church, aged 22 years, but
" without the indulgence of communing at the Lord's table
until she could more clearly ascertain her fitness for that
ordinance."

No. 194.

Benjamin Dudley Emerson, b. in Hampstead, April 4,
1781, son of Col. Benjamin and Ruth (Tucker) Emerson
(Nos. 190, 191). He was "admitted to the church May 5,
1799, aged 18, but without the indulgence of communing at
the Lord's table until he could more clearly ascertain his
fitness for that ordinance." He became a member in full
communion before 1830, and was dismissed to Boston in
1843. He was the founder of the Emerson High School of
Hampstead, and his will has been copied on p. 233, Vol. 1.
Also other mention of him on p. 233, and under "Educational
Work" in that volume. He was a graduate of Dartmouth
College, 1805, and was a teacher for many years in Boston
and vicinity. He died at Jamaica Plain, Oct. 1, 1872.

No. 195.

Mary Darling, b. in Amesbury, Mass., July 9, 1781, a
daughter of Lieut. John and Mary (Brown) Darling, of
Amesbury (No. 187). She married Joseph Noyes, as his
second wife, March 9, 1784, and was admitted to the church
June 23, 1799. She died about May, 1800, as "a request
for prayers was asked by Mr. Joseph Noyes of the congregation" at that date. She had no children (p. 357, Vol. 1).

No. 196.

Richard Kelly, b. in Amesbury, Mass., March, 1774, a son
of Stephen and Lois (Sargent) Kelly. His father lived on

the homestead of his father in Amesbury. He married his
cousin, Eunice Sargent (No. 211), and lived in Hampstead
several years, where his five children were born, and then
removed to Hopkinton, where he died, Nov. 21, 1843. He
was admitted to the church July 7, 1799, and was dismissed
to the Hopkinton church before 1823.

No. 197.

Ruth Wyman, b. in Woburn, Mass., Dec. 6, 1742, a
daughter of Capt. Benjamin and Esther (Richardson) Wyman, son of Benjamin and Elizabeth (Hancock) Wyman,
Jr., son of Francis and Abigail (Reed) Wyman, the emigrant
to America. Ruth Wyman married Jonathan Wright of
Woburn (Jacob 4, Jacob 3, Joseph 2, John 1), who was born
in Woburn, Aug. 16, 1735, a son of Jacob and Deborah
(Brooks) Wright. They were married Jan. 6, 1765, in Woburn. "She joined the First Church in Woburn, April 25,
1779, and was dismissed and admitted from that church by
letter to this church, Sept. 22, 1799." (Woburn church
records.)

Jonathan Wright was a soldier in the Revolutionary war.
He was a member of a troop of horse called out for service
during the French and Indian war, in 1757. He purchased
the island in the Island pond, in Hampstead, of Timothy
Dalton of Newburyport, Mass., in 1799, and Ruth, the
widow, sold it to the sons Jonathan and Edmund Wright,
who sold it to Thomas Huse in 1802. Their children were:

I.   Jonathan, b. in Woburn, March 5, 1766, of Boston, but at one
      time of Hampstead, and part owner of the Island in 1799.
II.   Ruth, b. May 17, 1767; m. Dea. Jacob Richardson, May 25, 1786;
      she d. March 13, 1844.
III. Jacob, b. April 7, 1769; m. Lucretia Richardson, Nov. 6, 1703.
IV.   Deborah, b. Feb. 15, 1770; m. Jacob Tidd, Nov. 16, 1795.
V.   Edmund, b. March 27, 1778; m. Rachel Dow, Dec. 9, 1804 (see
      owned the Covenant, No. 15). They had children, b. on the
      Island:—

1. Edmund, b. Oct. 4, 1805.
2. George, b. April 2, 1813; married, and resided in Atkinson, at the residence of a son, George Edmund; m. Mary Costello; a son, Fred P., m. Mary Knight, and resides in Atkinson; Josiah, married, and resides in Haverhill.

VI. Esther, b. Aug. 19, 1781; m., first, Samuel Bryant, Nov. 10, 1805; second, —— Winans, of Albany.

No. 198.

Mary Sawyer, b. in Haverhill, Mass., Oct. 29, 1758, a daughter of Jonathan and Elizabeth (Tenny) Sawyer of Haverhill. She married Capt. Joseph Smith, who d. in Hampstead, Jan. 27, 1816, aged 75 years. Joseph Smith was an adjutant in Lieut. Col. Welch's company, of Brig. Gen. Whipple's regiment, and joined the Continental army at Saratoga in 1777. Their children were :—

I. Timothy, resided in Hampstead.
II. James, mar. Sarah Colby (see p. 320, Vol. 1).
III. Maj. Isaac, b. May 31, 1793; mar. Mary, daughter of Nathaniel and Abigail (Clarke) Clarke (No. 318); mar., second, Sarah, daughter of Moses and Mary Clement, of Salisbury, Oct. 23, 1834; b. Dec. 9, 1795, and parent of children :—
    1. Rufus Clement Smith, b. June 19, 1836; mar. Helen M. Nichols (see No. 285, and Nos. 542, 586, Vol. 1).
    2. Joseph, b. March 12, 1839; d. June 17, 1839.
    Maj. Smith mar., third, Abigail Clarke (No. 494). He died in Hampstead, June 11, 1869.

Mary (Sawyer) Smith died in Hampstead, Dec. 7, 1804, aged 44 years. She was admitted from the church in North Parish, Plaistow, July 5, 1801.

No. 199.

Robert Chase, b. April 10, 1757, in Newbury, Mass., was a son of Samuel and Sarah (Stewart) Chase of Newbury, now West Newbury. He married Lydia Bodwell, Dec. 7, 1780, and was admitted to the church by letter from the church at Sandown, May 1, 1801. They had children on

Hampstead records (p. 408, Vol. 1), and Molly, b. Nov. 21,
1782; Ruth, b. Nov. 2, 1786, in Sandown. "He was frozen
to death on his own mill pond," in 1820. (From the Chase
Family Association Genealogical Collections, by John C.
Chase, president, of Derry.)

No. 200.

Samuel Little, b. in Atkinson, July 22, 1757, a son of
Samuel and Hannah (Sewell) Little (see Nos. 13, 14). He
married Elizabeth, daughter of Timothy and Elizabeth
(Huse) Stevens, of Hampstead (see No. 148), April 18,
1780. She died Sept. 15, 1794 (p. 311, Vol. 1). He married, second, Ruth, daughter of Rev. Henry and Ruth (Ayer)
True (No. 201). He married, third, Miriam French (No.
185). He was a prominent farmer in Chester, but later lived
in Hampstead, where he died, Jan. 27, 1842. He had no
children. He was admitted to the church from the church
at Chester, July 4, 1802.

No. 201.

Ruth Ayer True, b. in Hampstead, Feb. 16, 1764, a daughter of Rev. Henry and Ruth (Ayer) True (Nos. 1, 72). She
married Samuel Little (No. 200), and was admitted to the
church from the church at Chester, July 4, 1802. She died
in Hampstead, Oct. 4, 1811, and was buried in the village
cemetery.

No. 202.

Martha Webster, b. in Atkinson, April 4, 1742, a daughter of John and Hannah (Haines) Webster. She married
Eliphalet Knight, Feb. 27, 1768 (No. 251), and was admitted to the church from the church at Atkinson, May 8, 1804,
having been admitted to that church June 30, 1799. They
had children, b. in Atkinson :—

I.   Mary Webster, b. May 5, 1768; m. Col. William Page of Atkinson.

II. Elizabeth, b. June 11, 1771; m. Rev. Josiah Webster, Dec. 2, 1799. He was b. in Chester, June 16, 1772, a son of Nathan and Elizabeth (Clifford) Webster of Chester, and later of East Hampstead, where George Plummer now resides. He was a graduate of Dartmouth College in 1798, and Congregational minister at Essex, Mass., six years, when he was called to the Congregational Church at Hampton, in 1808, and remained until his death, March 27, 1837. Elizabeth (Knight) Webster, with Polly, daughter of Rev. Stephen Peabody, the first minister at Atkinson, were the first ladies to be admitted to the full course of study at Atkinson Academy in 1792. It is said "that they demanded liberty to be educated as fully as their brothers." She was admitted to the church in Atkinson, June 30, 1799. She died at the home of her son, Dr. Eliphalet Webster, at Boscawen, April 9, 1849. They had children :—

   1. Dr. Eliphalet Knight, b. May 1, 1802; m. Emily Webster, daughter of Col. Ebenezer Webster and wife Sarah, youngest sister of Hon. Daniel Webster. He practised medicine in Litchfield for a short time, then in Hill, from 1833 to 1840, and in Boscawen from 1844 to 1870. He d. in Pittsfield, Nov. 9, 1881. They had four children : 1, Daniel Dana, b. Feb. 1, 1835; m. Martha Pillsbury of Boscawen. 2, Sarah E., b. Sept. 3, 1837; m. Augustus Livingston. 3, Emily M., b. Jan. 17, 1844. 4, Edward Knight, b. Aug. 5, 1848.

   2. Josiah (No. 290), m. Mary Brickett (No. 300).

   3. Elizabeth Clifford, b. June 16, 1805; d. young.

   4. John Calvin, b. Jan. 10, 1810; m., first, Rebecca G. Runnels of Providence, R. I., and, second, m. Elizabeth Ripley Bouton, daughter of Hon. Nathaniel Bouton of Concord. He was a graduate of Dartmouth College in 1832, Theological Seminary, Andover, Mass., 1835; preached one year in Maine. In 1857 was chaplain to American and English seamen in Russia (Cromstadt); was installed pastor at Hopkinton, Mass., Dec. 19, 1863. In 1865, professor of logic, rhetoric, and belles lettres, at Eaton, Ill., Seminary, for twelve years; pastor of Congregational Church at Lisbon, Ill., from 1878 to 1881; D. D. at Dartmouth College, 1882. They had nine children, one adopted.

5. Joseph Dana, b. Aug. 25, 1811; m. Ann Elizabeth, daughter of John Wright of Chicago. He read law, but became clerk in the engineer and war department, at Washington, D. C. Was made a U. S. civil engineer in 1835, second lieutenant in U. S. topographical engineers in 1835. He was one year in the Mexican war, in 1840, and captain in 1853; was major and colonel of Illinois volunteers in U. S. army; chief of staff to Gen. Grant till 1862; was with Gen. Thomas at Hood's defeat in 1864; was with Gen. Sherman in his march to the sea, and was brevetted major general, leaving the service in 1865. They had five children.

6. Elizabeth Knight, b. Dec. 5, 1813; d. young.

7. Dr. Claudius Buchannon, b. Dec. 10, 1815; m. Mary Elizabeth, daughter of David Webster of Pembroke. He was a graduate of medicine in New York Medical School, and began practice in Northwood, and removed to Norwich, Conn., in 1845, and carried on a family school there for young ladies till 1863, when he took a position as assistant surgeon in the army, in which he served till September, 1865, when he was appointed by Gen. Grant U. S. consul at Sheffield, England, where he served for many years. He presented the Webster Memorial Chapel at Hampton, which was dedicated Dec. 23, 1894. He published a few of his poems in 1901, entitled "Four Score and Other Poems," which are greatly prized by his friends. He died in Concord, Sept. 7, 1902. He had no children.

III. Hannah, b. April 14, 1777; m. Rev. Moses Dow.

IV. Dr. James, b.   ; a physician in Hampstead many years, at what is now known as "Cobb's Corner."

No. 203.

Silas Tenney, b. in Bradford, Mass., Dec. 4, 1772, a son of Dea. Thomas and Hannah (Stickney) Tenney, of Bradford, where his father was deacon of the church from 1779 to his death in 1798. His sister Mary, b. in Bradford, April 27, 1769, mar. Moses Atwood of Haverhill, and were the parents of Harriet Atwood, who married the Rev. Samuel Newell, the celebrated missionary to the Isle of France, and died at

the age of 19 years and 4 months. He married Rebecca
Bailey (No. 204), and removed from Bradford, in 1804, to
Chester, at the old Tenney homestead, where Orlando Tenney
now resides. He was admitted to the church Sept. 7, 1806,
and was dismissed to the church at Chester, February, 1834,
and d. July 11, 1834.

No. 204.

Rebecca Bailey, b. in West Newbury, Mass., May 13, 1733,
a daughter of William and Anna (Stewart) Bailey of West
Newbury. She married Silas Tenney (No. 203), Oct. 2,
1795. She was admitted to the church Sept. 7, 1806, and
dismissed to the church at Chester, February, 1824. She died
in Chester, March 11, 1833, at the age of 99 years and 10
months. The children of Silas and Rebecca (Bailey) Tenney were all given superior educational advantages, four of
the six sons being graduates of Dartmouth College. They
were all baptized in Hampstead (see list of baptisms), the
first four children b. in Bradford, the others in Chester.

I.   Bailey. b. Jan. 7, 1797; d. Sept. 3, 1852; m., first, Jane Ware;
       second, Lydia Hawkes. No children.
II.   Rev. Thomas, b. Nov. 10, 1798; d. May 7, 1874; m. Martha T.
       Parker; daughter, Mary Eliza, m. Rev. Cyrus Hamlin, D. D.,
       founder of Roberts College, Constantinople, Turkey.
III.   Rev. Sewell, b. Aug. 27, 1801: d. June 6, 1890; m. Sarah M.
       Pearsons.
IV.   Sarah, b. Jan. 13, 1804; m., first, Rev. Jonathan Hale; second,
       Rev. J. R. Arnold. No children.
V.   William, b. July 13, 1807; m. Emeline J. Murray; resided at the
       homestead. Had children : Mary Atwood Tenney (see No.
       426), and Orlando M. Tenney, who resides at the homestead.
       William was a deacon of the church at Chester.
VI.   Mary, b. March 2, 1809; d. young.
VII.   Harriet, b. April 8, 1812; m. Hon. Thomas J. Melvin of Chester;
       d. March 17, 1870. Children : Rev. Charles Tenney, Con-
       gregational clergyman, deceased. 2, Harriet, graduate Mt.
       Holyoke college, teacher there; d. Dec. 21, 1897. 3. Sarah
       H., graduate Mt. Holyoke; teacher there twenty-five
       years, and d. there. 4, Josie Greenleaf, d. 1865. 5, John, of

Chester, and Helen Eliza, graduate Mt. Holyoke College, teacher there, missionary in the Girls' College, Constantinople, China, seven years.

VIII.   Rev. Charles, b. Sept. 3, 1814; m., first, Emily F. Parsons; second, Mary E. Kelly, daughter of Hon. John Kelly and widow Mary Chase of Atkinson. He d. Oct. 29, 1888, in Chester, where he was pastor of the Congregational Church.

IX.   Rev. Daniel, b. Dec. 10, 1810; m. Mary Adams Parker; died in San Diego, Calif., Oct. 24, 1892. Their children were : 1. Juliet, m. Rev. James Brand, D. D., of Oberlin Ohio. 2. Sarah, m. Rev. C. J. Ryder, D. D., of New York. 3. Charles Daniel, principal Atkinson Academy for a time after graduating from Dartmouth College; went as a missionary to China; was president of the American College at Tientsin until the Boxers came; is now at work in China. 4. William, a clergyman, graduated at Oberlin, O.; settled over Congregational Church in North Adams, Mass., president F. and A. College at Springfield, Mass. 5. Tilly, d. 1867, aged 19 years.

Among the descendants of Mr. and Mrs. Silas Tenney have been seventeen ministers, four sons, two sons-in-law, eleven grandchildren and great-grandchildren, among them Rev. William T. Bartley, now of Bennington (see 150th anniversaries of town and church, Vols. 1 and 2).

No. 205.

Mary Calfe, b. in Hampstead, June 25, 1765, a daughter of Hon. John and Lois (Calfe) Calfe (Nos. 107-108). She mar. John, son of David and Phebe (Carlton) Poor of Hampstead, June 25, 1795, who was b. Mar. 1, 1770, and moved to Corinth, Vt., in 1798, and returned to the vicinity of his birthplace, occupying some of his father's lands in Derry awhile, but d. in Hampstead, May 20, 1845. Mary (Calfe) Poor was adm. to the church Sept. 7, 1806, and d. in Hampstead, Oct. 8, 1844. They had children :—

I. John Calef, b. Aug. 30, 1707; m. Susan, daughter of Alexander
    and Susan (Stevens) Boyce of Londonderry, Nov. 22, 1822,
    and mar., second, Judith Corning. He was a cooper, then
    cabinet-maker, and later, a carpenter and builder; lived about
    one-fourth of a mile east of the station at Derry. He
    was chosen captain in the State militia, "but since his early
    days, was inclined to live a quiet life." Their children :—1.
    Lorenzo, m. Betsey Fitch; res. in Derry, and have three chil-
    dren. 2. George, lived for a time in California. 3. William
    Wallace, m. Clara Ann Brackett, P. M., and dealer in West
    India goods, for a long time in Derry; had six children b. in
    Derry. 4. John, d. young.

II. Jonathan Carlton, b. in Corinth, Vt., m. Mary, daughter of
    Caleb and Nancy (Cate) Hall, in Candia. A painter and
    wheelwright, in Derry; had children b. in Derry. 1.
    Charles, m. Louisa J. Eaton; lived in Weare, and New Boston,
    and had four children. 2. John, d. unm. 3. Eliza Ann,
    m. James Harvey, son of William and Abigail (Eastman)
    Kezer of Benton; had four children.

No. 206.

Mary Harriman, b. in Hampstead, June 5, 1790, a
daughter of Laban and Molly (Harriman) Harriman of
Hampstead (see No. 84). She was adm. to the church " by
faith and baptism," Sept. 7, 1806, " age 16 years." She
was afterwards " found to be inclined to Universalism," and
admonished in church meeting as follows from the church
records. " Samuel Little made complaint that Mary Harriman was neglecting the public worship and ordinances of
God's house, in consequence of which the church chose
Dea. Moses Little, Job Kent, and Lt. John Harriman, as a
committee to request Mary to meet the church, Nov. 27,
1810, at the house of the pastor, Rev. John Kelly, to give a
report of her neglect." She did not appear. The church
then chose Robert Chase and Dea. Little to wait on Mary,
and show her the nature and importance of the discipline of
the church, and to request her to attend the next church
meeting.

The committee reported that they had conversed with her upon the subject of duty, and sentiments and views were requested, one by one, to report to the church, what reasons Mary Harriman assigned, why she neglected her duty, and why she did not appear and answer for herself to the church. And from all that was said upon the subject, it appears evident to all that Mary Harriman was unwilling to be subject to the ordinances of the gospel, or to submit to the order or discipline of the Church of Christ. It also appeared that she was utterly opposed to the doctrines of grace, as they are revealed in the holy Scriptures, and held by this church.

And as she also neglected to hear the church after being repeatedly requested to attend and answer for herself, the church came to the unaminous vote that Mary Harriman be cut off from being a member of this church, as an incorrigible offender against Christ, and his church. The church then chose Deacon Moses Little and Mr. Abner Rogers to join with the pastor in addressing a letter to said Mary Harriman upon the subject of her excommunication. And concluded with prayer to God,

A copy of the letter sent :—

HAMPSTEAD, January 3d, 1811.

To Mary Harriman :—

This letter is to remind you that, in compliance with your earnest request, and in hopes that you would adorn the Christian profession by walking in all of the commandments and ordinances of the Lord in a blameless manner, you was admitted into the church of Christ, in Hampstead, on the 7th of Sept., 1806. But as you have for a long time neglected the public worship and ordinance of the gospel, and our brother, Samuel Little, having taken the steps with you as Christ has directed in the 18th of Matthew, and you having neglected to hear him and others, he has told it to the church.

The church has, therefore, according to the rules of the gospel, called upon you to give the reasons of the neglect of duty.

And for purpose of attending to this subject, they met at the house of the pastor, on the 27th of November, 1810; but you did not appear as you were requested by a letter of the committee.

The church, therefore, willing to treat you with all tenderness, and meekness, and love, sent another committee to converse with you, to show you the nature and use of the discipline of the gospel and to request you to attend the next church meeting which was to be held at the house of Deacon Moses Little, on the 25th of December, 1810.

But as you did not attend nor hear the church after solemn prayer, serious consideration and mature deliberation, the church came to their unaminous conclusion that you appeared to be determined not to do your duty, nor to submit to any order or discipline of the church, and therefore the church was under the necessity, in obedience to Christ, of cutting you off from being a member of this church.

For Christ says, "If he neglects to hear the church, let him be unto thee as an heathen man and publican," and the apostle says, "A man that is a heretic, after the first and second admonition, reject," Titus 3 : 10, 11.

An heretic is one whether man or woman who adheres to his or her own opinions, and rejects the Scriptures as being the word of God, and neglects duty contrary to his or her own solemn covenant engagements, see also Rom. 16 : 17, 18. Read also 2d Thes., 3d chapter, 6th and 14th verses, and you will see that if we obey Christ, and his inspired apostles, we must reject those who walk disorderly and openly neglect their duty, and will not hear the church.

But our earnest prayer to God is that you may be brought to see the sinfulness of your own heart and the evil of your ways, and that you may be brought to repentance of all of your sins, and humbly submit to the righteousness of God, through faith in the Lord Jesus Christ, and that you will give a proof of this by submitting to the rules and ordinances of the gospel, as he has commanded his people to observe them.

Should this be your happy case, then we should be under obligation to treat you as a true penitent disciple of Christ, accordingly as we are directed in Cor., 2d chap. and 2d Thes. 3 : 15.

But if you remain obstinate, and will not be admonished to hear the church, nor to return to God by humble repentance, and by faith in Christ, your case must be dreadful.

For Christ says to his church, " Verily I say unto you, whatsoever ye shall find on earth shall be found in heaven, and whatsoever ye shall lose on earth shall be lost in heaven."

Be persuaded to believe the words of Christ, and take warning and repent of your sins that you may be saved.

JOHN KELLY—Pastor.

DEA. MOSES LITTLE. }   <i>Church</i>
ABNER ROGERS.   }   <i>Committee.</i>

Mary Harriman was obdurate " and was dropped from the church rolls, Jan. 3, 1811." She mar. Isaac Sargent of Plaistow, May 21, 1812, and d. 1830, " a worthy wife and mother " of three children b. in Plaistow.

I.   Abigail, b. Sept. 14, 1813; d. young.
II.   Sarah, b. March 30, 1816.
III.   Gilbert, b. Sept. 3, 1827.

Isaac Sargent her husband, mar., second, in 1832, Ruth J. Rollins of Amesbury, Mass., and had daughter:—

IV.   Mary, b. May 30, 1835; m. Charles H. Christian, resided in Georgetown, Mass.; who had children. 1. Arthur C., b. 1860. 2. Ernest M., b. 1872; m. May Witham of Georgetown.

Ruth, wife of Isaac Sargent, d. 1841, and he then m., in 1844, Lydia J. Holt of Haverhill, Mass., and in 1848, m., fourth, Cynthia Sternes of Haverhill; who was drowned in Lake Michigan, Sept. 24, 1856. He d. June, 1850, in Haverhill, where he was a shoecutter.

No. 207.

Mary Gordon, b. in Hampstead, June 14, 1777, a daughter of John Gordon of Brentwood (who was a son of James and Lydia (Leavett) Gordon) and Mary (Polly) Johnson, his

wife, of Hampstead. She married Silas, son of John and
Martha (McKeen) Dinsmoor, of Londonderry. She was
admitted to the church May 27, 1808, and died in 1854. Mr.
Dinsmoor was a graduate of Dartmouth College in 1791. A
lieutenant in the U. S. army, and for a long time was employed as Indian agent by the U. S. govt. in Alabama and
Mississippi. Their son, Silas, bapt. in Hampstead, with his
mother, May 27, 1808 (p. 885, Vol. 1).

No. 208.

Capt. Simon Merrill, b. in Seabrook, April 10, 1753, the
seventh child of "Eliphe"[4] (doubtless meant Eliphalet) and
Lydia (Clough) Merrill. Eliphe was b. in Newbury, Mass.,
Oct. 7, 1717, a son of David. He was a joiner by trade,
and moved to Amesbury, Mass., and married Lydia Clough,
July 10, 1739, and had two children, b. in Amesbury. He
then moved to Hampton Falls, and thence to Kensington
and Seabrook, where eight other children were born. Simon
Merrill lived on Walnut Hill, in Chester. He was a soldier,
enlisting in Capt. Hezekiah Hutchens' company, in Stark's
regiment, June 9, 1775, in the Revolutionary war; received
the appointment of ensign Nov. 8, 1776, and of that of adjutant June 12, 1789, and of captain in the New Hampshire
militia Sept. 9, 1793. He was admitted to the church by
letter from the church in South Hampton (or Hampton),
Dec. 11, 1808. He was dismissed to the church at Chester
about 1818 (?). He died in Sandown, April 24, 1840, and
was buried in the cemetery at West Hampstead (p. 812,
Vol. 1). He was three times married—first, Betsey Ingalls;
second, Polly Colby; no children by either; third, Mary
Marston. Their children:—

I.   Mary C., m. Robert Rogers, and had no children.
II.   Simon, m. Hannah W. Kelly (No. 365).
III.   Austin Guy, m. Mary Canney and lived in Derry. He was a
       farmer and fruit raiser, and had three children :—

    1. Samantha C. (No. 444).
    2. Helen M., mar. Stephen J. Barker of Methuen, Mass.
    3. Alice Marian, a teacher in Somerville, Mass., English
       High School.
IV.   George W., mar. Mary A. Sleeper, and parents of :—
    1. George H.
    2. Albert J.; res. Walnut Hill, Chester.
    3. Helen F., d. unmarried; a teacher several years.
    4. Laura A., mar. Eugene L. Spinney (Nos. 640, 541).
V.   Betsey J., mar. Luther W. Hall, and had two daughters :—
    1. Mrs. Isabel Ryder of Manchester.
    2. Mrs. Rev. J. G. Robertson of Chester.

Mary, wife of Capt. Merrill, died April 12, 1850, and was
buried in West Hampstead cemetery.

No. 209.

Lucy Berry, b. in Middleton, Mass., June 12, 1778, a
daughter of Nathaniel and Susannah (Esty) Berry of Middleton; was admitted to be a member in full communion
with this church, Sept. 2, 1810. Nathaniel Berry was born
Sept. 16, 1736, and died in 1812. Susannah Esty was a
daughter of Jonathan and Susannah (Munroe) Esty, and was
born Jan. 26, 1741, and died May 27, 1827. The Berrys of
Middleton were farmers and highly respectable people,
reputed to be possessed of considerable means.

Lucy Berry married Isaac Colby, born in Derry, then
Londonderry, Feb. 15, 1777, at Middleton, where he was
working as a carpenter, on June 23, 1801. After a brief
residence in Danvers, Mass., they moved to Hampstead village. The land records of Rockingham county show that
"Isaac Colby, wheelwright, purchased from Daniel Kimball,
blacksmith, for $850, on Dec. 29, 1804, a tract of land partly
in Hampstead and partly in Londonderry, containing by
estimation forty acres, more or less, and bounded as follows,
viz. : Beginning at a stake and stone on the southerly side
of the road leading from Hampstead to Chester, and by land
of Joseph Brickett, thence southwesterly by said Brickett's

land 160 rods to a road leading to Londonderry, thence northerly by said road about 40 rods to land of Jabez Hoit, thence northwesterly by said Hoit's land, about 160 rods, to the aforesaid road, thence southeasterly by the road about 40 rods to the bound first mentioned."

The place thus described was the family home for the next seven years.

In 1811, Oct. 28, Isaac Colby bought of Thomas Huse, for $1500, Governor's Island, in Island Pond, and the old Wentworth mansion thenceforth was the home of the family, until he deeded the island to Lucy Everett, of Boston, Mass., Sept. 8, 1815.

The Colbys then moved to what is now known as Herrick farm and mill, between Derry Dock and Island Pond, which previously had been owned by the father (David, 2d), and the grandfather (David, 1st), of Isaac Colby, and there they dwelt until 1846.

Isaac Colby, though a wheelwright and farmer, was best known in the region as a builder, and according to tradition framed many of the best houses in Hampstead street and in East Derry, one of the last in the latter village being that known as the "Elms Hotel."

His wife having become a member of this church, Sept. 2, 1810, and having five children baptized in the church May 6, 1812, the family apparently worshipped in Hampstead until 1833. At that time Mrs. Lucy (Berry) Colby was dismissed from the church to the First Church at East Derry, with which church her daughter Lucy united in 1831, her son, James Knight, in 1833, and her son, George W., in 1838.

In 1846, when the infirmities of age led Isaac Colby and his wife to give up the management of the farm and mill (now Herrick) to their son, George Washington, they went to live, after a short stay in Boston, with their son, James K. Colby, in St. Johnsbury, Vt.

Isaac Colby joined the church by profession of faith, July

10, 1858. The few remaining years of their lives were spent peacefully and happily in the home of their son.

Lucy Berry Colby died after a brief illness, Nov. 7, 1854, aged 76 years. She was surrounded by her daughter Lucy, her sons, Nathaniel and James K., and when the latter asked her, shortly before her death, if she would like to recover, she replied, " No, why should I ? I have lived to a good old age," and then bolstered up in bed, surprised all by singing the verse beginning, " Fly swift around, ye wheels of time."

Isaac Colby died March 24, 1856, in his 80th year. The bodies of both Isaac Colby and his wife were buried in the Colby lot in the Mt. Pleasant cemetery in St. Johnsbury, Vt, where are also interred the bodies of their sons, Nathaniel B. and James K. Colby, and their wives.

The church records in Hampstead contain in the records of baptism the following entry, made while the Colby family dwelt in the Wentworth mansion on Governor's Island : " Nathaniel Baree- (should be Berry), Jesse Hoyt, Allen Lucy, and James Knight (known as James Kelsea Colby in his mature years, but evidently receiving his name from their family physician, Dr. James Knight) (see 202). Children of Isaac Colby, baptized on account of his wife, May 12, 1812."

The biographical record of these children is as follows :—

I.   Nathaniel Berry, b. in Hampstead, Sept. 13, 1803; was for many years master carpenter and superintendent of bridges of the Boston & Worcester Railroad. He died in St. Johnsbury Vt., July 5, 1864.

II.   Jesse Hoyt, b. on Governor's Island, March 20, 1806; was a wheelwright and mechanic. He died in Boston, Mass.; m. Nov. 23, 1826; and buried in the cemetery at East Derry.

III.   Allen Colby, b. on Governor's Island, Feb. 24, 1808; was a builder and carpenter, and had charge of the construction of the Kennebec & Portland Railway, between Brunswick and Bath, Me. Afterwards for twenty-five years he was roadmaster and superintendent of bridges of that railroad. Upon his retirement, for three years he was agent for the Brunswick cotton mills, and a manufacturer of yarn, and a railroad derrick which he invented. He died at Brunswick, Me., Jan. 3, 1890, and was buried at that place.

IV. Lucy Colby, b. on Governor's Island, Jan. 30, 1810; resided with her parents during their lives, and afterwards with her brother, James Knight. She married Alanson Lawrence, of Camden, Delaware, March, 1876, and died in Morestown, New Jersey, Oct. 3, 1887. She was buried in Monument cemetery, in Philadelphia, Pa.

V. James Knight, b. on Governor's Island, Jan. 31, 1812; studied at Pinkerton Academy, and was graduated from Dartmouth College in 1831. He taught in Petersburg, Va., in 1831 to 1839, studied in Lane and Andover Theological Seminary from 1839 to 1841, and was principal of the St. Johnsbury, Vt., Academy from its foundation, in 1842, till the date of his death, Aug. 13, 1866. He was buried in Mt. Pleasant cemetery, in St. Johnsbury, Vt. He was the father of Prof. James Fairbanks Colby, of the faculty of Dartmouth College, to whom we are indebted for family sketch. (See Memorial of James K. Colby, by Rev. Edward Taylor Fairbanks, 1867.)

VI. George Washington Colby, b. on Governor's Island, April 5, 1815; was for many years an agent of the Fairbanks Scale Co., in Philadelphia. He died in Morestown, N. J., April 2, 1890, and was buried in the Monument cemetery in Philadelphia, Penn.

No. 210.

Sarah Lake, b. in Topsfield, Mass., September, 1754, a daughter of Eleazer and Sarah (Perkins) Lake of Topsfield. She married Oliver Putnam of Danvers, Mass., who died May 10, 1814, in Hampstead, and buried in Hampstead, aged 59 years. She was admitted to be a member of this church, "on a bed of sickness, at her home, May 28, 1811." She died in Hampstead, Sept. 12, 1811, and was buried in the village cemetery. The tombstone bears the inscription:—
"Sacred to the memory of Oliver Putnam, b. in Newbury, Mass., Nov. 17, 1777 ; d. in Hampstead, July 11, 1826, aged 49 years." This was the Oliver Putnam, founder of the Putnam High School of Newburyport, Mass. (p. 331, Vol. 1). Other inscriptions on the stones in Hampstead are : "Charles Putnam, b. Jan. 26, 1793 ; d. Oct. 25, 1834." "Lucy, b.

July 16, 1795; d. July 6, 1839." (Sketch of the children of
Sarah (Lake) Putnam, on pp. 331, 332, 333 and 334,
Vol. 1.)

No. 211.

Eunice Kelly, b. in Amesbury, Mass., June 15, 1778, a
daughter of Hezekiah and Mary (Sargent) Sargent of Amesbury. She married Richard Kelly of Amesbury (No. 196)
her cousin, June 8, 1796, and was admitted to be a member
of this church, June 28, 1812. They lived in Hampstead
several years, and five children were born here, and then
lived in Hopkinton, where she died, Nov. 21, 1843. Their
children were :—

I.   Amos, b. Nov. 11, 1796; m. —— Evans, and lived in Buffalo, N.
      Y., and later in Hopkinton. He invented the "Kelly corn-
      popper."
II.   Judith, b. 1799; d. young.
III. Hannah, b. 1802.
IV.   Mary, b. Nov. 11, 1804; lived in the family of Nicholas Sargent,
      of West Amesbury, and later m. —— Evans, of Weymouth,
      Mass.
V.   Lois, b. March 8, 1807; when 15 years old weighed 300 pounds.
VI.   Belinda, unmarried.
VII. Rhoda, m. —— Dow, of Dunbarton.
VIII. Lucy, m. —— Judkins, of Unity.
IX.   Betsey, m. —— Knight, in Claremont.

No. 212.

Tamar Woodward, b.   She
married Robert Collins of Danville, and was admitted to
this church from the church at Hopkinton, June 29, 1812.
She had one child, b. in Hampstead—Loramah, b. May 8,
1790.

No. 213.

Joshua Eastman, Jr., b. in Hampstead, Oct. 24, 1797, a
son of Joshua and Sarah (Tucker) Eastman (Nos. 169, 170).
He married Susanna Chase (No. 230), and was admitted to

the church Nov. 1, 1812. He was elected deacon Nov. 12, 1848, and served until his death, June 15, 1859. " He was prominent in political, social, and religious interests, a Webster Whig in early life, later a free soiler." He resided where Mr. Orren Ranlett now resides.

No. 214.

John True, Esq., b. in Hampstead, Dec. 26, 1762, in Hampstead, son of Rev. Henry and Ruth (Ayer) True (Nos. 1 and 72). He mar. Mrs. Anna (Kimball) Parker (No. 249), and was adm. to the church May 2, 1813. He was elected deacon, May 2, 1816, and d. in Hampstead, Dec. 3, 1824. He left by will, " to the Congregational Society of Hampstead, $2000, the interest to be expended annually to support the ministry." (For inscription on tombstone, see p. 309, Vol. 1).

No. 215.

Susanna Emerson, b. in Hampstead, May 10, 1744, daughter of Benjamin and Hannah (Watts) Emerson (Nos. 37, 38). She mar. Ezekial Currier of Hampstead. She was adm. to the church Oct. 31, 1813, and had nine children. (see p. 406, Vol. 1).

No. 216.

Sarah Gould, b. in Rowley, Mass., daughter of Gideon and Hannah (Heath) Gould of Hampstead, 1790. She was adm. to the church by letter from the church at Topsfield, Mass., May 22, 1814.

No. 217.

Hannah True, b. in Hampstead, May 22, 1747, a daughter of Rev. Henry and Ruth (Ayer) True (Nos. 1, 72). She was adm. to the church May 7, 1815. She d. unmarried, April 19, 1824, and was buried in the True lot, in the village cemetery.

No. 218.

Henry True Kelly, b. in Hampstead, Aug. 13, 1794, a son of Rev. John and Abigail (Dearborn) Kelly (Nos. 164, 171). He was a graduate from Dartmouth College, 1819, and entered the Theological Seminary, at Andover, Mass., the same year; and was ordained at Parsonsfield, (with Newfield, Me.), June 15, 1825. He was installed at Kingsville, Ohio, in 1829. In Madisonville, Ohio, in 1836. He mar. Miss Clara Garland, at Parsonfield, Me., in 1830. He d. Sept. 9, 1840, at the Wilberforce Mission, at Chathem, Canada, West. He was adm. to this church Sept. 1, 1816.

The Congregational Journal soon after his death, remarked, "His early life was distinguished for sobriety, obedience to his friends, and a reverence for everything sacred and divine. As a metaphysician and theologian, few if any, of his day, stand before him, and his opinions and reasoning came to be respected. As a writer his thoughts were expressed in a clear and concise manner. His style was remarkably nervous and terse. He was retiring in his habits, and had little that was engaging in his manners, and was singularly averse to ostentation. He was diligent and conscientious in his discharge of the duties of his profession."

No. 219.

Joseph Welch, b. in Plaistow, May 5, 1778, a son of Col. Joseph and Hannah (Chase) Welch of Plaistow. Hannah Chase was b. in Newton, a daughter of Francis Chase. He mar., first, Martha Sargent (No. 168), and resided for a time where Joshua A. Richards resides in Atkinson, and later moved to near Sanborn's Corner, in Hampstead, where he owned, and run a fulling and dressing mill, on the shore of Island pond. He mar., second, Ruth Brown, Nov. 20, 1818. He was adm. to the church Sept. 22, 1816, but in March 13, 1835, an unpleasantness came up in some business matters, and he withdrew from the church.

No. 220.

Benjamin Garland, b. in Barrington, July 11, 1767, a son of John and Molly (Rand) Garland of Rye, who later resided on Green Hill, Barrington.

The Garland ancestry is as follows:—

1 Peter Garland and wife Elizabeth, came to Charlestown, Mass., 1838, a mariner. His son John², mar. Elizabeth Chapman; whose son Peter³, mar. Sarah Taylor; whose son John⁴, mar. ¦Elizabeth Dearborn, and resided in Rye. Their son John⁵, b. in Rye, May 18, 1719; mar. Molly Rand of Rye, 1744. He was assessor in Barrington, in 1753, 1755, 1758, and moderator in 1777, 1778, 1780, and 1785. He was commissioner in 1762 and 3. In 1778, he was chosen "to convene at Concord, June 10 next, for the purpose of forming government." In 1781, he "was chosen to represent Barrington, in the General Assembly at Exeter, for the ensuing year." March 30, 1785, he was a candidate for State senator, and had forty-eight votes from Barrington, and "a larger number from that town, than any other candidate ever had."

In the year 1770, John Garland and Samuel Brewster, in the behalf of the church and parish, asked the General Assembly, for authority to conduct the affairs of the church, independent of the town-meeting, setting forth as a reason, that certain inhabitants, who called themselves Quakers, and other separators from any religious body, and members of the church of England, cause a great confusion, whenever a town-meeting is held to settle a minister, according to the laws of the province." Which request was granted,

John and Molly (Rand) Garland, had twelve children b. in Barrington, of whom, Benjamin, the subject of this sketch, was the youngest. He mar. Polly Balch (No. 221). They owned the covenant, in Barrington. Nov. 21, 1790, and united with the church there, July 25, 1802. They moved to Hampstead, and resided at the "old James Noyes place," and later at the "old Garland house." He was adm. to the church by letter from Barrington, April 27, 1817. He was a cooper by trade, and served as tythingman for several years, much to the terror of the small boys in the neighborhood. He d. in Hampstead, Nov. 18, 1835, and was buried in the village cemetery.

No. 221.

Mary (or Polly) Balch, b. in Mendon, Mass., July 17, 1770, a daughter of Rev. Benjamin Balch, the pastor at Barrington, from Apr. 25, 1784 to 1815, when she d. aged 74 years. Rev. Benjamin, was b. in Dedham, Mass., Feb.

12, 1748; m. in 1764, Joanna O'Brien, b. in Scarboro, Me.;
d. in Barrington, 1820; who was a sister of the noted
Jeremiah, John and Joseph O'Brien, privateersmen in the
war of the Revolution.

Mary mar. Benjamin Garland (No. 220), Jan. 18, 1790,
and was adm. to the church here by letter from Barrington,
April 17, 1817, having been united with the church in Barrington, July 25, 1802, and owned the covenant, Nov. 21,
1790. She was dismissed by letter to Illinois (as she was to
take up her residence there), Sept. 20, 1837, and d. in Illinois, Aug. 1, 1855.

They had children, b. in Barrington :—

I.   Dennis J., b. May 27, 1790; m. Annie Ingly. They had two
        children :—
          1. Mary J., of 52 Chestnut St., Boston, Mass.
          2. Elizabeth A., m. —— Valentine, and resides in Cam-
             bridgeport, Mass.
II.   Benjamin Balch (No. 367); m. Mary H. Calef (No. 368).
III.   Joanna, b. Sept. 23, 1796.
IV.   Mary (No. 235), m. Ezra Davis (No. 234).
V.   Martha, b. March 6, 1802; d. 1802.
VI.   Susan, b. April 21, 1803; d. Sept. 2, 1838; m. Asa Wing of Hamp-
        stead, and moved to Joliet, Ill., and had two children, both
        of whom died there. He was a carpenter in Hampstead.
VII.   John Jay, b. July 21, 1806; m. Nancy Bagley, Dec. 21, 1831.
        They had four children, all dead. They resided in Joliet,
        Ill. He d. Sept. 4, 1845.
VIII.   Emily, b. March 24, 1815; m. Alanson Harris of Grand Rapids,
        Mich., December, 1838, and resided in Kent, Mich., where
        their two children lived. Both are now dead.

No. 222.

Mary Heath, b. in Hampstead, Feb. 24, 1800, a daughter
of Isaac and Susanna (Hall) Heath (p. 414, Vol. 1, for
birth of the seventeen children). She was bapt. and adm. to
the church membership, age 17, May 4, 1817. She married
Henry George (No. 239), and dismissed to the church in
Kingston, Mass., March 26, 1848.

No. 223.

Jesse Davis, b. in Hampstead, July 8, 1767, a son of Josiah and Dorothy (Colby) Davis. He married Lois Worthen of Hampstead, who d. Feb. 24, 1845, aged 77 years, and was admitted to the church " by owning the covenant," May 4, 1817. They had five children (see p. 409, Vol. 1). He married, second, Mrs. Mary (Marston) Merrill, who d. April 13, 1855. He married, third, Mrs. Mary Wells (No. 408), of Chester, who d. Feb. 18, 1878; Jesse Davis, d. in Hampstead, Feb. 18, 1859, aged 91 years.

No. 224.

James Brickett, b. in Newbury, Mass., Jan. 15, 1765, a son of Nathaniel and Anna (Woodman) Brickett, of Newbury. The Brickett ancestry was : Nathaniel Brickett, married, and had sons :—Nathaniel, John, James, b. Dec. 3, 1679, and Nathaniel 2d. James, b. Dec. 11, 1679 ; m.—— Pillsbury, and had son Nathaniel, who mar. Anna Woodman (above).

James Brickett married, first, Anna Wheeler (No. 225), and was admitted to the church May 10, 1817. His wife died in 1837, and he married, second, Mrs. Ruth (Chase) Smith of West Newbury (No. 385). He died in Hampstead.

No. 225.

Anna (or Nancy) Wheeler, b. in Salem, June 6, 1768, was a daughter of Jonathan Wheeler, b. in Rowley, Mass., 1733, and Esther Kimball, his wife, of Rowley. Jonathan Wheeler settled in Salem, and was a son of Stephen and Hannah (Heath) Wheeler, who was a son of Jonathan and Ann (Plummer) Wheeler, who was a son of Jonathan and Mary Wheeler, who was a son of David and Sarah (Wise) Wheeler. David was the son of John and Ann Wheeler of Salisbury, Eng. Esther Kimball, b. Aug. 1, 1735, was a daughter of Richard and Jemima (Gage) Kimball. Jemima (Gage) Kimball, widow, mar. John Webster of Plaistow. Richard Kimball was a son of Richard and Mehitable (Day) Kimball, who was a son of Benjamin and Mercy (Haseltine) Kimball (daughter of John Haseltine, who was among the first settlers in Bradford, Mass., then Rowley), who was a son of Richard Kimball, the emigrant to America, to Watertown, in 1634. Anna Wheeler married James Brickett of Hampstead (No. 224), March 16, 1766, and was admitted to the church, by " profession and baptism, May 4, 1817, by owning the baptismal covenant, with four children." She was a confirmed invalid for many years, and died in Hampstead in 1887. They had children, born in Newbury, Salem, and Hampstead :—

I.   Hannah (No. 409), mar. Edmund Mooers.
II.   Jonathan (No. 232), mar. Lydia Kent (No. 233).
III.   James, b. July 7, 1791; d. April 3, 1792.
IV.   Nathaniel, b. March 17, 1795; d. Jan. 17, 1796.
V.   Ralph (No. 376), mar. Sally Ordway (No. 275).
VI.   Anna, b. June 18, 1797; mar. Amos Little, son of Nathaniel and Mary (Carlton) Little of Hampstead (brother to No. 167), (see p. 361, Vol. 1). It is tradition in the family that when Nathaniel Little sold his farm in Plaistow and removed to Springfield, with his older sons, that he cleared land for all of his younger sons in Springfield, and that the Continental money received at the sale of his first farm depreciated so rapidly in his hands that finally all of it was given in exchange for a jar of butter. He returned to Hampstead in his later years, and died there in 1827. Amos Little, soon after his marriage to Ann Brickett, moved to Newport, after he had learned the trade of a hatter in Hampstead, and in 1818 went into business in Newport, which he continued until his death, in August, 1859. He served the town as selectman and representative, and was a devoted Free Mason, an active and prominent member of the Baptist church, and distinguished for his enterprise and social qualities. They had children :—
        1. Charles Henry, b. Jan. 10, 1820; m. Sarah Fuller of Chester, Vt., and had four children, b. in Newport, Vt., where he lives, and had been engaged in the

manufacture of hats. He was sergeant in the 9th N. H. Vols. in the civil war, and was severely wounded at Antietam. He is an active Free Mason and a worker in the temperance cause (see p. 208, Vol. 1); d. Mar. 1903.

2. Amos Brickott, b. Feb. 16, 1821; d., unmarried, 1862. He was educated at Meriden Academy and Brown University, was a lawyer by profession, and at his death chief examiner at the Patent Office, Washington, D. C., with which he had been connected twenty years.

3. Frances Ann, b. July 20, 1823; m. Joseph W. Parmelee of Newport, N. J., and had three children, residing many years in New York.

4. Mary Ellen, b. Sept. 12, 1828; d. Oct. 1, 1830.

5. George Edward, b. April 25, 1834; m. Sarah J. Welcome. He learned the trade of a hatter, and later was a clerk and paymaster for some railroad contractors in Vermont. Resides in Newport.

VII.   Della (No. 282), mar. first, Henry Welch; second, Simeon George.
VIII. Mary (No. 300), mar. Josiah Webster (No. 299).
IX.   James, b. in Hampstead, May 4, 1805; mar. Abigail C. Emerson (No. 280); second, mar. Mary C. Smith (No. 318).
X.   Richard Kimball (No. 201), mar. Abigail Kent (No. 203).
XI.   Louisa (No. 297), mar. Otis Little.
XII.   Moody H. (No. 292), mar. Laura A. Putnam (No. 381).

No. 226.

Anna Kimball, b. in Plaistow, Jan. 5, 1783, a daughter of Nathaniel and Susannah (Sawyer) Kimball of Plaistow. She married James Calef (No. 816), April 12, 1804, and resided in Saco, Me., where her first child was born, and then moved to Hampstead. She was admitted to the church by owning her baptismal covenant, May 4, 1817. She died in Hampstead, March 14, 1828, and was buried in Hampstead. She had children :—

I.   Horatio Gates, b. in Saco, Me., March 4, or 11, 1808; d. in Brooklyn, N. Y., May 10, 1891; m., first, in 1833, Julia Ann Patten, at Augusta, Me., who died Oct. 23, 1837, leaving one child, Abby Patten Calef, b. July, 1834. He married, second, Hannah Patten, May 30, 1838, who died Aug. 17, 1838. He married, third, Margaret S. Webster, daughter of Peter E. Web-

ster, of Salem, Mass., a niece of his stepmother (No. 814).
Their children were :—

    1. Julia Augusta, b. in Cambridgeport, Mass.

    2. Horace Webster, b. in Boston.

    3. James, b. in Boston.

II.   Almira Ann, b. May 15, 1810; d. young.

III.   James Albert, b. Dec. 12, 1812.

IV.   Harriet Newell (No. 385).

V.   Lois (No. 425).

VI.   Susannah Sawyer, b. June 24, 1835; d. young.

VII.   Infant, d. young.

Nabby Kimball, sister of Anna (above), married Joseph, brother of James Calef (see Nos. 107, 108). Their father was a farmer in Plaistow; ensign in the Revolution in 1776; afterwards quartermaster in Col. Joseph Cilley's regiment, and was a deputy sheriff in Rockingham county in 1784.

No. 227.

Phebe Poor, b. in Hampstead, June 4, 1775, a daughter of David and Phebe (Carlton) Poor. She married Capt. Jona. Carlton Little (No. 167), her cousin, as his second wife, Dec. 29, 1802. She was admitted to the church, by baptism, with her five children, Aug. 10, 1817. She died in Hampstead, Nov. 30, 1841. Her children were :—

I.   Meribah Farnum Hale (No. 448).

II.   Linus Lewis Carlton, b. Sept. 27, 1806; mar. Abiah L. Tewksbury (No. 302).

III.   David Poor (No. 270).

IV.   Phebe (No. 264).

V.   Nathaniel Hale, b. April 1, 1819; m. Almira Tewksbury (sister to 302). He was a cooper by trade. and spent the last part of his life in Lynn, Mass., where he died Dec. 30, 1877, Children :—

    1. Meribah Farnum (No. 448).

    2. Frank Henry (No. 488).

    3. Jonathan C. (No. 475).

    4. Mary Phebe, b. Sept. 1, 1852; m. John Dow, Jr., of Atkinson, Dec. 23, 1869; res. Danvers, Mass. Children: Ethelin May and John Carlton.

No. 228.

Irene Kelly, b. in Hampstead, April 27, 1800, daughter of Rev. John and Abigail (Dearborn) Kelly (Nos. 164, 171). She was admitted to the church May 3, 1818, and died in Hampstead, Aug. 27, 1831, unmarried.

No. 229.

Emma Chase, b. Feb. 8, 1766, in Newbury, Mass., daughter of Abel and Hannah (Campbell) Chase, of Newbury. She married Joseph Chase, who was born Nov. 8, 1758, son of Joseph[4] and Susanna (Bancroft) Chase of Newbury, Mass., and who d. April 2, 1836. She was admitted to the church March 21, 1819, and died May 11, 1831, and was buried in the village cemetery, aged 65 years, 3 months. They had children :—

I.   Hannah, b. Dec. 23, 1786; m. Moses Jaques of West Newbury, Mass.
II. Susannah (No. 230), m. Joshua Eastman, Jr. (No. 213).
III. Mary, b. Nov. 8, 1780; m. Thorndike Putnam (see p. 333, Vol. 1).
IV. Elizabeth S. (No. 460), m. John Ordway.
V.   Jonathan, b. Feb. 27, 1795, m. Hannah Harrington (No. 403).
VI. Emma, b. Feb. 21, 1797; m. Dea. William Tenney (No. 321).
VII. Dea. Joseph (No. 380), m. Elizabeth Morse (No. 308).

No. 230.

Susanna Chase, b. in Salisbury, Mass., March 4, 1788, a daughter of Joseph and Emma (Chase) Chase (No. 229). She married Joshua Eastman, Jr. (No. 213), and was admitted to the church June 13, 1819. She died in Hampstead, March 10, 1865, and was buried in the village cemetery. They had children :—

I.   Mary Putnam (No. 390), mar. Robert Henry Emerson (see Nos. 241, 242).
II. Edmund T. (No. 332).
III. John True, b. Nov. 27, 1823; d. Sept. 5, 1864. He was a merchant in Boston, Mass., and unmarried.
IV. Judith S. (No. 361).
V.   Joshua Chase, b. March 4, 1830; m. Nancy R. Marston (No. 456).

No. 231.

John Kelly, Jr., b. in Hampstead, Jan. 1, 1798, a son of Rev. John and Abigail (Dearborn) Kelly (Nos. 164 and 171). He entered Dartmouth College and spent one year there in 1816; but was graduated from Williams College in 1825. He studied medicine at the medical college in Fairfield, N. Y. He commenced the practice of medicine in Fultonville, N. Y., in 1832, from whence he went to Carlisle, N. Y., in 1837, and from there to Experience, N. Y., in 1851. He married Catherine Sweetman, of Carlisle, N. Y., in 1834. He died Jan. 15, 1872. They had seven children, of which the fourth (Henry) was a merchant in New York city, b. June 28, 1843. John Kelly, Jr., was admitted to the church in Hampstead June 13, 1819, and was dismissed to the Dutch Reformed Church in Coghuaneaga, near Johnston, N. Y., Feb. 23, 1834.

No. 232.

Jonathan Brickett, b. in Newbury, Mass., May 31, 1789, a son of James and Anna (Wheeler) Brickett (Nos. 224, 225). He married Lydia Kent (No. 233). He was admitted to the church Nov. 5, 1819, from the church in Exeter, and dismissed to the church in Londonderry (Presbyterian), "previous to Feb. 24, 1834," and continued there until his death, in Lowell, Mass., Dec. 19, 1872. He was buried in Londonderry.

No. 233.

Lydia Kent, b. in Hampstead, May 13, 1790, a daughter of Dea. Job and Elice (Little) Kent (Nos. 120, 121). She married Jonathan Brickett (No. 232), April 10, 1810. She was admitted to the church from the church in Exeter, and her five children bapt. in Hampstead, Nov. 5, 1819. She was dismissed to the Presbyterian Church in Londonderry, "previous to Feb. 24, 1834," and continued until her death,

March, 1870. She was buried in Londonderry. Their children were :—

I.   James, b. in Exeter; served in the civil war.
II.   Charles, served in the civil war, and died from disease contracted while in the service.
III. Henry W., res. in Concord.
IV.   Harriet, m. George Colby of Derry; d. at Philadelphia.
V.   Delia, m. Aaron Hardy of Derry; d. in Londonderry.
VI.   Elizabeth, unmarried; d. in Lowell; buried in Londonderry.
VII. Herbert, died in California, from the effects of a fall from his horse.

No. 234.

Ezra Davis, b. in Hampstead, Sept. 6, 1793, a son of Jesse and Lois (Worthen) Davis (No. 223). He married, first, Mary Garland (No. 235), by whom he had eight children. He was admitted to the church June 4, 1820, and died in Hampstead, Oct. 25, 1857.

No. 235.

Mary Garland, b. in Barrington, Sept. 9, 1799, a daughter of Benjamin and Mary (Balch) Garland, of Barrington and Hampstead (Nos. 220 and 221). She married Ezra Davis (No. 234), Dec. 25, 1817. She was admitted to the church July 30, 1820. She died in Hampstead, and was buried in the village cemetery. Their children were (p. 363, Vol. 1):

I.   Jesse Brooks (333).
II.   Joanna, b. Oct. 2, 1821; m. Hiram Withington of New Jersey.
III.   Charles Henry, d. young.
IV.   Mary E. (No. 429).
V.   Caroline Matilda, b. July 11, 1828; m. Wm. B. Blackwell of New Jersey.
VI.   Charles Ezra, b. Feb. 20, 1821, of Pennsylvania.
VII.   Emily Susan, b. June 14, 1834; m. Oscar H. Brown (No. 106).
VIII. William H. (No. 437).

No. 236.

Lydia Chandler, b. in Atkinson, March 1, 1789, daughter of Joseph and Elizabeth (Cook) Chandler, of Atkinson. Her father was b. in Andover, Mass., Jan. 8, 1743, and was brought up by his uncle Joseph, in Rowley. He served seven years in the Revolutionary war, and it is said came home so tattered and with such ill health that his own family could not recognize him. He lived where Alonzo Hall now resides in Atkinson. He died Jan. 8, 1834, aged 90 years. Lydia married Amos Baker of Campton, and she was admitted by baptism to the church, July 30, 1820. She was dismissed to unite with the church at Plymouth, in 1822, and from there she was dismissed to the Congregational Church in Lowell, Mass., Aug. 5, 1833.

No. 237.

Joseph Wentworth Batchelder, b.   .
He was adm. to the church by baptism, July 30, 1820.

No. 238.

Elizabeth Putnam, b. in Danvers, Mass., March 6, 1785, a daughter of Oliver and Sarah (Lake) Putnam (No. 210) She mar. Dr. Phillip Hackett of Hampstead, May 30, 1807. She was adm. to the church Aug. 20, 1820. She had children:—

I.   Robert Collins, bapt., Aug. 20, 1820.
II.   Henry George, bapt., Aug. 20, 1820.
III. Sarah Ann, b. Jan. 31, 1809.

No. 239.

Henry George, b. in Hampstead, August 9, 1798, a son of Jonathan and Hannah (Currier) George (No. 243). He mar. Mary Heath (No. 222), June 12, 1823. He was adm. to the church Aug. 20, 1820, and dismissed to the First Church in Haverhill, Mass., before "Feb. 24, 1834." He was admitted again to the church in Hampstead, Aug. 29, 1836, and dismissed to the church in Kingston, Mass., Mar. 26, 1848.

No. 240.

Sally Noyes, b. in Hampstead, June 23, 1785, a daughter of Joshua Hale and Sarah (Kimball) Noyes of Hampstead. She mar. Moses Heath (No. 244). She was adm. to the church Oct. 1, 1820. She had five children (see p. 419, Vol. 1).

No. 241.

John Emerson, b. in Hampstead, June 27, 1778, a son of Robert and Mary (Webster) Emerson (Nos. 186-187). He mar. Elizabeth Emery (No. 242). He was adm. to the church Oct. 15, 1820, and was elected deacon, March 2, 1821, and served till his death, May 5, 1848. He was buried in the village cemetery. Gravestone inscription, "I know that my Redeemer liveth." (See p. 868, Vol. 1.)

No. 242.

Elizabeth Emery, b. in Atkinson, Apr. 11, 1784, daughter of Benjamin and Mehitable (Ingalls) Emery of West Atkinson. She mar. Dea. John Emerson (No. 141), and was adm. to the church Oct. 15, 1820. They had children b. in Hampstead :—

I.   Jesse Emery (No. 308), m. Mary E. Morrisson (No. 354).
II. Alfred, b. Oct. 10, 1807.
III. John W. (No. 301), m. Abigail J. Page (No. 322).
IV. Robert Henry, b. Oct. 20, 1816; m. Mary P. Eastman (No. 396).
V.   Elizabeth (No. 397).
VI. Mary (No. 345).

She d. June 12, 1873, and was buried in the village cemetery; gravestone inscription, "Thou shalt come to thy grave in a full age, like a shock of corn cometh in its season."

No. 243.

Hannah Currier, b. in Hampstead, July 15, 1768, a daughter of Ezekial and Susanna (Emerson) Currier (No. 215). She mar. Jonathan George (No. 143). She was adm. to the church Nov. 5, 1820. She d. in Hampstead, and was buried in the village cemetery. Their children were : —

I.	Dudley (No. 379).
II.	Hannah, b. April 11, 1791.
III.	Sally (No. 350).
IV.	Henry (No. 239).
V.	Nabby, b. Aug. 5, 1800.
VI.	Mary (No. 276).

No. 244.

Moses Heath, b. in Hampstead, Oct. 18, 1779, a son of Jesse and Abiah (Kimball) Heath of Hampstead. He mar. Sally Noyes (No. 240). He was adm. to the church Jan. 7, 1821, "aged 41 years."

No. 245.

Jonathan Kent, b. in Hampstead, June 4, 1788, a son of Dea. Job and Alice (or Ellice) (Little) Kent (Nos. 120, 121). He mar. Clarissa Page (No. 247). He was adm. to the church Jan. 7, 1821 ; baptized in infancy. He was elected deacon, Dec. 24, 1824, and served till his death. He d. in Hampstead, at what is now the home of Mrs. Clara A. Clark, and was buried in the village cemetery (see p. 869, Vol. 1).

No. 246.

Clarissa Page, b. in Hampstead, June 13, 1790, a daughter of Jonathan and Abigail (Kimball) Page, who resided where Charles Damon now resides on the Chandler farm. Jonathan Page, d. in Hampstead, Aug. 6. 1832, aged 78 years,

DEA. JONATHAN KENT. NO. 245.

and wife Nabby Kimball, d. May 8, 1810. Jonathan Page, mar., second, Abigail Welch, mother of Dea. Ezra Welch of Hampstead, in Hampstead, Aug. 7, 1813; who d. in Hampstead, Feb. 5, 1856, aged 90 years and 6 mos. Clarissa mar. Dea. Jonathan Kent (No. 245), Oct. 8, 1807, and was adm. to the church by baptism, Jan. 7, 1821. They had nine children (see p. 369, Vol. 1), all of whom were members of the church in Hampstead. (Nos. 269, 294, 295, 329, 330, 331, 363, 523, 525).

No. 247.

Sarah True, b. in Hampstead, June 3, 1767, a daughter of Rev. Henry and Ruth (Ayer) True (Nos. 1, 72). She mar. John Howard of Haverhill, Mass., Feb. 23, 1797, and resided in Hampstead, where Mr. Aaron Smith now resides. She was adm. to the church Feb. 25, 1821, and dismissed to the church in Dunbarton, "before Feb. 24, 1834." She d. Feb. 21, 1841. Their children were :—

I.   Mary Ann, d. Nov. 1, 1829, aged 19 years.
II.   Ruth Ayer (No. 323).
III. Hannah True (No. 696).
IV.   Rev. Jabez True (No. 324).
V.   Henrietta.
VI.   Ann Maria Hazen, d. unmarried. A friend writes of her, "Ann was not a member of the church, but a sweet saint on earth, and did much good in her quiet way."

No. 248.

Mary Brown, b. in Hampstead, April 5, 1799, a daughter of Samuel and Hannah (George) Brown (Nos. 105, 106). She was adm. to the church by baptism, Aug. 26, 1821, and d. of small-pox, in Manchester; unmarried.

No. 249.

Anna Kimball, b. in Concord, June, 1773, a daughter of John Kimball of Bradford, Mass., and wife Anna Ayer of

Haverhill, Mass. She mar., first, Robert Parker of Litchfield; who d. Jan. 24, 1800. She then mar. Dea. John True (No. 214), Dec. 27, 1820, and was adm. to the church from the church at Litchfield, Oct. 28, 1821. She was dismissed to the church at Concord before Feb. 24, 1834. She d. in Concord, Dec. 3, 1834.

"Her parents moved from the Bradford homestead, when they were married, to Concord. Mr. Kimball united with the Bradford church when 18 years of age. A man of very strong religious convictions, and honored his Christian religion, during a long life. During thirty years, he was absent but once, from public worship."

No. 250.

Samuel Kelly, b. in Hampstead, Jan. 25, 1805, a son of John and Abigail (Dearborn) Kelly (Nos. 164, 171). After a course of study at Atkinson Academy, he completed his preparatory course, for the practice of medicine, but very soon after became deranged in intellect, and died a young man.

Dr. Isaac Tewksbury (No. 377), once wrote in a Boston paper, of Samuel Kelly, in regard to long fasting. "I have known of two persons, one of whom fasted fifty-five days, and the other forty-five days, but both died.

The first, was Samuel, son of Rev. John Kelly of Hampstead. He was of delicate constitution, and nervous temperament, and contrary to the advice of his physician, he studied medicine. After receiving his diploma, his health began to fail him, and he went west, where he remained two years, when becoming deranged, he returned to New Hampshire, and was found near Derry, fantastically attired, and a raving maniac. He was taken to an insane asylum, where he remained a few months, when he was returned to his father's home as incurable, and as he was daily becoming more violent, acting under the advice of his physician (Dr.

Tewksbury), his parents had a large cage constructed, and in this he was incarcerated. The cage was provided with a bed, and other needed conveniences, and although food was offered him, and placed in the cage at regular intervals, yet he persistently refused it for fifty-five days. He, however, drank a large quantity of water. At his death, he was greatly emaciated. A post mortem examination was held, and the interior organs were found to be greatly inflamed, no one more than the other. The physician who made the examination, found no evidence of food having been taken into the stomach for a long time, and as a strict watch was kept over him, both day and night, his long fast was attested to by the testimony of reliable persons."

Samuel Kelly was adm. to the church Feb. 8, 1824; d. Jan. 12, 1834, and was buried in the Hampstead village cemetery.

No. 251.

Eliphalet Knight, b. in Newbury, Mass., June 26, 1740, a son of Tristram and Elizabeth (Greenleaf) Knight, who moved to Atkinson, from " Pipe Stave Hill," in Newbury, in 1758, to near what is now the John Watson farm, near James M. Nesmith's. He mar. Martha Knight (Nos. 202), Feb. 27, 1768. He was adm. to the church Feb. 8, 1824, and lived in Hampstead, with his son, Dr. James Knight, at " Cobb's corner," where he died.

No. 252.

Jonathan Knight Little, b. in Hampstead, March 22, 1798, a son of Col. Jonathan and Dorothy (Little) Little. " He was adm. to the church May 8, 1825, on a sick and dying bed." He was a graduate from Dartmouth College, 1823. He taught school, at Belleville, Newburyport, Mass., and began the study of medicine, with Dr. Richard Spofford of Newburyport; died May 25, 1825; unmarried.

No. 253.

Hannah R. Rogers, b.

She mar. Jabez Hoyt, Jr., Dec. 4, 1823. Jabez Hoyt, was a son of Jabez and Charlotte (Little) Hoyt (see p. 415, Vol. 1), and grandson of Jabez and Abiah Hoyt. She was adm. to the church from the church at Chester, July 2, 1826. She was dismissed to the church in Chester, "previous to Feb. 24, 1834," but later moved to Coalville, Ohio. She had three children.

No. 254.

Mary Carlton, b. in Plaistow, a daughter of Capt. Jonathan and Susannah (Bartlett) Carlton. She mar. Nathaniel Little, Sen., 1768, son of Samuel and Dorothy (Noyes) Little of Atkinson. She was adm. to the church July 2, 1826, and d. in Hampstead, Feb. 13, 1832; buried in the village cemetery. Their children besides four, who d. young, were :

I.   Jonathan C. (No. 107).
II.   Nathaniel (No. 256).
III.   Susan. b. July 24, 1773; m. Capt. Osgood Taylor of Springfield, and d. Jan. 31, 1854. Her husband was an innkeeper, and lived at Springfield, Sandown, and Hampstead; where he died, Jan. 24, 1838, aged 68 years. They had children :—
       1. Lydia Taylor, m. Abner K. Kent. They resided for a time, where Mr. William Page now resides; they had children :—1. George Henry, m., first, Miranda H. Chase; second, Arabella B. Miller. 2. Louise M. (No. 443). 3. Elbridge Kimball, m. Julia F. Clark. 4. Frederick True, m., first, Ruth A. Dinsmore; second, Florence A. Gutterson. 5. Mary S. (No. 484). 6. Abner Kimball, Jr., m., first, Emma B. McNeil; second, Katherine M. Dinsmore. 7. Frank, m. Fannie Keyes; now Mrs. Wm. W. Wilder, Newton.
       2. True W. Taylor, m. Rhoda Ann Tewksbury of Hampstead.
       3. Jonathan C. Taylor, m. Betsey Wilson of Hampstead.
       4. John.
       5. Sarah Little, m. William Ayer of Hampstead.

6. Osgood Bartlett, m. Sarah S. Corner of Hampstead.
moved to Goffstown.

IV.   Samuel, b. May 20, 1778; m. Sally Pettengill; he resided in
Springfield, and they had children :—

    1. Hiram, m. Roxanna Carr, who, when a widow, mar.
Rufus Bean; he was a carriage-maker, and lived in
Cornish; they had a son, Hiram A., who d. unm., in
1869.

    2. Mary, d. unmarried.

    3. Eliza, m. Henry Webster of West Canaan.

    4. Phebe Malvina, m. Parker Carr of Oxford.

V.   Joseph, m. Sarah Webster of Salisbury. He was a sea captain,
and d. in 1820. Their children, b. in Salisbury, were :—

    1. Thomas Jefferson, m. Sarah Parsons. He was a lawyer
in Canton, Ill., and d. in 1855.

    2. Stephen Webster, m. Abigail Welch. He was a master
mechanic in Holyoke, Mass.; d. in 1852; they had
two children.

    3. Nathaniel Noyes, m. Sarah F. Plumer. He was a
contractor of stone work, and d. in Emmonsburg
N. Y., 1875. They had three children.

    4. Susan Webster, m. St. Clair Bean, who was a mill-
wright, in Holyoke, Mass. They had one child, who
was asst. postmaster at Holyoke, Mass.

VI.   Elizabeth, b. Oct. 9, 1787; m. John Hoyt of Springfield, and had
eleven children b. in Springfield.

VII.   John, b. June 17, 1789; d. unm., as a sailor, off the coast of
North Carolina, 1840.

VIII.   Sarah, b. Oct. 10, 1791; d. 1810.

IX.   Amos, b. Feb. 27, 1796; m. Ann Brickett (see Appendix).

No. 255.

Abiah Emerson, b. in Hampstead, March 31, 1774, a
daughter of Robert and Mary (Webster) Emerson (Nos.
186, 187). She mar. Nathaniel Little, Jr. (No. 256), and
was adm. to the church July 2, 1826. She d. in Hampstead,
Nov. 20, 1854, aged 80 years. They had children :—

I.   Polly (No. 399).

II.   Belinda (No. 277).

III.   Robert Emerson, b. Nov. 25, 1804; m. Clarissa, daughter of Dea.
James Pinkerton of Derry. He was educated at Atkinson
Academy, taught school in Essex, Mass., and after his mar-

riage, was engaged in mercantile work in Boston for
several years, and went to Illinois, where he was a real
estate dealer, and d. in 1842; they had one child,

 1. Henry Augustus, who was educated at Andover Phillips
  Academy, Amherst College, and Brown University,
  from which he received the degree of A. B. He
  taught in the Normal School in Lancaster, Mass.
  High schools in Reading, and Marblehead, Mass., and
  other places. In the military school at Worcester,
  and instructor of elocution, in New York City. "He
  has spelled his name Littel, and called as of Derry."

IV. George W. (No. 306).

No. 256.

Nathaniel Little, Jr., b. in Hampstead, May 5, 1771, a son
of Nathaniel and Mary (Carlton) Little (see No. 254). He
mar. Abiah Emerson (No. 255). He was adm. to the church
May 6, 1827, and d. in Hampstead, Dec. 4, 1857, and was
buried in the village cemetery. He resided at the homestead
of the late James Williams, was a cooper by trade, also a
farmer, and a very highly respected townsman. He was
chairman of the board of selectmen for thirteen years, and
town clerk for fourteen. "Fine penmanship and a musical
voice, fitted him for the last office. It is related that he had
a fine sense of the humorous side of life, and the publishment of marriage notices, or intentions, was proclaimed oral-
ly at the close of a Sabbath service, and often made much
merriment to the audience."

No. 257.

Jeremiah Jewett Tenney, b. April 17, 1805, in Topsfield,
Mass., son of Thomas and Elizabeth (Jewett) Tenney. He
mar. Patience Proctor of Derry, in 1833; b. Jan. 26, 1807;
d. 1877. They lived in Manchester, in Lawrence, Mass.,
1846, to the west, 1855. He was adm. to the church May
6, 1827. He was of Dedham, Mass., 1834.

No. 258.

Francis Welch, b. in Hampstead, March 29, 1801, a son of Joseph and Martha (Sargent) Welch (Nos. 219, 168). He married Harriette Conant of Ipswich, Mass. He was a graduate from Union College at Schenectady, N. Y., in 1832, and was admitted to the church May 6, 1827, and dismissed to be pastor of the church at Brentwood, April 6, 1835. He preached in Brentwood, Linebrook Parish, Ipswich, Mass., and in Perry, Me. He died in Haverhill, Mass., Feb. 17, 1894. They had children, all, except when death is noted, are now living in Haverhill, Mass. (1902), except Charles D., principal of the high school at St. Paul, Minn.

I.   Mary Webster, b. Nov. 25, 1840.
II.   Harriet Frances, b. Jan. 8, 1843.
III.   Abbie Eliza, b. July 20, 1845.
IV.   Sarah Louisa, b. Sept. 16, 1848; d. Jan. 7, 1872.
V.   George Henry, b. May 26, 1850; m. Clara Gould.
VI.   Charles Davis, b. Dec. 13, 1852.
VII.   Martha Ann, b. March 18, 1855.
VIII.   Eleanor Emerson, b. Aug. 13, 1857; d. June 16, 1891.
IX.   Frank Simons, b. Feb. 23, 1861.
X.   Elmer William, b. May 2, 1863.

No. 259.

Almira Ann Calef, b. in Hampstead, May 15, 1810, a daughter of James and Anna (Kimball) Calef (Nos. 316, 226). She was admitted to the church June 6, 1828, and d., unmarried, in early womanhood. The church records record the following : " A revival long expected in answer to the prayers of God's people visibly appeared towards the close of September, 1827, and twenty-nine persons were converted and united with the church ; mostly all were baptized in infancy."

No. 260.

Harriet Davis, b. in Hampstead, Nov. 26, 1804, a daughter of Jesse and Lois (Worthen) Davis (No. 223). She was admitted to the church Jan. 6, 1828.

No. 261.

Sarah Welch, b. in Hampstead, Aug. 29, 1797, a daughter of Joseph and Martha (Sargent) Welch (Nos. 219, 168). She married Henry Hubbard, June 13, 1819. She was admitted to the church Jan. 6, 1828, and died May 2, 1831. From the village cemetery we find a son, "George, d. 1831, an infant; Sally, aged 3 years"; Henry, b. Oct. 14, 1819, d. in Michigan.

No. 262.

Abigail Kelly, b. in Hampstead, July 6, 1808, a daughter of Rev. John and Abigail (Dearborn) Kelly (Nos. 164, 171). She was admitted to the church Jan. 6, 1828, and died in Hampstead in early womanhood, unmarried.

No. 263.

Abigail Kimball Kent, b. in Hampstead, Nov. 9, 1809, a daughter of Dea. Jonathan and Clarissa (Page) Kent (Nos. 145, 146). She married Richard K. Brickett (No. 291). She was baptized in infancy, and admitted to the church Jan. 6, 1828. She died in Hampstead, Jan. 7, 1891, and was buried in the village cemetery. They had children:—

I.   Lorenzo K., bapt. Jan. 6, 1832; d. young.
II. Mary Jane (No. 638).
III. William Henry, b. July, 1842; m. Rosa A. Morse. Their only daughter is Mabel J., of Manchester (see p. 345, Vol. 1).

No. 264.

Phebe Little, b. in Hampstead, March 23, 1811, a daughter of Jona. C. and Phebe (Poor) Little (Nos. 167, 227). She married Francis Sawyer (No. 271), Sept. 6, 1829. She was admitted to the church Jan. 6, 1828, having been baptized in infancy. She died April 27, 1880, in Haverhill, Mass., at the home of her youngest daughter, Mrs. Daniel Sawyer. She was dismissed to the church in Portsmouth

before 1834, and again admitted as a member of this church
from the church at Candia, Jan. 3, 1844. Their children
were :—

I.   Samuel S., d., unmarried, in 1852.
II.   Anna Elizabeth (No. 415).
III.   Henry L., d. young.
IV.   Harriet Colby, mar. Daniel Long Sawyer, of Haverhill, Mass.

No. 265.

Alice Kent, b. in Hampstead, March 23, 1781, a daughter
of Job and Alice (Little) Kent (Nos. 119, 120). She mar
ried Samuel Nichols of Hampstead, Sept. 17, 1805. She was
admitted to the church Jan. 6, 1828, and died in Hampstead
Sept. 8, 1868, and was buried in the village cemetery. Their
children were :—

I.   Stephen, b.   ; m. Mary Van Meter.
II.   Daniel (No. 290), m. Sallie Mynot.
III.   Moses, b.   ; m. Mary Ann Earle.
IV.   Hiram, b.   ; m. Louisa Hoyt (see p. 379, Vol. 1).
V.   Eliza Jane (No. 411).
VI.   Mary, d. young.

No. 266.

Mary Webster Welch, b. in Hampstead, March 8, 1797, a
daughter of Joseph and Martha (Sargent) Welch (Nos. 219,
168). She married James Nichols, of West Amesbury,
Mass., Nov. 29, 1828. His second wife (see No. 168) was
her sister, Martha S. She was admitted to the church Jan.
6, 1828, and was dismissed to the church at Amesbury " before Feb. 24, 1834," and d. in West Amesbury, March 20,
1835. Her children were :—

I.   Mary Webster, b. March 11, 1831; m. Daniel B. Foster, of Ha-
       verhill, Mass.
II.   Eliza Merrill, b. Dec. 28, 1834; m. Calvin W. Crowell of Haver-
       hill.
III.   Francis Welch, b. March 7, 1833; d. March 8, 1838.

No. 267.

Priscilla Gibson, b. in Nashua, May 4, 1804, a daughter of Samuel H. Gibson of Alstead, b. July 3, 1776, and his wife, Anna Webster, of Atkinson, married in 1799. She married Benjamin Sawyer (No. 395). She was admitted to the church Jan. 6, 1828, and d. in Hampstead, and was buried in the village cemetery. It is said of her that "she was the first woman that went over the bridge from Main street, Haverhill, to the Bradford side of the river, and that she once rode horseback from Hampstead to Alstead, N. H." (p. 378, Vol. 1). Their children were:—

I. Belinda Ann, b. Feb. 15, 1826; d. May 5, 1850, of small-pox, contracted while on a visit to Boston, Mass.
II. Benjamin Kimball, b. Aug. 23, 1828; d. young.
III. Caroline Priscilla, b. Dec. 20, 1831; d. May 23, 1833.
IV. Francis Harvey, b. Aug. 21, 1834; resides at the homestead (see p. 378, Vol. 1).
V. Horace Reuben (No. 529), m. Almira W. Bailey (No. 486).
VI. Sarah Elizabeth (No. 560), m. James Hunkins.

No. 268.

James Green, b. November, 1810, in Weare, a son of Col. James and Judith (Colby) Green, of Dunbarton. He was admitted to the church Jan. 6, 1828, aged 18, and was baptized in infancy. Moved to Goffstown.

No. 269.

Thomas Kent, b. in Hampstead, April 8, 1808, a son of Dea. Jonathan and Clarissa (Page) Kent (Nos. 245, 246). He married Mary Ann Mooers (No. 305). He was admitted to the church Jan. 6, 1828, having been baptized in infancy. He was dismissed to unite with the church at Pembroke, April 10, 1834, and again united with the Hampstead church from the Congregational Church at Concord, Mar. 26, 1848.

No. 270.

David Poor Little, b. in Hampstead, Nov. 1, 1808, a son of Capt. Jonathan C. and Phebe (Poor) Little (Nos. 167, 227). He married Martha Ann Ham (No. 392). He was admitted to the church Jan. 6, 1828, and was dismissed to the Third Church at Portland, Me., Nov. 29, 1835. He was an express and insurance agent, and resided at one time in Portsmouth, but died in Epping, Dec. 8, 1872.

No. 271.

Francis Sawyer, b. in Amesbury, Mass., July 30, 1806, a son of Wybird and Elizabeth (Williams) Sawyer of Amesbury. He was a cooper, and lived in Hampstead and Portsmouth, and about 1835 removed to Hampstead, where he resided a while, then to Candia, where he died, Nov. 7, 1843. He married Phebe Little (No. 264). and was admitted to the church Jan. 6, 1828, and was dismissed to the church at Portsmouth "before Dec. 24, 1834."

No. 272.

Mary Carlton Little, b. in Hampstead, Jan. 10, 1798, a daughter of Capt. Jonathan C. and Meribah Farnum (Hale) Little (No. 167). She was married by Rev. John Kelly to Capt. Jesse Ayer, a hat manufacturer in Ayers Village of Haverhill, who was b. in Hampstead, Feb. 24, 1798, and died in Methuen, Mass., August, 1880, and buried in Hampstead cemetery. They removed to Methuen, Mass., about 1854,· and sold their homestead to Dea. Charles W. Pressey in 1875. She was admitted to the church by baptism, Jan. 6, 1828. and was dis. and rec. to the Congregational Church at Methuen, April 10, 1862, and died in Merrimac, Mass., in 1884, but buried in the Hampstead cemetery. Their children :—

I.   Meribah Hale (No. 366), m. Henry Putnam of Hampstead.
II.   Albert William, b. Aug. 20, 1822; m., first, Ruth Merrill, who
       died, aged 10 years, by whom he had one son, Albert Harri-
       son Ayer, now living in Haverhill; and m., second, Lydia
       Ann Hoyt, daughter of Moses Hoyt, Esq., of Hampstead. He
       died in 1888, and she d. in Haverhill in 1899; both buried in
       Hampstead village cemetery. They had children :—
           1. Annie Elizabeth, b. in Hampstead; m. George G. Smith
               of Haverhill; had one son, Fred Albert, of Haver-
               hill, and a grandson, Philip Charlesworth Smith, b.
               January, 1901. Mrs. Smith d. May 13, 1901.
           2. Warren Perley; no children; d. Jan., 1890.
           3. Edward Horatio, m., and has children—Harry Edward
               and Clarence Lombard Ayer.
           4. Anson Burlingame, m., and has children—Forrest Dias,
               George Howard, and Marian Frances Ayer.
           5. Mary Allette, unmarried. (All residing in Haverhill.)
       Albert W. Ayer was interested in the Hampstead Musical So-
       ciety, being its chorister for nearly twenty years.
III.   Christopher Perley, b. Jan. 12, 1824; m., and lived in Ayers
       Village, Haverhill, and in Portland, Me.; had children—Mon-
       roe, Walter, Phineas, Kate, Annette, and others.
IV.   Mary Elizabeth Gibbon, b. July 21, 1829; m. Horatio Hoyt, and
       has one daughter, Emma, a teacher in Yonkers, N. Y., for
       several years; Mary E.; m., second, Frederick Nichols of
       Merrimac, Mass., where they now reside.
V.   Ebenezer Hale Little, b. July 1, 1834; m., and has sons, Jesse .
       R. and Russell S. Ayer. He resides in Detroit, Mich. (see p.
       196, Vol. 1).
VI.   Charles Richards, b. Jan. 22, 1837; m., and lived in Boston,
       Mass., where he was a messenger at the State House for a
       number of years. He d. in 1899.

No. 273.

Mary Noyes, b. in Hampstead, May 12, 1795, a daughter
of Joshua Hale and Sarah (Kimball) Noyes (No. 288). She
married Nathaniel Babb of Hampstead, who d. in Hampstead, April 27, 1822, aged 32 years. She was admitted to
the church " by confession and by baptism," Jan. 6, 1828,
and died in Hampstead, June 3, 1840, and was buried in the
village cemetery. Their children were :—

I.   Lorenzo II. (No. 383).
II.   Mary Ann, b. July 13, 1820; m. James M. Babson, Aug. 2, 1840,
        and had one child, Ed. Babson.

No. 274.

Hannah Noyes, b. in Windham, Jan. 1, 1790, a daughter
of Moses and Phebe (Richardson) Noyes of Windham, who
were the pioneers of the Noyes family in Windham. She
married Jonathan K. Brown, son of James and Alice (Ferren) Brown (see Nos. 105 and 106). She was admitted to
the church as a widow, "by baptism and by confession, Jan.
6, 1828." She died in Hampstead, Nov. 9, 1863. He died
Oct. 24, 1827. Both were buried in the village cemetery.
They had children, bapt. Jan. 6, 1828—Alice Frances and
Sarah.

No. 275.

Sally Ordway, b. in Hampstead, March 18, 1795, a daughter of John and Sally (Rogers) Ordway (see p. 334, Vol. 1).
She married Ralph Brickett (No. 876) (see Nos. 224, 225).
She was admitted to the church Jan. 6, 1828, and dismissed
and recommended to the church at Lawrence, Mass., Nov. 24,
1848, and from there was dismissed and recommended to the
Congregational Church at Atkinson, January, 1859. She
died in Atkinson, July 1, 1862, and was buried in the
Hampstead village cemetery. Their children were :—

I.   Sally Ann, d. young.
II.   An infant, d. young.
III.   Sarah O. (No. 741).
IV.   Augusta Ellen, d. unmarried.
V.   Ann Delia, d. young.
VI.   John James, d. young.

Sally Rogers was b. in Newbury, Mass., Feb. 22, 1763,
daughter of Abiel and Sarah (Woodman) Rogers of Newbury. She d. in Hampstead, Feb. 1, 1847. She was called

as a member of this church, but we did not find her name
on the records. Children were :—

I.   Polly, b. Jan. 7, 1788.
II.   Betsey (No. 880), m. Dudley George (No. 870).
III.   John, b. July 14, 1792; m. Eliza S. Chase (No. 466).
IV.   Sally (No. 275) (above).
V.   Nancy (No. 279).
VI.   Abigail, b. July 12, 1803; d., unmarried, in Hampstead.

No. 276.

Mary George, b. in Hampstead, July 8, 1803, a daughter
of Jonathan and Hannah (Currier) George (No. 243). She
was admitted to the church by confession and baptism, Jan.
6, 1828, and dismissed May 1, 1857, at her own request.
She d. in Hampstead, unmarried.

No. 277.

Belinda Little, b. in Hampstead, July 3, 1800, a daughter
of Nathaniel and Abiah (Emerson) Little (Nos. 255 and
256). She married Theodore Tarlton (No. 289), Aug. 12,
1831. She was admitted to the church Jan. 6, 1828, and
was dismissed to the church in " the Western country,"
probably Illinois.

No. 278.

Sarah Woodman Jaques, b. in West Newbury, Mass., Aug.
27, 1808, a daughter of Moses and Hannah (Chase) Jaques,
of West Newbury. She married Jacob Irving (No. 283),
Jan. 14, 1832. She was admitted to the church by confession and baptism, Jan. 6, 1828, and died Nov. 25, 1850.
Their children were :—

I.   John D., b. Sept. 10, 1833; m. Mary E. Kent (No. 523).
II.   Martha A., b. Jan. 14, 1835; d. June 30, 1845.
III.   Joseph C., b. Sept. 7, 1837.
IV.   Hannah E. (No. 482), m. John S. Titcomb (No. 451).
V.   Sarah E. (No. 514).
VI.   Jacob H., b. May 1, 1840.
VII.   Clara A. (No. 470), m. J. A. Davis.

No. 279.

Nancy Ordway, b. in Hampstead, April 25, 1800, a daughter of John and Sally (Rogers) Ordway (No. 275) and (p. 334, Vol. 1). She was admitted to the church Jan. 6, 1828, by confession and baptism, and died in Hampstead, Sept. 18, 1872, and was buried in the village cemetery.

No. 280.

Abigail Atkinson Emerson, b. in Hampstead, Nov. 18, 1810, a daughter of Robert and Sarah (Kent) Emerson (No. 296). She married James Brickett, Jr. (see No. 225). She united with the church May, 1828, and was dismissed to the church in Newport, Nov. 7, 1834. She died, and was buried in Claremont, April 25, 1852. James Brickett was for many years a member of the church at Claremont (see No. 318). He died April, 1864, and was buried in Claremont. They had four children, two of whom died young, and Robert and Louisa, who lived to young manhood and womanhood, and died of consumption.

No. 281.

Fanny Tufts,   said to have been a nurse in several families in town, and had brother William, who worked in Ralph Brickett's saw-mill for many years. She was admitted to the church by confession and baptism, Jan. 6, 1828.

No. 282.

Delia Brickett, b. in Hampstead, July 31, 1799, a daughter of James and Anna (Wheeler) Brickett (Nos. 224, 225). She married, first, Henry, son of Joseph Welch (No. 219). She was admitted to the church October, 1828, and was dismissed and recommended to the Congregational Church at East Haverhill, Mass., November, 1835. She married, second, Simeon George, of East Haverhill. She died in East Haverhill, and was buried there. She had children :—

I.   Moses Tyler, b. Nov. 25, 1834.
II.   Henry George and Delia Ann George, by second husband, b. in
        East Haverhill, Mass.

JACOB IRVING.   NO. 283.

No. 283.

Jacob Irving, b. in Londonderry, Oct. 10, 1808, a son of
David and Sally (Fern) Irving, of Londonderry and Hampstead. David Irving married, second, widow Hannah Marsh
of Fremont (No. 375). Jacob Irving married Sarah W.

Jaques (No. 278), and married, second, Mary M. Shirley (No. 497). He was admitted to the church, "aged 19, by confession and baptism, Jan. 6, 1828." He was dismissed to unite with the North Parish Church in Haverhill, Mass., July, 1854. From that church he was admitted as a member of the Congregational Church at Atkinson, and in 1868 again became a member of the church at Hampstead, and continued till his death, March 10, 1879. He was station agent at Atkinson Depot thirteen years, and resided three years in Atkinson Village, on the John Dow place, now occupied by Benj. R. Heald. He was chorister of the musical society eight years, and superintendent of the Sunday school twelve.

No. 284.

Thomas Kendrick Little, b. in Amesbury, Mass., May 2, 1807, a son of John and Susannah (Kendrick) Little. John Little was b. Nov. 13, 1873, and d. in Boston, Mass., July 9, 1812, and was one of the first persons to introduce carriage making into Amesbury. Susannah Kendrick was a daughter of Seth and Hannah Kendrick of Amesbury. She was b. June 17, 1779, and d. March 22, 1856. Thomas K. married Sarah Bennett, a daughter of John and Elizabeth H. (Reed) Burden, Dec. 28, 1834, who was b. Oct., 1811. He was a clothier, and resided in West Hampstead. He was admitted to the church, "aged 20, Jan. 6, 1828, by baptism and confession." He was separated from the church, by his own request, Nov. 6, 1835. They had children, b. in Hampstead :—

I. John William, b. Sept. 21, 1835; m. Lucy Ann Hall (No. 576).
II. Susan Elizabeth, b. Sept. 21, 1835; m. Moulton D. Pressey, and d. Nov. 14, 1864; Mr. Pressey mar. second Mary Jennie Little (see No. 605).

No. 285.

Daniel Nichols, b. in Hampstead, Dec. 6, 1811, a son of Samuel and Alice (Kent) Nichols. He married Sallie, b. Feb. 3, 1814, daughter of Martyn and Annie (Arnold) Minot, of East Hampstead. He was admitted to the church, "aged 16 years, by baptism and confession," Jan. 6, 1828. "He left the church upon a change of beliefs, Aug. 1, 1831." He was a mechanic by trade, and died in Hampstead, Oct. 16, 1885. Sallie (Minot) Nichols d. in Hampstead, 1902. (See photo of Mr. Nichols in Vol. 1.) They had children :—

I.   Helen M., m. Rufus C. Smith (p. 321, Vol. 1).
II.   Lucian, m. Maria Kelly; res. in Haverhill, Mass.
III. M. Iantha, b. Feb. 20, 1844.
IV.   Ada Eliza, b. Oct. 28, 1845.
V.   Moses E., d. aged 15 months.
VI.   Alice A., d. aged 10 months.
VII. Daniel, d. aged one year.

No. 286.

Josiah Franklin Heath, b. May 3, 1808, in Kingston, a son of Nathaniel and Sally (Patten) Heath, of Kingston and Hampstead. He was admitted to the church, "aged 20 years, by confession and baptism, Jan. 6, 1828."

No. 287.

Lyman Worthen, b. in Hampstead, 1808, a son of Oliver Worthen, b. in Vermont, and wife Lydia ——, b. in Maine. He was admitted to the church, " by confession and baptism, aged 20," Jan. 6, 1828. Their son, Lyman Worthen, resides in Haverhill, where he has for many years been connected with the fire department.

No. 288.

Sarah Kimball, b. in Hampstead, Feb. 1, 1764, a daughter of Moses and Sarah (Webster) Kimball. She married Joshua Hale Noyes of Hampstead, Dec. 17, 1778. She was

admitted to the church "·as a· widow, aged 64, March 2,
1828." They resided near the home of Benjamin W. Clark,
and had children :—

I.   Sally (No. 240).
II.   Clark, b. May 2, 1788; d. 1795.
III.   Polly, b. Sept. 15, 1790; d. 1795.
IV.   Stephen, b. Jan. 2, 1793; d. 1795.
V.   Polly (No. 278).
VI.   Clark, b. Sept. 10, 1795; d., unm., in Hampstead.
YII.   John, b. Oct. 0, 1806; m. Sarah A. Ball of Chester; lived in
        Lynn, Mass., and has sons in California.

No. 289.

Theodore Tarlton, b. in Exeter, son of John and Ruth
(Flander) Tarlton (see 307). He married, first, Belinda
Little (No. 277), and married, second, Mary Stevens (No.
311). He was admitted to the church by confession and
baptism, March 2, 1828. He removed to Peoria, Liverpool,
and Canton, Ill., where he was an agent for the sale of land.
The church passed the following letter, April 20, 1834 :
" This is to certify that Theodore Tarlton and Belinda, his
wife, are members of the Congregational and Orthodox or
Evangelical Church, in Hampstead, N. H., in good standing,
and as they are about to remove to the western country, or
into the State of Illinois, they are hereby recommended to
unite with any Evangelical, Congregational, or Presbyterian
church that may hereafter be found in the place of their
future residence. And whenever we have ascertained that
they have united with the church of Christ, to walk in all
the commandments and ordinances of the Lord, we shall
consider them as dismissed from this church. By order of
the church, John Kelly, pastor, and John Emerson, a deacon."

No. 290.

Daniel Nichols, b. in Hampstead, Sept. 1, 1811, a son of
Stephen and Sally (Ayer) Nichols (No. 272), of Hamp-

stead. He married Almira, daughter of Lorenzo Batchelder of Hampstead. He was admitted to the church, by confession and baptism, " aged 16 years, March 2, 1828, and was dismissed at his own request from change of views," April 21, 1833. He was a carpenter by trade, and lived and died, July, 1853, in Manchester, where he was buried.

No. 291.

Richard Kimball Brickett, b. in Hampstead, July 18, 1808, a son of James and Anna (Wheeler) Brickett (Nos. 224, 225). He married Nabby Kimball Kent (No. 263). He was admitted to the church as aged 19, by confession, March 2, 1828. He was a carpenter by trade, and d. in Hampstead, Aug. 3, 1881, and was buried in the village cemetery. (See photo of Mr. Brickett in Vol. 1.)

No. 292.

Moody Hill Brickett, b. in Hampstead, Oct. 10, 1813, a son of James and Anna (Wheeler) Brickett (Nos. 224,225). He married Laura A. Putnam (No. 384). He was admitted to the church by confession, Nov., 1828, and was dismissed and recommended to the church at Newport, Feb. 1, 1838 ; readmitted to the Hampstead church, 1840, and dismissed and recommended to the church in Claremont, April, 1841, and received again from the Claremont church, October, 1844, and dismissed to the Second Congregational Church in Haverhill, Mass., December, 1856, and received from the Winter Street Church in Haverhill, July 1, 1859, and dismissed to the North Church of Haverhill, December, 1864. He d. in Haverhill, May 23, 1887, and was buried in Hampstead village cemetery. He was a hatter by trade.

No. 293.

Phineas Carlton Balch, b. in Newburyport, Mass., June 20, 1797, a son of Jonathan and Abigail (Carlton) Balch.

He married, in 1820, Jane Kezer, b. May 24, 1787, a daughter of Samuel and Olive (Kezer) Merrill. He d. in Rowley, Mass. He was admitted to the church, by confession and baptism, March 2, 1828.

No. 294.

Lorenzo Kent, b. in Hampstead, Sept. 3, 1812, a son of Dea. Jonathan and Clarissa (Page) Kent (Nos. 245, 246). He married Susan Chapin, and resided in Woodstock, Vt. He was admitted to the church, age 15, by confession, March 2, 1828, and recommended to the church at Claremont, Aug. 27, 1841. They had six children, three d. young :—

I.   Henry C., died a young man.
II.   William Edwin, m. in California, living in San Dimas, Calif.
III.   Edwin William, m. at Lebanon; living in California, where they have two children.

No. 295.

Jonathan Page Kent, b. in Hampstead, Sept. 1, 1814, a son of Jonathan and Clarissa (Page) Kent (Nos. 245, 246). He married Ann Taylor, and resided in Boston, Mass. He was admitted to the church, as age 13, by confession, March 2, 1828. He was dismissed to unite with the church in South Boston, Aug. 21, 1836. They had children :—

I.   Elbridge L., m., first, Diantha Tidd. He was a baker of Lawrence, Mass. They had four children. He married, second, Emma Foye, of Methuen, Mass., and had three children.
II.   Annie, m. Minot Buckman of Woburn, Mass.; no children.
III.   Clara Ann, m. Herbert Fuller of Peterboro'.
IV.   Charles E., m. Harriet Wiggin; m. second, —— ——; both dead.
        Children :—
            1. Minot.
            2. Jonathan.
            3. Albert.
            4. Esther Belle (No. 714).
            5. Asa.

V.   Albert Lorenzo, m. first, Ellen Davis of Lawrence. Children :
          1, Carlia, m. Hugh Peckham in California; 2, Bessie, unmar-
          ried; 8, Genevieve, unmarried. He mar., second, "a Wis-
          consin lady." One daughter, Viola, resides in San Jose, Calif.

No. 296.

Sarah Kent, b, in Hampstead, May 22, 1786, a daughter
of Dea. Job and Alice (Little) Kent (Nos. 120, 121). She
married Robert Emerson, Jr., Nov. 26, 1807. She was admitted to the church as a widow, May 4, 1828. At church.
meeting it was voted, Nov. 7, 1734, "having removed to
Newport, and being a member of the church in Hampstead,
are, at their own request, hereby recommended to the Congregational Church in Newport, and on receiving intelligence that they are received there, they will be considered as
dismissed from this church." Their only child was : Abigail
Atkinson Emerson (No. 280).

No. 297.

Louisa Brickett, b. in Hampstead, March 8, 1811, a
daughter of James and Anna (Wheeler) Brickett (Nos. 224,
225). She mar. as the second wife of Otis Little, son of
Moses and Anna (Chase) Little of West Newbury, May 20,
1858. She was adm. to the church by confession, May 4,
1828, and at her request, was dis. and rec. to the First
Congregational Church, in West Newbury, Sept., 1858. She
d. in West Newbury, Dec. 28, 1858, and was buried there.

No. 298.

Caroline French, b. in Hampstead, Aug. 4, 1808, a
daughter of Joseph, Jr., and Molly (Tilton) French (Nos.
173, 174). She was adm. to the church by confession, May
4, 1828, dis. and rec. to the church at Kingston, N. H., July,
1853. She d. August 23, 1890, and was buried in Hampstead village cemetery. She never married.

No. 299.

Josiah Webster, b. in Essex, Mass., Oct. 25, 1803, a son
of Rev. Josiah and Elizabeth (Knight) Webster (see No.
202). He mar. Mary Brickett (No. 300), Dec. 2, 1799 (see
Nos. 224, 225). He was adm. to the church May 4, 1828,
dis. and rec. to the church at Amesbury, and Salisbury Mills,
Mass., Feb. 24, 1834. He d. Sept. 3, 1834, and was buried
in Princeton, Ill.

No. 300.

Mary Little Brickett, b. in Hampstead, Sept. 14, 1803, a
daughter of James and Anna (Wheeler) Brickett (Nos. 224,
225). She mar. Josiah Webster (No. 299), Nov. 29, 1826,
She was admitted to the church May 4, 1828, dis. and rec.
to the new church at Amesbury, and Salisbury Mills, Mass.,
Feb. 24, 1834. She d. in Concord, March 10, 1877, and
was buried there. They had children :—

I.   Calvin Clifford, b. Nov. 8, 1827; m., first, Jane Watkins Warner,
      Dec. 10, 1849; she was b. Oct. 14, 1827; d. Sept. 17, 1854. He
      mar., second, Eliza Fletcher, b. June, 1835; d. Sept. 27, 1877.
      He mar., third, Susan Chamberlain Marden; they reside at
      Concord. He has had children. By the first wife —1, Mary
      Frances, b. Nov. 1, 1850; 2, Abbie Jane, b. Dec. 12, 1853.
      By second wife :—3, Jesse Clifford, b. Sept. 19, 1856; 4,
      Edward Fletcher, b. Apr. 1; d. Nov. 10, 1858; 5, Eliza
      Fletcher, b. July 10, 1862; d. Oct., 1885.
II.   Ann Elizabeth, b. Oct. 2, 1829; m. Eliphalet W. Woodward of
      Conway; they have four children :—Charles Webster, Alice
      Livingston, Mary Allison, and Bartlett Woodman.
III. Josiah Crosby, b. Aug. 5, 1832; d. Nov., 1833.
IV.   Josiah Dana, b. Oct. 30, 1834; d. Nov. 25, 1836.
V.   Mary Frances, b. Nov. 24, 1836; d. Aug. 23, 1838.
VI.   Sophia Hill, b. May 11, 1841; m. Charles F. Swain of Gilmanton,
      and have one child.

No. 301.

John Webster Emerson, b. in Hampstead, Nov. 23, 1810,
a son of John, Jr., and Betsey (Emery) Emerson (Nos. 241,

242), He mar. Abigail J. Page (No. 822). He was adm.
to the church May 4, 1828, and "Oct. 9, 1837, dis. and
rec. to any church in the western country." He has resided in Cedar Rapids, Iowa, for many years, and was living
there, in April, 1902, aged 92 years (see p. 209, Vol. 1).

No. 302.

Abiah Tewksbury, b. in Hampstead, April 25, 1807, a
daughter of Ephraim and Rhoda (French) Tewksbury of
Hampstead. She mar. Lewis Linus Carlton Little, Jan. 22,
1832, and resided in Hampstead. She was adm. to the
church May 4, 1828, by baptism, and by confession. She
died in Hampstead, and was buried in the village cemetery
(see p. 351, 352, Vol. 1).

No. 303.

Hannah Johnson, b. in Hampstead, July 1, 1780, a daughter of Jesse and Priscilla (Kimball) Johnson. His parents
were Hon. John and Sarah (Haynes) Johnson, who were
among the first settlers, and proprietors of Enfield, and at
one time of Hampstead. Jesse was b. in the North Parish
of Haverhill, Mass., Oct. 20, 1732; d. Mar. 11, 1780. She
was adm. to the church May 4, 1828, by baptism and confession, and in Oct. 2, 1837, dis. and rec. to the church in
Methuen, Mass.

No. 304.

Lavina York, came to
Hampstead, a maiden lady, to work in Mr. Joseph Welch's
carding mill, from Exeter, and was adm. to the church by
baptism, May 4, 1828, dismissed and recommended to the
church in Exeter, under the pastoral care of Rev. Mr. Williams, Sept. 5, 1841.

No. 305.

Mary Ann Mooers, b. in Exeter, March 18, 1812, a
daughter of Edmund and Hannah (Brickett) Mooers (No.
409) of Hampstead. She was mar. to Thomas Kent (No.
269) by the Rev. John Kelly, May 12, 1831. She was adm.
to the church May 4, 1828, by baptism and confession, dis.
and rec. to the church at Pembrooke, April 10, 1834.   She
d. March 7, 1848, aged 86 years.   They had children.

I.   Ann Lucretia, d. at Concord, aged 9 years.
II.   Clara Ellen, m. Wilber A. Ladd of Newport.
III.   Laura Augusta, m. Dea. Daniel Hackett of Haverhill, Mass.
IV.   Mary Ann, m. Abner B. Chapin, at Cincinnati, O., where their
       children, George and Melvin are living.

No. 306.

George Washington Little, b. in Hampstead, Aug. 12,
1810, a son of Nathaniel and Abiah (Emerson) Little (Nos.
255, 256).   He mar. Louisa L. Lord of Lyman, Maine, Oct.
2, 1834.   He left Hampstead, at an early age, and went to
Boston, as a clerk in a store, and in 1834, moved to Farmington, Ill., where he resided until his death.

He was justice of the peace, and police magistrate many
years, school treasurer of the township for forty years, and
member of the church for about sixty years; after he was
admitted to the Hampstead church May 4, 1828, he was
dis. and rec. by a vote as follows: "April 20, 1834,
recommended by John Kelly, pastor:—   This is to
certify that George W. Little is a member of the Congregational and Orthodox, or Evangelical church, in Hampstead,
in good standing, and as he is about to remove into the
State of Illinois, he is hereby recommended to unite with
any Evangelical, Congregational, or Presbyterian church
that may be found, or that may hereafter be formed in the
place of his abode, and whenever we have ascertained that he
has thus united with the Church of Christ in all its com-

mandments and ordinances of the Lord, we shall consider him as dismissed from the church."

He was a member of the choir in Farmington, Ill., for a great many years as a leader. They had children:—

I.   Louisa Jane, b. July 10, 1835; m. Anthony W. Richards; a leading merchant in Farmington, Ill., for over twenty years, and had children—Carrie B., Walter C., and George L.

II.   Frances Helen, b. Dec. 13, 1836; d. young.

III.   Belinda Tarlton, b. May 11, 1839; m. Everett R. Breed of Farmington: had children—Stella H., Meta W., and Fred B.

IV.   Alfred Herman, b. March 8, 1841; d. young.

V.   Carrie Alice, b. Sept. 24, 1843; m. David Schoonmaker of Fayette, Iowa.   Children—Carrie and Fred.

VI.   Robert Franklin, b. March 27, 1845; m. Mary C. Browning, of Unionville, Missouri, and had children—Louisa B., Fanny R., Maria E., and Laura H.   At the age of seventeen he entered the Union army, and served till the end of the war.   He was a lawyer by profession, and was clerk of courts in Putnam county, Iowa.

VII.   Nathaniel, b. Sept. 27, 1846; m. Evangeline Croy, of Boone county, Iowa.   He served in the civil war.   They had children—Frank C., Florence B., George W., and Clifford.

No. 307.

Thomas Tarlton, b. in Exeter, December, 1809, son of John and Ruth (Flanders) Tarlton, of Stratham.   He was admitted to the church by baptism and confession, May 4, 1828; dismissed to the church at South Boston, Mass., "before Feb. 24, 1834."

No. 308.

Jesse Emery Emerson, b. in Hampstead, Oct. 29, 1805, a son of John, Jr., and Betsey (Emery) Emerson (Nos. 241, 242).   He married Mary E. Morrison (No. 354).   He was admitted to the church July 6, 1828.   Dismissed to the church in Canaan, July 10, 1835, and again received in the Hampstead church from the church in Canaan, Aug. 25, 1838 (see p. 368, Vol 1).   He died in Hampstead, at the home where his son, Alfred P. Emerson, now resides, Oct. 12, 1871, aged 66 years, and was buried in the village cemetery.

No. 309.

Nabby Kimball Calef, b. in Hampstead, June 6, 1810, a daughter of Joseph and Margaret (McKensie) Calef (see No. 108). She was admitted to the church July 6, 1828, and d. about 1850, unmarried.

No. 310.

Mary Dodge, b. in Londonderry, Feb. 12, 1776, a daughter of Parker and Mary (Little) Dodge (see No. 6). She married Hart Merrill, who married, as his first wife, Peggy Knight of Atkinson, who were parents of Haskell Merrill, of Lynn, Mass. ; living with his daughter, Mrs. Carrie H. Smith. She was admitted to the church as a widow, March 1, 1829, and d. in Derry, at an old age, about 1867.

No. 311.

Mary Stevens, b. in Hampstead, May 4, 1800, a daughter of Moses and Mary (Green) Stevens of Kingston. She married Theodore Tarlton as his second wife (No. 289). She was admitted to the church from the church at Corinth, Vt., May 8, 1829, and d. in Hampstead, Feb. 17, 1880, leaving a son George, baptized July 15, 1827.

No. 312.

James Mann, b. in Danbury, 1786, a son of John Mann, of Scotland, who d. in Hampstead, September, 1881, aged 75 years, and was buried in the village cemetery. He married Miriam French (No. 313), and removed to Hampstead to care for their relatives (No. 185), and was adm. to the church from Danbury, July 25, 1829, and dis. to Salisbury, N. H., before 1834.

No. 313.

Miriam French, b. in Hampstead, Dec. 21, 1789, a daughter of Joseph, Jr., and Molly (Tilton) French (Nos. 173 and 174). She married James Mann (No. 312), and was admitted to the church from Danbury, July 25, 1829. Dismissed to the church in Salisbury, Feb. 24, 1834. A daughter, Mary Jane, was baptized May 19, 1831.

No. 314.

Elizabeth Webster, b. in west precinct of Haverhill, Mass., July 20, 1791, a daughter of Jesse and Abigail (Eaton) Webster of West Haverhill. Jesse, son of Dr. Thomas and Ruth (Haseltine), son of Nathan and Sarah (Low), son of Stephen and Hannah (Ayer), son of John and Mary (Shatwell) Webster of Ipswich, Mass. She married, first, —— Cross, of Derry, and married, second, James Calef , (No. 316), March 17, 1829. She was admitted to the church from the church of Derry, May 30, 1830, and died in Hampstead, Dec. 20, 1867, and was buried in the Village cemetery.

No. 315.

Sarah Hidden Burnham, b. in Essex, Mass., daughter of Jacob, Jr., and Sally (Hidden) Burnham. Parents m. in Essex, Jan. 24, 1801. She m. as second wife of Humphrey C. Cogswell of Hampstead, July 19, 1825, who was b. in Ipswich, Mass., 1800. He built the " brick house " (see Parsonages). She was admitted to the church from the church at Essex, Sept. 5, 1830. Dismissed from this church to Essex church, May 10, 1840. She d. before 1856. They had children :—

I.   Henry Clay, b. Dec. 7, 1826.
II.   George William, b. Jan. 13, 1831.
III. Mary Virginia, b. March 27, 1835.
IV.   Sally Hidden, b. May 11, 1836.

No. 316.

James Calef, Esq., b. in Hampstead, Feb. 25, 1782, a son of Hon. John and Lois (Calef) Calef (Nos. 107, 108). He married, first, Anna Kimball (No. 226), and, second, married

MRS. TEWKSBURY. NO. 317.

Mrs. Elizabeth Webster (Cross) of Derry (No. 314). He was admitted to the church May 6, 1832. He died in Hampstead, Nov. 1, 1855, and was buried in the village cemetery. He was prominent in town and church affairs for several years.

No. 317.

Sabra Foster, b. in Andover, Mass., May 31, 1802, a
daughter of John Foster, b. in Andover, Mass., 1770, d.
April 13, 1846, and wife Mary, daughter of Samuel and Mary
(Toothaker) Danforth, b. March 1, 1780, in Billerica, Mass.,

MRS. COLBY. (SEE NO 317.)

d. Nov. 27, 1802, married 1799, and had two children, one
of whom, Sabra, married Dr. Isaac Tewksbury (No. 377),
Dec. 25, 1822, at Hudson, after completing her education at
Atkinson Academy. She was admitted to the church in

Hampstead May 6, 1832. She died in Lawrence, Mass.,
Nov. 25, 1858, and was buried in the Hampstead village cemetery. They had children, b. in Hampstead :—

I.   Herman Foster (No. 388).
II..   Isaac Adolphus, b. Dec. 15, 1826; d. August, 1885, in Elgin, Ill.,
        leaving a widow and two children.
III.   Sabra Frances, b. Nov. 15, 1827; m. Charles A. Colby of Law-
        rence, Mass.; d. July 25, 1891, in New York city, leaving hus-
        band and one son, Charles E. Colby, professor of organic
        chemistry, Columbia College; interred at Lawrence, Mass.
        Mr. Colby d. very suddenly, in New York, Oct. 23, 1902, aged
        nearly 83.
IV.   Jerome Danforth, b. Oct. 5, 1829; d. April, 1831; buried in
        Hampstead.
V.   Harriet Mary, b. March 10, 1831; d. August, 1847; buried in
        Hampstead.
VI.   Albion Danforth, b. May 19, 1833; d. September, 1833.
VII.   Elizabeth Merrill (No. 580).
VIII.   Helen Danforth (No. 421).
IX.   Sarah Abigail, b. March 31, 1838; d. in Hampstead, Aug., 1853.
X.   Mary Danforth, b. March 18, 1843; m. James Jackson, Jan. 17,
        1877. Mr. Jackson d. in Paris, France, July, 1895. Mrs.
        Jackson resides in Paris. The chandeliers for the church
        were her gift, and many tokens of remembrance have been
        received from her.
XI.   Clara Whittemore, b. Jan. 21, 1845; m. Samuel Hitchcock, of
        Aurora, Ill. Has two children—William F. and Alice M.

"The daughters of Dr. and Mrs. Tewksbury have remembered the church with generous gifts in many times of
need, which have been much appreciated." (Church records.)

No. 318.

Mary Clarke, b. in Plaistow, Jan. 21, 1800, a daughter of
Nathaniel and Abigail (Woodman) Clarke of Plaistow. She
married as the first wife of Isaac Smith of Hampstead (see
No. 198), July 18, 1822. She was admitted to the church
May 6, 1832, and died in Hampstead, June 6, 1833. They
had children :—

I.   Mary Clarke (No. 495).

II.   Isaac William, b. May 8, 1825; m. Amanda W. Brown (see p. 320 and account of the celebration of the one hundredth anniversary of Hampstead, p. 57 to 130, Vol. 1).

III. Nathaniel Clarke, b. Dec. 4, 1827; m., first, Elizabeth A. Heath (see p. 305, Vol. 1); second, m. —— ——. He was for several years an express agent from Newmarket to Boston, and died in Malden, Mass., Dec. 12, 1901, and had been manager of the American Express Co., at the North Union Station, Boston.

No. 319.

Mary Webster Emerson, b. in Hampstead, May 13, 1800, a daughter of Caleb and Betsey (Nichols) Emerson. She married Joseph Johnson of Hampstead. She was admitted to the church May 6, 1832, and d. in Hampstead about 1847.

No. 320.

Mary Dearborn Kelly, b. in Hampstead, July 6, 1806, a daughter of Rev. John and Abigail (Dearborn) Kelly (Nos. 168, 171). She was admitted to the church May 6, 1832, and d., unmarried, in Hampstead, May 28, or 29, 1841. "A lady of serious character and superior intellect."

No. 321.

William Tenney, b. in Topsfield, Mass., Jan. 6, 1797, a son of Thomas and Elizabeth (Jewett) Tenney of Topsfield. He married Emma Chase, b. in West Newbury, Mass., Feb. 21, 1797, daughter of Joseph and Emma (Chase) Chase (No. 219). They were married in Hampstead, Jan. 25, 1826. He was admitted to the church May 27, 1832, and the church records note, "William Tenney and *wife* were dis. and rec. to the church at Monson, Me., October, 1841." Date of Mrs. Tenney's admission to the church not given in the church records. He died in Monson in 1872, and Mrs. Tenney in Greenville, Me., in 1881. They had children :—

I.   Elizabeth, b. Jan. 21, 1827; d. in 1898.

II.   Laura Davidson, b. Jan. 20, 1828; resides in Greenville, Me.

III.   Albert William, b. June 25, 1829: a surgeon dentist in Stoneham,
        Mass. He writes of the memory of his parents: " But the
        path of the just is as a shining light that shineth more and
        and more unto the perfect day. So was their path. They
        have left a brightness in my memory which increases more
        and more as the days and the years go by."
IV.   Emma Ann, b. Sept. 30, 1830; d. in 1830.
V.   Herbert Franklin. b. Dec. 20, 1831; d. Nov. 0, 1865.
VI.   Enoch Pillsbury, b. June 10, 1835; d. Nov. 0, 1865.

No. 322.

Abigail Jane Page, b. in Salem, July 22, 1813, a daughter
of Joseph Wright and Jane (Little) Page, of Salem and
Hampstead. She married John W. Emerson (No. 301),
June 29, 1834, and was admitted to the church July 29,
1832. Resided in Cedar Rapids, Iowa. "March 31, 1836,
bapt. Elizabeth Kelly, their daughter."

No. 323.

Ruth Ayer Howard b. in Dunbarton, March 22, 1798, a
daughter of John and Sarah (True) Howard (No. 247). She
was a tailoress in Hampstead, and d., unmarried, about 1877,
and was buried in the village cemetery. She was admitted
to the church " by baptism, May 5, 1833."

No. 324.

Jabez True Howard, b. in Dunbarton, Aug. 22, 1804, a
son of John and Sarah (True) Howard (No. 247). He commenced his theological course at Gilmanton in 1838, and was
pastor of a church at West Charlestown, Vt., and also in
Holland, Vt., about twenty years. He left preaching a few
years before his death in Charlestown, where he was buried.
He was admitted to the church in Hampstead, " by baptism
and confession, May 5, 1833. Dis. and rec. to the
Christian Orthodox Church at Charlestown, Vt., Dec.
17, 1859." He married, first, Elizabeth S. Gilman of Meredith, and had one child, that d. young, and was buried in

Hampstead cemetery. His second wife was Mrs. Martha Page, of Albany, Vt. They had one daughter, Mrs. Belle Howard Cobb; lives in Morristown, Vt., and has two daughters. Mrs. Jabez Howard married, after Mr. Howard's death, Mr. Bernard, of West Charlestown, Vt.

No. 325.

Mary Jane Sargent, b. in Amesbury, Mass., June 3, 1803, a daughter of Ichabod Bernard and Ruth (Patten) Sargent, of Amesbury. She married Benjamin Pillsbury of Hampstead, Dec. 29, 1830, who d. 1884 (see p. 830, Vol. 1). She was admitted a member of the church from the church at Amesbury, Mass., July 10, 1835. Dis. and rec. to the First Congregational Church at Hyde Park, Mass., March 24, 1886. (See photos of Mr. and Mrs. Pillsbury in Vol. 1.) They had children :—

I.   Harlan H. (No. 410).
II. Daniel S. (No. 430).
III. M. Abbie (No. 433).
IV. Emma L. (No. 422).

No. 326.

Hannah K. ——, b. in York, Me. She married Isaiah P. Moody, Esq., lawyer, of Hampstead. She was admitted to the church from the church at York, Oct. 4, 1835. Dis. and rec. to the same church at York, Sept. 13, 1840. They had children :—

I.   Charles Isaiah, bapt. June, 1838.
II. Hannah Dow and Lydia Maria, bapt. Sept. 13, 1835.

No. 327.

Lavina W. Pevere, b. in Sandown, March 23, 1807, a daughter of Nathaniel Pevere, b. July 30, 1781, and wife, Mary Bennett, b. Feb. 2, 1784. The children of Nathaniel and Mary were :—

I. Page, b. July 22, 1805; mar. Hannah Irving (see p. 350, Vol. 1),
    daughter of David E. and Sally (Fern) Irving. Hannah Irv-
    ing was a member of the M. E. Church of Sandown. Their
    children were —

    1. Sarah, b. Sept. 24, 1830; m. Daniel Lane; resided in
        Illinois, where she d. in 1856.

    2. George, b. April 1, 1833; unmarried; resides in Derry.

    3. Lucinda, b. Sept. 30, 1834; d. young.

    4. Orrin, b. Sept. 27, 1835; m. Carrie Sleeper of Sandown.

    5. Perley, b. April 16, 1837; m. Susan Tilton; they reside
        in Hampstead, and have children : 1, S. Nellie, b.
        1861, unmarried, in Hampstead. 2, Gertie M., b.
        1871; m. Elmer Spollett of West Hampstead, and
        have one child : 1, Victor Brickett, b. Mar. 23, 1895.

    6. Mary, b. July 30, 1844; m. James Brooks; she is living
        in Pepperell, Mass.

II. Lavinia W. (No. 327).

III. Mary, b. June 5, 1810.

IV. Lucinda, b. Feb. 15, 1813.

V. Hazen, b. Sept. 27, 1816.

VI. Harriet, b. May 10, 1821.

No. 328.

Rev. John McClinch Bartley, b. in Londonderry, May 15,
1799. His father, Dr. Robert Bartley, graduated from the
University of Edinborough, in Scotland, and was one of the
colony of Scotch Presbyterians who settled in Londonderry.
His mother (Maria McClinch) was a lady of great refinement
and force of character. They had five children :—

I. Hugh, who was for many years a physician in Londonderry.

II. Robert, a resident of Windham, N. H., where he kept a country
    store most of his life. He was noted for strict integrity and
    usefulness as a citizen and officer in the Presbyterian church
    of that town.

III. Maria, who died in early womanhood; had a twin sister.

IV. Esther, who was known in Hampstead as " Aunt Esther "; had
    a high place in the hearts of the family of Rev. John McC.
    Bartley, her brother, as well as in the hearts of the Hamp-
    stead people generally. She became the wife of Rev. John
    Dickey, and went to reside in a village near Genesee, N. Y.,
    and died there about 1800. She was of a lovely character,
    generous, self-denying, and more than ready with ministra-
    tions to the needy and suffering.

V.   Rev. John McC. (above). He prepared for college at Pinkerton
        Academy, Derry, and entered Amherst College, but failing
        health prevented his completing the college course, but he was
        given the honorary degree of A. M. He took his theological
        course at Andover, Mass., where his most intimate friend was
        William G. Schauflaer, who afterwards was the well-known
        missionary at Constantinople. He married, first, Mary Ann
        Morrison, and, second, mar. Susan Dana (No. 355). He was
        admitted to the church by letter, Oct. 13, 1830, and ordained

REV. JOHN M. C. BARTLEY. NO. 328.

to preach as an evangelist on that date. He was dismissed
from the pastorate after serving twenty-one years, and died
in Kittery Point, Me., in 1860 (see Vol. 1, p. 324).

No. 329.

Elbridge Gerry Kent, b. in Hampstead, Feb. 8, 1817, a
son of Dea. Jonathan and Clarissa (Page) Kent (Nos. 145,
146). He married Martha Nutting, and resided in Holland,
N. Y. He was admitted to the church Nov. 11, 1836, and
was dismissed to the church in Holland, Oct., 1841. They
had children:—

I.   George Nutting, m. Mary Harvey, of Wales, N. Y. Have chil-
        dren, Maynard and Katie, unmarried.
II.   Mary Jane, m. Dr. Thomas Berry, of Spring Brook, N. Y. They
        have a son, Dr. Ray Kent Berry, of East Aurora, N. Y.
III.   Polly, unmarried.
IV.   John, unmarried.

No. 330.

Robert Emerson Kent, b. in Hampstead, March 28, 1820,
son of Dea. Jonathan and Clarissa (Page) Kent (Nos. 145,
146). He was admitted to the church Nov. 18, 1836, and
d., unmarried, at the age of 23 years.

No. 331.

Edwin Ahira Kent, b. in Hampstead, July 15, 1823, son
of Dea. Jonathan and Clarissa (Page) Kent (Nos. 145, 146).
He married Abbie F. Ward of Boston, Mass., in San Francisco, and resided in Jackson, Calif. He was admitted to the
church Nov. 18, 1836. They had children :—

I.   Walter E., m. in Cal.
II.   Eva Louise, unm., in Cal.
III.   Amy Foster, unm., in Cal.
IV.   Clara Ann, m. Edward Agard; resides in San Diego, Cal.

No. 332.

Edmund Tucker Eastman, b. in Hampstead, Nov. 6, 1820,
son of Joshua and Susanna (Chase) Eastman (Nos. 213,
230), (p. 323, Vol. 1). He was admitted to the church by
baptism, Nov. 18, 1836, and Sept. 5, 1845, he was dismissed
"to unite with the Congregational Church in Boston, under
the pastoral care of Rev. Mr. Rogers." He married Mrs.
Clara A. Eastman, and by her had one son, Edmund Chase
Eastman, of Brookline, Mass.

No. 333.

Jesse Brooks Davis, b. in Hampstead, Dec. 13, 1818, son
of Ezra and Mary (Garland) Davis (Nos. 234, 235). He

worked his way through the college course in the College of
New Jersey, where he was graduated in 1846. He was
graduated from the Theological School in Princeton, N. J.,
and ordained a minister over the church at Plattsburg, N.
Y., in 1849. His first pastorate was to Bridesburg, Pa.,
Presbyterian Church. He afterwards was located at Titusville, N. J., and at Hightstown, where he died. He resigned
October, 1887, on account of ill health, but was made pastor
emeritus. He was admitted to the Hampstead church Nov.
28, 1836. Dismissed, to unite with the church in New York
city under the pastoral care of Rev. Dr. Phillips, Nov. 1,
1848. He married Jane P. Voorhees, Sept. 11, 1849. They
had five children ; one died in infancy. The oldest, Mary
Edith, d. unmarried, in Hightstown, N. J., February, 1900.
Charles Edgar studied law, and later studied for the ministry, and preached in the West. Ada married John Endicott, a lineal descendant from Gov. Endicott of Massachusetts, and now resides in Atlantic City, N. J. The youngest,
Eva, married Samuel Dodd, and resides in Pittsfield, Mass.
Rev. J. B. Davis married, second, C. Matilda Hendrickson,
June 7, 1876.

No. 334.

James Brown, b. in Hampstead, November, 1768, son of
Joseph and Susanna (Johnson) Brown (Nos. 141, 142). He
married Alice Ferren, and was admitted to the church Nov.
28, 1838, and d. in Hampstead, and was buried in the village
cemetery (see p. 406, Vol. 1).

No. 335.

Harriet Newell Calef, b. in Hampstead, April 12, 1816, a
daughter of James and Anna (Kimball) Calef (Nos. 316,
226). She was admitted to the church Nov. 18, 1836, and
dismissed to the First Church in Derry, of which she was a
member at the time of her decease. She married Daniel J.

Day of Derry, Jan. 28, 1841, a prosperous farmer in Derry
(she was his third wife), and d. in Derry, January, 1896.
They had children :—

I.   Charles Henry, b. April 21, 1842; m. Martha Sanborn (No. 446).
II.   Lucy Elizabeth, b. Jan. 10, 1847; d. July 29, 1857.

No. 336.

Louisa Currier, b. in Hampstead in 1811, daughter of
John (son of Ezekiel and Susanna (Emerson) Currier (No.
215), of West Hampstead, and Hannah Gile, b. March 12,
1782, in Haverhill, daughter of James Gile and wife Deborah (Emerson) of Hampstead. She married Samuel Davis of
Atkinson, who d. a few years after their marriage, of consumption. She was admitted to the church Jan. 1, 1838, and
dismissed to the church in Atkinson, under the care of Rev.
Mr. Pierce, April 10, 1843.   They had two daughters :—

I.   Louisa, a graduate of Haverhill High School, and taught school
      several years in Quincy, Mass. She mar. George Kent, and
      d., aged 27.
II.   Lucy, graduate Haverhill High School, and d. soon after, aged
      16 years.

Mrs. Davis was a member of the Center Church in Haverhill at the time of her decease, in March, 1880. She, with
both of her daughters, were buried in the cemetery on the
hill in West Hampstead.

No. 337—No. 338.

Mr. and Mrs. Daniel Jones, were admitted to the church
from the Church of Christ, in West Newbury, Mass., May
5, 1838.

No. 339.

Martha Evans, b. in Townsend, Mass., May 5, 1810,
daughter of John and Susan (Mace) Evans. She married

Frank Kelly of Kingston. She was admitted to the church
by letter from the First Church of Lowell, Mass., June 15,
1838.

No. 340.

Nathaniel Ordway, b. in West Newbury, Mass., Jan. 19,
1803, a son of Nathaniel and Martha (Bartlett) Ordway, of
West Newbury. He married Ann W. Bolton (No. 393). He
was admitted to the church in Hampstead, July 1, 1838, and
dismissed May 1, 1857. They lived in Hampstead about
eight years, and removed to Bradford, Mass., where their
only daughter resides. He served in the civil war, a member of company G, 2d Mass. Heavy Artillery, and died of
yellow fever, at Newburne, North Carolina, Oct. 10, 1864,
and was buried there, aged 60 years.

No. 341.

Sarah Ayer, b. in Hampstead, April 25, 1792, a daughter
of Hezekiah and Thankful (Williams) Ayer (see No. 272).
She was admitted to the church July 1, 1838, and was a
member at her death, which occurred in Haverhill, Mass.,
Jan. 24, 1875. She was buried in the Hampstead village
cemetery. She married, first, Stephen Nichols, Oct. 25, 1810
(see No. 290), and had children:—

I.   Daniel (No. 290.)
II.   Hezekiah Ayer, b. Dec. 20, 1813; m. Maria Taylor of Fayette-
       ville, N. Y. He lived many years in the south, and d. Jan. 5,
       1890, in Connecticut.

She mar., second, Moses Harriman, May 17, 1817, and had
one child :—Adeline (No. 468).

No. 342.

Mrs. Harriet Illsley, a widow, lived for a time at what is
known as the Moody Brickett farm. She was admitted to

the church July 1, 1838, and was dismissed to unite with the
Congregational Church in Lowell, Mass., March 26, 1843.
Children : Moses Atkinson, Harriet Susan, Eunice and Jona.
Adams Illsley, who resided in Georgetown, Mass.

No. 343.

Ruth Kimball Conner, b. in Troy, N. Y., Dec. 8, 1808, a
daughter of James and Lydia (Brown) Conner, of Fremont.
Her mother was a daughter of Benjamin and Ruth (Kimball) Brown (see No. 21). She was educated in the public
schools of Cambridge, Mass., and had a good education for
the times, and retained a remarkable memory. She married
Daniel Emerson (p. 367, Vol. 1). She was admitted to the
church July 1, 1838, and was a member at her death, April
18, 1895. Her funeral was attended by Rev. R. P. Gardner,
and she was buried in the village cemetery, aged 87 years,
and 4 months. Their children were (see p. 367, Vol. 1) :—

I.   Jacob, d. young.
II.   Daniel Hazen, m. Sarah B. Richardson (No. 430).
III.   James Henry, m. Sarah A. Woodman.
IV.   Horatio Bartlett, m., first, Lizzie Ann Neal, May 23, 1862, b.
        Nov. 18, 1843, in Charlestown, Mass., and d. March 30, 1882,
        in Malden. He m., second, Sarah Augusta Jeffers, of Haver-
        hill, Dec. 21, 1882. Children :—
             1. George Horatio, b. Feb. 21, 1864; d. Aug. 24, 1867.
             2. David Benjamin, b. May 30, 1868; m., July 21, 1895,
                 Esther Agnes Doyle, b. April 9, 1871. They have
                 children : 1, John Horatio, b. Dec. 21, 1896; d. May
                 2, 1900. 2, Ruth Mary, b. Aug. 18, 1900.
             3. Chauncey Crafts, b. Nov. 29, 1873; mar., June 16, 1897,
                 Eliza E. Marden, who was b. Nov. 13, 1871.
             4. Lillian Mary, b. Dec. 21, 1875.
V.   William A. (No. 533), m. Abbie H. Dow (No. 534).

No. 344.

Mary True, b. in Hampstead, July 20, 1772, a daughter
of Rev. Henry and Ruth (Ayer) True (Nos. 1, 72). She
was admitted to the church July 1, 1838, and d., unmarried,

in Hampstead, and was buried in the village cemetery, in the family lot. It is related that Miss Mary had " her preparations all made, even to buying her china, but then decided not to marry." The same china is now in the possession of a grand-niece, Miss Helen Ayer Vose, of Chelsea, Mass.

No. 345.

Mary Emerson, b. in Hampstead, Aug. 20, 1823, daughter of John, Jr., and Betsey (Emery) Emerson (Nos. 241 and 242). She married John Bradley of Danville. She was admitted to the church July 1, 1838. They had children :—

I. Albert E., bapt. Sept., 1848; a teacher at present in Bryant & Stratton's Commercial School of Boston.
II. Mary E., bapt. July, 1853; m. Page Hunt of Danville.
III. Elizabeth (twin); d. young.
IV. Charles, resides in Dover.

No. 346.

Sarah George, b. in Hampstead, June 17, 1794, a daughter of Jonathan and Hannah (Currier) George (No. 243). She was admitted to the church July 1, 1838, and dismissed May 5, 1857. She d., unmarried, in West Hampstead, and was buried in the village cemetery.

No. 347.

Abigail Currier, b. in Hampstead in 1814, a daughter of John and Hannah (Gile) Currier (see No. 236). She married, late in life, John Webster, of Lawrence, Mass., and moved to North Andover, where she now (1902) resides, a widow. She was admitted to the church July 1, 1838, and is a present member of the church in North Andover, to which she was dismissed about 1856.

No. 348.

Amassa Eastman, b. in Hampstead, April 11, 1789, a son of Joshua and Sarah (Tucker) Eastman (Nos. 169, 170).

He married Betsey Edmunds of Sandown (No. 349), and resided on the old Eastman homestead at West Hampstead. He was admitted to the church July 1, 1838, and died in Hampstead.

No. 349.

Betsey Edmunds, b. in Sandown, Aug. 14, 1795, a daughter of Thomas and Mary (Hoyt) Edmunds, of Sandown. She married Amassa Eastman (No. 348), and was admitted to the church July 1, 1838, and d. in Hampstead, Nov. 20, 1855, very suddenly, while on the street, near West Hampstead.   Their children were:—

I.   Roxanna, b. Oct. 15, 1819; d. young.
II.   Jacob Edmunds, b. Dec. 8, 1820; d., unmarried, in Hampstead.
III.   George W., b. June 18, 1822; m. Mary A. Colby (No. 479).
IV.   Roxanna, b. May 14, 1824.
V.   Mary Elizabeth, b. Sept. 14, 1826.
VI.   Harriet Newell, b. Dec. 14, 1828; d. Dec. 31, 1832.
VII.   Charles Carroll, b. Aug. 31, 1832; m. Elizabeth Lunt, of Newburyport, Mass.; had two sons :—
         1.   Charles E., b. Feb. 14, 1860; m. Myra Hoyt of Sandown.
         2.   Albert S., b. May 28, 1861; m. Annie ——.
VIII. John Amassa, b. Oct. 20, 1835; d. Aug. 26, 1837.

No. 350.

Elbridge Gerry Little, b. in Hampstead, Nov. 11, 1817, a son of Joseph and Rebecca (Webster) Little. He married, first, Sarah E. Colman, of Newbury, Mass., in 1848, who d. 1851 ; married, second, Mrs. Sarah J. Weston, who d. 1854; married, third, Lucia F. Sanderson of Philadelphia. He was admitted to the church July 1, 1838, and later taught school in Hampstead and vicinity. He prepared for the ministry, being aided in his preparation for college by Benjamin Greenleaf of Bradford, Mass., and entered a year in advance in the college of New Jersey; Graduated in 1845, having supported himself by giving private lessons. November 1, 1842, he was dismissed to the New

York City Presbyterian Church, under Rev. Dr. Phillips. He studied theology at Princeton Seminary, and first settled over the church at Manayank, Pa., in September, 1850. He was called to Merrimac, Mass., "where he had a very successful pastorate, uniting ninety-seven persons to the church in five years." He was pastor of the church at Ashburnham, Mass., two years; in Middleton, Mass., ten years. From 1867 to his decease, Dec. 29, 1869, he resided in Wellesley, Mass., and was editor of Grey's Real Estate Journal. An obituary notice reads: "His ministry was marked by accuracy in scholarship and careful investigation. He was very instructive in his sermons and Bible classes, genial and affectionate in conversation, though inclined to the older type of Congregational theology, and very biblical in his statements and analysis." Their children were :—

I.   Edwin Coleman, b. July 5, 1850; m., first, Sarah E. Little; m., second, Catherine G. Goodwin. He has resided in West Newbury, Mass., and has children—Edwin, d. young; Harold and Charles.

II.   Sarah Isabel, b. Jan. 27, 1858.

III. Alexander Elbridge, b. Dec. 12, 1850.

IV.   Walter Sanderson, b. March 27, 1863.

No. 351.

Eunice Kelly, b. in Hampstead, Dec. 7, 1778, daughter of Samuel and Elizabeth (Heath) Kelly of Hampstead. She was a tailoress in Hampstead, and d., unmarried, in Dunbarton, in the family of Mrs. Mary Wilson, her niece, who was a daughter of Reuben and Ruth (Kelly) Mills (Nos. 176, 177), Sept. 17, 1849. She was admitted to the church July 1, 1838.

No. 352.

Weld Pecker, b. in Amesbury, Mass. He was admitted to the church July 1, 1838. He resided many years with Dr. J. C. Eastman's family, and died "at a good old age."

The funeral service was holden at the home of a sister, Mrs.
Dea. Colby, in Amesbury, where he was buried.

No. 853.

Betsey Emerson, b. in Hampstead, May 12, 1807, a daughter of Caleb and Betsey (Nichols) Emerson of Hampstead.
She married Eliphalet K. Heath (see p. 865, Vol. 1). She
was admitted to the church July 1, 1838, and was buried
in the village cemetery.

No. 854.

Mary Elizabeth Morrison, b. in Shapleigh, Me., April 15,
1811, a daughter of John and Mary (Perry) Morrison. She
married Jesse E. Emerson (No. 808), and was admitted to
the church by letter from the church in Canaan, Aug. 25,
1838. She d. in Hampstead, Jan. 8, 1892, aged 79 years,
and 10 months. They had an only child, Alfred P., b. July
26, 1841; m. S. Francena Diamond, b. Oct. 12, 1846 (p. 868,
Vol. 1). Their children :—

I.   Ada E. (No. 625), m. Charles W. Garland (No. 544).
II.   Albion D. (No. 652), m. Mary G. Calderwood (No. 755).
III.   John H. (No. 659).
IV.   George S. (No. 670).
V.   Fannie C. (No. 674).
VI.   Jesse E., b. Dec. 10, 1877.

No. 855.

Susan Dana, b. in Newburyport, Mass., Aug. 4, 1808, was
a daughter of Rev. Dr. Daniel Dana, who was pastor of the
church in Newburyport for fifty years, and great-grand-
daughter of Rev. Joseph Dana, D. D., pastor of the church
at Ipswich, Mass., for more than sixty years. Her mother
was Elizabeth, daughter of Capt. William Coombs, of Newburyport. Her early education was received in Boston, in
the family of her uncle, Hon. Israel Thorndyke, one of Boston's leading merchants, who, with Daniel Webster, resided

in a large double mansion on Summer street, where Susan, Dana, as a young girl, often met in society Josiah Quincy, Lafayette, and Daniel Webster. She married Rev. John McC. Bartley (No. 328), and was admitted to the church in Hampstead by letter from the First Church at Newburyport, June 1, 1838, and was dismissed and recommended to the Presbyterian Church at Newburyport, September, 1865. She d. in Malden, Mass., Jan. 16, 1900, aged 91 years and 5 months. Her funeral was held at her home in Malden, and another in the venerable church at Kittery Point, Me., where she was laid to rest beside her husband (see p. 324, Vol. 1). She is remembered as a woman "of very attrac-, tive personality, bright, highly cultured, with courteous manner, and for her strength and loveliness of Christian character." Their children were :—

I. Susan, d. July 10, 1844, aged 2 years.
II. John, d. May 31, 1854, aged 4 years.
III. Mary Ann, d. April 14, 1856, aged 8 years.
IV. William, b. 1830; was fitted for college at Phillips Academy, Andover, Mass.; entered Bowdoin College in 1850, and was graduated in 1854; after graduation he went south and became an Episcopal rector, and died, as pastor of a parish in Winchester, Tenn., in 1860 (see p. 324, Vol. 1).
V. Joseph Dana (No. 426).
VI. Susan Dana, b. July 10, 1844. She has been a resident of Malden for several years. For ten years she was a teacher in the Pinkerton Academy at Derry, but devoted herself to the care of her aged mother in her declining years. "The Mystic Side Congregational Church at Everett, Mass., owes much to her activity and good judgment."

No. 356.

James Gibson, b. in Nashua, Jan. 20, 1799, a son of Samuel Gibson, b. July 3, 1776, in Alstead, and his wife Anna, daughter of John Webster of Atkinson. He married, first, Sarah Webster (No. 357), and was admitted to the church Sept. 3, 1838; dismissed June 8, 1846 ; and d. in Hampstead. He was captain of the Hampstead Light Infantry, and was the contractor of the first church, built in 1837. He lived where Mr. Joseph Frost now resides, in the brick house. He m., second, Judith, daughter of Joseph and Elizabeth (Bartlett) Sargent of Sandown (see Appendix). They had a son, Kimball, who died young.

No. 357.

Sarah Webster, b. in Atkinson, May 21, 1797, a daughter of Ensign John and Sarah (Little) Webster. She married Capt. James Gibson (No. 356). She was admitted to the church Sept. 3, 1838, and d. in Hampstead. They had children :—

I.   Ezekiel Harvey Little, b. Aug. 9, 1827; a graduate from Dartmouth Medical College in 1850; d. April 11, 1851, in Hampstead.

II.   James Franklin, bapt. Sept., 1838; d., unmarried, in Hampstead, a young man.

No. 358.

John Heath, b. in Hampstead, Sept. 28, 1783, a son of Jesse and Abiah (Kimball) Heath (p. 365, Vol. 1). He married Abigail Wadleigh (No. 359). He was a captain of the Hampstead Light Infantry. He was admitted to the church Sept. 3, 1838, and d. in 1856.

No. 359.

Abigail Wadleigh, b. in Gilmanton, Sept. 7, 1787, a daughter of Jonathan and Abigail (Eastman) Wadleigh. Her mother died when she was seven years of age, and she came to Hampstead to live in the family of her grandfather, Peter Eastman. Her mother was b. June 9, 1756 (see p. 408, Vol. 1), (see p. 81, Eastman Genealogy, for sketch of Peter Eastman). She married Capt. John Heath (No. 358). She was admitted to the church Sept. 3, 1838, and d. in Hamp-

stead, Nov. 7, 1874. Their children (see p. 365, Vol. 1)
were :—

I.   Martha, b. Oct. 21, 1807; m. Capt. James Durgin of West Newbury, Mass.

II.   Eliphalet H., m., first, Betsey Emerson (No. 353); second, Alice Shannon.   -

III.   Louisa (No. 360).

IV.   Abigail R. (No. 450).

V.   Elizabeth A., b. June 12, 1820; m. Nathaniel C. Smith (see No. 318).

VI.   Mary Jane (No. 449), m. Dea. William Sanborn (No. 390).

No. 360.

Louisa Heath, b. in Hampstead, June 18, 1811, a daughter of Capt. John and Abigail (Wadleigh) Heath (Nos. 358, 359). She married James A., son of James and Anna (Kimball) Calef (Nos. 316, 226). She was admitted to the church Sept. 3, 1838. Dis. and rec. to the church in South Boston, Mass., Jan. 21, 1840, and died in Hampstead, April 26, 1891.

No. 361.

Judith Sawyer Eastman, b. in Hampstead, July 13, 1825, a daughter of Joshua and Susanna (Chase) Eastman (Nos. 213, 230). She was admitted to the church Sept. 3, 1838, and is the earliest member admitted, now on the church books. She resides in Danvers, Mass., in the family of Capt. John Peabody, and is unmarried.

No. 362.

Elizabeth Langmaid, b. in Atkinson, Feb. 16, 1799, a daughter of Reuben and Ruth (Kelly) Mills, of Atkinson (Nos. 176, 177). She mar. Thomas Langmaid, and d. in Dunbarton, Sept. 6, 1873. No children. She was admitted to the church Sept. 3, 1838. Dismissed to the church at Manchester, under the care of Rev. M. C. Wallace, in 1840, and from there dismissed to Dunbarton, March 30, 1846.

No. 863.

Ellen Gordon, b. in Hampstead, Aug. 11, 1823, a daughter of Jesse and Harriet (Conner) Gordon of Hampstead (p. 387, Vol. 1). She was admitted to the church Sept. 3, 1838. Dis. and rec. to the Congregational Church in Lowell, Mass., May 10, 1847, under the pastoral care of Rev. Mr. Blanchard.

MR. AND MRS. SIMON MERRILL.   NO. 365.

No. 364.

Benjamin Atwood, b. in Thornton, July 5, 1798, a son of Sylvanus and Mary (Leavitt) Atwood, son of James and Molly Lowell (see No. 74). He was admitted to the church in Hampstead Sept. 3, 1838, and d. soon after.

No. 365.

Hannah Worth Kelly, b. in Hampstead, Feb. 8, 1814, a daughter of Rev. John and Abigail (Dearborn) Kelly (Nos.

164, 171). She married Simon Merrill (see No. 208), and lived till late in life at the house built by her father, where Mrs. Emeline Mooers now resides. In 1885 they removed to Hyde Park, Mass. She was admitted to the church Sept. 3, 1838, and d. Nov. 11, 1898, and buried with her husband in the village cemetery. They had children :—

I.   Mary A. (No. 445).
II.   Hannah Eliza, bapt. Sept., 1847, aged 3 years; d. young.

Mr. Merrill d. Oct. 25, 1894.

No. 366.

Meribah Hale Ayer, b. in Hampstead, Nov. 8, 1820, a daughter of Capt. Jesse and Mary Carlton (Little) Ayer (No. 272). She married Henry Putnam (see p. 383, Vol. 1). She was admitted to the church Sept. 3, 1838, and d. in Hampstead, of cancer, Jan. 2, 1878, and was buried in the village cemetery. Their children were :—

I.   Helen Meribah, m. William E. Buck (p. 833, Vol. 1).
II.   Oliver (No. 717); m. Mary A. Little (No. 600).

No. 367.

Benjamin Balch Garland, b. in Barrington, Feb. 2, 1793, youngest child of Benjamin and Mary (Balch) Garland (Nos. 220, 221). He was a cooper by trade, and resided at the " old Garland homestead." He married Mary H. Calef (No. 868). He was admitted to the church Sept. 3, 1838, and d. in Hampstead, Aug. 8, 1872, and was buried in the village cemetery.

No. 368.

Mary Hazen Calef, b. in Hampstead, April 14, 1796, was a daughter of William and Mary (Little) Calef (No. 371), son of Hon. John and Lois (Calef) Calef (Nos. 107, 108). She married Benjamin B. Garland (No. 367), March 18,

1819. She was admitted to the church Sept. 3, 1838, and d. in Hampstead, March 22, 1879, and was buried in the village cemetery. They had children:—

I.   John William (No. 602); m. Emily A. Ring (No. 603).
II.   Mary A. (No. 386).

" A consistent and beloved member of the church for over forty years, and her long life of quiet usefulness and self-sacrificing devotion to others exerted a powerful influence for good in the world."

No. 869.

John Little, b. in Hampstead, Oct. 28, 1794, a son of Jonathan and Dorothy (Little) Little. He married Louisa Calef (No. 870). He was admitted to the church Sept. 3, 1838, and d. in Hampstead, June 27, 1852, and was buried in the village cemetery. He was a prominent lumber dealer and farmer in town. He resided at the home where Henry Noyes now resides.

No. 870.

Louisa Calef, b. in Hampstead, Nov. 17, 1798, a daughter of William and Mary (Little) Calef (No. 371). She married John Little (No. 869), Nov. 14, 1822, and d. in Hampstead, May 29, 1850, and was buried in the village cemetery. She was admitted to the church Sept. 3, 1838. They had children:—

I.   William Calef, b. Dec. 17, 1823; m. Julia E. (Harris) Haseltine (No. 480); m., second, Mrs. Emily J. (Harris) Greenough, M. D., widow of Elbridge G. of Atkinson, and later of Haverhill, Mass. (see p. 352, Vol. 1).
II.   Louisa, b. Feb. 7, 1830; m. Hazen Laurens Hoyt, May 20, 1852. She d. Sept. 14, 1863, leaving one son, George Wilbur, b. April 12, 1853, who, with his father, went to " the western country " to reside, after his mother's death.

No. 871.

Mary Little, b. in Hampstead, March 4, 1772, a daughter of Benjamin and Mary (Hazen) Little (see Nos. 80, 81 of list "Owned the Covenant "). She married William Calef (Nos. 107, 108), Nov. 11, 1795. She was admitted to the church Sept. 3, 1838, and d. in Hampstead, Feb. 25, 1855, and was buried in the village cemetery. Her husband d. in Hampstead, April 29, 1798, aged 25 years. Their children were :—

I.   Mary Hazen (No. 308); m. Benj. B. Garland (No. 307).
II.   Louisa (No. 870); m. John Little (No. 809).

No. 372.

Amos Nelson, b. in Georgetown, Mass., 1804, son of Moses and Abigail (March) Nelson, both of Georgetown. He m. Harriet Rollins (No. 373). He was admitted to the Hampstead church July 3, 1838, and dismissed to the church in South Danvers, Mass., April 3, 1839. He resided where Charles O. Cass now resides. He d. in 1892, and was connected with the Center Church in Haverhill, Mass.

No. 373.

Harriet Rollins, b. in Haverhill, Mass., Sept. 15, 1805, a daughter of John Rollins of Haverhill and wife Elizabeth, daughter of Maverick Johnson of Haverhill. She married, first, Daniel Black of Londonderry, in 1826, and had one daughter, Elizabeth, who married T. F. Griffin of Haverhill. She married, second, Amos Nelson (No. 372), Sept. 15, 1833, by whom she had children :—

I.   Miss Harriet O., for many years a teacher in Haverhill High School, and well known as a writer of many interesting articles in educational journals.
II.   Miss M. M. Nelson, for many years in Syracuse, N. Y., now of Boston.
III. William W. Nelson of Boston.

Mrs. Nelson was admitted to the church Sept. 3, 1838, and dismissed to unite with the Congregational Church at South Danvers, Mass., April 3, 1839, and later was connected with the Center church in Haverhill. She d. in Haverhill in 1874.

No. 374.

Mary French, b. in Hampstead, Dec. 18, 1796, a daughter of Joseph and Molly (Tilton) French (Nos. 173, 174). She married Joseph Hoyt of Hampstead. She was admitted to the church Sept. 3, 1838. She d. in Hampstead, April 11, 1832, aged 56 years. Their children were: Irene, Elizabeth, Daniel, and Arannah.

No. 375.

Hannah Johnson, b. in Seabrook. She married, first, Samuel Marsh of Fremont. She married, second, David Irving, as his second wife (see No. 283). They lived in Fremont for a time, where Mr. Irving had charge of a grist mill. She was admitted to the church Sept. 3, 1838. Samuel Marsh was a brother of Rev. John Marsh of Fremont, and son of Trueworthy Marsh.

No. 376.

Ralph Brickett, b. in Hampstead, Feb. 15, 1795, a son of James and Anna (Wheeler) Brickett (Nos. 224, 225). He married Sally Ordway (No. 275), April 16, 1823, and resided in Hampstead, Atkinson, and Lawrence, Mass. He was admitted to the church Sept. 3, 1838. Dismissed, to unite with the Church of Christ in Lawrence, Nov. 24, 1848, and from there united with the church at Atkinson, January, 1859. He d. in Atkinson, March 24, 1868, and was buried in the village cemetery. "The first belted saw-mill used in New Hampshire was built for him in 1836, in connection with a shingle mill in Atkinson to split the stuff. It had no counterbalance."

No. 377.

Dr. Isaac Tewksbury, b. in West Newbury, Mass., Jan. 18, 1795, a son of Jona. and Elizabeth (Merrill) Tewksbury, of West Newbury. (Note this correction from p. 325, Vol. 1, in the record of his birth and parentage.) He married Sabra Foster (No. 317), who d. Nov. 25, 1858; and he married, second, Harriet, the widow of Parker Smith, of Lawrence, Mass., in 1859. He was admitted to the church Sept. 3, 1838. He removed to Lawrence in 1847, and in 1881 returned to Hampstead, and d. here Jan. 25, 1885. He was buried in the village cemetery (see p. 325, Vol. 1, for sketch of his life work).

No. 378.

Albert Alphonso Little, b. in Hampstead, March 9, 1818, a son of Stephen and Betsey (Greenough) Little (see No. 370). He was admitted to the church membership, "on a sick and dying bed, having shown to be in feeble and declining health," in his room, Sept. 3, 1838. He d., unmarried, Feb. 25, 1839, and was buried in the village cemetery.

No. 379.

Dudley George, b. in Hampstead, May 7, 1789, a son of Jonathan and Hannah (Currier) George (No. 243). He married Betsey Ordway (No. 380). He was admitted to the church Nov. 11, 1838, and d. in Hampstead, Jan. 28, 1867, aged 77 years, 8 months. He was buried in the village cemetery. He resided at the "George homestead" at West Hampstead.

No. 380.

Betsey Ordway, b. in Hampstead, July 1, 1790, a daughter of John and Sally (Rogers) Ordway (see No. 275), (see p. 334, Vol. 1). She married Dudley George (No. 379), March 15, 1816. She was admitted to the church Nov. 11,

NO. 377.

1838. She d. in Hampstead, and was buried in the village cemetery. Their children were :—

I.   Warren Dudley, b. May 24, 1818; m. Sarah Tucker Griffin. He
        d. 1900, and was buried in the village cemetery. Widow liv-
        ing at West Hampstead. Children :—
          1. Ellen A. (No. 483).
          2. Charles (No. 472), m. Julia E. Batchelder (No, 477).
          3. Annie E. (No. 473).
II.   Sarah Elizabeth, b. June 27, 1821.
III.   Lucian, b. Aug. 22, 1824.
IV.   Isaac William (No. 471).

No. 381.

Laura Annette Putnam, b. in Hampstead, Aug. 20, 1818, a daughter of Thorndyke and Mary (Chase) Putnam (see p. 332, Vol. 1, and No. 222). She mar. Moody H. Brickett (No. 292). She was admitted to the church Nov. 11, 1838. She was received again from the Winter Street Church, Haverhill, Mass., July 1, 1859. She was dismissed and recommended to the North Church of Haverhill, December, 1864. She d. in Haverhill, June 4, 1885, and was buried in the village cemetery. They had children (p. 345, Vol. 1).

I.   Infant, d. young.
II.   James T. (No. 435).
III.   Albert Cushing, m. Annie Adams of Haverhill.
IV.   Calvin Webster, m. Fannie Furbush; resides in Haverhill.

No. 382.

Albert Grant, b. in Newbury, Mass., 1814, a son of Theodore and Susannah (Coffin) Grant. He married Clementine, daughter of Jacob and Lydia (Noyes) Emery, May 12, 1836. She was born June 24, 1807. He was a blacksmith by trade, and resided a few years in East Hampstead, and returned to West Newbury, where he d. of consumption, Sept. 5, 1849. He was admitted to the church by letter from the church in West Nembury, Nov. 11, 1838. Dismissed and recommended to the church in Georgetown, Mass., under the pastoral care of Rev. Mr. Branan, April 1, 1889. They had three children. The widow married, second, Joseph Brown, of Haverhill, Mass., and d. May 30, 1893.

No. 383.

Lorenzo Hale Babb, b. in Hampstead, Jan. 19, 1819, a son of Nathaniel and Mary (Noyes) Babb (No. 273). He married, and resided in Marysville, California, where he died, leaving three children and thirteen grandchildren. His daughter, Mrs. Mary A. Beever, resides in Bourneville, Yuba county, Cal. He was admitted to the church Nov. 11, 1838. Dismissed to the Church of Christ, on Bowdoin street, Boston, Mass., Feb. 6, 1841. He d. Sept. 18, 1888. A friend writes that " his business and church life in Marysville was uplifting to society."

No. 384.

Susan Eastman Putnam, b. in Hampstead, Jan. 19, 1820, a daughter of Thorndyke and Mary (Chase) Putnam (see No. 381). She married George Evan Merrill in 1851. She was admitted to the church Nov. 11, 1838, and dismissed to Center Church, in Haverhill, Mass. They had four children, three now living, two sons in the West, and Mary Putnam, a teacher in the public schools of Haverhill.

No. 385.

Ruth Chase, b. on " Meeting House Hill," in West Newbury, Mass., March 24, 1768, a daughter of Tristram and Priscilla Chase of Newbury. She married, first, Enoch Smith, Nov. 18, 1826, " when 58 years of age, as his second wife." She married, second, James Brickett of Hampstead (No. 224), Aug. 21, 1838, by the Rev. John Q. A. Edgell. She was admitted to the church by letter from the church in West Newbury, March 10, 1839, and d. in West Newbury, and was buried there.

No. 386.

Mary Ann Garland, b. in Hampstead, Sept. 28, 1820, a daughter of Benjamin B. and Mary H. (Calef) Garland (Nos. 220, 221). She married Frederick A. Pike of Hampstead, who d. Jan. 25, 1883. She was admitted to the church May 5, 1839, and d. at the home of her brother, J. W. Garland (where she had made her home since she became a widow), March 7, 1901, and was buried in the village cemetery. They had no children, but made a home for several young people until they married. Among them were: Miss Lizzie E. Smith (mar. George Hill of Plaistow), Carrie P. Noyes of Atkinson (mar. Edwin A. Chase of Haverhill), Alice A. Davis (mar. Prof. Forrest E. Merrill), Carrie A. Smith (mar. Andrew M. Moulton of Hampstead), and Arthur E. Bond of Waltham, Mass., who have had the kindest remembrance, with others, of "Auntie Pike," as she was called.

No. 387.

Belinda Little Merrick, b. in Hampstead, Sept. 21, 1825, daughter of Nathaniel and Sarah (Corliss) Merrick of Hampstead (see p. 355, Vol. 1). She married, and resided in Lowell, Mass. She was admitted to the church May 5, 1839. She had children, b. in Lowell.

No. 388.

Herman Foster Tewksbury, b. in Hampstead, May 16, 1824, a son of Dr. Isaac and Sabra (Foster) Tewksbury (Nos. 377, 317). He was admitted to the church May 5, 1839, and d. while serving in the civil war, March, 1863, leaving a widow and two children.

No. 389.

Dea. Joseph Chase, b. in Hampstead in 1801, a son of Joseph and Emma (Chase) Chase (No. 229). He married

Elizabeth Morse (No. 398). He was admitted to the church May 5, 1839, and d. in Hampstead, March 28, 1872. He was elected deacon of the church Aug. 16, 1859.

No. 390.

William Sanborn, b. in Chichester, Feb. 10, 1810, a son

WILLIAM SANBORN.   NO. 390.

of Jeremiah and Martha (Lake) Sanborn. His father was born in Chichester, Feb. 11, 1773, a son of Jeremiah Sanborn of Chichester. His mother, Martha Lake, was b. March 21, 1773, in Chichester, a daughter of Thomas Lake, who was b. in or near Portsmouth, England, in 1734, who, when 14 years of age, emigrated to Portsmouth, in 1748, going later to Rye, and in 1785 to Chichester, with his family, on a farm now owned by his great-grandson, Joseph T. Lake, situated on the road leading from the Pine Ground, so called, in Chichester, to Pittsfield village. He married Mrs. Eunice (Seavey) Davis, and d. March 6, 1816. The family of Jeremiah and Martha (Lake) Sanborn were :—

I. Anna, m. James Sanborn of Chichester.
II. Eunice, m. Abraham Stanlels of Chichester.
III. Mathew, m. Maria Moulton, and had a large family in Chichester.
IV. Betsey, m. Jacob T. Moulton of Chichester.
V. Josiah, m. Nancy Stanlels of Chichester.
VI. James Beverly, m. Mary Ann Babb of Effingham.
VII. Emma, m. John Fowler of Amesbury, Mass.
VIII. William (No. 390), m., first, Mary Greenleaf (No. 391); m., second, Lois Calef (No. 425); m., third, Mary J. Heath (No. 449).
IX. Jeremiah, m. Sarah Morrill of Portsmouth.
X. Lowell, m. and resided in Maine; d. 1890.

William resided with his first wife, in Pittsfield, for a time, then removed to Hampstead, about 1840. He was admitted to the church by letter from the church in Pittsfield, Oct. 30, 1840. He was elected deacon of the church Aug. 16, 1859, "after removing from his mind objections based on a personal unfitness, he accepted the office." (Church records.) "On Oct. 30, 1884, it was voted unanimously not to excuse Dea. Sanborn or grant his request of resigning his office at the expiration of his twenty-five years of service, but on Dec. 30, 1884, it was voted to accept it, and hereafter elect deacons once in three years." Dea. Sanborn d. in Hampstead, Sept. 18, 1893, and was buried in Hampstead.

No. 391.

Mary Greenleaf, b. in Canterbury, April, 1814, a daughter of Edmund and Lydia (Bartlett) Greenleaf of Canterbury. She married William Sanborn (No. 390), Sept. 20, 1837, and d. in Hampstead in 1844. She was admitted to the church by letter from the church in Pittsfield, Oct. 30, 1840. They had one daughter, Martha (No. 446).

No. 892.

Martha Ann Ham, b. in Portsmouth, Sept. 11, 1812, a daughter of William and Mary Langdon (Holbrook) Ham, of Portsmouth. She married David Poor Little (No. 270), Sept. 3, 1833. She was admitted to the church from the church in Portsmouth, Oct. 30, 1840. She d. in Chicago, Ill., Feb. 24, 1888, and was buried in Epping. They had children :—

I.   Ellen Harriet, b. Nov. 2, 1834; d., unmarried, in 1852.
II.   Albert William, b. March 17, 1836; m.; first, Maria E. Blackley of Pelham, and had two children :—
         1. Hattie Bell, b. April 25, 1865; m. Watson B. Scott of Chicago, Nov. 18, 1890.
         2. Arthur Waldo, b. July 27, 1868; d. young.
      He married, second, Ella Viola, daughter of Avender and Laura A. (Wheeler) Corson, of Hampstead (see p. 369, Vol. 1), and had children :—
         3. Florence Louise, b. June 17, 1886.
         4. Walter Avender, b. Feb. 2, 1889; d. June 10, 1899.
III. Eben Hale, b. Feb. 6, 1839; m., first, Mary Eliza, daughter of Hiram and Louis A. (Hoyt) Nichols (p. 379, Vol. 1); had one child :—Jesse May, b. Nov. 9, 1867; m. —— Tilton, of Bradford, Mass.
IV.   Martha Louisa, b. April 8, 1843; m. George Melvin Huntress of Portsmouth. They have children :—
         1. Ellen Louisa, b. 1863; d. young.
         2. Willie, b. July 29, 1865.
         3. Jennie Dodge, b. 1868; d. young.
         4. Albert Senter, b. July 3, 1873.
         5. Helen Webster, b. Jan. 20, 1878.
V.   Jay Plummer, b. March 11, 1843; m. Rosiline Wentworth, of Rumney. Their only child, Walter, d. in infancy.
VI.   Emma Placenta, b. July 31, 1847; m., Aug. 24, 1867, James Henry Rowe, a carriage manufacturer of Brentwood. They had children :—
         1. Annie Isabelle, b. July 26, 1868; m. Wm. C. Hoyt; d. March 11, 1891.
         2. John Melvin, b. June 22, 1872.

VII. Anna Isabel, b. July 18, 1849; d. young.
VIII. Frank Henry, b. March 20, 1852; m. Carrie M. Morrison of Waltham, Mass.
IX. Walter Langdon, b. March 28, 1854; m. Sarah Edgerly of Epping. They had one son : Guy Langdon, b. Feb. 12, 1878.

No. 393.

Ann W. Bolton, b. in Taunton, Mass., Dec. 12, 1807, a daughter of Enoch and Diana (Hewitt) Bolton of Taunton. She was married to Nathaniel Ordway (No. 340), Aug. 5, 1825, by the Rev. James Miltimore of the Belleville Parish, Newburyport. She was admitted to the church by letter from the church in West Newbury, Mass., Nov. 7, 1841, and d. in Bradford, Mass., March 25, 1874. They had six or seven children, some of whom died young and were buried in the Salem street cemetery of Bradford. "Andrew, d. in 1855, aged 22 years ; Enoch, d. aged about 45 years ; a daughter, Martha Ann, b. 1833, now Mrs. Lucian W. Ripley, resides in Bradford, Mass."

No. 394.

Belinda Helen Ayer, b. in Hampstead, October, 1819, a daughter of Hezekiah and Polly (Little) Ayer (No. 399). She was admitted to the church Oct. 25, 1841, at her residence, she being unable to attend church, and survived only three days, dying Oct. 28, 1841, and was buried in the village cemetery. She was unmarried.

No. 395.

Benjamin Sawyer, b. in Atkinson, Oct. 28, 1797, a son of Benjamin and Clarissa (Webster) Sawyer of Atkinson (Jonathan[4], Benjamin[3], Samuel[2], William[1]), (see p. 377, Vol. 1). He married Priscilla Gibson (No. 267). He was a carpenter by trade, and resided where his son, Francis H. Sawyer, now resides. He was admitted to the church May 1, 1841, and d. Feb. 16, 1884, and was buried in the village cemetery.

No. 396.

Mary Putnam Eastman, b. in Hampstead, Oct. 19, 1819, a daughter of Joshua and Susanna (Chase) Eastman (Nos. 218, 230). She married Robert Henry Emerson of Hampstead, as his second wife. She was admitted to the church May 1, 1841, and dismissed to Chelsea, Mass., where she now resides.

No. 397.

Elizabeth Emerson, b. in Hampstead, July 14, 1821, a daughter of Dea. John and Betsey (Emery) Emerson (Nos. 241, 242). She was admitted to the church May 1, 1841, and died, unmarried, in Hampstead, Feb. 13, 1845, aged 24 years, and was buried in the village cemetery. Gravestone inscription, "Blessed is the dead which die in the Lord."

No. 398.

Elizabeth Morse, b. in Derry, June 11, 1812, a daughter of Dea. Robert Morse, who was b. in Newbury, Mass., March 8, 1776, and who was deacon of the Presbyterian Church in Derry over thirty years, and his wife, Alice Dodge, b. in Derry, June 1, 1780, a daughter of Parker and Alice (Little) Dodge, and granddaughter of David and Martha (Esgate) Dodge (Nos. 6 and 7). Dea. Robert and Alice (Dodge) Morse were married by Rev. John Kelly, in Hampstead, March 24, 1801. Elizabeth Morse married Dea. Joseph Chase (No. 389), June 3, 1839, by the Rev. John M. C. Bartley. She was admitted to the church from the church in Derry, July 1, 1842, and d. in Hampstead, Aug. 8, 1862, and was buried in the village cemetery. Their children were:—

I.   Emma Alice, d. May 15, 1844, aged 1 year.
II.   Joseph, Jr., d. Nov. 25, 1869, aged 20 years.
III. Mary Lizzie (No. 458).

No. 399.

Polly Little, b. in Hampstead, July 9, 1798, a daughter of Nathaniel and Abiah (Emerson) Little (Nos. 255, 256). She married Hezekiah Ayer (see No. 272), Nov. 8, 1818. She was admitted to the church Nov. 1, 1841, from the church in Derry. She d. in Hampstead, April, 1858, leaving one child—Belinda Helen (No. 394).

No. 400.

Ann Augusta Wilson, b. in Derry, Sept. 22, 1822, a daughter of Capt. Leonard and Elizabeth (Cregg) (Warner) Wilson of Derry. Her father was drowned in the stream near his house in Derry, while returning home at noon, on March 20, 1868. He was a captain of militia in the war time of 1812. She married Dr. Josiah C. Eastman of Hampstead, May 2, 1843. She was admitted to the church from the First Church in Derry, Sept. 1, 1843. She d. in Hampstead, Feb. 17, 1850, and was buried there (see p. 342, Vol. 1). Their children were :—

I.   Mary B. (No. 442).
II.   Ella A., b. April 11, 1840; resides in Derry.
III.   Mahlon and Etta, d. young.

No. 401.

Caleb Emerson, b. in Hampstead, April 7, 1770, a son of Robert and Mary (Webster) Emerson (Nos. 186, 187). He married Betsey Nichols, and had children b. in Hampstead (see p. 411, Vol. 1). He married, second, Mrs. Mary Haselton (Wells) (No. 408). He was admitted to the church Jan. 2, 1844, and d. in Hampstead.

No. 402.

Hannah Smith, b. in Cornish, Vt., July 13, 1760, a daughter of Joseph and Sarah (Evans) Smith, of Vermont. She married Joseph Harrington of Woodstock, Vt. She was

admitted to the church by letter from the church in Cornish,
Vt., under the pastoral care of Rev. Mr. Spalding, October,
1844. She had a daughter, Hannah (No. 403).

No. 403.

Hannah Harrington, b. in Vermont, 1784, daughter of
Joseph and Hannah (Smith) Harrington (No. 402). She
mar. Jonathan Chase, son of Dea. Joseph and Emma (Chase)
Chase (No. 229), b. in West Newbury, Mass., later of Cor-
nish, Vt. She was admitted to the church by letter from
Cornish, October, 1844, and resided in Hampstead till Nov.
1, 1861, when she was dis. and rec. to the Congregational
Church in Hopkinton.

No. 404.

Hannah Emerson, b. in Weare (recorded on Hampstead
records, see p. 410, Vol. 1), Sept. 22, 1768, a daughter of
Caleb and Abigail (French) Emerson, and granddaughter of
Stephen and Hannah (Marden) Emerson (Nos. 15, 16). She
was unmarried, and lived in the family of Robert Emerson,
of Hampstead several years. She was admitted to the
church at Alstead, and from there was dismissed and united
with the Hampstead church, by letter, Jan. 3, 1844.

No. 405.

Helen Marr Davis, b. in Hampstead, Dec. 29, 1824, a
daughter of Jesse and Eliza (Stevens) Davis (No. 407), son
of Jesse and Lois (Worthen) Davis (No. 223). She was admitted to the church July 4, 1847, and d. in Hampstead,
Jan. 17, 1858.

No. 406.

Hannah French, b. in Hampstead, Jan. 15, 1764, a daughter of Joseph, Jr., and Judith (Diamond) French (Nos. 103,
104). She was admitted to the church Sept. 3, 1847, aged

84 years, and d., unmarried, in Hampstead, and was buried in the village cemetery.

No. 407.

Eliza Stevens, b. in Hampstead, Dec. 14, 1802, a daughter of Paul and Mary (Harriman) Stevens of Hampstead (see Appendix, Stevens). She married Jesse Davis (son of No. 223). She was admitted to the church Sept. 3, 1847, and d. in Hampstead Nov. 1, 1869. They had children:—

I. Helen M. (No. 405).
II. Paul, b. June 30, 1826.
III. Betsey Harriman, b. Sept. 19, 1828; m. John Abbott Follansbee, of West Newbury; Mass.; d. May 7, 1869.
IV. Oscar, b.   ; d. aged 2 years, 6 months.
V. Mary Stevens, b. Jan. 18, 1835; living in West Newbury.
VI. Eliza Frances, b. Nov. 22, 1829; m. Elbridge G. Wood, of West Newbury; d. Nov. 13, 1863.
VII. Josephine, b. Jan. 31, 1846; m. Elbridge G. Wood (above) as second wife. She now resides in West Newbury, a widow.

No. 408.

Mary Haselton, b. on " Walnut Hill," Chester, July 18, 1784, a daughter of John and Anna (Dearborn) Haselton. Anna was daughter of Peter Dearborn, an early settler of Chester. John Dearborn was son of Ephraim and Ruth, daughter of Samuel Ingalls of Chester, and grandson of Richard and Elizabeth (Chadwick Haseltine, a grantee of Chester). Mary Haselton married, first, John Wells of Chester, as his 2d wife, and had children :—

I. John Haselton Wells, b. Jan. 1, 1823; now residing in Portsmouth.
II. Emily, m. Moses Tilton of Portsmouth (deceased).

She was also a stepmother of Timothy Wells (see No. 731), and after the death of Mr. Wells married Caleb Emerson (No. 401), as his second wife, and later married, Jesse Davis (No. 223), as his third wife. She was admitted to the church by letter from the Chester church, March 29, 1848, and died in Portsmouth, Feb. 18, 1878, aged 93 years and 4 months. She was buried by the side of Mr. Davis in the village cemetery.

MRS. DAVIS. NO. 408.

No. 409.

Hannah Brickett, b. in Salem, Dec. 14, 1786, a daughter of James and Anna (Wheeler) Brickett (Nos. 224, 225). She was the oldest of their thirteen children, and moved to Hampstead when five years old. She married Edmund

Mooers, who was b. in Exeter, Oct. 22, 1786. They were married by the Rev. John Kelly, March 25, 1809. He was son of Edmund and Mrs. Mary (Hazen) (Little) Mooers, who was a daughter of Richard Hazen (No. 2), and wife of Benjamin Little (see No. 3), and had one son by Mr. Mooers, Edmund (above). Edmund, Sen., d. in Hampstead, Feb. 23, 1803. Hannah (Brickett) Mooers was admitted to the church March 4, 1849, and d. April 24, 1860. Her husband d. Dec. 16, 1830, and both were buried in the village cemetery. Their children were b. in Pembroke.

I.   William Calef, b. March 10, 1810; d. April 13, 1811.
II.   Mary Ann (No. 305), m. Thomas Kent (No. 200).
III.   Lucretia Little (No. 432).
IV.   Son and daughter (twins), b. Aug. 15, 1816; d. young.
V.   Edmund Brickett, b. March 23, 1818.
VI.   Son, b. Sept. 10, 1822; d. young.
VII.   Triphena Webster, b. July 4, 1825; m., first, Parmenas Pratt of Freeport, Me. One child :—Rosella Lucretia, m. Henry Chapin Sawin, for thirty years principal of the Bigelow School, Boston, Mass. They have a son, Edmund Chapin. Triphena W. married, second, Nathaniel M. Ladd of Newport, and had one son : Nathaniel Mooers, of Trenton, N. J., with whom Mrs. Ladd resides (see p. 100, Vol. 1). Mrs. Ladd is a present member of the church at Andover, Mass.

No. 410.

Harlan Henry Pillsbury, b. in Hampstead, May 15, 1833, son of Benjamin L. and Mary J. (Sargent) Pillsbury (No. 325). He was educated in the common schools of Hampstead, at Atkinson Academy, and at Dartmouth Medical College. He has practised medicine in Medford, Mass., New York State, and California. He married Harriet Foster of North Andover, Mass., June 29, 1859, and their family consisted of four children :—

I.   Carrie H., who d. in Auburn, Cal.
II.   Grace May (deceased).
III.   Ernest S., a physician of Los Angeles, Cal.
IV.   Arthur C., scenic photographer at Los Angeles, Cal.

Dr. Pillsbury united with the church May 2, 1849. He writes, June 18, 1902, from "The Tallac," Lake Tahoe, Cal.: "My first membership was with the Congregational church at Hampstead. Soon after our marriage we both united with the Kirk street church at Lowell, Mass. Three years later we joined Dr. Marvin's church at Medford, Mass, and were members of this church for sixteen years or more. Removing to Brooklyn, N. Y., we, with our oldest daughter, became members of the Lee Avenue Congregational Church, under the pastorate of Dr. Edward Eggleston. Ten years later, 1888, on account of the ill health of our daughter Carrie, we located at Auburn, Cal. Our membership continued with this church eighteen years. Our two sons became members at Auburn, and as they were educated at Stamford University, we were located in that vicinity for several years, and became members of the Third Congregational Church at San Francisco, and for one year members of the Congregational Church at Oakland, Cal. At present we are members of the First Congregational Church of Los Angeles. This is a large church, with a membership of over one thousand, and has two pastors, Dr. Day and son, but whether in a larger or smaller church, we have felt it our duty and privilege to do the little we can for the Master." (See p. 200, Vol. 1.)

No. 411.

Eliza Jane Nichols, b. in Hampstead in 1824, a daughter of Samuel and Alice (Kent) Nichols (No. 265). She was a teacher in Michigan and Virginia for several years, and was admitted by letter from the church in Alegan, Mich., April, 1851. She later married Leydenham Brooks of Virginia, and d. and was buried in Virginia in 1870.

No. 412.

Martha Barnard Peaslee, b. in Atkinson, Feb. 1, 1807, a

daughter of John and Martha (Barnard) Peaslee of Atkinson. Educated at Atkinson Academy, and a teacher. She
married Giles O. Marble of Hampstead in 1832. She was
admitted to the church May, 1851, and d. in Hampstead,
Sept. 14, 1854, aged 48 years, and was buried in the village
cemetery. They had children :—

I.   Giles F. (No. 665); m. Clementine F. Hoyt (No. 463).
II.   John W., b.   ; m. Emily A. Darling (No. 513).
III.   Martha E. (No. 507); m. Lewis Cass; second, Thorndike P. Lake.
IV.   Leonard A., b. June 18, 1842; m. Melissa A. McNiel (No. 512).
V.   Charles F. (see p. 362, Vol. 1).

No. 413.

Emma Eliza Ordway, b. in Hampstead, April 29, 1832, a
daughter of John and Eliza S. (Chase) Ordway (No. 466).
She was admitted to the church May, 1851, and d. in Hampstead, Jan. 30, 1857, unmarried, and buried in the village
cemetery.

No. 414.

Mary Jane Ela, b. in Derry, Sept. 29, 1815, the eldest
daughter of Dea. William Ela of Derry, and Mary Moore,
his wife, a native of Francestown (see No. 154). She married Capt. Amos Buck, with whom she resided in Hampstead from the time of their marriage, Dec. 1, 1836, to her
death, in Hampstead, April 22, 1879. She was admitted to
the church membership Aug. 7, 1851, and was known as "a
faithful and highly efficient wife, a loving and dutiful
mother, a sincere and consistent Christian." They had three
sons :—

I.   William Ela, b. in 1838; m., first, Helen M. Putnam (see No.
        366 and p. 333, Vol. 1); resides in Manchester, where he was
        superintendent of the city's public schools from April, 1877,
        to June, 1900, having previously served as teacher of public
        schools from 1859 to 1877 (see Vol. 1, p. 209).
II.   George Mitchell, d., aged nine years, April 24, 1850.
III.   Amos Henry, d., aged twenty-one years, Nov. 9, 1869.

No. 415.

Ann Elizabeth Sawyer, b. in Hampstead, Aug. 14, 1882, a daughter of Francis and Phebe (Little) Sawyer (Nos. 271, 264). She was admitted to the church September, 1851, and d., unmarried, Dec. 81, 1858, and was buried in the village cemetery.

No. 416.

James Burrill, b. in Hampstead, 1818, son of John and Lydia (Chase) Burrill of Hampstead. He was admitted to the church Feb. 4, 1852, and d. in Hampstead. They had children: Harrison, residing in Hampstead; Cynthia, m., and resided in Newburyport, Mass., 1878.

No. 417.

John Jackson, b. in Hampstead, 1818, a son of Robert Jackson, a mulatto, who served in the war of 1812; while confined as a prisoner in Dartmoor prison, was playing ball, which went over a fence, and when going over the fence after the ball, the guard immediately fired upon young Jackson, and shattered his leg, which had to be amputated. Robert afterwards married Peggy, daughter of Smith and Molly (Colby) Goodwin of East Hampstead, b. Dec. 14, 1778. John lived as a young lad in the family of Moses, father of Mr. Tristram Little, till he was 21 years of age, then for many years in the family of Dea. Chase, at West Hampstead. He married Mary Ferguson (No. 430), May 8, 1856. He was admitted to the church Feb. 4, 1852, and d. in Derry, 1900, and was buried in the cemetery at West Hampstead.

No. 418.

Caroline Mathews, b. in West Danville, Shipton, Canada East, March 24, 1824, the youngest of the thirteen children of Zenas Mathews, who was b. in Hartford, Conn., March

1, 1793, and who removed with his parents to Richmond, in
the town of Shipton, Canada East, when he was young, and
who d. in West Danville, March 20, 1869, and his wife, Bath
Leavitt (second cousin to Dudley Leavitt, famous for his
astronomical calculations), who was born in Littleton, Feb.
7, 1797, and went with her parents to Melbourne, Canada
East, when she was quite young. Her grandfather Leavitt
was in the Revolutionary war, and her parents were honest
and hard-working people, and raised eleven out of their
thirteen children. They were married Feb. 1, 1815, and
moved to Danville, Canada East. Caroline, their youngest
child, came to the United States in April, 1850, and was mar.
to Luther Chase of North Salem Jan. 29, 1852, and went to
Hampstead to reside, where the "old Chase place" stood,
near Joseph G. Brown's, and resided there till Jan. 20, 1892,
when they moved, to be near their son in North Salem,
where they now reside. She was admitted to the church by
letter from Danville Church of Christ, Dec. 12, 1852 (Shipton, Canada East). They had children, b. in Hampstead :—

I. Linus Leavitt, b. Dec. 7, 1859; m. Laura A. Hall of Atkinson
    Feb. 13, 1882. They have children :—
    1. Ethel Mabel, b. May 18, 1884.
    2. Alice Lillian, b. Nov. 21, 1888.
    3. Clarence Willard, b. March 28, 1892.
    4. Warren Edson, b. July 9, 1893.
II. Emma Frances (No. 556).

No. 419.

Dr. Francis Jewett Stevens. He writes : "Boxford,
Mass., July 29, 1902. I was born in Gilford, June 20, 1824,
the oldest son of John Sherburn and Lucy (Jewett) Stevens. My father was born in Kingston, and was a grandson
of Col. Ebenezer Stevens, who was for many years a prominent man in that place. My home during my minority was
on the farm, and my life was the same as other boys on a
farm. My parents had both been school teachers, and until

I was seven or eight years of age; they taught me at home, as the school was too far to run to go, especially in cold or stormy weather.

emies, in which I passed some three school years. I worked
on the farm, vacations, and taught school the winter before I
was twenty-one years of age. In May, 1845, I went to
Schenectady, N. Y., where I was a clerk in a book and
music store for several months, when the store changed
hands, and I soon began the study of dentistry, and for
about three years continued the study and practice, and commenced the study of medicine. I then went back to New
Hampshire, and continued the study of medicine with the
late Dr. G. W. Garland, of Meredith Bridge (now Laconia),
and received the degree of M. D. at the Albany Medical
College, in 1851.

In July (I think) of 1851, I commenced practice in Hampstead, where I remained four years. Jan. 1, 1852, I was
married to Susan Elizabeth Morrill, daughter of the late
Zebedee and Lucy (Potter) Morrill. She was born June 20,
1826, and died in Haverhill, Mass., February, 1873. Soon
after our marriage we took letters from the church at Meredith Bridge and united with the church at Hampstead (Dec.
26, 1852). Some time after moving to Haverhill (April,
1858), we transferred our church relations to the Center
church in Haverhill, and when the North Church was formed
we were among the charter members, from which I have not
withdrawn.

I was married, the second time, to Miss Lydia Helen
Gould, of Boxford, youngest daughter of the late Daniel
and Lydia (Batchelder) Gould, April 16, 1874.

I remained in Haverhill until the spring of 1878, when I
removed to Laconia, N. H., to care for my father, who was so
old and infirm that I felt it to be my duty to go and attend
to him. My health was also in such a condition that a
change to the open air was desirable. After his death, in
March, 1880, we moved to this town, November, 1880, at
the earnest solicitations of my wife's parents, who were very
old, and we still remain here. For some three or four years

after coming here I had an office in Haverhill, but finding it was affecting my health unfavorably, I gave it up, and have done but little professional work in dentistry or medicine, since we have as much land as I care for or am able to cultivate. I occasionally do a bit of dentistry for friends and prescribe for their ailments, and once in a while survey a piece of land, and write some and read quite a good deal, so that I am not idle ; I do not care to rust out.

I have never sought office, but I have held office a good deal of the time. I was a member of the school committee about three years in Hampstead, and for three years in Haverhill, and declined a re-election, and have nearly completed my twenty-first consecutive year on the school committee in this town ; a large part of the time I have been superintendent in this town. I was twice elected representative to the Massachusetts Legislature from Haverhill, and was for several years a coroner while in Haverhill, and I believe I can truly say that I never spent a day in 'lectioneering for myself.

In closing I will add that I have long felt that I would like to visit old Hampstead, where I have not been for more than twenty-five years. I received invitations to the town and church celebrations, and in both instances had to forego the anticipated pleasure, for in that town I spent four years as happily as in any place I have ever lived, and I remember many kind friends, many of them gone.

While I do not remember the " little school girl " whom I relieved of odontalgia, I do distinctly remember your father."

No. 420.

Susan Elizabeth Morrill (see No. 419 above).

No. 421.

·Helen Danforth Tewksbury, b. in Hampstead, May 16, 1836, a daughter of Dr. Isaac and Sabra (Foster) Tewks-

bury (Nos. 377 and 817). She married Joseph H. White,
at Manchester, Nov. 13, 1855. Mr. White is at present an
importer and dry goods commission merchant in Boston,
and president of the Elliot National Bank. They reside at
" Elmhurst," Brookline, Mass., and are members of the
Center Trinitarian Congregational Church, Boston. She is
a member of the " New Hampshire Daughters," and a " D.
A. R." Mrs. White was the first infant baptized in the
church, and was admitted to the church membership July 8,
1853. Dis. and rec. to the care and fellowship of the
Winter street church in Boston, under the pastoral care of
Rev. Mr. Richards, April, 1856. Mr. and Mrs. White have
four children :—

I.   Joseph Foster, unmarried.
II.   Harriet Foster, m. Arthur C. Smith of Omaha, Nebraska.
III. Helen Huntington, m. George J. Putnam of Boston.
IV.   Grace Sabra, m. John L. Batchelder, Jr., of Boston.

No. 422.

Emma Louisa Pillsbury, b. in Hampstead, June 7, 1838, a
daughter of Benjamin L. and Mary J. (Sargent) Pillsbury
(No. 325). She married Rev. James P. Lane, Jan. 1, 1861.
He was pastor of Congregational churches in East Wey-
mouth, Mass., Andover, Mass., Bristol, R. I., and Norton,
Mass. He died Jan. 6, 1889. Mrs. Lane was admitted to
the church membership in Hampstead July 3, 1853. Dis.
and rec. to the Congregational church in East Weymouth,
May 6, 1861. She now resides, a widow (May, 1902), in
Washington, D. C. They have children, now living :—

I.   Annie C., music teacher (piano).
II.   Gernard H., who is a proof reader in the government printing
      office, Washington.
III. John A., who is employed in the architectural department of
      the treasury building at Washington; a graduate from the
      Normal Art School of Boston, Mass.
IV.   May R., a graduate of Mt. Holyoke College, principal grammar
      school of Hinsdale.

No. 423.

Sophia Ann Greenleaf, b. in Salem, July 27, 1835, a daughter of William Greenleaf, who was born and died in what is now Bartlett, and his wife, Mary Harmon Dunlap, who was b. in Weare, May 8, 1806, and d. in Peabody, Mass., Oct. 15, 1890, and was buried there. Sophia went from her parents' home to live with Mr. Abiel and Miss Nancy Ordway, at West Hampstead, when she was nine years of age, and remained at their home until she was married, except as she taught school in Salem, Atkinson, and Hampstead, about nine years. She married Amos Clarkson Tappan of Bradford, April 19, 1868, where they now reside. She was admitted to the church in Hampstead May 7, 1854. Dis. and rec. to the Congregational church in Bradford, Mass., April 21, 1869. They have one adopted daughter: Carrie B., mar. Samuel J. Morse of Bradford, who have a son, Arthur Stanley Morse. Mrs. Tappan was much interested in the first Ladies' Charitable Society in Hampstead. She writes : " That society was very dear to us all ; we had nice times, and often over seventy persons to our suppers, and they were substantial suppers, before the days of chocolates and wafers. Few are now living of those who were so active then."

No. 424.

Sally Ward, b. July 22, 1793, in Plymouth, a daughter of Isaac and Polly (Thurlow) Ward of Plymouth. Mr. Arthur Ward Marshall, of Methchen, N. J., sends the following sketch of his parents, Nov. 15, 1901 (see pages 69 and 196, Vol. 1) :—

" My great-grandfather, Capt. William Marshall, came from Essex, Mass. He died in Hampstead, aged 96 years. My grandmother, Ruth Fellows Marshall, died at Kensington, at the age of 99 years and 8 months, and was buried at

Hampstead. She was a most excellent, Christian woman. My grandfather, Silas, was more than 90 years of age at his death. My mother, Sally Marshall (above), married Andrew Burnham, son of Silas and Ruth (Fellows) Marshall, Oct. 14, 1818, who d. in Hampstead in 1853. My mother was admitted to the church at Hampstead May 7, 1854, and d. in Still River, Mass., in her 95th year, April, 1888, and was buried in the village cemetery at Hampstead.

Andrew B. and Sally (Ward) Marshall had children, born in Hampstead :—

I.   William, b. Aug. 24, 1819; d. Aug. 30, 1841.

II.   Arthur Ward, b. April 9, 1822; m. Caroline Ward Trumbull, December, 1854, at Valparaiso, Chile. Miss Trumbull was a great granddaughter of Jonathan Trumbull, the first governor of Connecticut—"Brother Jonathan," so called by Gen. Washington. We had eight children, the two oldest b. in Valparaiso. My wife died May, 1892.

    1. Eliza Trumbull, b. September, 1855; is now my homemaker and housekeeper.

    2. William Burnham, b. April, 1858; d. of typhoid fever in Methchen; September, 1881.

    3. John Trumbull, b. January, 1860; lives at home, and is one of the leading men in the great Edison lamp factory, where they employ about 1000 persons.

    4. Nina Lovering, b. May, 1861; was graduated at Wellesley College, and is now teaching in the Ely School of New York city.

    5. Julia Campbell, b. January, 1863; d. October, 1881, of typhoid fever.

    6. James Arthur, b. May, 1864; d. in infancy (a member by baptism).

    7. David Trumbull, b. November, 1865; m., and is now practising medicine in New York city.

    8. Cornelius Bruyn, b. February, 1867; d. October, 1889, of typhoid fever.

The boys were all educated at Rutger College, New Brunswick, N. J. All of my children became members of the First Presbyterian Church at Methchen, N. J. Five of them are still living, and five have passed on to the other side. I

am one of this happy home of three, enjoying life, waiting
for the

> All beauty, bright and vernal,
> All glory, grand, eternal,
> When Jesus comes."

III.   Isaac Hill, b. Jan. 24, 1832.

No. 425.

Lois Calef, b. in Hampstead, Sept. 4, 1821, a daughter of
James and Anna (Kimball) Calef (Nos. 316, 226). She
married Dea. William Sanborn, Aug. 18, 1846, and d. in
Hampstead, May 11, 1876, and was buried in the village
cemetery. She was admitted to the church May 7, 1854.
They had children :—

I.   Mary Elizabeth, b. June 29, 1851; d. Aug. 25, 1804.
II.   James William (No. 548), m. Flora A. Corson (No. 549).
III.   Susan Emma, b. April 25, 1857; d. June 5, 1870.
IV.   John Calef (No. 598), m. Lillian R. Griffin (No. 580); second,
        Annie B. Fitts (No, 685).

No. 426.

Joseph Dana Bartley, b. in Hampstead, Sept. 17, 1838, a
son of Rev. John M. C. and Susan (Dana) Bartley (Nos.
328, 355). He was educated at Atkinson Academy, Williams College, and Princeton Theological School (p. 183,
Vol. 1). "He was admitted to the church in Hampstead
July 1, 1855, and was dis. and rec. to unite with the
church in New York city under the pastoral care of Rev. Mr.
Preston, Sept. 7, 1868." (Church records.)

Prof. Bartley writes, in 1902: "As for myself, I
have had a happy life of about thirty-seven years as a teacher,
and now it has been my good fortune to return to Burlington, the "Queen City" of Vermont, and of the whole
country as well, to teach in the same High School where,
twenty years ago, I was principal. The joy of such a return
to old scenes and to friends, new and old, I cannot express
in words.

Mrs. Tenney (Mary Atwood), daughter of Dea. William, son of Silas and Rebecca (Bailey) Tenney, and Emeline (Murray) Tenney (Nos. 203 and 204), is my cheery help-meet. Helen, our daughter, is with us, and William Tenney,

JOSEPH D. BARTLEY. NO. 426.

our son, is pastor of the Congregational Church at Salem, (see "Anniversary poems," by Rev. W. T. Bartley, Vol. 1). My son married Carrie Belle Webster of Salem, and has one son, Irving Dana, b. Aug. 30, 1902."

No. 427.

John Chesley Drew, b. in Brookfield, Dec. 2, 1802, was a son of Joseph and Susan (Hill) Drew, of Newfield, Me. Joseph Drew died in 1866, aged 88 years and 6 months. His wife Susan died in 1816. They had children : John Chesley (No. 427), Israel S., Joseph H., Sally, Susan, Lydia, Olive H. He married, second, Susan Gooding, and had two children, Mary L., and Ivory C., who is still living (1902),

MR. AND MRS. JOHN C. DREW. NOS. 427, 428.

aged 83 years. The father of Joseph Drew was a soldier in the Revolution and in the old French war. John Chesley Drew married Hannah Johnson (No. 428). He was admitted to the church in Hampstead by certificate, and also dis. and rec. from the church in Waltham, Mass., Feb. 29, 1854. He died in Salem, Sept. 5, 1884, while visiting his daughter.

No. 428.

Hannah Johnson, b. in Dunbarton, Oct. 15, 1810, a daughter of Joseph Johnson, who d. Sept. 10, 1852, aged 68 years, and his wife, Mary C. (Hoyt), who d. Nov. 20, 1883, aged 84 years. Both were buried in Hampstead. She was married to John C. Drew (No. 427), Feb. 26, 1835, by the Rev. Edw. L. Parker of Londonderry. She was admitted to the church by certificate from Waltham, Mass., Feb. 29, 1854. She d. in Derry, at the Drew homestead, May 31, 1881. The funeral was attended by Rev. Albert Watson. They had children:

I. Mary Susan, m. Nelson Burrill; they had three children—Etta Frances, Benjamin Franklin, and Clara Elizabeth.
II. Olive Frances, d. when five years of age.
III. Otis Almon, m. Sarah F. Wilson, and has children—George Clinton, Joseph Foster, John Wilson, Olive Frances, Mary Naomi, and William Harvey. Resides at the homestead in Derry.
IV. Anna Jane, m., first, Henry Reed, and had children—Ivan, Orrin, and Mabel. She mar., second, Joseph Long, of North Salem.
V. An infant, d. young.
VI. Jesse Walter, m. Annie E. Walker, and had children—Elbridge Walker, and an infant. He died Dec. 22, 1885, and his wife d. Feb. 21, 1887.

Mrs. Drew was ever an enthusiastic church worker, and in every part did her work well. She was the first president of the Ladies' Charitable Society, and as her son writes: "My mother was ever a very devoted Christian, and seldom was absent from church; even when she thought the travelling too bad for a team, she would walk, during the latter part of her life."

No. 429.

Mary Elizabeth Davis, b. in Hampstead, June 13, 1826, a daughter of Ezra and Mary (Garland) Davis (Nos. 234, 235). She married John Mount of Hightstown, N. J. She was admitted to the church by certificate from Rev. Dr. Cutter of the Methodist Episcopal Church at Portsmouth, July 6, 1856.   She has children :—

I.   Fred, a physician in Philadelphia, Pa.
II.   Carl, a lawyer in New Orleans, La.

No. 430.

Mary Furgerson, b. in Gloucester, Mass., moved to Derry, with the family of Beniah and Mary E. (Stacy) Titcomb (No. 451), and worked in their family until her marriage to John Jackson (No. 417), May 8, 1856. She was received by letter to the church from Gloucester Harbor, Mass., July 6, 1856. They had no children. (There is a defect on the Hampstead church records in regard to this entry and the two before it.)

No. 431.

Samuel Atwood, b. in Hampstead, May 1, 1796, son of Moses and Judith (Wadleigh) Atwood, of Alexandria, but of Hampstead until about 1800.   He resided a short time in Hampstead, and d. about 1867, "in the northern part of the state."   He was admitted to the church by confession, May 3, 1857.   (See No. 76 and Appendix.)

No. 432.

Lucretia Little Mooers, b. in Exeter, Dec. 11, 1818, a daughter of Edmund and Hannah (Brickett) Mooers (No. 409). She was married to John Jefferson of Pembrooke, June 18, 1840, by the Rev. John M. C. Bartley. He d. June 11, 1854. She was admitted to the church Jan. 2, 1857, and d. in Hampstead, Dec. 27, 1881, and was buried in the village cemetery.   They had children :—

I.   Triphena Pratt, b. March 2, 1845, in Pembroke; m., Dec. 1, 1866, Linus H., son of Linus Lewis and Abiah (Tewksbury) Little (No. 302), (see also No. 107). They have one child, Herbert C., b. Jan. 10, 1878. They reside in Haverhill, Mass.

II.   Hannah Ida, d. Oct. 4, 1853.
III.   Mary L., m. Fred J. Drinkwater of Haverhill, 1876; d. May 27, 1891.

No. 433.

Mary. Abbie Pillsbury, b. in Hampstead, a daughter of Benjamin L. and Mary J. (Sargent) Pillsbury (No. 325). She married Sylvanus Thurman, and resides in Redlands, Calif. She was admitted to the church July 1, 1857. Dis. and rec. to the First Congregational Church in Hyde Park, Mass., March 24, 1886. (See letter of greeting, 150th anniversary exercises of the church.)

No. 434.

Rev. Theodore Constantine Pratt, b. in South Weymouth, Mass., Jan. 3, 1829, a son of Ezra Pratt, of South Weymouth, who d. there, April, 1874, and his wife, Emeline Lincoln Vining, who d. in South Weymouth, April, 1869. He was educated in the public schools of Weymouth, and prepared for college at Worcester Academy, at Worcester, Mass. He took a partial course at Amherst College, and before entering the ministry he taught a grammar school in Weymouth three years. He married, first, Emeline Augusta Reed (No. 438), and, second, married Mrs. Mary Ann (Sanborn) Murray, of Auburn, Aug. 14, 1895. He was ordained a Congregational minister June 21, 1859, and that day was installed as pastor of the church in Hampstead. He was dismissed from the church Jan. 9, 1870, and was resident licentiate at Andover Theological Seminary over a year. He commenced work with the Congregational Church in Tilton, May 1, 1870, and was installed pastor Oct. 28, 1873, and dismissed June 13, 1875. He commenced labor with the Congregational Church in Hancock, July 11, 1875, and ceased March 18, 1877. Commenced work at Oxfordville Congregational Church, April 8, 1877, and dismissed March 5, 1882, and installed as pastor in Auburn April 1, 1882, and ceased March 31, 1892. Commenced work in Candia Congregational Church, April 1, 1892, and closed pastoral labor

REV. T. C. PRATT. NO. 434.

there March 31, 1901. He was admitted to the fellowship of the Hampstead church by letter from the church at

Weymouth, Mass., Aug. 30, 1861, and was dis. and rec. to
the Northfield and Tilton Congregational Church, April 8,
1875. Mr. and Mrs. Pratt reside in Candia, retired from
pastoral work.

No. 435.

James Thorndike Brickett, b. in Hampstead, April 5, 1841,
a son of Moody H. and Laura A. (Putnam) Brickett (Nos.
292, 381). He was admitted to the church by letter from
the Winter Street Church in Haverhill, Mass., July 1, 1859.
Dis. and rec. to the North Congregational Church at Haverhill, December, 1864. After serving in the civil war, he
married Mary Frances Parker, of Groveland, Mass., and settled in Haverhill, where they had three children born :—

I.   James Edward, m. Mary Moody; reside in Haverhill. Children :
      Margerite, Caleb, and Dorothy.
II.   Annette Putnam. After pursuing a course of training at North-
      field, Mass., and Chicago, has served as assistant pastor in
      Minneapolis, teacher in the Indian schools at Fort Berthold,
      North Dakota, and of the Neeees of Mississippi; mar. Dr.
      John Sturgis of Auburn, Me., Mar. 4, 1903.
III. Helen Louise, m. Dr. John Sturgis, of Auburn, Me., in 1895. She
      d., leaving an infant son, in 1900.

James T. Brickett was killed in the autumn of 1876.
"He was on his way to Groveland, where his wife was visiting, and as he stepped from the car it suddenly started,
throwing him under the wheels. He was so severely injured
that he died in a few hours."

Dr. Crowell of Haverhill spoke of him at his death: "In
all of the walks and relations of life Mr. Brickett proved
himself consistent. His convictions of duty were clear and
decided, and based upon a consciousness of high moral obligations. Governed by this principle, he entered the service
of his country in the hour of its great peril, and proved true
to his professions of loyalty. In his Christian experience he
was modest, humble, and sincere, but bold and uncompromis-

ing in his defence of truth, taking as his standard the revealed word of God, always ready to give a reason for the
faith that was in him. His relation to the church, the Sunday school, to his associates and to his family, were strong
and constant, tenderly endearing him to all who came under
his influence. His funeral was largely attended by relatives
and friends, members of his Sunday school class, with their
teacher, and fellow-workmen." Dr. Kingsbury of Bradford
conducted the funeral service.

No. 486.

Daniel Sargent Pillsbury, b. in East Hampstead, May 5.
1886, a son of Benjamin L. and Mary J. (Sargent) Pillsbury,
of Hampstead (No. 325). He was educated in the common
schools of Hampstead, Phillips Academy, Andover, Mass.,
and a graduate from the Bridgewater State Normal School.
He married, first, Sarah J. Tisdale, of Middleton, Mass.
They had two daughters, Anne Mary and Mildred Sarah. He
m., second, Mary F. Goldthwaite of Medford, Mass., Feb. 4,
1874. "He was admitted to the church Sept. 4, 1859. Dis.
and rec. to the 18th Presbyterian Church in New York city,
under the pastoral care of Rev. Dr. Burchard, Aug. 12,
1866." He died Feb. 18, 1902. The following, from a
clipping at the time of his death, dated Mount Vernon, N.
Y.: " Daniel Sargent Pillsbury, for forty years a stationer,
printer, and wholesale paper dealer in New York city, with
offices formerly at 680 Sixth Avenue, and later at 25 Maiden
Lane, died this morning, at his home on Chester Hill, Mt.
Vernon. The cause of his death was heart disease, brought
on by an attack of the grip. Mr. Pillsbury had a hobby for
the collection of brass musical instruments, and owned the
largest and most complete assortment of them known to
artists in the world. Part of his collection, consisting of 175
instruments, had recently been on exhibition at Chickering's,
in Boston. Mr. Pillsbury had nearly as many more instru-

ments and musical curios in his Mt. Vernon home. Mr. Pillsbury leaves a wife and two daughters. The funeral was held from his late home, No. 162 Rich Avenue, Chester Hill, Mt. Vernon, and attended by Rev. Crandall J. North

DEA. W. H. DAVIS. NO. 437.

of the M. E. Church, assisted by Rev. Owen B. Lovejoy of the First Congregational Church. Burial was temporary at Woodlawn." (See photo, Vol. 1.)

No. 437.

William Henry Davis, b. in Hampstead, Dec. 16, 1836, a

son of Ezra and Mary (Garland) Davis (Nos. 234, 235).
He married, first, Lizzie E. Wadleigh (No. 502), and married, second, R. Jane Taylor (No. 699). He was admitted
to the church Sept. 4, 1859, and was elected a deacon Dec.
30, 1896, which office he now holds. He has served in the
choir fifty-two years and many years as chorister. He served
in the civil war. He is a worker on shoes in Hampstead.

No. 438.

Emeline Augusta Reed, b. in Sterling, Mass., Feb. 23,
1834, a daughter of Elbridge Gerry Reed, who resided
many years in Sterling, where he died, June, 1870, and his
wife, Mary Ann Rice, who d. in Erving, Mass., December,
1880. She married Rev. T. C. Pratt (No. 434). She was
admitted to the church by letter from the Baptist church in
Sterling, Mass., Sept. 4, 1859. Dis. and rec. to unite with
the church at Northfield and Tilton, April 3, 1875. She d.
in Candia, Feb. 8, 1894, and was interred in the Hampstead
village cemetery. They had children :—

I.   Melissa Ann, now residing in Candia.
II.   Eugene Meader, b. July 31, 1860; d. Oct. 7, 1865.
III.   Ella Boardman, b. March 9, 1862; d. Oct. 7, 1865. (One funeral
     service was held, and the last two children laid in one wide
     grave.)
IV.   Albert Wallace, b. Sept. 3, 1864; d. Oct. 13, 1865 (last three born
     and baptized in Hampstead).
V.   Lester Channing, b. in Tilton, April 15, 1873; was a graduate
     from Pinkerton Academy, Derry, in June, 1894, and was
     admitted to Amherst College in September of that year, but
     was obliged to leave in one week on account of ill health, and
     died of quick consumption, June 8, 1895, in Candia.

These four children were buried in the family lot, with
their mother, in Hampstead village cemetery.

No. 439.

Sarah Bagley Richardson, b. in Groveland, Mass., Aug. 7,
1828, a daughter of John Richardson, of Groveland, Mass.,

and his wife, Lavina, daughter of Dea. Stephen Bailey, of West Newbury, Mass. She married Daniel H. Emerson, April 27, 1852 (see p. 367, Vol. 1). She was admitted to the church Sept. 4, 1859, and is a present member. They have children:—

MRS. PRATT. NO. 438.

I.   Laura Ann, bapt. in Hampstead.
II.   Albert H., m. Susie Stimson.
III.   Emma E. (No. 656).

No. 440.

Mary Ann Tilton Brown, b. in Hampstead, Feb. 1, 1815,

a daughter of Joseph and Sally (Greenleaf) Brown. She was admitted to the church by letter from the Baptist church of Lynn, Mass., Oct. 30, 1857; and d., unmarried, at the home of her brother, Joseph G. Brown, Feb. 2, 1860, and was buried in the village cemetery.

REV. GEO. O. JENNESS. NO. 441.

No. 441.

George Osborne Jenness, b. in Methuen, Mass., April 14, 1837, a son of Elijah Jenness, a local Methodist minister, and his wife, Deborah L. Batchelder, who married, second, Moses Hoyt, Esq., of Hampstead, in 1848. He was educated in the common schools of Methuen, Mass., and Hampstead, at Atkinson Academy, and at Richmond College in Virginia. He was ordained to the gospel ministry at Gill's Grove Baptist Church, Chesterfield, Va., in 1861, and was admitted to the church by a letter from that church, Dec. 22, 1859. He began work as a home missionary of the Congregational Church, under the direction of the New Hampshire Home Missionary Society, at the Congregational Church at Wakefield. He was dis. and rec. from the Hampstead church to unite with the church at Wakefield, July 3, 1879. He was subsequently pastor of the following churches: Attleboro Falls, Mass.; Beechwood, Mass.; West Gloucester and Magnolia, Easton and Charlton, Mass. All but nine and a half years have been spent in home missionary work. The pastorate in Charlton, Mass., began July, 1896, where he now resides. He married Mary Abbie Merrill (No. 445).

No. 442.

Mary Bartlett Eastman, b. in Hampstead, Feb. 15, 1844, a daughter of Dr. Josiah G. and Ann A. (Wilson) Eastman (No. 400). She was admitted to the church Jan. 1, 1860. Dis. and rec. to the Westminster Presbyterian Church in South Brooklyn, N. Y., under the pastoral care of Rev. Mr. Carpenter, Oct. 28, 1866. She married Lavoser Hill, of the firm of Hill & Palmer, San Antonio, Texas. Mrs. Hill died in Derry, after a few days' illness, but was an invalid for twenty-five years, Oct. 14, 1902. They had children: Dr. Eugene W., of Newton, Mass., and Walter E., of Derry. (See pp. 341-2, Vol. 1.)

No. 443.

Louisa Maria Kent, b. in Hampstead, Nov. 11, 1828, a daughter of Abner K. and Lydia (Taylor) Kent (see 255). She married John D. Ordway, Nov. 28, 1850. She was admitted to the church March 1, 1860, d. in Hampstead, Nov.

3, 1877, and was buried in the village cemetery. "She was beloved by all who knew her." (See p. 337, Vol. 1). They had children :—

I.   John Kent, m. Carrie Cox; resides in Dorchester, Mass. She d. March 20, 1900, leaving daughters :—

MRS. J. D. ORDWAY.   NO. 443.

1.   Ruth Louise, b. Dec. 4, 1889.
2.   Emelie Marjorie, b. Jan. 30, 1894.

II.   Da...s F., m. Eleanor T. Randall (No. 564).
III.   Ch...les E., b. Sept. 25, 1865; d., aged 3 years.
IV.   Ge...ge E., b. Oct. 30, 1867; d. July 11, 1872.
V.   Em...a Louisa, b. April 24, 1870; d. July 22, 1885.

No. 444.

Samantha Currier Merrill, b. in Derry, a daughter of Austin Guy and Mary (Ganney) Merrill, and granddaughter of Capt. Simon and Mary (Marston) Merrill (No. 208). She was admitted to the church by baptism, March 1, 1860. Dis. and rec. to the First Church in Derry, Sept. 7, 1863. She has been a teacher in Adams Female Academy at Derry, and for several years a teacher in the Brackett Academy in Greenland. At present a writer of Sunday school literature and for religious magazines, and resides in Malden, Mass.

No. 445.

Mary Abbie Merrill, b. in Hampstead, May 80, 1843, a daughter of Simon and Hannah W. (Kelly) Merrill (No. 865), and granddaughter of Rev. John (No. 164) and Abigail (Dearborn) Kelly (No. 171). She married Rev. George O. Jenness (No. 441), June 18, 1870. She was admitted to the church March 1, 1860. Dis. and rec. to unite with the Congregational Church in Wakefield, July 8, 1879. They have had children :—

I.   Ella Pratt, d. Sept. 15, 1870, an infant.
II. Eddie Osborne, d. Sept. 6, 1871, an infant.
III. Alice Mary, d. April 2, 1874, an infant.
IV. Annie Mary, b. Nov. 15, 1875; at present a teacher in Rutland, Mass.
V.   Manora, b. in Wakefield, April 15, 1877; mar. George F. Howard, physical director in the Y. M. C. A. at Montclair, N. J., June 25, 1901 (see p. 160, Vol. 1).

No. 446.

Martha Sanborn, b. in Hampstead, July 29, 1841, a daughter of Dea. William and Mary (Greenleaf) Sanborn (Nos. 890, 891). She mar. Charles Henry Day of Derry (see No. 335), Nov. 24, 1864. She was adm. to the church March 1, 1860. Dis. and rec. to unite with the Congregational Church, in Derry, under the pastoral care of Rev. Mr. Bremner, June 3, 1871. They had children, b. in Derry :—

I.   Lucy Elizabeth, b. July 31, 1866; d. March 7, 1870.
II.   Mary Harriet, b. Oct. 27, 1872, a teacher in Springfield, Mass.
III.   John Walter, b. June 10, 1877, resides with his parents, in
        Derry.

No. 447.

Hannah Maria Little, b. in Hampstead, Aug. 28, 1843, a
daughter of Linus L. C. and Abiah F. Tewksbury (No. 302).
She mar. Frank M. Brown of Haverhill, b. in Wilmot, June
4, 1879. She was adm. to the church "by baptism, March
1, 1860. Dis. and rec. to unite with the Center Church of
Haverhill, Mass., April 5, 1888." She d. in Haverhill, Aug.
29, 1892; buried in Hampstead village cemetery (see p.
851, Vol. 1). Their son, Henry Gibbon Brown, m. and has
one child, Henry Raymond Brown.

No. 448.

Meribah Farnum Little, b. in Hampstead, May 8, 1841, a
daughter of Nathaniel H. and Almira (Tewksbury) Little
(see No. 167). She mar. Gardner B. Reynolds of Lynn,
Mass., Oct. 8, 1872, and d. in Oct., 1875, leaving one child,
Lorenzo Theodore, b. Feb. 6, 1875, that d. in infancy. She
d. Oct. 18, 1875. She was admitted to the church May 6,
1860.

No. 449.

Mary Jane Heath, b. in Hampstead, June 12, 1826, a
daughter of Capt. John and Abigail (Wadleigh) Heath
(Nos. 858, 859). She was adm. to the church by baptism,
May 6, 1860. She mar. Dea. William Sanborn, Oct. 11,
1876 (No. 390). A present member of the church (see p.
365, Vol. 1).

No. 450.

Abigail R. Heath, b. in Hampstead, Jan. 14, 1824, a
daughter of Capt. John and Abigail (Wadleigh) Heath
(Nos. 858, 859), (p. 365, Vol. 1). She was adm. to the

church by baptism, May 6, 1860 ; d. unm. in Hampstead, Sept., 1896, and was buried in the village cemetery.

No. 451.

John Stacy Titcomb, b. in Gloucester, Mass., Feb. 1, 1836, a son of Beniah and Mary Elizabeth (Stacy) Titcomb of Gloucester. He mar. Hannah E. Irving (No. 482). He was adm. to the membership of the church May 6, 1860, and united with the Center Church in Haverhill, Mass., where he is a present member.

No. 452.

Caroline Ela, b. in Derry, Dec. 14, 1815, a daughter of Dea. William and Mary (Moore) Ela of Derry (see Nos. 154, 415). She mar. Ebenezer Buck of Hampstead. She was adm. to the church by letter from the M. E. Church at North Salem, Sept. 2, 1860, "the first afternoon that was devoted to communion service." She was dis. and rec. to the care of the North Church at Haverhill, Dec., 1864 ; she d. in Haverhill, July 30, 1891, and was buried in Hildale cemetery; "a most estimable woman." They had children :—

I. Marietta, mar. James Hall, late contractor and builder in Haverhill; they had several children, b. in Haverhill.
II. Alva, who d. unmarried.

No. 453.

Huldah A. Hoyt, b. in Sandown, Dec., 1838, a daughter of Eben and Mary (Clark) Hoyt of Sandown. She mar. —— Merserve of Danville. She was adm. to the church Nov. 4, 1860. She d. about 1878, leaving a daughter Mary.

No. 454.

Elizabeth Perkins Choate, b. in Derry, May 1, 1823, a daughter of Humphrey Choate, who resided in that part of Londonderry (now Derry), and his wife Betsey Low, who was b. in Londonderry, on the General Stark place, where she lived till her marriage.   Elizabeth P. mar. Nelson Ordway of Hampstead, Mar. 21, 1851 (see p. 335, Vol. 1, and No. 466). She was adm. to the membership of the church by letter

MRS. ELIZABETH P. ORDWAY.   NO. 454.

from the Congregational Church in Derry, Jan. 3, 1862. She d. in Winchester, Mass., March 31, 1900, while on a visit to her son ; burial in Hampstead village cemetery ; they had children :—One son d. in infancy, and Henry C. (No. 659).

Nelson Ordway died suddenly at his home early Thursday morning, April 9, 1903. He was educated in the public schools of the town, at Pinkerton Academy, and at Plymouth. For many years he was engaged in mercantile business, and in 1846, he became a member of the firm of John Ordway and Son, and later carried on the business in company with his brother, the late John D. Ordway. For several years he was a director of the Derry National Bank. He was a valued trustee of Hampstead High School for about twenty years. He founded Hampstead Public Library in 1888.

Mr. Ordway was a life-long resident of Hampstead, and was always interested in its welfare, and has served it in various capacities, being its representative to the Legislature in 1862, and again in 1863. He was a man of strict integrity, and his judgment and counsel were held in high esteem. (See photo, Vol. 1.)

No. 455.

Lydia Currier Jones, b. in South Hampton, June 5, 1812, a daughter of Joseph, Jr., and Mary A. (Bradbury) Jones of South Hampton, and granddaughter of Joseph and Miss (Blaisdell) Jones of Newburyport, Mass. She mar., first, Amos Ring, who was b. in Amesbury, Mass., May 1, 1810, and d. in Hampstead, Jan. 13, 1875. He was a son of Jonathan Ring, who was b. in Amesbury, Oct. 18, 1775, and d. 1855, and his wife Priscilla (Martin), who was b. Feb. 25, 1774, and d. 1857, in Amesbury. Amos and Lydia (Jones) Ring, settled first in Ware, Mass., later in Atkinson, and moved to Hampstead, where Amasa Hunt now resides. She was adm. to the church March 2, 1862. They had children :—

I.   Emily A. (No. 603), m. John W. Garland (No. 602).
II.   Anson Jones, b. Aug. 13, 1837; m., first, Delana J. Corson (see
      p. 809, Vol. 1); they had children :—

1. Carrie Ellen, b. Nov. 2, 1864, in Hampstead; m. Benjamin F. Tripp, Oct. 17, 1889, who was b. in Liming-
   ton, Me., Oct. 17, 1867; they reside in Newton, Mass.
   and have children. Mary Delanie, b. June 23, 1894.
   Robert Henry, b. Feb. 7, 1898.
2. Walter Sherman, b. April 13, 1867, in Hampstead, m.
   June 1, 1898, Margaret Phelan, who was b. in Sack-
   ville, Canada, Sept. 5, 1867; their child, Irma Priscilla,
   b. April 8, 1901, in Brighton, Mass.

Lydia mar., second, Ebenezer Follansbee of Hampstead
(see No. 601), Jan. 1, 1883, and d. in Hampstead, April 29,
1887 ; was buried in the village cemetery.

No. 456.

Nancy Rogers Marston, b. in Sandown, Feb. 1, 1830, a
daughter of Amos and Susan (Flanders) Marston of Sandown. She was mar. to Joshua C. (Hamilton C.) Eastman
(see Nos. 213, 230), Dec. 13, 1865, by the Rev. Alfred Emerson of Fitchburg, Mass., pastor of the First Congregational
Church. She was adm. to the church Mar. 2, 1862 ; she d.
in Hampstead, Sept. 9, 1891, and was buried in the village
cemetery. They had children :—

I.   Henry Lincoln, b. Nov. 3, 1871; m. Annie L. Griffin (No. 604).
II. John Marston, b. Oct. 27, 1868; m. Annie E., daughter of Asa
     and Hannah (Noyes) Worthen of East Hampstead. They
     have children :—
     1. Mary Agnes, b. Nov. 3, 1893.
     2. John Edgar, b. Nov. 6, 1899.

No. 457.

Elvira P. Wheeler, b.   She
mar. Parker Howe, and lived for a time where John C.
Sanborn now resides. She was adm. to the church by letter
from the Appleton St. Church in Lowell, Mass., May 2,
1862. Dis. and rec. to unite with the First Congregational
Church in Lowell, under the pastoral care of Rev. Horace
James. They had a daughter, Elvira.

No. 458.

Mary Elizabeth Chase, b. in Hampstead, 1847, a daughter of Dea. Joseph and Elizabeth (Morse) Chase (No. 398). She mar. Silas W. Tenney of Chester. She was adm. to the church Sept. 2, 1862, and d. in Danville, N. Y., Nov. 4, 1875; she was buried in the village cemetery, aged 28 years. She had children:— Leroy S., d. Nov. 22, 1872; aged 3 years, and "A daughter, now living in New York State."

No. 459.

Maria M. ——, b. in Woburn, Mass. She mar. Isaac Hale of Atkinson, for his third wife. She was adm. to the church by letter from the church in Woburn, Jan., 1864. Dis. and rec. to unite with the Baptist Church in Chelmsford, Mass., Oct. 30, 1884.

No. 460.

Elizabeth Maria Dearborn, b. Feb., 1826, a daughter of Leonard Dearborn of Lowell, Mass. She mar. Horace Locke of Winchester, Mass., and was adm. to the church in Hampstead by letter from the Congregational Church in Winchester, June 11, 1865. She d. Oct. 6, 1892, and was buried in the village cemetery. She had a daughter b. in Winchester. Sarah Lizzie, b. Jan. 19, 1854; mar. William A. Little (see p. 352, Vol. 1), their son, Horace Walter (No. 718).

No. 461.

Syrena Brown, b. in Hampstead, Feb. 1, 1818, a daughter of Joseph Brown (see No. 141, 142) and wife Sally Greenleaf, b. in Haverhill, Mass., and was a member of the First Baptist Church. Syrena mar. Nathan Johnson of Atkinson, June 2, 1842. She united with the church in Hampstead, July 2, 1865, and d. in Hampstead, June 21, 1894. She was buried in the family lot in the village cemetery. Her husband d. in 1884. They had children :—

I.   John Franklin, b. March 4, 1843; served in the civil war at its
     close. He is unmarried, and resides in Concord.
II. Abbie Ann (No. 402).
III. Lucy Sarah (No. 550).
IV. Mary, b. August 8, 1852; d. in infancy.
V.   Alice, b. March 8, 1854; d. in 1864.

No. 462.

Abbie Ann Johnson, b. in Hampstead, March 24, 1846, a
daughter of Nathan and Syrena (Brown) Johnson (No. 462).
She was educated in the public schools, and at Atkinson
Academy. She taught school for several years. She was
united with the church July 2, 1865. Dis. and rec. to unite
with the Mystic Side Congregational Church at Everett,
Mass., Nov. 1, 1894; she is at present a member of the
Center Congregational Church at Haverhill, Mass., where
she resides.

No. 463.

Clementine Hoyt, b. in Sandown, Feb., 1835, daughter of
Ebenezer and Mary (Clark) Hoyt of Sandown. She mar.
Giles F. Marble (No. 665). She was adm. to the church
July 2, 1865, and d. in Hampstead. They had children :—

I.   Frank Giles, d. aged 4 years.
II. Dana Giles, b. in 1862, educated in the public schools of Hamp-
     stead, attended Phillips Academy at Exeter, and graduated
     from Dartmouth College, in 1884; he d. in 1885, while teach-
     ing in Hillsboro Academy, of pneumonia, and would have
     been adm. to the bar in three weeks; he was unmarried.
III. Charles E., mar. Bertha Pressey; resides in Haverhill; was
     educated in the Hampstead High School, Pinkerton Academy,
     and attended Dartmouth Medical Lectures. Had son Dana.

No. 464.

Alice Carlton Merrill, b. in Danville, Ill., Dec. 13, 1843,
an only child of Guy Merrill, who moved to Danville early
in life, and his wife Annie M. Kingsbury of Danville, but a
native of Massachusetts. She died when Alice was eleven

years of age, who was cared for by her aunt Mrs. Swan, mostly in the east, and for a time lived in Hampstead. She was educated at Bradford Academy, and after living in Danville, taught school. She was adm. to the church July 2, 1865, and was dis. and rec. to unite with the Presbyterian Church in Danville, Dec. 27, 1868, and at present a member of the same church. She mar. George B. Yeomans, who d. in Danville, May 11, 1871; she has five children, three daughters and two sons.

No. 465.

Anna Louisa Heath, b. in Hampstead, April 18, 1848, a daughter of Eliphalet K. and Alice H. (Shannon) Heath (p. 365, Vol. 1). She was educated in the common schools and at New Hampton Academy, and taught school for one year. She married Calvin A. Merrick (No. 734), June 29, 1872. She was admitted to the church July 2, 1865, and is a present member. She has no children.

No. 466.

Eliza Sanborn Chase, b. in Newbury, Mass., Feb. 27, 1792, a daughter of Joseph and Emma (Chase) Chase (No. 229). She came with her parents to Hampstead when twelve years old. She married John Ordway, Esq., Jan. 19, 1819 (see p. 834, Vol. 1). She was admitted to the church by baptism, Sept. 3, 1865, and d. in Hampstead, Jan. 21, 1873, and was buried in the village cemetery. They had children :—

I. Elvira, b. Oct. 3, 1819; d. May 22, 1857, unmarried.
II. Nelson, b. July 31, 1821; m. Elizabeth P. Choate (No. 454).
III. Dana, b. Nov. 23, 1823; d. aged three years.
IV. John Dana, b. Aug. 3, 1828; m. Louisa M. Kent (No. 443).
V. Daniel Henry, b. Oct. 7, 1829; graduate Dartmouth College, class of 1852; d. July 14, 1854.
VI. Emma Eliza (No. 413).

No. 467.

Rebecca Sanborn, b. in Sandown, April 27, 1804, a daughter of Jonathan Collins Sanborn, who was b. in Sandown,

MRS. ELIZA S. ORDWAY.   NO. 466.

Feb. 24, 1765, and d. there, Dec. 27, 1840, who married
Molly Hunkins, Dec. 29, 1790, who was b. in Sandown in

1769, and who d. April 25, 1852. Rebecca married Enos
Colby, Aug. 31, 1826, who was b. in South Danville, Aug.
20, 1802, and who d. in West Hampstead, Feb. 21, 1855.
Mr. and Mrs. Colby kept an old-fashioned hostelry at West
Hampstead, the house later purchased by Mr. William Fellows and his son-in-law, Edson S. Pressey. They had the
honor of entertaining many prominent people of the day,
among them the governors of New Hampshire, and many
times Daniel Webster, on his trips to this part of the State.
Mrs. Colby is said to have possessed a very retiring disposition, yet was a great worker in all directions, and her remarkable skill as a cook made the house of Colby famous to
the travelling public. She was admitted to the church by
baptism, Sept. 3, 1865, and d. in Hampstead, Aug. 11, 1878.
They had children, b. in Hampstead :—

I.   Mary Ann (No. 479).
II.   Clarissa Ayer, b. Nov. 17, 1820; m. Rufus G. Morrill. They had
      a daughter :—
           1. Ellen F., m. Curtis Leavitt, and d. Jan. 12, 1900.
III. Annette, b. July 1, 1833; mar. William Kershaw of Lawrence,
      Mass. They had children :—
           1. Nellie, mar. William Kershaw (deceased).
           2. Eva, mar. C. W. Whittier, of Broadway, Lawrence.
IV.   Julia Ann, b. Aug. 3, 1838; mar. Mason Hall (deceased).
V.   Emily Maria, b. Sept. 20, 1840; d. Aug. 17, 1841.
VI.   Emma Frances, b. Jan. 13, 1846; m. John T. Little (No. 605); d.
      in Hampstead, April 16, 1894. Their son, Arthur H., mar.
      Ruth A. Emerson (No. 680).

No. 468.

Adeline Harriman, b. in Hampstead, Feb. 23, 1818, a
daughter of Moses and Sally (Ayer) Harriman (No. 341).
She married Dr. Joseph Eastman, Feb. 3, 1841, who was b.
in London, Jan. 29, 1814, a son of Dr. Joseph and Miriam
(Calef) Eastman. He d. in Candia, May 2, 1853. Dr.
Eastman was a student of medicine with his brother, Dr.
Josiah C. Eastman of Hampstead, and later attended lectures

at Dartmouth Medical College, and settled for practice in Candia about 1840. In 1846 ill health compelled him to sell his practice to Dr. Richard Page of Atkinson, whose son, Frank E. Page, now occupies the late Eastman homestead in Candia. Adeline Eastman was admitted to the church by baptism, Sept. 3, 1865, and died Nov. 22, 1865, aged 47 years, 9 months, and was buried in Hampstead. Their children were :—

I.   Frank Scott, b. Dec. 28, 1841; mar. Susan Brown of Haverhill, July, 1875.
II.   Helen Ayer, b. June 23, 1844; mar. Elmer S. Harris of Hampstead, now of Worcester, Mass., Dec. 28, 1871. Their son :—
        1. Elmer Eastman, b. Feb. 26, 1874; student in Harvard College.
III. Ann Bremer, b. Aug. 13, 1846; d. Oct. 2, 1848.

No. 469.

Juliette Harris, b. in Haverhill, Mass., Dec. 28, 1828, a daughter of Stephen Harris, son of Hubbard Harris, of Canaan, and his wife, Mary Jane Colby, of Haverhill.   Mr. and Mrs. Harris resided in Hampstead about fifteen years, where Sylvester Ayer now lives, on the " old Harriman farm," and were constant attendants of the church in Hampstead for some years.   They later moved to Hanover, where they both died.   They had children, b. in Haverhill :—

I.   Julia E. (above); mar., first, Ralph Harris Haseltine, of West Haverhill, Mass., and had daughters :—
        1. Mary Ida, b. Sept. 9, 1852; mar. Fred W. Noyes of Atkinson. They have no children, and reside in Melrose, Mass.
        2. Emma Harris, b. in 1853; mar., first, Herbert W. Clark of Hampstead, and has daughters :—1, Eva M., mar. David Bailey (see p. 366, Vol. 1). 2, Marion, d. young. She married, second, Lorenzo Frost, of Haverhill, Mass., where they now reside.
      Julia E. married, second, William O. Little, May 4, 1856 (see Nos. 369, 370). They had children :—
        3. Orrie Belle (No. 587).
        4. Alice M. (No. 585).

She was admitted to the church by baptism, Sept. 3, 1865, and d. in Hampstead, Sept. 27, 1875, and was buried in the village cemetery. She was for several years a prominent leader in the church music.

II.   Emily Jane, mar. Elbridge G. Greenough of Atkinson, and had a daughter, Amy, who d. young; she mar., second, her sister's husband, William C. Little, April 25, 1878, and d. in Haverhill in 1890. She was a graduate of the College of Physicians and Surgeons, in Boston, and practised medicine in Hampstead and Haverhill for some years.

III.   Leander, m., first, Emily J. Hunt, and had two daughters :—

    1. Annie S., mar. George H. Levia, b. in Georgetown, Mass. Their children : 1, Edgar H., b. in Haverhill, Mass., March 31, 1881. 2, Louis W., b. in Haverhill, Mass., Feb. 8, 1884. 3, Mabel A., b. June 29, 1885.

    2. Josie H., m. Alphonso B. Ladd, b. in Deerfield, now residing in Hampton Falls. Their children : 1, Perley E., b. in Haverhill, May 15, 1885. 2, Walter A., b. in Hampton Falls, Aug. 28, 1887.

  He married, second, Lizzie Colby, his cousin, of Haverhill. They reside in Hampton Falls.

IV.   Margaret, mar. Edward Tozier of Haverhill, and had child— Ned H., a druggist, of Haverhill and Elmer.

V.   Joseph K., mar. Clara Sargent of Enfield. Have children— Hayden, organist at Center church, and Disa. He has for many years been connected with church choirs in Haverhill.

VI.   Elmer S., mar. Helen A. Eastman (see No. 408).

VII.   Henry H., mar. Lois Leavett of Hanover, where they now reside and have children.

VIII.   George W., d. in the civil war,

And other children that d. young.

No. 470.

Lucy Ann Farwell, b. June 14, 1829, in West Bethel, Me., daughter of Melvin and Anna Farwell of Londonderry. She married, first, —— Anderson, of Londonderry, by whom she had four children, two now living. She married, second, Horace Adams of Hampstead (p. 378, Vol. 1). She was admitted to the church by letter from the Presbyterian church in Londonderry, Oct. 3, 1865. She is a present member. Children, by second husband : Charles F. (chairman selectmen of Hampstead, 1902), m. Ella F. Page ; George H., d. 1900 ; and Lucy J., d. young.   Mr. Adams d. April 10, 1903.

No. 471.

Isaac William George, b. in Hampstead, Sept. 12, 1831, a son of Dudley and Betsey (Ordway) George (Nos. 879, 380, 144, 145). He married Mary G. Emerson (No. 487). He was admitted to the church Nov. 5, 1865, and d. in Hampstead, Aug. 11, 1901. His funeral was attended by Rev. R. P. Gardner, and he was buried in the village cemetery. He lived on the land purchased of Ebenezer Kezar in 1752 by the George family, in the West village.

No. 472.

Charles Warren George, b. in Hampstead, August, 1845, a son of Warren D. and Sarah Tucker (Griffin) George, of West Hampstead (see No. 380). He married, first, Juliette B. Batchelder (No. 477), and had four children. He married, second, —— ——, and resides in West Hampstead, on the old George homestead (see No. 471). He was admitted to the church Nov. 5, 1865, and was dis. and rec. to the Grace M. E. Church, at Haverhill, March 3, 1882.

No. 473.

Annie Elizabeth George, b. in Hampstead, Aug. 31, 1848, a daughter of Warren D. and Sarah T. (Griffin) George (No. 380). She was educated in the public schools and at Pinkerton Academy, Derry, and has been a successful teacher for more than thirty years, at present a teacher in Boston (see p. 364, Vol. 1). She was admitted to the church Nov. 5, 1865.

No. 474.

George Henry Titcomb, b. in Gloucester, Mass., a son of Beniah and Mary Elizabeth (Stacy) Titcomb of Gloucester (see No. 451). He married Mary Alma, daughter of Charles

H. Osgood, of Hampstead (see p. 354, Vol. 1). He was admitted to the church Nov. 5, 1865, and dismissed Feb. 26, 1886. They reside at West Hampstead. They have a son, George Mahlon, b. Dec. 19, 1883; graduate H. H. S., class 1900.

JONA. C. LITTLE.   NO. 475.

No. 475.

Jona. Carlton Little, b. in Hampstead, Aug. 19, 1847, a son of Nathaniel H. and Almira (Tewksbury) Little (see Nos. 167, 227). He married Lucy Ann Sawyer, July 26, 1870, who was b. in Boston, Mass. He was a cooper by trade. He was admitted to the church Nov. 5, 1865. As

a young man he always took a great interest in everything
that would further the work for good in every department
of the church. In the Sabbath school in which he was a
teacher, he was beloved by the little children of his class,
and left loving messages to them in his last hours. For the
older members he was always thoughtful, and ready to step
aside to give a welcome. He was chosen leader of the choir
in 1868, and held the place as long as he lived. His father
had been chorister many years before. John C. Little was a
noble-hearted, Christian man. It has been said by a friend,
" It was John C. Little's life that led me in the right way."
Truly " His works do follow him." He died at the home of
his brother, in Atkinson, March 5, 1874.

No. 476.

Clara Ann Irving, b. in Hampstead, March 22, 1848, a
daughter of Jacob and Sarah W. (Jaques) Irving (Nos.
283, 278). She married James A. Davis of Sandown (see
No. 737). She was admitted to the church Nov. 5, 1865, and
resides at West Hampstead. A present member.

No. 477.

Juliette Bond Batchelder, b. in Derry, Jan. 20, 1850, a
daughter of Albert A., son of David and Sarah (Abbott)
Batchelder, of Raymond, and his wife Clarissa, daughter of
Daniel Tappan, son of —— Bond and Ann Hilton (of Eng-
land), grandson of John and Juda (Dow) Bond (Nos. 55, 56).
Albert and Clarissa (Bond) Batchelder had daughters :—

I.   Annie, mar. Willard F. Williams of Hampstead (see p. 377, Vol.
       1), whose only son, Walter, is at present stationed at Fort
       Warren, in the U. S. army.
II.   Juliette B., married Charles W. George (No. 472), and d. in
       Haverhill, Mass., Jan. 24, 1897. She was admitted to the
       church Nov. 5, 1865. Dis. and rec. to unite with the Grace
       M. E. Church at Haverhill, March 30, 1882. They had chil-
       dren, all of whom reside in Haverhill :—

1. Arthur Phillips, b. Oct. 18, 1868; a physician. (See p. 364, Vol. 1.)
2. Forrest Leighton, b. July 20, 1871; d. Feb. 18, 1872.
3. Allison Eugene, b. Oct. 30, 1872.
4. Alice Marion, b. Jan. 11, 1878; a teacher in the Currier School.

MRS. DAVIS. NO. 476.

No. 478.

Anna R. Bartlett, b. in Hampstead, Oct. 6, 1817, a daughter of John, Jr., and Mary (Morrill) Bartlett of Hampstead. She mar. Ithamar Eaton, and d. in Hampstead, April 2, 1887, and was buried in the village cemetery. She was adm. to the church Nov. 5, 1865. They had an only child :—

I. "Edwina M., b. April, 1848; mar. Charles W. Peasley, who d.
in Hampstead, "March 27, 1881, aged 40 years." (Cemetery
inscription). She d. April 26, 1869, aged 21; both buried in
the village cemetery. In a letter dated Nov., 1856, from
Lucinda Peasley, the mother of Charles W., says, "I am now
living in South Paris, Me., where I moved two weeks ago
from Buffalo, N. Y. I mar. Mr. Peasley in March last.
Charles is my oldest son, b. in Lowell, Mass., March, 1843.
I have two other sons, for whom I have found good homes
in Paris, Me. My first husband was Thomas L. Walker, and
was the father of my children. I put my son Charles out to
live in the family of Mr. Benjamin Sargent, in Hampstead,
when he was ten years old. His name is Charles Walker, not
Charles W. Peasley."

No. 479.

Mary Ann Colby, b. in Hampstead, Sept. 17, 1828, a
daughter of Enos and Rebecca (Sanborn) Colby (No. 467).
She mar. George Whitefield Eastman, in Derry, N. H., July
4, 1848 (see No. 848 and 349). He d. in Derry, April 18,
1880. She was adm. to the church Nov. 5, 1865. She was
"dis. and rec. to unite with the Second Congregational
Church in Exeter, under Rev. Dr. Street's pastoral care, Nov.
28, 1889." They had children, b. in Derry.

I.   Harriet Ella, b. July 24, 1853; d. March 18, 1855.
II.   Frank Hurbert, b. Sept. 5, 1856; d. Oct. 6, 1856.
III. Mary Etta, b. Oct. 9, 1857; d. Jan. 16, 1858.
IV.   Laurietta Ada, b. Dec. 3, 1858; graduated P. A., Derry; mar.
      George W. Libby of Nottingham, Dec. 25, 1879. They reside
      in Melrose, Mass., and have children.
      1. George Eastman, b. Nov. 17, 1881; a student in Institute
          of Technology.
      2. Harold Moses, b. May 30, 1886.

Mr. and Mrs. Eastman were members of the choir
for many years, and constant attendants at the church,
not missing a Sunday for a year at a time. Mr. E.
was chorister fourteen years, and connected with the
Hampstead Musical Society, thirty-one years. Mrs. E. pos-

sessed a fine alto voice, and upon one occasion, was soloist at a cantata, which embraced the best singers in four towns.

After the death of Mr. E., she removed to Haverhill, Mass., for a time, then removed to Exeter, where she resided the remainder of her life. She was an active member of the Second Congregational Church until her death, April 12, 1895. Her remains were interred in the old family lot in Hampstead Center.

No. 480.

Sarah Stanwood Flanders, b. in East Hampstead, July 15, 1828, a daughter of Thomas and Mrs. Harriette Sawyer (Horton) Flanders of Hampstead. She married David L. N. Hoyt of Hampstead, Feb. 4, 1849, and was a life long resident of Hampstead. She united with the Congregational Church Nov. 5, 1865, and a member of the home department since its organization. She was a patient sufferer for more than twenty years, and from a dislocated hip for many months, the last seven not able to leave her bed; d. May 8, 1902. Her funeral was attended by Rev. W. H. Woodsum.

Their only child, Caroline Estelle, b. Oct. 26, 1856; d. Mar. 3, 1864.

No. 481.

Sarah Maria Noyes, b. in Deering, March 9, 1834, a daughter of Parker and Dorcas (McCoy) Noyes of Atkinson. She mar. Samuel Johnson of Boston, Dec. 6, 1854, at Haverhill, Mass. She was adm. to the church Nov. 5, 1865, and was dismissed Jan. 4, 1883. They had children:—

I.   Ella F., b. in Atkinson, Nov. 11, 1856; mar. James C. Merrill of North Parish, Haverhill, and have children.

        1. Lucy Carlton, b. Aug. 5, 1878, educated at Atkinson Academy, and Miss Wheeler's private school; m. John Greenleaf Howe of Flint, Mich., June, 1900. A daughter, Madeline Frances, b. Dec. 14, 1902.

2. Ann Wainwright Cushing, b. Aug. 13, 1880, attended
    private school, and Wheaton Seminary. Graduated
    from the Bradford Seminary, in 1901; teacher in the
    public schools of Plaistow.
3. James Cushing, Jr., b. Nov. 5, 1881; Durham Agricul-
    tural College.
4. Giles Watson, b. May 11, 1883; Atkinson Academy
    student.

II.   James, b. in Atkinson, June 3, 1858; d. March 9, 1859.
III.   George A., b. in Salem, Nov. 5, 1859; m. Alice M. Howard. He
       resides in Epping.
IV.   Mary C., b. in Hampstead, Dec. 29, 1867; mar. George W. Berry.
       She d. in Amesbury, Mass., Mar., 1903, leaving a daughter.
       1. Annie Elizabeth, b. April, 1893.
V.   Samuel Gilbert, b. in Hampstead, March 11, 1872; m. Viola Eva
       Coburn; resides in Amesbury.

No. 482.

Hannah Eliza Irving, b. in Hampstead, July 28, 1841,
a daughter of Jacob and Sarah W. (Jaques) Irving
(Nos. 288, 278). She mar. John S. Titcomb (No. 481).
She was adm. to the church Nov. 5, 1865, and later united
with the Center Congregational Church of Haverhill, Mass.,
of which she is a present member. They had children:—

I.   Charles Stacy, bapt. in Hampstead, Sept., 1866; m. Aug. 27,
      1902, Marion E., daughter of Mr. and Mrs. Arthur E. Hoyt
      of Atkinson Depot. He is cashier of the Second National
      Bank of Haverhill.
II.   Henry Irving, b. Dec. 9, 1871; d. Aug. 15, 1888.
III. Sarah Woodman, at home in Haverhill.

No. 483.

Ellen Angeline George, b. in Hampstead, Jan., 1848, a
daughter of Warren D. and Sarah T. (Griffin) George (see
379, 380). She mar. Samuel James Hersum, and died in
West Hampstead, April 7, 1869, and was buried in the village cemetery. She was adm. to the church Nov. 5, 1865.
They had children:—Infant son, d. May 22, 1861, aged 4
mos., and Samuel, who now resides in Haverhill.

No. 484.

Mary Susan Kent, b. in Hampstead, in 1838, a daughter of Abner Kimball and Lydia Gordon (Taylor) Kent of Hampstead (see No. 254). She mar. Elbridge M. Clark of

MRS. SAWYER. NO. 486.

Methuen, for his second wife. She was adm. to the church Nov. 5, 1865, and was dis. at her own request, April 14, 1878, died in Methuen, Mass., Jan. 22, 1892. No children.

No. 485.

Elizabeth Gibbon Little, b. in Hampstead, Feb. 17, 1848, a daughter of Linus L. C. and Abiah F. (Tewksbury) Little (No. 302). She mar. Samuel S. Corliss of Haverhill, Mass., Jan. 18, 1874, where they now reside. She was adm. to the church Nov. 5, 1865, and was given a letter of dismissal, July 2, 1896. (See photos of Mr. and Mrs. Little, Vol. 1.)

No. 486.

Almira Webster Bailey, b. in Salem, March 11, 1840, a daughter of Moores and Ann (Webster) Bailey of Salem. She mar. Horace R. Sawyer (No. 529), August 20, 1862. " She was adm. to the church by letter from the Congregational Church in Salem, Jan. 5, 1866, and was dis. to unite with the Riverside Congregational Church in Haverhill, Mass., June 28, 1895," of which she is a present member. They had children :—

I.   Clarence L., b. May 25, 1866; m. Annie Graham (No. 643).
II.   Annie L. (No. 690).
III.   Edward G., b. March 10, 1870; m. Annie Hooper; resides in Haverhill; no children.

No. 487.

Mary G. Emerson, b. in Chester,   She mar. I. W. George (No. 471). She was adm. to the church March 4, 1866, and "asked for dismissal to the North Church in Haverhill, Mass., Jan. 2, 1875."

No. 488.

Frank Henry Little, b. in Hampstead, Oct. 18, 1843, the eldest son of Nathaniel Hale and Almira (Tewksbury) Little (see No. 255, 256). He served in the 11th N. H. Reg. three years in the civil war, and was discharged as first sergeant. He was a carpenter by trade ; resided several years in Danvers Centre, Mass. He was adm. to the church Nov. 5, 1865.

Dis. and rec. to unite with the Congregational Church in Atkinson, April 27, 1876. He mar. Helen Matilda, daughter of John and Matilda (Atwood) of Atkinson, May 6, 1869. He d. in Danvers, Mass. Sept. 5, 1891. Rev. Harry C. Adams, his pastor in Danvers, attended the funeral,

FRANK H. LITTLE. NO. 488.

which was under the charge of the G. A. R. About fifty of the comrades, with as many members of the Relief Corps, and many Sons of Veterans attended. Ward Post No. 90, G. A. R. adopted the following resolutions at his death.

"Again the angel of death has taken one of our members, this time from among those comparatively young, one who was active and hopeful for our future life as a Post, and one on whom we had gladly placed the rank of senior vice commander. With saddened hearts we commemorate his virtues, therefore, be it

Resolved, That in the death of our senior vice commander, we have lost a true friend and comrade, the faithful soldier, the active worker, the good and upright neighbor. We tender to the family of the deceased, our sympathy in this hour of grief, and pray for heaven's blessing upon his wife and children. Their grief is our burden, and we will do all in our power to help and comfort them.

Reminded by our loss that we must work while it is day, we will renew our efforts for the best interest of our Post, remembering the sick, and gladly ministering to their needs with a soldier's zeal and kindness, awaiting the summons that must come to us all, in humble trust in God, our Father, who doeth all things well.

Resolved, that this minute be placed upon our records, and a copy be sent to the family of our late worthy and respected comrade, Frank H. Little. George J. Sanger. W. W. Eaton, and William T. Damon."

His friends were many, as they found him always the same kind man, with a cheerful word for all. He always looked on the bright side, and even when near his end of life would always say, "I shall be better in a few days."

Mr. and Mrs. Little had children :—

I.   Ernest Hale, b. April 18, 1870; m. Mabelle Blackmore of Lynn, Nov. 11, 1894; is an engineer on the B. & M. R. R.
II.   Frank Weston, b. Aug. 26, 1872; is a carpenter, unmarried.
III.   Helen Josephine, b. Nov. 3, 1873; d. July 21, 1897.
IV.   Jonathan Carlton, b. June 29, 1875; d. Aug. 18, 1875.
V.   George Henry, b. Nov. 28, 1876; d. Aug. 29, 1877.
VI.   Emma Louisa, b. March 24, 1878.
VII.   Mary Elizabeth, b. June 30, 1880.
VIII.   Harriet Atwood, b. Dec. 23, 1882; m. Herbert M. Flint of Danvers, Oct. 16, 1901.
IX.   Henry Curtis, b. Feb. 12, 1885.
X.   Minnie Almira, b. Oct. 13, 1886.
XI.   Jay Carlton, b. July 22, 1891; d. Feb. 16, 1893.

No. 489.

Dianna H. Pillsbury, b. in Hanover, Nov. 21, 1800, a daughter of Samuel and Mary (Currier) Pillsbury. Her parents, after the Revolutionary war, settled in Sandown one year, and moved to Hanover, where they resided fifteen years, then returned to Sandown, where the father died, May 4, 1857. He was an officer in the town, as town clerk, selectman many years, auditor, and justice of the peace. She was admitted to the church July 7, 1867, and d., unmarried, in Sandown, Aug. 15, 1884, at the old Pillsbury homestead, and was buried in Sandown.

No. 490.

Martha Hutchens Gordon, b. in Landaff, Nov. 26, 1839, a daughter of George W. and Mary Ann (Sargent) Gordon, of Landaff. She married Caleb W. Williams (No. 515), Sept. 4, 1859, at Landaff. She was admitted to the church July 7, 1867, and d. in Hampstead, Nov. 27, 1890. Burial was in the " Eastman cemetery." " A true and worthy wife and mother." They had children :—

I.   George G. (No. 553).
II.   Nellie R. (No. 581).
III.   Mary A. (No. 575).
IV.   Fannie B. (No. 642).
V.   Lester A. (No. 689).

No. 491.

Albert Robinson, b. in Johnson, Vt., April 11, 1804, son of John and Lydia (Heath) Robinson, of Johnson. He resided on the Bailey homestead in Windham, ten years, then moved to Methuen in 1848, where he was a butcher and dealer in sheep and cattle. May, 1853, moved to Lawrence, and to Hampstead in 1866. He married Phebe Bailey (No. 492). " He was admitted to the church Dec. 29, 1867, by letter from the M. E. Church in Lawrence, Mass., and was dismissed to unite with the Center church in Haverhill, under the care of Rev. Mr. Hyde, March 17, 1872." He d. Feb. 17, 1883, and was buried in Pine Grove cemetery in Salem.

MRS. WILLIAMS. NO. 490.

No. 492.

Phebe Bailey, b. in Haverhill, Mass., April 17, 1801, daughter of Woodbridge and Abigail (Lowell) Bailey of West Haverhill. She married Albert Robinson (No. 491), May 6, 1823, and was admitted to the church by letter from

the M. E. Church in Lawrence, Mass., Dec. 29, 1867, and
was dis. to unite with the Center church in Haverhill, March
17, 1872. She d. Aug. 31, 1888, and was buried in Pine
Grove cemetery, Haverhill.   They had children :—

I.   Ezra Albert, b. April 13, 1831; d., unmarried, March, 1877; bur-
      ied in Pine Grove cemetery.
II.   Harriet A. (No. 493).
III. Calvin Brewster, b. Jan. 8, 1837; m. Mary E. Pettengill (No.
      496).
IV.   Harlin Milton, b. 1847; d. 1851.

No. 493.

Harriet Ann Robinson, b. in Haverhill, Mass., March 19,
1832, a daughter of Albert and Phebe (Bailey) Robinson
(Nos. 491, 492). She married Richard Lake of Fall River,
Mass., and d. Feb. 3, 1899. They had no children. She was
admitted to the church by letter from the M. E. Church in
Lawrence, Mass., Dec. 29, 1867, and was dis. to unite with
the Center Church in Haverhill, March 17, 1872.

No. 494.

Abigail Clarke, b. in Plaistow, April 5, 1795, a daughter
of Nathaniel and Abigail (Woodman) Clarke of Plaistow.
She married, first, her double cousin, David, son of David
and Anna (Woodman) Clarke, of Sandown, October, 1817.
They had children :—

I.   Elizabeth Abby, b. May 14, 1819; m. George W. Worthen of
      Lowell, Mass., and had daughters : Frances Abby, m. Chas.
      H. Burbank; Susan, d. young; Elizabeth Clarke, d. young;
      and Janet Wright.
II.   John, b. April 4, 1822; d. young.
III. Nathaniel, b. May 10, 1823; d. young.
IV.   David (twin to above); d. young.
V.   Susan Moody, b. June 20, 1824; d. young.
VI.   David, b. Feb. 29, 1828; d. May 2, 1859. "He was educated in
      the public schools of Lowell and Nashua. Learned the
      printer's trade of Hon. Albin Beard, editor of the Nashua
      Telegraph, and later studied the management of steam ma-

chinery, and took charge of a large sugar plantation in Cuba
for several years, where he contracted consumption. In the
spring of 1859 he returned to Lowell and died. Judge Smith
referred to him as a young man of much promise and noble
qualities."

David Clarke died Nov. 24, 1834, and the widow, Abigail,
married, second, Maj. Isaac Smith, of Hampstead, March 20,
1867, as his third wife (see Nos. 318, 198). " She was adm.
to the church by letter from the Kirk Street Church in Lowell, Jan. 8, 1868, and was dis. to the same church Dec. 15,
1869." She died Aug. 27, 1879.

No. 495.

Mary Clarke Smith, b. in Hampstead, Sept. 16, 1823, a
daughter of Isaac and Mary (Clarke) Smith (Nos. 198, 318).
She married James Brickett, Jr., Sept. 3, 1853 (see Nos·
224, 225). She was admitted to the church by letter from
the church in Claremont, Feb. 28, 1868. She was organist
for the church for several years. She d. in Newmarket,
Aug. 27, 1879. They had no children.

No. 496.

Mary Elizabeth Pettengill, b. in Haverhill, Mass., in 1841,
a daughter of Dea. Isaac and Judith Bartlett (Coffin) Pettengill, of the West Parish of Haverhill. She married Calvin B. Robinson (see No. 492), May 26, 1864. She "was
admitted to the church by letter from the West Haverhill
Congregational Church, July 2, 1869, and was dismissed to
unite with the Center Church in Haverhill, under Rev. Mr.
Hyde, March 17, 1872." At present is a member of the
Congregational Church of Merrimac, Mass. Mr. Robinson
became a member April, 1877. He d. Feb., 1903. They
had no children.

No. 497.

Mary Morrison Shirley, b. in Chester, Nov. 29, 1823, a

daughter of John and Mary (Grimes) Shirley, of Chester. She married Jacob Irving, as his second wife (No. 283). "She was admitted to the church by letter from the Atkinson Congregational Church, Feb. 28, 1868. She died Feb. 18, 1903, and was buried in the village cemetery. Their children :—

REV. EBENEZER W. BULLARD. NO. 498.

I.   Hattie, b. Nov. 10, 1864; d. Jan. 27, 1874.
II.   Martha M. (No. 536).

No. 498.

Rev. Ebenezer W. Bullard, b. in Sutton, Mass., Nov. 9 1809, a son of Dr. Artemas and Lucy Ann (White) Bullard,

whose youngest daughter, Eunice, married Rev. Henry Ward
Beecher. Rev. Mr. Bullard prepared for college at the Boston Latin School, took a partial course at Amherst College,
and finished at Miami University, Ohio, where he also took
the theological course under Dr. Lyman Beecher. His first
pastorate was in Fitchburg, Mass., where he was settled
twenty years. His second was at Royalston, Mass., where
he lived eighteen years, and the last at Hampstead, where he
was installed Dec. 14, 1870, and was dismissed from that
pastorate Oct. 25, 1875, on account of ill health. He was
admitted to the church by letter from the church in Royalston, Mass., July 2, 1871, and was dismissed to the church
in Stockbridge, Mass., Nov. 6, 1875. He was twice married,
first to Margaret P. Smith, of Hadley, Mass. They had no
children. He married, second, Harriet N. Dickinson (No.
499). He died at the home of his daughter (Mrs. Bullock),
in Kilbuck, N. Y., Feb. 4, 1898, and was buried in the family lot in Laurel Hill cemetery, in Fitchburg, Mass.

No. 499.

Harriet Newell Dickinson, b. in Hadley, Mass., March 5,
1818, a daughter of William and Dorothy (Warner) Dickinson, of Hadley. She married Rev. Ebenezer W. Bullard
(No. 498), and d. Oct. 4, 1883. She was admitted to the
church by letter from the Congregational Church in Royalston, Mass., July 2, 1871, and was dismissed to unite with
the Congregational Church in Stockbridge, Mass., Nov. 6,
1875. They had five children :—

I.   Harriet M. (Bullock.)
II.   Caroline (Hoffman), of Stockbridge, Mass.
III. Lucy Ann (No. 500).
IV.   Dr. William E. (No. 501).
V.   Edward Dickinson, of San Francisco, Cal.

Mrs. Bullock writes: "My recollections of my father's
home in Hampstead are most pleasant. We were all very

happy there. Then sorrow had not entered our circle. My own dear little Margaret was born there. She lived only eighteen years. Ellen Hassel, a little girl with my mother in Hampstead, is now with me. She has been a firm and cherished friend and helper all these years."

MRS. BULLARD. NO. 499.

No. 500.

Lucy Ann Bullard, b. in Fitchburg, Mass., Aug. 31, 1849, a daughter of Rev. E. W. and Harriet N. (Dickinson) Bullard (Nos. 498 and 499). She was admitted to the church from the Congregational Church in Royalston, Mass., July 2, 1871, and was dismissed to unite with the church in

Stockbridge, Mass., Nov. 4, 1875. She d. in Stockbridge, Oct. 8, 1877, unmarried.

No. 501.

Dr. William E. Bullard, b. in Fitchburg, Mass., Jan. 20, 1852, a son of Rev. E. W. and Harriet N (Dickinson) Bullard (Nos. 498, 499). He was graduated from Dartmouth Medical College in 1873, and College of Physicians and Surgeons in New York, in 1874. He practised medicine in New York city for a number of years, but at present is located at Larchmont, on Long Island Sound, in the summer, and at Nassau, Bahama Island, as physician to the Flagler Hotels, in the winter. He married Fanny Atwood Higgins, of New York, and has no children. He was admitted to the church by letter from the Congregational Church in Royalston, Mass., July 2, 1871. He was for several years a deacon in the Fourth Avenue Presbyterian Church of New York city.

No. 502.

Elizabeth C. Wadleigh, b. in Kingston in 1844, a daughter of Daniel Wadleigh, who was b. in Kingston, Aug. 14, 1793, a son of Daniel and Polly (Bartlett) Wadleigh. He was a blacksmith and farmer, as was his father. " A strong, resolute, and vigorous man." He held the commission of captain in the Light Infantry, and took great interest in soldiery. He was always called " Capt. Daniel." He d. July 31, 1862. Her mother, Sally, daughter of John and Betsey (Kimball) Davis, of Kingston, was a woman of more than ordinary executive ability, and, as a widow, twenty years managed the farm and educated their children, Lizzie (above), and Daniel, who resided on the old Wadleigh homestead in Kingston, until he went to Kansas, where he is now extensively engaged in lumbering and business. Elizabeth C. was educated at Kingston and Sanbornton Academies, and was a successful teacher for several years. She married William H. Davis (No. 437), as his first wife. She was admitted to the church by letter from the Congregational Church in Kingston, July 2, 1871, and d. in Hampstead, June 20, 1874, and was buried in Kingston. They had no children.

No. 503.

Sarah Ann Lowe, b. in New York city, March 31, 1830, a

MRS. ROWE. NO. 503.

daughter of John J. Lowe, a farmer, shoe manufacturer, and storekeeper in Derry, and wife, Mary Parker Boynton, of Derry. Both died about thirty years ago in Derry. She married Benjamin Frank Rowe, in Lynn, Mass., Oct. 3, 1850, who was b. in Franklin, son of Joseph and Elizabeth (Wadleigh) Rowe. She was admitted to the church from the

Congregational Church in Derry, May 7, 1872, and is a
present member. They have children :—

I.   George Henry, b. in Derry, March 10, 1854; m. Marietta York;
        resides in Haverhill, Mass. Children :—
        1. Frank Elmer, b. May 3, 1886.
        2. Charles Ernest, b. June 26, 1889.
        3. George, b.   ; d. young.
        4. Edson Dewey, b. May 18, 1898.

II.   Ida Mary, b. Jan. 2, 1858, in Derry; m. Charles W. York; re-
        sides in Haverhill. Their daughter :—
        1. Alice Cleveland, b. Nov. 10, 1884.

III. Katie Bell, b. April 20, 1861; m. George A. Davis. Children:
        1. Charles Herbert, b. March 17, 1878; m. Florence B.
           Kenny, of Wolfboro, Oct. 16, 1901.
        2. Ethel May, b. July 29, 1881; d. young.

IV. John Gilbert, b. Nov. 26, 1867; m. Mary Ellen Favor; reside in
        Newton. They have children :—
        1. Edgar Cecil, b. June 10, 1900.
        2. Willis Merton, b. April 25, 1902.

No. 504.

Abigail Hale Jaques, b. in West Newbury, Mass., Feb. 17,
1805, a daughter of Moses and Hannah (Chase) Jaques, of
West Newbury (a sister to No. 278). She married Isaac
Morrill Heath, Oct. 20, 1829. They resided in Danbury
until about 1870, when they moved to Hampstead. She
was admitted to the church by letter from the church in
Danbury, Nov. 2, 1870. Mr. Heath d. in Hampstead,
July 20, 1871, and wife died Oct. 28, 1885. They had
no children.

No. 505.

Abbie Marilla Stevens, b. in Chester, Feb. 5, 1841, a
daughter of Calvin and Nancy (Coffin) Stevens (see No.
555). She was admitted to the church Nov. 3, 1872, and is
a present member.

No. 506.

Agnes Craig Millar, b. in Stonehouse, Scotland, daughter

of Gavin and Agnes (Shearer) Millar, of Stonehouse. She
was a member of the family of Mr. Nelson Ordway for several years, and was admitted to the church Nov. 2, 1872, by
letter from the church in Stonehouse, and is a present member.

No. 507.

Martha Elizabeth Marble, b. in Hampstead, Jan. 1, 1838,
a daughter of Giles O. and Martha B. (Peaslee) Marble (No.
412), (see p. 362, Vol. 1). She married, first, Lewis, son of
Davis and Mary (Sargent) Cass, of Danville, Dec. 8, 1858,
by whom she had one child:—

I.   Charles O. Cass (No. 574); m. Inez A. Wilson (No. 572).

She married, second, Thorndike P. Lake, and had children :

II.   George E. (No. 626).
III. Mary C. (No. 622); m. Charles H. Sweet (No. 634).
IV.   Helen P. (No. 646); m. Harry A. Tucker (No. 669).

She was admitted to the church Aug. 22, 1873, and was
dismissed to unite with the Free Will Baptist Church, in
Haverhill, Mass., July 26, 1900.

No. 508.

Lizzie Patten Sargent, b. in West Amesbury, Mass., May
9, 1841, a daughter of Orlando and Abigail (Patten) Sargent, of Merrimac. Her father was a deacon in the Congregational Church at Merrimac for several years, and was a
farmer. Both parents were buried in Merrimac. She married Alden Eaton Pillsbury, of Sandown, where they now
reside, and where Mr. Pillsbury is a farmer, has been a
member of the selectmen, member of the school board, collector of taxes, etc., in Sandown. Mrs. P. was admitted to
the church by letter from the church at Merrimac, Aug. 22,
1873, and is a present member. Their children :—

I.   Frank Newton, b.   ; m. Mary A. Cutter (No. 761).
II. Gertrude S. (No. 713).

No. 509.

Sarah Jane Hall, b. in Newburyport, Mass., Feb. 19, 1841, a daughter of Moses W. and Abigail (Hawkins) Hall. Her father was b. in Salem, and mother in Centre Harbor. She

MRS. BROWN. NO. 509.

married, first, Jesse Sweet Bean, of Windham, Aug. 7, 1858, and had one daughter:—

I.   Mary Jane, b. in Salem, March 17, 1860; m. Benj. W. Clark of Hampstead, Dec. 11, 1878 (see p. 374, Vol. 1). They have children, b. in Hampstead :—

1. Lillian Josephine, b. Oct. 6, 1879; m. Adin Everett Poor of Atkinson, and have Adin Eugene, b. Mar. 14, 1901, and Bernice Lillian, b. Mar. 18, 1903.
2. Ora Etta, b. Jan. 16, 1881.
3. Ida May, b. Oct. 24, 1883.
4. Charles Henry, b. Aug. 5, 1885.
5. Alice Mabel, b. April 6, 1888.
6. Emma Florence, b. March 12, 1890.
7. Annie Cora, b. April 28, 1891.
8. Esther Viola, b. April 2, 1892.
9. Walter Fred, b. Jan. 21, 1895.
10. Eugene George, b. Feb. 10, 1901.

She married, second, Joseph G. Brown (No. 528), July 13, 1866. She was admitted to the church July 2, 1874, and is a present member.

No. 510.

Mary Amanda Little, b. in Hampstead, July 9, 1836, a daughter of Linus L. C. and Abiah F. (Tewksbury) Little (No. 302). She married John W. Tabor (No. 618), April 12, 1857. She was admitted to the church Jan. 3, 1875, and is a present member. (See photos of Mr. Tabor and Mr. and Mrs. Little in Vol. 1.) They had children :—

I. Ida M. (No. 511).
II. Henry W., b. Sept. 9, 1860; m. Abbie M. Corsen (No. 624).
III. Mary E. (No. 556); m. W. Amos Fitts (No. 667).
IV. Edward Ellsworth, b. April 13, 1863; d. young.
V. Annie J. (No. 599).
VI. Fanny M. (No. 647).
VII. John Ellsworth, b. March 18, 1869; m. Laura A. Bailey; resides in Haverhill, Mass.
VIII. Ellery Edward, b. Jan. 16, 1873; m. Josephine F. Hyde (No. 722).

No. 511.

Ida May Tabor, b. in Hampstead, Oct. 2, 1858, a daughter of John W. (No. 618) and Mary A. (Little) Tabor (No. 510). She married Dwelly Elgin, son of George and Emeline (Buttrick) Simpson, a farmer in Pelham, Feb. 24,

1878. She was admitted to the church Jan. 3, 1875; dismissed to unite with the Congregational church in Pelham, April 27, 1881. They have an adopted daughter, Grace (Jones).

No. 512.

Melissa McNiel, b. in Haverhill, Mass., June 25, 1838, a daughter of Edmund and Abigail S. (Cronk) McNiel, of Atkinson, where both parents died. She married Leonard A. Marble (see No. 412), Dec. 25, 1866. He died in Hampstead, March 26, 1878, and was buried in Hampstead. They had children :—

I.   Mary Abbie, b. Dec. 14, 1869; m. Dr. John F. Jordan of Ward
      Hill, Haverhill, Mass. She was a school teacher several
      years. Their children are :—
          1. Esther Mary, b. Dec. 6, 1895.
          2. Mendell Franklin, b. Feb. 28, 1897.
          3. Arthur Cheever, b. Feb. 26, 1899.
          4. Agnes Melissa, b. Jan. 17, 1901.
II.   Leonard Eugene, b. May 29, 1873; m. Mary Edna Haseltine, who
      was a teacher for several years in Ayers Village, Haverhill.
III. William Oscar, b. March 9, 1876; unmarried; a civil engineer
      and draughtsman.

Mrs. Marble married, second, Orren Hall (No. 617), and now resides in Ayers village, of Haverhill. She was admitted to the church March 5, 1872, and was dismissed to unite with the Congregational Church at West Haverhill, June 28, 1894.

No. 513.

Emily Augusta Darling, b. in Haverhill, Mass., Aug. 15, 1840, a daughter of Leonard and Elizabeth (Dustin) Darling, who resided at what is now called the Williams, or Hurd, farm on North Main street, Haverhill. Elizabeth was in a direct line from Hannah Dustin, the Indian heroine. She married John W. Marble, son of Giles O. and Martha B. (Peaslee)

Marble (No. 412), (see p. 362, Vol. 1). She was admitted to the church March 5, 1878, and is a present member. They have children :—

I.   Edward G., m. Maggie ——; she died in 1901.   One son, Ralph.
II.   Fred D. (No. 658),
III. Walter J.

No. 514.

Sarah Ellen Irving, b. in Hampstead, May 12, 1843, a daughter of Jacob and Sarah W. (Jaques) Irving (Nos. 288, 278). She was educated in the public schools and Atkinson Academy. She was a teacher from 1860 to March, 1873, in the district schools of New Hampshire and in the schools of Haverhill and Bradford, Mass. She married William Shirley Cowdery, of North Andover, Mass., June, 1873, as his second wife, who died in 1891, in North Andover. She was admitted to the church March 5, 1872, and was dismissed to unite with the Trinitarian Church in North Andover, Sept. 17, 1873, and is a present member there. She resides in Haverhill, a widow (see p. 206, Vol. 1).

No. 515.

Caleb Washington Williams, b. in Plaistow, April 15, 1836, a son of Benjamin and Hannah (Rowell) Williams of Plaistow (see Nos. 77, 78). He married, first, Martha H. Gordon (No. 490). He married, second, Mrs. Rosazina Harriman, widow of Hiram Hadley; and, third, married Mrs. Mary E. (Johnson) Carter, widow of Tappan Carter, late of East Hampstead. They reside at the old Johnson homestead (see p. 381, Vol. 1, and Appendix to this volume, Williams). Mr. Williams was admitted to the church May 7, 1872, and elected deacon Aug. 31, 1872. He was dismissed to unite with the Center Church in Haverhill, Mass., Dec. 17, 1891, and again united with the Hampstead church April 20, 1893, and is a present member.

No. 516.

Margaret Bly Williams, b. in Plaistow, Nov. 20, 1839, a daughter of Benjamin and Hannah (Rowell) Williams (see Nos. 77, 78). She married, first, Silas M. Marshall, son of

CALEB W. WILLIAMS. NO. 515.

Caleb and Asenath (Morse) Marshall, of East Hampstead, in 1854, who d. March 17, 1865, in Washington, D. C. She was admitted to the church May 7, 1872, and dismissed March 1, 1883. They had children:—

L.   Charles Levi, b. Sept. 2, 1855; d. Feb., 1856.
II.   Silas William, b. May 18, 1857; d. Nov. 19, 1857.
III.   Rose Asenath, b. Jan. 22, 1859; m., Sept. 10, 1876, Hiram F., son
        of Nathan and Harriet Newell (Mason) Russell, of East Ha-
        verhill and Atkinson. She d. Feb. 4, 1882. They had chil-
        dren :—

    1. Lilla May, b. June 14, 1877; m. George A. Granton,
        Dec. 8, 1897, of Haverhill, Mass., and have chil-
        dren—Irina Nichols and Russell Alexander.
    2. Henry Milton, b. Sept. 28, 1879.
    3. Ada Lillian, b. May 12, 1881.

IV.   Silas Caleb, b. June 23, 1861, in Argyle, Me.; d. July 23, 1882,
        in Hampstead.
V.   Willie, b. Sept. 29, 1863; d. Dec. 24, 1864, in Hampstead.

Mrs. Marshall married, second, William P. Russell, of
Solon, Me., March 9, 1882. They reside in Bradford, Mass.

No. 517.

Belinda Gibson Atwood,ꞏ b. in Hampstead, Sept. 3, 1840,
a daughter of Amos and Mary C. (Mills) Atwood (see Nos.
532, 59 and 60). She married William Burnham Wilson.
She was admitted to the church May 7, 1875, and is a present member. They have children :—

I.   Inez A. (No. 572); m. Charles O. Cass (No. 574).
II.   Annie J. (No. 695).
III.   Will C. (No. 650).

No. 518.

Edwin Sydney Pressey, b. in Fremont, Nov. 12, 1856 (see
Nos. 557, 558). He was educated in the public and high
schools of Hampstead ; graduate Phillips Academy, Andover ; a graduate from Williams College in 1885; Union Theological College in New York, in 1888. His first pastorate
was in Brooklyn, N. Y. From there he went to Springfield,
Vt., August, 1890, and remained two years, until August,
1892. He was installed pastor of the Congregational church,
in Elmwood, Ill., December, 1892, and remained till November, 1896, when he went to St. Anthony Park, St. Paul,

Minn., where he is a faithful, earnest, Christian worker. He married Orrie Belle Little (No. 537), of Hampstead.

REV. ALBERT WATSON. NO. 519.

He was admitted to the church May 1, 1875, and was dismissed Oct. 26, 1875.

No. 519.

Rev. Albert Watson, b. in England, Aug. 3, 1845, a son of William and Ann (Lockhart) Watson. He married Mary A. Priestley (No. 520). He was admitted to the church by letter from the church in Albany, Vt., May 7,

MRS. WATSON. NO. 520.

1876. He was installed pastor in Hampstead, March 23, 1876, and continued until June 11, 1893. He was dismissed to unite with the Mystic Side Congregational Church, Everett, Mass., June 11, 1893. At present is pastor Pres. church, Windham, N. H.

No. 520.

Mary Miranda Priestley, b. in England, Jan. 12, 1845, a daughter of John and Priscilla (Hooson) Priestley. She married Rev. Albert Watson (No. 519). She was admitted to the church by letter from the church in Albany, Vt., May 7, 1876, and was dismissed to unite with the Mystic Side Congregational Church, Everett, Mass., Aug. 17, 1893. They have children :—

I.   John W. (No. 651).
II.   Mabel A. (No. 662).
III.   Albert P. (No. 671).

No. 521.

John Fernandez Brown, born at sea, on the Mediterranean, July 4, 1831, a son of Lt. Brown of the U. S. navy, and wife (Miss Moore), who d. at his birth. He was cared for during his childhood by Dea. Grant of Boston, and when of age removed to Haverhill, Mass., where he married Annie Smith (No. 522). He was admitted to the church by letter from the North Church in Haverhill, May 5, 1876, and was dismissed to unite with the Grace M. E. Church in Haverhill, May 29, 1884. He is a sole leather cutter by trade, and works in Haverhill. Homestead on the late Moody H. Brickett place in Hampstead.

No. 522.

Annie Smith, b. in Brentwood, June 23, 1834, daughter of Edward Tuck, son of John and Mercy (Tuck) Smith, of Brentwood, and his wife, Lavina G. Langley, b. in Gilford. She married John F. Brown (No. 521), in 1860. She was admitted to the church by letter from the North Church of Haverhill, May 5, 1876, and was dismissed to unite with the Grace M. E. Church in Haverhill, July 24, 1884. They have children :—

I.   Mabel Alice, b. in Haverhill, Sept. 1, 1861. At home.

II.   George Edward, b. Feb. 15, 1864; m. Lucy A. Nichols of North Salem, July 2, 1800. Children :—

MRS. EASTMAN. NO. 523.

1. George Ernest, b. in Salem, Oct. 5, 1891.
2. Edward Arthur, b. in Salem, Aug. 11, 1893.
3. Mildred Gertrude, b. in Haverhill, Nov. 27, 1895.

No. 523.

Mary Elizabeth Kent, b. in Hampstead, April 26, 1833, a daughter of Dea. Jonathan and Clarissa (Page) Kent (Nos.

ALBERT L. EASTMAN.   (SEE NO. 523.)

245, 246). She married, first, John D. Irving (see p. 350, Vol. 1, and No. 278). They had children :—

I.   Henry Albert, b. Oct. 8, 1863.

II.   Nabbe and Clara (twins), b. Aug. 11, 1865; both d. in infancy.

Mrs. Irving married, second, Albert L. Eastman (see Nos. 348, 349). She has served as president of the Ladies' Aid

JOHN H. CLARK. NO. 524.

Society many years, and is always ready to do more than "her part" in every department of the church work. She was admitted to membership July 1, 1876, and is a present member.

No. 524.

John Henry Clark, b. in Derry, Jan. 22, 1826, a son of
Joshua and Eliza (Spollett) Clark, of Derry. He married

MRS. CLARK. NO. 525.

Clara A. Kent (No. 525). He was admitted to the church
July 1, 1876, and d. in Hampstead, Feb. 16, 1900, and was
buried in the village cemetery.

No. 525.

Clarissa Ann Kent, b. in Hampstead, Dec. 8, 1826, a daughter of Dea. Jona. and Clarissa (Page) Kent (Nos. 245, 246). She married John H. Clark (No. 424). She was

MOSES B. LITTLE. NO. 526.

admitted to the church July 1, 1876, and is a present faithful worker. They had children:—

I.   Clarence L., d. young.
II. Mary E. (No. 547); m. John S. Corson (No. 546).
III. Frank, d. young.

No. 516.

Margaret Bly Williams, b. in Plaistow, Nov. 20, 1839, a daughter of Benjamin and Hannah (Rowell) Williams (see Nos. 77, 78). She married, first, Silas M. Marshall, son of

CALEB W. WILLIAMS. NO. 515.

Caleb and Asenath (Morse) Marshall, of East Hampstead, in 1854, who d. March 17, 1865, in Washington, D. C. She was admitted to the church May 7, 1872, and dismissed March 1, 1883. They had children:—

I.   Charles Levi, b. Sept. 2, 1855; d. Feb., 1856.
II.   Silas William, b. May 18, 1857; d. Nov. 19, 1857.
III.   Rose Asenath, b. Jan. 22, 1859; m., Sept. 10, 1876, Hiram F., son
        of Nathan and Harriet Newell (Mason) Russell, of East Ha-
        verhill and Atkinson. She d. Feb. 4, 1882. They had chil-
        dren :—
              1. Lilla May, b. June 14, 1877; m. George A. Granton,
                  Dec. 8, 1897, of Haverhill, Mass., and have chil-
                  dren—Irina Nichols and Russell Alexander.
              2. Henry Milton, b. Sept. 28, 1879.
              3. Ada Lillian, b. May 12, 1881.
IV.   Silas Caleb, b. June 23, 1861, in Argyle, Me.; d. July 23, 1882,
        in Hampstead.
V.   Willie, b. Sept. 29, 1863; d. Dec. 24, 1864, in Hampstead.

Mrs. Marshall married, second, William P: Russell, of
Solon, Me., March 9, 1882. They reside in Bradford, Mass.

No. 517.

Belinda Gibson Atwood,' b. in Hampstead, Sept. 3, 1840,
a daughter of Amos and Mary C. (Mills) Atwood (see Nos.
532, 59 and 60). She married William Burnham Wilson.
She was admitted to the church May 7, 1875, and is a present member. They have children :—

I.   Inez A. (No. 572); m. Charles O. Cass (No. 574).
II.   Annie J. (No. 695).
III.   Will C. (No. 650).

No. 518.

Edwin Sydney Pressey, b. in Fremont, Nov. 12, 1856 (see
Nos. 557, 558). He was educated in the public and high
schools of Hampstead ; graduate Phillips Academy, Andover ; a graduate from Williams College in 1885 ; Union Theological College in New York, in 1888. His first pastorate
was in Brooklyn, N. Y. From there he went to Springfield,
Vt., August, 1890, and remained two years, until August,
1892. He was installed pastor of the Congregational church,
in Elmwood, Ill., December, 1892, and remained till November, 1896, when he went to St. Anthony Park, St. Paul,

No. 524.

John Henry Clark, b. in Derry, Jan. 22, 1826, a son of Joshua and Eliza (Spollett) Clark, of Derry. He married

MRS. CLARK. NO. 525.

Clara A. Kent (No. 525). He was admitted to the church July 1, 1876, and d. in Hampstead, Feb. 16, 1900, and was buried in the village cemetery.

No. 531.

Nellie Rose Williams, b. in Bath, Jan. 31, 1862, a daughter of Dea. Caleb W. and Martha H. (Gordon) Williams (Nos. 515, 490). She married Charles A. Trow of Haverhill, Mass., Oct. 14, 1897, where she has been, for several years, connected with shoes as forelady or stitcher. She was educated in the public schools of Hampstead, and was a teacher for a time. She is a present member of the church, having been admitted July 1, 1876. She has no children.

No. 532.

Mary Caldwell Mills, b. in Dunbarton, Sept. 8, 1821, a daughter of Amos Mills, who was a son of Reuben, son of James (Nos. 59, 60), and his wife, Betsey Mills, daughter of Thomas, and son of Thomas, who was a son of Nos. 59 and 60. Her grandfather, Thomas Mills, was a lieutenant in the Revolutionary army, and one of the first settlers of Dunbarton, in 1751. She married Amos, son of James and Molly (Lowell) Atwood (No. 76), Sept. 29, 1839, who d. in 1899. Mrs. Atwood united with the church by letter from the M. E. Church at West Hampstead, July 1, 1876, and is a present member. They had children :—

I.   Belinda G. (No. 517).
II. Charles Edwin, b. Nov. 1, 1842.

No. 533.

William Alonzo Emerson, b. in Hampstead, Sept. 7, 1842, a son of Daniel and Ruth (Corner) Emerson (No. 343). He married Abbie H. Dow (No. 534). He is a shoe manufacturer. He was admitted to the church Sept. 8, 1876, and is a present member (see p. 868, Vol. 1, and photos Vol. 1).

No. 534.

Abbie Hannah Dow, b. in Atkinson, Aug. 26, 1844, a daughter of Francis Vose Dow of Atkinson, and wife, Me-

No. 524.

John Henry Clark, b. in Derry, Jan. 22, 1826, a son of
Joshua and Eliza (Spollett) Clark, of Derry. He married

MRS. CLARK. NO. 525.

Clara A. Kent (No. 525). He was admitted to the church
July 1, 1876, and d. in Hampstead, Feb. 16, 1900, and was
buried in the village cemetery.

No. 525.

Clarissa Ann Kent, b. in Hampstead, Dec. 8, 1826, a daughter of Dea. Jona. and Clarissa (Page) Kent (Nos. 245, 246). She married John H. Clark (No. 424). She was

MOSES B. LITTLE. NO. 526.

admitted to the church July 1, 1876, and is a present faithful worker. They had children:—

I.   Clarence L., d. young.
II. Mary E. (No. 547); m. John S. Corson (No. 546).
III. Frank, d. young.

No. 516.

Margaret Bly Williams, b. in Plaistow, Nov. 20, 1839, a daughter of Benjamin and Hannah (Rowell) Williams (see Nos. 77, 78). She married, first, Silas M. Marshall, son of

CALEB W. WILLIAMS. NO. 515.

Caleb and Asenath (Morse) Marshall, of East Hampstead, in 1854, who d. March 17, 1865, in Washington, D. C. She was admitted to the church May 7, 1872, and dismissed March 1, 1883. They had children:—

I.   Charles Levi, b. Sept. 2, 1855; d. Feb., 1856.

II.   Silas William, b. May 18, 1857; d. Nov. 19, 1857.

III.   Rose Asenath, b. Jan. 22, 1859; m., Sept. 10, 1876, Hiram F., son of Nathan and Harriet Newell (Mason) Russell, of East Haverhill and Atkinson. She d. Feb. 4, 1882. They had children :—

      1. Lilla May, b. June 14, 1877; m. George A. Granton, Dec. 8, 1897, of Haverhill, Mass., and have children—Irina Nichols and Russell Alexander.

      2. Henry Milton, b. Sept. 28, 1879.

      3. Ada Lillian, b. May 12, 1881.

IV.   Silas Caleb, b. June 23, 1861, in Argyle, Me.; d. July 23, 1882, in Hampstead.

V.   Willie, b. Sept. 29, 1863; d. Dec. 24, 1864, in Hampstead.

Mrs. Marshall married, second, William P. Russell, of Solon, Me., March 9, 1882. They reside in Bradford, Mass.

No. 517.

Belinda Gibson Atwood,' b. in Hampstead, Sept. 3, 1840, a daughter of Amos and Mary C. (Mills) Atwood (see Nos. 532, 59 and 60). She married William Burnham Wilson. She was admitted to the church May 7, 1875, and is a present member. They have children :—

I.   Inez A. (No. 572); m. Charles O. Cass (No. 574).

II.   Annie J. (No. 695).

III.   Will C. (No. 650).

No. 518.

Edwin Sydney Pressey, b. in Fremont, Nov. 12, 1856 (see Nos. 557, 558). He was educated in the public and high schools of Hampstead; graduate Phillips Academy, Andover; a graduate from Williams College in 1885; Union Theological College in New York, in 1888. His first pastorate was in Brooklyn, N. Y. From there he went to Springfield, Vt., August, 1890, and remained two years, until August, 1892. He was installed pastor of the Congregational church, in Elmwood, Ill., December, 1892, and remained till November, 1896, when he went to St. Anthony Park, St. Paul,

Westley Flanders of Sandown. She mar. Rodney C. Haseltine of Hampstead, July 3, 1873, who d. of consumption.
They had one child. She was adm. to the church Sept. 3,
1876. She mar., second, Alfred Farrer, and resides in Derry.

MRS. CORSON. NO. 547.

No. 546.

John Sullivan Corson, b. in Great Falls, Jan. 20, 1856, a
son of Avender and Laura A. (Wheeler) Corson (see p. 369,
Vol. 1). He mar. Mary E. Clark (No. 547). He was adm.
to the church Sept. 3, 1876, and is a present member.

No. 547.

Mary Elizabeth Clark, b. in Hampstead, Oct. 27, 1856, a daughter of John Henry and Clara A. (Kent) Clark (Nos. 524, 525). She mar. John S. Corson (No. 546), in 1875, and was adm. to the church Sept. 8, 1876. She is a present member. They have children :—

I. Edwin Leroy (No. 720).
II. Harold Eugene, b. July 23, 1877.

No. 548.

James William Sanborn, b. in Hampstead, April 30, 1858, a son of Dea. William and Lois (Calef) Sanborn (Nos. 390, 425). He mar. Flora A. Corson (No. 549). He was adm. to the church Sept. 8, 1876, and is a present member (see p. 371, Vol. 1.) (See photo Vol. 1.)

No. 549.

Flora Amanda Corson, b. in Hampstead, Dec. 14, 1858, a daughter of Avender and Laura A. (Wheeler) Corson (see p. 369, Vol. 1). She mar. James W. Sanborn (No. 548), Feb. 6, 1876. She is a present member; adm. Sept. 8, 1876 ; they have a daughter, Ethel Lois (No. 701).

No. 550.

Mary Etta Tabor, b. in Hampstead, March 14, 1862, a daughter of John W. and Mary A. (Little) Tabor (Nos. 613, 510). She was educated in the public and high schools of Hampstead, and Atkinson Academy, and taught school eight years in Hampstead, Atkinson, and Sandown. She mar. W. Amos Fitts (No. 667), Feb. 22, 1889. She was adm. to the church Sept. 8, 1876, and is a present member. She is also a member of the Foreign Mission, Cent Society, Ladies' Aid, Christian Endeavor, and was sent to Chicago as a delegate to the National Society, in 1888. They have had children :—

I.   Ray Everett, b. Jan. 23, 1890; d. April 3, 1895.
II. Lee Mahlon, b. July 24, 1891; d. Sept, 7, 1894.
III. Mabel Gertrude, b. Dec. 8, 1892; d. April 3, 1895.
IV. Clara Emma, b. Aug. 19, 1895.

No. 551.

William A. Love, b. in Cold Springs, N. Y., about 1861.
He was an orphan at an early age, and placed in an orphan's
home in N. Y., from where he found a home in the family
of Benjamin and Mary L. (Sargent) Pillsbury (No. 325) at
East Hampstead.

He united with the church Sept. 3, 1876, and was dis.
and rec. to unite with the Park St. Church in Boston, June
14, 1883. He has been a worker in the Sunday schools of
Boston, Somerville, and Everett. He is at present a member of the Presbyterian Church at Windham, and teacher in
that Sunday school. He mar. Lizzie F. Bryant of Salem, in
1884, and has one child, Bernard A., b. 1885.

No. 552.

William Johnson, b. in Hampstead, son of James and
Angelia (Canny) Johnson of Hampstead (see p. 381, Vol 1).
He mar. in Haverhill, Mass., Maggie Hughes, where he re-
sides. He united with the church Sept. 2, 1876, and dis.
Jan. 4, 1883.

No. 553.

George Gordon Williams, b. in Bath, Jan. 18, 1861, a son
of Dea. Caleb W. and Martha H. (Gordon) Williams (Nos.
515, 490). He mar. Mrs. Annie M. (Allen) Pettengill of
Haverhill, Oct. 21, 1893. His occupation has practically
been on some part of the shoe industry since his school days,
which were in the public and high schools of Hampstead.
They reside in Haverhill, Mass., and have one child, Helen
Gordon, b. Dec. 20, 1898. He was adm. to the church
Sept. 3, 1876, and was dis. to unite with the Grace M. E.
Church in Haverhill, March 3, 1897.

No. 554.

William Alonzo Griffin, b. in Sandown, Dec. 23, 1841, a son of Capt. William and Miriam (Colby) Griffin of Hampstead. He mar. Mary E. Stevens (No. 555). He was adm. to the church Nov. 5, 1876, and is a present member, and resides in Hampstead.

No. 555.

Mary Elizabeth Stevens, b. in Chester, Oct. 10, 1835, a daughter of Calvin and Nancy (Rodgers) Stevens, of Chester. She married William A. Griffin (No. 554), in 1862. She was admitted to the church Nov. 5, 1876, and is a present member. They have children :—

I.   Lillian R. (No. 589); m. John C. Sanborn (No. 598).
II.   Louise B. (No. 645).
III. Will Sawyer (No. 709).

Calvin and Nancy (Rodgers) Stevens of Chester had children :—

I.   Luther C.
II.   H. Maria Louisa, b. Oct. 10, 1834; m. George C. Fitts, who was
      b. Dec. 19, 1832.
      1. Carrie M. (No. 684); m. Edward F. Perot (No. 676).
      2. William Elmer, b. Sept. 16, 1861; m. Annie P. Clark.
      3. George Arthur, b. Sept. 7, 1866; m. Mary E. Sanborn.
      4. Minnie M. (No. 742).
      5. Annie B. (No. 685); m. John C. Sanborn (No. 598).
      6. Charles Albert, b. Jan. 3, 1874; m. Alice C. Bisbee (No.
          757).
III. Mary E. (twin to above) (No. 655); m. W. A. Griffin (No. 554).
IV.   William Rodgers Stevens.
V.   Abbie M. (No. 505).
VI.   Martha A. (No. 618).
VII. Albert Ayer Stevens.
VIII. Ella Nancy, m. —— Coombs.

No. 556.

Emma Frances Chase, b. in Hampstead, Sept. 18, 1862, a daughter of Luther and Caroline (Mathews) Chase (No.

418). She was educated in the public and high schools of
Hampstead. She taught school for a time, but the work not
being congenial to her, she left that occupation to work in a
shoe shop, and later married John H., son of Lewis and
Ruth (daughter of Obediah Dustin of Salem) Hunt of
Salem, April 9, 1899. She united with the church Nov. 5,

DEACON PRESSEY. NO. 557.

1876, and was dismissed to unite with the M. E. Church at
Salem Depot, July 2, 1896. They had children :—

I.   Mabel Emma, b. April 27, 1890.
II.   Leslie Myron, b. Jan. 21, 1892.
III.   Mildred Ruth, b. Jan. 18, 1897.

She died at Salem Depot, of pneumonia, Jan. 31, 1901. Her funeral was attended by Rev. Mr. Quimby of the M. E. Church and Rev. Albert Watson of Windham.

No. 557.

Charles Wilbur Pressey, b. in Sandown in 1834, a son of

C. PARK PRESSEY. (SEE NO. 558.)

Henry Moulton and Mary (Ingalls) Pressey, of Sandown. He married Mrs. Clementine (Wood) Sleeper (No. 558). He was admitted to church membership by letter from the church in Sandown, Nov. 5, 1876. He was elected a deacon Dec. 31, 1884. He is a present member (see p. 856, Vol. 1).

No. 558.

Clementine Wood, b. in Sandown in 1834, a daughter of Joseph Gardner and Polly (Pressey) Wood, of Sandown.

MRS. S. LIZZIE (SAWYER) HUNKINS.   NO. 560.

She married, first, in 1855, Joseph C. Sleeper, who d. in 1858. One son, Edwin S., b. 1856. She married, second, Charles W. Pressey (No. 557), and was admitted to the church by letter from the church in Sandown, Nov. 5, 1876. She is a present member. Her children :—

I.   Edwin S. (No. 518); m. Orrie B. Little (No. 537).
II.   Henry Mahlon, b. 1857; d. 1868.

MRS. SAWYER. NO. 267. (SEE P. 451.)

III.   Charles Park, b. in 1869; was educated in the public and high schools of Hampstead, Exeter Phillips Academy, Williams College, 1893; now manager of the Boston Branch of the Educational Register.

No. 559.

Lucy Sarah Johnson, b. in Hampstead, Nov. 4, 1850, a daughter of Nathan and Syrena (Brown) Johnson (No. 461). She was educated in the public schools of Hampstead, and was admitted to the church Jan. 14, 1877, and was dismissed to unite with the Union Congregational Church in Haverhill, Mass., of which she is a present member, Nov. 1, 1894.

No. 560.

Sarah Elizabeth Sawyer, b. in Hampstead, April 4, 1839, a daughter of Benjamin and Priscilla (Gibson) Sawyer (No. 267). She received her education in the common schools of Hampstead and at Atkinson Academy, and was a teacher in the public schools for several years. She also was educated in music under private teachers, and was organist several years in the church. She married James Hunkins of Sandown. She was admitted to the church March 4, 1877. She died in Hampstead, Nov. 2, 1901. Her funeral was attended by Rev. Mr. Pratt, her former pastor. Their daughter:—

I.   Etta M. (No. 657).

No. 561.

Mary Amanda Smith, b. in Concord, Nov. 29, 1846, a daughter of Abel C. Smith, of Concord, a shipbuilder, and his wife, Sarah Elizabeth Cummings. She married Orren E. Follansbee (No. 601), June 12, 1867. She was admitted to the church by letter from the church in Goffstown, March 4, 1877, and was dismissed to unite with the Congregational Church in Methuen, Mass., Jan. 30, 1895, and is at present a member of the First Church in Bradford, Mass., adm. May 4, 1899. Their daughter :—

I.   Nettie May (No. 606).

No. 562.

Sarah Elizabeth Heald. It was a pleasure to call on Mrs. Chandler, the oldest member of the church, Oct. 24, 1901, at her cosy home, No. 10 Union street, Haverhill, Mass., and hear from her the life story of her ninety years. Showing very few of the infirmities of age, and with a remarkable memory, with heartfelt greeting, and with the deepest interest in my work of compiling the church family history, she said: " I was born in Carlisle, Mass., in poverty and want, Nov. 13, 1811, of poor, but highly respectable parents. My father, Paul Heald, was a carpenter by trade, and died in or near Buffalo, N. Y., of typhoid fever, in 1811, five weeks before I was born. My mother, Sarah (Nutting) Heald, died in Carlisle, and was buried there, in 1851, aged 67 years. My parents had three children. Paul married Elizabeth Richards of Atkinson, and had children: John, now of Springfield, Mass., Isaac (deceased), and Benjamin R. Heald, of Atkinson. Benjamin Hurd Heald married Francis Bowers of Billerica, Mass., and resided there until his death, in 1897, aged 89 years. He was a farmer and stone mason. He was a fine singer, and led the choir at the Unitarian Church in Billerica for a number of years. They had no children. My parents were very much devoted to music, an art which has descended to their posterity.

I united with the Merrimac Street Congregational Church in Lowell, Mass., in 1828, the year the church was built. I was about seventeen years of age, and remember the words used the day I was admitted, "Sanctify through thy truth, Thy word is truth." I was a leader in the church choir for several years in Rev. Mr. Blanchard's church, with Miss Abbott, an aunt of Emma Abbott, the celebrated singer. I was a member of the Handel and Haydn Society.

I married, first, Deacon Liberty Frost, in 1836, a son of John and Sarah (Adams) Frost, of Jaffrey, N. H., where he was born. He was an overseer in the dressing room in a Lowell

mill, and died from a cold taken while washing sheep in
Jaffrey, in 1838. He was a deacon in the Second Baptist
Church in Lowell several years, a leader in the singing class,
superintendent of the Sunday school, and a member of the
old Mechanics' Association of Lowell. Dea. Frost was one

MRS. NOYES.   NO. 563.

of those Christians who exhibit the truth of the gospel.
There was scarcely a meeting, either on the Sabbath or during the week, in which he was not in his seat, and his solemn
exhortation and fervent prayer was not soon forgotten. He
left behind a bright example of consistent piety, of fidelity

and affection, which it would be well for Zion were it more extensively imitated.

We had one child, Lemuel Porter Frost, b. May, 1836, and d., aged six weeks. He was named for our minister.

I married Abner Woodman Chandler, b. in Atkinson,

WASHINGTON NOYES. (SEE NO. 563.)

April 6, 1815, a son of Joseph and Polly (Woodman) Chandler, in 1840. I bought the farm of Dea. Jonathan Kent in 1849, and moved there (now known as the Charles Damon place in Hampstead). The place is historic in interest, because of the Kent ancestors of Revolutionary times.

I united with the Congregational church in Hampstead by letter from the Lowell church, May 6, 1877, and am a present member there. I was always connected with the musical work of the church until we moved to Haverhill, in 1889. We had two children:—

I.   Orren Porter, b. Jan. 20, 1841; d., of consumption, unmarried, April 26, 1881.

II.   Abbie Frances, b. Feb. 9, 1849. She was educated in the public schools of Hampstead, and at Atkinson and Pinkerton Academies. Of natural musical ability, she was further educated in music at the Boston Conservatory of Music, and under such private teachers as Charles R. Adams and Guilmette. She was connected with musical circles in Hampstead, and sang at the North Church in Haverhill for sixteen consecutive years. She is now my faithful, self-sacrificing daughter, devoted to me in my feeble age." (See p. 132, Mem. Hist., Vol. 1, and the account of the 150th anniversary exercises of the church in this volume.)

No. 563.

Sabrina Drew Corson, b. in Lebanon, Me., Dec. 22, 1840, a daughter of Nathaniel and Mary (Fernald) Corson (see pp. 369, 358, Vol. 1). She married Washington Noyes, in 1868, who d. in Hampstead, Oct. 25, 1888, aged 63 years. She was admitted to the church May 6, 1877, by letter from the Free Will Baptist Church at Great Falls, having joined that church when about 16 years old. She is connected with the ladies' societies, and in other ways is an earnest worker for the church. She is favorably known as a writer of verse for neighborhood entertainments, and among her rhymes are " The Old Elm," " Wiwurna Cottage," and " The Sewing Circle."

No. 564.

Eleanor True Randall, b. in Derry, July 18, 1860, a daughter of Isaac Randall of Chester, and wife Sarah A. (Bartlett) (No. 592). She married, first, Daniel F. Ordway (see

p. 337, Vol. 1). She married, second, H. Parker Williams, of Bradford, son of Harrison Williams (see No. 78). She was admitted to the church July 1, 1877, and was dis. and rec. to the Congregational church in Bradford, Mass., Feb. 12, 1891. They have no children.

No. 565.

Sarah Ann Graham, b. in Glasgow, Scotland, a daughter of John and Margaret (McClain) Graham, and granddaughter of Donald and Sarah (Stewart) Graham, of Scotland. The parents emigrated to Brooklyn, Prince Edward's Island, and several of the family of children came to the States. The family were :—

I. Katherine, m. James Scott, of Belmont, Mass. (dead).
II. Charles, m. Katie McDonald.
III. Sarah A. (above); m. Jesse B. Shirley (No. 530). She was admitted to the church July 1, 1877, and was dismissed to unite with the First Congregational Church in Methuen, Mass., March 8, 1897, and have son :—
    1. Clarence.
    2. An adopted daughter, Mary S. (No. 726).
IV. Jennie, m. Moses Young, of Hudson, Mass.
V. Christina M. (No. 668).
VI. Annie (No. 645).
VII. Mary, m. Andrew McGilvary, of Boston.
VIII. Donald, d., aged 17 years.
IX. Effie, m. John McDonald, of Pictou, N. S.

No. 566.

Loren Mandanow Chase, b. in Waithfield, Vt., March 10, 1846, a son of Josiah and Polly (Chase) Chase. He married Addie M. Bragg (No. 567). He served in the civil war, in Co. A, 4th Mass. Cavalry, from Nov. 13, 1863, to Nov. 14, 1865. He was admitted to the church Sept. 2, 1877, and dismissed, at his own request, June 28, 1883. Resides at East Hampstead (see p. 354, Vol. 1).

No. 567.

Mary Adelaide Bragg, b. in Hampstead, May 28, 1851, a daughter of Oliver R. and Sarah (Whittier) Bragg, of Hampstead (see p. 858, Vol. 1). She married Loren M. Chase (No. 566). She was admitted to the church Sept. 2, 1877, and was dismissed at her request, June 28, 1888. They have a son :—

I.   Oliver Adelbert, b. Nov. 12, 1869; m. Myra L. Roque; have children :—
    1, George Loring, b. Aug. 81, 1900.
    2. Mattie A., b. Nov, 18, 1902.

No. 568.

Nettie Catherine Maryott, b. in Jewett City, Conn., Oct. 13, 1844, a daughter of James and Lucy (Smith) Maryott, of Connecticut. She married Thomas M. Arnold, of Hampstead, who d. in Haverhill, Mass. She was admitted to the church Sept. 2, 1877, and dismissed Jan. 4, 1883. She d. in Haverhill, Nov. 27, 1902. They have an only son, John William, residing in Haverhill.

No. 569,

Elizabeth Hutchinson Johnson; b. in East Hampstead, June 24, 1859, an only child of the late Moses D. and Sarah Moody (Arnold) Johnson, both of Hampstead, on Central street, at the home now occupied by Mr. Faxon. She married Horace T. Littlefield, of Haverhill, Mass., Nov. 20, 1881. She was admitted to the church Sept. 2, 1877, and was dis. and rec. to unite with the Center Church in Haverhill, April 24, 1884, and is a present member there. They have no children.

No. 570.

Ezra Warren Foss, b, in Alton, July 4, 1889, a son of Dearborn Foss of Strafford, who lived with the son in East

Hampstead, aged 93 years; d. Nov. 28, 1902, and his wife Betsey Wentworth of Wakefield, N. H.

Ezra W. was a member of Co. I, 11th N. H. Regt. on detailed duty as teamster from Dec. 20, 1862, and engaged in the battle of Fredericksburg, Va. He is now a farmer and shoemaker. He mar., first, Nancy J. Haynes. They had no children. He mar., second, Lydia W. (Lang) Haynes (No. 571), and have no children. He was adm. to the church by letter from the M. E. Church in West Hampstead, Sept. 2, 1877; and was dis. to unite again with the M. E. Church at West Hampstead, Oct. 29, 1882, and was again received to the church membership, 1890, and are present members.

No. 571.

Lydia Williams Lang, b. in Deerfield, May 21, 1830, a daughter of John Lang of Candia, and wife Relief Brown of Danville. She mar., first, Oliver S. Haynes of Candia, in 1849, and had children :—

I.   Angeline R., b. Sept. 17, 1849; m. George J. Penneo (see No. 705).
II.   Dea. Bradley N. (No. 744).
III.   Arthur O., b. May 24, 1856; m. Jennie Patten of Candia; resides in Manchester.
IV.   John E., b. Oct. 7, 1858; m. Annie Kidder of Newton; resides in Haverhill.

She mar., second, Ezra W. Foss (No. 570), July 8, 1877. She was adm. to the church by letter from the M. E. Church at West Hampstead, Sept. 2, 1877, and was dis. to unite again with the M. E. Church in West Hampstead, Aug. 19, 1882, and in 1890 was again received to the Congregational Church, and is a present member.

No. 572.

Charles Ordway Cass, b. in Danville, Sept. 6, 1859, a son of Lewis and Martha E. (Marble) Cass (No. 507). He mar. Inez A. Wilson (No. 273). He was adm. to the church Sept. 2, 1878, and was dis. Sept. 2, 1886.

No. 573.

Inez Amanda Wilson, b. in Hampstead, Dec. 5, 1862, a daughter of William B. and Belinda G. (Atwood) Wilson (No. 517). She mar. Charles O. Cass (No. 572). She was adm. to the church Sept. 1, 1878, and is a present member. They have an only child, Howard Clinton, b. Oct. 6, 1885.

No. 574.

Mary Ann Williams, b. in Hampstead, Feb. 19, 1866, a daughter of Dea. Caleb W. and Martha H. (Gordon) Williams (Nos. 515, 490). She was educated in the public and high school of Hampstead, and mar. Otis Masterson of Haverhill, April 10, 1887. She was adm. to the church Sept. 1, 1878, and is a present member. They reside in Haverhill, Mass., and have one child, Ilda Mae, b. August 12, 1899.

No. 575.

Sarah R. Fitts, b. in Lynn, Mass., a daughter of Josiah and Sarah R. (   ) Fitts, who united with the church in Atkinson, March 27, 1859. She was adm. to the church by letter from the Congregational Church in Chester, Sept. 1, 1878, and was dis. and rec. to unite with the Congregational Church in Chester, Dec. 18, 1884. She united with the church in Atkinson, March 27, 1859. She mar., first, W. W. Sawyer; had a son, Fitts Sawyer. She mar., second, Gordon ; mar., third, Moses Hoyt, Esq., of Hampstead, and fourth, Seth Bruce (No. 653). She d. in Chester, in 1901.

No. 576.

Lucy Ann Hall, b. in Haverhill, Mass., Nov. 4, 1838, a daughter of Moses W. Hall of Salem, and wife Abigail (Hawkins), b. in Center Harbor (see No. 509). She mar. John W. Little (see No. 284), Nov. 4, 1857. She was adm. to the church by letter from the Garden St. M. E. Church in Lawrence, Mass., Sept. 1, 1879, and was dis. to unite with the M. E. Church at West Hampstead, Aug. 19, 1882.

Mrs. Little has from early womanhood been an earnest and enthusiastic adherent of the Methodist denomination; becoming a resident of Hampstead, she united with the Congregational Church as " a church home." She, however, true to her faith, was instrumental in having Methodist services, and a Sunday school, in No. 4 school house, as often as convenient, and about June, 1882, she mentioned to her Sunday school class the hope that some day they would have a building of their own in which to hold services, and asked who would bring the first ten cents towards it, which was brought the next Sunday by Estelle, the little daughter of Benjamin and Elizabeth (Carr) Huston of West Hampstead. From then on, Mrs. Little used every effort to secure contributions, and succeeded in raising $500 before any others helped her in the work of collecting funds, and herself raised $800 of the $1100 of which their church building, which was dedicated in 1884, cost. She has been president of the Ladies' Aid Society of that church two years. They have children :—

I.   William French, b. Dec. 28, 1858; m. Mary Lizzie Kelly of Waltham, Mass., May 4, 1890. He is station agent at West Hampstead. They have children :—
            1.   Marion Isabelle, b. Feb. 10, 1891.
            2.   Forest Ellsworth, b. June 25, 1894.
II.   Grace May (Thompson), adopted; mar. Earl O. Fitts of Danville. (See p. 353, Vol. 1.)

No. 577.

Abbie Rogers Randall, b. in Derry, Jan. 18, 1863, a daughter of Isaac and Sarah A. (Bartlett) Randall (No. 592). She was educated in the public and high school of Hampstead, and at Framingham, Mass., Normal School, and was a teacher seven years in Amesbury, and Haverhill, Mass. She mar. Fred M. Rice (No. 663), and at present resides in New Rochelle, N. Y. They have children :—

I.   Miriam Sarah, b. Sept. 3, 1897.
II.   Elizabeth Randall, b. May 24, 1900.

She united with the church May 4, 1879, and was dis. to unite with the Brick Presbyterian Church in New York City, Jan. 27, 1895.

No. 578.

Christie L. Graham, b.   She mar. Rufus McNeil (No. 591), April 30, 1880. She was adm. to the church May 4, 1879, and is a present member, but resides in Chelsea, Mass. They have one child, Carrie E. (No. 716).

No. 579.

Francis W. Coaker, b. in Tourquay, England; d. in Manchester, Jan. 15, 1900. He had five children by his first wife, two of whom were:—

I.   Catherine E. (No. 581).
II.   Emma J. (No. 582).

He married, second, Elizabeth M. Tewksbury (No. 580). He was admitted to the church Jan. 5, 1879, and was dismissed to unite with the Franklin Street Congregational Church at Manchester, Jan. 4, 1894. He was buried in Lawrence, Mass.

No. 580.

Elizabeth Merrill Tewksbury, b. in Hampstead, July 16, 1834, a daughter of Dr. Isaac and Sabra (Foster) Tewksbury (Nos. 377, 317). She married, first, R. H. Colby, in Lawrence, Mass., in 1851. Their son, John F. Colby, m. Henrietta Stacy, in Boston, January, 1884, and they reside in Jamaica Plains, Mass., and have children:—Elizabeth E. b. Dec. 1, 1885; Annah May, b. Dec. 16, 1892; Laura Gladys, b. Nov. 27, 1895.

Elizabeth M. married, second, L. A. Ostrom, at Chicago, in 1867, and had a daughter :—Laura Annette, who resided many years in Paris, France; mar. Ferdinand d'Azevedo, Nov. 29, 1885. They reside in Brussels, Belgium, Mr.

MRS. COAKER. NO. 580.

d'Azevedo being ambassador from Portugal. They have a daughter, Marie Elizabeth, b. Oct. 29, 1896.

She married, third, Francis W. Coaker (No. 579), of Chicago, in 1875. She now resides in Boston, Mass. She was admitted to the church by letter from the Congregational Church in Chicago, Ill., Jan. 5, 1879, and was dismissed to unite with the Franklin Street Congregational Church in Manchester, Jan. 4, 1894.

No. 581.

Catherine E. Coaker, b. in England, a daughter of Francis W. Coaker (No. 579). She was admitted to the church Jan. 5, 1879, and was dis. and rec. to unite with the Grace Church in Oswego, N. Y., Dec. 3, 1886.

No. 582.

Emma Jane Coaker, b. in England, a daughter of Francis W. Coaker (No. 579). She was admitted to the church Jan. 5, 1879, and was dis. and rec. to unite with the Franklin Street Congregational Church in Manchester, Jan. 4, 1894.

No. 583.

Myron P. Dickey, b. Feb. 19, 1852, in Derry. He was educated in the common schools of Derry, and was a graduate of Pinkerton Academy, class of 1870, and of Dartmouth College, 1874. He taught school at Palmer, Mass., and for four years was principal of the Hampstead High School. He graduated from Yale Theological School in 1883, and was pastor of the Congregational Church in Ludlow, Mass., ten years. Called to Milton, April, 1893, where he is at present (see p. 370, Vol. 1). He was admitted to the church in Hampstead by letter from the Congregational Church in Derry, Jan. 5, 1879. He married Louise R. Shumway (No. 584). (See photo, Vol. 1.)

No. 584.

Louise Ripley Shumway, b. in Three Rivers, Mass. She married Rev. Myron P. Dickey (No. 583), Aug. 3, 1876. She was admitted to the church Jan. 5, 1879. They have children :—

I.   Maurice Woodburn, b. in Hampstead, Oct. 28, 1878; graduate of the Nute High School, in Milton, 1895; Dartmouth College, 1899.

II.   Orinda Sophia, b. in Ludlow, Mass., June 22, 1883.

III.   Mark Shumway, b. July 2, 1885.

No. 585.

Alice Marion Little, b. in Hampstead, May 16, 1862, a daughter of William C. and Julia E. (Harris) Haseltine Little (No. 469). She was educated in the public and high school of Hampstead, graduating in class of 1880, the first class that received a diploma from the high school. She was a student at Mount Holyoke Seminary and at the Moody School at Northfield, Mass. She was admitted to the church Jan. 5, 1879, and was dis. and rec. to unite with the Union Church at Haverhill, Mass., July 16, 1891. She resides with her father on North Main street, Haverhill.

No. 586.

Alice Nichols Smith, b. in Hampstead, Sept. 7, 1865, a daughter of Rufus C. and Helen M. (Nichols) Smith (see Nos. 285, 318). She was educated in the common and high schools of Hampstead. She married Charles H. Pearson of Boston, July 16, 1890. She was admitted to the church Nov. 3, 1878. They have children:—

I.   Philip Kimball, b.

II.   Daniel Nichols, b.

III.   Clement Smith, b.

No. 587.

Nellie L. Perley, daughter of Augustus and Almira (Johnson) Perley (No. 607). She was admitted to the church Nov. 3, 1878, and dismissed June 18, 1894. She married George F. Carlton, of Haverhill, Mass., where they reside.

No. 588.

Lizzie I. Tabor, b. in Hampstead, a daughter of Eben and Lizzie (Roundy) Tabor (see No. 480 and p. 875, Vol. 1). She married Clarence Bray, of Haverhill, Mass. They had five children. She was admitted to the church Nov. 3, 1878. She d. in Haverhill.

No. 589.

. Lillian Rogers Griffin, b. in Hampstead, Nov. 7, 1864, a daughter of William A. and Mary E. (Stevens) Griffin (Nos. 554, 555). She married John C. Sanborn (No. 598), Nov. 12, 1885. She was admitted to the church Nov. 3, 1878. She died in Hampstead, May 2, 1897.

No. 590.

Helen Adelaide Ranlett, b. in Hampstead, Oct. 21, 1863, a daughter of Charles H. and Susan P. (Tabor) Ranlett (see pp. 875, 887, Vol. 1). She was educated in the public and high schools of Hampstead, and married Charles E. Page, of Haverhill, Mass. She was admitted to the church Nov. 3, 1878, and was dis. and rec. to unite with the Winter Street Free Will Baptist Church in Haverhill, Feb. 10, 1887. They have children :—

I.   Mary Elizabeth, b. Nov. 3, 1883.
II.   Emily A., b. July 27, 1885.
III. Helen M., b. Sept. 14, 1887.
IV.   John J., b. Nov. 8, 1889.
V.   Carrol Snow, b. June 3, 1891.
VI.   Doris L., b. April 12, 1896.

No. 591.

Rufus McNiel, b. in Haverhill, Mass., a son of Edmund and Abigail S. (Cronk) McNiel, of Atkinson, where both parents died (see No. 512). He married Christie L. Graham (No. 578). He was admitted to the church March 2, 1879, and is a present member, but resides in Chelsea, Mass.

No. 592.

Sarah Ann Bartlett, b. in Salisbury, Mass., March 31, 1827, a daughter of Jacob Bartlett of Amesbury, and Mary True of Salisbury, his wife. She married Isaac Randall, of Chester, July 14, 1846 (see p. 347, Vol. 1). She was admitted to the church March 2, 1879, and is a present member. They had children :—

I. Mary Ann, b. March 12, 1848; m. Ladd Richardson, of Hampstead.

II. Sarah Frances, b. Dec. 18, 1850; m. Alfred W. Foote. They had children :—
 1. Ola, who d. Oct. 7, 1894, in young womanhood.
 2. Charles F. (No. 719).
 3. Esther, who d. Feb. 22, 1898, a young lady.
 4. Mark, d. Nov. 6, 1902, aged 14.
 5. Guy.

III. Isaac, b. July 6, 1853; d. in infancy.

IV. Jacob, b. Feb., 1855; d. in infancy,

V. Jane Worth, b. Aug. 22, 1857; m. Melvin Cooke of Haverhill.

VI. Isaac, b. Oct. 4, 1858; m. Alice H. Spollett (No. 657).

VII. Eleanor True (No. 564).

VIII. Abbie R. (No. 577).

IX. Laura Taylor, b. Feb. 7, 1865; d. in infancy.

No. 593.

Flora Jane Harris, b. in Plaistow, May 13, 1851, a daughter of Gilman and Susan (Kimball) Harris, of Plaistow. She was educated in the common schools of Plaistow and at the New Hampton Academy. She was a successful teacher for several years in Plaistow, Kingston, and Hampstead. She married Albert H. Little (No. 604), Jan. 5, 1876. She was admitted to the church March 2, 1879, and d. in Hampstead, of consumption, April 22, 1881. Her funeral was attended by Rev. Albert Watson. She was buried in the village cemetery. She had no children.

No. 594.

Mary Ann Tabor, b. in Chester, Oct. 16, 1834, a daughter

of Eben and Sarah (Jack) Tabor, of Chester and Hampstead (see p. 376, Vol. 1). She married George W. Bragdon (No. 609), October, 1856, who d. in Hampstead, June
4, 1885. She was admitted to the church July 6, 1879, and
is a present member. They had children :—

I.   George L., b. June 2, 1859, of Hampstead, unmarried.
II.   Sarah H., b. Sept. 7, 1804; m. Charles M. Woodward, of San-
        down. Their children : Laura E., b. March 5, 1887; Charles
        Herbert, b. March 5, 1889; George C., b. in 1891; Willie A.,
        b. 1893; Elmer E., b. 1895; Frank B., b. Sept., 1898; and Etta
        May, b. April 24, 1902.
III.   Mary L., b. Aug. 6, 1875; m. Daniel O. Coombs, of Derry. They
        reside in Hampstead, and have children :—
        1. Burton Leroy, b. May 11, 1808.
        2. Vera May, b. Aug. 10, 1900.

No. 595.

Charlotte Ela Carr, b. in Derry, Nov. 26, 1833, a daughter
of Moses and Almira (Murray) Carr, of Derry. She married, first, Charles Robie, and had one child :—

I.   Charles Edward, b. Dec. 17, 1850.

She married, second, Jacob Townsend, of Hampstead, and
had children :—

II.   Myra C. (No. 596).
III.   Minnie Copp (No. 623).
IV.   Jacob Arthur, b. Oct. 7, 1868, in Hampstead; m., and has a son,
        William A , b. Oct. 4, 1891.
V.   Linnie Murray, b. Oct. 6, 1871, in Hampstead; m., June 15,
        1892, George S. Norton. They have a daughter, Hazel Ge
        nerva, b. Sept. 30, 1894; resides in Hampstead.

She was admitted to the church Jan. 6, 1879. She d. in
Hampstead, Aug. 22, 1893, and was buried in Wakefield,
Mass.

No. 596.

Myra Charlotte Townsend, b. in Wakefield, Mass., Oct. 6,
1864, a daughter of Jacob and Charlotte (Carr) Townsend

(No. 595). She was educated in the public and high school of Hampstead. She married Elmer E. Ranlett, Dec. 22, 1884, and resides in Haverhill, Mass. She was admitted to the church July 6, 1879. They have children :—

MRS. TOWNSEND. NO. 595.

I.   Alice, b. Aug. 14, 1886.
II.   Maud T., b. Oct. 4, 1889.
III.   Guy Everett, b. Dec. 10, 1891.
IV.   Clyde Berkeley, b. Oct. 9, 1893.
V.   Charlotte Carr, b. Dec. 22, 1899.

No. 597.

Annie Maybelle Tabor, b. in   a daughter

JOHN C. SANBORN. NO. 598.

of Albert Lombard and Mary J. (White) Tabor, son of
Pardon and Roxanna (Colby) Tabor (No. 630). Her mother

married, after the death of Mr. Tabor, Mr. Theodore Shores of Haverhill. Annie was admitted to the church July 6, 1879, and was dis. and rec. to unite with the Center Church in Haverhill, Mass., July 22, 1889.

No. 598.

John Calef Sanborn, b. in Hampstead, Sept. 29, 1863, a son of Dea. William and Lois (Calef) Sanborn (Nos. 390, 425). He was educated in the common and high schools of Hampstead. He united with the church July 6, 1879, and is a present member, being clerk of the church and society. He was elected a deacon Dec. 31, 1902. He married, first, Lillian R. Griffin (No. 589), who d. May 2, 1897; and married, second, Annie B. Fitts (No. 685), June 22, 1899.

No. 598.

Annie Janette Tabor, b. in Hampstead, April 27, 1865, a daughter of John W. and Mary A. (Little) Tabor (Nos. 613 and 510). She was educated in the common and high school of Hampstead, and married George B. Dennett of Gilmanton. She was admitted to the church Sept. 7, 1879, and d., of consumption, June 11, 1892. She was buried in the village cemetery. They have children :—

I.   Vera Abbie, b. in Haverhill, Mass., June 14, 1888.
II.   Earl Ephraim, b. Sept. 13, 1889.

No. 600.

Mary Emma Mooers, b. in Atkinson at the place now owned by Mrs. Cynthia Alexander (set off to Hampstead in 1857), Feb. 24, 1850, a daughter of Edmund and Emeline (Ela) Mooers (No. 608). She mar., first, Adin T. Little (see No. 302), Nov. 30, 1869, who d. April 11, 1871. They had one child :—

I.   Adin Sidney, b. Oct. 12, 1870; m. Fannie C. Emerson (No. 674).

She mar., second, Oliver Putnam (No. 717). May 12, 1878, and had children :—

II.   Helen May, b. May 5, 1881; d. Oct. 15, 1881.
III.   Thorndyke, b. Aug. 12, 1882; a farmer on the Putnam Place (see p. 333, Vol. 1).
IV.   Howard, b. Oct. 5, 1886.
V.   Maud, b. May 4, 1888.

No. 601.

Orren Eaton Follansbee, b. in New Boston, April 7, 1844, a son of Ebenezer and Lorania (Barnard) Follansbee. His father later moved to Hampstead, where Mr. Amasa Hunt resides (see No. 455), where he d. Sept. 4, 1887; mother d. in Hampstead, July 6, 1882. Orren is a shoe packer by occupation; at present resides in Bradford, Mass. He mar. Mary A. Smith (No. 561). He was adm. to the church Jan. 4, 1880, and was dis. to unite with the Congregational Church in Methuen, Mass., Jan. 30, 1896, and is at present a member of the First Church of Christ in Bradford, where he united May 4, 1899.

No. 602.

John William Garland, b. in Hampstead, Feb. 15, 1828, a son of Benjamin B. and Mary (Balch) Garland (Nos. 367, 368). He mar. Emily A. Ring (No. 603). He was adm. to the church Jan. 4, 1880, and is a present member. He was elected deacon, Dec. 30, 1891 (see pp. 373, 374, Vol. 1.)

No. 603.

Emily Ann Ring, b. in Ware, Mass., Oct. 30, 1833, a daughter of Amos and Lydia C. (Jones) Ring (No. 455). She mar. John W. Garland (No. 602). She was educated in the common schools of Atkinson and Hampstead, and Atkinson Academy. She was a teacher for several years. She united with the church Jan. 4, 1880, and d. in Hampstead, Feb. 23, 1901, after patient suffering for several years with a broken hip and others complications; was buried in the village cemetery. They had children :—

JOHN W. GARLAND. NO. 602.

I.   Willie, b. Sept. 23, 1858; d. in infancy.
II.   Charles W. (No. 544).

The writer has the most kindly remembrance of this quiet, unassuming little woman, since her first term in school

TRISTRAM LITTLE. (SEE NO. 605.)

in the old red schoolhouse in District No. 1, when three and a half years of age. A beloved teacher then, and a friend always.

No. 604.

Albert Hazen Little, b. in Hampstead, June 17, 1852, a son of Tristram and Betsey (Peaslee) Little (No. 605). He was educated in the common school of Hampstead, and at Atkinson and Pinkerton Academies. He mar., first, Flora

MRS. BETSEY P. LITTLE. NO. 605.

J. Harris (No. 593); second, mar., Abbie I. Gale (No. 631). He was adm. to the church March 5, 1880, and is a present member. He is a farmer in Hampstead, and resides on the old homestead of his fathers.

No. 605.

Betsey Peaslee, b. in Newton, N. H., Sept. 5, 1819, a daughter of Obediah and Hannah (Bartlett) Peaslee of Newton. She mar. Tristram Little, Oct. 10, 1839 (see p. 850, Vol. 1). She was adm. to the church March 5, 1880.

MRS. GRIFFIN. NO. 606.

She d. in Hampstead, Mar. 4, 1898, and was buried in the village cemetery. They had children :—

I.   Moses Hazen, b. July 26, 1840; d. Jan. 16, 1841.

II.   John Tristram, b. Jan. 12, 1844; m. Emma Frances Colby (see
       No. 467), Nov. 20, 1866; she d. April 16, 1894. Their only
       child :—
            1. Arthur Herbert, b. Oct. 10, 1867; m. Ruth A. Emerson
               (No. 680.)
III.   Mary Jane, b. Jan. 6, 1848; m. Moulton D. Pressey of Haverhill
       (see No. 284), Jan. 20, 1869; they reside in Haverhill, Mass.,
       and have had children :—
            1. Wilbert Pressey, b. Sept. 16, 1870; resides in Haverhill.
            2. Carl Forest, b. Sept. 28, 1878; d. in infancy.
IV.   Albert II. (No. 604), m. Flora J. Harris (Nos. 593, 631).

No. 606.

Hannah Bartlett Little, b. in Hampstead, March 19, 1832,
a daughter of David and Louisa (Peaslee) Little, of Hampstead. (See No. 570.) She mar., first, Amos Clark of
Hampstead, Nov. 25, 1858 ; she mar., second, Capt. William
Griffin (see No. 554). She had no children. She was adm.
to the church March 5, 1880, and is a present member.

No. 607.

Almira Johnson, b. in Newbury, Mass., daughter of
Stephen Johnson of Newbury. She mar. Augustus Perley,
and resided in Hampstead, where Orren V. Ranlett now resides ; later moved to Haverhill, Mass. She was adm. to the
church May 1, 1880, and dis. June 28, 1894. Children :—
two sons and Nellie L. (No. 586).

No. 608.

Emeline Ela, b. in Derry, Feb. 8, 1822, a daughter of
Dea. William Ela of Derry, and wife Mary Moores from
Francestown. She mar. Edmund Brickett Mooers, by the
Rev. E. L. Parker of Derry, May 4, 1847 (see No. 409).
They resided at the " old Brickett place," and on the island,
and built the house now known as the Matavey place near
" Copp's Corner," which was in Atkinson until 1857. She
was adm. to the church by letter from the First Church in

Derry, May, 1880, and is a present member. They had children :—

I.   Mary E. (No. 600).
II. Ella, d. August 15, 1858, aged 5 years and 11 mos.

No. 609.

George Washington Bragdon, b. in Milton, July 12, 1827, a son of Ivory and Zilphia (Ricker) Bragdon, who was son of Amos Bragdon, of York, Me. He married, first, Laura A., daughter of Pardon and Roxanna (Colby) Tabor (No. 680). He married, second, Mary A. Tabor (No. 594). He was admitted to the church July 4, 1880, and d. in Hampstead, June 4, 1885.

No. 610.

Frederick Spollett, b. in Derry, Aug. 30, 1822, a son of Frederick and Hannah (Nichols) Spollett, of Derry. He married Abbie Bartlett (No. 611). A carpenter by trade, he built the house now occupied by Carlos W. Noyes, and moved from Walnut Hill, in Chester, to Hampstead, in 1880, and later built the house where he now resides, in the Center village. He was admitted to the church by letter from the church at Chester, Sept. 2, 1880, and is a present member. He first united with the church in Derry. He served in the civil war three years, from Sept. 25, 1861, to Sept. 25, 1864, a member of the 1st N. H. Light Battery, which won a noble record for faithful and distinguished service to the nation. Mr. Spollett participated in the battles of Rappahannock Station, Sulphur Springs, Groveton, second Bull Run, Antietam, Upperville, Fredericksburg, Chancellorville, Gettysburg, Brandy Station, Mine Run, Wilderness, Spottsylvania P. O., North Anna River, Petersburg, Amelia Court House, Appomattox Court House, Lee's surrender, Sailor's Crest, Sheldon's Cross Road, Tolopotomy, Cold Harbor, Deep Bottom, White Oak Church, and Boynton Plank Road.

No. 611.

Abbie Bartlett, b. in Chester, May 6, 1819, a daughter of
Peter and Mary (Dearborn) Bartlett, of Chester. She married Frederick Spollett (No. 610), March 20, 1845. She
united with the church in Chester in 1836, and from that
church she was admitted to the church in Hampstead by
letter, Sept. 2, 1880; d. in Hampstead, Jan. 27, 1890, and
was buried in the village cemetery. Their daughter: Mary
E. (No. 612).

No. 612.

Mary Ella Spollett, b. in Chester, April 20, 1856, a
daughter of Frederick and Abbie (Bartlett) Spollett (Nos.
610, 611). She was educated in the public schools of Chester, Atkinson Academy, and the grammar schools of Haverhill, Mass., and was graduated from the Chester Normal
Institute. She commenced teaching at the age of fifteen
years, and taught twelve years in the common schools of
Chester, Hampstead, Atkinson, and Sandown, when she
retired to care for her parents. She united with the church
in Chester, Jan. 4, 1874, and was admitted to the church in
Hampstead by letter, Sept. 2, 1880, and is a present member. She has served as president of the Ladies' Aid Society
one year, ten years as secretary and treasurer of the same
society, superintendent of the home department of the Sunday school since its organization in 1898, secretary and treasurer of the Rockingham County Sunday School Convention
since 1898, and still holds the position. She has served as
president of the Y. P. S. C. E., and president of the King's
Daughters. In 1899 she was elected district secretary of
the New Hampshire State Christian Endeavor Union, and
was re-elected in 1901. In 1899 she was elected one of the
sixteen delegates from New Hampshire to represent the
State at the Sunday School International Convention at
Atlanta, Ga.

No. 618.

John William Tabor, b. in Dunbarton, March 22, 1836, a

MISS SPOLLETT.   NO. 612.

son of Pardon and Roxanna (Colby) Tabor (No. 630), (p. 375, Vol. 1).   He married Mary A. Little (No. 510), and d.

in Hampstead, November, 1898. Buried in the village cemetery. He was admitted to the church March 3, 1881. (See photo, Vol. 1.)

No. 614.

Wallace Bailey, b. in Salem, a son of Jesse Ordway Bailey, b. Dec. 26, 1810, in Salem, and wife Sarah, grandson of Phineas and Lydia Bailey, of Salem. He married Laura A. Tabor (No. 548), daughter of Eben and Lizzie (Roundy) Tabor (see No. 630). He was admitted to the church March 3, 1881, and was dismissed to unite with the Union Congregational Church, at Haverhill, Mass., June 28, 1894. They reside at present in Haverhill.

No. 615.

Ebenezer Hoyt, b. in Hampstead, March 1, 1812, a son of Eliphalet and Lois (Hunt) Hoyt. His father was a soldier in the war of 1812, stationed at Portsmouth Harbor. He married Eunice A. Shannon (No. 616). He was a shoemaker by trade. Admitted to the church by letter from the M. E. Church in Haverhill, Mass., March 3, 1881. He died in Hampstead, May 16, 1896, and was buried in the village cemetery.

No. 616.

Eunice Ann Shannon, b. in Hampstead, Oct. 1, 1820, a daughter of Joseph P. and Alice (Nichols) Shannon, of West Hampstead. Eunice married Ebenezer Hoyt (No. 615), and was admitted to the church by letter from the M. E. Church of Haverhill, Mass., March 3, 1881, and is a present member. They had children :—

I.   Mary Alice, b. in 1843; m. Rev. Calvin B. Griffin, of Danville. They had children :—
        1. Annie L. (No. 664).
        2. Edith S. (No. 700).

II.   Porter H., b. in 1845; mar., first, Ida F. Hoyt; mar., second, Myra Gurley, of Haverhill, Mass.

III.   William, b. in 1847; m. Marie J. Cate, and had children :—
        1. Carlton.
        2. Harry.
        3. Hazel.
IV.   Etta L., b. in 1850; d., aged 12 years and 10 months.

No. 617.

Orren Hall, b. in Strafford, May 19, 1836, a son of Elisha
and Betsey (Crickett) Hall, of Strafford. He married, first,
Mary O. Bean, and had five children. He married, second,
Marilla Badger, and had five children. He married, third,
Melissa (McNiel) Marble (No. 512). He was admitted to
the church Sept. 4, 1881, and was dis. and rec. to unite with
the West Parish Congregational Church of Haverhill, Mass.,
June 28, 1894. He has been a deacon of the Union Evangelical Church, in Ayers Village, three years, where he now
resides.

No. 618.

Martha Augusta Stevens, b. in Chester, June 11, 1848, a
daughter of Calvin and Nancy Coffin (Rogers) Stevens (see
No. 555). She was admitted to the church by letter from
the Portland Street Baptist Church of Haverhill, Mass.,
March 4, 1882, and is a present member.

No. 619.

Russell Alexander Woodward, b. in East Townsend, Vt.,
son of Amassa and Mary Ann (Evans) Woodward. He
married Barberie G. Harriman. He was admitted to the
church May 5, 1882, and is a present member. Son :—

I.   Ethelbert B. (No. 632).

No. 620.

Esther Sophia Morrill, b. in Epping, March 7, 1849, a
daughter of John Morrill, b. in Centre Harbor, and Lydia
Hall, his wife, b. in Nottingham. She married Charles Bas-

sett, b. in Pittsfield. She was educated in the public schools
of Epping and high school of Fremont, and was admitted to
the church May 5, 1882, and is a present member. They
had children:—

I.   Cora M. (No. 621).
II.   Grace M. (No. 703).

No. 621.

Cora Maybell Bassett, b. in Danville, Aug. 11, 1867, a
daughter of Charles and Esther S. (Morrill) Bassett (No.
620). She was educated in the public and high school of
Hampstead and in music under private instruction. She was
admitted to the church May 5, 1882, and is a present member.

No. 622.

Mary Carrie Lake, b. in Hampstead, Feb. 17, 1868, a
daughter of Thorndyke P. and Martha E. (Marble) Lake
(No. 507). She was educated in the public and high school
of Hampstead and Boston Conservatory of Music, and has
taught music for several years. She married Charles H.
Sweet (No. 634). She was admitted to the church May 5,
1882, and was dis. and rec. to unite with the College Congregational Church at Hanover, March 2, 1899. They have
children :—

I.   Lillian Lake, b. April 18, 1890.
II.   Marion Helen, b. July 19, 1892.
III. Roxanna Elizabeth, b. March, 1897.
IV.   Charles Henry, b. March, 1900.

No. 623.

Minnie Copp Townsend, b. in Derry, a daughter of Jacob
and Charlotte E. (Carr) Townsend (No. 595). She was
educated in the common and high school of Hampstead,
class of 1885, and at Plymouth Normal School, 1888 and

1889; taught school in Atkinson in 1889, and Hampstead two years, until her marriage to Dr. Minot A. Steele, Dec. 29, 1891. She was admitted to the church May 5, 1882, and was a member of the church choir ten years. They reside in Portsmouth, R. I. No children.

MRS. TABOR. NO. 624.

No. 624.

Abbie May Corson, b. in Hampstead, Dec. 18, 1864, a daughter of Avender and Laura A. (Wheeler) Corson (see p. 369, Vol. 1). She was educated in the public and high school of Hampstead. She was admitted to the church May

5, 1882, and is a present member. She married Henry W. Tabor (see Nos. 510, 613). They have children :—

MRS. GARLAND.   NO. 625.

I.   Forrest Harold, b. Sept. 25, 1890.
II.   Flora Amanda, b. Aug. 20, 1893.

No. 625.

Ada Eldesta Emerson, b. in Hampstead, Dec. 25, 1865, a daughter of Alfred P. and S. Francena (Diamond) Emerson of Hampstead (p. 368, Vol. 1, and No. 354). She was educated in the public and high schools of Hampstead. She married Charles W. Garland (No. 544), April 21, 1885; was admitted to the church May 5, 1882, and is a present member. They have children:—

I.   Leona C. (No. 759).
II.   Mildred Ring, b. June 5, 1887.
III. John Alfred, b. June 6, 1889.

No. 626.

George Edward Lake, b. in Hampstead, June 13, 1866, a son of Thorndike P. and Martha E. (Marble) Lake (No. 507). He married Laura F. Davenport, of New York city, Sept. 19, 1899. He was admitted to the church July 2, 1882, and was dismissed to unite with the Congregational Church at Patten, Me., as pastor, March 30, 1899. He was educated in the public and high school of Hampstead, 1875. In 1888 he entered Phillips Andover Academy, and graduated in 1892. At Phillips he was president of the Y. M. C. A.; also at Dartmouth College he held office in the Y. M. C. A. Was a graduate of the class of 1896. He was a member of the Delta Kappa Epsilon fraternity, and worked in several missionary enterprises near Hanover. In 1893 he spent the summer under the aid of the college Y. M. C. A. in New York city, in connection with St. Bartholomew's Parish House. In September, 1896, he entered the Bangor Theological School, from which he was graduated May, 1899. One week later he was installed as pastor over the Congregational church in Patten, Me. He is at present pastor of the churches in Newfields and Stratham, since Jan. 1, 1901, and president of the Exeter local union, Y. P. S. C. E. He sends a feeling tribute to Rev. R. P. Gardner, his pastor in

REV. GEO. E. LAKE. NO. 626.

Hampstead, for the kindly encouragement, help and friendship during his preparatory years.

No. 627.

Mary Elizabeth Blake, b. in Newton, a daughter of Charles H. and Angelina (Carlisle) Blake (Nos. 628, 629). She married Fred S. Sargent in 1881, now of Loudon, and was admitted to the church, on her death bed of consumption, May 19, 1882, d. May 20, 1882, and was buried in the village cemetery.

. No. 628.

Charles Henry Blake, b. in Kensington, son of Charles Blake. He married Angelina Carlisle (No. 629). He was admitted to the church July 2, 1882, and was dismissed to unite with the Baptist church in Brentwood, June 28, 1894. He married a second time in Brentwood. Lived in Hampstead, at what is known as the "Isaac Heath place."

No. 629.

Angelina Carlisle, b. in Newton, Jan. 11, 1829, a daughter of Jacob Carlisle of Exeter. She married Charles H. Blake (No. 628). She was admitted to the church July 2, 1882. She died Dec. 12, 1888, and was buried in the village cemetery. They had children:—

I.   Mary E. (No. 627).
II.   Clara A., b. in 1859; d. Sept. 22, 1895; buried in Hampstead village cemetery.

No. 630.

Roxanna Colby, b. in Dunbarton, Sept. 19, 1808, a daughter of Clark and Susanna (Morse) Colby, both of Methuen, Mass., who moved, soon after their first child was born, to Hooksett. (Some members of the family say Roxanna was born in Methuen, Mass.; town records of Dunbarton record her there.) She married Pardon Tabor. She was admitted to the church Nov. 2, 1882. She d. in Hampstead, July 5, 1900. Her funeral was attended by Rev. R. P. Gardner.

She was buried in the village cemetery. They had six children and nearly a hundred descendants at the time of her death (see pp. 337, 375, Vol. 1). (See photos, Vol. 1).

MRS. LITTLE. NO. 631.

No. 631.

Abbie Isadore Gale, b. in Kingston, June 19, 1859, a daughter of Franklin and Ann (Rowell) Gale, of Kingston, both natives of Newton. She was educated in the public schools of Kingston and at Kingston Academy. She taught school several years in Kingston, Danville, and Hampstead. She was educated in music under private teachers, Prof. Hartwell and others. She has been a member of the church choir nineteen years. Was elected chorister Dec. 31, 1902, and is a member of the various church societies. She married Albert H. Little (No. 604), July 18, 1882, and was admitted to the church Jan. 7, 1883. They have children:

I.   Myrta A. (No. 758).
II.   Edith Marion, b. Jan. 13, 1893.

No. 632.

Ethelbert B. Woodward, b. in Lowell, Mass., in 1861, a son of Russell A. and Barbary G. (Harriman) Woodward (No. 619). He was admitted to the church July 2, 1883, and is a present member. He is a butcher, at present residing in Hampstead.

No. 633.

Seth Bruce. He married Mrs. Sarah K. Hoyt (No. 575), and also married the widow of John Nichols, of Derry, in 1901. He was admitted to the church Feb. 24, 1884, and was dismissed to unite with the Congregational church in Chester, Dec. 18, 1884. Resides in Derry.

No. 634.

Charles Henry Sweet, b. in Derry, Aug. 16, 1862, son of Charles H. and Roxanna (Griffin) Sweet. He married Mary C. Lake (No. 622). He was admitted to the church Feb. 24, 1884, and was dis. and rec. to unite with the College Church at Hanover, March 2, 1899.

No. 635.

Osman Cleander Baker Nason. He writes from Medway, Mass., Jan. 6, 1902:—" I was born in Taunton, Mass., Sept.

14, 1858. My father was Rev. Charles Nason, a Methodist Episcopal clergyman, and my mother Sarah (Nason) Nason. I was educated principally in the public and high schools of Providence, R. I., where I fitted for Brown University, from which I was graduated in 1882. After five years as a teacher in various public and private schools, among which was one year in the Hampstead High School, I entered upon the study of medicine at Boston University, graduating from its medical department in 1891. After practising medicine for ten years in Reading, Mass., I took a post-graduate course of medical study at Harvard University, passed the examinations of its under-graduate course, and received its degree of M. D. in 1901.

I am at present practising my profession in Medway, Mass. I married Medora Taggard Barber, who was born in Bellingham, Mass., Feb. 28, 1856, her parents being Adams J. and Elizabeth (Taggard) Barber. We are at present members of the Congregational Church, Medway."

Dr. and Mrs. Nason united with the church in Hampstead by letter from the M. E. Church at East Blackstone, R. I., September, 1884, and were dis. and rec. to unite with the Church at Woonsocket, R. I., July 16, 1885.

No. 636.

Medora Taggard Barber (see No. 635).

No. 637.

Alice Harriet Spollett, b. in Derry, Sept. 16, 1860, a daughter of Hazen N. and Martha J. (Adolphus) Spollett, of Derry. She was educated in the public schools of Derry, Adams Female Academy, and later at Pinkerton Academy. She married Isaac Randall, Feb. 24, 1889 (p. 347, Vol. 1). She was admitted to the church by letter from Chester, July 18, 1884, and is a present member, and connected with the various societies of the church. They have children:—

I.   Eleanor True, b. May 5, 1893.
II.   Maurice Isaac, b. Aug. 17, 1895.
III. Evelyn Worth, b. Nov. 5, 1899. (See cradle roll.)

No. 638.

Mary Jane Brickett, b. in Hampstead, March 31, 1835, a daughter of Richard E. and Nabby (Kent) Brickett (Nos. 291, 268). She married, first, James Hamilton Hoyt, of Hampstead, and, second, William Fellows, of Hampstead, as his second wife, who died in Hampstead, Dec. 12, 1902, aged 83 years. She was admitted to the church Jan. 4, 1885, and d. in Hampstead, Aug. 19, 1901, after a long illness. Her funeral was attended by Rev. R. P. Gardner, and interment was in the village cemetery. She had no children.

No. 639.

Henry Choate Ordway, b. in Hampstead, Aug. 8, 1856, a son of Nelson and Elizabeth P. (Choate) Ordway (No. 454). He was educated in the common schools of Hampstead, and fitted for Yale College at Andover Phillips Academy, graduating from Yale in 1880, Columbia Law School in 1882, and was admitted to the New York bar in 1882. He married Fannie Haines Scudder, Oct. 20, 1885. He was admitted to the church Jan. 4, 1885, and was dis. and rec. to unite with the First Congregational Church at Winchester, Mass., Dec. 17, 1885, and joined there in 1886. He has been a member of the church committee from January, 1901, to the present time. (See p. 837, Vol. 1.) (See photos, Vol. 1.) They have children :—

I.   Philip Scudder, b. March 14, 1887; joined the Congregational
      church in Winchester, Nov. 3, 1891.
II.   Elizabeth Irving, b. Dec. 30, 1888; joined the Congregational
      church in Winchester, Nov. 3, 1901.
III. Katherine Lewis, b. July 20, 1890.
IV.   Helen Frances, b. Oct. 2, 1893.

No. 640.

Eugene Leroy Spinney, b. in Londonderry, Nov. 19, 1849, a son of John D. and Zillah M. (Taylor) Spinney (both deceased), of Londonderry. He married Laura A. Merrill (No. 641). He was admitted to the church by letter from the M. E. Church of East Pepperell, Mass., March 1, 1885, and is a present member.

No. 641.

Laura Anna Merrill, b. in Chester, Jan. 6, 1856, a daughter of George Washington Merrill, who was b. in Sandown, a son of Capt. Simon Merrill (No. 208), and received his name from the fact that his father, Capt. Merrill, shook hands with Gen. Washington on the battlefield in the Revolutionary war, and ever held him ´ in great esteem. He married Mary A. Sleeper, a native of Derry. Laura A. married Eugene L. Spinney (No. 640). She was admitted to the church by letter from the Congregational Church in Chester, March 1, 1885, and is a present member. She was educated in the common schools of Chester and at the State Normal School at Salem, Mass. She taught school several terms. They have children:—

I. Helen Ethel (No. 700).
II. Alice Gertrude (No. 725).
III. Grace Marion, b. Jan. 25, 1885.
IV. Laura Merrill, b. June 25, 1887.
V. Gladys Lillian, b. Oct. 12, 1892.
VI. Doris Madelene, b. July 31, 1897.

No. 642.

Fannie Belle Williams, b. in Hampstead, Sept. 14, 1872, a daughter of Dea. Caleb W. and Martha H. (Gordon) Williams (Nos. 515, 490). She was admitted to the church March 1, 1885, and was dis. and rec. to unite with the Trinitarian Congregational Church at Northfield, Mass., Oct. 18, 1894. Miss Williams writes: "Carney, Lincoln County,

Oklahoma, March 29, 1902: After teaching for five years subsequent to my graduation from the Hampstead High School, in 1889, I went to Northfield Seminary in 1894, where I studied for two years. Here a desire to do Christian work was fostered and developed, and in December, 1896, the Lord thrust me forth to active service. At that time I went to Barrington, where I remained in evangelistic work until the following September, when I was permitted to extend my preparation for more active service by going to

MISS WILLIAMS. NO. 642.

the Bible Institute founded by D. L. Moody in Chicago. While in the Bible Institute I studied and had different forms of Christian work assigned to me for every week, such as house to house visitation, meetings for policemen at the police stations, cottage prayer meetings, women's meetings, children's meetings, Sunday school classes. From there I went at once into evangelistic effort, and was engaged in Bible teaching for some evangelists. In June, 1899, I went to Kansas to engage in missionary and evangelistic work. While in Kansas I supplied one church for three months and another for seven months in the capacity of pastor, or partially so. I worked in other churches, too, but in those others my work was more like that of an evangelist.

In May, of 1901, I came to Oklahoma, where my summer was spent in working in two small, weak churches, and teaching the day and Bible school. In October I began my duties as principal of the school here in Carney, which is a small town. One of the churches is located here, and I have been acting as pastor of it, as well as teaching this winter. I was called to the pastorate last fall, and was formally approbated in October, 1901.

I am glad of the help that the church in Hampstead gave me when I was younger. May God still use it in forming character and developing a Christian life for many another one."

Nov. 29, 1902, Miss Williams writes from Alvaretta, Okla., where she is stationed doing enjoyable work, and also is corresponding secretary of the Y. P. S. C. E. of the Territorial Union of Oklahoma and Indian Territories, and sent the following original lines as "quite true to her life."

"THE MAGIC TOUCH.

The earth was dark, and dead, and cold,
And bleak and desert the barren wold;
No trace of life, no beauty fair,
No charm of Nature to hold me there.

The soft rains fell, and soft winds blew,
The touch was gentle, but each root knew,
A thrill of life came rushing then,
And earth burst forth into life again.

My life was dark, and dead, and cold,
While back on itself it inward rolled;
No trace of love that brightens life,
No kindly action, but discord, strife.

My soul was swept by breath divine,
And to that barren, cold heart of mine,
A burst of love and kindness came,
And earth its sisterhood then could claim".

No. 643.

Annie Graham, b. in Brooklyn, Prince Edwards Island, April 24, 1862, a daughter of John and Margaret (McClain) Graham (see No. 565). She married Clarence L. Sawyer (see Nos. 529 and 496). She was admitted to the church March 1, 1885, and is a present member. They have no children.

No. 644.

Mary Lillie Hoyt, b. in Hampstead, May 20, 1862, a daughter of Daniel N. and Martha (McDuffee) Hoyt (p. 849, Vol. 1). She was educated in the public and high school of Hampstead. She was admitted to the church March 1, 1885, and is a present member. (See photo, Vol. 1.)

No. 645.

Louise Belle Griffin, b. in Hampstead, Sept. 8, 1869, a daughter of William A. and Mary E. (Stevens) Griffin (Nos. 554, 555). She was educated in the common and high school, class of 1887. She married Everett William Boyd, Sept. 1, 1898, and resides in Somerville, Mass. She was admitted to the church March 1, 1885, and is a present member. They have children:—

I. Byron Griffin.
II. Frances.

No. 646.

Helen Putnam Lake, b. in Hampstead, May 26, 1870, a daughter of Thorndike P. and Martha E. (Marble) Lake (No. 507), (p. 362, Vol. 1). She was educated in the public and high school, and Salem, Mass., Normal School. A teacher four years. She married Harry A. Tucker (No. 669). She was admitted to the church March 1, 1885, and was dis. and rec. to unite with the Free Will Baptist Church

in Haverhill, Mass., July 26, 1900. They have an only
child :—

I.   Mildred Lake, b. Sept., 1889.

No. 647.

Fannie Maria Tabor, b. in Hampstead, June 27, 1867, a
daughter of John W. and Mary A. (Little) Tabor (Nos.
613, 510). She was educated in the public schools of
Hampstead. She united with the church March 1, 1885, and
was dis. and rec. to unite with the Congregational Church in
Chester, June 28, 1894, and again received in the Hampstead church by letter from Chester, June 29, 1899. She
married Oliver M. Edwards, of Chester, Feb. 19, 1888.
They had children :—

I.   Alta E., b. Nov. 6, 1889.
II.   Ethel E., b. June 9, 1892.
III. Leon F., b. Nov., 1893.
IV.   Carl, b. April, 1897; d. in 1898.

No. 648.

Charles M. Colby, b. in Lawrence, Mass., April 25, 1849,
a son of John and Susan E. (Whitten) Colby, of Lawrence.
He married Sarah J. Brown (No. 649), in 1872. He was
admitted to the church March 1, 1885, and dis. Sept. 2, 1886.

No. 649.

Sarah Julia Brown, b. in Lowell, Mass., May 5, 1856, a
daughter of Benjamin and Mary Brown, of Ayers Junction,
Mass. She married Charles M. Colby (No. 648), in 1872,
and moved from Lawrence to Hampstead in 1882. She was
admitted to the church March 1, 1885, and was dis. to unite
with the Congregational Church in Munda, Ill., March 8, 1888.
She died in 1901.

No. 650.

Will Clarence Wilson, b. in Deerfield, Feb. 23, 1864, a
son of William B. and Belinda G. (Atwood) Wilson (No.
517). He is married, and resides in Philadelphia. He was
admitted to the church in Hampstead March 1, 1885, and
dis. April 30, 1891, to unite with the Fairhail Baptist Church
in Philadelphia (p. 200, Vol. 1).

No. 651.

John William Watson, b. in Lawrence, Mass., July 8,
1870, a son of Rev. Albert and Mary M. (Priestly) Watson
(Nos. 519, 520). He was educated in the public schools of
Hampstead, graduating from the high school class of 1866;
continued and completed a preparatory course at Phillips
Exeter Academy; graduate Dartmouth College, 1893; post
graduate course, with degree A. M.; graduate Baltimore
Medical College of Physicians and Surgeons, 1900, where
he was resident physician of the Presbyterian Eye, Ear,
Nose and Throat Hospital of Baltimore, Md. He is at present practising his profession at West Hartford, Vt. He
married, Sept. 3, 1901, Cassius May Jones. He was admitted to the Hampstead church March 1, 1893, and dis. to the
Mystic Side Congregational Church in Everett, Mass., Aug.
17, 1893.

No. 652.

Albion Diamond Emerson, b. in Hampstead, Feb. 29,
1868, a son of Alfred P. and S. Francena (Diamond) Emerson (see p. 868, Vol. 1). He was educated in the public
and high school, graduating class of 1886. He married
Mary G. Calderwood of Atkinson (No. 755). He was admitted to the church May 2, 1885, and is a present member.

No. 653.

Fred Darling Marble, b. in Hampstead, July, 1864, a son

MR. AND MRS. A. D. EMERSON. NOS. 652, 755.

of John W. and Emily A. (Darling) Marble (No. 513, and p. 362, Vol. 1). He was educated in the public and high

school of Hampstead. He mar. Lizzie Shrenan and resides
in Hampstead, where they have children :—Ethel, Mamie
and Agnes. He was adm. to the church May 2, 1885, and
dis. Feb. 5, 1897.

No. 654.

' Dana Giles Marble, b. in Hampstead, 1862, a son of Giles
F. and Clementine (Hoyt) Marble (Nos. 665, 463). He
was educated in the public and high schools of Hampstead,
graduating in class of 1881. He continued his studies at
Phillips Exeter Academy; graduated from Dartmouth College in 1884, and studied law; he would have been adm. to
the bar in three weeks, but while teaching at Hillsboro
Academy he contracted a cold, which resulted in his death,
in 1885; unmarried. He was adm. to the church July ·5,
1885 (see p. 362, Vol. 1). (See photo, Vol. 1.)

No. 655.

Kate Fuller Chaples, b. in Haverhill, Mass., Jan. 13, 1865,
a daughter of Andrew F. and Lydia Augusta (Hoyt)
Chaples. Her mother married, second, Dea. John Badger of
Plaistow. Kate mar. John B. Haseltine, son of William
Haseltine of Plaistow. She was adm. to the church July 5,
1885, and was dis. and rec. to unite with the North Parish
Congregational Church in Haverhill, Oct. 31, 1886. They
have children :—

I.   Clifton, b. April 17, 1887.
II.   Christine, b. Nov. 28, 1889.
III. Hope, b. Jan. 26, 1891; d. March 20, 1901.

No. 656.

Emma Eliza Emerson, b. in Hampstead, Feb. 4, 1865, a
daughter of Daniel H. and Sarah B. (Richardson) Emerson
(No. 439). She was educated in the public and high school
of Hampstead, graduated in class of 1882, and was a suc-

cessful teacher for several years.   She mar. Elwin E. Edgerly of Haverhill, Mass., Sept. 10, 1889.   She was adm. to the

MRS. M. ETTA TUPPER.   NO. 657.

church July 5, 1885, and was dis. and rec. to unite with the
Center Congregational Church in Haverhill, Feb. 20, 1890.
They have children :—

I.   Hazel Louisa, b. Jan. 11, 1895.
II.   Janet Sarah, b. Oct. 20, 1897.

No. 657.

Etta Maria Hunkins, b. in Hampstead, July 13, 1865, a daughter of James and S. Elizabeth (Sawyer) Hunkins (No.

J. HERBERT EMERSON. NO. 659.

560). She was educated in the public and high school of Hampstead, and a musical education under private teachers; she was organist at the church for five years. She married William Tupper. She was admitted to the church July 5,

1885, and is a present member. They reside in South Rye-gate, Vt.

MRS. EMERSON. (SEE NO. 659.)

No. 658.

Edward Elmer Bradley, b. in Stockbridge, Mass., Feb. 8,

1862, son of George Patten and Lydia (Rogers) Bradley, residing in Stockbridge. He mar. Sarah Allen White Phillips. He was principal one year, 1884-85 of Hampstead High School. He was adm. to the church by letter from the Congregational Church at Stockbridge, March, 1885. Dis. and rec. to unite with the M. E. Church in Baltimore, Md., Oct. 31, 1886. He was settled as clergyman, in Lincoln, Mass., 1893. They have one child, Phillips Bradley.

No. 659.

John Herbert Emerson, b. in Hampstead, July 28, 1869, a son of Alfred P. and S. Francena (Diamond) Emerson (Nos. 308, 354 and p. 368, Vol. 1). He was educated in the public and high school, class 1887, and at Comer's Commercial School, Boston. He married, Emma Josephine Hill of Derry, June 9, 1898, who was b. June 9, 1874. He was adm. to the church May 2, 1886, and was dis. and rec. to unite with the Berkeley St. Temple Church of Boston, Oct. 28, 1896. Their son, Horace Albert, b. Nov. 29, 1902.

No. 660.

Emma Jane Brown, b. in Rochester, mar. William, son of Ezra Card of Atkinson. She was adm. to the church July 4, 1886. Dis. and rec. to unite with the Grace M. E. Church in Haverhill, Mass., Dec. 27, 1888. They reside in Haverhill.

No. 661.

Edward S. Smith (called Colby on church records), b. in Salisbury (a nephew of Mrs. Charles B. Moulton, East Hampstead). His mother died when he was an infant, and he was reared by his grandparents, Mr. and Mrs. Seth N. Colby of Salisbury. He resided in the No. 7 district a few years. He was baptized in the Angly Pond by Rev. Albert Watson, and was admitted to the church September 5, 1886. Dis-

missed and recommended to unite with the Congregational
Church at West Concord, February 28, 1887, where he was
a member, January 6, 1903, but his residence was unknown
by the pastor of that church. He went from West Concord
to Boston, and enlisted in the U. S. Navy, and not heard
from since.

No. 662.

Mabel Alice Watson, b. in Albany, Vt., August 29, 1878,
a daughter of Rev. Albert and Mary M. (Priestly) Eaton
(Nos. 519, 520). She was educated in the public and high
school of Hampstead, graduating in the class of 1889. She
continued her studies, and completed her preparatory course
at Kimball Union Academy at Meriden; was graduated
from Mt. Holyoke College, in 1896. She is at present a
teacher in the high school at Peabody, Mass. She was admitted to the church September 5, 1886, and was dis. and
rec. to unite with the Mystic Side Congregational Church
at Everett, Mass., August 17, 1893.

No. 663.

Fred Martin Rice, b. in Natick, Mass., July 6, 1861, a son
of Martin and Mary Celia (Pray) Rice, both of Natick.
He was a graduate from Williams College, in 1883, as A.
M., and studied at Yale Divinity School, 1888-9. He was
principal of Hampstead High School from 1886 to 1888, and
a teacher in the Allen School, in New York City, from 1889
to the present time (1902). He married Abbie R. Randall
(No. 577). He was admitted to the church by letter from
the Second Presbyterian Church at Cranberry, N. J., September 22, 1886, and was dis. and rec. to unite with the
Congregational Church at Natick, Mass., Aug. 2, 1888. He
is at present a deacon of the Second Presbyterian Church
in New Rochelle, N. Y., where he resides.

No. 664.

Annie Lyle Griffin, b. in East Andover, Oct. 29, 1870, a daughter of Rev. Calvin B. and Mary Alice (Hoyt) Griffin (see Nos. 616, 617). Rev. Calvin B. Griffin was b. March, 1841, and moved to Danville when an infant. He made a public profession of religion and united with the church in 1862. He was in the 8th N. H. Vol., and went with his regiment to New Orleans, and was dismissed on account of ill health. In 1866 he entered the theological school at New Hampton, N. H., and remained nearly three years, when failing health compelled him to leave the school. In 1869 he received a call to the church at East Andover. While he was there the church edifice was burned, and through his efforts mainly and his encouragement a more commodious structure was erected. In 1872 he went to Chicago, Ill., where he received a call, but the climate being unfavorable, he came to Boston in September of 1872, and entered on a pastorate of three years. There he effected the sale of the church property on North Bennett street, and secured a place farther up town for their church, the Freeman place chapel, where he preached the last part of his pastorate. In April, 1877, he again went to East Andover, in hopes that the climate might be beneficial, but preached two Sundays, and died Aug. 7, 1877. He married Mary Alice Hoyt. They had four children, two of whom died in infancy, and—

I.   Edith S. (No. 700).
II.   Annie Lyle (above); m. Henry L. Eastman (see No. 456), Dec. 21, 1895. She was a graduate from Hampstead High School, class of 1886. She was admitted to the church Dec. 20, 1880, by letter from the Christian Baptist Church at Danville. Dis. to unite with the St. Peter's Presbyterian Church, Rochester, N. Y., Sept., 1902. Resides in Rochester, N. Y. They have children :—
        1. Alice Warren, b. April 29, 1897.
        2. Helen Darthea, b. April 22, 1900.

No. 665.

Giles Francis Marble, b. in Hampstead, Sept. 4, 1834, a son of Giles O. and Betsey B. (Peaslee) Marble (No. 412). He married Clementine Hoyt of Sandown (No. 463), Oct. 31, 1833. He was admitted to the church March 3, 1887, and is a present member (p. 362, Vol. 1).

No. 666.

Nettie May Follansbee, b. in Dunbarton, May 19, 1869, only daughter of Orren E. and Mary A. (Smith) Follansbee (Nos. 601, 561). She was educated in the public and high school of Hampstead, and after teaching one year, entered Kimball Union Academy at Meriden. Ill health compelled her to leave school before completing the preparatory course for college. She was admitted to the church March 3, 1887, and was dis. and rec. to unite with the First Congregational Church at Methuen, Mass., Jan. 30, 1895, and is at present a member of the First Church of Christ in Bradford, Mass., having been admitted by letter from Methuen, May 4, 1899. She married L. Lyman Campbell, of Bradford, June 26, 1901. Their daughter, Caroline Mary, b. July 14, d. 18, 1902.

No. 667.

Will Amos Fitts, b. in Candia, a son of William Garland Fitts, a soldier in the civil war, and wife, Martha A. Brown, both of Candia. He was educated in the common and high school of Candia. He married Mary E. Tabor (No. 550), Feb. 21, 1889. He was admitted a member of the church by letter from the Congregational Church in Candia, March 3, 1887, and is a present member.

No. 668.

Christina Mabel Graham, b. in Brooklyn, Prince Edwards Island, in 1859, a daughter of John and Margaret (McClain)

Graham (see No. 565). She married Buchanan Shirley of Chester. She was admitted to the church at the home of her sister, Mrs. Jesse Shirley (No. 565), "seriously ill,"

DR GEO. S. EMERSON. NO. 670.

Sept. 11, 1887. She died a few days later. Her husband d. ——. They had one daughter:—

I.   Mary S. (No. 726).

No. 669.

Harry A. Tucker, b. in Somerville, Mass., Sept., 1869, a son of Mason Warren and Arvilla (March) Tucker. He was educated at New Hampton Academy. He married

MRS. EMERSON. (SEE NO. 670.)

Helen P. Lake (No. 646). He was admitted to the church
May 6, 1888, and was dis. Dec. 29, 1890.

No. 670.

George Short Emerson, b. in Hampstead, Sept. 7, 1871, a son of Alfred P. and S. Francena (Diamond) Emerson (see Nos. 308, 354, and Vol. 1, p. 363). He was educated in the common and high school of Hampstead, class of 1888 ; from the Baltimore Medical College, and is at present physician and surgeon in Fitzwilliam. He married Ella May Hill, of Derry, June 9, 1898, who was b. June 9, 1874. He was admitted to the church May 6, 1888, and was dis. and rec. to unite with the Congregational Church in Fitzwilliam, Dec. 20, 1898. Their son :—

I.   Reginald Hill, b. Jan. 2, 1903.

No. 671.

Albert Priestley Watson, b. in Barrington, Nov. 12, 1875, a son of Rev. Albert and Mary M. (Priestley) Watson (Nos. 519, 520). He was educated in the public and high school of Hampstead, graduate from Kimball Union Academy of Meriden, and entered Dartmouth College, from which institution he was graduated in 1897 ; Andover Theological School, 1900. Ordained as pastor of the Presbyterian Church at Bedford, Sept. 25, 1900. He was admitted a member of the Hampstead church May 6, 1886, and was dis. and rec. to unite with the Mystic Side Congregational Church at Everett, Mass., Aug. 17, 1893.

No. 672.

Carlton Hoyt Barnes, b. in Sandown, Nov. 3, 1855, a son of Luther and Roxanna (Hoyt) Barnes, of Sandown. He married Dora A. Brown (No. 673). He was admitted to the church July 1, 1888, and is a present member.

No. 673.

Dora Annie Brown, b. in Sandown, June 27, 1860, a daughter of Jonathan Nay Brown, of Sandown, and wife,

Dorcas] D. Brewster, of Farmington, Me. She married Carlton H. Barnes (No. 672). She was admitted to the church July 1, 1888, and is a present member. They have children :—

ADIN S. LITTLE. (SEE NO. 674.)

I. Nelson Eugene (No. 721).
II. Marion Fitzgerald, b. Jan. 14, 1882; educated at Raymond; works in Quincy, Mass.
III. Clinton Nay, b. Jan. 14, 1883; at home.

No. 674.

Fannie Casandria Emerson, b. in Hampstead, March 23,

1873, a daughter of Alfred P. and S. Francena (Diamond) Emerson (see Nos. 308, 354), (p. 368, Vol. 1). She was

MRS. LITTLE. NO. 674.

educated in the public and high school of Hampstead. She mar. Adin Sidney Little (See No. 600), Sept. 11, 1892. She was admitted to the church July 1, 1888, and is a present member. They have children :—

I.   Adin Edmund, b. Oct. 28, 1898.
II.   Perry Ellsworth, b. April 12, 1901.
III. Francena M., b. April 30, 1903.

No. 675.

Edwin Hunt Whitehill, b. in South Wilbraham, Mass. (now Hampden), Oct. 30, 1865, a son of John and Clara Joanna (Hunt) Whitehill. Graduate Amherst College, 1881, and since that time has been in charge of high schools at West Barnstable, Mass., '87, '88; Hampstead, '88, 90 ; Medford, Mass., '90-'92 ; Woodstock, Vt., '92 to '98 ; Bridgewater, Mass., 1898 to the present year, 1902. He married Caroline Thayer Manning, at Andover, Mass., Aug. 30, 1889 ; b. Nov. 6, 1865, a daughter of John Hart and Lois Ann (Batchelder) Manning, of Andover. They have a daughter, Gladys Marion. Mrs. Whitehill taught school five years before marriage. She spent one year of special study at Smith College. She taught a Sunday school class, and was a leader of a " ten " of King's Daughters in Hampstead. He was admitted to the church by letter from the Church of Christ, at Amherst College, Mass., Sept. 13, 1888, and was dis. and rec. to unite with the Second Congregational Church, at Medford, Oct. 23, 1890.

No. 676.

Edward Foster Perot, b. in Plympton, Mass., April 11, 1855, in the home where he now resides, a son of Joseph Edward Perot, now deceased, and his wife, Mary Davis Pope, b. in Middleboro, Mass., in 1840, who now resides with the son Edward, at the old family homestead. He is a market gardener, milkman and farmer in Plympton. He married, first, Hattie Crocker, in 1876, who d. in 1888. They had children :—

I.   Charles Foster, b. March 16, 1877; married, and resides in Ray-
          nan, Mass.
II.   Estelle D., b. May 28, 1882; works in a paper-box factory in
          Middleboro; a working member in the Society of C. E.

He married, second, Carrie M. Fitts (No. 684). He was
admitted to the church Sept. 1, 1889, and dis. to unite with
the Congregational Church at Plympton, Mass., Dec. 22,
1892. He has lived in Hampstead and Haverhill, Mass.

No. 677.

Anna Maria Bartlett, b. in Raymond, March 19, 1836, a
daughter of Peter and Mary (Dearborn) Bartlett (see No.
611). She was educated at Atkinson Academy and at Mt.
Holyoke Seminary, and in the summer schools of Illinois.
She has been engaged in teaching school forty-one years in
Vermont, New Hampshire, and Massachusetts, including
twenty years in Evanston and Chicago, Ill., sixteen years of
educational work in Chicago in the first to seventh grades
inclusive, but principally in the fourth and fifth grades. She
was admitted to the church by letter from the Leverett
Street Congregational Church of Chicago, Dec. 12, 1888,
having united with the First Congregational Church in
Chelsea, Mass., in 1855. She is a present member.

No. 678.

Carrie Etta Ranlett, b. in Hampstead, June 28, 1873, a
daughter of Charles H. and Susan P. (Tabor) Ranlett (p.
375 and 337, Vol. 1). She was educated in the public and
high school of Hampstead, class of 1890. She married
Lyndell Pressey. She was admitted to the church March 2,
1890, and is a present member. They have children :—

I.   Edna, b. June 23, 1895.
II.   Zelda L., b. Oct. 15, 1898.

No. 679.

Minnie Estelle Stevens, b. in Plaistow, June 26, 1865, a daughter of Moses Brown and Emily Augusta (Heath) Stevens. Her parents moved to Atkinson in June, 1870. She¯was educated in the public schools of Atkinson and at

MRS. EMERSON. NO. 679.

Atkinson Academy. She was a successful teacher several years in Atkinson and Salem, and a "natural musician." She has been organist at the church since 1887. She was married to Frank W. Emerson, by Rev. Mr. Alexander of Atkinson, now of Newport (see Nos. 533, 534), Sept. 12, 1886. She was admitted to the church May 4, 1890, and is a present member, and connected with the various societies of the church, with especial work in the local C. E. Union. A teacher in the Sunday school, in the same class since 1890, a class consisting of young women, whose ages range from 18

FRANK W. EMERSON. (SEE NO. 679.)

to 30 years. She has also held several important offices in the county Sunday school work. She has no children.

No. 680.

Ruth Ann Emerson, b. in Hampstead, Dec. 22, 1866, a daughter of James H. and Sarah Ann (Woodman) Emer-

son (p. 368, Vol. 1). She was educated in the public and
high school, graduating class of 1885. She married Arthur
Herbert Little, May 27, 1891 (see Nos. 467 and 605), p.
351, Vol. 1). She was admitted to the church May 4, 1890,
and is a present member. Their son :—

I. Maurice Emerson, b. May 14, 1892; d., aged 7 days.

No. 681.

Mary Lizzie Emerson, b. in Hampstead, Dec. 16, 1871, a
daughter of James H. and Sarah Ann (Woodman) Emerson
(see No. 680). She was educated in the public and high
school of Hampstead, class of 1889, and taught school five
years in Hampstead before her marriage to Harry Isaac
Noyes, of Atkinson, Oct. 17, 1894. She was admitted to the
church May 4, 1890, and is a present member. They have
children :—

I.   Caroline Ruth, b. Dec. 8, 1895.
II.   Harold Emerson, b. March 12, 1897.
III. Roland Isaac, b. Sept. 15, 1898.
IV.   James Marlon, b. Sept. 12, 1901.

No. 682.

Thomas H. H. Knight. He was admitted to the church
by letter from the Congregational Church at Melrose High-
lands, Mass., Sept., 1891. Dis. and rec. to unite with the
Congregational Church at Duxbury, Mass., June 17, 1892.
He writes : " I was educated in the Boston schools (the
old Brimmer and the English High) and Doane College.
Previous to my teaching in Hampstead I had taught in
Weeping Water Academy and at Cotuit, Mass. I was principal of Hampstead High School only one year, and since
that time, 1891, I have taught seven years at Duxbury,
Mass., as principal of Partridge Academy, and for the past
four years I have been junior master of the Girls' High
School in Boston."

No. 683.

John Pease, b. in Cornish, Me. He was admitted to the church by letter from the Congregational Church in Cornish, Dec. 18, 1890, and was dis. and rec. to unite with the Union Congregational Church at Haverhill, Mass., July 21, 1892.

No. 684.

Carrie M. Fitts, b. in West Newbury, Mass., Sept. 9, 1857, a daughter of George Calvin Fitts, b. in West Newbury, and wife, Hannah Maria Louisa Stevens, b. in Chester, and who d. in Hampstead, Jan. 26, 1898 (see No. 555). She was educated in the public schools and at the high school of Hampstead. She writes, under date of Feb. 27, 1902, Plympton, Mass.: "My parents moved to Hampstead from West Newbury when I was very young, and I lived there most of my life, except when working away. I united with the Trinitarian Congregational Church at North Andover, Mass., with twenty others, Jan. 9, 1883, under the pastor, Rev. Horace H. Leavett, now of Somerville, Mass. From there I was admitted to the church in Hampstead, under Rev. Albert Watson, by letter from the North Andover church, Jan. 1, 1891. I was married by Rev. Mr. Watson to Edward F. Perot, then of Hampstead (No. 676), Sept. 30, 1890. We have lived in Hampstead two years, in Haverhill, Mass., a few years, and at present in Plympton. We have no children. I am a member of the C. E. Society here, as is also my step-daughter. We have a flourishing society, and we each try to do our part in the meetings. Wishing the church in Hampstead success and prosperity in the future, as in the past, and a hope for your personal success in the great task which you have undertaken, I can say the Lord has given me strength in my trial, and I have never been sorry that I accepted him. I only regret that I had not sooner in life."

No. 685.

Annie Belle Fitts, b. in Chester, Feb. 28, 1870, a daughter

MRS. SANBORN. NO. 685.

of George C. and H. Maria (Stevens) Fitts, of Hampstead (see No. 555). She was educated in the public and high

school of Hampstead, class of 1887. She married John C. Sanborn (No. 598). She was admitted to the church March 1, 1891, and is a present member. They have children :—

I. , Marjory, b. April 7, 1900.
II.   Donald Fitts, b. Sept. 13, 1902.

LESTER A. WILLIAMS.   NO.   .

No. 686.

Lester Alonzo Williams, b. in Hampstead, June 11, 1880, a son of Dea. Caleb W. and Martha H. (Gordon) Williams (Nos. 515, 490). He was educated in the public schools of

Hampstead and Haverhill, Mass., and was a graduate from
the Hampstead High School, class of 1898. He continued
his studies at the French and American College, at Springfield, Mass., and entered Dartmouth College two years in
advance, Sept., 1901, in preparatory to enter the ministry.
He was adm. to the church when ten years of age, April 30,
1891 (see No. 758), and was dis. and rec. to unite with the
Center Congregational Church in Haverhill, Dec. 17, 1891,
and was again received to the Hampstead Church April
20, 1893, and is a present member.

No. 687.

Ezra Willard Pepper, b. in Washington, Vt., June 18,
1833, a son of Willard and Rachel (Taylor) Pepper of
Washington. He was a carpenter and shoemaker by trade.
He married Susan E. Hyde (No. 691), and died at the late
Dr. Tewksbury's home, July 30, 1900. He was admitted to
the church September 1, 1891.

No. 688.

Susan Everline Hyde, b. in Newmarket, Jan. 6, 1847, a
daughter of Lorenzo Dow Hyde, b. in Tamworth, and his
wife Mary Smith Thompson, b. in Gilford, who moved to
Hampstead, about 1856, and both died here. Susan was
educated in the public schools, and for several years was a
member of the church choir. She married Ezra W. Pepper
(No. 687), July 30, 1865. She was admitted to the church
September 1, 1891, and is present member ; they have no
children.

No. 689.

Annie Sophia Knight, b. in Atkinson, Sept. 16, 1857, a
daughter of Joseph Kimball Knight of Atkinson, and his
wife Orphia Tuthill, of Westminster, Vt. She married
Herbert W. Mills of Hampstead, son of John and Sarah

(Cowell) Mills, Nov. 29, 1878. She was admitted to the church September 1, 1891, and is a present member, and connected with the societies of the church. They have a son, Carlisle Wellington, b. Feb. 8, 1892.

No. 690.

Annie Louise Sawyer, b. in Hampstead, July 7, 1868, a daughter of Horace and Almira W. (Bailey) Sawyer (Nos. 529, 486, and p. 378, Vol. 1.) She was educated in the public and high school. She mar. John E., son of John and Sarah (Cowell) Mills of Hampstead. She was admitted to the church Nov. 1, 1891. Dis. to unite with the Center Church at Haverhill, Mass., October, 1902. They have no children.

No. 691.

William D. Rich, b. in   He was principal of Hampstead High School the year of 1891, 1892. He was admitted to the church by letter from the Congregational Church in Ware, Mass., Nov. 1, 1891.

No. 692.

Forrest Eugene Merrill, b. in Georgetown, Mass., August 2, 1858, a son of Moses Merrill, Jr., deceased, and wife Laura Susan Watson, living in Georgetown. He was educated in the public schools of Georgetown, and at Atkinson Academy and Dartmouth College. Principal of Hampstead High School, 1879 to 1884, and from 1891-'2 to June, 1902. He mar. Alice M. Averill (No. 693). He was admitted to the church by letter from the Provo Congregational Church, Utah, Oct. 6, 1892. He was elected a deacon of the church Dec. 30, 1896 (see p. 848, Vol. 1).

No. 693.

Alice Melisse Averill, b. in Charlestown, Mass., March 3,

FORREST E. MERRILL. NO. 692.

1865, a daughter of Charles and Eliza Ann (Ballard) Averill, both now deceased, of Boston, Mass. She married

Forrest E. Merrill (No. 692). She was educated in the common and high school of Hampstead, living for several years with Mrs. Mary A. (Garland) Pike (No. 386). "She has an enviable musical talent, and was especially pleasing at the 150th anniversary exercises." She was admitted to the church by letter from the Provo Congregational Church at Utah, October 6, 1892. They have children :—

I.   Francis Eugene, b. March 31, 1885; d. Jan. 11, 1888.
II.   Laura E. (No. 763.)
III.   Mary Alice, b. Oct. 16, 1888.
IV.   Florence Margaret, b. April 3, 1890.
V.   Charlotte Ruth, b. March 8, 1892.
VI.   Jeanette Edith, b. Oct. 21, 1893.

No. 694.

Mary Story Fuller, b. in Dunbarton, March 12 ,1837, a daughter of Jared and Thankful (Story) Fuller of Dunbarton, now both deceased. Jared Fuller was a son of Stephen Fuller, who served in the Revolutionary war, and he, with two other soldiers, in running the blockade, carrying provisions to our troops at Charlestown, Mass., were fired upon. One man lost his head, and the spent bullet took off the thumb of Mr. Fuller.

Mary S. Fuller was educated at Pinkerton Academy, Derry. She married Aaron Smith, who was a soldier in the civil war. He enlisted first from Worcester, Mass., in Co. E, 42 Reg. of Infantry, for nine months. The second time in the Mass. Heavy Artillery, Co. D, 4th Reg., and served until the close of the war, being discharged at Fort Richardson, Vt., June 17, 1865. She was admitted to the church by letter from the Pilgrim Church at Dorchester, Mass., December 15, 1892, and is a present member. They had children :—

I.   Harriet Davenport, b. in Bridgton, Me., Feb. 1, 1872; d. June 11, 1874.
II.   Elizabeth M. H. (No. 715).

No. 695.

Annie Imogene Wilson, b. in Deerfield, May 22, 1866, a
daughter of William B. and Belinda G. (Atwood) Wilson
(No. 517).   She was adm. to the church by letter from the
St. James M. E. Church of Manchester, Jan. 13, 1893, and
is a present member.

MISS RANLETT.   NO. 697.

No. 696.

Hannah True Howard, b. in Hampstead, Sept. 14, 1801, a
daughter of John and Sarah (True) Howard (see No. 172,
347).   She was a tailoress by trade, and made many of the

clothes of the residents of Hampstead, in her younger days. She was adm. to the church (unable to be present at the church) at her home, Feb. 19. 1893. and d. Jan., 1895, aged 94 years. She was unmarried, and was buried in the village cemetery.

MRS. SNOOK.   NO. 698.

No. 697.

Lillian Davis Ranlett, b. in Hampstead, May 9, 1876, a daughter of Charles H. and Susan P. (Tabor) Ranlett (see pp. 375, 337, Vol. 1). She was educated in the public school and graduated in the high school class of 1894. She was adm. to the church July 1, 1894, and is a present member.

No. 698.

Carrie Elsie Davis, b. in Hampstead, Nov. 2, 1876, a

MRS. DAVIS. NO. 699.

daughter of William H. and Jane R. (Taylor) Davis (Nos. 437, 699). She was educated in the public schools, and graduated from high school class of 1894, and had a musical education under private teachers. She has resided in Titusville, N. J., for a few years. She was admitted to the church

July 1, 1894, and was dismissed to unite with the church at Titusville, Dec. 7, 1899. She m. Theodore Snook, May 19, 1903.

No. 699.

Jane Rachel Taylor, b. in Washington, Vt., July 3, 1848, a daughter of David and Sophia (Wiley) Taylor of Wash-

H. CLINTON DAVIS.   (SEE NO. 699.)

ington. She was educated at the Normal School in Vermont, and was a very successful teacher in Vermont and Hampstead, before her marriage to William H. Davis, June 23, 1875 (No. 437). She was admitted to the church July 1, 1894, and is a present member, and helpful in the various forms of church work. They have children:—

I.   Carrie E. (No. 698).
II.   Henry Clinton, b. June 26, 1878; who was educated in the public and high school. A member of the choir.
III.   Mary G. (No. 723).

MISS SPINNEY. NO. 700.

No. 700.

Helen Ethel Spinney, b. in Haverhill, Mass., May 1, 1880, a daughter of Eugene L. and Laura A. (Merrill) Spinney (Nos. 645, 641). She was educated in the public and high school, graduating in class of 1897, and at the summer schools of Plymouth. She was educated in music by private teachers. She has taught school four years in Hampstead and Charlton, Mass. She was admitted to the church July 1, 1894, and is a present member.

No. 701.

Ethel Lois Sanborn, b. in Hampstead, Feb. 22, 1878, a daughter of James W. and Flora A. (Corson) Sanborn (Nos. 548, 549). She was educated in the public and high school graduating in class of 1894, and at Northfield, Mass. · She was adm. to the church July 1, 1894, and is a present member.

No. 702.

· Edith Selina Griffin, b. in Boston, Mass., Dec. 29, 1873, a daughter of Rev. Calvin B. and Mary Alice (Hoyt) Griffin of Danville, N. H. (see Nos. 664, 616). She was a graduate of class of 1890, high school. She married Will S. Griffin (No. 709). She was admitted to the church by letter from the M. E. Church at West Hampstead, July 1, 1894, and was dis. to unite with the Center Church at Haverhill, Mass., Jan. 1, 1901.

No. 703.

Grace Melvina Bassett, b. in Hampstead, Oct. 26, 1877. a daughter of Charles and Esther S. (Morrill) Bassett (No. 620). She was educated in the public and high school of Hampstead, graduate of class of 1894, at Groton Academy and at Haverhill Business College, graduate of class of 1902, and in music under private teachers, both vocal and instrumental. She has taught school in Candia seven years, and is a present teacher there. She was adm. to the church July 1, 1894, and is a present member.

No. 704.

Kimball Kent Clark, b. in Haverhill, Mass., May 31, 1878, a son of Harlan P. and Josephine A. (Silloway) Clark

(Nos. 710, 711). He was educated in the public and high school, class of 1898, French and American College at Springfield, Mass., and private teachers. He mar. Lillian G. George (No. 769), and was ordained as pastor of the M. E. Church at East Deering, 1901, and transferred to Fitzwilliam, 1902. He was adm. to the church July 1, 1894, and dis. to unite with the M. E. church at Deering, July 25, 1901; located at Lakeport, 1903.

No. 705.

George Jay Pinneo, b. in Hampstead, July 25, 1878, a son of George Jay Pinneo, b. in Boston, Mass.; d. in Hampstead, March 22, 1901, and his wife Angeline Relief Haynes of Candia, N. H. (see No. 571). He entered the Hampstead High School at the age of twelve years, and graduated in class of 1894; entered Phillips Andover Academy, and remained until the spring of 1896, when he entered the New Hampshire College of Agriculture and Mechanic Arts at Durham, and was graduated in June, 1901, in the agricultural course, taking the degree of B. S. He mar. Lulu Warren of Lee, June, 1901. He was adm. to the church July 1, 1894, and is a present member.

No. 706.

Rev. Rufus Parker Gardner, b. in Orland, Me., Sept. 14, 1858. His early education was in the town of Orland, and from his eleventh year in the schools of Castine, where he was a graduate from high and State Normal Schools. He received a business training from Howe's Commercial School at Worcester, Mass., and was a graduate from Bryant and Stratton's Business College, Boston. He pursued a classical course of college work under private tutors, taught two years in the district schools, and two years as an instructor in East Maine Conference Seminary at Bucksport, Me. After serving two and a half years on missionary work in eastern Maine, he entered Bangor Theological Seminary, from which he was graduated May 25, 1886, and June 2d

REV. RUFUS P. GARDNER.   NO. 706.

of that year was installed pastor of the First Congregational Church at Waldoboro, Me.   He was called from there, Sept.,

1888, to the First Congregational Church at Marion, Mass. In the midst of a very successful pastorate he was called, Oct., 1893, to the church in Hampstead. Resigned to take charge of the New Hampshire State Orphan's Home, Franklin, Sept. 16, 1901. He has served in all the church and

' MRS. GARDNER. NO. 707.

Endeavor work in Rockingham county, as moderator and scribe, and in the larger work of the state, two years as president of the State Sunday School work, and declined a third term. A member of the finance committee, and State superintendent of the junior work. Two years as president of the Christian Endeavor Society, and as scribe of the Congregational and Presbyterian Churches of New Hampshire, and in 1901 preached the annual sermon at Rochester, before the state body. He has served fifteen successive years as secretary of the business committee of Tabor Academy Corporation at Marion, Mass. He is a trustee of the industrial school at Manassah, Va., and president of Sanborn Academy at Kingston, N. H. He was twice married, second, to Belle Clement (No. 707). His daughter (No. 708). He was adm. to the church membership from the church at Marion, Mass., July 1, 1894, and united with the Congregational Church at Franklin, March 8, 1902.

No. 707.

Belle Clement, b. in Knox, Me., May 18, 1867, a daughter of George and Hannah (   ) Clement. Her parents died when she was quite young, and she was educated in the public schools and academy at Freedom, Me. She married. Rev. Rufus P. Gardner (No. 706), June 8, 1886. She was admitted to the church by letter from the Congregational church at Marion, Mass., July 1, 1894, and united with the Congregational church at Franklin, March 8, 1902. Their son :—

I.   Harold Parker, b. Dec. 23, 1890.

No. 708.

Addie Besse Gardner, b. in Edmunds, Me., April 23, 1881, daughter of Rev. Rufus P. Gardner. (No. 706). She was a graduate of the Hampstead High School, class of 1898, and N. H. State Normal School, June, 1902. She taught in Hampstead five terms, and at present is teaching in the third and fourth grades at Lisbon. She was admitted to the church July 1, 1894, and was dis. and united with the Congregational church at Franklin, March 8, 1902.

No. 709.

Will Sawyer Griffin, b. in Hampstead, Oct. 6, 1874, a son of William A. and Mary E. (Stevens) Griffin (Nos. 554, 555). He married Edith S. Griffin (No. 702). He was

MISS GARDNER. NO. 708.

admitted to the church July 1, 1894, and was dis. Nov. 1, 1900.

No. 710.

Harlan Page Clark, b. in Derry in 1841, a son of

Joshua and Eliza (Spollett) Clark, of Derry (see No. 524). He married Josephine A. Silloway (No. 711). He was a soldier in the civil war, in the 1st Regt. of N. H. Vol. Infantry, for three months. He was admitted to the church by letter from the First Baptist Church, at Haverhill, Mass., Aug. 3, 1894. He died March 11, 1903, in Hampstead.

MRS. TABOR. NO. 712.

No. 711.

Josephine Ayer Silloway, b. in Haverhill, Mass., in 1847, a daughter of Luther and Sarah (Bean) Silloway, of Kingston. She married Harlan P. Clark (No. 710). She was admitted to the church by letter from the First Baptist Church at Haverhill, Aug. 3, 1894, and is a present member. They have had children:—

I.   Georgia, b. 1867; m. Eugene Burpee, of Haverhill.
II. Willie Westley, d. young.

III. Sadie Eliza, d. young.
IV. Kimball Kent (No. 704); m. Lillian G. George (No. 709).
V. Eddie Harland, d. young.

No. 712.

Olivia Abbie Wiggin, b. in Stratham, Nov. 16, 1838, a daughter of Ambrose and Abbie (Brown) Wiggin, of Stratham. She married, first, Charles E. Young, of Portsmouth, Sept. 15, 1862, who d. in Haverhill, Mass., Jan. 25, 1881. They had children :—

I. Alice Mary, d., aged 22 months.
II. Abbie Eloise; resides in Groveland, Mass.
III. Alice Crosby, d., aged 4 years and 3 months.

She married, second, Job Tabor (see No. 630), Oct. 9, 1889. She was admitted to the church by letter from the First Baptist Church, Aug. 30, 1894, and is a present member.

No. 713.

Gertrude Sargent Pillsbury, b. in Sandown, Oct. 7, 1877, a daughter of Alden E. and Lizzie P. (Sargent) Pillsbury (No. 508). She was educated in the public and high school, graduating in class of 1897. She was admitted to the church Nov. 4, 1894, and is a present member.

No. 714.

Esther Belle Kent, b. in Lawrence, Mass., Jan. 25, 1879, a daughter of Charles Edwin Kent, of Lawrence, son of Jonathan, and grandson of Dea. Jona. and Clarissa (Page) Kent (Nos. 245, 246). As an orphan, she came to live in Hampstead when about eight years of age, and attended the common schools, and one year at the high school. She then attended, with a cousin, the Northfield, Mass., Seminary, and remained three years. She now resides in Lawrence. She was admitted to the church Nov. 4, 1894, and is a present member.

No. 715.

Elisabeth Maria Howard Smith, b. in Bridgton, Me., June 9, 1877, a daughter of Aaron and Mary S. (Fuller) Smith (No. 694). She was a graduate of the high school class of 1895, and a student at the N. H. Normal School at Plymouth. She has taught several terms. She has, besides the great-grandfather, Stephen Fuller (see No. 694), a great-grandfather, James Packard, who fought in the Revolutionary war, enlisting from Bridgewater, Mass. She was admitted to the church Nov. 4, 1894, and is a present member.

No. 716.

Carrie E. McNiel, b. in Hampstead, a daughter of Rufus and Christia (Graham) McNiel (Nos. 591, 578). She was educated in the public schools, graduating from the high school class of 1897. She was admitted to the church Nov. 4, 1894, and was dis. and rec. to unite with the First Baptist Church at Chelsea, Mass., April 6, 1899.

No. 717.

Oliver Putnam, b. in Hampstead, March 1, 1844, a son of Henry and Meribah H. (Ayer) Putnam (No. 366). He married Mary E. (Mooers) Little (No. 600). He was admitted to the church Feb. 28, 1895. He d. in Hampstead, Oct. 6, 1897 (see p. 332, Vol. 1). (See photo, Vol. 1).

No. 718.

Horace Walter Little, b. in Hampstead, Nov. 2, 1878, a son of William A. and S. Lizzie (Locke) Little (see No. 460 and p. 352, Vol. 1). He was educated in the common and high school, was graduated from class of 1899, and continued his studies at the college (French and American) at Springfield, Mass. He was admitted to the church Feb. 28, 1895, and is a present member. (See photo, Vol. 1).

No. 719.

Charles F. Foote, b. in Hampstead, Nov. 20, 1874, a son of Alfred W. and Sarah F. (Randall) Foote (see No. 592). He was educated in the public and high school of Hamp-

MRS. TABOR. NO. 722.

stead. He was admitted to the church Feb. 28, 1895, and is a present member. He resides in Haverhill, Mass.

No. 720.

Edwin Leroy Corson, b. in Hampstead, Dec. 7, 1875, a son of John S. and Mary E. (Clark) Corson (Nos. 546,

547). He was educated in the public and high school, class of 1894, and at a commercial school in Boston. He was admitted to the church Feb. 28, 1895, and is a present member. He resides in Boston.

MISS DAVIS. NO. 723.

No. 721.

Nelson Eugene Barnes, b. in Sandown, Nov. 19, 1880, a son of Carlton H. and Dora A. (Brown) Barnes (Nos. 672, 673). He was educated in the public and high school, class of 1898. He was admitted to the church Feb. 28, 1895, and dismissed Nov. 25, 1897. A clerk in Haverhill, Mass.

No. 723.

Mary Garland Davis, b. in Hampstead, Aug. 9, 1880, a daughter of William H. and Jane R. (Taylor) Davis (Nos. 437, 699). She was educated in the public and high school of Hampstead, class of 1898, and had a musical education

AMASA W. HUNT.   NO. 727.

under private teachers (see 150th anniversary exercises). She was admitted to the church Feb. 28, 1895, and is a present member.

No. 724.

Alice Rinda Osgood, b. in Hampstead, July 18, 1880

daughter of Charles H. and Francella (Eastman) Osgood, of Hampstead. She married Alfred C. Davis, Aug. 25, 1898 (see No. 737). She was admitted to the church Feb. 28, 1895, and is a present member.

MRS. HUNT. NO. 728.

No. 725.

Alice Gertrude Spinney, b. in Haverhill, Mass., Jan. 20, 1883, a daughter of Eugene L. and Laura A. (Merrill) Spinney (Nos. 640, 641). She was educated in the public and high school of Hampstead, and to within a few weeks of graduation class of 1897. She was admitted to the church Feb. 28, 1895, and is a present member.

No. 726.

Mary S. Shirley, b. in Hampstead, Dec. 13, 1886, a daughter of Buchanan and Christina M. (Graham) Shirley (No. 668). She was educated in the common and high school of Hampstead, and was a teacher, student Normal School, Salem, Mass., 1902. She was admitted to the church Feb. 28, 1895, and was dis. and rec. to unite with the First Congregational Church in Methuen, Mass., March 8, 1897.

No. 727.

Amasa Warren Hunt, b. in Marshfield, Mass., Feb. 5, 1856, a son of Isaac N. Hunt, a farmer, of Marshfield, and his wife, Jerusha W. Bourne, both deceased. He married Lois J. Reynard (No. 728). He was admitted to the church Feb. 28, 1895, by letter from the Baptist church in Chester, and is a present member.

No. 728.

Lois Jane Reynard, b. in Kempville, Yarmouth, N. S., Feb. 13, 1862, a daughter of Henry G. F. and Deborah (Roberts) Reynard, of Yarmouth, both deceased. She married Amasa W. Hunt (No. 727). She was admitted to the church Feb. 28, 1895, by letter from the Baptist church in Chester, and is a present member. A daughter, Pearl Marston, b. Oct. 3, 1883, was educated in the public and high school of Hampstead.

No. 729.

Mercy Ann Conner, b. in Gilford, Me., April 27, 1834, a daughter of James Conner, of Cambridgeport, Mass., and wife, Esther Ford, of Montville, Me. She married William H. Woods (she is a niece of No. 843). She was admitted to the church Feb. 28, 1895, by letter from the Walnut Street M. E. Church, of Chelsea, Mass., and is a present member. They have children:—

byterian Church, of Lowell, Mass., and is a present member. They had children :—

I.   Walter (deceased).
II.   Ethel May, b. in 1890.

No. 731.

Lydia Maria Sargent, b. in Chester, March 28, 1827, a daughter of Abraham and widow Sarah (Underhill) (Greenough) Sargent, of Chester. She married Timothy Wells, of Chester, Nov. 28, 1846, who died Dec. 9, 1872. She was admitted to the church by letter from the First Congregational Church at Bradford, Mass., Feb. 28, 1895, and is a present member. Mrs. Wells was matron at the Bradford Female Seminary, Bradford, eight years, from 1873 ; one year in a young ladies' parlor school at Boston ; four years at the New Hampshire State Normal School at Plymouth ; one year at Tilton Seminary; five years at St. Mary's Episcopal School, Concord, and two years at Tabor Academy, at Marion, Mass. They had children :—

I.   Mary Sargent, b. Nov. 12, 1847; m. Andrew D. Norcross of
      Athol, Mass.; she died leaving one child.
         Mary M., m. Harry Justin Colburn, a teacher at Wilbra-
           ham Academy.
II.   Sarah Greenough, b. Dec. 16, 1849; m. Amos Brown of Auburn,
      (deceased); no children.
III. Clement Henry, b. Oct. 20, 1852; m. Lora M. Moore; resides in
      Chester; they have children :—·
         1. Charles Timothy, b. April 23, 1874; m. Clara A. Leigh-
             ton, and have Josephine Lura, b. July 25, 1899.
         2. Sadie Merrill, b. Oct. 2, 1880.
         3. Wilson Sargent, b. Oct. 21, 1882.
         4. Annie Susia, b. Dec. 17, 1888; d.
         5. Clementine Moore, b. March 25, 1893.
IV.   Edson Howard, b. Sept. 16, 1854; d. young.

No. 732.

Richard Winters, b. in St. John, New Brunswick, June 22, 1875, son of Frederick and Margeret (Patchell) Winters,

b. in London, England. He resided for a number of years
in the family of Mr. and Mrs. Spinney (Nos. 640). He enlisted in the U. S. Navy, and served in the Spanish-American war. He was at Annapolis Naval Academy two years.
He is married, and has children; a resident of Chicago. He
was admitted to the church by letter from the First Church
at Brockton, Ill., Feb. 28, 1895, and is a present member.

No. 783.

Lizzie S. Hoyt, b. in Sandown, a daughter of Eben Hoyt
of Sandown, and wife, who was widow of James Hoyt of
Sandown. She was admitted to the church by letter from
the M. E. Church of Sandown, Feb. 28, 1895, and was dis.
May 3, 1900, to unite with the St. Paul's M. E. Church at
Manchester.

No. 784.

Calvin Abner Merrick, b. in Salem, July 8, 1850, a son
of Abner Merrick, of North Salem, and his wife, Eliza
(Nightingale), of Roxbury, Mass. He married Annie L.
Heath (No. 465), June 20, 1872, and moved to Hampstead.
He was admitted to the church March 8, 1895. He resides
in Hampstead.

No. 785.

Charles Henry Whittier, b. in Danville, May 12, 1850, a
son of George and Eunice (Locke) Whittier, of Danville.
He married Lilla H. Page (No. 736). He is a shoemaker
and barber in Hampstead. He was admitted to the church
June 28, 1895, and was dis. Nov. 23, 1899.

No. 736.

Lilla Hannah Page, b. in Mechanic Falls, Me., June 12,
1856, a daughter of John O. Page, of Windham, Me., and
wife, Harriet Faunce, of Oxford, Me. She married Charles
H. Whittier (No. 785). She was admitted to the church by

letter from the M. E. Church at Mechanic Falls, Me., June 28, 1895, and is a present member.   They have children :—

I.   Lottie May, b. Nov. 5, 1884; m. George, son of Asa and Hannah
       F. (Noyes) Worthen of East Hampstead, Aug. 30, 1902.
II.   Grace Emma, b. April 2, 1887.
III.   Lewis Bryon, b. Dec. 2, 1889.
IV.   Jacob Henry, b. May 10, 1892.

No. 787.

Fannie Faith Davis, b. in Sandown, June 13, 1879, a daughter of James A. Davis, who was born in Hubbardston, Mass., May 27, 1850, and who married, July 15, 1874, Martha Lois Chase, who was born in Haverhill, Mass., March 7, 1853, and died in Lynn, Mass., Oct. 10, 1887, and buried in West Hampstead cemetery.   Martha L. Chase was a daughter of Ephraim and Sarah (Eaton) Chase, of Sandown.   Mrs. Chase now resides in West Hampstead, with her son-in-law and second wife, Clara A. Irving (No. 476), in her 92d year.   She is a daughter of Samuel Eaton, b. about 1760, son of Joseph, son of Thomas, son of Thomas Eaton, Jr., all of Haverhill, whom tradition says was killed by the Indians in the Haverhill massacres.   Mrs. Chase has the deeds of land to Thomas Eaton and to Joseph Eaton, dated Dec. 6, 1682, and another dated Nov. 25, 1717 ; also a captain's commission to Joseph Eaton, dated April 8, 1776. James A. and Martha L. (Chase) Davis had children :—

I.   Alfred Chase, b. Sept. 15, 1875; m. Alice R. Osgood (No. 724).
II.   Fannie F. (above). She was educated in Meriden Academy, and
       at present is a trained nurse in Connecticut. She was adm.
       to the church June 28, 1895, and is a present member.
III.   Mary Hurbert, b. Aug. 15, 1881.   Graduate of Hampstead
       High School, class 1899. Student at Pinkerton Academy.

No. 738.

Ada Mabelle Ranlett, b. in Hampstead, May 19, 1871, a daughter of Charles H. and Susan P. Ranlett (see p. 337, Vol. 1).   She was educated in the public and high school of

Hampstead. She was admitted to the church June 28, 1895, and is a present member.

Nos. 739 and 740.

Mr. and Mrs. John T. Whiteley, of England, were admitted to church membership by letter from the Center Congregational Church, at Haverhill, Mass., Dec. 31, 1896, and were dismissed to unite with the Congregational church at Derry, March 6, 1902. P. O. address, West Derry, N. H., Dec., 1902.

No. 741.

Sarah Ordway Brickett, b. in Hampstead, Feb. 16, 1827, a daughter of Ralph and Sally (Ordway) Brickett (Nos. 376, 275), (p. 344, Vol. 1). She was educated in the public schools of Hampstead, Wentworth Academy, and Stevens Academy, at Claremont, and under private instruction at Lawrence, Mass., and Boston. She began teaching in the Oliver grammar school in Lawrence in 1848, in the Bowdoin School in Boston in 1868, where she continued till 1889, when she returned to Hampstead to make her home. She was a member of the board of education from 1891 to 1897. She was admitted to the church by letter from the Mt. Vernon Congregational Church in Boston, Mass., Nov. 7, 1897, and is a present member. (See photo, Vol. 1.)

No. 742.

Minnie Maria Fitts, b. in Hampstead, Jan. 21, 1868, a daughter of George C. and H. Maria (Stevens) Fitts (see No. 555). She was educated in the public schools of Hampstead. She was admitted to the church from the M. E. Church at West Hampstead (which she joined March 18, 1888), Sept. 6, 1897, and is a present member.

No. 743.

Walter Alfonso Johnson, b. in Haverhill, Mass., March 24, 1880, a son of Gideon W. and Ida A. (Vincent) Johnson (see p. 381, Vol. 1). He was educated in the public and high school, graduate of class of 1899, and at Brewster

MISS FITTS. NO. 742.

Academy at Wolfboro, where he was a graduate of class of 1901. He entered Dartmouth Medical School in 1901. He was admitted to the church May 7, 1899, and is a present member. (See photo, Vol. 1.)

I.   Carrie Mabel, resides with her grandparents in Candia.
II.   Albert E. (No. 746); m. Daisy B. Eldredge (No. 747).
III.   Hattie M. (No. 748).

No. 746.

Albert Eugene Haynes, b. in Hampstead, April 4, 1876, a
son of Bradley N. and Sarah A. (Barker) Haynes (Nos.
744, 745). He married Daisy B. Eldredge (No. 747), and
resides in Hampstead. He was admitted to the church by
letter from the Riverside Congregational Church, June 26,
1898, having been admitted there June 3, 1892, and is a
present member.

No. 747.

Daisy Belle Eldredge, b. in Methuen, Mass., Nov. 4, 1876,
a daughter of William S. and Ella Jane (Fish) Eldredge.
She married Albert E. Haynes (No. 746), Aug. 10, 1895.
She was admitted to the church June 26, 1898, and is a
present member. They have children :—

I.   Earle Loburton, b. Feb. 27, 1896.
II.   Lester Albert, b. June 21, 1900; d. young.

No. 748.

Hattie May Haynes, b. in Newton, Nov. 11, 1881, a
daughter of Bradley N. and Sarah A. (Barker) Haynes
(Nos. 745, 746). She married Burton H. Cheney, of Danville, June 24, 1899, and resides in Kingston. She was admitted to the church by confession, June 26, 1898 ; dis. to
unite with the M. E. church at Kingston, Oct., 1902. Their
daughter :—

I.   Edna Jane, b. Feb. 20, 1901.

No. 749.

Mary Frances Heath, b. in Hampstead, May 18, 1881, a
daughter of John H. and Frances F. (Rolfe) Heath (see Nos.
858, 859), (p. 365, Vol. 1). She was educated in the public

schools, and graduated from class of 1898. She has taught school one year in Sandown, three in Epping, where she is at present a teacher. She was admitted to the church June 26, 1898, and is a present member.

MISS HEATH. NO. 749.

No. 750.

Grace M. Robins. She was admitted to the church June 26, 1898, and was dis. and rec. to unite with the Congregational church in Pawtucket, R. I., March 2, 1899.

No. 751.

Ora Louise Ordway, b. in Haverhill, Mass., Nov. 23, 1879, a daughter of Charles Richard Ordway, of Newburyport,

Mass., and wife, Jennie Sarah Quimby, of Sandown. She was educated in the public and high school, graduate of class of 1895, and has taught school in Atkinson several terms. She was admitted to the church May 7, 1899, and is a present member.

No. 752.

Richard Ordway, b. in Hampstead, Dec. 18, 1881, a son of Charles R. and Jennie S. (Quimby) Ordway. He married Edna L. Clark, of Dunstable, Mass., June 16, 1902. He was educated in the public schools of Hampstead. He was admitted to the church May 7, 1899, and is a present member.

No. 753.

Mabelle Estelle Mills, b. in Sandown, Oct. 28, 1875, a daughter of Elwin C. Mills and Sarah A., daughter of Giles and Mary (Plummer) Davis, who was a daughter of Samuel Plummer, of Hampstead. Giles Davis married, first, Sarah Hoyt (see No. 615). Mabel E. was educated in the public schools of Sandown, and three years at Pinkerton Academy, Derry. She has taught school two years in Sandown, and five at East Hampstead. Her musical education was under Mrs. Crawford, of Chester, and Azro Dow, of Haverhill, Mass., and she has taught music very acceptably for some years. She married Clinton C. Buttrick, of East Hampstead, June 22, 1901, and now resides at East Hampstead. She was admitted to the church July 2, 1899, and is a present member.

No. 754.

Abbie Catherine Nutting, b. in Quincy, Mass., Sept. 18, 1864, a daughter of John D. and Sarah Elizabeth (Pratt) Nutting, now of Quincy. She was educated in the public schools of Quincy. She married Joseph Frost, " the popular clerk at the grocery store of Isaac Randall." She was admitted to the church by letter from the M. E. church at West Quincy, July 2, 1899, and is a present member.

No. 755.

Mary Grace Calderwood, b. in Atkinson, Aug. 17, 1873, a daughter of Charles V. and Julia (Thomas) Calderwood, of Atkinson. She was educated in the public schools and academy of Atkinson, and was a teacher for several years. She was admitted to the church Nov. 5, 1899, and is a present member. She married Albion D. Emerson (No. 651), Sept. 6, 1899, and has children :—

I.   Hollis Albion, b. Feb. 4, 1901.
II.   Roland Charles, b. Feb. 15, 1902.

No. 756.

Caroline P. Hills, b. in Chester, Nov. 5, 1852, a daughter of Francis and Martha L. (Kimball) Hills, of Chester. She married Carlos W., son of Walter H. and Maria (Quimby) Noyes, of Londonderry, in 1888. She was admitted to the church by letter from the Congregational church in Chester, Nov. 5, 1899, having united with the Chester church in 1875, and is a present member. No children.

No. 757.

Alice Cary Bisbee, b. in Plympton, Mass., March 31, 1876, a daughter of John Thomas and Rosina (Sherman) Bisbee, both now deceased. She mar. Charles A. Fitts (see No. 555). She was admitted to the church by letter from the Congregational church in Plympton, Mass., May 5, 1899, and is a present member. Their children :—

I.   Freeda Rosina, b. July 21, 1900.
II.   Charles Albert, Jr., b. Jan. 9, 1902.

No. 758.

Myrta Alice Little, b. in Hampstead, Jan. 15, 1888, a daughter of Albert H. and Abbie I. (Gale) Little (Nos. 604-

631). She is a member of the class of 1903, H. H. S. As a writer of children's stories she has shown much talent, as in "Miss Violet's Thirteen," "Him that cometh unto Me I will in no wise cast out," "Theresa." She was admitted to the church by confession, Nov. 5, 1899, and is the youngest

MISS LITTLE. NO. 758.

member ever admitted to the church (the next younger being No. 686).

No. 759.

Leona Casandria Garland, b. in Hampstead, April 22, 1886, a daughter of Charles W. and Ada E. (Emerson) Garland (Nos. 544, 625). She is a member of H. H. S.,

class of 1903. She was admitted to the church by confe
sion, Nov. 5, 1899, and is a present member.

No. 760.

Mary Ellen Sherman, b. in Chester, Sept. 30, 1885,

MISS GARLAND. NO. 759.

daughter of George Levi Sherman, b. in Roxbury, Mass.
and wife, Nettie Waterman Batchelder (deceased). Sh
belonged to the class of 1903, H. H. S. She was admitte:
to the church by confession, Nov. 5, 1899, and is a presen
member.

No. 761.

Mary Alice Cutter, b. in Hyde Park, Mass., Jan. 11, 1875, a daughter of Frank Eben Cutter, of Newburyport, and wife, Alice Ann Colby. She married Frank N., son of Alden

JESSE E. EMERSON. (SEE NO. 354.)

and Lizzie B. (Sargent) Pillsbury (No. 508). She was admitted to the church by letter from the St. Paul's Episcopal Church, in Newburyport, Jan. 6, 1900, and is a present member. Their son:—

I.   Ernest Colby, b. Oct. 19, 1900.

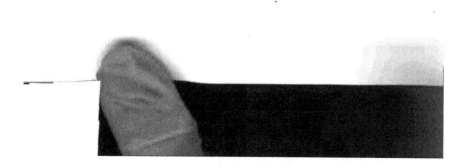

No. 762.

Maggie Cregg, b. in New Boston. She married Frank M.
Conner (cousin of No. 729). She was admitted to the
church Jan. 6, 1900, and is a present member, living at
present in St. Louis, Mo. They have a daughter, May, m.

MISS OSGOOD. NO. 764.

Louis Robinson, living in Schenectady, N. Y., with children,
Dorothy and Frank.

No. 763.

Laura Eliza Merrill, b. in Park City, Utah, Jan. 30, 1887,
a daughter of Forrest E. and Alice M. (Averill) Merrill
(Nos. 692, 693). She is a member of the H. H. S. She

was admitted to the church by confession, Nov. 4, 1900, and is a present member.

No. 764.

Agnes Francella Osgood, b. in Hampstead, June 4, 1883, a daughter of Charles H. and Francella (Eastman) Osgood,

MISS OSGOOD. NO. 765.

of Hampstead (see p. 354, Vol. 1). She was educated in the public and high school of Hampstead, graduate of class of 1901. She was admitted to the church by confession, Nov. 4, 1900, and is a present member. She is a clerk in her father's store at West Hampstead.

No. 765.

Mildred Blanche Osgood, b. in Hampstead, May 13, 1885, a daughter of Charles H. and Francella (Eastman) Osgood. She was educated in the public and high school of Hampstead, graduate of class of 1901. She was admitted to the church by confession, Nov. 4, 1900, and is a present member. She is housekeeper in her father's family.

No. 766.

Elsie Gertrude Bartlett, b. in West Hampstead, July 1, 1884, a daughter of Nathaniel E. and Lizzie (Hart) Bartlett. She is at present housekeeper in her father's family. She was educated in the public and high school of Hampstead, graduate of class of 1901. She was admitted to the church by confession, Nov. 4, 1900, and is a present member.

No. 767.

Caroline Elizabeth Sherman, b. in Chester, June 3, 1883 (sister of No. 760). She was admitted to the church by confession, Nov. 4, 1900, and is a present member. She was educated in the public schools of Hampstead.

No. 768.

Esther Gertrude Bailey, b. in Hampstead, April 6, 1881, a daughter of Charles W. and Ruth J. (Dustin) Bailey. She was educated in the public and high school, graduate of class of 1897, and from the State Normal School in Bridgewater, Mass., June, 1900. A teacher in Hampstead in 1899; at present in Reading, Mass. She was admitted to the church by confession, Nov. 4, 1900, and is a present member.

No. 769.

Ida May Clark, b. in Hampstead, Oct. 24, 1883, a daughter of Benjamin W. and Mary J. (Bean) Clark (see p. 874, Vol. 1, and No. 509). She was educated in the public schools. She was admitted to the church by confession, Jan. 6, 1901, and is a present member.

No. 770.

Lillian Gertrude George, b. in Danville, Oct. 24, 1884, a.

MISS CLARK. NO. 769.

daughter of Albert Monroe and Hattie (Hall) George, of Danville. She married Kimball K. Clark (No. 704), June 3, 1901. She was admitted to the church by confession, May 5, 1901, and was dis. to unite with the M. E. church in East Deering, July 25, 1901.

Mass. He married Florence M. Eldridge (No. 771). He united with the church March, 1902, by letter from the Free Will Baptist Church in Haverhill, Mass., and is a present member.

MRS. WOODSUM. NO. 774.

No. 772.

Florence Mabel Eldridge, b. in Lawrence, Mass., Feb. 23, 1879, a daughter of William S. and Ella J. (Fish) Eldridge (see No. 747). She married George A. F. Picard (No. 771) She was admitted to the church by letter from the Free Will

Nos. 77, 78, Benjamin Little and wife, Mary Hazen.
" 79, 80, William Page and wife, Sarah Silver.
" 81, 82, Alpheus Goodwin and wife, Abiah Heath.
" 83, Widow Rachel (Rowell) Morse.
" 84, 85, David Hadley and wife, Mary Gile.
" 86, 87, Joseph Knight and wife, Sarah Merrill.
" 88, 89, Caleb Johnson and wife, Ruth Eastman.
" 90, 91, Ezekiel Currier and wife, Susanna Emerson.
" 92, 93, Moses Little and wife, Mary Stevens.
" 94, 95, John Trussell and wife, Mary Johnson.
" 96, 97, John Chase and wife, Ruth ——.
" 98, 99, Richard Heath and wife, Mehitable Copp.
" 100, 101, Moses Brown and wife, Sarah Kimball.
" 102, 103, Joshua Kelly and wife, Deborah Page.
" 104, 105, Levi Stevens and wife, Dolly French.
" 106, 107, James Clement and wife, Elizabeth Little.
" 108, Susanna ( ) Perry.
" 109, 110, Thomas Cheney and wife, Hannah Worthen.
" 111, 112, Job Rowell and wife, Priscilla Emerson.
" 113, Ruth (Atwood) Little.
" 114, 115, Joseph Webster and wife, Mary Sawyer.
" 116, 117, Benjamin Pillsbury and wife, Mary Kelly.
" 118, 119, Benjamin Hale and wife, Lydia White.
" 120, 121, Obednum Hall and wife, Mary Kimball.
" 122, David Poore.
" 123, 124, Moses Clark and wife, Molly Clark.
" 125, Mary (Johnson) Therrill.
" 126, 127, Moses Chase and wife, Anna Webster.
" 128, 129, Jacob Chase and wife, Mary (Colby) Worthen.
" 130, 131, Anthony Taylor and wife, Priscilla ——.
" 132, 133, Jacob Currier and wife, Hannah Morrill.
" 134, Hannah Grove.
" 135, 136, Samuel Worthen and wife, Mehitable Worthen.
" 137, 138, Parker Dodge and wife, Mary Little.
" 139, Molly Stevens.
" 140, Elizabeth Stevens.
" 141, 142, Moses Stevens and wife, Mary Heath.
" 143, 144, Nathaniel Flanders and wife, Mary ——.
" 145, 146, Jonathan Taylor and wife, Dolly French.

SKETCHES OF THOSE PERSONS WHO "OWNED THE COVENANT."

Nos. 1 and 2.

Lemuel Davis, b. in Amesbury, Mass., May 6, 1697.

Son of John and Mary (Page) Davis, of Newbury and Salisbury; married Sarah Green, b. in 1704, daughter of James and Nancy (Brown) Green. They owned the covenant September, 1752.

Nos. 3 and 4.

John Mudgett, b. in Haverhill, Mass., in 1724.

A son of William and Dinah (Peasley) Mudgett of Haverhill. Widow Mudgett married, second, Ensign James Heath, of Hampstead (see No. 70, ch. mem.). He married Sarah Palmer, b. in Haverhill, Mass., Sept. 8, 1730, a daughter of Joseph and Sarah (Lull) Palmer, of Haverhill. They had six children, b. in Hampstead (see p. 421, Vol. 1). They owned the covenant October, 1752, and later moved to Goffstown, N. H. Widow of James Heath married, third, —— Robertson.

Nos. 5 and 6.

Moses Hale, Jr., born in Rowley, Mass.

Son of Moses and Elizabeth (Wheeler) Hale (Nos. 57, 58, ch. mem); married Abigail Emerson (No. 6), born in Hampstead, Nov. 20, 1730, daughter of Stephen and Hannah (Marden) Emerson (Nos, 15, 16, ch. mem.). He removed to Rindge from Hampstead about 1760, where he was a selectman in 1771, and held various town offices. He was coroner of Cheshire county in 1778 and 1783, and afterwards county treasurer. "He was a substantial and respected citizen, but not as prominent in politics as his brothers, Enoch and Nathan" (see No. 58). He d. in Rindge, N. H., March 2, 1799; wife d. Aug. 27, 1821; both buried in Rindge. They had children, first four buried in Hampstead, others in Rindge.

I.   Sarah, d. young.
II.   David, m. Maria Russell; second, Bathsheba Barker.
III.   Abigail, d. young.

(718)

IV.	Moses, m., first, Sarah Adams; second, widow Sybil (Howe)
		(Stone) Sawtelle.
V.	Sarah, m. Nathan Ingalls, of Chester.
VI.	Abigail, m. Nathan Hunt.
VII.	Jesse, d. young.
VIII.	Enoch, d. young.
IX.	Jesse, d. young.
X.	Elizabeth, b. Oct. 31, 1776.

Nos. 7 and 8.

Otho Stevens, Jr., born in Gloucester, Mass., in 1722.

Son of Otho and Abigail (Kent) Stevens (Nos. 63, 64, ch. mem.); married Abigail Emerson, b. March 20, 1737, daughter of Benjamin and
Hannah (Watts) Emerson (Nos. 37 and 38, ch. mem.), Oct. 28, 1752.
They owned the covenant, April, 1754. He died Sept. 21, 1759, aged 37
years. He was with Wolfe at the storming of Quebec, and while
climbing the Heights of Abraham his foot slipped, and he fell to the
bottom, which caused such injuries as to result in his death, and he was
taken back to Oswego, where he died. Capt. Jacob Bayley's Journal
reads, "Oswego, Friday, Sept. 21, 1759, Cool morning, but pleasant.
About 2 o'clock in the afternoon dies Otho Stevens after a long and
tedious illness of 22 days, much lamented by his relations and friends,
he being a loving brother and a faithful friend. He was sensible to the
last breath he drew, and sensible of his approaching near another world,
which did not in the least ruffle his spirits. But he seemed to have his
hope firmly placed in God." They had children, b. in Hampstead :—

I.	Abiah, b. Aug. 23, 1753.
II.	Simon, b. March 14, 1755; mar. Elizabeth Boynton. He died
		June 10, 1825. She was born Nov. 10, 1754, and d. Feb. 9,
		1846. They lived and died in Canterbury, where they had
		twelve children, of whom John, who married Submit New-
		comb, was one, who moved to Boscawen (now Webster),
		where their eight children were born, and his wife, Submit,
		died and was buried there. He married a second time, and
		moved to Illinois, with his sons. They have descendants in
		Princeton, Ill.
III.	Jesse, b. Jan. 22, 1757.
IV.	Jacob, b. March 16, 1759; d., aged one year.

After Otho Stevens' death, in 1757, Abigail, his wife, married Deacon
David Morrill, of Canterbury, Dec. 28, 1763, and moved there with her
children. The old house is still standing, and owned by a descendant,
Mr. Charles Sargent, of Canterbury, and is in good condition. Abigail
(Emerson) (Stevens) Morrill died June 30, 1833, aged 95 years and seven

months, and was buried in the Center cemetery at Canterbury. She
has been noted as "a remarkably fine woman." Her children, b. in Canterbury, were :—

V.   Reuben Morrill, b. Oct. 18, 1764.
VI.   Hannah, b. Oct. 21, 1767.
VII. David, b. Dec. 5, 1768; d. in 1770.
VIII. Betty, b. May 30, 1770.
IX.   Sarah, b. May 17, 1772.
X.   Abigail, b. Dec. 23, 1774.
XI.   Ruth, b. Feb. 8, 1776.

No. 9.
Hannah Hazen, born in Haverhill, Mass.

A daughter of Richard and Sarah (Clement) Hazen, of Haverhill and
Hampstead (see Nos. 2 and 3, list of ch. mem.). She married John
Mooers of Londonderry. She owned the covenant, April, 1754. Her
daughter, Hannah, was b. in Hampstead, Nov. 2, 1756.

Nos. 10, 11.
Joseph Terrill, b. in Salisbury, Mass., in 1703.

Son of John and Susanna (Page) Terrill, of Salisbury; married Martha
Thurston, b. in Amesbury in 1707, daughter of James and Fanny (Gile)
Thurston. They owned the covenant, July, 1754, and removed to Coos
county in 1762.

Nos. 12, 13.
Theopolis Colby, born in Amesbury, Mass., in 1713.

Son of Theopolis and Elizabeth (Harvey) Colby, of Amesbury; married Elizabeth Hastings, of Haverhill, Oct. 18, 1750, and m., second,
Priscilla Stevens, March 28, 1752, in Hampstead. They had children,
b. in Haverhill :—

I.   Molly, b. April 28, 1752.
II.   Elizabeth, b. Feb. 5, 1757.

Theopolis and Priscilla (Stevens) Colby owned the covenant July,
1754, and had children, b. in Hampstead. Susanna, bapt. 1754.

No. 14.
Paul Pressey, b. in 1729, in Amesbury, Mass.

A son of John and Elizabeth (Weed) Pressey, of Amesbury. John was a son of William and Elizabeth (Jameson) Pressey, of Amesbury, who was a "shoe man " in 1708, and died in 1737, in Amesbury. William was a son of John and Marsh (Gouge) Pressey, who came to Salisbury in 1639. Paul was a resident of Kingston, and owned the covenant August, 1754, " in his own house in Kingston, before several persons, apprehending himself as near death."

Nos. 15, 16.

Abraham Dow, born in Haverhill, Mass. (in that part now Atkinson, at the Dow homestead, now residence of George P. Dow, Esq.), Feb. 23, 1732.

A son of John and Mehitable (Haines) Dow, who settled in Atkinson in 1728, and was one of the first settlers in that part of the town. He married Susannah Hoyt, born in 1734, a daughter of Micah and Susanna (Colby) Hoyt, of Haverhill and Newtown. They lived near the Salem line, and afterwards in Salem. He was called " Esquire," and married some couples in Hampstead. He was the owner of the mills, afterwards called " Clendennin's mills," on the upper stream of the Spicket river, in Salem. They owned the covenant in 1755, and had children :—

I.   Thomas. b. Sept. 18, 1781; mar. Elizabeth Jones; lived in Atkinson and Salem, and had children :—
    1. Moses, who mar. ——— ———, and lived in Atkinson, and were the parents of Amos, Hezekiah (now of California), Clarissa, who mar. John W. Follansbee, and others.
    2. Relief, mar. James Poor, of Atkinson, and were parents of Johnathan, who mar. Eliza Currier, of Pelham; Charles A., mar. Persis Howard, and, second, Sara P. Wetherbee, and resided in Boston; and Benjamin Kimball Poor, who mar. Sophia P. Noyes, of Atkinson, and parents of Charles Herbert of Haverhill, Ellen R., who mar. Rufus P. Clement, now of Merrimac, Mass., and Persis H., who d. in 1882, unmarried, a successful teacher in Hampstead and Salem for several years.
II.   Susan, mar. Robert Clendennin; of Salem. She died, leaving a son, Robert, b. Sept. 10, 1804; mar. Phebe Wyman Bailey.
III. Mary, mar. Amos Mills of Hampstead (No. 172, ch. mem.).
IV.   Rachel, mar. Capt. Edmund Wright, son of Jonathan and Ruth Wright (see No. 197, ch. mem.).

Nos. 17, 18.

Archelaus Stevens, born in Gloucester, about 1706.

A son of Otho and Abigail (Kent) Stevens (Nos. 63, 64, ch. mem.), married Hannah Emerson, Aug. 11, 1753. She was born in Hampstead; Nov. 29, 1738, a daughter of Benjamin and Hannah (Watts) Emerson (Nos. 37, 38, ch. mem.). They owned the covenant, May, 1754, and had eight children, b. in town (see p. 427, Vol. 1).

Nos. 19, 20.

Ebenezer Mudgett, born in Salisbury, Mass., in 1720.

A son of William and Dinah (Eastman) Mudgett, of Salisbury; married Miriam Johnson, born in Londonderry, a daughter of Michael and Mary (Hancock) Johnson, of Haverhill, Mass., and Londonderry. They owned the covenant, August, 1855, and had six children (see p. 422, Vol. 1), and others born in Goffstown, one of whom was Eben, who married, and has descendants living there now. "A brother of Eben Mudgett was 'Bill Mudgett,' who settled over the mountain in Weare, and has many descendants in that region." Miriam Mudgett, as a widow, married Capt. Wm. Marshall, of Hampstead.

Nos. 21, 22.

Elijah Heath ("commonly called Joshua Heath"), born in Haverhill, Mass., in 1730.

Son of John and Frances (Hutchens) Heath; married Hannah Dearborn, who was born in Chester, Oct. 13, 1731, daughter of Ebenezer, commonly called Ebenezer, Jr., and wife, Huldah (Nason) Dearborn, who lived on the Jesse R. Gordon place, in Chester. Elijah and Hannah (Dearborn) Heath had children :—

I.   Nanna, b. in Hampstead, Oct. 21, 1755; mar., Sept., 1775, Jeremiah Underhill, who was a son of John and Joanna (Healey) Underhill, of Chester, whose daughter, Sarah, married Capt. Moses Greenough, of Atkinson. Jeremiah and Anna (Heath) Underhill lived on what is now called Bunker Hill, in Auburn, and "had nine children, who were all raised in a house with one large room and a bedroom." He died suddenly, Sept. 16, 1794; she d. May 19, 1844. Their children were :—
   1. David, b. in 1756.
   2. Elijah, m. Molly White.
   3. Benjamin, m. Polly Green.
   4. Betsey, m. Samuel Davis, who d. at Concord, in the U. S. service, April 7, 1813. They lived at Hooksett.
   5. Reuben, m. Hannah H. Chase.

6. Anna, mar. Joseph, son of Samuel Noyes and Abigail (Coffin) Little. A successful farmer of 'Newbury Hill, in Atkinson, where Washington B. Wason now resides. They had children : Samuel Noyes Little, who married, in 1837, Hannah Knight, of Atkinson; who married for her second husband, Albert Noyes, of Atkinson; her daughter, Marinda A., married W. B. Wason, and has one child, George A., mar. Anna G., daughter of Dea. Albert and Sarah A. (Greenough) Emerson, of Haverhill.

7. James, m. Elizabeth Chase.

8. Samuel.

9. John, b. Nov. 26, 1703; m. Molly Chase.

II.   Elijah, d. in 1784.

III.   Levi.

IV.   Stephen, mar. Mary Aiken; went to Pennsylvania.

V.   Hannah.

VI.   James.

VII.   Miriam.

VIII.   Huldah, m. Samel White.

Elijah Heath, the father, d. about 1776. All of the above children were under fourteen years old in 1779. Elijah Heath and wife owned the covenant, in town, Dec., 1755.

Nos. 23, 24.

Nathaniel Knight and wife, Abigail Merrill.

Owned the covenant before the "Church of Christ," in Hampstead, Dec., 1755 (No. 120, ch. mem.).

Nos. 25, 26.

Jacob Eaton and wife, Mary (Breed),

Owned the covenant before the church, January, 1756 (see Nos. 73, 74, ch. mem.).

Nos. 27, 28.

Nichodemus Watson, born in Lynn, Mass., in 1705.

A son of John and Ruth (Jameson) Watson, of Lynn; married Betty Harriman, b. in Haverhill, Mass., in 1709, a daughter of Mathew, of Haverhill. They owned the covenant January, 1756, and had children, b. in town (p. 430, Vol. 1).

No. 29.

Elizabeth Ring, born in Salisbury, Mass., in 1718.

A daughter of David and Sarah (Osgood) Ring, of Salisbury; married Paul Dustin of Salem. She owned the covenant May 9, 1756.

Nos. 30, 31.

John Kezer, born in Haverhill, Mass., July 6, 1678.

A son of John and Hannah (Davis) Kezer, who were killed by the Indians in 1696-7; was probably the first settler in the part of Hampstead that once belonged to Kingston, or the "Peak" (see pp. 152, 361, Vol. 1). He married Judith Heath, b. in Haverhill, Mass. They owned the covenant July 25, 1756. They had ten children (p. 419, Vol. 1). Judith, d. in Hampstead, Oct., 1756. John Kezer m., second, Ruth Terrill (No. 88, ch. mem.).

No. 32.

Abigail Kezer, born in Hampstead, Feb. 14, 1738.

A daughter of John and Judith (Heath) Kezer, of Hampstead (see Nos. 30, 31). She married Joseph Hancock, Aug. 15, 1754. She owned the covenant, in town, July 25, 1756, and removed to Londonderry. She had several children that went to Ohio to live.

Nos. 33, 34.

Stephen Colburne, born in 1720, in Weare.

A son of Asa and Lucy (Brown) Colburne, of Weare; married Mary Emerson, b. in Haverhill, Mass., a daughter of Stephen and Hannah (Marden) Emerson, of Hampstead (Nos. 15 and 16, ch. mem.). They owned the covenant July 16, 1755, and moved "up country."

Nos. 35, 36.

Jonathan Clark, born in Haverhill, Mass., April 28, 1696.

Son of Daniel and Mary (Gutterson) Clark, of Haverhill. He married Martha Ela, who was born in Haverhill, June 7, 1715, a daughter of Samuel and Hannah (Clark) Ela, of Haverhill, and removed to Hampstead. They owned the covenant April 10, 1757, and died in Hampstead. She had two children, Amos and Martha, that d. young. He then married, second, Priscilla Whittaker, and had children :—

I.   Amos (No. 49, ch. mem.).
II.   John, m. Susanna Sinclear, and had eight children, b. in town (p. 407, Vol. 1).

Nos. 37, 38.

Benjamin Little, born in Hampstead, March 18, 1737 (see Nos. 32, 33, ch. mem.).

Married Hepsibah Poor, who was born in Rowley, Mass., July 16, 1738, and died in Bradford, Vt., July 9, 1808 (see Nos. 32 and 33). They owned the covenant April 23, 1758.

Nos. 39, 40.

John Colby, born in Chester, Jan. 18, 1731.

Son of Beniah and Mary (Webster) Colby, of Chester. He married Mary Wells, daughter of Thomas and Ruth Wells, of Chester, her father being killed by John Talford in 1773. They owned the covenant May 7, 1758, as of Chester.

No. 41.

Mary Stevens (widow), (see No. 63, ch. mem.)

Married Otho Stevens as his second wife, who died in Hampstead, May 21, 1758. She died in Hampstead, April 4, 1771. "Voted, that the expense of the widow Stevens' funeral shall be paid by the town, and that the said widow's household furniture and wearing apparel shall not be taken towards defraying said charges, but shall be given to her youngest daughter." (Town records.)

Nos. 42, 43.

Joseph Sawyer and wife, Judith Kelly (Nos. 117, 118, ch. mem.).

Judith Kelly Sawyer owned the covenant July 30, 1758, and Joseph Sawyer Dec. 6, 1758.

Nos. 44, 45.

Edmund Colby, born Dec. 6, 1725, in Amesbury, Mass.

A son of Jacob and Hannah (Hunt) Colby, of Amesbury. Married Mary ——. They "owned ye covenant before ye church here," May 6, 1759.

Nos. 46, 47.

Ebenezer Hale, b. in Haverhill, Mass., Aug. 15, 1786.

A son of Thomas and Mary (Smith) Hale. His father was settled as early as 1734 in Plaistow, the part now Atkinson, on a farm which he received in a deed dated 1734, of one hundred acres of land. His father was a selectman of Plaistow, in Haverhill District, before the incorporation of the town, in 1745. The son Ebenezer married Susanna Roberts, April 28, 1758. She was a daughter of Jonathan Roberts, of Hampstead. They settled in Hampstead soon after marrirge, on the farm now a part of Daniel Ayer's farm, as given by his father (above). He died at the house of Ebenezer Ladd, in Haverhill (apparently while on a visit), early in 1774. They owned the covenant May 13, 1760. He was in the French war. He was buried in the Hampstead village cemetery. They had children, b. in Hampstead :

I. Susannah, b. Nov. 20, 1758; m. Isaac Tewksbury.
II. Jonathan Roberts, b. Nov. 5, 1760; m. Lydia Johnson.
III. Ebenezer, b. Nov. 8, 1763; d. young.
IV. Meribah Farnum, b. April 6, 1768; m. Jonathan C. Little (No. 167, ch. mem.).

The widow, Susanna, m., second, Maj. Edmund Mooers, of Hampstead, March 14, 1776, and d. in Hampstead, June 25, 1782.

Nos. 48, 49.

Ezekiel Foster and Mary Roberts.

Were m. in Hampstead, May 10, 1755, and owned the covenant April 20, 1760.

Nos. 50, 51.

Isaac Foster and wife, Mehitable Worthen.

Were married in Hampstead, Oct. 31, 1754, and owned the covenant April 20, 1760.

No. 52.

Abraham Johnson, b. in Haverhill, Mass., May 30, 1739.

Son of Zachariah and Susanna (Chase) Johnson (p. 381, Vol. 1). He served in the Revolutionary war, and married Priscilla Colby. They owned the covenant Nov. 16, 1760, and had children, b. in Hampstead. (p. 416, Vol. 1).

Nos. 53, 54.

David Hale, b. in Newbury, Mass., Sept. 30, 1729.

Son of Daniel and Judith Hale, of Newbury. He married, in Hampstead, Dec. 13, 1757, Mehitable, daughter of Peter Hale and Elizabeth (Harriman) Eastman, b. June 28, 1737. By his father's will he received 100 pounds and "the remaining lands in ye Narragansett." Daniel Plummer bought lands of him (No. 178, ch. mem.), both of Gloucester, Dec. 1, 1756. They had seven children, b. in Hampstead (pp. 413, 414, Vol. 1). "David Hale was a soldier in the Revolutionary war, Col. Moses Nichols as commander, and many descendants point with pride to his service." (Mrs. G. F. Gilkey, Oshkosh, Wis.)

Nos. 55, 56.

James Emerson and wife, Lydia Hoyt.

Owned the covenant Jan. 11, 1761 (Nos. 149, 150, ch. mem.).

Nos. 57, 58.

Joshua Merrill, b. in Amesbury, Mass., Feb. 20, 1722.

A son of Stephen and Mary (Carr) Merrill, of Amesbury. He married Mehitable Kelly (widow of Peter Merrill, of Salisbury), b. Aug. 18, 1816, a daughter of Abiel and Rebecca (Davis) Kelly, of Amesbury. They owned the covenant Jan. 10, 1761, and moved from town before 1782 "up country."

Nos. 59, 60.

Col. Robert Johnson, b. in Haverhill, Mass., Sept. 8, 1738.

Son of Michael and Mary (Hancock) Johnson (see No. 110); married four times, 1st Abigail Hadley. They owned the covenant April 19, 1761, and settled in Newbury, Vt., called Johnston there.

Nos. 61, 62.

Caleb Heath, b. in Haverhill, Mass., June 8, 1704.

A son of John and Frances (Hutchens) Heath, of Haverhill. He married Mary Kezer, born in Hampstead, June 12, 1736, a daughter of John and Judith (Heath) Kezer. They owned the covenant May 16, 1761. They had a daughter, Judith, b. April 4, 1756.

Nos. 63, 64.

Jeremiah Kent, b. in Gloucester, Mass., Feb. 27, 1741.

A son of John and Mary (Godfrey) Kent, of Gloucester and Hampstead. He married Jemima Philbrick, b. Oct. 29, 1737, in Hampstead, a daughter of Benjamin and Sarah (Chute) Philbrick (p. 424, Vol. 1). They owned the covenant June 21, 1761. They had children:—

I.   Mary, b. Aug. 4, 1760.
II.   John, b. Nov. 2, 1762.

No. 65.

Elizabeth Plummer, b. in Hampstead, March 4, 1739.

A daughter of Samuel and Ann (Lunt) Plummer. She married Jonathan Atwood (No. 76, ch. mem.). She owned the covenant Sept. 20, 1761.

Nos. 66, 67.

Simeon Goodwin, b. in Amesbury, Mass.

He married Susanna Heath, b. in Haverhill, Mass., July 27, 1738, a daughter of Ensign James and Dinah (Mudgett) Heath (Nos. 3, 4). They had four children, b. in Hampstead (p. 412, Vol. 1). They owned the covenant June 13, 1761).

Nos. 68, 69.

Daniel Stevens, b. in Newbury, Mass., in 1742.

A son of Otho and Abigail (Kent) Stevens (Nos. 63, 64). He married Hannah Hill, of Newbury (No. 67, ch. mem.). They had children :—

I.   Hannah, b. May 5, 1762.
II.   Daniel, b. July 19, 1764.

They owned the covenant June 13. 1761. She d. in 1765. He married, second, Elizabeth Bryant (see No. 407).

Nos. 70, 71.

Micajah Morrill, b. in Amesbury, Mass., in 1738.

A son of Micajah and Mary (Greeley) Morrill, of Amesbury. His father d. in 1755, and widow Mary m. Henry True, of Amesbury. He married Hannah Hackett, Jan. 30, 1752, of Amesbury. They owned the covenant June 27, 1761. They seem to have lived a short time in Hampstead, and moved to Londonderry. Several children, b. in Amesbury and Salisbury, Mass.

Nos. 72, 73.

Joshua Copp, b. in Haverhill, Mass., in 1740.

A son of Moses and grandson of Aaron and Mary (Heath) Copp, of Hampstead. He married Sarah Poor, in Hampstead, a daughter of Samuel and Elizabeth (Searl) Poor (Nos. 37, 38). They owned the cov-

enant Nov. 28, 1761. They had twelve children (eleven of whom are recorded on p. 408, Vol. 1). An account of each child is found in Poore Genealogy, p. 201.

No. 74.

John Merrill, b. in Plaistow (now Atkinson), in 1740.

A son of Abel and Abigail (Stevens) Merrill, of Atkinson. They reside at the farm formerly known as the "Merrick place," on the East road. He married, first, Mary Emery, and had children :—

I. Stephen, b. Jan. 22, 1767; he was a deaf and dumb mute; settled at the old homestead.
II. Abel, b. Nov. 10, 1763; m. Tamar Kimball; second, Abigail, widow of Samuel Noyes, of Landaff.
III. Hannah, b. April 22, 1762; m. Joshua Poor, of Atkinson (see p. 202, Vol. 1).
IV. Ruth, b. May 5, 1764; m. John Davis; settled on the old homestead of her father in Atkinson.
V. Joshua, b. June 26, 1769; m. —— Richardson; settled in Corinth, Vt.
VI. Polly, b. Sept. 30, 1771; m. —— Smith, and d., aged 21 years, leaving a daughter.

Nos. 75, 76.

James Little, b. March 18, 1737.

A son of Samuel and Dorothy (Noyes) Little, of Atkinson. He married Tamar Roberts. They had eight children. He d. April 23, 1783. The widow married, second, Thomas Muzzey, later of Hampstead. They resided on the bank opposite the residence of Frank W. Greenough, on "East Road," Atkinson. They owned the covenant Nov. 28, 1761.

Nos. 77, 78.

Benjamin Little, b. Nov. 4, 1732.

A son of Moses and Sarah (Jaques) Little. He married Mary, daughter of Col. Richard Hazen (No. 2, ch. mem.). They owned the covenant Jan. 16, 1763. Mr. Little was a farmer and prominent citizen of Hampstead; d. April 18, 1777. Mary, the widow, married, second, Maj. Edmund Mooers, by whom she had one son (No. 409, ch. mem.). Their children were :—

I. Micajah, b. Nov., 1762; m. Sarah Noyes, of Atkinson; resided in Union and Rockland, Me.; had five children.

II.   Charlotte, b. Aug. 9, 1765; m. Jabez, son of Jabez and Abigail Hoyt, of Hampstead. He was b. Jan. 15, 1765; and m., second, Rhoda Scarlett. The children of Jabez and Charlotte Hoyt were :—

    1. Hazen, b. Jan. 12, 1791; m. Mehitable Wheeler, and had six children, one of whom, Hazen, m., first, Louisa Little (see Nos. 369, 370, ch. mem.).

    2. Abigail, b. Sept. 10, 1793; m. Isaac Spofford.

    3. Charlotte, b. April 4, 1797; m. Lorenzo Batchelder, of Hampstead.

    4. Jabez, twin to above; m. Hannah R. Rogers (No. 253, ch. mem.).

    5. Sophia, b. April 18, 1799; m. Hazen Webster, of Haverhill, Mass.

III.   Walter, b. May 30, 1766; m. Sarah Little. He lived in Boston the last twenty-five years of his life. Their children were :—

    1. Sarah, d. unmarried.

    2. Walter, m. Jerusha Richardson, of Northfield, Vt., and had three children.

    3. Meribah Hale, m. Charles C. McDonald, of Exeter, N. H.; and, second, Charles Shaw, of New York city. Had seven children.

    4. Tamar, b. in Atkinson; d. in Boston in 1874.

    5. Mary, d., unmarried, in 1806.

    6. Benjamin, d. in Hampstead, unmarried, in 1825.

    7. James Henry, b. in Exeter, d. in Boston, unmarried; a book-binder.

    8. Eliza, d., unmarried, in 1899, in Boston.

IV.   Richard Hazen, b. Jan. 14, 1769; m. Ruth Cochran, of Pembroke; had twelve children.

V.   Mary (No. 371, ch. mem.).

VI.   Dudley, b. Jan. 1, 1775; d., by an accident, unmarried, Jan. 8, 1827.

Nos. 79, 80.

William Page, b. in Haverhill, Mass., in 1737.

A son of Joseph and Mary (Thomson) Page, of Plaistow (now Atkinson). He married, first, in 1760, Martha, daughter of Joseph and Martha (Barker) Parker, and was b. in Andover, Mass., in 1739. He married, second, Oct. 20, 1761, Sarah Silver, who was bapt. in Amesbury. They had children, b. in Haverhill :—

I.   Martha, b. Aug. 28, 1761.

II.   William, b. May 17, 1762.

III.   Sarah, b. March 24, 1764.

IV.   Eunice, b. June 25, 1768.

V.   Lewis, b. in 1772, in Hampstead.

They owned the covenant April 17, 1763.

Nos. 81, 82.

Alpheus Goodwin, b. July 20, 1741.

A son of Nathan and Rhoda (Colby) Goodwin (Nos. 47, 48, ch. mem.).
He married Anna Heath, b. in Hampstead in 1745, daughter of Jesse
and Dinah (Mudgett) Heath. They owned the covenant April 14, 1763.

No. 83.

Widow Rachel (Rowell) Morse,

Owned the covenant May 24, 1763 (No. 95, ch. mem.).

Nos. 84, 85.

David Hadley and wife, Mary,

Daughter of Daniel and Joanna (Heath) Gile, b. Oct. 12, 1741, in
Plaistow (p. 413, Vol. 1).

Nos. 86, 87.

Joseph Knight, b. in Atkinson, Oct. 14, 1735.

Son of Nathaniel and Sarah (Somersby) Knight, who were, as far as
research shows. the first couple to move to Atkinson (then Plaistow),
in 1722, to the farm now owned by John K. Mason (East Road). He m.
Sarah Merrill, b. in Atkinson, daughter of John Merrill, in 1761. They
owned the covenant Aug. 23, 1763. They had nine children, b. in Atkinson.

Nos. 88, 89.

Caleb Johnson, b. in Haverhill, Mass., June 4, 1738.

A son of John and Hannah (Haynes) Johnson, of Hampstead. He
married Ruth Eastman, Nov. 28, 1759. They had eleven children from
1761 to 1784.

Nos. 90, 91.

Ezekiel Currier and wife, Susanna Emerson,

Owned the covenant Sept. 4, 1768 (see No. 215, ch. mem.).

Nos. 92, 93.

Moses Little, b. in Hampstead, Aug. 8, 1742.

A son of Capt. George and Mary (Kimball) Little, of Hampstead and New Boston. He lived in Hampstead until about 1767, when they removed to Goffstown, where he d., Sept. 5, 1813. He served in the Revolutionary war, was first lieutenant in company 9, of Gen. Stark's regiment, and took part in the battle of Bunker Hill. He was a justice of the peace for many years, and prominent in town affairs. He m. Mary Stevens, a sister of Jacob Stevens of Hampstead, Mrs. Butterfield and Mrs. Annis of Goffstown, and daughter of Timothy and Elizabeth Stevens of Hampstead. They owned the covenant Oct. 16, 1763. They had nine children, three b. in Hampstead.

Nos. 94, 95.

John Trussell, b. in Amesbury,

Son of Henry and Hannah (Weed) Trussell, of Amesbury, and later of Hampstead. He mar. Mary Johnson. They owned the covenant Nov. 20, 1763, and moved to Weare, and later to Corinth, Vt.

Nos. 96, 97.

John Chase, b. in Newbury, Mass.

Married Hannah Ela, in Haverhill, Oct. 27, 1741. Had children: Sarah, Jacob, and Rachel. Married, second, Ruth ———. They owned the covenant Nov. 20, 1763.

Nos. 98, 99.

Richard Heath, b. in Haverhill, Mass., Dec. 27, 1701.

Son of Bartholomew and Mary (Bradley) Heath, of Haverhill. He married Mehitable Copp, daughter of Aaron Copp, of Haverhill. They owned the covenant Nov. 27, 1763.

Nos. 100, 101.

Moses Brown, b. in Newbury, Mass.

Son of Joseph and Hannah (Pike) Brown (see ch. mem., 105, 106). He married Sarah Kimball (No. 106, ch. mem.). They owned the covenant Feb. 19, 1764.

Nos. 102, 103.

Joshua Kelly, b. in Amesbury, Mass.

Son of John and Hannah (Somes) Kelly. He married Deborah, daughter of Col. David Page, of Atkinson, and granddaughter of Col. Edmund and Abigail (Page) Page. They owned the covenant July 22,

1704. Joshua Kelly lived in his youth in the family of Capt. John Sawyer, of South Amesbury (Merrimac), Mrs. Sawyer (Elizabeth Kelly) being an aunt. Afterwards he moved to Atkinson, and after the birth of two children he moved to Conway. He was induced, with others, to go to that place, which was included in the "Pequaiket country," by the glowing descriptions given of the richness of the soil, abundance of game, and other attractions of that region. He was a soldier in the Revolutionary war, as a private. He lived in Atkinson as late as 1795. He d. May 1, 1822.

Nos. 104, 105.

Levi Stevens, b. in Newbury, Mass.

Son of Otho and Abigail (Kent) Stevens; m. Dolley French in 1759 (see No. 64, ch. mem.); and m., second, Lydia Hills, and had children (p.428, Vol. 1). Levi and Dolley Stevens owned the covenant Aug. 28, 1764. Lydia Hills was b. in Newbury, Mass., Oct. 13, 1740, daughter of Joshua and Hannah (Hunt) Hills (No. 67, ch. mem.).

Nos. 106, 107.

James Clement, b. in Plaistow, April 2, 1737 ; d. Feb. 8, 1812.

Was a respected citizen in Dunbarton for many years, and deacon of the church there. He m. Elizabeth Little, b. March, 1744, a daughter of Thomas and Mary (Bond) Little, of Atkinson. They owned the covenant Oct. 21, 1764. They had ten children, b. in Dunbarton.

No. 108.

Susanna, wife of Benjamin Perry,

Owned the covenant Oct. 28, 1764.

Nos. 109, 110.

Thomas Cheney and wife, Hannah Stevens, of Haverhill (see No. 124, ch. mem.).

Owned the covenant Nov. 18, 1704, and had son Ephraim, who mar. Mary Ela (see No. 156, ch. mem.),

Nos. 111, 112.

Job Rowell, probably son of Job and Bethia Brown, of Amesbury.

Benjamin, on the death of his father, in 1759, succeeded to the care of his mother and younger sisters. Before the Revolutionary war he was a first lieutenant of a troop of horse in the N. H. militia. On the alarm at Lexington he literally left his plow in the furrow, and started for the scene of action, and was in active service at Bunker Hill, though not regularly enrolled. He m. Lydia, b. July 2, 1738, daughter of Nicholas White, of Plaistow, and granddaughter of Hon. John Gilman, of Exeter, Dec. 9, 1762. When the Revolutionary war broke out he was father of six children, ranging from one to ten years of age, and with his family he could not enlist, as he would, but more than half of the whole term of war he was, in one form or another, connected with the service of his country. He was present and took part in the battle of Saratoga, in 1777, and assisted in conducting the prisoners to their permanent quarters.

They owned the covenant in Hampstead, Dec. 15, 1765, and in June, 1780, joined the North Parish Congregational Church at Haverhill, and in November of the same year was chosen the first deacon of the Congregational church in Atkinson, under Rev. Stephen Peabody. In the summer of 1781 his health began to fail, and he died, of scrofulous disease of the throat, December, 1781. His wife died in Newbury, Vt., Nov. 14, 1791. Benjamin Hale made a will just before his death, which was proved in the probate court at Exeter, Jan. 8, 1782, in which he made his wife sole executrix, and the residue to his sons, Joshua and Nicholas, they paying debts, and a certain sum to the other children. He was supposed to be possessed of much property, but the losses caused by the war, it was charged through the bad faith of a neighbor who was the chief adviser of the family, they were left almost penniless, and an insolvent estate. Their negro servant, Cato, was given his freedom. The widow remained with her daughter, Hannah, in Atkinson, till 1789, when she was given a home with a bachelor brother in Newbury (Dr. Samuel White). Here she lived till her death, in 1791. "She was a woman of rare excellence, of sweet and gentle disposition, combined with great firmness and energy of character." They had children, b. in Atkinson :—

I.   Joshua, b. Dec. 31, 1764; d., unmarried, 1838.
II. Nicholas, b. Oct. 14, 1766; m. Hannah Knight.
III. Lydia Gilman, b. July 28, 1769; m. James Meserve.
IV. Mary, b. May 10, 1771; d., unmarried, 1803.
V.   Thomas, b. June 23, 1773; m.. first, Alice Little; second, Mary Little.
VI. Ebenezer, b. Oct. 4, 1774; m. Lucy (Balch) French.
VII. Hannah, b. March 2, 1777; m. Joseph Knight, of Atkinson.
VIII. Benjamin, b. Nov. 4, 1779; d. young.

Obednum Hall, b. in Amesbury, Mass., Dec. 1, 1744.

Son of Henry and Joanna (Sargent) Hall, of Amesbury; mar. Mary, daughter of Benjamin and Mary (Eaton) Kimball, of Hampstead (see Nos. 21, 22, ch. mem.). They owned the covenant May 25, 1706. They settled in Candia, and were the first settlers in the north part of the town, about the time of the beginning of the Revolutionary war. It is related of Mary Hall that "once when her husband was sick or lame, that she threshed a grist of rye and caught and saddled a horse and rode to Trickling Falls, in East Kingston and back, about twenty-five miles, to mill." They had twelve children, baptized in Hampstead. He d. Sept. 8, 1805; she d. Dec. 25, 1799, in Candia.

No. 122.

David Poore, b. in Plaistow, July 24, 1745.

A son of Daniel and Sarah, daughter of Humphrey and Elizabeth (Little) Noyes, of East Road, Atkinson. David learned the trade of a cooper when young, and all of his sons and grandsons had the same trade. He m. Phebe, daughter of Capt. Jona. and Susannah (Bartlett) Carlton, b. May 9, 1747; d. Aug. 1, 1816. He was a lieutenant in the Revolutionary war, and helped defeat Burgoyne. After the battle a British officer, being without money to purchase food for his son, who was hungry, gave to Mr. Poore his watch for some bread, and that watch was recently in the possession of a great-grandson, William W. Poore, of Derry. Mr. Poore settled on land of his father, purchased of Hon. Charles Johnson (No. 110, ch. mem.), in the northwestern part of Hampstead, near the Derry line, and another of his farms was known as the Hugh Mills farm, in Derry. They had children :—

I. John, b. March 1, 1770; m. Mary Calef (No. 205, ch. mem.).
II. Sarah, b. March 9, 1772; m. Moses Green, of Plaistow. (See Poore Genealogy, p. 107.)
III. David, b. Sept. 9, 1773; m. Betsey Sawyer.
IV. Phebe (No. 227, ch. mem.).
V. Anna, b. June 9, 1777; m. Richard Sawyer.
VI. Mary, b. Sept. 9, 1779; d., unmarried; a teacher for many years.
VII. Hannah, b. July 13, 1781; d. young.
VIII. Daniel, b. Aug. 31, 1783; d., unmarried, in 1824.
IX. Susannah Bartlett, b. Aug. 24, 1778; d., unmarried, in 1802.

Nos. 123, 124.

Moses Clark and Mary Clark, both of Amesbury, Mass.

Were published in Hampstead, March 16, 1754. They owned the covenant Aug. 13, 1769.

No. 125.

Mary Johnson, b. in Hampstead, Oct. 1, 1744.

A daughter of Stephen, Jr., and Susannah (Lovekin) Johnson (Nos. 23, 24, ch. mem.). She mar. Jesse Thurrell, and as a widow owned the covenant, Oct. 20, 1769. She had three children (p. 420, Vol. 1).

Nos. 126, 127.

Moody Chase and wife, Anna Webster.

Owned the covenant Nov. 10, 1769. Moody Chase was b. in Chester, Oct. 7, 1744, tenth child of Joseph Chase, of Chester; m. Anna, daughter of John and Elizabeth (Lunt) Webster, of Hampstead, b. May 26, 1749; mar. Oct. 20, 1768. They resided in Chester. Chase's History says : "Thanksgiving day, in 1806, Samuel Graham carried his bass viol into the meeting-house, and no sooner did he begin to sound it than Dea. William Wilson took his hat and left in hot haste, and Moody Chase followed, who came into my grandfather's after meeting, being nearly ready to burst, and gave vent to the bile."

Nos. 128, 129.

Jacob Chase and wife, Mary (Colby) Worthen.

Owned the covenant Dec. 10, 1769. Jacob Chase was b. in Chester, Dec. 25, 1727, a son of Joseph and Mary (Morse) Chase, of Chester. He was a very prominent man in Chester, being frequently moderator. He was very active in Revolutionary times. He m., first, Prudence, daughter of Benjamin Hills, Sen., of Chester, who d. in 1765. They had children :—

I. Sarah, m. Moses Richardson.
II. Stephen, m. Rhoda Blake; removed to Springfield.
III. Josiah, m. Lydia Blaisdell, of Grantham.

Jacob Chase m., second, Mary Colby, widow of David Worthen. He d. Dec. 12, 1803.

Nos. 130, 131.

Anthony Taylor and wife, Priscilla.

Owned the covenant June 22, 1770.

Nos. 132, 133.

Jacob Currier and wife, Hannah Morrill.

Owned the covenant July 14, 1770, both of Amesbury, Mass. (see No. 13, ch. mem.).

Hannah Grove, " of Stratham of late."

Owned the covenant Nov. 17, 1770.

Nos. 135, 136.

Samuel Worthen and wife, Mehitable Heath.

Owned the covenant June 7, 1772.

Nos. 137, 138.

Parker Dodge and wife, Mary Little.

Owned the covenant July 4, 1777 (see Nos. 6, 7, ch. mem.).

Nos. 139, 140.

Molly and Elizabeth Stevens,

Owned the covenant Oct. 30, 1774. They were daughters of Samuel and Susannah (Griffin) Stevens, of Hampstead (see Nos. 63, 64).

Nos. 141, 142.

Moses Stevens and Mary Heath, his wife,

Owned the covenant Feb. 19, 1775 (p. 427, Vol. 1, and No. 63, ch. mem.).

Nos. 143, 144.

Nathaniel Flanders and his wife Mary, both of Sandown.

Owned the covenant Feb. 19, 1775.

Nos. 145, 146.

Jonathan Taylor and wife, Dolly French.

Who were mar. in Hampstead, Feb., 1779, owned the covenant Jan. 12, 1782.

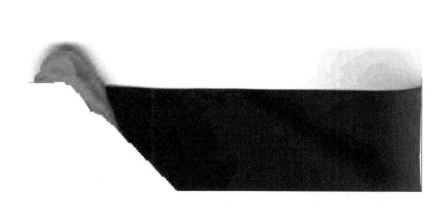

APPENDIX.

ADDITIONS AND CORRECTION TO THE MEMORIAL HISTORY OF HAMPSTEAD, VOL. 1.

When the illustrations were inserted in Volume 1 an un-avoidable circumstance made it impracticable to give the page on which they might be found. The following list in the order of insertion in the Town Memorial, with the page preceding the groups of pictures, may be an aid to us all.

NO. 5.

NO. 6.

The school-houses in Nos. 5 and 6 were, by error omitted to print in Vol. 1. They appear in the "Hour of Rest."

Additions to Vol. 1 and corrections not given on page 469 of the Memorial History :—

Page 10, read, Spaulding for "Spaulding," Guy S. Rix for "Guy V.," Frances I. Wallace for "Francis," Morrill for "Morrell."
Page 11, read in the last line of the quotation, loom for "helm."
Page 19, read Hutchen for "Hutch."
Page 132, read William H. Davis for "William A."
Page 133, read in the first line, The centuries old, etc., for "Century's old." Third verse, read, Our fathers' God, for "Our father's God," and has managed all for "has arranged all." Last line in the fifth verse read, and lean wolves hungry pack, for "and leave wolf's hungry pack."
Page 134, read, fifth verse, last line, Of Little. Noysey Ayers that bring, instead of "Of little Noyse'y Ayers, that bring."
Page 135, second line of second verse, While through the Morsey path, for "while through the Morse'y path."
Page 140, read Esther G. Bailey for "Esther J."
Page 161, read Charles Ranlett for "Randlett"; also on p. 172, read Ranlett.
Page 207, in the greeting by Mrs. Cowdery, the first two lines of the third verse were omitted. Read :
　　　　　　"There rest in quiet slumber,
　　　　　　The patriots, grand and brave."
Page 214, We have been told by our English cousins that "the article on Hampstead, England, is remarkably correct in detail, but with a few mistakes in spelling of names." We are now unable to correct only on page 228, that the poetess, Joanna Baillie, did not have a sister Agnes, who was a poetess, as the sentence reads. Read Wordsworth for "Wadsworth," Sir Francis Palgrave for "Palgrane."
Page 222, Sir Walter Besant, M. P.
Page 230, read Lancashire for "Lancestershire."
Page 233, class 1880, cross out "Mrs. Henry Merrick Danville."
Page 239, class of 1886, read "Henry L. Eastman" for "Henry C." Class of 1890, read Edith S. Griffin, mar. Will S. Griffin, for "Henry L. Eastman." Read Ranlett for "Rundlett."
Page 240, class 1894, read Lillian D. Ranlett.
Page 242, the name of Nelson Ordway was omitted from the list of former trustees.
Page 248, read Charles Boynton, M. D., for "John."

Page 201, read Ranlett for "Rundlett."

Page 263, in the list of Sunday School officers, after Asst. Supt., read, Supt. Home Department, Miss Mary E. Spollett.

Page 300, An impression might be given from the reading of the sentence, that the stone with inscription referred to was on a footstone at the grave of Mr. Hadley, and omitted to be recorded. No stone is found, or any mark to denote his burial spot. The inscription noted is to be read in connection with the sentence following on the rude stone at the grave of Mrs. Mary Ayer.

Page 325. In the sketch of Dr. Tewksbury, read 1705 for 1805, as birth date; and read, son of Jonathan and Elizabeth (Merrill) Tewksbury, for "Isaac and Susannah (Hale) Tewksbury."

Page 328. In the first verse of "Lake Wentworth," read, third line, rushes glide, for "waters glide." Fourth verse, second line, read, O'er its waves, for "on its waves." Fifth verse, fourth line, read, songs confessed, for "lungs confessed." Sixth verse, second line, read, Old Governor's Isle, for "Old Gunner's isle." Eighth verse, first line, read, Escumbuets, for "Escomorswets," and fifth line, Bay, for "bay." Ninth verse, read, Redgates for "Red-gates."

Page 334, in the third line from the bottom, read, July 14, for July 4.

Page 335, read, Daniel H., d. 1854, for "1864."

Page 337, read Helen Frances, for "Emma Frances." Read, Eugenia Safford, for "Eugenis Safford," and "Charles Edwin Ordway, b. Sept. 25, for "Aug. 25." Read Ranlett for "Randlett," and add Charles Henry Ranlett, b. Feb. 17, 1838; see also additions in Nos. 506 and 500, ch. mem.

Page 341, add: John F. and Nettie Belle (Carter) McCollester had children :—

I.   A daughter, who d., aged four years.
II.   Josie, d. 1900, aged 10 years.
III.   Frank C., b. June, 1883.
IV.   Katie, b. Nov., 1885.
V.   Lottie M., b. Nov., 1890.
VI.   Ruby G., b. April, 1807.

Josie G. and Susie Isabelle (Carter) Norman had children :—

I.   Child, d. young.
II.   Clarence A., b. May, 1892.
III.   Maurice H., d., aged 2 years.
IV.   Nellie F., b. Nov., 1897.
V.   Alice E., b. Aug., 1890.
VI.   Hazel W., b. June, 1902.

Page 343, read a correction to the item, Widow Hannah Hills, in No. 67, ch. mem.

Page 344, read, Sarah O. Brickett, b. Feb. 18, for "Feb. 10," and in the line below read, Ralph Brickett was the fifth of the twelve children, etc.

Page 350, read, David Irving mar., second, widow Hannah Marsh (No. 375, ch. mem.).

Page 350, read, fifth line from the bottom, great-great-grandson, for "great grandson."

Page 352, read Elizabeth Gibbon Little, for "Gordon."

AYER.

Peter Ayer, b. in Nottingham, England, a son of John Ayer, of that place, came to Haverhill, Mass., in 1646; mar. Hannah Allen. Their son, Samuel, b. in Haverhill, Sept. 28, 1669, had a son Peter, b. Oct. 1, 1696, who had children—Joseph, Lydia, Phineas, Hannah, Pearley, Sally, and William.

Pearley, son of Peter, was b. in Haverhill, Sept. 30, 1732, and his son, Hezekiah, b. in Haverhill, May 25, 1769, mar. Thankful Williams in 1791, and moved to Hampstead, where their children were born.

I.   Sally (No. 341, ch. mem.).
II.   Fanny, b. Oct. 23, 1793; m. Thomas Rundlett, and lived in Manchester; an only daughter, Lucy, who is now deceased.
III.   Hezekiah, b. May 23, 1796; m. Polly Little; d., and was buried in Hampstead (No. 399).
IV.   Jesse, b. April 24, 1798; mar. Mary C. Little (No. 272).
V.   Charles, b. June 5, 1800.
VI.   William, b. June 4, 1803; mar. Sarah Little Taylor (see No. 254, ch. mem.). Their children were: Sarah Adeline, b. March 2, 1831; William Herman, b. Aug. 26, 1832; and others.
VII.   Christopher, b. March 3, 1806; was chorister in the musical society for many years.
VIII. Perley (twin to above); lived in Boston, where he died about 1808.

CURRIER.

Samuel Currier, b. in Haverhill, Mass., Feb. 4, 1716, a son of Samuel and Abigail (Kelly) Currier, settled in Hampstead, and later became a Baptist minister, said to be the first minister in the town of Wentworth. His grandson, Aaron, went to Plymouth in 1819, and reared a family of nine children, who are among the most influential families of that town and Wentworth.

Asa Currier mar. Rebecca Plummer, in Hampstead, March 22, 1759, and removed to Sanbornton. He served in the Revolutionary war at Bunker Hill, and d. at West Point in 1781.

HOYT.

John Hoyt was of Amesbury in 1647. He mar. Frances ——, and had eight children, of whom his oldest son, John, married Mary Barnes, who was a member of the training band, and was killed by the Indians in Andover, on the road to Haverhill, Aug. 13, 1696. John and Mary had ten children, of whom the third was John, b. in 1663; mar. Elizabeth Chellis, of West Amesbury, who had three children, the youngest, Daniel, b. March 2, 1690, mar. Sarah Rowell, and resided in West Amesbury, where they had son, Eliphalet, who mar. Mary Peaslee, resided in Kingston. Their son, Ebenezer, b. in Amesbury, June 15, 1754, lived awhile in Newburyport and Amesbury, mar. Sarah Nichols, July 3, 1779, and settled at Hoyt Corner, in Hampstead. Ebenezer Hoyt, with his daughter, Mehitable, were baptized in West Amesbury in 1780, then called of Hawke. He served in the Revolutionary war in a Massachusetts regiment. He d. in Hampstead, Dec. 19, 1836, and his wife d. Feb. 18, 1854, aged 100 years and 7 months. Their children were :—

I.   Mehitable, b. Sept. 10, 1779; m. Samuel Dexter, son of "Lord"
     Timothy Dexter, of Newburyport.
II. William H., b. July 5, 1782; m. Betsey French, of South Hampton; settled in Sandown; and parents of Ebenezer, m., first,
     Mary Clark; Clementine (No. 463); Huldah (No. 453); and
     Lizzie S. (No. 733), were daughters.
III. Ebenezer, b. March 12, 1785; m., first, Mary Wells; second, Mary
     Hoyt; lived in Sandown.

.   Daniel Nichols, b. March 5, 1789.

Eliphalet, b. May 19, 1791; m. Lois Hunt, and had children :—
1. Sarah, m. Giles Davis, of Sandown.
2. Ebenezer (No. 614); m. Eunice A. Shannon (No. 615).
3. Stephen, b. Oct. 7, 1818; mar., May, 1849, Olive Whittier, who d. Feb. 9, 1854, leaving two children : 1, Luella, b. Sept. 6, 1850; mar., July, 1870, Moses II. Sargent; he d. July, 1871; she mar., second, in 1878, Fred M. Seavey, of Hampstead; their children : Charles F., b. Jan., 1879; Mary O., b. August, 1882; and Etta M., b. July, 1889. 2, Charles A., b. Aug. 21, 1852; resides in East Hampstead; mar. Eleanor A. Whitaker, of Atkinson, Oct., 1880; she d. April, 1884; their daughter, Leortie A., b. Dec. 12, 1881. Stephen Hoyt mar., second, Mary J. Winslow, of Kingston, May, 1855, who d. Feb., 1868; their children : 3, Emma J., b. July 17, 1856; mar. George Plummer, of Sandown, June, 1876; they reside in East Hampstead. 4, Mary O., b. June 19, 1859; mar. Fred E. Collins, of Danville; their children : Bert E., b. Nov., 1881; d. Feb., 1895; Perley L., b. Nov., 1887. 5, Martha W., b. Sept. 10, 1861; resides in East Hampstead; mar. Joseph G. Norman, of Boston, Feb., 1880; she d. Dec., 1881; one child, Mary F., b. Sept. 18, 1880; mar. Hersey C. Mooers, of Plaistow, Nov., 1898. Stephen Hoyt resides in East Hampstead, with son Charles.
4. Moses, b. June 5, 1824; mar., first, Marion Miner, b. in Rochester, N. Y., in 1830. They were married in Hampstead, Dec. 23, 1852. She d. in Watson, Mich., June, 1868. They had children, first two b. in Hampstead, last three in Watson, Mich.: 1, Lucy Frances, b. Jan., 1854; mar. William C. Ames, of Haverhill, Mass.; they have daughters, Eva, Eldora, and Minnie. 2, Ida Florence, b. Aug., 1855; mar. Porter Hoyt (see No. 615); they had daughters : Alta M., d. young; and Ethel B., mar. Clarence Harvey, of Virginia; married, second, Fred Shannon, of Plaistow. 3, Leonard Miner, b. Dec., 1856; married, first, Abbie Carter; one daughter, Annie Marion, b. March, 1879; he married, second, Flora M. Heath, of Hampstead; they have children, Alta, Maud, Lena, Grace, b. Jan., 1888; Clifton M., b. March, 1890; Herbert L., b. July, 1892; Walter E., b. Aug., 1898.

Moses Hoyt mar., second, Ellen J. Lowry, of Kingston, April 5, 1887; both living in East Hampstead.

      5. Leonard, d. unmarried.
      6. Mehitable, m. Luther Webber, of Hampstead (p. 347,
         Vol. 1).
      7. Joseph, m. Mary French (No. 374).
VI. Joseph, b. Oct. 2, 1704.
VII. Moses, b. Aug. 7, 1707; m., first, Hannah Williams, who was b.
      Oct. 29, 1709; daughter of Moses and Mehitable (Atwood)
      Williams (see p. 420, Vol. 1). She d. Dec. 22, 1841. They
      had children :—

          1. Mehitable, b. Sept. 17, 1821; m. Francis V. Dow, of
             Atkinson. He d. Jan. 7, 1893. They had children :
             1, Abbie H. (No. 534); m. Wm. A. Emerson (No.
             533). 2, Josephine, m. Martin Dow, of Hampstead;
             resides in Haverhill, Mass. 3, Annie. 4, Lizzie. 5,
             Frank (deceased). 6, Moses H., of Haverhill. 7,
             Lucy, m. George Ordway. 8, William, m. Emma
             Hamlin; resides in Haverhill.
          2. Sarah, b. June 10, 1823; m. Josiah Emerson; resided in
             Haverhill. They had children : Daniel H. and Wil-
             lard F. (deceased), and Charles W.
          3. Lydia Ann, b. Feb. 1, 1825; m. Albert Ayer (see No.
             272).
          4. Daniel Lowell Nichols, b. Jan. 1, 1827; m. Sarah S.
             Flanders (No. 480).
          5. William Howard, b. Oct. 13, 1828; m. Mary F. Ranlett;
             she d. Aug. 18, 1902. They had children : Jose
             phine, William (deceased).
          6. Philena W., b. April 22, 1830; m. William Eaton, of
             West Haverhill. They have children : Belle, m.
             Frank Emerson; Lizzie, William, Lucy, Gertrude
             and Walter.
          7. Caleb J., b. Dec. 15, 1832; d. June 27, 1900; m. Hannah
             Jane Wheeler, who d. Nov., 1891. They had chil-
             dren : Hattie C. (deceased), and Charles M., of Brad-
             ford, Mass.
          8. Daniel N., b. Aug. 15, 1834; m. Martha McDuffee; she
             d. July 6, 1887. Children (see p. 349, Vol. 1) : 1, Mary
             Lillie (No. 644). 2, Eugene, b. Jan. 18, 1865; d. Aug.
             8, 1865. 3, George A., b. Feb. 20, 1870; m. Lizzie
             Gilmore; resides in Hampstead.
          9. Moses H., b. June 19, 1837; d. young.
        10. Hannah E., b. Aug. 16, 1839; d. young.

Esq. Moses Hoyt m., second, Joan Brown; no children.
He m., third, Deborah Jenness (see No. 441). They had
children :—

11. Charles C., b. July 22, 1849; m. Ada Roundy. They have children : Inez, Caroline, Martha, Eugenia.
12. Henry H., b. Sept. 21, 1855; m. Eliza Flanders; have one daughter, Olive Deborah.

Mrs. Deborah Jenness Hoyt d. Sept., 1876; and Moses Hoyt m., fourth, Mrs. Sarah R. Gordon (No. 575).

LITTLE.

Samuel Little, oldest son of Daniel and Abiah (Clement) Little (No. 13, ch. mem.), married, first, Sarah Sewell, in 1736, and, second, Sarah Follansbee, Dec., 1738. He resided in Atkinson, on the farm of the late Greenleaf Clarke, and later moved to Hampstead, where he died, Jan. 16, 1798. He was a prominent citizen in town, and served as selectman many times, and as moderator twelve times. He was an active patriot, and a member of the Provincial Congress. He also held a magistrate's commission, and did much legal business in town. He was a member of the church at North Parish, having been admitted May 22, 1737. A letter written by him to his daughter Sarah, when he was over eighty years of age, is of interest : " I, your aged father, have great cause to bless God for giving me so many likely children, and in so good credit in the world, and granting them so comfortable and affluent circumstances with respect to things of this life, and so virtuously disposed to secure a better life when this life shall end. May the best of blessings rest upon them and theirs to the latest posterity is the unceasing prayer of their affectionate father."

The children of Samuel and Sarah (Follansbee) Little were :—

I.   Moses, mar. Mary Noyes (see Nos. 180 and 181).
II. Joshua, b. Sept. 17, 1741; mar., first, Lydia Brown; second, mar. Mrs. Ruhannah (Burnham) Blaisdell. He served in the Revolutionary war as lieutenant, at Castine and Crown Point, and as captain in the State militia. He was one of the first settlers in Whitefield, Me., where he was an extensive lumber merchant. They had five children, all b. in Whitefield.

III.   Mary, b. Aug. 10, 1743; mar. Stephen, son of Deacon Stephen
        Webster, of Haverhill, Mass. He was an officer in the Rev-
        olutionary war, and also took part in the battle of Bunker
        Hill. She was the mother of nine children, three of whom
        d. young. The oldest, Stephen Peabody Webster, mar. Mary,
        daughter of Rev. Stephen Peabody, the first minister of At-
        kinson. She was one of the two first ladies who demanded
        an equal education at Atkinson Academy, in 1793. The
        youngest daughter, Lydia, mar. John Vose, Esq., and were
        grandparents of John Vose Hazen, professor of civic engi-
        neering and graphics at Dartmouth College.

IV.   Abigail, b. Sept. 15, 1745; mar. Gen. Nathaniel Peabody, of At-
        kinson (see biographical and other sketches by William
        Cleves Todd, pub. 1901).

V.   Sarah, b. Aug. 20, 1747; mar. Enoch, son of Edmund Sawyer
        (see No. 45). They resided in Hampstead, later in Goffs-
        town, and died in Antrim, Dec. 5, 1829. She was the mother
        of ten children. She has been spoken of as a noble Christian
        woman, who left her impress upon her children, all of whom
        were church members, and nearly every one of her many
        grandchildren.

VI.   Daniel, b. March 19, 1750; mar. Hannah Mooers, daughter of
        John, of Hampstead. He was a farmer, and died Jan. 13,
        1841. Their children were:—

        1.   John. b. March 24, 1776; mar. Sarah Little, and re-
              moved to Union, Me., where he was engaged in the
              manufacture of lime casks. He died there, without
              issue, Dec. 21, 1855.

        2.   Moses, b. March 15, 1778; m. Mary Johnson, of Hamp-
              stead. He was a carpenter and builder, also a farmer,
              at the homestead of Mr. Tristram Little, his son.
              He died March 10, 1831. They had children:

              1.   Abigail Peabody, b. Feb. 17, 1808; mar. Thomas Run-
                    nels Wheeler, of Haverhill, Mass., and later lived in
                    Hampstead, where Edw. F. Noyes now resides. Mr.
                    Wheeler mar., second, Hannah F., daughter of Capt.
                    Jonathan and Susanna (Noyes) Moulton, of Hamp-
                    stead. She resides now (1902) as an inmate of the
                    Old People's Home, in Charles City, Iowa. Abigail
                    (Little) Wheeler had children: 1, Mary Phebe, b.
                    Dec. 24, 1829; m., first, in 1848, John S. McNiel, of
                    Andover and Amesbury, Mass., and had daughter,
                    Emma Estelle, mar. Horatio Dennett, of Lawrence,
                    Mass.; mar., second, Benjamin G. Currier, of Salem,
                    and had children, Marion D., Milton and Clinton

(twins, the latter d. young); she now resides in Lawrence, Mass. 2, Laura A., b. in Haverhill, June 15,
1834; mar. Avender Corson (see p. 309, Vol. 1, and
ch. mem., Nos. 545, 548, and 622).

2. Daniel Hazen, b. Sept. 25, 1813; d., aged two years.
3. Tristram, b. Dec. 12, 1815; mar. Betsey Peaslee, of
Newton (No. 604).

3. Sally, b. July 10, 1780; d., unmarried, at the home of
her nephew, Mr. Tristram Little, March 26, 1870.
4. Abigail Peabody, b. Nov., 1782; d., aged five years.
5. Tristram, b. May 4, 1785; m. Phebe Heustis, of Mt.
Pleasant, N. Y. He was educated at Atkinson and
Phillips Academy at Exeter. Was a teacher and
trader in White Plains, N. Y., and county superintendent of schools many years. He died in 1844.
They had seven children, of whom the sixth was
Sally Ann, b. April 13, 1827; a graduate from Rut-
gers College, in New York city; and married, in
1861, to Dr. Richard Harris. Mrs. Harris was also a
graduate from the Women's Medical College, and
resides at White Plains.

VII. Elizabeth, b. May 9, 1752; m. Eliphalet Poor, of Hampstead.
They lived in Hampstead until their first eight children were
born; then at Hopkinton and Dunbarton. He was a farmer,
also had a grist mill. He was in the Revolutionary war.
They had eleven children.

VIII. Tristram, b. Jan. 20, 1755; d. in 1778, while on his way home
from the army, in Rhode Island.

IX. Samuel, b. July 22, 1757 (see No. 200).

X. Abiah, b. April 6, 1760; m. Ezra, son of Capt. Joseph French,
of Hampstead (No. 100). He resided in Sandown, where he
was a prominent citizen, and held many town offices. They
had five children, b. in Sandown. She died July 9, 1721.

Jonathan and Dorothy (Little) Little were residents of
Hampstead, where he was a large farmer and land owner;
also a good military officer. He served in the State Legislature three terms, and was several times selectman. He was
born in Newbury, Mass., April 6, 1760, son of Stephen and
Judith (Bailey) Little, of Newbury. They had children, b.
in Hampstead:—

I. Joseph, b. July 26, 1788; m. Rebecca Webster; resided in Hampstead, and later in Atkinson. Their children, b. in Hampstead, were :—

1. John W., b. Aug. 27, 1812; resided in Haverhill until his death.
2. Elbridge G. (No. 850).
3. David Webster, b. Nov. 14, 1820; m. Mary F. Stevens; resided in Atkinson, where they had eight children, most of whom d. young.
4. Laurania Rebecca, b. March 15, 1834; m. John Q. A. Perry, of Atkinson, and have children: Elbridge G., m. Susan O. Ellis, resides in Atkinson; Ella J., m. Samuel French, of Atkinson; Charles E. A., m. in California; and George H. G., d. young.
5. Joseph F., b. Aug. 20, 1837; resides in Haverhill, Mass.

II. Stephen, b. April 20, 1792; m., first, Betsey Greenough; second, Mrs. Mary J. (Pemberton), of Groveland, Mass.; resided in Hampstead, Bradford, and Groveland. Their children, by first wife, were :—
1. Albert A. (No. 378).
2. Mary Jane, b. 1824; d. unmarried.
3. Elizabeth Albina, b. in 1832; m. William R. Little, of Atkinson, whose daughter, Albina M., m. John H. Smith, and has daughter Verta A., of Atkinson.

III. John (No. 369).
IV. Jonathan K. (No. 252).
V. David, b. Aug. 1, 1803; m. Louisa, daughter of Obediah and Hannah Peaslee of Newton. He resided in Hampstead, where John Mills now resides (later in Newburyport, where he d., and was buried in the Hampstead village cemetery.) Their children were .—
1. Hannah B. (No. 606).
2. Jonathan Peaslee, b. May 7, 1839; m. Mary Adelaide Jewell; resided in Amesbury, Mass., an only child : Annie Louisa, b. Oct. 10, 1874; m. George Ashley Woodsum, Dec. 28, 1897. Their children : Helen Jewell, b. Jan. 8, 1899; Jewell Douglass, b. April 8. 1901.
3. Jacob Edward, b. Nov. 15, 1843; d., unmarried, July 30, 1872.
4. Moses Bartlett (No. 526).

Page 353, read, as addition to the Bragg family: Children of George and Almena (Bragg) Page :—

I. Ethel Gertrude, b. Jan. 5, 1876.
II. Charles Sydney, b. May 19, 1884.
III. Willie Forrest, b. March 7, 1886.
IV. Sarah Lydia, b. Aug. 6, 1893.

DAVID LITTLE.

J. PEASLEE LITTLE AND GRANDDAUGHTER HELEN J. WOODSUM

MRS. ANNIE (LITTLE) WOODSUM.

Page 354, omit "widow of the late," as Elisha Richardson (m. Mary
H. Shannon), and are both living at West Hampstead.

SHANNON.

Thomas Shannon, born near Dublin, in Ireland, or, as
some say, near the river Shannon, emigrated to America
about 1722, settled at the Isle of Shoals, and later went to
Rye, where he married Mary Rand, and soon after moved to
lot 38, in Chester, where they resided a short time, and
before the incorporation of Hampstead had settled in Hampstead, on the farm now called the Ezra W. Foss place, in
East Hampstead.   They had children, as below, and perhaps
others :—

I.   William, mar. Hannah Holmes, widow of Nathan Lane, who
      had children : Dea. Josiah, who m. Sarah Sargent, and re-
      sided in Candia; Sarah, wife of Moses Sargent; and Jane,
      wife of Jona. Worthen.
II.   Samuel, m., first, Lydia Taber; second, Lydia (Leavett) Griffin.
      He d. in 1813.   They had children : Lydia, m. Josiah Morse;
      Thomas, m. —— Davis; and Sarah, who m. Thomas Chase.
III. Joan, m. Jacob Griffin.
IV.   Thomas, b. in 1750, in Hampstead; m., first, Sally Pillsbury, in
      1788; she d. in 1816, as oldest daughter of Joseph and Mary
      (Kelly) Pillsbury; second, Dolly Locke, widow of Josiah
      Moore.   Their children were :—
  1.   John, who was a sailor and followed the seas till his death in
        Roxbury.
  2.   Ebenezer, b. Nov. 27, 1796; m. Betsey, daughter of Timothy
        Smith, of Hampstead.   They had children, and lived at the
        farm now John F. Brown's :—
    1.   Stephen Smith, b. in 1825; m. Lucy T. Baldwin, of
          Thetford, Vt., March 20, 1850, and who d. in 1862.
          Children :   Edgar Francis, m., first, Lizzie, daughter
          of Joseph and Orphia (Tuthill) Knight, of Atkinson,
          and had daughter, Amy; m., second, Lizzie A.,
          daughter of John and Sarah (Kent) Little, of Atkin-
          son; Leslie Emerson, m. Miss Jones, and has a son,
          Bernard, of Lynn, Mass.; Mary Jane, m. John Ben-
          nett, of Alton, had daughter, Lucy, and son, d.
          young; Nettie Inez, m. Frank J. Paine, of Plaistow,
          and has daughter, Alice; Winifred, m. George Mor-
          rison, of Lynn.   Stephen S. Shannon m., second,
          Harriet Woodbury, of Salem, in 1864, and who d. in

STEPHEN S. SHANNON.

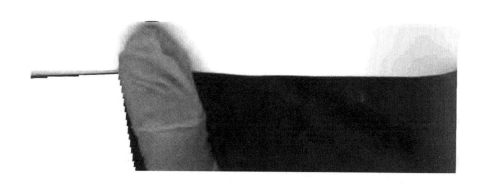

1876, and had children: Charles Woodbury, m. Mrs. Arnold; Annie Gordon, who is unmarried; and Bessie, d. young. He mar., third, Lois Ann Taylor, of Salem; they reside in Salem.

2. Sarah, b. in 1827; m. Samuel Morse, of Hampstead.
3. Charles Otis, b. in 1829; m. Sarah Brierly, of Windham; resides in Edgerton, Wis., and have several children, residing in the west.
4. Martha, b. in 1831; m. James M. Davis, of Plaistow; no children.
5. George Ebenezer, b. in 1835; wounded on the battle-field of Fredericksburg, Va., after taking part in sixteen engagements, and lived six months; he was unmarried.
6. Frank Welch, b. in 1839; m. Augusta Wood, of Sandown; had children: Frances; Kate, m. George A. Donacour, of Plaistow; Fred, m. Mrs. Ida F. Hoyt; Ernest, and Pearl.
7. Walter S., b. in 1845; m. —— Flanders; resides in Malden, Mass.
8. Henry M., b. in 1847; resides in Haverhill, Mass.

3. Joseph Pillsbury, m. Alice Nichols, and had children :—
 1. Eunice (No. 616), m. Ebenezer Hoyt (No. 615).
 2. Alice, m. Eliphalet Heath (see No. 358).
 3. Abby, m. Lewis Hale.
 4. Stephen Nichols; unmarried; resides at West Hampstead.
 5. Mary H., m. Elisha Richardson.
 6 Perley H. (No. 540).
 7. Frank; d. unmarried.
 8. Charles; m. Caroline Webster. He was killed in the civil war, and had son, Charles, of Manchester.

V. Mary, m. —— Hawes; lived in Roxbury, Mass.

In the sketch of Osgood read Francella Eastman for Francena; read Mildred for " Nellie."

OSGOOD.

Charles Henry Osgood, b. in Sandown, July 24, 1838, a son of Ephraim and Ruth (Gile) Osgood. Ruth Gile was b. in Haverhill, Mass., June 18, 1793, a daughter of Amos Gile and Ruth Foster. He had children by first marriage :—

I. Mary E., b. March 22, 1862; m. George H. Titcomb (No. 474).
II. Charles Henry, Jr., b. Oct. 18, 1864; unmarried.

He married, second, Francella Eastman, who was b. in Hampstead, Feb. 11, 1863, and d. July 12, 1890. They had children.

III.   Rinda Alice (No. 724).
IV.   Sadie Mildred, b. Feb. 4, 1882; d. Dec. 20, 1883.
V.   Agnes F. (No. 704).
VI.   Mildred B. (No. 705).
VII.   Freeman, b. Aug. 18, 1886; d. Sept. 6, 1891.

Page 355, Mary, mar. Samuel Dalton; moved to Northfield, where she
     d. July 18, 1820.

Page 355, read, Joseph Merrick was of the fourth generation, for
     "third," in line fourth.

MERRICK.

James Merrick, b. in Wales, in 1612, in St. David's, Pembrookshire; was
     in Charlestown, Mass., in 1632.   He was a fish packer and cooper
     by trade, and owned his own place of business in Charlestown, on
     the water front.   He mar. Margaret ——, and died in Newbury,
     Mass., before 1708.   His son, Timothy, mar. Mary Lancaster, of
     Amesbury, in 1696; lived in Newbury, where a son, Timothy, was
     born in 1704, who mar. Mary Bodwell, who lived in Methuen for
     some time, where most of their eight children were born, except
     the seventh, Joseph, b. in Hampstead, Dec. 30, 1749, and mar.
     Judith Little.   (p. 335, Vol. 1).

Page 335, read niece for "sister of Gen. Bailey."

Abner Little, son of Joseph and Judith (Little) Merrick, m. first, Betsey
     Steele.   A son b. in Salem.

I.   Abner, b. Dec. 14, 1803; mar. Eliza Nightingale, and resides in
       Salem.   They had children,   Eliza, m. Charles E. Bailey;
       Albert T., m. Louise Goodhue; Porter C., m. Harriet Newell;
       Caroline J., m. George A. Goodhue, and were the parents of
       Laura A., Emma F. (Mrs. Ford), and Lizzie E.; Mary J.; Julia
       F., m. David W. Ingalls; Elizabeth M., m. Samuel T. New-
       ell; Adeline II., and Calvin A. (No. 734).
          Abner Little Merrick mar., second, Martha Corliss, and had
       children :—b. in Hampstead.
II.   Jonathan Little, b. Oct. 10, 1807; mar., first, Nancy Morse; sec-
       ond, Marion Watts; third, Cynthia (Cummings) Ayer. Chil-
       dren, all by first wife, were : Arthur L., m. Selina George;
       Harriet, m. —— Durant, of Derry; John Randolph, m., in
       Middleboro, Mass.; Laura Ann, m. Aaron H. Davis, of
       Hampstead; Mary B., m. John K. Mason, of Atkinson; and
       Ridgeley R., m. Charlotte L. Copp, resides in Derry.
III.   'Nancy Pillsbury, b. Aug. 6, 1809; d., unmarried.
IV.   Susan, b. in 1811; d. young.
V.   [Susan Shannon, b. Sept. 26, 1814; m. Tappan S. Carter (see p.
       339, Vol. 1).

VI.   Stephen Little, b. May 6, 1818; m. Harriet Bagley; resided in
      Hampstead and Danville. Their children were : Harriet E.,
      m. Nathan Webster, of Haverhill; Joseph G., m. Rose
      Brown; Edward N.; Alice G., d. young; Henry W., m. Jennie
      Mayley; Andrew B., m., and resides in Sandown; Merrill B.;
      Abbie; and Mary, m. John Matavia, of Danville.
VII. Joshua Corliss, b. April 28, 1821; m., April 24, 1845, Nancy
      Morse Campbell. Children, all b. in Hampstead, were :—
         1. Charles Byron, b. Jan. 24, 1846; d. in 1861.
         2. Adelia, b. Dec. 16, 1850; d. in 1854.

MRS. MARTIN.

         3. Delia Ann, b. Dec. 29, 1855; m. Willard W. Merrick.
         4. Flora Ada, b. Oct. 5, 1858; m. Orlaton L. Whittaker, of
            Atkinson. Six children.
         5. Charles Beecher, b. Aug. 17, 1862; m. Lora Spaulding;
            resides in Sandown; three children.
         6. Mary Silloway. b. Jan. 15, 1867; m., second, Willard
            W. Merrick (above).
VIII. Julia Adeline, b. Aug. 21, 1824; m. Allen B. Martin; she resides
      in East Hampstead. Children :—
         1. Ellen Frances, b. Aug. 3, 1854; m. Melvin Cook; she d.
            in 1876, leaving a son, Allen, d., aged two years.

2. Hamlin
    maste
Nathaniel and
  children: J
  April 27, 183
Nancy (Pear
stead, in 18
    1. Belin
        N
    2. Joh

6. Abbie, d., aged 13.
7. Flora, d. young.
8. Willie, d. young.

II.   Herbert W., b. Jan. 25, 1855; m. Annie S. Knight (No. 689).

III.   Flora E., b. Jan. 22, 1856; m. Daniel W. Knight; resides in Dorchester, Mass. Children: Howard V., b. July 6, 1883; student Dartmouth College, 1905; and Lloyd W., b. July 20, 1889.

ISAAC HEATH.

IV.   Cynthia S., b. Dec. 15, 1860; m. Walter W. Knight, of Dorchester, a brother to Daniel W. and Annie S. (see No. 689).

V.   John Everett, b. Nov. 25, 1866; m. Annie L. Sawyer (No. 690).

ISAAC HEATH.

Second son of Stephen and Mollie (Chandler) Heath. Born in Sandown, N. H., March 3d, 1798. His early life

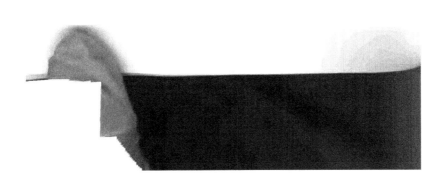

different bodies, also represented ward four in the board of aldermen. July 11, 1883, he married Elizabeth Ayer Newcomb, of Haverhill, who died July 8, 1898. In 1898 he joined his brother-in-law, O. H. Smith, in the purchase of the Calvin Taylor farm, at East Derry, N. H.

Isaac William Heath, born July 3, 1846; left home in 1868 to engage in railroading in the West, settling in Galesburg, Illinois. He accepted a position on the C., B. & Q. R. R. May 2, 1872, he united in marriage with Laura Lyford Austin, to whom three children were born, Emma Almira, Charles, and Isaac William, the latter living but one year and seven months. In 1883 ill health compelled a relinquishment of his position on the railroad, and moving to Foster, Pierce county, Neb., purchased a farm, and soon became popular with his fellow-citizens, for soon after his settlement there he was elected sheriff of Pierce county, and re-elected for three terms in succession, but died Sept. 22, 1889, only a few days before the expiration of his office. Their children: Emma A. is a successful teacher in the public schools of Osmond, Nebraska; Charles remaining on the farm left by his father.

Page 306, the tenth child of Charles W. and Ruth J. (Dustin) Bailey was omitted. Read:

X. Ruth Nancy, b. May 18, 1802. Read: V. Lillian May, mar. Arthur E. Mills, of Sandown, 1900.

Page 306, read, Charles Hamilton Grover, for " Charles Henry," as father of Charles Hanson Grover, for " Charles Henry, Jr."

GROVER.

Edmund Grover, b. in England, in 1600, was of Salem, Mass., in 1633. He was made a freeman in 1678. His wife was Margaret ——. They had daughters, Mary, Naomi, and Lydia, bapt. May 17, 1646, and Deborah, 1648, who married John Bennett, 1671; a son, Nehemiah, who was administrator of his father's estate in 1688. They lived on

the Beverly side of the river. The son, Nehemiah, was made a freeman in Beverly in 1678. He married, first, Ruth Haskell; second, Abigail ——. Nehemiah and Ruth (Haskell) Grover had children, among them a son, Edmund, who,

FREDERICK S. C. GROVER.

about 1719, moved from Beverly with a family and settled at Sandy Bay, Gloucester, where, upon the organization of the church, he was made a ruling elder. His wife was Mary ——, who died in 1757, aged 78 years. He died Feb. 5, 1761, "at an advanced age."

A son, Josiah, b. in 1792, in Beverly; mar., in 1719,

Hannah, daughter of Richard Dolliver, of Gloucester. Nov.
12, 1724, Elias Elwell, mariner, and wife, Dorcas, of Gloucester, sold to Richard Dolliver, of Jamestown, in the same
county, yeoman, for thirty-seven pounds and sixteen shillings, two lots, or parcels of land, in the town of Gloucester,
one on the western side of the "Cutt," so called, the other
lying below "Salem Path," so called, and June 12, 1736,
Richard Dolliver and wife Hannah deeded the same lots of
land and others, described as follows: "Two pieces of land
on the south side of the way that leads to the house of William Davis, deceased, being about five or six acres, bounded
northerly by said way, and southerly by Joseph Coward's
land, southeasterly where the stone wall stands on the hill,
then coming up the hill, as the fence now is, to the said way
to the first bounds." A second lot at "the head of the
marsh," and a third parcel "containing about five acres,
where his house now stands, and also a small garden spot now
being improved near Long Rock." It was deeded "for the
love and affection which I have and bear for my son-in-law,
Josiah Grover, now of Gloucester, and his wife, my daughter Hannah, and to their son Joseph after them, to hold forever."

Josiah and Hannah (Dolliver) Grover owned and lived
near the tract called "Norman's Woe Pasture," now the site
of the Gloucester Fishery. They had four sons, by one of
whom only has the name been perpetuated, and that Joseph,
born in Gloucester before 1736. He was a mariner, and
married Sarah Page, of Haverhill, May 19, 1757. They
resided at Fresh Water Cove until three children were born,
then moved to East Haverhill, Mass., near their uncle Singletary's estate, and on March 5, 1777, purchased of his
father-in-law. Nathaniel Page, ninety acres and buildings
thereon, for £200, lawful money, in Atkinson. The house
was situated a short distance from the present Grover homestead in Atkinson, and in 1779 Joseph Grover built the house

lately removed by Stillman H. Grover, to make way for his present residence. The Grover farm descended by deed from Josiah to sons Edmund and Josiah in equal shares, April 9, 1804, and from Josiah, Jr., who had purchased his brother's part, to his son Joseph Grover, and thence to the only descendant of the name in Atkinson by inheritance, Stillman H. Grover, to whom I am much indebted for many facts of the Grover family. Joseph and Sarah (Page) Grover had twelve children, three born in Gloucester, seven in East Haverhill, and the youngest two in Atkinson, as follows :--

I.   Joseph, b. in 1758; was in Capt. Jesse Page's company during the Revolutionary war. and was lost while privateering after the close of the war. He was unmarried.

II.   A daughter.

III.   A daughter.

IV.   Josiah, b. April 5, 1764; mar. Susannah, daughter of Dea. Jeremiah Jewett, of Rowley, June 4, 1795; settled on the farm of his father, in Atkinson, except for a few years in Hampstead, at the farm of the late Isaac Heath, where the second, third, and fourth child was born. He died in 1856, aged 92 years. Their children were :—

    1. Betsey, b. Sept. 18, 1796; mar. Thomas Arnold.

    2. Sarah, b. April 5, 1798; mar. Caleb Jackson, Jr.

    3. Susanna, b. Aug. 14, 1799; a teacher in Gloucester and Rockport many years; d., unmarried, in Atkinson, aged 90.

    4. Dr. William, b. Feb. 20, 1802; mar. Sarah Taylor; resided in Barnstead, where they had a daughter, d. young, and Alcina.

    5. Rev. Nathaniel, b. Sept. 13, 1805; mar. Sarah, daughter of Hon. John Vose, of Atkinson; resided in Grand Haven, Mich.; had children : John, d. young; Martha, mar. —— Hudson; Henry, William J., and Carrie, mar. —— Mertz, and resides in Spokane, Wash. Rev. Nathaniel Grover was the author of the toast, which is as widely known as is the town of Atkinson. He sent the toast to the alumni of Atkinson Academy, at its celebration, Aug. 25, 1859, as follows :— "Atkinson—long known as the POOR, LITTLE, NOYES-EY town, inscribed upon some obscure

PAGES of history, overshadowed by the darkness of
many KNIGHTS; yet her POOR men have enjoyed
an abundance of the good things of earth; many of
her LITTLE men have been almost giants; her
NOYES-ES have not been empty sounds. She has
produced PAGES of sufficient size and importance to
honor any author, and her very KNIGHTS have been
employed to enlighten the youthful mind."

6. Joseph, b. Feb. 23, 1808; mar. Sarah Page; settled at
the old homestead, and had children : Harlan, d.
young; Loren, d. aged three years; and Stillman H.;
Joseph d. Jan. 26, 1899, aged 90.

7. Phebe, b. Oct. 1, 1811; mar. Rev. William Page, of Atkinson, and were the parents of S. Lizzie, of Atkinson, and Amelia, who died in young womanhood.

V. Nathaniel, b. Jan. 21, 1766; moved to Wells, Vt.

VI. Timothy Eaton, b. Oct. 14, 1767. He lived in Atkinson till
about eighteen years of age, when he moved to Boston and
engaged in the trucking business, which he followed many
years, and later moved to Sandown, where he died. He
married Rhoda Bennett, of Hampstead, pub. in town Aug. 17,
1805. Their children were Eleazer, Irene, John, who settled
in Sandown, and parents of Charles and Horace T., now of
Sandown, and Charles, who married Abigail, daughter of
John Bartlett, of Hampstead. Charles was killed by the
blasting of a quarry in Quincy, Mass., Feb., 1848, and the
widow married, second, John Reed, of Haverhill, Mass.
Their son, Charles Hamilton, b. Feb. 26, 1848, a few days
after the death of his father, mar. Lois, daughter of Hanson
and Clarissa (Chase) Whitehouse, and resides in Hampstead,
where their children were born, as follows : Charles Hanson,
mar. Alma E. Sears; Bessie G., mar. E. Cecil Mills; Frederick S. C. (see cut); and Abbie C. (see p. 367, Vol. 1).

VII. Ruth, b. Dec. 24, 1769; m. —— Sloan.

VIII. Hannah, b. May 6, 1771.

IX. Phebe, b. May 18, 1772.

X. Edmund, b. June 8, 1773; mar. Dorcas ——; lived for a time at
the half of the homestead in Atkinson, where two children
were born : Roxanna, b. April 3, 1803; Stephen, b. Dec. 11,
1804. They had sons, who moved to Massachusetts, and were
manufacturers of tinware, and both died of typhoid fever,
unmarried, in young manhood. Edmund moved to Canterbury about 1807.

XI. An infant, d. young.

XII. John, b. in 1778, his mother dying at his birth. He followed the sea, and was an owner of a vessel which was washed away in a storm. His sea chest is now owned by Stillman H. Grover, in Atkinson. The following letter, written by his brother, Timothy E. Grover, to Josiah, records the date of his death : " May 9, 1805. John died in Boston, on Hanover street, at Mrs. Barynes' boarding house. He was under the care of Dr. Danforth in his sickness. He was siqk twenty-seven days of fever, and then died. He died Nov. 15, 1804." In the same letter Timothy writes : " Josiah, take your horse and go to Hampstead and inform Miss Bennet of the death of your brother John, and ask her to write me a letter. Then you take the letter and you write me one, and wrap one in the other and send to me at Boston, at Asa Lawrence's, corner Merchant's row."

Page 367, read Stimson for Stimpson. Read that it was John B. Richardson who was b. in Groveland and d. in Hampstead, not his daughter, Sarah B., as might be inferred.

Page 371, read Dea. William Sanborn mar., third, Mary J. Heath.

Page 372, add to Moulton family Caleb Harriman Moulton, b. Oct. 3, 1777, not 1787. He d. in 1845. His wife d. in 1883, aged 91 years. Their son, Caleb, b. in Hampstead, Jan. 3, 1818, d. May 17, 1878; mar. Abigail A. Morse, who was b. in Hampstead, April 13, 1819, daughter Abbie, b. Feb. 4, 1857; d. Jan. 25, 1864. Son Andrew, d. Aug. 7 (not June). Carrie A. Smith, b. June 26, 1853.

Frank E. and Clara E. (Moulton) Darling had children :—
I.   Louis C., b. Feb. 26, 1898.
II.   Elwin M., b. May 29, 1900; d. Sept. 15, 1901.
III.   Caroline, b. Sept. 18, 1901.

David Moulton (p. 442), b. in Hampstead, June 1, 1805, m. Marcia L. Conner, Nov. 6, 1827. He was a printer and publisher of books at Sanbornton, and at one time a newspaper editor. He moved west and entered the U. S. service at St. Louis. He d. April 23, 1834. His daughter, Marcia, married Shrevel Lorain, a nephew of Leigh Hunt, the English author, from Hampstead, Eng., and who was first cousin to Benjamin West, the artist.

Page 374, read Amos Clark, mar. Hannah Stevens, and d. Feb. 13, 1835, aged 84.

Page 375, read, third line from bottom, John Ellsworth for "John William." Read Ellery Edward for " Ellery Ellsworth."

ATWOOD.

Mr. Charles Atwood, distinguished scholar and prominent lawyer, who died in Boston in 1887, made an extensive research of the Atwood family in England and America. From his MS., in the possession of Mrs. George W. Warren, of Somerville, Mass., a niece of Mr. Atwood, we read: "The name of Atwood originated in Coulsdon, a parish in Surrey county, twelve miles south of London, and adjoining Croydon and Sanderstead. As early as 1313 tenants of estates of the Abbey of Cherster were Peter, John, and Geoffrey Atte-Wodee, named from their residence "at the wood." This estate had 150 acres of land, and had been in the family 150 years. The first Atwood buried in the church in the village of Sanderstead was in 1520, A. D.

Nicholas, the third son of John Atwood of Sanderstead, served Queen Elizabeth from the second year of her reign, May 14, 1586, leaving a wife, Olive Harman, and sons, Harman, John, Nicholas, Thomas, James, John, 2d, or Jonathan, Richard, daughters Alice and Susan.

John Atwood, who came to Plymouth in 1635, was the second son of Nicholas and Olive (Harman) Atwood, and his nephew, Harman Atwood, was first mentioned as a freeman in Boston, Dec. 26, 1642. He was a member of the Ancient and Honorable Artillery company in 1644. He married Ann, daughter of William Copp, and lived near Court House Square, in Boston. They had a son, John, baptized in Boston, Sept. 5, 1647, " when five days old." He married Sarah ——. He was a deacon of the North Church in Boston twenty-one years, and a member of

the Ancient and Honorable Artillery in 1673. He died in 1714, according to a stone in Copp's Hill burying ground. It was the opinion of Mr. Charles Atwood, and also of A. Burnside Atwood, now of the engineering department, Boston City Hall, to whom we are indebted for much of this sketch, that James Atwood, born in Boston in 1673, had a son, John, b. in 1714, in one of the surrounding centres of Boston, that the son James was deceased before 1729, when the estate of the father, John Atwood, was disposed of on Middle street, Boston, and that the son John was brought up by his half uncle, John Atwood, who mar. Hannah Bond, and settled in Bradford, Mass. John and Hannah (Bond) Atwood were the parents of Joseph Atwood, mar. Sarah Chresdee, whose son, Moses, mar. Mary Tenney, and were the parents of Harriet Atwood, later the wife of Rev. Samuel Newell, the missionary. The Atwood family of Atkinson were descendants of John and Hannah (Bond) Atwood.

John Atwood, son of James, b. in 1714, was the pioneer of the family in Hampstead, being one of the original petitioners for the township in 1744, and probably came to the town in 1742. He built the house now known as the Horace Adams home, and it was one of the seven farms in town mentioned by Judge Smith, in 1849, as having been in the possession of the same family for one hundred and fifty years. This house descended from John Atwood to his son James, who married Molly Lowell, and then to their son, Moses, who sold it to Mr. Adams in 1851. Moses Atwood, son of John and Ruth (Whittaker) Atwood, built a house on the corner near by, about 1780, which was burned in 1884.

John Atwood married, first, Abigail Sanders, in Haverhill, Mass., Jan. 7, 1735, and had children :—

I.   Abigail, b. Aug. 13, 1735; mar. Alexander Hoog, Dec. 27, 1754, and resided in Alexandria.

II.   Jonathan, b. Sept. 29, 1736; bapt. April 27, 1737; mar., first, Elizabeth Plummer, Oct. 5, 1758; mar., second, Dolly Wells; removed to Weare, where he resided with his second wife. Children :—

      1. Elizabeth, b. Oct. 30, 1760 (see bapt. in Hamptead); mar. Thomas Colby, and removed to Sutton, Vt.

2. Joshua, b. April 16, 1762; m., first, Susan Cram; second, Mrs. Anna Russer; lived in Antrim, and had sixteen children, the second of whom married and lived in Weare; Dolly m. Squire Gove, and Rhoda m. Jesse Gove.

3. Ruth, b, July 13, 1764.

4. Philip, b. July 29, 1766; m. Sarah Dustin, and had one child, William D., b. 1789; mar. Sally Simonds, of Antrim; lived in Antrim until 1823, when he removed to Bridgewater, Vt., where he lived to a great age.

5. John, b. May 18, 1768; m., Oct. 9, 1791, Dolly Prescott, b. Jan. 17, 1773, daughter of Joshua Prescott and wife, Ruth Carr. He died at West Campton in 1832.

6. Dolly, b. in 1768; d. young.

7. Peter, b. June 9, 1771.

8. Jonathan, b. Oct. 9, 1772; m. Mary, dau. of John and Mary Cheney of Methuen, and they had nine children, Roxana the eldest, b. May 26, 1793, m. Alexander Thrall 1819, they had George and Roxana ; Roxana, b. in Granville, Licking Co., Ohio, Dec. 14, 1822, m. Chas. Sherman in Berkshire, Del. Co., Apr. 18, 1844. They had seven children; Mary Emily, b. Feb. 28, 1846, m. in Placerville Co., Cal., Kirke White Taylor, Oct. 20, they had three children, Marion, b. Oct. 30, 1866 ; Ida, b. July 13, 1874, d. Nov. 24, 1877 ; Emily Marcia, b. July 14, 1879. Marion, m. in Martinez, Reuben Leonard Ulsh, Apr. 3, 1899. They have one child, Emily, b. June 17, 1901.

9. Dolly, b. Oct. 2, 1774.

10. Elijah, b. May 7, 1777; m. Polly Dustin, and had a child, Peter P., b. May 12, 1796.

11. Jessey, b. July 10, 1779.

12. David, b. July 6, 1781; m. Polly Barnard, 1802.

13. Mehitable, b. March 7, 1784; d. unmarried.

14. Sarah, b. Dec., 1786; m. William Eastman.

III. Caleb, b. Dec. 28, 1738.

IV. Joshua (twin to Caleb); died a soldier in the French war.

V. Joanna, b. July 7, 1740.

VI. Ruth, b. May 20, 1742; mar. Bond Little (see list of those who " owned the covenant ").

VII. Sarah, b. March 20, 1746; m. —— Straw.

VIII. John, b.   ; m. Merideth Roberts, of Hampstead, Sept. 28, 1769; removed to Weare, and settled on lot 76, range 2; he sold out early and returned to Hampstead. They had one child, b. in Weare, Daniel, b. June, 1770.

Abigail, wife of John Atwood, died Nov. 9, 1750, and he married Ruth Whittaker (see No. 76, ch. mem.).

Caleb, son of John and Abigail (Saunders) Atwood, had children :—

I. Samuel, b. Sept. 22, 1763; m. Lydia Persons in 1787, and settled in Bradford.
II. Abigail, b. Sept. 3, 1765; m. Charles Colburn.
III. Caleb, b. Sept. 25, 1767; m. Hannah Persons.
IV. Mehitable, b. Dec. 4, 1769; m. Hezekiah Emerson.
V. Elizabeth, b. Nov. 6, 1772.
VI. Eunice, b. Sept. 16, 1774; m. William Rowe in 1704.
VII. Stephen, b. March 27, 1777; m. Fanny Seal.
VIII. Joshua, b. June 26, 1779; m. —— Patten; resides in Deering.
IX. Moses, b. Sept. 21, 1781.

Caleb Atwood bought, Feb. 4, 1760, lot 60, range 2, in Weare, of his father, John Atwood, of Hampstead, for 42 Spanish milled dollars. His father bought of Moses True, Jan. 30, 1760, the same lot, for 12 pounds lawful money. Young Caleb Atwood moved to Weare from Hampstead in the spring of that year, and built a cabin on the side of Mt. Dearborn, the highest house in town. It stood just south of the house at present owned by Josiah G. Dearborn, which is now the flower garden, and was one mile west of Meadow Brook, on the road over the hill to Deering, "and was on the west side of the way," and soon after it was built a gale took the roof off, carried it over the road, and laid it down softly in the stumpy field.

Mr. Caleb Atwood was a prominent man in Weare, a soldier in the Revolution, active in town matters, and a member of the First Church. In his old age he went to live with his son Joshua, in Antrim. After that he lived in Deering, where he died, aged 76 years.

John Atwood, the father, died in Hampstead, Jan. 1, 1812, aged 97 years and 7 months. The story is told of him that "he weighed about 260 pounds, and was over six feet, and lifted a barrel of cider in his hands, and carried 500 feet of lumber up a hill."

James, the tenth child of John and Ruth Atwood, married Molly Lowell. Their fourth child, Levi, b. Nov. 4, 1781, mar.

Betsey Francis, of Sandown, July 27, 1806. They resided the last part of their life in Nashua, where they both died. Their son, Amos, b. in Thornton, Jan. 15, 1812, m. Mary C. Mills (No. 531), and parents of—

I.   Belinda G. (No. 516).
II. Charles Edwin; a soldier in the 1st N. H. Regt. of Vol., 1864 to 1865.

Sylvanus, eleventh child of James and Molly (Lowell) Atwood, married Mary Leavitt, of Washington, Vt., and died in Andover, at the age of 74 years. He was a wheelwright by trade, and an earnest member of the Methodist church. They had one daughter and a son :—

I.   Laura Ann, m. George W. Cilley, of Hebron; d. in Andover, June 11, 1902, at the age of 77. They had eight children, six of them dying in infancy, and are buried in Andover. The two surviving children were Mrs. Rozanna F. Elkins of Andover and Mrs. Mary S. Peabody of Nashua.
II. Moses, m. Mary Ann Emery, of East Andover; one child, d. young.

John, the seventh child of James and Molly (Lowell) Atwood, b. June 9, 1787, was drowned.

STEVENS.

William Stevens, from Gonsham, Oxford county, England, came to Newbury, Mass., probably in the ship "Confidence," in April, 1638. He married Elizabeth ——, in Newbury, in 1645, and had children, b. in Newbury, of whom the eldest son was John, born Nov. 19, 1650, married Mary, daughter of Aquilla Chase. John and Mary (Chase) Stevens had children :—

I.   Mary, b. Feb. 10, 1670.
II. John, b. March 23, 1673; m. Hannah Currier, and had two children who d. young; and, second, m. Mary Bartlett, and had eleven children; and, third, m. Miriam Jackman, and had one child. Children were :—
      1. Child, d. young.
      2. Child, d. young.
      3. Abigail, b. July 4, 1701.
      4. Moses, b. Nov. 13, 1702; m. Molly Heath. Three children, b. in Hampstead (see p. 427, Vol. 1).

5.   Hannah, b. March 16, 1704; m.
6.   Jonathan, b. March 25, 1707; m. Eleanor Heath, and settled in Atkinson about 1741, where he sold to Jonathan Whittaker, in 1774, farm now known as the " Joseph Whittaker place."
7.   Joseph, b. July 12, 1709; m. Ruth Heath; settled in Hampstead (see p. 427, Vol. 1, for some of their children).
8.   Mary, b. April 4, 1711.
9.   John, b. July 26, 1713.
10.   Susanna, b. May 17, 1716.
11.   Samuel, b. March 29, 1718.
12.   Timothy (No. 148).
13.   Ruth, b. Feb. 20, 1724.
14.   Ann, b. May 13, 1729.

III.   Thomas, b. July 13, 1676.
IV.   Moses, b.
V.   Aaron, b. April 7, 1685; m. Mary Harris, of Haverhill (see No. 18).
VI.   Joseph, b. Nov. 19, 1689.
VII.   Benjamin, b. Jan. 25, 1693; m. Abigail Johnson; lived in Hampstead (see p. 428, Vol. 1).
VIII.   Sarah, b. Sept. 7, 1680; m.
IX.   Hannah, b.
X.   Samuel, b. in 1699.
XI.   Otho, b. in 1702; m. Abigail Kent (Nos. 63 and 64).
XII.   William, m. Mary Tucker; second, Elizabeth Dodge; third, Lydia Gile (No. 122).

Daniel Stevens m. Elizabeth Bryant (see No. 64), Jan. 26, 1768 (see Cov. list, Nos. 68, 69). Their children were :—

I.   Elizabeth, b. Oct. 28, 1768.
II.   Tamar, b. Nov. 5, 1770.
III.   Susannah, b. April 27, 1773.
IV.   Paul, b. April 27, 1775; m. Mary Harriman (see No. 407, ch. mem.).
V.   Daniel, b. May 29, 1778.
VI.   Prudence, b. Jan. 3, 1782.

Paul Stevens m. Mary Harriman, Jan. 28, 1799. She was b. Jan. 28, 1771, and d. Jan. 1, 1837. He built the house about 1796, and occupied it until his death, Feb. 3, 1819, where Joshua F. Noyes now resides. Their children :—

I.   Eliza (No. 407).

II.   Moses, b. Feb. 19, 1806; m. Sophia Lyford, of Hampstead, by
       Rev. John Kelly, March 24, 1831. She d. in Groveland,
       Mass., April 8, 1809; b. Feb. 6, 1810. He d. July 17, 1877.
       Their children :—

        1.   Orin Wallace, b. Sept. 9, 1832; d. Feb. 17, 1806; m.
              Susan R. Jackson, b. in Carlisle, Mass., Sept. 4, 1830;
              m., in 1855, at Lawrence, Mass.; widow resides in
              Woburn, Mass. (1902). Children, b. in Woburn:—
              1, Fred Harris, b. Feb. 6, 1856; d. young. 2, Caddie
              Mariah, b. Aug. 18, 1857; d. young. 3, Charles Harri-
              man, b. June 3, 1860; m. Mary E. Anderson, of West
              Dalhousia, N. S., Oct. 11, 1856. 4, Orin William, b.
              Oct. 1, 1862. 5, Benjamin Franklin, b. June 16, 1865;
              m. Eulila Whitman, of Inglisville, N. S., Oct. 10,
              1893, b. Aug. 24, 1869. 6, Flora Adeline, b. July 21,
              1867; m. George Weston Dinsmore, of Woburn. 7,
              Carrie Amanda, b. Aug. 12, 1872; m. Herbert E.
              Lord, of Woburn.
        2.   Amanda Melvina, b. in Atkinson, July 24, 1834; m. Dea.
              Moses C. Kimball, Oct. 18, 1863 (see No. 183); son
              Charles William, b. Feb. 17, 1865; d. Jan. 29, 1870.
        3.   Oscar Fitsalen, b. in Hampstead, May 3, 1839; m. Mrs.
              Sarah (Wallis) Dennis, July 6, 1868. Children : 1,
              Oscar Edwin, b. June 27, 1870; d. young. 2, Louis
              Edwin, b. Sept. 19, 1880.
        4.   Edwin Therion, b. Feb. 28, 1841, in Hampstead; d. Oct.
              15, 1873. He was in the civil war as sergeant of Co.
              D, 3d Mass. Heavy Artillery.

Page 380, read Rebecca Carlton for " Priscilla Carlton."

Research shows that the first two children of Peter and Tamosine Hale Morse were b. in Newbury, and the last three in
Hampstead, and that they moved to the town in the spring of
1734. The sixth child was Moses, mar. Rachel Goodhue.

The genealogy of the Hampstead family, beginning with the
family of Lieut. Edmund and Rachel (Rowell). Children (see
p. 421, births).

I.   Jacob, b. March 31, 1751; mar. Naomi Sykes; second, Mehitable
       Williams; resided in Wakefield, Mass. Children : Clarissa,
       m. Rev. Mr. Lyman, resided in Hartford and Colchester,
       Conn. James, m. Frances Douglass; children: Charles and
       James, of Wakefield. Harvey, d. unmarried, in Port-au-
       Prince. Elizabeth, m. Rev. Stephen Taylor, D. D., of Rich-

mond, Va. Henry, m., first, Drusilla Day; second, Maria.
Boggs; resided in Trenton, N. J. Edmund, m. Catherine
Tice; resided in New Haven, Conn. Theodore, resided in
Baltimore, Md. Mary, m. Tilly Merrick, of New Haven,
Conn. Naomi, unmarried, a teacher in New Haven.

The fourth child, Daniel, mar. Mary Eastman, and resided in
Hanover. They had a son, Daniel, who mar. Sarah Ann Morse,
and had five children.

Edmund and Rebecca Carlton's children :— .

I. John, mar. Sally Williams, and resided in Hampstead, where he
    d. in 1820.
II. Moses, m: Mary Carlton, of Haverhill, Mass.
III. Molly, m. Abiel Kelly.
IV. Ebenezer, d., unmarried, in the West Indies.
V. Samuel, m., first, Sally ——, who d. in 1805, aged 25 years; had
    five children; second, m. Nancy Page. He was called Esquire
    Morse. Children were:—
    1. John F., d. aged two years.
    2. Rebecca P., b. in 1799; d., unmarried, in 1830.
    3. Edmund, b. June 8, 1801; m. Sally Moulton; resided in
        Hampstead and Atkinson. Had children : Thomas
        W., b. June 20, 1837; now residing in Sandown. Ed-
        win A., b. in 1843; d. young. Florence A., b. March
        20, 1845. Frances A., b. April 13, 1847.
    4. Asenath, mar. Caleb Marshall, of Hampstead.
    5. Samuel, d. young.
    6. Sally, d., unmarried, in Haverhill.
    7. Hannah P., d. young.
    8. Hannah P., 2d, mar. Moses Clark, of Haverhill.
    9. Polly F., d. young.
    10. Samuel, mar. Sarah Shannon (see p. 380, Vol. 1.)
    11. Abigail A., mar. Caleb Moulton (see p. 372, Vol. 1).
    12. Polly P., mar. Rev. John K. Chase; resided in South
        Hampton. He mar., second, Miss Laura A. Graves,
        of East Hampstead, and died there, while attending
        a prayer meeting, Jan., 1902.

Joseph, the youngest child of Edmund and Rebecca Carlton,
was born in 1773; d., unmarried, in Hampstead, in 1838.

Page 381, read William Johnson, son of James, resides in Haverhill,
Mass., for "resides in Hampstead."

JOHNSON.

Luther Johnson, b. in Hampstead, July 3, 1792 ; mar. Dorcas
J. Hardy, b. in Danville, Vt., May 29, 1803. They had children :—

I.   James, b. Dec. 14, 1825; mar. Angelina Canny. He is a carpen-
       ter, and resides in East Hampstead. They had children :
       Gideon, mar. Ida Vincent, and had children; Walter A. (No.
       743); and Blanche, mar. —— Hoyt, of Bradford, Mass.; Mr.
       and Mrs. Hoyt are both dead; William L. (No. 552); and Ad-
       die, mar. Geo. H. Hunt, of Somersworth.
II.   John, b. Feb. 10, 1828; d. in 1900, in East Hampstead. He was
       a carpenter and builder; mar., Mina A. Lane; had children,
       Luther L., of East Hampstead, Newton L., and Annie R.
III.   William, b. April 19, 1833; a machinist and inventor; m. Sarah
       M. J. French; resides in Cleveland, Ohio. They had
       children : Charles H., Frank L., Willie H., Elmer L., Carrie
       B., Grace L., and Florence M., and several grandchildren.
IV.   Mary, b. May 15, 1839; m., first, Tappan S. Carter, of East
       Hampstead; m., second, Dea. Caleb W. Williams (No. 515).

John Johnson, of Haverhill, Mass., mar., first, Sarah Haynes ;
second, Sarah Morse. He was one of the first settlers in that
part of Atkinson set off to Hampstead, near Copp's Corner.
Their children, rec. in Hampstead as on page 417, Vol. 1, of
whom Hannah married James Knight, of Atkinson, and John,
b. Feb. 2, 1760 (called Col. John), married, first, Ruth Emerson,
and had children ; second, Dolly Knight (but no children by
second marriage) ; Mary, b. June 20, 1784 ; mar. Moses Little,
of Hampstead (see p. 350, Vol. 1), and Moses, b. Feb. 25, 1786,
mar. Sarah Webster, resided at the homestead of his father.
They had eight children .—

I.   Bethiah Webster, b. Aug. 13, 1809; mar. Col. Nathan Richard-
       son, of Vermont. They resided in Lowell, Mass., and Tren-
       ton, N. J., and had children: Sarah Elizabeth, d. young;
       Charles Henry, now living in Philadelphia.
II.   Hannah, b. in 1811; mar. Moses Webster, of Methuen, Mass.
       No children.
III.   Adeline, d. young.
IV.   Sarah, d. young.
V.   Nathan, b. in 1818; m. Syrena Brown (No. 461)

VI. Sarah Ann, b. in 1820; mar. Harris Wilson, of Topsham, Vt., in 1846; they resided in Hampstead. Children: Hannah Adeline, b. in 1848; reside in Haverhill, Mass.; and Albert, b. in 1853, of Haverhill.

VII. Bailey Davis, b. in 1822; mar. widow Caroline Follansbee. Children: Leonard, b. in 1853, d. in Haverhill, Dec., 1902; Cora M., mar. James Howard, resides in Gorham, Me.; and Harlan, of Haverhill.

VIII. Moses Hazen, b. in 1825; m. Nancy, daughter of John Ames, of Atkinson; a schoolmaster for many years; moved to Trenton, N. J., in 1864; d. in 1883. They had children: Milton H., b. in 1842; Mary Frances, b. in 1851; and Charles H., all mar., in Trenton, N. J.

Attention has been called to dates of birth, marriage, or publishment, which vary from those recorded in family Bibles, or other records; some misprints varying from the records on the town books, and also that the town books have other or fuller dates in some instances.

Page 410, read, Moses, son of James and Lydia (Hoyt) Emerson, b. in 1760.

Page 411, read, second line, Caleb and Betsey (Nichols) Emerson, for Betsey (Tucker).

Page 423, read, Abial for "Abiah" Ordway; b. July 13, 1803, for "July 12."

Page 464, Ordway, John, add 335 and 336.

DEXTER.

Lydia Marsh, b. in Haverhill, Mass., Dec. 9, 1744, a daughter of Jonathan Marsh, mar. David Dexter, who was b. Feb. 18, 1748, and called of Atkinson Aug. 27, 1767. They lived in Haverhill, Mass., Hampstead, and Pembroke. He died in Boston, Nov. 24, 1821. She died in Hampstead, Dec. 30, 1785. Their home in Hampstead was situated nearly on the spot where the residence of the late Elbridge H. Noyes stands, and is still known as the "Dexter farm."

Elizabeth Dexter, daughter of David and Lydia, married Micajah Emerson, b. Jan. 29, 1798, a son of Stephen and Hannah (Marden) Emerson (No. 16). She was b. Feb. 28, 1773, and d. in Boston, Mass., June 12, 1848. They moved to Piermont.

Lydia Dexter, daughter of David and Lydia, b. Dec. 14, 1782, m. Abraham Richards, of Atkinson, April 24, 1800, and were the parents of Leverett E. P. Richards, late of Atkinson and Hampstead, Mrs. Cynthia Alexander of Hampstead, and nine other children. She lived to be one hundred years of age.

HAZEN.

Moses Hazen, a brother of Richard Hazen, Esq., of Hampstead, was one of the first land-owners in Hampstead, and an early proprietor, as well, of the settlement of Pennycook (now Concord). He was born in Haverhill, Mass , May 17, 1701, son of Lieut. Richard and Mary, daughter of Capt. John and Hannah (Andrews) Peabody. He married Abigail, daughter of John and Lydia (Gilman) White. "The Worshipful William White," the first proprietor of Haverhill, was grandfather of John White. Their children were:—

I.   Abigail, b. Jan. 7, 1729; m. Moses Moors. Gen. Benjamin Moors
.   of Plattsburg, N. Y., was a son.
II.   John, b. Aug. 11, 1731; m. Anne Sweet, Nov. 30, 1752, daughter
       of Timothy and Anne (Merrill) Sweet. Mrs. Anne Sweet
       (widow) became the second wife of Capt. Hezekiah Hutchens
       of Hampstead (see sketch of Capt. Hutchens). John Hazen
.   was active in the settlement of Hampstead, and when the
       French and Indian war broke out distinguished himself for
       good service. He was a lieutenant in Capt. Jacob Bailey's
       company in the Crown Point expedition, in 1757, in Col.
       Meserve's regiment from New Hampshire. In 1758 he was a
       captain in Col. Hart's regiment, and in 1760 he was a captain
       in Col. Goff's regiment. After the war he and Col. Bailey
       joined in the enterprise of settling the rich Coos country, and
       in 1761 became the first settler in Grafton county, at Haver-
       hill. His wife died Sept. 29, 1765. They had children, b. in
       Hampstead : John and Sarah, and two who d. in infancy.
       Their son, John, b. Nov. 29, 1755, m. Priscilla, daughter of
       Dr. William and Priscilla (Leonard) McKinstry. They had
       twelve children, and went to New Brunswick with an uncle,
       William Hazen.
III. Moses, b. June 1, 1733; was in the old French war, and severely
       wounded on the Plains of Abraham, where he distinguished
       himself. He was retired on "half pay" for life by the Brit-
       ish army. He settled at St. John, Canada. He mar. Char-

lotte La Sausee. They had no children. He then joined the patriot cause in the Revolutionary war, and sacrificed a large estate and his half pay for life. He raised a regiment of Canadians, recruited from all quarters as the war proceeded, variously known as Congress' Own," or "Hazen's Own." The traitor Arnold honored him by baseless charges of subordination, but the record proves his good conduct. He was a brigadier-general at the close of the war. He cut the military road through northern Vermont, from Peacham to Hazen's Notch, in Montgomery, which still bears his name.

IV.　Anna, b. July 30, 1735; m. Robert Peaslee, son of Amos Peaslee of Dover, one of the first settlers of Gilmanton.

V.　William, b. July 17, 1738; moved to New Brunswick, Canada, from the establishment of the province. He married Sarah, daughter of Dr. Joseph and Sarah (Leonard) Le Baron, of Plymouth, Mass. They had sixteen children, among whom was Elizabeth, who married Hon. Ward Chipman, Judge of the Supreme Court, and acting Governor of New Brunswick at his death, in 1824. They had sons, William, Robert, an officer in the British army, a daughter, Sarah Charlotte, mar. Gen. Sir John Foster, member of the British Parliament, and Frances Amelia, who married Col. Charles Drury, of the English army, whose two sons were generals and resided at St. John, N. B.

VI.　Sarah, b. Nov. 1, 1741; mar. Major Nathaniel Merrill, of Haverhill.

HARRIMAN.

Thomas Harriman m. Martha Pool, moved from Hampstead to Plymouth. They were married at Rowley, Mass., Sept. 26, 1766. They had children, b. in Hampstead.

I.　Jane, b. Jan. 28, 1770; mar. Benjamin Gould, of Plymouth, Aug. 11, 1791.

II.　Miriam, b. Oct. 18, 1771; m. Nehemiah Snow, of Plymouth, April 9, 1789.

III.　John, b. Feb. 2, 1774; m. Hannah Green, March 20, 1799.

IV.　Anna, b. April 15, 1776.

V.　Thomas, b. May 15, 1778.

They had one child born in Manchester, and six more in Plymouth, N. H.

John Hogg, or Hoog, doubtless was a North Ireland man, who came to Londonderry, N. H., after 1719, and from there to Hampstead. His name appears on the early petitions for a township in 1743, and other places on the early records. He married Elizabeth Hambleton in 1739, possibly from Kittery, Maine. He refused to pay his rates towards the support of the minister, in 1752 [p. 26, Vol. 1]. They resided at the "old James Smith" house in West Hampstead, and both were buried in the village cemetery [see inscription of the tomb, p. 310, Vol. 1]. From the family Bible, printed in 1734, in the handwriting of John Hoog, is taken the following :—

"My own birth and marriage; the names and ages of my children. I, myself, born September, 1704. I was married to Elizabeth Hambleton, Nov. 6, 1729."

"My son, Samuel Hoog, born Aug. 13, 1730.
" daughter, Elizabeth Hoog, born April 29, 1732.
" " Agnes Hoog, born Sept. 2, 1734.
" " Ann Hoog, b. July 4, 1736.
" son, John Hoog, born Oct. 29, 1739.
" daughter, Mary Hoog, born May 7, 1742.
" son, David Hoog, born March 5, 1745.
" " Abasser Hoog, born May —, ——.
" " Caleb Hoog, born Nov. 22, 17—."

The son, John, mar. Agnes ——, Feb. 19, 1767. His descendants settled in Henniker, and changed their names to Raymond. It is recorded by some historians that ".John settled in Dunbarton in 1752, with John S. Stinson and Thomas Mills, his brother-in-law, but it seems to some members of the family more probable that it was Samuel who settled in Dunbarton in 1752 than John."

John Hoog, Esq., senior, was a prominent man on the committees of Londonderry in the first years of the settlement of Dunbarton, although he resided in Hampstead. " He may have lived in Londonderry from 1752 for a few years."

MARSHALL.

" In the first generation of New England people were many families by the name of Marshall." Edmund Marshall was of

Salem, Mass., in 1636. He was a freeman in Massachusetts, May 17, 1637. He had lands granted him there in 1638. In 1650 he bought lands at "Kettle Cove," about one half a mile from Gloucester boundary, upon which is now built the summer residence of the Hon. T. Jefferson Coolidge, late minister to France. In 1651, with his son John and other Cape Ann people, he went to New London, Conn., in company with Rev. Mr. Blinman, but after a short stay returned to Gloucester. After 1657 he was of Ipswich, and later of Newbury, Mass. He was a weaver. Edmund Marshall and wife Millicent had children.

I.   Naomi, bapt. Jan. 24, 1637.
II.   Ann, b. April 15, 1638.
III.   Ruth, b. May 3, 1640.
IV.   Sarah, b. May 29, 1642.
V.   Edmund, b. June 16, 1644.
VI.   Benjamin, b. Sept. 27, 1646; m. Prudence Woodward, Nov. 2, 1677, in Ipswich. Had children, b. in Ipswich : Benjamin, b. Nov. 15, 1684, m. Bethia Goodhue; Anna, m. Samuel Page, of Hampton; Mary, b. July 21, 1686; m. Ralph Butler, of Hampton; Abigail, unmarried; Sarah, b. Dec. 2, 1693; Rachel, b. Dec. 28, 1695; Edmund, Ezekiel, John, and Joseph.

Benjamin Marshall and Bethiah Goodhue were published Nov. 24, 1711, in Ipswich. He d. Oct. 1, 1747. His will was admitted to probate Oct. 19, 1747. It commences :—

"In the name of God, Amen, I, Benjamin Marshall, of Chebacco Parish, in Ipswich, Yeoman." "He appoints his sons, Benjamin and Joseph, to be executors, mentions wife Bethiah, and daughters, Elizabeth, wife of David Burnham, Jr., Bethiah, wife of John Burnham, of Chebacco, Susannah, wife of Abner Day of Gloucester, and Anna." "To son Moses land in Cheshire and a cow and steers when he comes of age. He divides his homestead between sons Benjamin and Joseph, and to the son William, b. in Ipswich, April 3, 1720, as follows : "I give and bequeath to my son William, and his heirs and assigns forever, the whole of my land and interest in Almsbury Peak (so called), within the Province of New Hampshire. I also give to said William one cow and one pair of steers (upon demand) after my decease. The bequest to William is in every part in fee simple."

The son mentioned, William Marshall, m. Sarah Buswell, of Salisbury, Mass., moved to "Almsbury Peak," that part now

Hampstead. He built the house in East Hampstead at "Marshall's Corner," as seen in the cut following p. 320, Vol. 1, owned and occupied by the Marshall family from 1726 to the death of Miss Ellen Augusta Marshall, in 1901.

Capt. William and Sarah (Buswell) Marshall had children, b. in Hampstead :—

I.   Caleb, b. June 23, 1750; m. Zuruh Harriman (see No. 84, ch.
       mem.); moved to Northumberland, and had children : Benja-
       min, Sarah, Abigail, William, Betsey, Caleb, Susannah, Rho-
       da, Nancy, Fanny, Silas, and Mary, who mar. Joseph Dyer,
       and later joined the Shakers at Enfield, and ran away from
       the company, and became the author of several works ex-
       posing the teachings of Ann Lee. One of her works was
       published in 1847, entitled "The Rise and Progress of the
       Serpent from the Garden of Eden to the Present Day, with
       Discourse of Shakerism."
II.   Betty, b. June 3, 1753; d. young.
III.   Molly, b. July 30, 1754.

Sarah, wife of Capt. William, d. in 1755, and he m., second, Abigail Burnham, a cousin, of Essex, Mass., Jan. 1, 1756. They had children, b. in Hampstead :—

IV.   Sarah, b. May 4, 1757; m. Joshua Stevens, of Enfield,
V.   Silas, b. Jan. 1, 1763; m. Ruth Fellows, and were the parents of
       the nine children recorded on p. 422, Vol. 1, whose son,
       Andrew Burnham, was father of Arthur Ward Marshall (see
       sketch No. 424, ch. mem.).
VI.   Betty, b. Dec. 31, 1764.
VII.   Samuel, b. June 3, 1766; m. Lydia Eaton, of Plaistow; moved to
       Landaff. They were the parents of James Marshall, who m.
       Mary Dudley of Brentwood, and d. in Kingston in 1858, who
       were parents of James Frank Marshall, m. Mary Miranda
       George, whose son, Rev. Harold Marshall, of Porto Rico, m.
       Bertha Hills.
VIII. Ann, or Abigail, b. in 1768.

Capt. William Marshall m., third, Feb. 3, 1790, Miriam Johnson, widow of the late Ebenezer Mudgett, of Hampstead and Weare (see Nos. 19 and 20, list of cov. mem.). He died in Hampstead, June 23, 1822, aged 96 years, 4 months, and 10 days. He was buried in an orchard near the old homestead.

He served in the Revolutionary war, "although in his fiftieth year when the battle of Lexington was fought," and was the first representative to the General Court under the new constitution. His granddaughter, Mrs. Mary Marshall Dyer (author referred to above), says of her grandfather in her book, "When I was sixteen years of age I spent two years at my grandfather's home in Hampstead to be near the seashore for my health. My grandfather, Capt. William Marshall, was much of a business man. Previous to the Revolution he had been a commanding officer in the King's Regiment. He was also a worthy merchant. He had a large farm where he lived, and owned rights in a number of towns. While in this situation the Americans began to be dissatisfied with British oppression. The stamp act began to arouse the inhabitants. He soon exclaimed, "We can be an independent nation.' He renounced his gold-laced coat and hat ; he would wear nothing but home-made manufacture, and abolished all costly ornaments in his family, of apparel or furniture, and declared himself independent of foreign powers. His influence had a good effect. In the time of the Revolution, he, with my father (Caleb), did much for the soldiers and suffering in Coos county. He continued an unflinching patriot through life. He was a large and robust man, and much was said about him because he wore his grey cloth clothes. He had a strong and persevering mind. His last counsel when he parted with his friends was, ' You must be honest and always speak the truth, let your circumstances be what they will ; truth and justice will carry you through all difficulty.' "

(We are indebted to Charles H. Whittier, of Hampstead, for the gift of the book, by Mrs. Mary Marshall Dyer, referred to above. To Mr. Thomas Hills, of South Boston, President Hill's Family Association, for many items connected with the family of Marshall.)

In his " Reminiscences of Seventy Years," delivered by Dr. Jeremiah Spofford, in the First Church of Groveland, Mass., June 22, 1867, is found the following in reference to his home in Hampstead :—

" June, 1813, I made my second visit to Boston. Then I found it greatly agitated by the news, just arrived from Halifax, of the death of

Captain Lawrence, and the circumstances of the capture of the Chesapeake, which had so mysteriously disappeared from off the harbor a few days before, after a single blockade. British ships of war were lazily blockading the port. Soldiers were parading the Common, which was well filled with piles of cannon balls, staked arms, and munitions of war.

After two days in Boston I took passage for Salem, and spent the night at Danvers, and arrived at my father's the next day (Groveland). After remaining at my father's a few weeks, and assisting him in his haying, I was induced to visit Hampstead, about nine miles north of Haverhill, Mass., where the kind attentions of Rev. John Kelly and J. True, Esq., principally conduced to my stay and settlement in that town, where I was kindly received, and found a remarkably steady, industrious people, among whom I spent three and a half years, with pleasure and advantage.

As I was not burdened with practice, in October I visited Dartmouth College, and attended the medical lectures. President Wheelock, the son of the founder, was spending his last years in office. The unfortunate quarrel which removed him soon after was already in progress, and my wonder was that he remained there so long. Dr. Perkins lectured on anatomy and physiology, Dr. Noyes of Newburyport on theory and practice of physic, and Dr. Graves on chemistry.

I received a certificate to practice in the State from Dr. Nathan Smith, the founder of the medical school there, and president of the New Hampshire Medical Society, then about to remove to New Haven.

Upon this journey I visited Jaffrey, N. H., where I was married, Oct. 25, 1813, consummating a union which had been five years in contemplation, and which has had an important bearing upon all the subsequent transactions of my life, a course of action which many would pronounce imprudent, but which I recommend to every industrious and prudent young man prepared to go into business, and especially to every young physician.

The according January we commenced housekeeping in Hampstead, which, with the blessing of God, which always rests upon a wise use of his institutions, still continues.

Hampstead, like all other towns at that time which had a good portion of active, intelligent men, was greatly agitated with politics. It was difficult even to acquire the personal friendship of a political opponent. I had opinions, and scorned to conceal them. The town was about equally divided, and my predilections were no sooner known than half the people were my firm friends and patrons, but as there was a Democratic doctor in town, it will be perceived that it was a difficult task to gain the other half.

Thinking outspoken honesty the best policy, but carefully avoiding all political discussions while attending the sick, I openly advocated my own views in social conversations and public occasions, but during

the sickly season of 1815 politics were forgotten, and I had the patronage of many of the strongest Democratic families in the town.

With this circle of intelligent and active friends I remained three years and a half, and just about paid my expenses. In connection with my father, I built a good house and barn, which I furnished and occupied from November, 1815, to 1817, in full expectation of a more permanent residence. These buildings the present owner has finished and improved, so as to do no discredit to my plans or his own, and I did what few do with buildings they put up, sold them for the cost when I removed to this town (now, 1902, known as the Titcomb place, in West Hampstead).

For the people of Hampstead I have ever entertained the highest regard. They received us with great kindness; myself and my wife were made happy in our residence among them, and we left them with much regret. Mr. Kelly was my firm friend and warm adviser and patron, and his friendship did not cease when I removed; his frequent visits were welcome to my home, till he went to his reward in his extreme old age.

In December, 1816, Dr. Elias Weld informed me that Dr. Eben Jewett, then physician here (Groveland, or as it was then East Bradford), was in the last stages of consumption, and advised me to step into the vacancy soon to be made. I decidedly preferred a residence in Massachusetts to equal advantages in New Hampshire, but to leave my excellent friends, my newly acquired homestead, and throw myself, with the encumbrance of two families (my father and mother lived with me) upon the uncertain ties of a new location, and trust to acquiring new friends, these considerations bore heavily upon my mind, and cost many hours of deepest consideration. In March I visited this place, and in April I removed my family.

I never saw a light or fire in any church previous to 1821, save once at Hampstead, to close a town meeting, though I was then thirty years of age, and had resided in different towns and states.

I have been a constant attendant of the ancient Congregational Orthodox service in all places where I have resided since I was ten years old. Myself and wife were admitted to the church Nov. 7, 1819. I have no bigoted attachment to any denomination. I have not adhered to that in which my fathers worshipped because they did so, but because, whatever individuals or local churches may have done, I do not see that others, as a whole, do any better, and all other things being equal, I prefer that religious connection which was earliest and has done the most to make New England and the country what they are.

To the people of Hampstead and Groveland and vicinity I have been under infinite obligation. Of the departed I would express my high estimate of their thousand acts and kindness; to the living my grateful thanks."

Timothy Sargent, b. in Haverhill, Mass., Aug. 11, 1747; m. Anna Whittier, of Amesbury; second, m. Deborah Smith. He d. in Hill, where he moved. Two of his children were born in Salem; next three, John, Abigail, and Moses Sargent, were born in Hampstead, from 1788 to 1799.

Phineas Sargent, b. in Amesbury, Mass., July 3, 1750, m., first, Rebecca Wells; m., second, Hannah Colby. He was one of the original settlers of Hill, and the father of twenty five children, twelve by first wife, and thirteen by the second. Resided in Hampstead from 1771 to 1780.

Joseph Sargent, b. in Sandown, March 18, 1802, m. Elizabeth Bartlett, of Amesbury. Children :—

I.   Benjamin, b. Feb. 9, 1825; m. Maria E. Johnson in 1840. Children :—
        1. Ellen M., b. in 1852.
        2. Warren B., b. in 1855.
        3. Mary E., b. in 1855.
        4. Henrietta, b. in 1857.
II.   Judith, b. Oct. 10, 1826; m. James Gibson.
III.   Almira B., b. June 12, 1828; m. Lorenzo Frost, of Haverhill.

James Woodward went from Hampstead to Haverhill in 1763, and purchased a farm, at 20 cents an acre. In 1764 he married Hannah Clark, and it was the first marriage service performed in Grafton county. He was prominently connected with the affairs of the new town, serving as an officer, committee, etc. In 1782 he became judge of the Court of Common Pleas. In 1783 he was chosen to represent the town of Haverhill in the General Assembly at Concord. Hannah (Clark) Woodward died Oct. 21, 1805, and he married, second, Elizabeth Hale, a daughter of Rev. John Hale, a surgeon in the Revolutionary army. Elizabeth Hale was married, first, to Dr. Samuel Poor, her father's assistant surgeon. James Woodward had a son, Joshua, a prominent man in town and church affairs in Haverhill. He was an Abolitionist, being a colleague of William Lloyd Garrison, Parker Pillsbury, and others. James Woodward died in 1821.

ERRATA AND ADDITIONS.

Page 6, read, last line, plastering for "plaitering."

Page 8, read 1600 for "1700."

Page 10, read, last line, Nichols for "Nickols."

Page 37, read that "Mr. Pratt lived for a time in the Townsend house, and later in the 'Brick house,' which he purchased for himself."

Several accounts of the Townsend house as a parsonage have been given the writer. An authority says the true facts are the house never was a parsonage. Mr. Pratt, when he first came to Hampstead, boarded for a time in the family of Dea. Jona. Kent, and later moved to the Townsend house, which was owned by a company consisting of Mr. Amos Buck, Henry Putnam, and R. Kimball Brickett, who controlled all of the land from the church to the Chase house, now occupied by Ellery Tabor. After a short time Mr. Pratt moved to the "Brick house," which he purchased for himself. The company of owners sold land to John W. Little, who built the house where Frank W. Emerson now resides, and sold the present Townsend house to Maj. Isaac Smith, and it was occupied by the son, Rufus C., until he moved to Haverhill, when it was purchased by Mr. Townsend.

Page 127, read Mrs. Fannie C. Little for "Fannie E."

Page 128, read Mrs. for "Miss" Alice C. Fitts.

Page 134, read Mrs. W. P. Noyes for C. P.

Page 145, read Emily S. for Emily J. Davis.

Page 191, read Joshua for Jonathan, son of John Ingalls.

Page 225, read "with the spirit," for saith the spirit.

Page 342, cross out "No. 59," as the sketch of Nathan Hale is under No. 58.

Page 361, read Maroa, for Maria Bowles.

Page 416, read *wife* Mary Chase, for widow Mary Chase, fifth line.

Page 420, last line but one, read *where he*, for "when she."

Page 431, read Dec. 3, for 11, in No. 224.

Page 444, read in No. 251, Martha *Webster*, for Knight.

Page 510, read Stanford, for Stamford University.

Page 521, read Mrs. Bartley, for Tenney, in the first line.

Page 527, read marriage of Annette Brickett as *May 4.*

Page 533, read Josiah C., for Josiah G. Eastman.

Page 561, read, fifth line, Pine Grove Cemetery, Salem.

Page 588, sketch No. 534, read Myron E. Emerson as fourth son of Abbie H. Emerson, b. 1883, not as fourth child of his brother, Arthur M., and b. 1893.

Page 610, read Otis *Masterman*, for Masterson.

Page 622, read Mary (Calef), for Balch, in No. 602.

Page 627, read Orren *B.* Ranlett for Orren V.

Page 703, read Ora L. Ordway, No. 751, mar. June 10, 1903, H. Walter Little, No. 718, on page 688.

Page 708, read Lizzie P. Sargent, for Lizzie B.

Page 727, read, second line, Peter Morse, not Peter Hale Morse.

Page 743, read, Joseph G. Norman, for Josie G.

Page 755, read Mary A. Osgood, for Mary E.

Page 756, read Mary Merrick m. Samuel Dalton.

Page 756, read Mary E. Merrick m. John K. Mason, for Mary B.

Page 766, read that Clarissa (Chase) Whitehouse mar., second, Zimri Bragdon, of Atkinson, and the parents of Miss Apphia, of Hampstead.

INDEX.

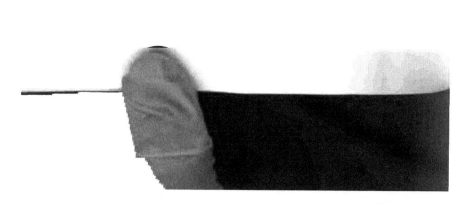

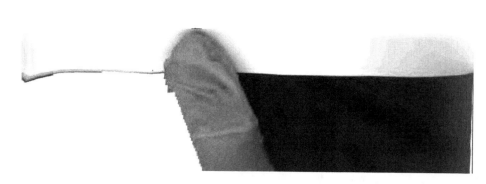

WADLEIGH, Abigail, 357,
    368, 488, 489, 530.
Aaron, 101.
Daniel, 566.
Elizabeth, 566, 567.
Ephraim, 193.
Henry, 196.
Jona., 30, 488.
Judith, 187, 354, 524.
Lizzie E., 530.
Mary, 343.
Moses, 189.
Thomas, 171, 189, 191,
    194, 196, 354.
WAKEFIELD, Jona., 383.
WALLACE, M. C., 489.
WALKER, Anson E., 523.
Charles, 552.
Cyrus, 199.
Elbridge, 523.
George, 193.
Thomas, 192, 552.
WARD, Abbie F., 478.
Isaac, 518.
John, 6, 7, 288.
Nathaniel, 5, 6.
Sally, 518, 519.
WARE, Jane, 415.
WARNER, Dorothy, 564.
Jane, 464.
Richard, 352.
WARREN, Lulu, 681.
George W., 768.
WASHINGTON, 331.
WASON, George A., 723.
Huldah, 722.
Sarah J., 590.
Thomas, 590.
Washington B., 723.
WATERS, Abigail, 343.
WATERMAN, Nettie,
    707, 711.
WATTS, 167, 244.
Hannah, 333, 407, 408.
Marion, 427, 719, 722.
    756.
Samuel, 333.
Sarah, 327.
WATSON, Abijah, 184.
Albert, 25, 38, 107,
    108, 112, 113, 114,
    123, 153, 156, 159,
    161, 163, 211, 231,
    260, 265, 270, 272,
    273, 288, 302, 304,
    523, 576, 577, 598,
    599, 617, 648, 655, 668.

Watson, Albert P., 211,
    219, 260, 578, 654, 660.
Caleb, 186.
Daniel, 182.
Ithamar, 188.
John, 723.
John W., 289, 304,
    444, 578, 648.
Laura S., 672.
Mabel A., 157, 101,
    304, 578, 655.
Miranda, 212, 302.
Nichodemus, 182, 184,
    186, 188, 723.
Ruth, 327.
William, 577.
WAGNER, R., 219, 220.
WEARE, Hannah, 305.
WEBBER, Leonard, 740.
Luther, 747.
WEBSTER, 241.
Abbie J., 464.
Abigail, 333.
Abiah, 192, 303.
Anna, 363, 451, 487, 737.
Ann E., 200, 464, 556.
Asa, 366.
Caleb, 179, 303.
Calvin C., 200, 464.
Carrie B., 521.
Charles H., 112.
Clarissa, 503.
Caroline, 755.
Daniel, 413, 486, 487,
    545.
Daniel D., 413.
David, 414.
Ebenezer, 367, 413.
Edward K., 413.
Elizabeth, 296, 303,
    414, 464, 469.
Elizabeth C., 413.
Eliphalet, 413.
Emily, 413.
Ephraim, 193, 194,
    296, 300, 307, 386.
Hannah, 414.
Hazen, 730.
Henry, 446.
James, 414.
Jesse C., 464, 469.
John, 15, 32, 179, 363,
    407, 412, 432, 469,
    483, 487, 488, 734, 737.
John C., 413.
Joseph, 192, 195, 196,
    363, 734.

Webster, Josiah, 30, 200,
    207, 297, 413, 464, 761.
Josiah C., 464.
Josiah D., 416, 464.
Martha, 412.
Margaret S., 433.
Mary, 191, 200, 299,
    300, 309, 407, 439,
    440, 505, 725.
Mary E., 414.
Mary T., 404.
Moses, 194, 307, 776.
Nathan, 418, 469, 757.
Peter E., 433.
Phebe, 296, 306.
Philena, 355.
Rebecca, 484, 750.
Samuel, 366, 386.
Sarah, 193, 195, 196,
    303S, 67, 371, 446,
    459, 483, 488.
Sophia H., 404.
Stephen, 194, 469.
Stephen P., 749.
Susanna, 366.
Thomas, 469.
WEED, Elizabeth, 720.
Hannah, 732.
WELLS, Annie S., 690.
Charles T., 690.
Clement H.
Clementine M., 696.
David, 191.
Dorothy, 356, 357.
Dolly, 769.
Edson H., 686.
Eleazer, 191.
Emily, 507.
Hannah, 188.
Jacob, 183.
Jemima, 182, 296, 357.
John, 507.
John H., 507.
Josephine L., 690.
Lydia M., 128, 134, 139,
    142, 162, 305, 357.
Luke, 356.
Mary, 191, 725, 745.
Mary H., 431, 505.
Mary S., 690.
Moses, 188.
Obediah, 182, 296,
    356, 357.
Rebecca, 786.
Ruth, 725.
Sarah, 357.
Sarah G., 690.

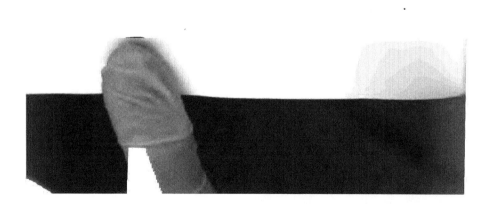

3741

16